Cryobanking the Genetic Resource

Wildlife conservation for the future?

Edited by

P. F. Watson

Professor of Reproductive Cryobiology
The Royal Veterinary College, London, UK

W. V. Holt

Senior Research Fellow
The Institute of Zoology, The Zoological Society of London,
Regent's Park, London, UK

London and New York

First published 2001 by Taylor & Francis
11 New Fetter Lane, London EC4P 4EE

Simultaneously published in the USA and Canada
by Taylor & Francis Inc,
29 West 35th Street, New York, NY 10001

Taylor & Francis is an imprint of the Taylor & Francis Group

© 2001 P. F. Watson and W. V. Holt

Typeset in Stone Serif by Exe Valley Dataset Ltd, Exeter
Printed and bound in Great Britain by
T J International Ltd

Every effort has been made to ensure that the advice and information in
this book is true and accurate at the time of going to press. However,
neither the publisher nor the authors can accept any legal responsibility or
liability for any errors or omissions that may be made. In the case of drug
administration, any medical procedure or the use of technical equipment
mentioned within this book, you are strongly advised to consult the
manufacturer's guidelines.

British Library Cataloguing in Publication Data
A catalogue record for this book is available
from the British Library

Library of Congress Cataloguing in Publication Data
Cryobanking the genetic resource: wildlife conservation for the future?/edited by P. F. Watson,
W. V. Holt.
   p.   cm.
Includes bibliographical references.
ISBN 0-7484-0814-2 (hbk.: alk. paper)
   1. Germplasm resources, Animal. 2. Vertebrates–Germplasm
resources–Cryopreservation. I. Watson, P. F. II. Holt, W. V.

QH432.C77 2000
333.95'4–dc21   00–057712

ISBN 0–748–40814–2

Cryobanking the Genetic Resource

Cryobanking the Genetic Resource
Wildlife conservation for the future

Preface

The stimulus for this book arose as a result of a Concerted Action project, funded by the European Commission under the Framework III BIOTECH initiative. The objective of the project was to draw together a framework of principles governing the way in which genetic resource banks in general should be organised. Not all participants within the project were cryobiologists or reproductive biologists. In fact, many different disciplines were represented within the group of colleagues, and they addressed issues such as taxonomy, genetics and the generation and storage of cell lines from threatened wildlife, as well as cryopreservation of germplasm. The European Commission requested, however, that we should produce a wide-ranging review of germplasm cryopreservation methods, which generated so much information that we decided to publish it in the form of this book.

The first half of the book is devoted to the science of genetic resource banking and the associated disciplines that are required for a full informed approach to the subject. In the second half we have attempted to review the current literature on gamete and embryo cryopreservation. This is by no means exhaustive, especially in those groups of animals where there is a large literature (cattle, sheep, mouse); in this case we have tried to exercise judgement as to what is really helpful in developing robust methodology that is well attested by fertility results. In those groups where the literature is less conprehensive we have referred to what is published so that our readers can see for themselves what has been published. We hope that the chapters will form a way into the science for those for whom it is a new venture. It is our expectation that this book will become a reference text for those who plan to get involved in conservation ventures. We hope it will signal the pitfalls in such activity and help to develop good practice and realistic expectations amongst those who wish to contribute to addressing the issues of the maintenance of biodiversity.

In reflecting on the development of genetic resource banking, we became aware that there were differences of emphasis expressed by workers in different parts of the world. Elaborating our own philosophy through this process has been a rewarding and stimulating exercise, and we offer the results of our thinking for critical appraisal and to stimulate others to join the venture.

We would like to thank our contributors for the patience and persistence. (They revised their work at least once during the long delays occasioned in the gestation of the volume). We are indebted to their expertise in ensuring that this work stands up to scrutiny. They are all acknowledged experts in the field and have made their own significant contribution in the areas of their expertise.

We thank the publisher, Taylor and Francis, for their support and belief in the worthwhile nature of the content. We trust that the work will strengthen their reputation in the area of scientific technology addressing issues confronting the modern world.

Finally, we express our gratitude to the European Commission for enabling this work to be undertaken.

P. F. Watson
W. V. Holt
March 2000

Foreword

There is a growing awareness of a worldwide reduction in biodiversity and the urgent need to develop ways to redress the problem. For this reason the editors of this book were recently involved in organizing a series of conferences as part of a European Commission Concerted Action Project on Genetic Resource Banking. Various strategies for the conservation of genetic diversity based on the preservation of biological materials were considered, but the predominant theme was the storage of gametes and embryos for use in animal breeding. This book arose as a result of these discussions.

In consideration of where genetic resource banking fits into the overall strategy for maintenance of genetic diversity, it is clear that it is no answer to the increasing destruction of ecosystems and natural habitats and the loss of species within them. Restoration and protection of these habitats must surely be the best solution in the long run. In the mean time, however, genetic resource banking can play an important role in supporting breeding programmes in small populations of endangered animals kept in captivity in anticipation of future opportunities for reintroduction to the wild.

The roots of genetic resource banking go back more than fifty years to the time when a method was first discovered for preservation of spermatozoa at very low temperatures. There followed a revolution in animal breeding, particularly in cattle, caused by a widescale application of artificial insemination and the use of semen long-stored in the frozen state. This prompted the remark from Sir Alan Parkes, a pioneer of cryobiology, that 'time and space had been abolished in cattle breeding'. This concept might be regarded as the basic principle of genetic resource banking particularly since it is time and space for breeding that are running out for endangered animals. It has not been difficult to envisage opportunities to extend this concept on a wider scale. An early application in farm animals was by the Rare Breeds Survival Trust in the UK, who established banks of frozen spermatozoa to augment their efforts to conserve endangered breeds. Initially these sperm banks were seen as an insurance policy against a catastrophic loss of live animals, but later it was appreciated that they could also be an aid to maintenance of genetic diversity in small breeding populations. The further discovery of methods for freezing and storage of embryos extended the scope of genetic banking to conservation of the whole genome rather than just the spermatozoa.

Development of methods for freezing spermatozoa and embryos of wild animals relies heavily on results obtained in domestic and laboratory species. But experience in cryobiology has shown that there are frequently important species variations in the reaction of cells to low temperatures and these must therefore be determined. In addition it is always the case that application of reproductive technologies for breeding are more complex in wild than in domestic animals. In the past, however, the spermatozoa of several different species of wild animals have been successfully frozen and occasionally used for breeding. More recently the birth of live young following embryo transfer has also been achieved in some captive wild animals. But these have been relatively isolated cases and it is stressed in this book that a store of gametes and embryos in itself is not particularly useful as a genetic resource bank. It is only when this resource is integrated and used within an ongoing breeding programme that it can make a real contribution to genetic conservation. This is the important message that this book conveys and it brings together the various strands of knowledge and information currently available in order to promote the use of genetic resource banks in effective breeding programmes.

Of primary importance are the principles which must be understood to make informed decisions about the proper use of a stored resource. Specifically these are concerned with the selection of individuals for storage and use in order to maximize genetic diversity in small populations. There is also a need to select the most appropriate species for storage to meet conservation goals. Another important aspect is the reproductive technologies involved in the efficient use of stored gametes and embryos and how best to apply them in species in which very little is known about their basic reproductive physiology. It is encouraging, for example, that useful practical aids are being developed for the identification and control of reproductive cycles. Some of the difficulties actually encountered in practice are well exemplified in Dr Holt's experience of trying to establish a genetic resource bank in support of a breeding programme for three endangered gazelle species in Spain. There are also many technical and practical issues involved in the safe and efficient use of stored gametes and embryos. All these aspects are covered in this book.

Present strategies for genetic resource banking are based almost entirely on cryogenic storage of spermatozoa and embryos because this technology has been extensively tried and tested in animal breeding. By contrast, reference is also made to the great expansion in reproductive technology that has occurred in recent years. This has led to new developments, most of which are associated with the manipulation of eggs and embryos. They include, for example, the preservation of oocytes, *in vitro* fertilization and embryo culture, sex selection, nuclear transfer and embryo multiplication. Some of these technologies will undoubtedly play an important part in future developments of genetic resource banks, especially, perhaps, the opportunity for cloning by nuclear transfer from conserved somatic cells. Most of these technologies, however, require much further development before they can be applied effectively in practice.

I commend this book as a timely contribution to all those concerned for the conservation of genetic diversity in this world and particularly to those who might become involved in the practical establishment of a genetic resource bank. It contains much useful information and advice from authors who are all experts in their fields. But it also highlights some of the present limitations to genetic resource banking, not least of which is the paucity of knowledge concerning the physiology of reproduction in many species. There is a crucial need, therefore, for more extensive financial support not only to develop genetic resource banks on an international scale, but also for basic research.

The destruction of any species due to the activities of humans is an important loss. But for anyone who has seen animals such as the beautiful gazelles which have been saved from extinction and kept in the south of Spain, efforts directed to genetic conservation are more poignantly appreciated. It is good to know that some of these animals have now been returned to their original habitat.

Professor C. Polge, FRS
April 2000

Contributors

Teresa Abaigar, Consejo Superior de Investigaciones Científícas, Estación Experimental de Zonas Áridas, c/. General Segura 1, 04001 Almería, Spain.

Sylvie P. A. Beekman, Department of Herd Health and Reproduction, University of Utrecht, PO Box 151, 3508 Utrecht, The Netherlands.

Peter M. Bennett, The Institute of Zoology, Zoological Society of London, Regent's Park, London NW1 4RY

R. Billard, Muséum National d'Histoire Naturelle, Laboratoire d'Ichtyologie, 43 rue Cuvier, 75231 Paris Cedex 05, France.

C. J. Candy, Department of Anatomy, St George's Hospital Medical School, Cranmer Terrace, London, SW17, 0RE

Ben Colenbrander, Department of Herd Health and Reproduction, University of Utrecht, PO Box 151, 3508 Utrecht, The Netherlands.

B. J. Fuller, Academic Department of Surgery, Royal Free and University College Hospital School of Medicine, Pond Street, London NW3 2QG, UK

Gary C. W. England, Department of Farm Animal and Equine Medicine and Surgery, Royal Veterinary College, Hawshead Lane, North Mimms, Hatfield, Herts AL9 7TA, UK.

Denise A. Hewitt, Department of Farm Animal and Equine Medicine and Surgery, Royal Veterinary College, Hawshead Lane, North Mimms, Hatfield, Herts AL9 7TA, UK.

J. K. Hodges, Department of Reproductive Biology, German Primate Centre, Kellnerweg 4, 37077 Göttingen, Germany

W. V. Holt, The Institute of Zoology, The Zoological Society of London, Regent's Park, London NW1 4RY, UK

S. D. Johnston, School of Veterinary Science and Animal Production, University of Queensland, Brisbane, Queensland 4072, Australia.

James K. Kirkwood, Universities Federation for Animal Welfare, The Old School, Brewhouse Hill, Wheathampstead, Herts AL4 8AN, UK.

J. D. Millar, Department of Basic Veterinary Sciences, The Royal Veterinary College, London, NW1 0TU, UK

J. M. Morrell, German Primate Centre, Kellnerweg 4, 37077 Göttingen, Germany

Joyce M. Parlevliet, Department of Herd Health and Reproduction, University of Utrecht, PO Box 151, 3508 Utrecht, The Netherlands.

L. M. Penfold, White Oaks Conservation Center, 3823 Owens Road, Yulee, FL 32097, USA

P. F. Watson, Department of Veterinary Basic Sciences, The Royal Veterinary College, London, NW1 0TU, UK

G. J. Wishart, Avian Reproduction Group, University of Abertay Dundee, Bell Street, Dundee DD1 1HG, Scotland, UK

M. J. Wood, Department of Anatomy, St George's Hospital medical School, Cranmer Terrace, London, SW17, 0RE, UK.

Tiantian Zhang, Department of Biology, Research Centre, University of Luton, Luton LU1 5DU, UK.

Abbreviations

AI	Artificial insemination
ART	Assisted reproductive technology
AV	Artificial vagina
BES	*N,N*-bis(2-Hydroxyethyl)-2-aminoethanesulphonic acid
BSA	Bovine serum albumin
BWW	Biggers, Whitten and Whittingham medium, An embryo culture medium modified from Tyrode's medium (Biggers *et al.*, 1971 in Daniel, J.C. (ed.) *Methods in Mammalian Embryology*, San Francisco: Freeman and Co. pp. 86–116)
CL	Corpus luteum
CPA	Cryoprotectant additive
DI	Donor insemination
DMA	Dimethyl acetamide
DMSO	Dimethyl sulphoxide
eCG	Equine chorionic gonadotrophin
EG	Ethylene glycol, ethanediol
EDTA	Ethylenediaminetetraacetic acid a divalent cation chelator
EGTA	Ethyleneglycol-bis(ß-amino- ethyl ether)-*N,N,N´,N´*-tetraacetic acid, a divalent cation chelator but more specific for calcium than is EDTA
Equex STM	Sodium triethanolamine lauryl sulphate
ET	Embryo transfer
EYC	Egg yolk citrate
FBS	Fetal bovine serum
FCS	Fetal calf serum
FSH	Follicle-stimulating hormone
GnRH	Gonadotrophin-releasing hormone
GV	Germinal vesicle stage oocyte
hCG	Human chorionic gonadotrophin
HEPES	4-(2-Hydroxyethyl)-1-piperazine ethane sulphonic acid
HES	Hydroxyethyl starch
hMG	Human menopausal gonadotrophin
ICSI	Intracytoplasmic sperm injection
IUI	Intrauterine insemination
IVF	*In vitro* fertilization
IVM	*In vitro* maturation
LH	Luteinizing hormone
LN_2	Liquid nitrogen
MI and MII	Metaphase I and II, stages of oocyte development
MOET	Multiple ovulation and embryo transfer
NCS	Newborn calf serum

OES	Orvus ES paste, sodium triethanolamine lauryl sulphate
PBS	Phosphate-buffered saline
PMSG	Pregnant mare's serum gonadotrophin
PN	pronuclear stage
PrOH	1,2–Propanediol, propylene glycol
PVA	Polyvinyl alcohol
PVP	Polyvinyl pyrollidone
SD	Standard deviation
SEM	Standard error of the mean
SOF	Synthetic oviductal fluid
STLS	Sodium triethanolamine lauryl sulphate
TALP	
TCM 199	Tissue culture medium 199, a commercially available cell culture medium
TES	2-[tris(Hydroxymethyl)-methylamino-1-ethane]sulphonic acid
TEST	TES and Tris semen diluent
Tris	tris(Hydroxymethyl)-aminomethane

Introduction

P. F. WATSON

Department of Veterinary Basic Sciences, The Royal Veterinary College,
London NW1 0TU, UK

Contents

1.1   WHAT THIS BOOK SETS OUT TO DO

The concepts of genetic resource banking (GRB) are beginning to be banded around in the general media as a potential solution to the perceived problem of maintaining genetic diversity. While we would argue GRB has a place in the arsenal of means to tackle this global problem, it is not of itself the answer to the problem. We believe it is time to produce a statement of the collected expertise within the subject and to articulate our own understanding of how these concepts fit into the overall strategy.

We have therefore devoted the first half of this book to the various principles involved in the application of GRB in maintaining genetic diversity. The reader will find chapters on the principles of cryostorage of gametes and embryos, on the genetic considerations that must be in the forefront of decisions to store and to use the stored material, and the ancillary procedures that will be required when use is intended.

The second half of the book contains reviews of the literature, which will enable newcomers to the field to make intelligent decisions in the light of published research. We recognize that in this field it is probable that specific studies will not have been performed on a species of interest, and therefore decisions will have to be made based on studies of nearest similar species. Our contributors have generally been chosen because of their expertise and involvement in these areas, and have been directed to review the most important observations. Clearly this is a difficult decision in the case of species where there is much published work, such as the agricultural species, the laboratory mouse and the human. In other species, where the literature is more sparse the contributors have been more able to give an overview of the entire literature.

1.2   WHAT IS GENETIC RESOURCE BANKING?

This term, genetic resource banking, has been coined within the last decade to encompass the activity of storing gametes and embryos for future use in breeding. So-called artificial breeding using frozen semen has been used in the agricultural world for the best part of fifty years, and the extension of these concepts to address problems of human infertility are also well established. Indeed, the potential application of these techniques in wildlife conservation was recognised around some twenty-five years ago (Watson, 1978).

What has changed is the way in which science has extended cryopreservation to embryos and more recently oocytes, and the growing recognition of the importance of these concepts in preserving biodiversity. Reproductive technology has developed apace in the last fifteen years. Not only are we now able to preserve embryos from many species with a reasonable chance of success, but the technological advances have enabled us to cryopreserve the female gamete for use in *in vitro* fertilization. While these techniques at the present are not sufficiently reliable to be considered routine, progress has been such as to invite confidence that a solution is within reach. The difficulties with mature gametes and the possibilities presented with immature gametes in the treatment of human infertility have led to attempts to cryopreserve ovarian and testicular germ cells. The possibilities created by these approaches suggest that gamete cryopreservation has not yet reached its full potential.

Combined with these extraordinary developments in the last few years has been the increasingly widely recognized problem of a dwindling genetic biodiversity. Geneticists have been predicting that the expansion of humankind with the destruction of habitats cannot continue without having a profound impact on the fauna and flora of our world. With the developments in genetic identification we are now able to study the process of evolution and predict the consequences for a species of narrowing the genetic diversity. At last, Western society is aware of its responsibility for the elimination of species at a rate higher than ever before on this planet. With that has come an awakening of a sense of duty to address the problem with the powers that science has given to us. The combination of these factors has given rise to the need to coin a new phrase which encompasses the wider concepts. So genetic resource banking is born!

The term genetic resource banking implies the manipulation of the genetics of a species for the benefit of that species. The use of the word resource suggests that here is a commodity, which can be squandered or conserved, and the idea of a bank conveys the concept of deposits and withdrawals as necessary. If such is managed well, then the value of the resources can be amplified through the storage process. While the terms are helpful in giving a general impression of what is implied, their detailed application requires some adaptation. For example, the banking involves elaborate procedures for ensuring identity, security and continued viability. Unlike a financial bank, actions cannot be reversed, and the bankers bear a responsibility concerning the uses to which the resources are put. Moreover, losses can still arise from situations beyond our control, and cannot simply be restored by monetary compensation. However, GRB remains the best term to convey the particular combination of concepts and their applications. This book is intended to flesh out the concepts and lead the reader realistically into the subject.

There are differences of approach in the field and we have chosen to focus on our own interpretations. For example, in such activities, where should the 'power' lie? Does it reside with the country of origin of the experts, those who have the expertise to effect the results, or does it lie with the country of origin of the species? The resolution of such reflections helps to define the sort of strategies one chooses. We hope it will become apparent to our readers where we believe there are important considerations of this nature.

We have limited this book to a consideration of vertebrates only since it is a very large subject. However, when one investigates the gamete preservation literature there is an emphasis on the orders we have decided to encompass. The plant kingdom was well catered for in the recent book by Benson (1999).

1.3 FUTURE APPLICATIONS

The expansion of reproductive technology in recent years has already been mentioned. Indeed, there is now less need to preserve viability in sperm cells since it has been shown that spermatozoa can be freeze dried and then subsequently used for intracytoplasmic sperm injection with the production of live births (Wakayama and Yanagimachi, 1998). In the last five years, the possibility of using stored spermatogonia (undifferentiated male germ cells) for repopulating the testis of a common 'host' species in order to obtain spermatozoa for IVF has become a reality (Avarbock *et al.*, 1996; Clouthier *et al.*, 1996). In the female, the prospect of employing oocytes from primordial follicles in stored ovarian tissue came a step nearer with studies published in the 1990s (Newton *et al.*, 1996). As our ability to manipulate cells in culture increases we may expect to see primitive germinal stem cells cultured to maturity for subsequent use in genetic resource banking. With these processes, genetic manipulation will also increase, leading to the possibility of targeted insertion and/or deletion of particular gene constructs. Where such activities will fit into GRB remains unclear, but they will surely raise new areas for discussion.

Furthermore, with the development of cloning technology, a move away from the need to preserve reproductive cells becomes possible. Within a few years, individuals may be generated from tissue cells in storage, extending the concept of GRB from simply reproductive germ cells and embryos to any viable cell population or tissue. That is clearly much further away but the progress to date suggests that such possibilities may well be within our grasp in a shorter rather than a longer timescale. However, at the heart of GRB is the concept of genetic conservation, and the recombination of genes associated with meiosis and syngamy contributes to this goal in no small measure. We should be hesitant to bypass this process in our enthusiam to achieve short-term success.

The limits to GRB activity may depend not on science but on politics. When humanity is able to control genetics on such a scale as we have been envisaging, it remains to be seen whether we will have the will to bring about genetic resource management and to bring under control the loss of habitats and their species. Unless this activity is positively chosen, destruction of the planet will keep on apace and no scientific discovery will reverse it.

1.4 HOW TO USE THIS BOOK

We suggest that if these concepts are new, the reader is advised to read through the first half of the book. If they are familiar, then we recommend dipping into chapters which deal with species close to one's own interest. Subsequent reference to particular concepts may help to refresh ideas and to direct approaches for the future.

■ CHAPTER 1 ■

REFERENCES

AVARBOCK, M. R., BRINSTER, C. J. and BRINSTER, R. L. (1996) 'Reconstitution of spermatogenesis from frozen spermatogonial stem cells', *Nature Med.* **2**, 693–696.

BENSON E. E. (1999) *Plant Conservation Biotechnology*, London: Taylor and Francis.

CLOUTHIER, D. E. AVARBOCK, M. R. MAIKA, S. D., HAMMA, R. E. and BRINSTER R. L. (1996) 'Rat spermatogenesis in mouse testis', *Nature, Lond.* **381**, 418–421.

NEWTON, H., AUBARD, Y., RUTHERFORD, A., SHARMA, V. and GOSDEN, R. (1996) 'Low temperature storage and grafting of human ovarian tissue', *Hum. Reprod.* **11**, 1487–1491.

WAKAYAMA, T. and YANAGIMACHI, R. (1998) 'Development of normal mice from oocytes injected with freeze-dried spermatozoa', *Nature Biotechnol,* **16**, 639–641.

WATSON, P. F. (ed.) (1978) *Artificial Breeding of Non-Domestic Animals, Symposium of the Zoological Society of London, No. 43*, London: Academic Press.

Part A:

Considerations Pertinent to Genetic Resource Banking

Genetic Resource Banking and Maintaining Biodiversity

W. V. HOLT

The Institute of Zoology, The Zoological Society of London,
Regent's Park, London NW1 4RY, UK

Contents

2.1 INTRODUCTION

2.1.1 Why conserve biodiversity?

The word 'biodiversity' is now so widely used that few people stop and seriously consider its meaning. In fact, the concept of biodiversity has probably come to mean different things to different groups. Some use the word as a way of referring to the variety of organisms which currently exist; others extend its usage more widely to include the ecological complexes in which the organisms occur, and alternative definitions span genes, species and ecosystems. This latter definition implies an inclusive collection of hierarchically ordered entities, such as Soulé's (1991) 'biospatial hierarchy', but leaves out the processes of life that include gene and energy flow. When these aspects are included, biodiversity begins to encompass the dynamics of living systems, including the temporal changes that occur as a result of evolution and natural selection. Gaston (1996), who recently reviewed the biodiversity concept in detail, collected nine alternative definitions, each with a slightly different emphasis.

Regardless of the exact nature of its definition, biodiversity as a concept is an abstraction and a descriptor. In other words it is a neutral concept which makes no value judgement about nature conservation. Nevertheless, there is a commonly held perception that use of the term biodiversity somehow implies 'a conservation need'; indeed, some use the term 'biodiversity' as a synonym for 'nature conservation' (Bowman, 1993).

In a book devoted to evaluating techniques and concepts for the preservation of biological resources and hence biodiversity, it is fair to provide a reasoned justification for the view that conservation in a broad sense is worthwhile, and that species and gene conservation is a valid component of the entire scheme. Most authors who have considered the coherent justifications for conservation emphasize the direct benefits humanity gains from diverse ecosystems and species. For example, Wilson (1992) stated that 'biological diversity is the key to the maintenance of life as we know it'. Arguments range from the beneficial influences of forests on the control of floodwater and atmospheric quality, to the potential exploitation of particular species for food, drugs and industrial chemicals. Especially important is the argument that functional ecosystems are able to transform solar energy into the biochemical substances which are responsible for maintaining the life of nearly all species, including humans (Wildt, 1997). The role of life–the biosphere–in optimizing environmental conditions on the earth and oceans and in the atmosphere has been expounded as the Gaia hypothesis (Lovelock, 1989). This somewhat unconventional hypothesis takes the view that life adjusts the environment to suit itself, rather than evolving to suit the prevailing conditions.

CHAPTER 2

The economic potential of wildlife in attracting tourists and thus strengthening local economies in developing countries is a further important motive for conservation, albeit of a particular subset of species regarded as aesthetically attractive. It is considerably more difficult to develop strong arguments for the preservation of species whose exploitable value may not be immediately apparent. Important biologically based arguments include the need to conserve options for the further evolution of species; indeed, sound and logically based strategies for conservation can be developed from this foundation. As this argument is not primarily driven by the desire for immediate profits it can be regarded as unselfish and justifiable on moral grounds. It is thus an extension of the view that we should act as guardians of the planet and the biodiversity it contains. Unfortunately arguments based on moral principles carry little weight when they need to be backed with financial investment and there is also a tendency, even among biologists, to dismiss the moral argument on the grounds of its subjectivity (Kunin and Lawton, 1996). Furthermore, Soulé (1991) pointed out that many of the most urgent conservation needs exist in less developed areas whose governments are simply too poor to invest in them; if anything, these countries are most vulnerable to overexploitation of their resources. Thus arguments formulated on both scientific and moral principles run the risk of being viewed as esoteric luxuries in conditions of social deprivation, and regrettable though it may be, the anthropocentric arguments for biodiversity conservation are likely to remain the most readily justifiable.

There is a continuing discussion and some disagreement about the relative merits of the different approaches to conservation. The most profound differences are between adherents of the ecosystem-based, *in situ* approach and the *ex situ*-based approach. Conservation through the protection of ecosystems is clearly a desirable strategy. The principle of this approach is to set aside and manage natural areas based on systems of landscape classification that will capture as much species and ecological diversity as possible. By its very nature this approach requires the cooperation of land-owners, governments and local communities. Moreover, except in affluent societies direct benefits must be perceived by these different interested parties before this approach is feasible, and political instability may indeed rule it out where it is most desirable.

Ex-situ conservation mainly addresses the maintenance of single species by attempting to optimize breeding success while simultaneously minimizing the deleterious effects of inbreeding. Optimization may involve population control through contraception and sterilization, as well as the development of efficient husbandry techniques for animal breeding. Ideally, individuals managed through the *ex-situ* conservation modality could be reintroduced to their original habitat, and this is the stated aim of such programmes (Ginsberg, 1994). Where habitat destruction has occurred, this will clearly be impossible in the short term, but species are often then maintained in captivity in the hope that an opportunity for their reintroduction will arise at some unspecified future time (see, e.g. Wildt, 1992).

Some advocates of ecosystem-based conservation view the *ex-situ* approach as irrelevant since the organisms being conserved are no longer in their natural habitat. However, although in practice the potential for reintroduction is very limited, some successes have been recorded and these would have been impossible without the contribution of *ex-situ* conservation (Stanley-Price, 1989). One example is that of the southern white rhino, *Ceratotherium simum* (Burchell). Early in the twentieth century its population had declined to about ten animals, but after strict protection in South Africa the population increased to 120 by 1930, and by the 1980s there were sufficient animals to permit translocation to other parts of southern Africa (Smithers, 1983). Another, more recent example is that of the Mohor gazelle (*Gazella dama mhorr*), one of several species of the genus *Gazella* from the Western Sahara which has been bred successfully in captivity. No wild individuals have been observed since 1968, but about 190 animals are currently held in several zoos in Europe and the United States. The captive population was founded in 1971 when four male and thirteen female gazelles were taken to the Estación Experimental de Zonas Aridas (EEZA) in southern Spain; the history of this population has been described by Alados *et al.* (1988). Recently it has been possible to reintroduce Mohor gazelles into protected areas in Tunisia, Morocco and Senegal, where they are thriving (see Chapter 8).

In a wide-ranging and thoughtful review of conservation tactics, Soulé (1991) argued the case for 'eight paths to biotic survival', saying that different conservation strategies should not be regarded as conflicting, but rather should complement each other, thus providing a degree of synergism. The eight paths were defined as follows:

1   In situ. Conservation systems based on bounded wild areas with little human disturbance.
2   Inter-situ *conservation systems*. These can occur in regions where native species persist, but which are outside the bounds of established protected areas. Land in this category is typically infertile and unsuitable for farming.
3   *Extractive reserves*. Here, certain kinds of sustainable resource harvesting can be implemented. This could include rubber tapping, collection of fruit, thatch grasses and logging and hunting.
4   *Ecological restoration projects*. These would incorporate intensive management activities intended to increase species richness or productivity in degraded habitats. Political and institutional stability are essential for such activities.
5   *Zooparks*. These are facilities in secure locations where a mix of local and exogenous species can be maintained under semi-natural conditions. They can act as sanctuaries for a variety of sensitive species, even those which might never be returned to their original habitats.
6   *Agroecosystems and agroforestry projects*. These represent highly managed, production-orientated systems with a wide range of dependence on artificial chemical and

CHAPTER 2

energy inputs. It can be argued that in the appropriate context sound agroecological practices create a healthy environment and contribute to self-sufficiency and the maintenance of crop genetic resources. In addition they may reduce wood collecting, hunting and other pressures on nearby wildland.

7   *Living* ex-situ *programmes*. These include zoos, aquaria and botanical gardens whose aim is to maintain and propagate living organisms for non-commercial purposes, i.e. education and research, as well as conservation.

8   *Suspended* ex-situ *programmes*. In these, living material is metabolically arrested and maintained in seed banks and collections of cryopreserved germplasm (sperm, oocytes, embryos). Tissue culture collections are included under this heading, but it is important to recognize that such collections cannot normally be used for the propagation of animals, even though this may not be true for plants.

2.2   THE ROLE OF GENETIC RESOURCE BANKS IN CONSERVATION, AGRICULTURE AND BIOTECHNOLOGY

Soulé (1991) emphasized the value of *ex-situ* conservation as a way of maintaining species through the 'demographic winter', a centuries-long interval during which humans will eliminate essential habitat for many space-intensive species. Despite the growing environmental movement there is still overwhelming pressure on land use for human-oriented purposes and there is no pressing reason to reverse this pessimistic view. Applications of reproductive biotechnology have therefore been viewed as being able to make a potentially important contribution to species conservation, supporting the viability of extant populations through genetic management. The possibility of setting up genetic resource banks for the conservation of wild species or rare agricultural species has been suggested as a way of contributing towards these aims.

The concept that underlies the establishment and use of germplasm resource banks is essentially very simple. If gametes are maintained in a state of metabolic arrest, currently using cryopreservation, they could be used to support natural breeding programmes. If the frozen gametes were available for use within breeding programmes, and given the availability of reliable associated reproductive technologies, they could be regarded as additional genetic members of the breeding groups and would therefore increase the effective population size. With proper storage, the stored gametes have the advantage that they survive long after the death of the gamete donor, and thereby continue to augment the effective population size. The importance of maximizing 'effective population size' is in countering the trend towards loss of genetic diversity within small populations, and therefore inhibiting the potential tendency towards loss of fitness through inbreeding depression effects (Frankham, 1996). Considerable efforts have been made to provide a theoretical framework, mainly drawn from the field of population biology, within which to operate breeding programmes that minimize inbreeding (Mace and Ballou, 1990). Many captive breeding programmes have formal plans to manage small captive populations which attempt to minimize inbreeding and other processes that are believed to cause extinction. For example, a common goal is to maintain a minimum of 90% genetic diversity in a demographically stable population for 200 years (Soulé *et al.*, 1986). A range of management strategies have been established to achieve this. It is common for coordinators of captive breeding programmes to calculate statistics that estimate the degree of relatedness between individuals and subsequently to plan matings cooperatively between zoos and other organizations. More complex methods for estimating gene losses from wild-caught founder animals are also used, and management strategies are employed to minimize predicted losses of rare alleles (see Chapter 4).

The successful development of captive breeding programmes, including the applications of reproductive technologies and genetic resource bank (GRB) programmes, will depend upon advances in knowledge about the biology of the species in question. In this context increasing our knowledge of the reproductive biology of different species must be viewed as an essential activity; this view has been elaborated at some length by Wildt and his colleagues (for example, Wildt and Wemmer, 1999). Funding such research, which may be seen as lacking industrial and scientific importance, presents a major problem. It is salutary, however, to ask who will take on the responsibility?

2.3   AIMS OF GENETIC RESOURCE BANK PROGRAMMES

Genetic resource bank programmes can be organized with two rather different objectives in mind. One is the development of a collection of preserved somatic tissues, cell lines and DNA samples from diverse species, primarily for taxonomic, demographic and medical research. Here, there is no intention to breed new individuals with this material, and it can thus be stored in a variety of ways. Cryopreserved cell lines are the ideal material for this type of bank as they can be sampled non-destructively by regenerating the material whenever it is used. However, frozen tissue and blood samples are suitable for genetic analysis, and extensive use can now be made of alcohol-stored and desiccated tissues found in museums. A recent survey of centres holding cell lines and tissues from animal species (Palacios and Perez-Suarez, personal communication) showed that more than 150 centres hold organized collections of animal tissues, primarily set up for their own research purposes. Most of these were in government or university laboratories and were individually supported by institutional funds or research grants.

The alternative objective, and that which underpins this book, is explicitly aimed towards animal breeding, whether in the future or in a geographically distant location. Clearly, this type of genetic resource bank necessarily contains gametes and embryos;

however, the recent demonstration of mammalian cloning from adult cell lines implies that there is new potential for recreating individuals from cryopreserved cell lines. This is still an inefficient experimental technique, which relies upon the availability of conspecific oocytes as recipients for nuclear transfer, and so is unlikely to offer much potential for animal breeding from rare species. Laboratory and agricultural species may be more amenable to reproduction by this approach, and the inclusion of cell lines within this type of genetic resource bank programme may grow in importance. Technological advances are developing at such a pace that the need for semen cryopreservation may diminish as novel methods of assisted conception are implemented. In particular, the advent of intracytoplasmic sperm injection (ICSI), where individual spermatozoa are injected directly into the egg cytoplasm, may allow the generation of viable offspring from sperm that are incapable of normal fertilization. This may theoretically be the case, but will only be possible if reliable oocyte collection or preservation protocols are available, and if the microinjected oocytes proceed to normal development. Neither caveats are true for most species; some, but not all, recent genetic analyses indicate that ICSI-derived human embryos have a higher than normal rate of sex chromosome abnormalities (Meschede *et al.*, 1998; Aran *et al.*, 1999).

For the present time, therefore, the practical implementation of genetic resource bank programmes should concentrate on using technologies that are available today, whilst ongoing research programmes address the more esoteric possibilities. Even with this down-to-earth view, there are many associated aspects of reproductive technologies that require development, especially when dealing with unusual and rare species. The aim of this book will be to highlight these aspects, indicate methodologies that have proved successful, and point out where further research is needed.

Given that space and finance for genetic resource bank programmes will inevitably be limited, choices of gamete donors from among the population at large will have to be made. Only in the case of very small populations will it be possible to sample every individual. However, for conservation purposes this would be an ideal aim as the intention is maintenance and support of genetic diversity. Selection of gamete donors, or donor lineages, is therefore an important consideration. Johnston and Lacy (1995) addressed this issue by modelling the genetic consequences of managing captive populations of okapi, golden-headed lion tamarin, Siberian tiger and gaur with the aid of different genetic resource bank strategies. In their study, they demonstrated that although maximal retention of allelic diversity was achieved by banking genes from all living animals, nearly optimal retention of allelic and gene diversity was obtained by a selection strategy based on minimizing mean kinships. The frequency with which stored germplasm is used and replenished still requires consideration; for example, would it be better to maintain constant interchange between the banked semen and the extant population or should this only be done every few generations?

Within the framework of genetic resource banking for animal breeding, different objectives can be identified which influence the way in which such banks are set up and operate. The main categories are (1) banks for animal conservation, (2) banks for the preservation of agricultural species, and (3) banks for medical research. There are fundamental differences in concept and intention between these banks which influence the choice of materials to be stored.

The objectives of genetic resource bank programmes for agricultural and bio-technological use are considerably simpler than those for the conservation of threatened species. Here the aims are to preserve specific genetic lines without any introgression from others. Extensive experience of embryo cryopreservation now exists for laboratory mouse colonies; the number of inbred strains is now so numerous that it has become impractical to maintain separate living populations. Some arrangements for semen preservation from rare breeds of agricultural animals, mainly cattle and pigs, have been set up, for example by the Rare Breeds Survival Trust in the UK. Although the physical organization and security of these collections is somewhat *ad hoc*, the Trust has developed a genetically based policy for integrating decisions on the collection and storage of the spermatozoa from individual animals into its breeding programmes. In this instance, the individual samples are treated as if they were animals.

2.4   CONCLUDING REMARKS

Reproductive biology as a discipline operates within a conceptual framework of ideas and knowledge, developed over many decades. However, hi-tech applications that catch media attention, such as cloning and interspecies embryo transfer, are often perceived as the only benefits arising from our knowledge of reproduction. Cryobiology also has both conceptual and biological depth, such as understanding how life survives naturally in low-temperature environments, but this discipline has also developed a wide-ranging set of techniques for preserving live tissues and cells for prolonged periods. Genetic resource banking combines the practical aspects of both disciplines for specific, but widely applicable reasons. The applied nature of this topic should not, however, overshadow the fact that extensive research into the natural history and fundamental biology underpinning these disciplines is necessary if the applications are to be widely and reliably used.

REFERENCES

ALADOS, C. L., ESCOS, J. and VERICAD, J.-R. (1988) 'Captive populations of northwest African antilopinae and caprinae at the Estacion Experimental de Zonas Aridas', in Dixon A, and Jones D. (eds) *Conservation and Biology of Desert Antelopes*, Bromley: Christopher Helm, pp. 199–211.

CHAPTER 2

ARAN, B., BLANCO, J., VIDAL, F., VENDRELL, J. M., EGOZCUE, S., BARRI, P. N., EGOZCUE, J. and VEIGA, A. (1999) 'Screening for abnormalities of chromosomes X, Y, and 18 and for diploidy in spermatozoa from infertile men participating in an *in vitro* fertilization-intracytoplasmic sperm injection program', *Fertil. Steril.* **72**, 696–701.

BOWMAN, D. M. J. S. (1993) 'Biodiversity; much more than biological inventory', *Biodivers Lett.* **1**, 163.

FRANKHAM, R. (1996) 'Relationship of genetic variation to population size in wildlife', *Conserv. Biol.* **10**, 1500–1508.

GASTON, K. J. (1996) 'What is biodiversity?', in Gaston, K. J. (ed.) *Biodiversity. A Biology of Numbers and Differences,* Oxford: Blackwell Science, pp. 1–9.

GINSBERG, J. (1994) 'Captive breeding, reintroduction and the conservation of canids', in Olney, P., Mace, G. and Feistner, A. (eds) *Creative Conservation: Interactive Management of Wild and Captive Animals,* London: Chapman and Hall, pp. 365–383.

JOHNSTON, L. A. and LACY, R. C. (1995) 'Genome resource banking for species conservation selection of sperm donors', *Cryobiology* **32**, 68–77.

KUNIN, W. E. and LAWTON, J. H. (1996) 'Does biodiversity matter? Evaluating the case for conserving species', in Gaston, K.J. (ed.) *Biodiversity. A Biology of Numbers and Differences,* Oxford: Blackwell Science, pp. 283–308.

LOVELOCK, J. E. (1989) 'Geophysiology, the science of Gaia' *Rev. Geophys.,* **27**, 215–222.

MACE, G. M. and BALLOU, J. D. (1990) 'Population management for conservation'. *TREE* **5**, 102–104.

MESCHEDE, D., LEMCKE, B., EXELER, J. R., DEGEYTER, C., BEHRE, H. M., NIESCHLAG, E. and HORST, J. (1998) 'Chromosome abnormalities in 447 couples undergoing intracyto-plasmic sperm injection–prevalence, types, sex distribution and reproductive relevance', *Hum. Reprod.* **13**, 576–582.

SMITHERS, R. I. N. (1983) *The Mammals of the Southern African Subregion,* Pretoria: University of Pretoria.

SOULÉ, M. E. (1991) 'Conservation tactics for a constant crisis', *Science* **253**, 744–749.

SOULÉ, M., GILPIN, M., CONWAY, W. and FOOSE, T. (1986) 'The Millennium Ark–How long a voyage, how many staterooms, how many passengers?', *Zoo Biol.* **5**, 101–113.

STANLEY-PRICE, M. R. (1989) *Animal Reintroductions: the Arabian Oryx in Oman,* Cambridge: Cambridge University Press.

WILDT, D. E. (1992) 'Genetic resource banks for conserving wildlife species: justification, examples and becoming organized on a global basis', *Anim. Reprod. Sci.* **28**, 247–257.

WILDT, D. E. (1997) 'Genome resource banking. Impact on biotic conservation and society', in Karow, A. M. and Critser, J. (eds) *Reproductive Tissue Banking,* New York: Academic Press, pp. 399–439.

WILDT, D. E. and WEMMER, C. (1999) 'Sex and wildlife: the role of reproductive science in conservation', *Biodivers. Conserv.* **8**, 965–976.

WILSON, E. O. (1992) *The Diversity of Life,* London: Allen Lane/The Penguin Press.

CHAPTER 2

Principles of Cryopreservation of Gametes and Embryos

P. F. WATSON[1] AND B. J. FULLER[2]

[1]Department of Veterinary Basic Sciences, The Royal Veterinary College, London NW1 0TU, UK; [2]Academic Department of Surgery, Royal Free and University College Hospital School of Medicine, Pond Street, London NW3 2QG

Contents

3.1 INTRODUCTION

The cryopreservation of reproductive cells and embryos embraces a science in which there is a considerable background of theory. Since the discovery of the cryoprotective actions of glycerol (Polge *et al.*, 1949), a wealth of experience of freezing and thawing a great variety cells and tissues has been accumulated, not least that associated with cryostorage of spermatozoa and embryos. The oocyte, on the other hand, has so far largely evaded a satisfactory solution, presenting as it does a large cell which is highly differentiated and arrested part-way through the reduction divisions of meiosis in which the genetic information is mixed and the chromosome complement is halved. Its specialization implies that the unique features peculiar to its state must be preserved in order for it to carry out its purpose. While this can also be true of spermatozoa, their number allows less than optimal procedures to be acceptable *pro tem*. Oocytes, however, are available in strictly limited numbers; thus, cryopreserving protocols have to be very successful before they become very useful. In this chapter, the basic considerations to be borne in mind when freezing cells are briefly considered.

For cryopreservation of reproductive cells, the final storage temperature has often been dictated by practicalities of the nature of the cooling agent available. Early studies (Polge *et al.*, 1949) used solid carbon dioxide (at a temperature of $-79°C$), but with the increased availability of liquid nitrogen from the late 1950s, this has become the cryogen routinely used for storage (at a temperature of $-196°C$ in the liquid phase, or within the range -140 to $-160°C$ if samples are stored in the vapour just above the liquid surface).

3.2 BASIC CRYOBIOLOGICAL THEORY

For successful low-temperature storage, cells need to be cooled below about $-100°C$, and under these conditions they may remain viable for many years (Mazur *et al.*, 1981). They also need to be protected from the effects of freezing by adding particular 'antifreezes' or cryoprotectants (see Section 3.4.1) to avoid irreparable damage. The biological and biophysical responses that occur when cooling from normal ambient temperatures to these ultra-low temperatures are complex, and our understanding of these has only gradually increased over the past fifty years (Mazur, 1984). Many parts of the puzzle remain to be pieced together, but we have provided the following brief summary as an introduction to what will follow in subsequent chapters. More detailed explanations can be found elsewhere (Mazur, 1990).

When a solution is cooled below its freezing point, it is initially supercooled, i.e. it remains liquid at a temperature colder than the 'true' or equilibrium freezing temperature. This is an unstable condition and as the temperature is lowered further the probability of ice nucleation increases and crystals begin to form. The solution

CHAPTER 3

therefore becomes more concentrated as pure water crystallizes out as ice and the proportion of solution remaining liquid is reduced. As cooling proceeds further, so more of the liquid water crystallizes and the solution becomes ever more concentrated, reaching osmolality values greater than 20 times isosmotic at temperatures approaching $-40°C$ (Mazur et al., 1981). Below this temperature range, the small, highly concentrated residual solution finally becomes a solid as the eutectic temperature of the mixture is passed.

If the solution contains a suspension of cells as ice crystallization progresses, the more concentrated extracellular solution results in water being drawn out of the cell by osmosis, and the cell volume diminishes. If cooling is sufficiently slow, the intracellular water content remains in equilibrium with the extracellular solution such that no ice forms within the cell. However, if the cooling rate is significantly faster than this equilibrium rate, sufficient water does not have time to leave the cell during cooling to avoid excessive intracellular supercooling of the intracellular liquid and the same process of ice crystal nucleation and growth can then take place inside the cell. Should this occur, the cell will not survive.

The recovery of viable cells from cryopreservation depends on many variables, but concentrating only on the effects of cooling rate, it has been noted that for many cells, maximum survival was associated with the use of a specific range of cooling rates. Recoveries were poorer if either slower or faster rates were applied (producing an inverted 'U'-shaped survival curve). These observations led to the formulation of a 'two-factor' hypothesis to explain cell survival during freezing in a quantitative fashion (Mazur, 1965), in which intracellular ice formation is the factor dictating cell death at the high end of the cooling rate curve.

At the low end of the cooling rate curve are the so-called 'solution effects' experienced by the cells during freezing, i.e. the exposure of cells to the changing hypertonic liquid environment as ice crystallizes out of solution (Mazur, 1965). During very slow cooling, cells will be exposed to the extreme hypertonic conditions in the residual liquid fraction for a sufficiently long period to experience damage before reaching the 'safe' ultra-low temperatures used for storage. Whether the solution effects are due to the high salt concentration per se, the physical reduction in liquid space compacting the cells, the physical relationship between the cells and the surrounding ice matrix, pH fluctuations with temperature and concentration of buffers, or to some other aspect of the events, has not been satisfactorily demonstrated.

For spermatozoa it has been difficult to test some aspects of the 'two-factor' hypothesis because of the small size, the irregular shape and the relative fragility of the plasma membranes, although in the last few years methods have been developed to examine these phenomena. However, the large size and regular structure of oocytes and early-stage embryos has made them an ideal target for direct microscopical study of the effects of cell cryopreservation. From such observations, and measurements of the cell membrane permeability to water, it proved possible to extrapolate the observed cooling rates at which intracellular ice formed (Leibo *et al.*, 1974) or extreme dehydration took place (Leibo, 1977) to those predicted from Mazur's equations, and a close fit was achieved, strengthening the acceptance of the 'two-factor' hypothesis (see Mazur, 1985; Watson, 1990; Critser *et al.*, 1997; Paynter *et al.*, 1997).

Some aspects of the freezing process are worthy of further comment. In practice, reproductive cells are often cooled at rates yielding a quasi-equilibrium state, resulting in a minute amount of intracellular ice which is still compatible with cell survival providing warming rates are rapid (Mazur, 1990). This does not allow time for ice crystal growth, a process known as recrystallization, which may become lethal for cells.

The initiation of ice crystal growth during freezing is important. Because of the physical requirements of crystal formation, molecules in solution need to be ordered in particular configurations to start the process. Crystals tend to grow from nucleation centres, such as other crystalline material or solid particles. In cell suspensions, there are few such nucleation centres, and thus unless the initiation of ice crystallization is controlled it may not take place until cooling has proceeded by more than 10°C below the equilibrium freezing point, particularly in a solution with added cryoprotectant, resulting in a considerable fluctuation in the cooling profile of the sample as the latent heat of ice formation is released at this stage of the cooling profile. There is some evidence that this may be detrimental to spermatozoa (Critser *et al.*, 1987; Fiser, 1988; Ritar *et al.*, 1990) but the gain in eliminating the temperature fluctuation has not necessarily been shown to be consistently beneficial (Watson and Martin, 1975; Fiser *et al.*, 1991).

However, there is certainly considerable evidence that oocytes can be damaged if ice crystal formation is not controlled, and this may relate to the initiation of sites of intracellular freezing (Trad *et al.*, 1998). Similar concerns about the negative effects of uncontrolled ice nucleation during embryo cryopreservation have also been raised (Trounson, 1990). Thus, most groups involved in oocyte and embryo cryopreservation take specific precautions to control ice nucleation. Spontaneous nucleation can be achieved by pausing the cooling protocol just below the equilibrium freezing point of the mixture and touching the container with a metal instrument, such as forceps, cooled in liquid nitrogen (the most common method), by pulsing an extra short flux of liquid nitrogen into the cooling machine, by a Peltier localized cooling device in the freezing rack, by vibration or by proprietary seeding agents. The method is often dictated by practical considerations – for example, it is easy to deal with a few samples containing embryos by the forceps method, but if a large number of samples are being frozen at one time, it can be time-consuming and difficult to coordinate. It is essential to ensure that seeding has indeed been initiated and that the sample has stabilized before proceeding with cooling.

■ CHAPTER 3 ■

Another major issue to consider is the method of rewarming the cryopreserved cells from deep subzero temperatures. In general, it has been considered that it is best to reverse the temperature profile as quickly as possible, because of the concerns about intracellular freezing taking place during rewarming. Although at face value this sounds an unlikely scenario, this has been demonstrated during rewarming of mouse embryos (Rall, 1987) and spermatozoa (Watson *et al.*, unpublished). It is thought to occur by water molecules 'adding on' to small nucleation sites within the cells which formed during cooling but were unable to grow in the time of the freezing protocol. As water molecules become more mobile at higher subzero temperatures (above about −60°C), it is kinetically favourable for small ice nuclei to merge and grow into larger crystals, and if this takes place intracellularly, it may be lethal.

In some specialized cases, cryopreservation has been attempted under conditions where the formation of ice crystals is either severely limited or inhibited altogether, producing a 'glassy' solid at very low temperatures (Rall and Fahy, 1985), a process known as vitrification. This requires a combination of specific additives and control of cooling and warming. It is not universally accepted as a reliable method for cryo-preserving reproductive cells, but has been used in a variety of recent work (Paynter *et al.*, 1997; Kuleshova *et al.*, 1999).

3.3 THE CAUSES OF CRYOINJURY

The responses to cryopreservation within the reproductive cells of interest in this text are essentially dictated by the biology of each cell type.

3.3.1 Spermatozoa

The spermatozoon is a highly specialized end-differentiated cell. Its cytoplasm is limited and its surface area:volume ratio is considerable due to the long extension of the tail. Many common organelles are absent (e.g. the Golgi apparatus, ribosomes), but specialized organelles are present with particular functions during the processes leading to fertilization and early development, such as the acrosome and the proximal centriole (Figure 3.1). Moreover, its plasma membrane is regionally specialized. Such considerations are important for cryopreservation since spermatozoa cannot be considered as typical somatic cells.

3.3.2 Oocytes

The female gamete, the oocyte, is a much larger cell and by the time of ovulation, in most mammalian species, it has a diameter of close to 100 μm (Bernard, 1991). At this stage, it has undergone maturation within the ovarian follicle to achieve reductive division, and is ovulated at the stage of metaphase of the second meiotic division (MII). This has particular relevance to many of the concerns surrounding cryopreservation, because at MII the chromosomes are arranged in a particular configuration on the

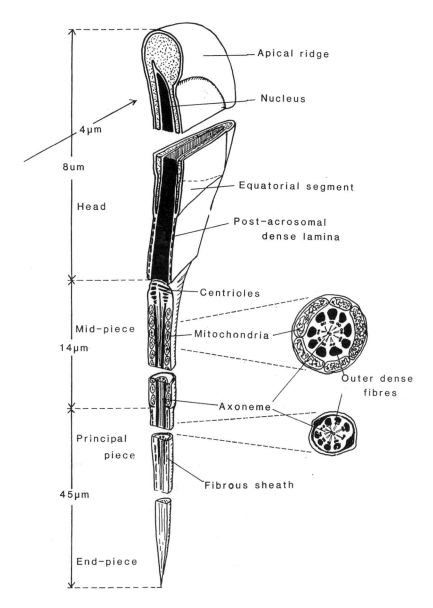

Figure 3.1: Diagrammatic drawing of the structure of ram spermatozoa. Note the extreme dorso-ventral flattening and the regionalization of the acrosome, nucleus, mitochondria and axoneme. All mammalian spermatozoa are constructed on a similar organization, although the shape varies due to the variations in the shape of the nucleus and acrosome. In electron microscopical sections, only the cut edge is generally seen, which can be misleading to the inexperienced eye.

meiotic spindle, and are not protected by a nuclear envelope. Also, the oocyte is surrounded by a proteinaceous coat (the zona pellucida), which plays an important role in normal fertilization, and is another target for cryopreservation damage. There have been several important studies on the sensitivity of these highly specialized structures to cooling, addition of cryoprotectant solutions and ice formation which can be found in recent reviews (Bernard and Fuller, 1996; Critser *et al.*, 1997). It is nevertheless worth highlighting a few of the more important consequences of these effects on the oocyte. Both reduction in temperature (even before the point of ice formation) and the addition of cryoprotectant solutions have been shown to cause disassembly of the meiotic spindle (Pickering and Johnson, 1987; Vincent *et al.*, 1990) with potential displacement of maternal chromosomes leading to concerns about genetic damage post-fertilization. Figure 3.2 shows two mouse oocytes stained by immunocytochemical techniques to visualize the meiotic spindles with their associated chromosomes. It is easy to appreciate how individual chromosomes could be lost if the spindles were severely disrupted. However, it is possible to select protocols that minimize or circumvent some of these effects (Bernard and Fuller, 1996), and there is also the potential for spindle reorganization during a period of culture after these stresses (George and Johnson, 1993), but these problems should always be borne

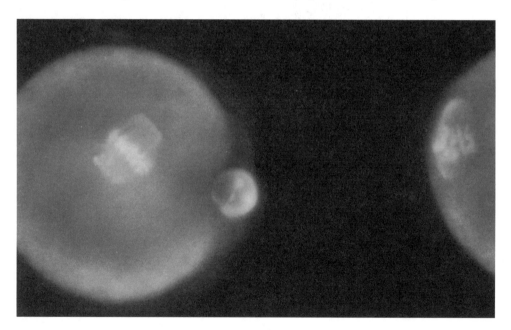

Figure 3.2: Photomicrograph of two adjacent mouse MII oocytes, stained with fluorescent antibodies against tubulin to visualize the meiotic spindle. In the left-hand oocyte, a normal barrel-shaped spindle can be seen with chromosomes aligned along the central plate. The small, brightly staining cells to the edges of both oocytes are the extruded first polar bodies, which define the MII state of maturation. Reproduced from O'Neil *et al.* (1997b), with permission from *Cryo-Letters*.

in mind when approaching oocyte cryopreservation. Indeed, there have been some studies relating post-cryopreservation genetic aneuploidy to these effects (Kola *et al.*, 1988), although considering the large number of studies now performed on mammalian oocyte cryopreservation, particularly in laboratory and domestic species, the number of such reports remain encouragingly low. However, there is no room for complacency, and more detailed, long-term follow-up on offspring from cryopreserved oocytes will be essential.

Another major concern in oocyte cryopreservation is the sensitivity of the zona pellucida. During normal fertilization, after the sperm and oocyte have fused, there are special structures in the cortex of the oocyte (the cortical granules), which release enzymes to act on the zona effectively 'toughening' the coat and reducing the ability of other spermatozoa to penetrate the protective layer. Again, the various stresses associated with cryopreservation can lead to an abnormal early release of the enzymes before fertilization (Vincent *et al.*, 1990), making the oocyte unfertilizable. There are ways to modify the culture medium to minimize this risk (Carroll *et al.*, 1993), and due to recent technical advances there are now ways to inject sperm directly into the cryopreserved oocyte (Gook *et al.*, 1995). Nevertheless, it will be obvious that in many species, successful cryopreservation of MII oocytes remains a significant challenge.

It should be pointed out that there are theoretical grounds favouring cryo-preservation of the immature oocyte, i.e. before germinal vesicle breakdown and while the chromosome complement is still surrounded by the nuclear membrane. Immature oocytes have been successfully cryopreserved in some species such as mice (Candy *et al.*, 1994). However, such approaches also increase the complexity of the strategies for assisted reproduction because they depend upon the ability to mature the recovered immature oocyte *in vitro* up to a stage where normal fertilization can be achieved (Figure 3.3).

Another approach to cryopreservation of immature oocytes is that of cryo-preserving slices of ovarian tissue, which contain growing oocytes within the various stages of primary and secondary follicles within the tissue. It has been known for some forty years that some follicles within ovarian tissue can survive cryopreservation (Parrot, 1960) and go on to develop normally after grafting into the ovarian bursa in mice. Tissue cryopreservation in theory allows the option of either grafting the thawed tissue to establish fertility (but tissue transplantation between individuals is subject to the same allo-immune rejection as any other donor graft) or isolating immature oocytes from the tissue for subsequent maturation in culture for normal *in vitro* fertilization (IVF) procedures (but this depends on the availability of sophisticated culture methods to promote follicle development over many days). Nevertheless, several groups have undertaken studies on ovarian tissue cryopreservation, and the results have been recently reviewed (Paynter *et al.*, 1997; Ludwig *et al.*, 1999). A live birth was reported in a sheep given cryopreserved ovarian tissue as an autograft

CHAPTER 3

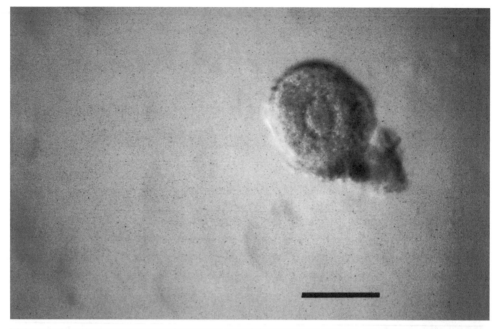

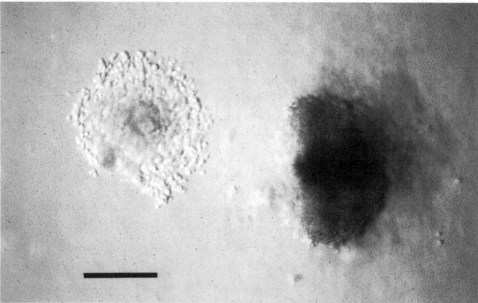

Figure 3.3: Photomicrographs of isolated murine follicular complexes. (A) A freshly isolated follicular/granulosa cell complex at the preantral stage with some theca attached and a centrally located immature oocyte. (B) The same individual culture after 6 days, showing an extruded cumulus/oocyte complexes (on the left-hand side), and leaving an empty follicular cell mass (on the right-hand side). Note that the cumulus/oocyte complex has grown to a larger size than the original follicle during the culture period (scale bars 100 μm). Kindly provided by P. Ashley, University of Wales College of Medicine, UK.

(Gosden *et al.*, 1994), and the same group have recently reported a restoration of folliculogenesis following autografting ovarian tissue into a young woman who had been previously been rendered infertile following bilateral oophorectomy for a medical condition (Oktay *et al.*, 1999). However, much further work will be required to accomplish consistent success with ovarian tissue cryopreservation, not least because normal oocyte growth within the follicle depends upon a set of complex interactions between the surrounding follicular cells and the gamete which could easily be disrupted by the freezing process.

3.3.3 Embryos

After fertilization and the completion of the second meiotic division, subsequent developmental changes in preimplantation embryos tend to improve their resilience to cryopreservation. In many species there is an early change in membrane permeability to cryoprotective agents (Jackowski *et al.*, 1980) which makes their addition and removal less hazardous, whilst consecutive cell divisions increase the number and reduce the size of the blastomeres. In this situation, it is possible to 'lose' a number of blastomeres in multicellular embryos to cryopreservation damage and still achieve embryonic development. However, excessive blastomere loss is associated with reduced embryo survival (Alikani *et al.*, 1993) and may point to the use of a suboptimal cryopreservation protocol (Lehn-Jensen and Rall, 1983). Nevertheless, It has generally been acknowledged that in most species, embryos are 'easier' to cryopreserve than oocytes (Gelety and Surrey, 1993). However, 'easier' is a relative term, and attention still needs to be paid to all aspects of a cryopreservation programme to achieve consistent success. Embryonic stages from the single cell through to blastocyst stages have been preserved in a variety of species (Bernard, 1991). It is, nevertheless, worth commenting on a few points of concern in embryo cryopreservation. During early preimplantation development, the blastomeres are still surrounded by the zona pellucida, and this acellular structure can also be damaged by the rigours of cryopreservation. Cracks or splits in the zonae of cryopreserved embryos have been noted for some time and have been termed fracture damage (Rall and Meyer, 1989). In some studies, zona fracture has been found to impact negatively on the outcome of embryo cryopreservation (Van den Abbeel and Van Steirteghem, 2000).

3.4 THE STRESSES OF CRYOPRESERVATION

Moving on from the specific biological factors of reproductive cells which impact on cryopreservation, essentially, there are three stresses to which cells are exposed as they are frozen and thawed to the temperature of liquid nitrogen (−196°C). These are, first, the adverse effects of dilution in cryopreserving media; second, the effects of the changing temperature; and third, the effects of the consequences of freezing water out of solution as ice during cooling and dissolving it again during thawing. Although for much of the protocol these latter two occur simultaneously, they should be regarded as separate sources of injury.

3.4.1 Cryoprotectant effects

It has been known for a long time that glycerol is toxic for spermatozoa of many species. Nevertheless, it remains the most beneficial cryoprotectant additive for spermatozoa (see Watson, 1990) and therefore its toxic effects have to be balanced against its beneficial effects. Concentrations of approximately 0.5—1.5 M (~4—10% v/v) are usual, although, because of an extreme sensitivity to the toxicity of glycerol, an even lower concentration of 2% has been used for boar spermatozoa (Paquignon, 1985). The perceived role of glycerol is to mix throughout the water phase of the diluent and to reduce the amount of ice at any temperature below the freezing point.

This so-called colligative action results in a lower salt concentration at any given temperature below the freezing point in the presence of glycerol. However, it is a permeating cryoprotectant and therefore penetrates the cell membrane and may also have a range of other effects on living cells (Hammerstedt and Graham, 1992). Depending on the permeability of the cell membrane, glycerol may exert transitory osmotic effects on the cell that may cause cell volume fluctuations incompatible with survival (Gao et al., 1995). Awareness of such stresses is essential in order to institute steps in the protocol to minimize their influence, for example, by subdividing the addition and removal into a series of steps (Gao et al., 1995). For spermatozoa, however, since the concentrations of glycerol generally tend towards the lower end of the spectrum (−0.5 M) the effects are likely to be relatively less severe. Nevertheless, this is a matter to be borne in mind in devising a protocol for a new species.

Other aspects of sperm cryopreservation diluents have been thoroughly reviewed, including the addition of egg yolk and milk as protective agents and the use of glucose or lactose as osmotic agents with the addition of sodium choride and other common ions to provide sufficient ionic strength (see Watson and Martin, 1975; Watson, 1990). One particularly noticeable aspect of stallion sperm preservation is the need to reduce the concentration of seminal plasma, especially if entire rather than fractionated ejaculates are preserved. Stallion seminal plasma appears to compromise the storage of spermatozoa (see Amann and Pickett, 1987).

In the case of oocytes, problems with the interaction of cryoprotectant solutions and the ultrastructural components of the specialized cell have been mentioned above. However, there are targets additional to the microtubules of the spindle, and these include the microfilament network in the cortex of the oocyte, which can also suffer disruption by chemical interaction with the cryoprotectant (Vincent and Johnson,

1992). Several cryoprotective agents have been investigated for both oocytes and embryos, but the most frequently used include dimethyl sulphoxide (DMSO), 1,2-propanediol (PrOH) and, to a lesser extent, glycerol and ethylene glycol (EG) (Bernard, 1991; Paynter *et al.*, 1997). Because high concentrations of the solutes (typically in the range of 1–2 M) are required, osmotic damage can easily be induced during removal and addition of the agents. For example, exposure of oocytes to cryoprotectants such as DMSO causes rapid volume reduction as water is drawn out of the cells by osmotic forces (Figure 3.4). The oocyte cell volume returns towards normal only as the cryoprotectant and associated water start to diffuse back into the cell. The influx is dictated by the cell membrane permeability to the cryoprotectant, and is slower at lower temperatures (Figure 3.4).

Methods have been developed to reduce damage from anisovolumetric changes, particularly during removal from cryoprotectant, by performing gradual step-dilution and by incorporating an osmotic buffer such as sucrose in the washing steps (Bernard and Fuller, 1996). The temperature and time of exposure to the cryoprotectant solutions are also carefully controlled to reduce chemical toxicity. This is particularly important when non-equilibrium rapid cooling or vitrification techniques are being used (Critser *et al.*, 1997), where concentrations of agents such as DMSO are as high as 6 M (Wood *et al.*, 1993). In some cases, to achieve an overall high concentration of

CHAPTER 3

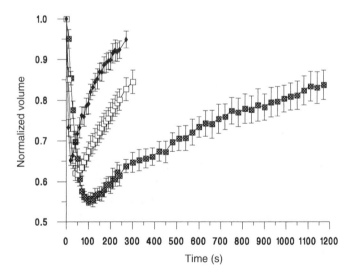

Figure 3.4: Volume changes in human oocytes following exposure to cryoprotectant DMSO at different temperatures (♦, 10°C; □, 24°C; ■, 30°C). It can be seen that exposure to DMSO at 1.5 M caused a rapid osmotic shrinkage at all temperatures. Oocyte volumes returned towards normal values as cryoprotectant and associated water diffused back into the cells, and this occurred at faster rates when higher exposure temperatures were used. Reproduced from Paynter *et al.* (1999) with permission from Human Reproduction and Clarendon Press, Oxford.

cryoprotectant for vitrification whilst avoiding individual chemical toxicity, mixtures of several agents have been used (Rall and Fahy, 1985).

For cryopreservation of preimplantation embryos, the same general principles apply for avoiding cryoprotectant damage. It is worth noting, however, that glycerol may be an efficient additive for embryos (Bernard and Fuller, 1983), and seems particularly useful for cryopreserving late-stage embryos such as blastocysts (Menezo *et al.*, 1992). A recent area of interest has been the use of growth factors to reverse some of the cryopreservation-induced damage in blastocysts (Desai *et al.*, 2000).

3.4.2 Temperature effects

Temperature effects can be separated from the ice crystal effects by considering responses in the temperature range above the temperature at which water freezes. Mammalian spermatozoa show a variable degree of adverse response to reduced temperature depending upon species, and this can be illustrated by the susceptibility to cold shock which is an extreme form of temperature stress. Ungulate spermatozoa are especially sensitive to cold shock although differences in degree of sensitivity exist between species; consequently, most authors recommend slow cooling from ambient temperature to +4°C (see Watson, 1979, 1990). It is still not clear why the faster cooling rates are more damaging to spermatozoa of many species, although most studies link it to the question of phase events in the membranes (Watson, 1981). Watson and Morris (1987) suggested that it could be due to loss of membrane integrity because of multiple packing faults in the lipid bilayer as a result of phase changes in the lipids.

The injury is manifested as a loss of the barrier function of the plasma membrane, and is therefore probably associated with the change in phase of the membrane lipids as the temperature is lowered. More subtly, it may also relate to the differences in lipid phase between the outer and the inner leaflet and to the variability in the fatty acids in the different phospholipid classes. The range of temperature that is most damaging invariably appears to be the same range at which profound phase changes are also demonstrable, i.e. between 20°C and 0°C. Those species in which cold shock is most profound display the most pronounced phase events, e.g. pig (Drobnis *et al.*, 1993).

The phenomenon of cold shock has not been universally recognized in the cooling of embryos and oocytes, even from those species whose spermatozoa show most sensitivity. However, there are some exceptions. Most notable is the example of the pig, whose gametes and embryos all show extreme sensitivity to cooling below about 18°C. However, this is temperature sensitivity *per se* rather than a cold shock sensitivity, since it is unrelated to the rate of cooling. In general, it is common, in cooling gametes and embryos from all species from room temperature to 0–4°C, to avoid very rapid temperature change. More recently, however, attention has been paid to a possible cold shock phenomenon in bovine oocytes, but in this case it has been suggested that very rapid cooling rates should be used during cryopreservation to try to 'outpace' the cold shock (Martino *et al.*, 1996).

It is a well-attested phenomenon that in any given species there are very real differences between individuals in the response of their spermatozoa to cryo-preservation. This is apparently widely applicable but is accentuated more in some species than others. Among mammals, it is very evident in horse and pig spermatozoa. In recent years, it has been recognized between strains of mice and thus may have a genetic basis which is currently being investigated. The same concerns have been voiced about cryopreserving embryos and oocytes, although little evidence currently exists. In embryo freezing, however, there may be differences for post-thaw recovery between embryos within the same cohort (Wood, 1997), which may relate to differences in embryo maturation at ovulation, or the condition of each embryo in culture before cryopreservation (i.e. the number of fragmented blastomeres already present).

3.4.3 Ice formation and dissolution effects

Much attention has been devoted over the past few years to understanding the causes of cell injury during ice formation and dissolution. The maximum cooling rate consistent with the avoidance of intracellular ice is determined by the water permeability of the plasma membrane and its activation energy, the cell surface area and the volume of intracellular water, as demonstrated by Mazur's original cell dehydration model (Mazur, 1963). With the exception of rabbit spermatozoa (Curry *et al.*, 1995), the permeability values of the plasma membrane of a number of species are remarkably high (see Watson, 1995). Using these values in formulae originally proposed by Mazur (1963) to predict the movement of water across the cell membrane at various cooling rates, attempts have been made to model the dehydration of mammalian spermatozoa and to predict the maximum cooling rate permitting preservation without the formation of intracellular ice (Duncan and Watson, 1992; Noiles *et al.*, 1993; Gilmour *et al.*, 1995). Comparisons with empirically determined cooling rates giving optimal survival can then be used to determine the accuracy of the model. Curry *et al.* (1994) found that the model gave predictions three orders of magnitude faster than empirically determined rates for ram and human spermatozoa, and concluded that the model did not relate to the true causes of cell injury in spermatozoa. In the presence of cryoprotectant the water permeability of the sperm membrane was much lower (Gilmour *et al.*, 1995) and also perhaps below the freezing point of the external medium, suggesting possible explanations of the discrepancy. A further discussion of these phenomena can be found in Watson (2000).

Further studies (Gao *et al.*, 1993; Curry and Watson, 1994) led to the conclusion that an important additional component in the cryopreservation of spermatozoa was the osmotic stress across the cell membranes induced by the increasing osmolarity of the external medium. This factor assumes major importance given the centrality of membrane events in the subsequent function of spermatozoa. The phenomenon is related to the inward passage of water to the cell, rather than the outward passage, and is apparently proportional to the volume of water moving in unit time, i.e. the rate of passage; osmotic injury is therefore probably manifested during warming and rehydration rather than during cooling (Gao *et al.*, 1993; Curry and Watson, 1994; Holt and North, 1994). Given the high permeability of sperm membranes to water, injury is probably not due to structural disruption from water flow, that is, so-called 'frictional' injury (Muldrew and McGann, 1994), but may be due to disruption of cytoskeletal elements by too rapid movement of the membrane to accommodate the increased volume. This evidence is supported by the conclusions from other studies that have tended to stress the importance of thawing injury. Attention should thus be focussed on ways in which the osmotic stress might be modified, or alternatively, how the membrane might be made more resistant to the osmotic stresses.

Embryos and oocytes are equally susceptible to osmotic events induced during conventional slow freezing methods and thawing. Considerable efforts have been made to quantitate the permeability of these cells to water and cryoprotectant additives (Jackowski *et al.*, 1980; Mazur, 1990; Hunter *et al.*, 1992; Paynter *et al.*, 1997) so that cryopreservation protocols can be proposed which avoid the twin perils of osmotic damage and intracellular ice formation. Permeability studies of these cells can be made by direct volume measurements from real-time microscopy during cryoprotectant exposure or ice formation (Toner *et al.*, 1990; Paynter *et al.*, 1999) and modelled to quantitative transport equations. These derived variables can then be used to predict the rates of cryoprotectant exposure and cooling which will have the best chances of avoiding damage. Such prospective modelling has already shown promise in developing an optimized cryopreservation protocol for mouse oocytes (Karlsson *et al.*, 1996). Because of the dimensions and small surface:volume ratio, both oocytes and embryos must be cooled slowly during conventional cryopreservation in order to allow adequate dehydration to prevent intracellular freezing. Early studies for both embryos (Whittingham *et al.*, 1972) and oocytes (Whittingham, 1977) established a protocol based on slow cooling to temperatures below $-60°C$ before transfer to liquid nitrogen, together with slow rewarming, and such approaches have consistently been found to be successful (Cooper *et al.*, 1998). However, success has been equally achieved in some studies by terminating cooling at higher subzero temperatures (-30 to $-40°C$) and then rewarming as quickly as possible (Paynter *et al.*, 1997). Much depends upon the propensity of each particular oocyte or embryo type to succumb to either osmotic dehydration during freezing or intracellular ice nucleation.

3.5 VITRIFICATION

Because of the difficulties with managing the ice formation and cellular dehydration, an alternative preservation approach was developed in the 1980s. In this method, high levels of cryoprotectant are introduced (up to 6 M) and cooling is carried out relatively rapidly. The extracellular medium and the intracellular solution undergo glass transition, forming a stable solid structure without ice formation. As long as rewarming is carried out carefully (generally rapidly), no ice formation occurs and the cells are returned to ambient temperature without the considerable cellular distortion seen with conventional freezing. However, it is generally recognized that the state which can be achieved by cooling biological samples such as embryos or oocytes is, in effect, a quasi-vitrified state, containing potential intracellular ice nuclei, which is why rewarming has to be as rapid as possible. The addition of such high concentrations of cryoprotectants causes a degree of dehydration prior to cooling which may be temporary or prolonged, depending on whether the cryoprotectants are permeating or non-permeating. The permeating cryoprotectants generally considered are glycerol, DMSO, EG, PrOH, and the non-penetrating agents are polyvinyl pyrollidone (PVP), sugars or (PEG) and hydromethyl starch (HES). Generally, combinations are preferred because this reduces the final concentration of any one cryoprotectant and thus its potential toxicity.

Such methods have been established for embryos (Rall and Fahy, 1985; Trounson, 1990) and, more recently, for oocytes (Wood *et al.*, 1993; Kuleshova *et al.*, 1999). The 'glassy' state of the samples at low temperatures is especially fragile. It is possible to fracture the sample through embryos or oocytes during handling or rewarming, and to cause problems such as zona fracture. The inclusion of high concentrations of macromolecules partially avoids this problem (O'Neil *et al.*, 1997a) perhaps by stabilizing the glass. To date, these methods have not been successfully introduced for spermatozoa because of their sensitivity to the toxicity of the high cryoprotectant concentrations necessary for vitrification.

3.6 OTHER CONSIDERATIONS OF CRYOPRESERVATION

3.6.1 Subtle effects of cooling

Membrane injury sets in train the processes of oxidative damage by free radicals. So-called reactive oxygen species (ROS) become involved in cyclical processes that can rapidly destroy viability in cells. Such damage has been implicated in cryopreserved spermatozoa (Bilodeau *et al.*, 2000), and is a potential danger in any cell suffering membrane injury during freezing and thawing.

Apart from the question of gross injury to membranes with the resulting loss of cell viability, it has also become apparent in the past few years that surviving cooled or frozen thawed spermatozoa are not in the same condition they were before cooling. This is manifested by a number of observations of their subsequent function, as reviewed by Watson (1995). In summary, cooled and rewarmed spermatozoa resemble capacitated spermatozoa in that they are more readily induced to undergo the acrosome reaction and have a less stable membrane and a shorter life expectancy. In addition, motility patterns are different, and poorer than those of fresh spermatozoa. Fertility *in vitro*, however, is comparable with that of fresh spermatozoa on a equal sperm number basis, indicating that given close association with the oocyte, penetration and fertilization will occur. Thus the poor fertility of cryopreserved spermatozoa inseminated via the cervix is due to failure to sustain survival for long enough for passage in the female tract rather than any inherent impairment of the fertilizing capacity. Much less is known about the likelihood of ROS effects in the cryopreservation of oocytes or embryos.

3.6.2 Packaging

Originally, spermatozoa were packaged for freezing in glass ampoules (~ 1 ml). These have generally given way to plastic straws (0.5 or 0.25 ml) sealed by a variety of means (PVA plug, steel or plastic ball bearings, heat) or to pellet freezing, where a $50–150\,\mu l$ drop of diluted semen is frozen in a pit on the surface of a block of dry ice (solid CO_2, $-79°C$). Straws allow for satisfactory fast freezing because of their high surface:volume ratio, and can be clearly and permanently marked with their contents. For semen packaging of larger volumes, larger straws (5 ml) have been used or flat plastic packs (Bwanga *et al.*, 1991). Pellets are to be discouraged for genetic resource banking because of their tendency to disintegrate with long-term storage, their difficulty with identification and their lack of container to restrict disease spread.

Oocytes and embryos have often been frozen in glass or plastic ampoules, cryotubes (special plastic tubes of ~ 2 ml capacity with a tight screw-sealed lid) or plastic straws (see above). With straws it is possible to package one or more embryos/oocytes in a small volume of cryoprotectant media separated by an air bubble in the straw from a thawing solution containing sucrose to counteract the tendency for the cells to swell as they are diluted out of cryoprotectant (Rall and Wood, 1994). On thawing, the contents are rapidly mixed as the ice melts, allowing for a rapid onset of equilibration with non-cryoprotectant solution.

The type of container influences the rewarming profile because its size and composition determines thermal conductance. For example, it has been shown that the type of container (straw versus plastic tube) may affect the final outcome of embryo cryopreservation (Van den Abbeel and Van Steirtgehem, 2000).

If the samples are stored in the liquid phase of the cryogen, there is a potential for liquid nitrogen to permeate into the sample, and on rewarming this will rapidly transform into the gaseous state, which may crack or shatter the container (this was an early dangerous consequence of using glass vials which had not been properly sealed), and has also caused straws to shatter during vitrification experiments. This may be avoided by holding the straw in the vapour phase for a brief period initially to allow a slightly slower initial warming rate. This also may avoid the propensity for some straws to shatter during rapid rewarming because of problems of thermal conductance in the plastic, which is fragile at low temperatures. A second consideration of influx of liquid nitrogen is the potential for carriage of infection – liquid nitrogen is not a sterile fluid. Such considerations have not been given high priority so far in the cryopreservation of animal oocytes and embryos, but are raising questions currently in human reproductive cell banking (Wood, 1999).

3.7 CONTROLLED COOLING AND THAWING

Spermatozoa have conveniently been frozen in straws 4 cm over the surface of liquid nitrogen. This is the commercial method and it allows for a rapid throughput of large numbers of straws. Pellets are dispensed manually and frozen on dry ice and require little equipment. However, they are difficult to handle. Flat packs and larger straws are frozen in controlled freezing machines that have programmable cooling rates. This method of freezing is also preferable for controlled rate freezing of embryos and oocytes. The freezers are limited in the maximum rate of controlled cooling ($\sim40°C/min$) they can achieve, and the control being determined by chamber temperature rather than within a dummy sample. However, for slower freezing rates they are excellent, if expensive. For vitrification or ultra-rapid cooling of embryos and oocytes, direct plunging into liquid nitrogen is often employed.

Thawing is occasionally performed in a controlled rate freezer (particularly if slow rewarming is used from temperatures in the range from $-80°C$ to $0°C$; Cooper *et al.*, 1998) but is more commonly achieved by one of a number of methods: exposure to ambient air, a water bath at 5, 25, 37 or 70°C, depending on the packaging and the rate of warming desired. Combinations of these methods allow considerable flexibility in the rates of rewarming. Pellets are thawed either in a dry tube or by dilution directly into warm thawing solution.

3.8 ASSESSMENT

There is much debate about how to assess the survival of cells after thawing. Spermatozoa have traditionally been assessed by subjective estimation of the proportion motile and the quality of the motility. While this is simple, there is little evidence that it relates to fertility. Even more recent sophisticated computer-assisted motility analysers have not been clearly demonstrated to assess the fertilizing potential of a sample of frozen semen. Other assessments are morphological, relating to the appearance of the sperm structures (e.g. tail conformation, acrosome integrity) or the embryonic cell appearances (cell size, shape, fragmentation).

More recently, with the appearance of fluorescent markers of cell functional ability, sperm assessments have been made of viability, ability to penetrate the zona, calcium uptake, intracellular pH, mitochondrial function, etc. The ability to swell in an hyposmotic environment, the so-called HOS test, is widely used. It indicates a functional plasmalemma acting as a semi-permeable membrane. While such approaches are preferable to the earlier morphological assays, there is a problem in that they rarely correlate closely with fertilizing ability. For fertilization to be achieved there must be a minimum of fully functional cells present. Since the inseminate generally contains more than the critical number, it is not until a profound failure in cryopreservation is present that fertilizing ability is noticeably impaired.

For oocytes and embryos, developmental competence is assessable in the laboratory, and probably is related to the ability to develop *in vivo*. However, laboratory culture conditions are presently suboptimal for the majority of species. This means that although success indicates that cryopreservation is promising, failure does not necessarily imply that the cryopreservation protocol is at fault.

In the end, the only convincing evidence that cryopreservation has yielded functional cells is that given by the production of viable offspring. Even that is now questionable in the case of sperm, when even damaged cells can be used by ICSI to produce embryos that appear to be normal! Live-births of normal offspring remain the 'gold standard' for assessing cryopreserved oocytes and embryos.

3.9 CONCLUSIONS

The profound temperature effects giving rise to dramatic phase separations and the severe osmotic forces driving water across cell membranes together result in a substantial membrane damage and loss of viability in the sperm population. In some species there is a subpopulation of vulnerable spermatozoa that do not survive cryopreservation (Curry and Watson, 1994). By careful optimization of the cryo-preservation protocol, together with attention to all the interacting factors, the non-surviving population can be minimized. In some species, selection of males whose spermatozoa display better cryosurvival can also improve overall results, although this is contrary to the principles of genetic banking, where a wide range of unselected genetic representatives of the population is required.

For the female gamete and embryo preservation, there is still much to be done to optimize protocols for successful cryopreservation in all but a few species. Whether immature oocytes come to be the cell of choice for female gamete cryopreservation depends upon the establishment of good *in vitro* maturation protocols for post-thaw use.

There is no evidence that cryopreservation induces genetic changes which result in increased embryonic malfunction. It remains to be established whether the lower fertility seen with cryopreserved cells is due to failure of fertilization or whether it can in part be attributable to increased early embryonic death. The recent surge in success in the use of cryopreserved human oocytes with establishment of pregnancies and ensuing live-births (Paynter, 2000) will ensure that this area of reproductive biology remains at the forefront of scientific scrutiny.

REFERENCES

ALIKANI, M., OLIVENNES, F. and COHEN, J. (1993) 'Microsurgical correction of partially degenerate mouse embryos promotes hatching and restores their viability', *Hum. Reprod.* **8**, 1723–1728.

AMANN, R. P. and PICKETT, B. W. (1987) 'Principles of cryopreservation and a review of cryopreservation of stallion spermatozoa', *Equine Vet. Sci.* **7**, 145–173.

BERNARD, A. (1991) 'Freeze preservation of mammalian reproductive cells', in Fuller, B. and Grout, B. (eds) *Clinical Applications of Cryobiology*, Florida: CRC Press, pp. 149–168.

BERNARD, A. and FULLER, B. (1983) 'Cryopreservation of *in vitro* fertilised 2-cell mouse embryos using a low glycerol concentration and normothermic cryoprotectant equilibration: a comparison with *in vivo* fertilised ova', *Cryo-Letters* **4**, 171–183.

BERNARD, A. and FULLER, B. (1996) 'Cryopreservation of human oocytes: a review of current problems and perspectives', *Hum. Reprod. Update* **2**, 193–207.

BILODEAU, J. F., CHATTERJEE, S., SIRARD, M. A. and GAGNON, C. (2000) 'Levels of antioxidant defenses are decreases in bovine spermatozoa after a cycle of freezing and thawing', *Mol. Reprod. Dev.* **55**, 282–288.

BWANGA, C. O., EINARSSON, S. and RODRIGUEZ-MARTINEZ, H. (1991) 'Cryopreservation of boar semen. II: Effect of cooling rate and duration of freezing point plateau on boar semen frozen in mini- and maxi-straws and plastic bags'. *Acta Vet. Scand.* **32**, 455–461.

CANDY, C., WOOD, M., WHITTINGHAM, D., MERRIMAN, J. and CHOUDRY, N. (1994) 'Cryopreservation of immature mouse oocytes', *Hum. Reprod.* **9**, 1738–1742.

CARROLL, J., WOOD, M. and WHITTINGHAM, D. (1993) 'Normal fertilization and development of frozen-thawed mouse oocytes: protective effect of certain macromolecules', *Biol. Reprod.* **48**, 606–612.

COOPER, A., PAYNTER, S., FULLER, B. and SHAW, R. (1998) 'Differential effects of cryopreservation on nuclear or cytoplasmic maturation *in vitro* in immature mouse oocytes from stimulated ovaries', *Hum. Reprod.* **13**, 971–978.

CHAPTER 3

CRITSER, J. K., HUSE, B. A., AAKER, D. V., ARNESON, B. W. and BALL, G. D. (1987) 'Cryopreservation of human spermatozoa. I. Effects of holding procedure and seeding on motility, fertilizability, and acrosome reaction', *Fertil. Steril.* **47**, 656–663.

CRITSER. J, AGCA, Y. and GUNASENA, K. (1997) 'The cryobiology of the mammalian oocyte', in Karow, A. and Critser, J. (eds) *Reproductive Tissue Banking,* New York: Academic Press, pp. 329–358.

CURRY, M. R. and WATSON, P. F. (1994) 'Osmotic effects on ram and human sperm membranes in relation to thawing injury', *Cryobiology* **31**, 39–46.

CURRY, M. R., MILLAR, J. D. and WATSON, P. F. (1994) 'Calculated optimal cooling rates for ram and human sperm cryopreservation fail to conform with empirical results', *Biol. Reprod.* **51**, 1014–1021.

CURRY M. R., REDDING, B. and WATSON, P. F. (1995) 'Determination of water permeability coefficient and its activation energy for rabbit spermatozoa', *Cryobiol.* **32**, 175–181.

DESAI, N., LAWSON, J. and GOLDFARB, J. (2000) 'Assessment of growth factor effects on post-thaw development of cryopreserved mouse morulae to the blastocyst stage', *Hum. Reprod.* **15**, 410–418.

DROBNIS, E. Z., CROWE, L. M., BERGER, T., ANCHORDOGUY, T. J., OVERSTREET, J. W. and CROWE, J. H. (1993) 'Cold shock damage is due to lipid phase transitions in cell membranes: a demonstration using sperm as a model', *J. Exp. Zool.* **265**, 432–437.

DUNCAN, A. E. and WATSON, P. F. (1992) 'Predictive water loss curves for ram spermatozoa during cryopreservation: comparison with experimental observations', *Cryobiology* **29**, 95–105.

FISER, P. S. (1988) 'Effect of induced nucleation (seeding) at −6°C on motility and acrosomal integrity of ram spermatozoa', *Cryobiology* **25**, 566–567.

FISER, P. S., HANSEN, C., UNDERHILL, K. L. and SHRESTHA, J. (1991) 'The effect of induced ice nucleation (seeding) on the post-thaw motility and acrosome integrity of boar spermatozoa', *Anim. Reprod. Sci.* **24**, 293–304.

FULLER, B. and BERNARD, A. (1984) 'Successful in vitro fertilization of mouse oocytes after cryopreservation using glycerol', *Cryo-Letters* **5**, 307–312.

GAO, D. Y., ASHWORTH, P. E., WATSON, P. F., KLEINHANS, F. W., MAZUR, P. and CRITSER, J. K. (1993) 'Hyperosmotic tolerance of human spermatozoa: separate effects of glycerol, sodium chloride and sucrose on spermolysis', *Biol. Reprod.* **49**, 112–123.

GAO, D. Y., LIU, J., LIU, C., MCGANN, L. E., WATSON, P. F., KLEINHANS, F. W., MAZUR, P., CRITSER, E. S. and CRITSER, J. K. (1995) 'Prevention of osmotic injury to human spermatozoa during addition and removal of glycerol', *Hum. Reprod.* **10**, 1109–1122.

GELETY, T. and SURREY, E. (1993) 'Cryopreservation of embryos and oocytes : an update', *Curr. Opin. Obstet. Gynaecol.* **5**, 606–614.

GEORGE, M. and JOHNSON, M. (1993) 'Cytoskeletal organization and zona sensitivity to digestion by chymotrypsin of frozen-thawed mouse oocytes', *Hum. Reprod.* **8,** 612–620.

GILMOUR, J. A., McGANN, L. E., LIU, J., GAO, D. Y., PETER, A. T., KLEINHANS, F. W. and CRITSER, J. K. (1995) 'Effect of cryoprotectant solutes on water permeability of human spermatozoa', *Biol. Reprod.* **53,** 985–995.

GOOK, D. A., SCHIEWE, M. C., OSBORN, S. M., ASCH, R. H., JANSEN, R. P. and JOHNSTON, W. I. (1995) 'Intracytoplasmic injection and embryo development of human oocytes cryopreserved using 1,2 propanediol', *Hum. Reprod.* **10,** 2637–2641.

GOSDEN, R., BAIRD, D., WADE, J. and WEBB, R. (1994) 'Restoration of fertility to oophorec-tomised sheep by ovarian autografts stored at −196°C', *Hum. Reprod.* **9,** 597–603.

HAMMERSTEDT, R. H. and GRAHAM, J. K. (1992) 'Cryopreservation of poultry sperm: the enigma of glycerol', *Cryobiology* **29,** 26–38.

HOLT, W. V. and NORTH, R. D. (1994) 'Effects of temperature and restoration of osmotic equilibrium on the induction of plasma membrane damage in cryopreserved ram spermatozoa', *Biol. Reprod.* **51,** 414–424.

HUNTER, J., BERNARD, A., FULLER, B., McGRATH, J. and SHAW, R. W. (1992) 'Plasma membrane permeabilities of human oocytes: the temperature dependence of water movement in individual cells', *J. Cell Physiol.* **150,** 175–179.

JACKOWSKI, S., LEIBO, S. and MAZUR, P. (1980) 'Glycerol permeability of fertilized and unfertilized mouse ova', *J. Exp. Zool.* **212,** 329–341.

KARLSSON, J. O., EROGLU, A., TOTH, T. L., CRAVALHO, E. G. and TONER, M. (1996) 'Fertilization and development of mouse oocytes cryopreserved using a theoretically optimized protocol', *Hum. Reprod.* **11,** 1296–1305.

KOLA, I., KIRBY, C., SHAW, J., DAVEY, A. and TROUNSON, A. (1988) 'Vitrification of mouse oocytes results in aneuploid zygotes and malformed fetuses', *Teratology* **38,** 467–474.

KULESHOVA, L., MacFARLANE, D., TROUNSON, A. and SHAW, J. (1999) 'Sugars exert a major influence on the vitrification properties of ethylene glycol-based solutions and have low toxicity to embryos and oocytes', *Cryobiology* **38,** 119–130.

LEHN-JENSEN, H. and RALL, W. (1983) 'Cryomicroscopic evidence of cattle embryos during freezing and thawing', *Theriogenology* **19,** 263–277.

LEIBO, S. (1977) 'Cryobiology of embryos and ova', in Elliott, K. and Whelan, J. (eds) *The Freezing of Mammalian Embryos*, Ciba Foundation Symposium 52, New York: Excerpta Medica, pp. 69–92.

LEIBO, S., MAZUR, P. and JACKOWSKI, S. (1974) 'Factors affecting cell survival of mouse embryos during freezing and thawing'. *Exp. Cell Res.* **89,** 79–88.

CHAPTER 3

Ludwig, M., Al-Hasani, S., Felberbaum, R. and Diedrich, K. (1999) 'New aspects of cryopreservation of oocytes and embryos in assisted reproduction and future perspectives', *Hum. Reprod.* **14** (Suppl. 1), 162–185.

Martino, A., Songsasen, N. and Leibo, S. (1996) 'Development to blastocysts of bovine oocytes cryopreserved by ultra-rapid cooling', *Biol. Reprod.* **54**, 1059–1069.

Mazur, P. (1963) 'Kinetics of water loss from cells at sub-zero temperatures and the likelihood of intracellular freezing', *J. Gen. Physiol.* **47**, 347–369.

Mazur, P. (1965) 'Causes of injury in frozen and thawed cells', *Fedn. Proc.* (Suppl. 15) **24**, S175–S182.

Mazur, P. (1980) 'Fundamental aspects of freezing cells with emphasis on mammalian ova and embryos', in *IX International Congress on Animal Reproduction and Artificial Insemination (Madrid).* Vol. 1, pp. 99–114.

Mazur, P. (1984) 'Freezing of living cells: Mechanisms and implications', *Am. J. Physiol.* **247**, C125–C142.

Mazur, P. (1985) 'Basic concepts in freezing cells', in Johnson, L. A. and Larsson, K. (eds) *Deep Freezing of Boar Semen,* Uppsala: Swedish University of Agricultural Sciences, pp. 91–111.

Mazur, P. (1990) 'Equilibrium, quasi-equilibrium, and non-equilibrium freezing of mammalian embryos', *Cell Biophys.* **17**, 53–92.

Mazur, P., Rall, W. F. and Rigopoulos, N. (1981) 'Relative contribution of the fraction of unfrozen water and of salt concentration to the survival of slowly frozen human erythrocytes', *Biophys. J.* **36**, 653–675.

Menezo, Y., Nicollet, B., Herbaut, N. and Andre, D. (1992) 'Freezing co-cultured human blastocysts', *Fertil. Steril.* **58**, 977–980.

Muldrew, K. and McGannm L. E. (1994) 'The osmotic rupture hypothesis of intracellular freezing injury', *Biophys. J.* **66**, 532–541.

Noiles, E. E., Mazur, P., Watson, P. F., Kleinhans, F. W. and Critser, J. K. (1993) 'Determination of water permeability coefficient for human spermatozoa and its activation energy', *Biol. Reprod.* **48**, 99–109.

Oktay, K., Karlikaya, G, Gosden, R. and Schwartz, R. (1999) 'Ovarian function after autologous transplantation of frozen-banked human overian tissue', *Fertil. Steril.* **72** (Suppl. 1), S21.

O'Neil, L., Paynter, S., Fuller, B. and Shaw, R. (1997a) 'Vitrification of mature mouse oocytes : improved results following addition of polyethylene glycol to a dimethyl sulphoxide solution', *Cryobiology* **34**, 295–301.

O'Neil, L., Paynter, S., Fuller, B. and Shaw, R. (1997b) 'Murine cytoskeletal changes, fertilization and embryonic development following exposure to a vitrification solution', *CryoLetters* **18**, 17–26.

Paquignon, M. (1985) 'Freezing and thawing extenders for boar spermatozoa', in Johnson, L. A. and Larssen, K. (eds) *Deep Freezing of Boar Semen*, Uppsala: Swedish University of Agricultural Sciences, pp 129–145.

Parrot, D. M. (1960) 'The fertility of mice with orthotopic ovarian grafts derived from frozen tissue', *J. Reprod. Fertil.* **1**: 230–241.

Paynter, S. (2000) 'Current status of the cryopreservation of human unfertilised oocytes', *Hum. Reprod. Update* (in press).

Paynter, S., Cooper, A., Thomas, N. and Fuller, B. (1997) 'Cryopreservation of multi-cellular embryos and reproductive tissues', in Karow, A. and Critser, J. (eds) *Reproductive Tissue Banking*, New York: Academic Press, pp. 359–398.

Paynter, S., Cooper, A., Gregory, L., Fuller, B. and Shaw, R. (1999) 'Permeability characteristics of human oocytes in the presence of the cryoprotectant, dimethyl sulphoxide', *Hum. Reprod.* **14**, 2338–2342.

Pickering, S. J. and Johnson, M. H. (1987) 'The influence of cooling on the organization of the meiotic spindle of the mouse oocyte', *Hum. Reprod.* **2**, 207–216.

Polge, C., Smith, A. U. and Parkes, A. S. (1949) 'Revival of spermatozoa after vitrification and dehydration at low temperatures', *Nature, Lond.* **164**, 666.

Rall, W. (1987) 'Factors affecting the survival of vitrified mouse embryos', *Cryobiology* **24**, 387–402.

Rall, W. and Fahy, G. (1985) 'Ice free cryopreservation of mouse embryos at −196°C by vitrification', *Nature, Lond.* **313**, 573–575.

Rall, W. and Meyer, T. (1989) 'Zonae fracture damage to mammalian embryos during cryopreservation and its avoidance', *Theriogenology* **31**, 683–692.

Rall, W. and Wood, M. (1994) 'High in vitro survival of day 3 mouse embryos vitrified or frozen in a non-toxic solution of glycerol and albumin'. *J. Reprod. Fertil.* **101**, 681–688.

Ritar, A. J., Ball, P. D. and O'May, P. J. (1990) 'Examination of methods for the deep freezing of goat semen', *Reprod. Fertil. Dev.* **2**, 27–34.

Toner, M., Cravalho, E. G. and Armant, D. R. (1990) 'Water transport and estimated transmembrane potential during freezing of mouse oocytes', *J. Membr. Biol.* **115**, 261–272.

Trad, F., Toner, M. and Biggers, J. (1998) 'Effects of cryoprotectants and ice-seeding temperature on intracellular freezing and survival of human oocytes', *Hum. Reprod.* **14**, 1569–1577.

Trounson, A. (1990) 'Cryopreservation', *Br. Med. Bull.* **46**, 695–708.

Van den Abbeel, E. and Van Steirteghem, A. (2000) 'Zona pellucida damage to human embryos after cryopreservation and the consequences for their blastomere survival and in vitro viability', *Hum. Reprod.* **15**, 373–378.

■ CHAPTER 3 ■

VINCENT, C. and JOHNSON, M. (1992) 'Cooling, cryoprotectants and the cytoskeleton of the mammalian oocyte', *Oxford Rev. Reprod. Biol.* **14**, 73–100.

VINCENT, C., PICKERING, S. and JOHNSON, M. (1990) 'The hardening effect of dimethyl sulphoxide on the mouse zona pellucida requires the presence of an oocyte and is associated with a reduction in the number of cortical granules present', *J. Reprod. Fertil.* **89**, 253–259.

Watson, P. F. (1979) 'The preservation of semen in mammals' *Oxford Rev. Reprod. Biol.* **1**, 283350.

WATSON, P. F. (1981) 'The effects of cold shock on sperm cell membranes', in Morris, G.J. and Clarke, A. (eds) *Effects of Low Temperatures on Biological Membranes*, London: Academic Press, pp. 189–218.

WATSON, P. F. (1990) 'Artificial insemination and the preservation of semen', in Lamming, G. E. (ed.) *Marshall's Physiology of Reproduction.* 4th edn, Vol. II, London: Churchill Livingstone, pp. 747–869.

WATSON, P. F. (1995) 'Recent developments and concepts in the cryopreservation of spermatozoa and the assessment of their post-thawing function', *Reprod. Fertil. Dev.* **7**, 871–891.

WATSON, P. F. (2000) 'The causes of reduced fertility with cryopreserved semen', *Anim. Reprod. Sci.* **60–61**, 481–492.

WATSON, P. F. and MARTIN, I. C. A. (1975) 'Effects of egg yolk, glycerol and the freezing rate on the viability and acrosomal structures of frozen ram spermatozoa', *Aust. J. Biol. Sci.* **28**, 153–159.

WATSON, P. F. and MORRIS, G. J. (1987) 'Cold shock injury in animal cells', in Bowler, K and Fuller, B. J. (eds) *Temperature and Animal Cells,* Soc. Exp. Biol. Symp. no. 41, Cambridge: The Company of Biologists, pp. 311–340.

WHITTINGHAM, D. (1977) 'Fertilization and development to term of unfertilised mouse oocytes previously stored at −196°C', *J. Reprod. Fertil.* **49**, 89–94.

WHITTINGHAM, D., LEIBO, S. and MAZUR, P. (1972) 'Survival of mouse embryos frozen to −196°C and −269°C', *Science* **178**, 411–414.

WOOD, M. J. (1997) 'Embryo freezing : is it safe?', *Hum. Reprod.* **12** (Suppl. 2), 32–37.

WOOD, M. J. (1999) 'The problems of storing gametes and embryos', *Cryo-Letters* **20**, 155–158.

WOOD, M., BARROS, C., CANDY, C., CARROLL, J., MELENDEZ, J. and WHITTINGHAM, D. (1993) 'High rates of survival and fertilization of mouse and hamster oocytes after vitrification in dimethyl sulphoxide', *Biol. Reprod.* **49**, 489–495.

Establishing Animal Germplasm Resource Banks for Wildlife Conservation: Genetic, Population and Evolutionary Aspects

PETER M. BENNETT

The Institute of Zoology, The Zoological Society of London,
Regent's Park, London NW1 4RY, UK

Contents

4.1 INTRODUCTION

To see a World in a Grain of Sand,
And a Heaven in a Wild Flower,
Hold Infinity in the palm of your hand,
And Eternity in an hour.

A Robin Redbreast in a Cage
Puts all Heaven in a Rage.

(From *Auguries of Innocence*, William Blake, 1803)

These inspirational opening lines from Blake's famous poem contain a surprisingly simple metaphor which questions the keeping of wild songbirds in captivity for our amusement, a practice that is still common in many areas of the world. Today conservationists emphasize the importance of maintaining animals from threatened populations in secure conditions to protect them from human activities. The maintenance of closely managed and protected populations in zoos, ranches or nature reserves provides an insurance against catastrophic events that can cause extinction in populations of free-living animals. However, even these populations are not secure from threats such as disease epidemics, war and natural disasters. In recent years, advances in genetic and reproductive technologies for animal breeding have provided an extremely secure means of assisting vulnerable populations–the long-term storage of their gametes in germplasm resource banks.

Genetic resource banking is defined as the storage of gametes (sperm and oocytes) and embryos from threatened populations with the deliberate intention to use them in a breeding programme at some future occasion (Holt *et al.*, 1996a). This activity, in combination with assisted reproductive techniques, offers the prospect of substantial benefits in species conservation programmes that require active management of isolated populations (Holt and Moore, 1988; Ballou, 1992; Conservation Breeding Specialist Group, 1992, 1994; Holt *et al.*, 1996a). Currently, there is general agreement that artificial insemination (AI) using frozen semen offers the greatest practical benefits. Therefore, in this chapter, I will concentrate on how the disciplines of population and evolutionary biology can assist in defining strategies for the effective storage, management and use of frozen semen banks to meet certain defined goals. Specifically, I will discuss the selection of individuals for storage to maximize genetic diversity and thereby help meet population survival goals, and the selection of species for storage to help meet biodiversity conservation goals.

CHAPTER 4

4.2 DEFINING GOALS FOR GENETIC RESOURCE BANKS

Limited resources are available for the establishment and maintenance of GRBs. It is essential, therefore, that the goals of a banking programme are defined as clearly as possible from the outset.

When considering the goals of animal GRBs, it is informative to examine how seed banks have been established to conserve plant diversity (Hoyt, 1988; Bennett, 1998). The Royal Botanic Gardens, Kew (London, UK), have established and maintained a bank of stored seeds at Wakehurst Place in Sussex since 1974. Kew maintain hundreds of millions of seeds from over 4000 plant species which are stored in air-tight containers in large deep-freezes. However, even this capacity is not sufficient to store seeds from the around 250 000 species of flowering plants thought to exist. Instead, specific goals for seed banking projects are defined. For example, one project aims to help conserve native British flora by storing their seeds, while another aims to conserve seeds from 10% of the world's flora from the arid tropics under optimal storage conditions for over 200 years. Providing quantitative goals such as these is extremely useful because the scope and limits of the plant germplasm resource banking programme are clearly defined.

How can the goals of animal GRBs be defined? The first step is to be clear about the aims of the banking project. To illustrate this Table 4.1 lists some of the possible reasons why particular species may be chosen to be included in animal GRBs. Economic, political, social and scientific goals are listed but it is important to recognize that these goals can be interdependent. For example, frozen semen banks are used routinely to breed dairy cattle by artificial insemination in many parts of the world, an activity that has benefits for all these spheres of human endeavour. In this chapter I concentrate on the goal of conserving diverse wildlife resources, another activity that has multiple benefits. However, germplasm banks provide a path of 'least regret'

TABLE 4.1
Some examples of possible goals for animal GRBs

Economic	to preserve rare domesticated breeds
	to enable multiple inseminations from the fittest males
	to increase productivity of food sources for human consumption
	to help conserve diverse wildlife resources
Political	to help meet demands of conservation and environmental legislation
	to conserve flagship species or national emblems
	to meet the demands of non-governmental organizations
Social	to conserve species of cultural or religious significance
	to conserve species of educational or recreational importance
	to conserve species of known or suspected medical importance
Scientific	to conserve species that support pure or applied research

because while the goals may change over time the stored material does not. Therefore, regardless of the original reason for storage, a germplasm resource bank has the potential for multiple uses, some of which may not be currently envisaged.

4.3 GENETIC PROBLEMS IN SMALL, ISOLATED POPULATIONS

Populations of threatened species are often small, declining and inhabit restricted ranges such as nature reserves or islands. For example, populations of threatened free-living animals are often fragmented and widely separated because of habitat destruction or degradation. Populations of threatened species maintained in captive or semi-captive conditions, such as zoos or ranches, are restricted by cages and fences and are also separated by large distances. These barriers to animal movement restrict gene flow and the potential for population replenishment. Unfortunately, these problems can lead to the extinction of small isolated populations even in the absence of any other external threat. This is because small populations are especially susceptible to chance fluctuations in gene frequencies, size, and age- and sex-structure. These processes have been reviewed in numerous publications and therefore are only briefly discussed here.

Small populations lose genetic variability through random processes (Frankel and Soulé, 1981; Lacy, 1987). This can be seen by quantifying genetic variability using the amount of heterozygosity (*H*) – the percentage of loci that are heterozygous in the average individual of a population. Figure 4.1 shows the effect of population size on loss of heterozygosity over 200 generations. The smaller the population, the more

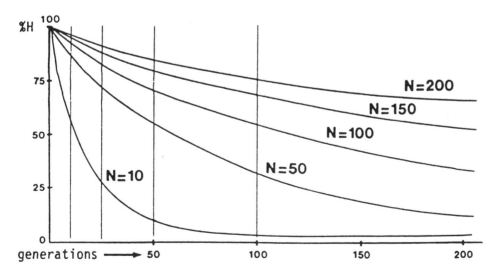

Figure 4.1: Loss of percentage heterozygosity (%*H*) over 200 generations in populations of different size (*N*).

rapidly heterozygosity is lost due to random sampling. One way of explaining this is that the more individuals there are in the population, the larger the probability that a given allele (which by chance is not transmitted by one individual) is transmitted by one of the others (de Boer, 1989). Another critical factor that influences loss of genetic variability is the size of the founder population. Models show that a founder population of 50 individuals may retain 99% of original heterozygosity, while 6 founders retains only 92% of original heterozygosity (de Boer, 1989). Thus, small founder numbers result in inevitable losses of genetic diversity because of random sampling of founding individuals who represent a proportion of the total hetero-zygosity in the original source population. This process is known as the founder effect.

A variety of mechanisms have evolved in natural populations to avoid inbreeding, such as dispersal from the natal group. This is because inbreeding, matings between relatives, can be harmful (Frankel and Soulé, 1981). It increases homozygosity in the population and thus is another process that reduces genetic variability. It also increases the probability that deleterious recessive alleles will be expressed. Inbreeding depression results, a phenomenon that affects survivorship (especially if lethal alleles are expressed) and reproductive characters (e.g. reduction of fertility). Small isolated populations must be managed to avoid or minimize inbreeding.

Loss of genetic variability is also influenced by the rate of growth of the population after its foundation, generation time, biases in the sex ratio and family size, and fluctuations in population size. Small populations are especially prone to these processes and I will consider how GRBs can be used to help minimize some of them below

4.4 COORDINATED BREEDING PROGRAMMES

A number of conservation biologists working in zoos have used these insights drawn from the discipline of population biology to define goals for animal breeding programmes (Foose, 1983; Foose and Ballou, 1988). Their specific aim was to coordinate breeding programmes for endangered species, for example the tiger and the lion tamarins, to manage problems such as loss of genetic diversity and inbreeding. Formal breeding plans were established to manage small captive populations which attempted to minimize these and other processes that are believed to cause extinction. A common goal of these plans is to maintain a minimum of 90% of genetic diversity in a demographically stable population for 200 years. A range of management strategies and tools have been established that aim to achieve this. It is common for coordinators of captive breeding programmes to publish studbooks that aim to list all the living individuals of a species kept in captivity along with their ancestors back to the original wild-caught animals. Software tools have been developed to calculate statistics that estimate the degree of relatedness between individuals and allow matings between animals in different zoos and other organizations to be planned in order to minimize the loss of genetic diversity (for example, the animal management software packages produced by ISIS (1989). More complex methods for estimating gene losses from wild-caught founder animals are also used, and management strategies are employed to minimize predicted losses of rare alleles.

To date, the achievements of these breeding programmes, as measured by captive-bred animals returned to the wild, have been modest (IUDZG/CBSG, 1993). This situation, along with the long time-scales of these programmes, makes it difficult to evaluate the effectiveness of the population management strategies employed to maximize factors such as genetic diversity. Nevertheless, systematic use of GRBs in animal breeding programmes offers the potential to ease some of the processes that precipitate the extinction of species and it is useful to review these.

4.5   ADVANTAGES OF GENETIC RESOURCE BANKS FOR MANAGING SMALL, ISOLATED POPULATIONS

What are the potential benefits of using GRBs for supporting threatened animal populations? Of course, GRBs and assisted reproductive techniques cannot be used to replace living animal populations whether in the wild or captivity. Instead, they allow new opportunities for integrating the management of isolated populations (wild and/or captive) of threatened species in planned species recovery programmes, a process that has been termed 'metapopulation management'. Usually, these benefits will only accrue if living animal populations can be maintained so that stored material can be used.

A range of potential benefits of using stored frozen germplasm for conservation programmes requiring metapopulation management have been identified (e.g. Ballou, 1984, 1992; Benirschke, 1984; Dresser, 1988; Holt and Moore, 1988; Mace, 1989; Johnston and Lacy, 1991; Rall, 1991; CBSG, 1992, 1994; Mace *et al.*, 1992). These were reviewed by Holt *et al.* (1996a) and are summarized here:

- *Increased security*. Storing germplasm from a relatively small number of individuals per species enables a high proportion of genetic diversity to be preserved indefinitely. This benefit provides some protection against catastrophes causing local extinctions of genetically important living populations.
- *Unlimited space*. A large number of species can be banked and is limited only by the number of containers in the banks. This benefit is very important for banking programmes aiming to conserve species diversity for particular taxonomic groups or regions, because space for live animals both in the field and in captive conditions is becoming increasingly limited.
- *Increased gene flow*. Managed breeding or species recovery programmes are facilitated because transportation of frozen gametes has many advantages over moving live

animals. For example, the opportunities for gene flow within and between small isolated wild and/or captive populations will be greatly enhanced. This is especially true in the context of our increasing knowledge of disease transmission risks, as well as the welfare and financial costs, of moving live animals.

- *Minimize introgression*. Storage of germplasm from animals of known provenance can secure the integrity of a genepool against the threat of introgression. The introduction of foreign genes through hybridization is increasingly being recognized as a problem by wildlife managers, especially when it involves introduced species. Cade (1983) reviewed examples of hybridization between bird species. A recent example is the white-headed duck (*Oxyura leucocephala*) which is threatened globally (Tucker and Heath, 1994). The population of around 1000 individuals remaining in Spain is threatened by hybridization with the ruddy duck (*Oxyura jamaicensis*), a species introduced to Europe from North America, where it is common. Culling programmes for the ruddy duck are now being recommended for the UK and other areas in order to protect the white-headed duck from extinction by introgression.

- *Extend generation times*. The genetic lifespan of an individual is extended for as long as its germplasm is viable and the GRB is maintained. This means that natural generation times (the average time between conception and first breeding) can be artificially extended. This intervention would reduce chance losses of alleles (genetic drift) through genetic recombination and therefore smaller population sizes are required to meet genetic goals. It has been argued that more space is therefore made available for breeding threatened species in captivity (Ballou, 1992).

- *Maximize genetic diversity*. GRBs facilitate genetic management. Managers can attempt to maximise genetic diversity by, for example, storing and using germplasm from genetically unrepresented potential founder animals, descendants of under-represented founders or doomed wild animals (see below).

- *Minimize inbreeding*. Inbreeding can be minimized by restoring germplasm to unrelated or the most distantly related animals (see below).

- *Manage effective population size*. The effective population size (N_e) is usually much less than the census number of animals because only a proportion of animals of a given generation breed and pass their genes on to the next generation. This is particularly the case in herd-living species where one male may sire the majority of offspring for many years. A small effective population size leads to increased loss of genetic diversity, particularly of rare alleles. GRBs provide a means to manage N_e by using stored germplasm from unrelated males, by helping to equalize family sizes, by manipulating age-specific fertility rates and by attempting to control sex ratios.

- *Minimize selection*. In farm animal production and in the preservation of rare domesticated breeds artificial selection is used to breed from animals with desired traits. This practice of artificial selection causes changes in quantitative traits and, in general, it must be avoided in conservation programmes for threatened wild species because it reduces genetic diversity. Stored germplasm of donor animals has a 'hidden phenotype' and its utilization would help to minimize the effects of keeper selection in living populations. Likewise, some of the effects of local adaptation to unnatural habitats could be countered because evolution is suspended while gametes are stored in frozen banks. In some cases, however, it may be necessary to select against deleterious traits with a known genetic basis that lower survivorship or fertility. This is especially likely when these traits have occurred artificially due to genetic drift, inbreeding, introgression or unnatural selection. A strategy combining detailed pedigree analysis to choose donor males using GRBs would assist in this process.

- *Mutation.* In small populations harmful mutations may become fixed through random genetic drift and cause extinction (Lande, 1994). Recent estimates suggest that the rate at which deleterious mutations occur in the genomes of humans and the great apes is much higher than previously believed. For humans a recent conservative estimate is that the rate is 4.2 mutations per person per generation with a deleterious rate of 1.6 (Eyre-Walker and Keightley, 1999). This rate is extraordinarily high and suggests that GRBs by extending generation lengths may assist in decreasing the load of harmful mutations.
- *Reproductive failure.* Husbandry problems, such as incompatible pairs that fail to breed, could be circumvented by interventions using AI. Reproductive failure is a common problem in captivity and appears to be especially prevalent in species where the sexes maintain long-term bonds, such as in macaws. The opportunity to choose between a number of potential mates can be difficult to provide for logistical reasons, and therefore AI can be used to help circumvent this problem.
- *Future benefits.* As further advances in reproductive biology and biotechnology are made, and as long as stored germplasm exists, there will be the potential for treating infertility in genetically important animals, screening for disease, restoring 'lost genes' or choosing the sex of offspring. Cloning of genetically important animals is also possible but it will not increase genetic diversity because clones are equivalent to identical twins.

Many of these potential benefits would be substantial. In particular, the economic, legal, administrative, disease and welfare advantages of transporting frozen germplasm instead of live animals would reap enormous immediate benefits in wildlife conservation programmes. In the longer term, the increased opportunities for gene flow between isolated populations will be vitally important for the success of many species recovery programmes. Of course, there are also problems associated with maintaining germplasm for long periods in the absence of evolutionary processes such as selection and mutation. These will result in genetic changes in the living population

CHAPTER 4

but not in the stored material. This genetic divergence could be important in the longer term and lead to lowered viability when stored germplasm is utilized (Mace *et al.*,1992). Managers of GRBs will need to ensure that the process of collection and use of stored germplasm is a dynamic process such that the offspring produced are able to survive the challenges of their 'natural' habitats, which are continually changing due to biotic and abiotic factors, and the globally destructive activities of humans.

4.6   GENETIC MANAGEMENT IN PRACTICE

I have reviewed some of the potential benefits of semen banking for conservation programmes with genetic goals. As discussed above, a common goal in coordinated captive breeding programmes is to maintain a minimum of 90% of genetic diversity (i.e. population heterozygosity) in a demographically stable population for 200 years. But how can this be achieved in practice? Various genetic management strategies can be employed to minimize the loss of heterozygosity in a population. The next section considers these in more detail and offers some examples of how semen banking can assist in carrying out these actions to minimize the loss of genetic variability in small populations.

To some extent, management practices such as the culling of dominant males in herd-living species represent a form of genetic management. These males are likely to have sired a majority of the offspring in the herd and thus will be well-represented in the local genepool. However, genetic management using reproductive technologies is only practical under very closely managed populations such as domesticated food animals and those wild animals that are maintained in captivity, ranches or reserves.

Three main prerequisites are required before GRBs can be used effectively in genetic management. First, the animals from which germplasm is collected for storage must be well characterized taxonomically. This problem is not straightforward because for many taxa there are disputes about the distinctiveness of populations within 'species'. This is especially the case when populations are geographically separated and are unable to interbreed. The applications of molecular genetic techniques to quantify differences between species are helping to resolve some of these disputes. However, it is a complex problem and it becomes even more difficult when germplasm is also collected from captive animals where the geographic origins of founder animals are often obscure. Second, individual animal identification must be possible (for example, using tags or microchip implants) and records of birth, death and parentage must be kept both for living animals and for their ancestors (see below). Molecular genetic techniques may assist in resolving pedigree uncertainties when the number of generations is small and DNA can be obtained from a range of putative parents/ ancestors. Third, to use stored germplasm effectively it is necessary to have a good understanding of the basic reproductive biology of the species being assisted, including knowledge of hormonal cycles in females to plan the optimal time for AI. Unfortunately, for most threatened species these prerequisites have yet to be established. Considerable research effort is required, together with improvements in recording schemes to enable routine use of GRBs for genetic management of populations of vulnerable species.

4.7 MAXIMIZING GENETIC DIVERSITY

Once we are in a position to establish a GRB to assist a species recovery programme we can formulate a strategy for maximizing genetic diversity. Table 4.2 lists some of the aims we might wish to achieve by carefully selecting donors and recipients. How do we achieve these aims? The first step is to calculate a number of useful statistics from pedigrees, including the number of founder animals, representation of founder genes in living animals and mean kinship values. This is done by using software for managing studbooks such as the GENES pedigree analysis software which is distributed with the SPARKS package produced by ISIS (1989) or more laboriously by using algorithms and worked examples published in various textbooks (e.g. Schonewald-Cox *et al.*, 1983) and manuals (e.g. de Boer, 1989). Careful pedigree analysis will be essential for successful genetic management using GRBs. A number of conservation programmes already use these analytical methods, including the model GRB project on the endangered Mohor gazelle (Holt *et al.*, 1996b).

To maximize allelic diversity we might choose a dual strategy of increasing founder representation and minimizing mean kinship values. Studies of captive populations have shown that they are often founded by a surprisingly small number of original wild-caught animals. Thus, even before individuals from a newly founded managed population have bred, there has been a reduction of genetic diversity because only a proportion of the total species', genepool will be represented in these founder animals. Rare alleles are especially at risk of loss due to this population 'bottleneck' known as the founder effect (see above). In some cases, where a species went extinct in the wild, such

TABLE 4.2
Strategies for maximizing genetic diversity in small isolated populations

---

Maximize effective population size
Maximize number of founders
Equalize founder representation among living animals
Minimize inbreeding
Maximize generation length
Minimize artificial selection
Maximize gene flow between subdivided populations
Equalize the numbers of males and females (sex ratio)
Equalize family sizes (number of offspring per individual)
Minimize fluctuations in population size

CHAPTER 4

as the Arabian oryx, it is not possible to increase founder representation but it is still possible to equalize the genetic representation of founders amongst living descendants.

Storing and using semen from GRBs can help to alleviate the problem of low founder numbers in a number of ways. First, it is common to find that a number of potential founder animals or early generation founders have never bred and left surviving descendants. It is critical that these males are identified and that semen is collected from them before they die and their genomes are lost. Another possibility is that males are sometimes regarded as 'doomed' in the wild because, for example, they are old, diseased or become permanently separated from other individuals. Semen can be collected from these males to increase founder numbers in managed populations. Another frequent problem in closely-managed populations is to find that, after a number of generations, some founder animals are very successful at breeding and have left many surviving descendants while others may have left only a few. It is important to try to equalize the representation of founder genes in the living population to prevent gene losses, and this can be assisted by storing and using semen from the descendants of under-represented founders.

How many founder animals are necessary to preserve the evolutionary potential of a species? This will depend on a number of factors, including the length of the conservation programme, the degree of relatedness of the founders, and the amount of genetic diversity remaining in the source population.

Inbreeding depression can be severe in normally outbred small populations. This can be minimized by using mean kinship values which estimate the degree of relatedness between all animals in a population. It is essential that these statistics are used to plan matings between unrelated or the most-distantly related animals. Where pedigree analysis is not possible then molecular genetic techniques may assist in establishing the degree of relatedness of animals. In the absence of any pedigree information, moving animals between small isolated populations should help to reduce inbreeding. Storage and utilization of semen in GRBs can help to minimize inbreeding when potential donors and recipients are identified by pedigree analysis. Donor males for GRBs must be selected using a strategy that minimizes mean kinship values among semen samples. Female recipients can be chosen that are either unrelated to the donor males or have the lowest mean kinship values.

GRBs can also be used to help equalize the number of offspring produced by an individual. In addition, progress is being made in developing an effective method for separating X and Y sperm to preselect sex (e.g. Welch and Johnson, 1999). This would allow much greater control of the population sex ratio. Biases in these demographic parameters (family size and the sex ratio) reduce the effective population size and increase gene losses through drift.

How many donor animals are required for banking to meet genetic and demographic goals? How often should stored gametes be used? Quantitative questions such as these have been examined by using computer simulations to look at the consequences of different options. They work by simulating the changes in gene frequencies per generation that might be expected given alternative strategies for storage and utilization of gametes in GRBs. These models have proved useful in establishing systematic practical procedures for integrating the use of GRBs in captive populations of threatened species. For example, the tiger species recovery plan estimates that gametes from between 25 and 50 individuals should be stored in a GRB to conserve with 95% probability any allele with a frequency greater than 0.05 in the source population (CBSG, 1992). In addition, it was estimated that four offspring (in two litters) would need to be produced per generation by AI from the tiger GRB to retain over 90% of genetic diversity in the living captive population. While these models help to establish best practice, it should be emphasized that they are relatively simple, with many untested assumptions. In addition, they need to be developed separately for each species in a GRB.

Johnston and Lacy (1995) used simulation techniques to evaluate four different selection strategies for identifying the most genetically important sperm donors. They used four pedigrees from North American captive populations. The selection strategies were: (a) all males in the population; (b) only living founders and early generation descendants; (c) males that remained after 'culling' to reduce mean kinship; and (d) only males remaining after 'culling' to minimize kinship reduced to the number of living founders. They evaluated the effectiveness of each strategy by comparing genetic variation in the stored GRB population with that in current living population. Not surprisingly, they found that retention of allelic diversity was greatest when sperm from all males was collected. However, nearly optimal retention of genetic diversity was also achieved by using the strategy of minimizing mean kinship values. Thus, this strategy of minimizing mean kinship coefficients appears to be a useful way of selecting donors and recipients for GRBs.

4.8 RECORDING SCHEMES AND DATABASES

For GRBs to meet their goals effectively it is essential that donors and recipients are selected in a systematic manner. For genetic management, detailed analyses of pedigrees are necessary so that mean kinship values can be minimized both in the stored and living populations. Computer databases greatly facilitate this task and Table 4.3 gives some examples of how they can assist in managing GRBs. Table 4.4 lists examples of the information that is essential for effective genetic management using GRBs.

4.9 ORGANIZATION OF GENETIC RESOURCE BANKS

Rall (1991), CBSG (1994) and Holt *et al.* (1996a) have considered how GRBs can be used to integrate the management of wild and captive populations. The first consideration

CONSIDERATIONS PERTINENT TO GENETIC RESOURCE BANKING

is that GRBs should be located in different geographic areas to increase security. Support systems can fail for a variety of reasons and while backup power, liquid nitrogen and other requirements can be kept in reserve, they will not protect against fire or flood. This means that germplasm from important individuals or species should be duplicated and stored in geographically separated banks.

CBSG (1994) distinguished between three types of GRB. GRB no. 1 is to store germplasm in sufficient quantity to represent a high proportion of genetic diversity in a living species and thereby preserve indefinitely its evolutionary potential. This GRB is meant to serve as a backup to be accessed in the case of near extinction of the species. GRB no. 2 is another bank representing maximum genetic diversity but is meant to be used actively to manage wild and captive populations. GRB no. 3 is for providing biological samples for research that will assist in the conservation of a species.

One problem with using donor males from a captive population is that their genetic integrity is often questionable because the geographic origin of their wild-caught ancestors is often unknown and they have undergone a number of generations of artificial selection. For these reasons it may be wise to consider three separate banks based on the origin of the sperm donors. Donors from wild populations of known provenance should be stored in a 'Wild bank' and such material can be utilized in both wild and captive populations. Donors from captive populations should be stored

TABLE 4.3

Computer applications for managing GRBs

Facilitate basic recording of samples using unique identifiers
Facilitate routine management of banks
Ensure essential data is recorded in a standard agreed format
Facilitate data sharing and aggregation on central database/website
Incorporate algorithms to assist optimal:
    sampling of living populations (from whom? When and where? How many? How much?)
    management of stored materials (quality control over space and time)
    utilization of stored materials (to whom? When and where? How much?)
Incorporate algorithms for population modelling and projections

TABLE 4.4

Examples of essential information for effective genetic management

Geographic origin of founders
Degree of relatedness of founders
Degree of relatedness of living animals
Pedigrees to calculate founder representation, gene loss and mean kinship coefficients
Unique and permanent identity for each animal
Current location and movement history of each animal
Effective and census population size
Sex and age structure of population

separately in a 'captive bank' and this material should probably only be given to captive recipients. This is because there is a risk of introgression and outbreeding depression in wild populations if the integrity of the germplasm from captive donors is not well established. Material collected from both captive and wild donors can be stored in a third 'reserve bank' which would provide an insurance against loss of the main banks. This scheme is shown in Table 4.5.

Holt *et al.* (1996a) used this scheme for organizing GRBs to illustrate how the collection, storage and subsequent utilization of frozen germplasm can facilitate genetic management in conservation programmes for threatened species (Figure 4.2). GRBs provide a means to create artificial 'corridors' that enable genetic material to be exchanged between geographically isolated populations. By careful planning of the movement of germplasm between wild, captive and stored populations over time, such schemes have great potential for maintaining genetic diversity and recruitment in small isolated populations.

4.10 SPECIES SELECTION FOR GENETIC RESOURCE BANKS

Currently, the criteria for selecting species for conservation programmes are poorly defined and controversial. Often the issue is avoided and in some quarters there is a belief that biologists should not be 'playing God' by choosing some species for conservation efforts at the expense of others. This debate is especially relevant to the use of GRBs in wildlife conservation because species must be selected for storage and use of germplasm. It is clear that the resources available for conservation activities are finite and therefore we must prioritize species for effort. However, as discussed above, while there has been considerable work addressing population-level questions such as ways to minimize losses of genetic diversity, there has been very little effort put into strategies for deciding which species to conserve in the first place.

In my experience a range of criteria have been used for selecting particular species for conservation effort. Some examples are listed in Table 4.6. However, it must be emphasized that it is common to find that no particular reason was given for selecting a particular species or phylogenetic group for captive breeding programmes, especially in the past.

TABLE 4.5
A scheme for organizing GRBs

Collection from	Storage in	Utilization to
Wild populations ———————	Wild bank ———————	Wild populations
	Reserve bank	Captive populations
Captive populations ———————	Captive bank ———————	Captive populations
	Reserve bank	

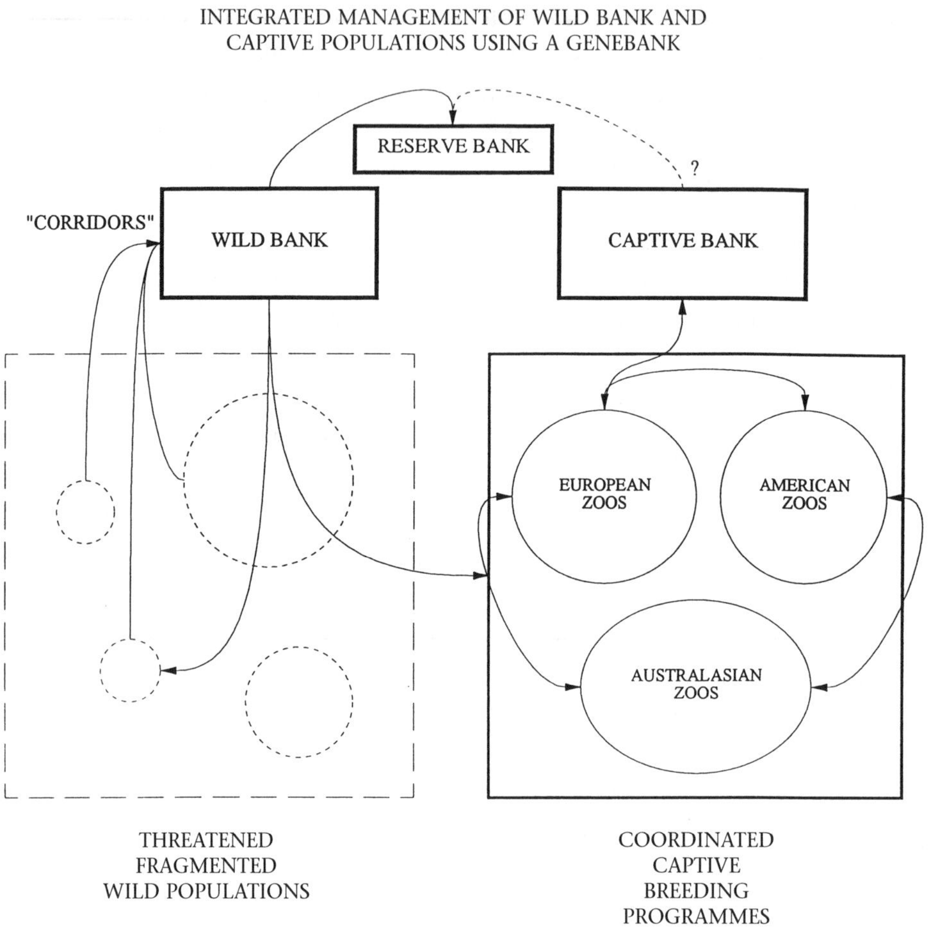

INTEGRATED MANAGEMENT OF WILD BANK AND
CAPTIVE POPULATIONS USING A GENEBANK

Figure 4.2: Scenario for integrated management of small wild and captive populations using a GRB. Reproduced from Holt *et al.* (1996a) with permission of the publisher.

When explicit reasons are given for conservation programmes, the level of threat is often used. However, even when this criteria is used there are over 2000 species of threatened mammals and birds alone, with 337 given the highest level of endangerment (WCMC, 1996). Even if we restricted ourselves to these species and attempted to bank semen from them it would be a huge task and we might wish to rationalize it in some way. One problem with current methods for ranking the importance of particular species for conservation effort is that they ignore how distinctive a species is in relation to other species. No attempt is made to prioritize above the species level. The consequence is that multiple races/subspecies from the same species, or multiple species from the same genus, may be conserved at the expense of highly distinctive taxa with no living close relatives.

TABLE 4.6
Examples of species-selection criteria for conservation effort

By level of threat to species (Critical, endangered, vulnerable)
By area or range (e.g. Africa, Philippines, island endemics)
By 'charisma' (e.g. elephant) or 'cuddliness'
By availability (e.g. accessible in wild, already in captivity)
By level of educational or exhibit interest (e.g. giraffes in zoos)
By level of scientific interest (e.g. Partula snails)
By perceived agricultural importance (e.g. exotic Bovidae)
By availability of funds to support work on particular species

4.11 AN EVOLUTIONARY APPROACH TO SPECIES SELECTION FOR GENETIC RESOURCE BANKS

One way to address this issue is to consider three questions. First, how distinctive (or similar) is a selected species in comparison to other selected species in a GRB? Second, what traits should be used to evaluate quantitative differences between species? Third, how much diversity in the traits of interest is sampled by the selected species? Birds are a useful group to consider these questions. This is because semen collection and AI are routinely used to assist breeding in some groups such as birds of prey and cranes, a molecular phylogeny is available for the entire class (Sibley and Ahlquist, 1990), they are exceptionally well-known (life histories, morphology, etc.) and their vulnerability to extinction has been assessed for the entire class (Collar *et al.*, 1994). In fact, 11% of all bird species are threatened, as shown in Table 4.7. This is a large number, so how do we choose which species to conserve?

Owens and Bennett (2000) used the Comparative Analysis by Independent Contrast (CAIC) method (Purvis and Rambaut, 1995) to investigate this problem. This statistical method can assess the magnitude and direction of evolutionary changes ('contrasts') for any trait at each branching point ('node') in a phylogeny. It allows us to assess when diversity in a trait evolved in the evolutionary history of a group and to calculate the relative 'phylogenetic distinctiveness' of taxa with respect to patterns of phylogenetic branching. Owens and Bennett (2000) used this method to develop a new approach to measuring the relative contribution of different taxa in representing

TABLE 4.7
The number of bird species at risk of extinction

No. of species	Level of threat	Risk of extinction
168	Critical	50% chance of going extinct in 10 years
235	Endangered	20% chance of going extinct in 20 years
704	Vulnerable	10% chance of going extinct in 100 years

Data from Collar *et al.* (1994).

■ CHAPTER 4 ■

phenotypic diversification. This method is based on the use of independent contrasts to measure the amount of phenotypic change that occurs when lineages diverge and to quantify the extent to which a taxon represents the phenotypic diversification that has occurred in the past. They illustrated the method by using an analysis of variation in clutch size across 133 avian families, and found that not all families contribute equally to representing clutch size diversification. The top ten avian families in terms of representing clutch size diversification are the mesites (Mesitornithidae), cranes (Gruidae), bustards (Otidae), New World quail (Odontophoridae), seriemas (Cariamidae), finfoots (Heliornithidae), swallows (Hirundinidae), megapodes (Megapodiae) and guans (Cracidae). The 217 species in these ten families (2.3% of all bird species, 7.5% of families) represent 19.3% of diversification in clutch size.

What is the potential value of this method to species selection for GRBs that aim to conserve biodiversity? Owens and Bennett (2000) found that 17% of overall clutch size diversification is represented by taxa that are currently threatened by extinction. The ten families which represent the greatest proportion of overall clutch size diversification threatened by extinction are the mesites (Mesitornithidae), kagu (Rhynochetidae), cranes (Gruidae), kiwis (Apterygidae), New World quail (Odontophoridae), megapodes (Megapodiae), cassowaries (Casuariidae), finfoots (Heliornithidae), guans (Cracidae) and logrunners (Orthonychidae). Remarkably, the 42 threatened species (0.5% of all bird species, 3.8% of all threatened bird species) in these ten families encompass 53% of the overall representation of clutch size diversification threatened by extinction. These results suggest that this type of analysis could potentially help to prioritize and rationalize speciesbased conservation effort by identifying those taxa that contribute most towards representing biodiversity.

For birds, most variation in life history traits evolved over 40 million years ago and this accords with recent fossil evidence and molecular extrapolations (Owens and Bennett, 1995). Species selection criteria for conservation programmes ignore this fact and therefore there is a danger that conservation efforts that concentrate on saving many representatives from speciose groups may be neglecting unique sources of diversity in other lineages. We must develop algorithms such as that proposed by Owens and Bennett to maximize diversity by sampling species for GRBs from across the whole phylogeny. In this way we sample and conserve the results of millions of years of evolution and not just the last few thousand or few million years.

4.12 CONCLUSIONS

There are many advantages in using GRBs in conservation programmes that require active management of isolated populations of threatened species. The advantages for promoting gene flow alone are substantial, especially in the face of increasing restrictions on the movement of live animals. However, perhaps the greatest benefit is providing security against the increasing pressures facing living populations. Major funding is required to establish internationally planned GRBs that can help meet the objectives of biodiversity conservation programmes. Work is needed to establish the precise goals of these programmes and to determine how these can be translated into criteria for selecting species for GRBs. Phylogenetic approaches to species selection performed on a regional/national basis may assist with developing quantitative goals for GRBs to meet conservation objectives. In addition, considerable research effort is required for each species chosen for inclusion in GRBs to enable effective selection of donors and recipients to meet genetic goals. Furthermore, procedures for optimal storage and utilization of germplasm between stored and living populations need to be developed and tested. There is also a need to consider how GRBs for threatened habitats and ecosystems that integrate plant seed banks and animal germplasm banks can be developed.

REFERENCES

BALLOU, J. D. (1984) 'Strategies for maintaining genetic diversity in captive populations through reproductive technology', *Zoo Biol.* **3**, 311–323.

BALLOU, J. D. (1992) 'Potential contribution of cryopreserved germplasm to the preservation of genetic diversity and conservation of endangered species in captivity', *Cryobiology* **29**, 19–25.

BENNETT, M. D. (1998) 'Plant genome values: how much do we know?' *Proc. Natl. Acad. Sci. USA* **95**, 2011–2016.

BENIRSCHKE, K. (1984) 'The frozen zoo concept', *Zoo Biol.* **3**, 325–328.

CADE, T. J. (1983) 'Hybridization and gene exchange among birds in relation to conservation', in Schonewald-Cox, C. M., Chambers, S. M., MacBryde, B. and Thomas, L. (eds) *Genetics and Conservation: A Reference for Managing Wild Animal and Plant Populations*, California: Benjamin/Cummings, pp. 228–309.

CBSG (Conservation Breeding Specialist Group) (1992) *Population Biology Aspects of Genome Resource Banking*, Workshop Report, CBSG/SSC/IUCN, Apple Valley, MN, USA.

CBSG (Conservation Breeding Specialist Group) (1994) *Genome Resource Banking for Conservation in Africa*, Workshop Report, CBSG/SSC/IUCN, Apple Valley, MN, USA.

COLLAR, N. J., CROSBY, M. J. and STATTERSFIELD, A. J. (1994) *Birds to Watch 2: The World List of Threatened Birds*, Cambridge: Birdlife International.

DE BOER, L. E. M. (1989) 'Genetics and breeding programmes', in *EEP Co-ordinators Manual*, Amsterdam: National Foundation for Research in Zoological Gardens, Chapters I–V.

DRESSER, B. L. (1988) 'Cryobiology, embryo transfer, and artificial insemination in ex situ animal conservation programmes', in Wilson, E. O. and Peter, F. M. (eds) *Biodiversity*, Washington DC: National Academy Press, pp. 296–308.

EYRE-WALKER, A. and KEIGHTLEY, P. D. (1999) 'High genomic deleterious mutation rate in hominids', *Nature* **397**, 344–347.

FOOSE, T. (1983) 'The relevance of captive populations to the conservation of biotic diversity', in Schonewald-Cox, C. M., Chambers, S. M., MacBryde, B. and Thomas, L. (eds) *Genetics and Conservation: A Reference for Managing Wild Animal and Plant Populations*, Menlo Park, CA. Benjamin/Cummings, pp. 374–401.

FOOSE, T.J and BALLOU, J. (1988) 'Management of small populations.' *Int. Zoo Yearbook* **27**, 26–41.

FRANKEL, O. H. and SOULÉ M. E. (1981) *Conservation and Evolution,* Cambridge: Cambridge University Press.

HOLT, W. V. and MOORE, H. D. M. (1988) 'Semen banking–is it now feasible for captive endangered species', *Oryx* **22**, 172–178.

HOLT, W. V., BENNETT, P. M., VOLOBOUEV, V. and WATSON, P. F. (1996a) 'Genetic resource banks in wildlife conservation', *J. Zool., Lond.* **238**, 531–544.

HOLT, W. V., ABAIGAR, T. and JABBOUR, H. N. (1996b) 'Oestrous synchronization, semen preservation and artificial insemination in the Mohor gazelle (*Gazelle dama mhorr*) for the establishment of a genome resource bank programme', *Reprod. Fertil. Dev.* **8**, 1215–1222.

HOYT, E. (1988) *Conserving the Wild Relatives of Crops,* Rome: IBPGR, IUCN and WWF.

ISIS (International Species Information System) (1989*) SPARKS–Single Population Animal Record Keeping System*, Software and Manual, Apple Valley, MN, USA.

IUDZG/CBSG (1993) *The World Zoo Conservation Strategy; the Role of Zoos and Aquaria of the World in Global Conservation*. Illinois: Chicago Zoological Society.

JOHNSTON, L. A. and LACY, R. C. (1991) 'Utilization of sperm banks to maintain genetic diversity in captive populations of wild cattle', in Armstrong D. L. and Gross, T. S. (eds) *Proceedings of the Wild Cattle Symposium*, Omaha: Henry Doorly Zoo, USA, pp. 107–118.

JOHNSTON, L. A. and LACY, R. C. (1995) 'Genome resource banking for species conservation–selection of sperm donors', *Cryobiology* **32**, 68–77.

LACY, R. C. (1987) 'Loss of genetic diversity from managed populations: interacting effects of drift, mutation, immigration, selection and population subdivision', *Conserv. Biol.* **1**, 143–158.

LANDE, R. (1994) 'Risk of population extinction from fixation of new deleterious mutations', *Evolution* **48**, 1460–1469.

MACE, G. M. (1989) 'The application of reproductive technology to endangered species breeding programmes', *Zool. J. Linnean Soc.* **95**, 109–116.

MACE, G. M., PEMBERTON, J. M. and STANLEY, H. F. (1992) 'Conserving genetic diversity with the help of biotechnology–desert antelopes as an example', *Symp. Zool. Soc. Lond.* **64**, 123–134.

OWENS, I. P. F. and BENNETT, P. M. (1995) 'Ancient ecological diversification explains life-history variation among living birds', *Proc. R. Soc. Lond. B,* **261**, 227–232.

OWENS, I. P. F. and BENNETT, P. M. (2000) 'Quantifying biodiversity: a phenotypic perspective', *Conserv. Biol.* **14**, 1014–1022.

PURVIS, A. and RAMBAUT, A. (1995), 'Comparative Analyses by Independent Contrasts (CAIC): an Apple Macintosh application for analysing comparative data', *Comput. Appl. Biosci.* **11**, 247–251.

RALL, W. F. (1991) 'Guidelines for establishing animal genetic resource banks: biological materials, management and facility considerations', in Armstrong, D. L. and Gross, T. S. (eds) *Proceedings of the Wild Cattle Symposium*, Omaha: Henry Doorly Zoo, pp. 96–106.

SCHONEWALD-COX, C. M, CHAMBERS, S. M., MACBRYDE, B. and THOMAS, W. L. (1983) *Genetics and Conservation: A Reference for Managing Wild Animal and Plant Populations*, Menlo Park, CA: Benjamin/Cummings.

SIBLEY, C. G. and AHLQUIST, J. E. (1990) *Phylogeny and Classification of Birds*: *A Study in Molecular Evolution*, Stanford, CT: Yale University Press.

TUCKER, G. M. and HEATH, M. F. (1994) *Birds in Europe: Their Conservation Status*, Cambridge: BirdLife International.

WCMC (1996) World Conservation Monitoring Centre 1996 IUCN Red List of Threatened Species, Cambridge, UK.

WELCH, G. R. and JOHNSON, L. A. (1999) 'Sex preselection: laboratory validation of the sperm sex ratio of sorted X- and Y-sperm by sort reanalysis for DNA', *Theriogenology* **52**, 1343–1352.

CHAPTER 4

Disease Control Measures for Genetic Resource Banking

JAMES K. KIRKWOOD[1] **AND BEN COLENBRANDER**[2]

[1]Universities Federation for Animal Welfare, The Old School,
Brewhouse Hill, Wheathampstead, Herts AL4 8AN, UK

[2]Department of Herd Health and Reproduction, University of Utrecht,
PO Box 151, 3508 Utrecht, The Netherlands

Contents

5.1 INTRODUCTION

Conservation strategies for some endangered species involve captive breeding programmes. It is important that, as far as possible, these are coordinated and managed so as to preserve the genetic constitution of the founder populations (Seal *et al.*, 1994; Ballou and Foose, 1996). Animals involved are often maintained in subgroups at a number of locations including zoos and other animal collections. This is because the number of individuals that can be kept at any one place is almost always limited by the availability of space and other resources. This dispersed subgroup structure has some advantages and some disadvantages. Keeping animals in separate subpopulations reduces the risk of catastrophic epidemic disease or any other disaster killing the entire stock at a stroke. On the other hand, there can be significant logistical problems in genetic management when the population exists as small subgroups dispersed around the globe. In this situation, movement of germplasm rather than whole animals offers several advantages. It avoids the stresses that transport and introduction into new environments and social groups can impose on sentient animals, it greatly reduces the risk of some types of disease transmission that can accompany animal translocations (Kirkwood, 1997a), and it can be cheaper and easier than moving animals.

The long-term cryopreservation of germplasm of endangered species offers further flexibility in genetic management (Holt, 1994; Holt *et al.*, 1995; Bainbridge and Jabbour, 1998; Howard, 1999) and also further security against any disasters that may affect subpopulations. This technology may prove, therefore, to have an important role in the conservation of some species. However, there are several risks to be guarded against including (a) those from accidental transmission of infectious diseases via germplasm and (b) any adverse impacts on the welfare of the animals involved. Although there are strict controls on this technology in some countries, aimed at minimizing these risks (Kirkwood, 1997a; Bell and Paul, 1998), it is essential that both issues are very carefully considered in all cases. Whether germplasm is stored for use at another place or in the same place at another time, it is most important to minimize the risk of accidental storage of infectious agents with it. This chapter aims to provide an overview of the risks of germplasm resource banking in relation to infectious disease and how these can be minimized.

5.2 THE POTENTIAL IMPACT OF INTRODUCTION OF INFECTIOUS DISEASE

The introduction of exotic organisms into ecosystems is generally considered to have been one of the major causes of extinctions and loss of biodiversity in recent times (Pimm, 1991), and accidental or deliberate introductions remain a major threat.

Animals are frequently hosts to large and diverse communities of symbiotic, parasitic and opportunist organisms and the risks of accidental introductions of such agents when animals, or their products, are moved from one ecosystem to another have often been underestimated. This threat has received considerable discussion in recent years (e.g. Woodford, 1993; Woodford and Rossiter, 1993; Cunningham, 1995; Kirkwood, 1996, 1997b). Infectious diseases can affect host species in one or both of two ways: they may affect the dynamics and viability of the populations in which they occur and/or they may affect the welfare, the quality of life, of affected individuals.

The development of mathematical approaches to the study of host/parasite interactions (Anderson and May, 1992) has led to substantial advances in understanding the potential impact of infections on host population density, and these methods have begun to be used to explore the potential effects of infections on endangered species (Scott, 1988; Lyles and Dobson, 1993; McCallum and Dobson, 1995). An infectious disease may have no effect on its host population size or density, it may lead to fluctuations or a temporary or sustained depression of population size or density, or it may lead directly or indirectly to extinction (Kirkwood, 2000a). Infectious diseases generally present a greater threat to small, high-density populations (as those being managed for conservation often are) than to large, extensive populations. Not only are the direct effects of mortality or reproductive depression caused by an infectious disease likely to be more disastrous to small populations (perhaps leaving very few breeding individuals at all) but, residual, very small populations are then at even greater risk of extinction through chance demographic or other events.

In many cases, the introduction of infectious disease presents a greater threat to animal welfare than to population viability. This is well illustrated by myxomatosis in rabbits in Europe. This New World virus was introduced into rabbits, *Oryctolagus cunniculi*, in Europe in about 1950. Since that time, over fifty years ago, it has caused severe disease lasting for days or weeks, and almost certainly causing severe pain and distress, in millions of rabbits each year. The disease is not a significant threat to the viability of the European rabbit population but has a huge impact on the welfare of vast numbers of animals (Kirkwood *et al.*, 1994; Sainsbury *et al.*, 1995).

Infectious disease can have serious consequences for individual animal welfare and for species conservation and every effort must be made, when translocating animals or their products, not to transport infectious agents too. There is evidence that a wide range of infectious agents can occur in semen (Philpott, 1993) and a number of cases have been documented in which infectious diseases have been unintentionally spread through artificial insemination. For example, tuberculosis occurred in a large number of cattle inseminated with semen from a bull subsequently discovered to have the disease (Raumy, 1966), equine viral arteritis has been disseminated via samples of horse semen (Wood *et al.*, 1995), and, in humans, T-cell lymphotrophic virus type III has been transmitted via artificial insemination (Stewart *et al.*, 1985).

5.3 DISEASE RISKS WITH GERMPLASM BANKING AND USE FOR CONSERVATION

The risk of disease transmission associated with the movements of gametes and embryos is generally lower than that associated with animal translocation (Woodford and Rossiter, 1993). Translocating germplasm rather than animals blocks the possibility of transmission of many infectious diseases such as those caused by macroparasites (arthropods, helminths, etc.). Although some microparasitic agents (e.g. viruses and bacteria) can be present in germplasm, there are many diseases caused by micro-parasitic agents that are very unlikely to be transmitted via semen or ova, providing appropriate precautions are taken in animal management and during collection. Similarly, using the International Embryo Transfer Society's approved protocols, it has been found, in domesticated animals, that when transferring seven-day-old blastocysts, the risk of transmission of many bacterial and viral diseases is relatively small and, indeed, may offer a route to the elimination of some endemic infections (Philpott, 1993; Wrathall, 1995; Parker *et al.*, 1998). However, some important diseases can be transmitted via germplasm and, since semen samples, for example, can be used to inseminate many animals there is the potential for wide dissemination of disease if samples carry infection from the donor animal or become contaminated by contact with other samples during storage (Tedder *et al.*, 1995; Russell *et al.*, 1997).

Philpott (1993), Hare (1985) and Singh (1988) have provided valuable reviews of disease transmission risks associated with artificial insemination and embryo transfer. These papers consider germplasm technology in domestic species and it must always be considered that there could be differences with wild animals. There have been few attempts to investigate disease transmission via germplasm in wild animals (but see Howard *et al.*, 1995; Robison *et al.*, 1998) or to consider specifically the disease risks associated with germplasm banking in wild animals (but see Diseases and Medical Concerns Working Group, 1994).

5.3.1 Diseases that can be transmitted via semen

A wide range of infectious diseases can be transmitted via artificial insemination. These include bacterial, viral and other diseases. The lists in Tables 5.1 and 5.2 are largely based on diseases of domesticated animals since little information is available for other species. It is likely that a wide range of virus and other diseases in other taxa would be likely to be transmissible via semen. Risk assessments would need to be done on a case-by-case basis using up to date information on the known or possible infections of the species.

5.3.2 Diseases that can be transmitted via embryo transfer

Using approved protocols of embryo handling (International Embryo Transfer Society, 1990), it has been demonstrated that there is very much less danger of transmitting virus or bacterial diseases through embryo transfer than by artificial insemination (Philpott, 1993). It has recently been demonstrated that embryo transfer can provide an effective barrier against the transmission of sheep pulmonary adenomatosis from

TABLE 5.1
Virus diseases that can or probably could be transmitted by artificial insemination

Virus disease	Host species
Foot and mouth disease	Various artiodactyla
Rinderpest	Various artiodactyla
Peste de petite ruminants	Various artiodactyla
Vesicular stomatitis	Pigs
Bluetongue	Various artiodactyla
Epizootic haemorrhagic disease of deer	Deer
Rabies	Mammals
Malignant catarrhal fever	Various artiodactyla
Encephalomyocarditis	Various
Lumpy skin disease	Various artiodactyla
Rift Valley fever	Various artiodactyla
Sheep pox	Various artiodactyla
Scrapie	Sheep (prion diseases in other species?)
Enzootic bovine leucosis	Bovids
Infectious bovine rhinotracheitis	Bovids
Bovine virus diarrhoea	Bovids
African swine fever	Pigs
Classical swine fever	Pigs
Swine vesicular disease	Pigs
Teschen disease	Pigs
Aujeszky's disease	Pigs
Various parvoviruses	Pigs, carnivores
Blue ear disease	Pigs
Equine infectious anaemia	Horse
Glanders	Horse
African horse sickness	Horse
Equine viral arteritis	Horse
Equine herpes viruses	Horse
Simian, feline, other immunodeficiency virus	Various
Hepatitis B	Primates
Feline infectious peritonitis	Felidae
Feline infectious enteritis	Felidae
Feline rhinotracheitis	Felidae
Feline leukaemia virus	Felidae
Feline immunodeficiency virus	Felidae
Canine distemper	Various carnivora
Avian influenza	Birds
Newcastle disease	Birds

Sources: Foster *et al.* (1992); Philpott (1993); Diseases and Medical Concerns Working Group (1994); Royal College of Pathologists (1995); Tedder *et al.* (1995); Jordan *et al.* (1996); Glossop (1998).

TABLE 5.2
Bacterial and other diseases that can or probably could be transmitted by artificial insemination

Bacterial disease	Host species
Tuberculosis	Mammals, birds
Paratuberculosis	Various mammals
Salmonellosis	Vertebrates
brucelosis	Various mammals
Leptospirosis	Various mammals
Haemophilus diseases	Various
Campylobacter diseases	Various
Chlamydiosis	Various
Mycoplasma diseases	Various
Trichomoniasis	Various

Sources: Philpott (1993); Diseases and Medical Concerns Working Group (1994); Glossop (1998).

affected donors (Parker *et al.*, 1998). Although final results are not yet available, preliminary observations suggest that embryo transfer might also provide an effective barrier against transmission of bovine spongiform encephalopathy from affected donors (Wrathall *et al.*, 1994). However, in contrast, Foster *et al.* (1992) found in an embryo-transfer study that scrapie (another form of transmissible spongiform encephalopathy) did pass from dams to their offspring via the preimplantation embryo.

5.3.3   Cross-contamination in liquid nitrogen freezers

The potential for cross-contamination with infectious agents among samples stored in liquid nitrogen was demonstrated not long ago in an unfortunate incident in which six human patients undergoing cytotoxic treatment developed hepatitis B after perfusion with cryopreserved bone marrow or peripheral-blood stem cells (Tedder *et al.*, 1995). Leakage from a storage bag had led to contamination of the liquid nitrogen tank. Following this incident, the hazards of contamination of cryopreserved samples in liquid nitrogen storage tanks has received further attention (e.g. Department of Health, 1997; Fountain *et al.*, 1997; McLaughlin *et al.*, 1999). In one study it was found that seven of 583 thawed components were contaminated with a variety of environmental or waterborne organisms and that one freezer was heavily contaminated with *Aspergillus* species (Fountain *et al.*, 1997).

Disease risks to and from humans

It is important to note that there are many infectious diseases of wild animals that can also affect humans. Protocols for collecting, handling and storage of germplasm should be designed to protect against any such risks. Particular care should be taken when handling germplasm from species (e.g. a number of non-human primates) that quite commonly carry infections (e.g. in the case of non-human primates: herpesvirus simiae, hepatitis A and B, yellow fever, monkey pox, simian immunodeficiency virus) that can or may cause serious or fatal disease in humans (Ott-Joslin, 1993; Weber *et al.*, 1997). Conversely, a range of human infections can cause disease in non-human primate species and great care should be taken to prevent infection of germplasm by human pathogens during collection and handling. There are various publications that may help in devising appropriate occupational health protocols (e.g. National Research Council, 1997).

5.4   HYGIENIC COLLECTION AND HANDLING OF SEMEN, OVA AND EMBRYOS

As a tool for species conservation, germplasm banking remains largely in the experimental stage at present (but see Howard, 1999; Pope and Loskutoff, 1999). The techniques are well established in domestic animal production and the protocols for the collection and handling of semen, ova and embryos that have been developed in this industry (e.g. OIE, 1992; Glossop, 1998) provide good models for the conservation community.

For example, in the management of pig herds for semen production, it is recommended that a stringent biosecurity policy must be followed based on knowledge of the diseases that may pose a risk (Glossop, 1998). This includes consideration of control of all potential sources of infection, including windborne, incoming animals, attendants, feed and water, and arthropod and other wildlife vectors. Likewise, the infectious disease status of wild animals maintained for collection of germplasm that may be used in geographically or temporally separated populations, should be as well defined as possible and the animals should be kept as isolated as possible from potential sources of infection.

5.4.1 Management of donor animals

Donor animals should be in good health, free of infectious diseases, and managed in such a way as to minimize the risks of exposure to infectious agents and that will meet the conditions required to permit the international transport of germplasm. The animals, and the facilities in which they are kept, should be maintained in isolation from other animals, be under close veterinary supervision and subject to regular routine checks for health and hygiene practices. Donor animals should have been resident at the premises for at least 30 days before any collections are made. Prior to collections an assessment should be made of infectious diseases that the species could carry or be affected by and specific measures should be made to eliminate the risk of the presence of these agents by appropriate testing and/or prophylactic treatment, isolation, and other methods as appropriate. Entry of visitors to the site should be strictly controlled and all persons entering should observe high standards of hygiene.

5.4.2 Hygienic collection and handling of semen

During collection of semen, careful attention should be paid to hygiene with rigorous disinfection of the collecting equipment used and, where necessary, thorough cleaning of the preputial orifice. Collecting tubes should be sterile. Semen samples should be handled according to the codes of hygiene provided by the Office International des Epizooties (OIE, 1992). The OIE also sets out methodologies for counting micro-organisms in semen samples and these may be used to help monitor semen quality. Any diluents used must be free of pathogens.

Straws of semen should be carefully and permanently labelled and the records for each sample should include data that may be important for assessment of the health or carrier status of the donor at such time, possibly in the quite distant future, when the sample comes to be used. Data recorded should include details of the origin, age and full history of the donor animal, listing the places it had been kept previously and the animals it had been in contact with, and also providing full details of health assessment and quarantine measures and specific screening tests undertaken and their results.

At the time of semen collection and two weeks subsequently, blood samples should be collected for serum samples for storage. These may be used for screening tests at the time, but aliquots should also be kept to be stored with the semen, for possible use in infectious disease screening that may be deemed appropriate at the time the sample comes to be used in the future. Knowledge of the infectious diseases of wild animals is scant and it is likely that new infectious diseases will be discovered and also that better tests will be developed for screening against some of the diseases that are already known.

It has been shown that there is potential for cross-infection between semen packaging straws due to leakage from the straws with some methods of filling and sealing (Russell *et al.*, 1997), and the resulting potential contamination of liquid nitrogen storage dewars (Tedder *et al.*, 1995). Russell *et al.* (1997) found that the risk of leakage can be minimized by careful practice and the use of a secondary seal of adhesive tape on straws. The Working Party of the Royal College of Pathologists (1995) has recommended, in order to minimize the risk of cross-infections, the storage of cryopreserved human materials in screw-top cryovials secondarily sealed in cryoflex tubing or, ideally, storage in the gaseous phase of cryopreservation tanks (in the vapour above the liquid nitrogen). Further recommendations, including the hygienic maintenance of freezers, have been given by the Department of Health (1997). The advantages and difficulties of storage of samples in the gaseous phase have been recently discussed at a cyberspace (internet) meeting (McLaughlin *et al.* 1999).

5.4.3 Hygienic collection and handling of embryos and ova

For domesticated animals, the Office International des Epizooties recommends (OIE, 1992) that the embryo collection team should be supervised by a veterinarian and that all team personnel should be trained in principles and techniques of infectious disease control. At the time of embryo collection, and two weeks subsequently, serum samples should be collected and stored, as described in the above section on semen collection, as a resource for further infectious disease screening, should it be deemed appropriate, at the time embryos or ova come to be used.

The International Embryo Transfer Society (1990) recommends, for domesticated species, that each embryo is examined using at least $50 \times$ magnification, over its entire surface in order to be certified free of adherent material. The IETS code also requires that embryos are washed according to standard protocols and certified to have intact zonae pellucidae both before and after washing. As for semen samples, cryopreserved ova and embryos must be clearly and permanently labelled, stored with due care, and full records relevant to the assessment of the health status of the donors in the future should be maintained (see above).

5.5 LEGISLATION COVERING THE COLLECTION AND INTERNATIONAL MOVEMENT OF GERMPLASM

The international movement of germplasm is covered under two branches of legislation (Kirkwood, 1997a). The CITES (Convention on International Trade in Endangered Species) legislation imposes restrictions on international movements of endangered animals and tissues and products from them. For international movements it is necessary to have certification from both the exporting and importing countries. Since 1993 there has been no requirement for CITES certification for movements between European Union (EU) countries, but some EU countries still expect or require certification following this and it remains advisable to check the situation before arranging shipments between countries within the EU.

The other branch of legislation regulating international shipment of germplasm is the animal health legislation. This is primarily focused on the prevention of importation of infectious diseases of importance to human and production animal health. It should not be assumed that meeting the requirements of existing animal health legislation indicates disease-free status and for non-domesticated species there may be a need for extra provisions and responsibility for considering this falls on those involved in the movement. The importation of germplasm is strictly regulated in many countries and international shipment is highly unlikely to be permitted unless freedom from certain diseases can be certified by the state veterinary service of the exporting country.

The animal health requirements governing trade within and imports into the EU of semen, embryos and ova from animals not covered by other existing legislation (e.g. Directive 90/429/EEC covering porcine semen, Directive 88/407/EEC covering bovine semen, and Directive 89/556/EEC covering bovine embryos) are laid out in the 'Balai' (catch-all) Directive 92/65/EEC of 13 July 1992. This covers all primates (except humans), ungulates (including zoo ruminants, deer and Suidae), bees, rabbits and hares, ferrets, mink and foxes, cats and dogs and other rabies-susceptible animals, and semen ova and embryos of the ovine, caprine and equine species (Directive, 1992). The implementation of this directive, or at least parts of it, has proved somewhat problematic, and the rate of progress has varied between EU member states. It is wise to seek advice from the state veterinary authorities about restrictions and requirements for certification well in advance of planned shipments of germplasm from wild animals between countries (within the EU and elsewhere). Apart from restrictions on international movements, there may be local, within-country restrictions under some circumstances for disease control reasons. If in doubt, advice should be sought from appropriate regional or state veterinary authorities.

It is pertinent to note here that there are also, in the UK and in other countries, legislation and codes of conduct covering animal welfare aspects of the collection of semen, ova and embryos from live animals and relevant to the transport of cryopreserved material (Kirkwood, 1997b). The collection and reimplantation of germplasm from live animals is unlikely to be to the welfare advantage of the animals involved. Prior to deciding to undertake any intervention for species conservation which may harm the welfare of the individual animals involved: (a) the conservation benefits should be weighed carefully against potential welfare costs, and (b) where, on the basis of this ethical review, the decision is taken to proceed, protocols should be refined so as to minimize any adverse impact on the welfare of the animals involved (Kirkwood, 2000b).

5.6 CONCLUSION

The cryopreservation of germplasm may become a valuable part of the conservation programme of some species in the future. However, since accidental introduction of infectious agents can have catastrophic consequences on population viability and on the welfare of individual animals, great care needs to be taken to ensure that cryopreserved germplasm does not harbour infections. There are quite stringent codes and regulations covering the hygiene aspects of the collection, transport and use of

CHAPTER 5

semen, ova and embryos of domesticated animals in some countries (the efficacy of which has recently been discussed by Bell and Paul, 1998), and these rules provide a valuable basis from which to proceed in the development of special techniques and measures for wild animals. Furthermore, unless these codes are observed closely, countries are unlikely to issue import permits for cryopreserved germplasm. However, since most national and international animal health legislation is focused on diseases of domestic livestock, it should not be assumed that meeting these legislative requirements equates to the germplasm having disease-free status. It remains the responsibility of those involved in the collection, shipping and use of cryopreserved germplasm from wild animals, to assess carefully the infectious disease risks associated with these activities. In addition to rigorous measures to avoid storage of germplasm that may carry infection (which cover all aspects from husbandry of donor animals to treatment of samples collected), it is strongly recommended that full health records are maintained of donor animals and that paired sera are also cryopreserved as a resource for further screening tests that may be deemed appropriate at the time of use of the germplasm.

REFERENCES

ANDERSON, R. M. and MAY, R. M. (1992) *Infectious Diseases of Humans: Dynamics and Control*, Oxford: Oxford Science Publications.

BAINBRIDGE, D. R. J. and JABBOUR, H. N. (1998) 'Potential of assisted breeding techniques for the conservation of endangered mammalian species in captivity: a review', *Vet. Rec.* **143**, 159–168.

BALLOU, J. D. and FOOSE, T. J. (1996) 'Demographic and genetic management of captive populations', in Kleiman, D. G., Allen, M. E., Thompson, K. V. and Lumpkin, S. C. (eds) *Wild Mammals in Captivity*, Chicago: University of Chicago Press, pp. 263–283.

BELL, R. A. and PAUL, R. A. (1998) 'Disease risks associated with international movement of semen and embryos'. *J. Anim. Breeding* **2**, 14–17.

CUNNINGHAM, A. A. (1995) 'Disease risks of wildlife translocations', *Conserv. Biol.* **10**, 349–353.

DEPARTMENT OF HEALTH (1997) *Guidance Notes on the processing, Storage and Issue of Bone Marrow and Blood Stem Cells*. London: UK Department of Health.

Directive (1992) Council Directive 92/65/EEC. *Official Journal of the European Communities* **L264**, 54–65.

DISEASES AND MEDICAL CONCERNS WORKING GROUP (1994) Report of the diseases and medical concerns working group, in *Genome Resource Banking for Conservation in Africa, Workshop Report June 19–21 1994*. Pretoria, Republic of South Africa: Pan

African Association of Zoological Gardens, Aquaria and Botanical Gardens/IUCN Captive Breeding Specialist Group, pp. 13–19.

FOSTER, J. D., MCKELVEY, W. A. C., MYLNE, M. J. A., WILLIAMS, A., HUNTER, N., HOPE, J. and FRASER, H. (1992) 'Studies on maternal transmission of scrapie in sheep by embryo transfer', *Vet. Rec.* **130**, 341–343.

FOUNTAIN, D., RALSTON, M., HIGGINS, N., GORLIN, J. B., UHL, L., WHEELER, C., ANTIN, J. H., CHURCHILL, W. H. and BENJAMIN, R. J. (1997) 'Liquid nitrogen freezers: a potential source of microbial contamination of hematopoietic stem cell components', *Transfusion* **37**, 585–591.

GLOSSOP, C. (1998) 'AI in pigs: the production of quality-assured, healthy semen', *In Practice* **20**, 182–188.

HARE, W. C. D. (1985) *Diseases Transmissible by Semen and Embryo Transfer Techniques*, OIE Technical Series No.4, Paris: Office International des Epizooties.

HOLT, W. V. (1994) 'Reproductive technologies', in Olney, P. J. S., Mace, G. M. and Feistner, A. T. C. (eds) *Creative Conservation: Interactive Management of Wild and Captive Animals*, London: Chapman and Hall, pp. 144–166.

HOLT, W. V., BENNETT, P. M., VOLOBOUEV, V. and WATSON, P. F. (1995) 'Genetic resource banks in wildlife conservation', *J. Zool.* **238**, 531–544.

HOWARD, J. (1999) 'Assisted reproductive techniques in nondomestic carnivores', in Fowler, M. E. and Miller, R. E. (eds) *Zoo and Wild Animal Medicine: Current Therapy*, 4th edn, Philadelphia: W.B. Saunders Co, pp. 449–457.

HOWARD, J., WILDT, D., JORDAN, H., KENNEDY-STOSKOPF, S. and TOMPKINS, W. (1995) 'Transmission of feline immunodeficiency virus in domestic cat by artificial insemination: model for seminal transmission of FIV in nondomestic felids', *1995 Proceedings of the American Association of Zoo Veterinarians*, 450–451.

INTERNATIONAL EMBRYO TRANSFER SOCIETY (1990) *Manual of the International Embryo Transfer Society. A Procedural Guideline and General Information for the Use of Embryo Transfer Technology Emphasising Sanitary Procedures*, Champaign, Illinois: International Embryo Transfer Society.

JORDAN, H. L., HOWARD, J.-G., SELLON, R. K., WILDT, D. E., TOMPKINS, W. A. and KENNEDY-STOSKOPF, S. (1996) 'Transmission of feline immunodeficiency virus in domestic cats via artificial insemination', *J. Virol.* **70**, 8224–8228.

KIRKWOOD, J. K. (1996) 'Special challenges of maintaining wildlife in captivity in Europe and Asia', *Rev. Sci. Techn. l'Office Int. Epizooties* **15**, 309–321.

KIRKWOOD, J. K. (1997a) 'Import and export of semen, ova and embryos: legislation concerning the collection and movement of genetic material (embryos, semen and

CHAPTER 5

ova) of wild animals into and within the European Community', *J. Br. Vet. Zool. Soc.* **2**, 14–18.

KIRKWOOD, J. K. (1997b) 'Disease risks with translocations of wild animals into, out of, and within Europe', *J. Br. Vet. Zool. Soc.* **2**, 3–4.

KIRKWOOD, J. K. (2000a) 'Helminth diseases and wildlife conservation', in Chowdhury, N. and Aguirre, A. A. (eds) *Helminths of Wildlife*, New Delhi: Oxford and IBH Publishing Co Pvt Ltd., pp. 397–408 (in press).

KIRKWOOD, J. K. (2000b) 'Veterinary considerations and ethical dilemmas in vertebrate reintroduction programmes', in Langenhorst, T. and Wakefield, S. (eds) *Bringing Back the Bison: Proceedings of a Symposium,* jointly organized by Marwell Zoological Park, The Defence Evaluation and Research Agency and The Wildlife Conservation Foundation, *1–2 October 1998, Farnborough, UK.* Colden Common, Winchester: Marwell Preservation Trust, pp. 30–35.

KIRKWOOD, J. K., SAINSBURY, A. W. and BENNETT, P. M. (1994) 'The welfare of free-living wild animals: methods of assessment', *Anim. Welf.* **3**, 257–273.

LYLES, A. M. and DOBSON, A. P. (1993) 'Infectious disease and intensive management: population dynamics, threatened hosts, and their parasites', *J. Zoo Wildlife Med.* **24**, 315–326.

McCALLUM, H. and DOBSON, A. (1995) 'Detecting disease and parasite threats to endangered species and ecosystems', *Trends Ecol. Evol.* **10**, 190–194.

McLAUGHLIN, E., PACEY, A. and ELLIOTT, T. (eds) (1999) *Safe Cryopreservation of Gametes and Embryos. World-Wide Conferences on Reproductive Biology,* Perth: Ladybrook Publishing.

NATIONAL RESEARCH COUNCIL (1997) *Occupational Health and Safety in the Care and Use of Research Animals,* Washington DC: National Academy Press.

OIE (Office International des Epizooties) (1992) *International Animal Health Code: Mammals, Birds and Bees,* Paris: Office International des Epizooties.

OTT-JOSLIN, J. E. (1993) 'Zoonotic diseases of non-human primates', in Fowler, M.E. (ed.) *Zoo and Wild Animal Medicine: Current Therapy,* 3rd edn, Philadelphia: W.B. Saunders Co, pp. 359–373.

PARKER, B. N. J., WRATHALL, A. E., SAUNDERS, R. W., DAWSON, M., DONE, S. H., FRANCIS, P. G., DEXTER, I. and BRADLEY, R. (1998) 'Prevention of transmission of sheep pulmonary adenomatosis by embryo transfer', *Vet. Rec.* **142**, 687–689.

PHILPOTT, M. (1993) 'The dangers of disease transmission by artificial insemination and embryo transfer', *Br. Vet. J.* **149**, 339–369.

PIMM, S. L. (1991) *The Balance of Nature?* Chicago: University of Chicago.

POPE, C. E. and LOSKUTOFF, N. M. (1999) 'Embryo transfer and semen technology from cattle applied to nondomestic artiodactylids', in Fowler, M.E. and Miller, R.E. (eds) *Zoo and Wild Animal Medicine: Current Therapy*, 4th edn, Philadelphia: W.B. Saunders Co, pp. 597–604.

RAUMY, B. (1966) 'Une epizootie de tuberculose bovine transmise par insémination artificielle', *Rec. Méd. Vét.* **142**, 729–741.

ROBISON, C. D., DAVIS, D. S., TEMPLETON, J. W., WESTHUSIN, M., FOXWORTH, W. B., GILSDORF, M. J. and ADAMS, L. G. (1998) 'Conservation of germ plasm from bison infected with *Brucella abortus*', *J. Wildlife Dis.* **34**, 582–589.

Royal College of Pathologists, Working Party of (1995) *HIV and the Practice of Pathology*, London: Marks and Spencer Publications Unit of the Royal College of Pathologists.

RUSSELL, P. H., LYARUU, V. H., MILLAR, J. D., CURRY, M. R. and WATSON, P. F. (1997) 'The potential transmission of infectious agents by semen packaging during storage for artificial insemination', *Anim. Reprod. Sci.* **47**, 337–342.

SAINSBURY, A. W., BENNETT, P. M. and KIRKWOOD, J. K. (1995) 'The welfare of free-living wild animals in Europe: harm caused by human activities', *Anim. Welf.* **4**, 183–206.

SCOTT, M. E. (1988) 'The impact of infection and disease on animal populations: implications for conservation biology', *Conserv. Biol.* **2**, 40–56.

SEAL, U. S., FOOSE, T. J. and ELLIS, S. (1994) 'Conservation assessment and management plans (CAMPS) and global captive action plans (GCAPS)', in Olney, P. J. S., Mace, G. M. and Feistner, A. T. C. (eds) *Creative Conservation: Interactive Management of Wild and Captive Animals*, London: Chapman and Hall, pp. 312–325.

SINGH, E. (1988) *Potential of Embryos to Control Transmission of Disease: A Review of Current Research*, Nepean, Ontario: Animal Disease Research Institute.

STEWART, G., TYLER, J. P. P., CUNNINGHAM, A. L., BARR, J. A., DRISCOLL, G. L., GOLD, J. and LAMONT, B. J. (1985) 'Transmission of human T-cell lymphotrophic virus type III (HTLV III) by artificial insemination by donor', *Lancet* ii, 581–584.

TEDDER, R. S., ZUCKERMAN, M. A., GOLDSTONE, A. H., HAWKINS, A. E., FIELDING, A., BRIGGS, E. M., IRWIN, D., BLAIR, S., GORMAN, A. M., PATTERSON, K. G., LINCH, D. C., HEPTONSTALL, J. and BRINK, N. S. (1995) 'Hepatitis B transmission from contaminated cryo-preservation tank', *Lancet* **346**, 137–140.

WEBER, H., BERGE, E., FINCH, J., HEIDT, P., HUNSMANN, G., PERETTA, G. and VERSCHUERE, B. (1997) 'Sanitary aspects of handling non-human primates during transport', *Lab. Anim.* **31**, 298–302.

WOOD, J. L. N., CHIRNSIDE, E. D., MUMFORD, J. A. and HIGGINS, A. J. (1995) 'First recorded outbreak of equine viral arteritis in the United Kingdom', *Vet. Rec.* **136**, 381–385.

WOODFORD, M. H. (1993) 'International disease implications for wildlife translocation', *Journal of Zoo and Wildlife Medicine* **24**, 265–270.

WOODFORD, M. H. and ROSSITER, P. B. (1993) 'Disease risks associated with wildlife translocation projects', *Rev. Sci. Techn. l'Office Int. Epizooties* **12**, 115–135.

WRATHALL, A. E. (1995) 'Embryo transfer and disease transmission in livestock: a review of recent research', *Theriogenology* **43**, 81–88.

WRATHALL, A. E., BROWN, K. F. D., PULLAR, D. and BASTIMAN, B. (1994) 'Embryo transfer (ET) from cattle affected with bovine spongiform encephalopathy (BSE): preliminary report', *Theriogenology* **41**, 337.

CHAPTER

6

Reproductive Technologies Necessary for Successful Applications of Genetic Resource Banking

J. K. HODGES

Department of Reproductive Biology, German Primate Centre,
Kellnerweg 4, 37077 Göttingen, Germany

Contents

6.1 INTRODUCTION

The potential impact of germplasm resource banking is dependent not simply upon successful methods for collecting and preserving gametes and embryos, but also on related technologies for manipulating reproductive processes and/or function in order to facilitate the utilization of banked material. Since the ultimate objective is the (re)introduction of genes into a given population through the production of reproductively viable offspring, the power of germplasm resource banking is thus effectively limited by the extent to which such related technologies are available for a given number of species and situations.

Key among these technologies are those for monitoring and controlling reproductive function. Timing of reproductive events is essential for the collection of gametes and embryos for cryostorage and their later use for establishing pregnancies. This involves not only reliable monitoring of natural events, but also the use of procedures for exerting external control over their timing and frequency. Of the other assisted reproductive technologies, those concerned with the *in vitro* production of embryos are of particular significance for germplasm banking, in that they offer a high degree of flexibility and potential for manipulation of gametes, provided current technical limitations can be overcome. The efficiency of the collection and transfer (insemination) procedures themselves is clearly also important in determining the effective utilization of banked material, as too is their ability to function under extensive and varied management conditions. Furthermore, since the use of anaesthesia often cannot be avoided, a knowledge of the potential effects of anaesthetic agents on various reproductive processes is essential. In all these aspects, the challenges presented when working with non-domestic animals are confounded by the diversity of species in question and the variation in reproductive control mechanisms, responsiveness to treatment and sensitivity to procedural disturbance which they display.

6.2 MONITORING REPRODUCTIVE STATUS

Methods for determining reproductive status provide essential support for germplasm banking technologies by facilitating not only the collection of gametes and/or embryos but also their subsequent use for the establishment of pregnancy and production of offspring (Figure 6.1). Information on preovulatory follicular status and timing of impending ovulation is necessary for scheduling recovery of oocytes in both stimulated and non-stimulated cycles. Timing of ovulation is also crucial to the success of AI. Since the lifespan of both gametes is limited, particularly that of the egg, which usually needs to be fertilized within 12 hours of ovulation, timing of insemination in relation to follicular rupture needs to be precisely regulated. It should also be

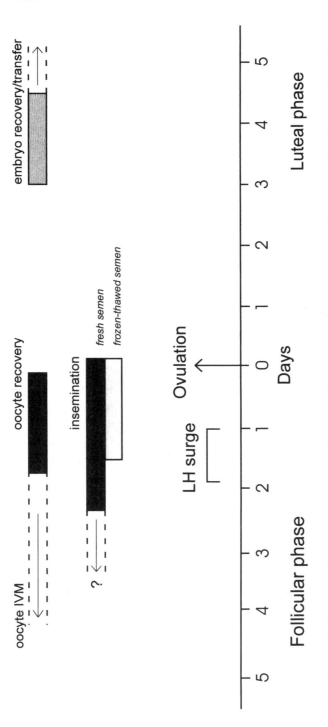

Figure 6.1: Schematic diagram indicating the timing of various assisted reproduction procedures in relation to ovulation. Insemination with fresh sperm should normally be scheduled within the 48 hours preceding ovulation, and as close to the event as possible. In some (rare) cases, sperm may remain viable in the female tract for longer periods. The lifespan of frozen-thawed sperm is reduced, while that of the ovulated oocyte is usually less than 12 hours. *In vivo* matured oocytes are normally recovered after the onset of the mid-cycle LH surge, and within the 24-hour period before ovulation. In conjunction with IVM, oocytes may theoretically be recovered at any stage of the reproductive cycle and even during quiescence. Preimplantation embryos are recoved from the uterus at the four-cell to early blastocyst stages, usually between 3 and 7 days after ovulation, depending on species.

remembered that survival of cryopreserved-thawed spermatozoa is usually reduced compared with fresh spermatozoa, thus further curtailing effective gamete lifespan (see Chapter 3). Since the consequences of failure to inseminate within a relatively short window include not just lack of fertilization but also increased likelihood of genetic and/or developmental abnormalities arising from fertilization with post-mature (aged) gametes (e.g. German, 1968), prospective information enabling accurate prediction of the time of ovulation is critical.

Knowledge of the time of ovulation is also necessary for scheduling embryo recovery and/or transfer procedures since, in general, the detection of pregnancy itself is not possible at the early (preimplantation) stages. In this case, retrospective detection of ovulation suffices. Pregnancy detection, however, is necessary for determining the outcome of assisted breeding attempts, and information at an early stage is important if repeat procedures are to be scheduled, or for determining the incidence and timing of embryonic losses.

A number of methods exist which can be applied to obtain information of the nature described above. In addition to reliability and accuracy of information, practicability is a major consideration when working with non-domesticated species, and since capture and restraint are often stressful to the animal, methods which require repeated handling are unsuitable for many species. Of the various options, laparoscopy has been used extensively and successfully for scheduling insemination and/or oocyte retrieval in a number of species, most notably Felidae (e.g. Wildt, 1980; Wildt *et al.*, 1992), but as a monitoring method has largely been superseded by less invasive procedures.

6.2.1 Ultrasound

Real-time ultrasonography can be used to monitor follicular development and early pregnancy and is the method of choice for monitoring both natural and induced cycles in domestic and some laboratory species. Ultrasound enables direct visualization of reproductive organs, providing a high degree of resolution, but without the need for surgical intervention. The principal drawback is that handling is required and so the method is suitable for repeated application only in animals which are tame or which can be conditioned to the procedure without the need for anaesthesia. In the larger ungulate species, conditioning to stand in a crush device for non-sedated transrectal scanning is, however, possible (e.g. Adams *et al.*, 1991; Radcliffe *et al.*, 1997), whilst, with training, smaller animals will often tolerate manual restraint for the abdominal surface approach (e.g. Oerke *et al.*, 1995; Hildebrandt and Göritz, 1995).

Since ultrasound enables direct visualization of ovarian structures, individual follicles and corpora lutea down to sizes of 1–2 mm can be readily identified. Probes of 5–7.5 MHz are commonly used, but for smaller species (e.g. Callitrichid primates)

CHAPTER 6

frequencies of 10 MHz are necessary to provide sufficient resolution (Oerke *et al.*, 1996). Single scans can be useful for indicating general level of ovarian activity, for discriminating pre- and postovulatory stages of the cycle, and for confirming the presence of preovulatory structures indicating impending ovulation. Meaningful interpretation of results, however, requires access to a database on cyclic changes in the presence and appearance of different ovarian structures and, in particular, on range of follicle size in relation to stage of development. Since for most non-domestic species, this is not yet available, accurate assessment of follicular status or prediction of ovulation usually requires repeated scanning and in situations where this is impractical, ultrasound is best performed as an adjunct to other procedures such as hormone measurement.

In contrast, a single scan is usually sufficient to enable detection of pregnancy at a relatively early stage. The presence of a distinctive endometrial echo or fluid-filled embryonic vesicle can often be visualized within 2–3 weeks of conception, allowing confident diagnosis at a stage comparable to (if not earlier than) that achievable by standard endocrine methods. Ultrasound also provides valuable information on the number of embryos (useful after ovarian stimulation or multiple embryo transfer) and detection of heart beat also confirms fetal viability.

In recent years, the use of ultrasound as a diagnostic tool in non-domestic species has increased considerably and its application to monitoring ovarian function and detection of pregnancy has now been described for a wide range of species, including Old and New World monkeys (e.g. Oerke *et al.*, 1995, 1996; Tarantal and Hendrickx, 1988; Tarantal, 1992; Jaquish *et al.*, 1995), great apes (Loskutoff *et al.*, 1991a), diverse ungulate species (Adams *et al.*, 1991; Bravo *et al.*, 1992; Skidmore *et al.*, 1996), carnivores (Göritz *et al.*, 1996), elephants (Hildebrandt and Göritz, 1995), rhinoceros (Adams *et al.*, 1991; Schaffer *et al.*, 1994; Radcliffe *et al.*, 1997), marine mammals (du Boulay and Wilson, 1988; Stone, 1990) as well as several non-mammalian species (Hildebrandt and Göritz, 1995; Casares, 1997; Göritz, 1996).

6.2.2 Hormone analysis

Since most reproductive processes are associated with characteristic changes in hormone production, endocrine-based methods provide the most effective indirect approach to monitoring reproductive status. Whereas historically (in laboratory or domestic species) this has been most conveniently achieved through the assay of blood plasma, such an invasive approach is usually undesirable or simply not possible for many non-domestic species. Hormone determination in urine and faeces offers a non-invasive alternative by which sample collection, even on a frequent basis, can be performed without the need for animal handling. Although much of the information on reproductive cycles in endangered species derives from urine analysis, determination of hormonal profiles through faecal analysis has recently generated increased interest, primarily due to its advantages in terms of sample collection from animals in group-living or free-ranging situations.

The most commonly used endocrine approach to reproductive assessment is based on the determination of oestrogen and progesterone profiles. In this way (at least in most mammals) the measurement of elevated levels of progesterone or its excreted metabolites indicates the postovulatory or luteal phase of the cycle. An increase in levels above a defined threshold is normally used to signal (usually to ±one day) the onset of the luteal phase, one day after ovulation. In most species this will correspond to day 1 of pregnancy, which can then be used to schedule the day of embryo collection and/or transfer. Information on follicular development in the preovulatory phase of the cycle is provided by measurement of oestrogens (oestradiol and its excreted metabolites), which are almost exclusively of preovulatory follicular origin. Measurement of gonadotrophins (usually luteinizing hormone (LH)) enables more precise timing of ovulation, the onset of the mid-cycle LH surge usually preceding follicular rupture (in mammals) by about 24–36 hours.

Pregnancy is generally indicated by maintenance of elevated luteal phase levels of progestogens and thus by the absence of a continuing cyclic pattern. A variety of other hormones, including oestrogens, inhibin, relaxin and prolactin show pregnancy-associated elevations of a species-specific nature and which may be of diagnostic value. In some species, pregnancy-specific hormone secretion can be detected, and amongst simian primates, for example, the measurement of the early postimplantation rise in the glycoprotein hormone chorionic gonadotrophin, either in plasma or in urine, provides a reliable and highly convenient method of pregnancy detection.

In general, information derived from hormone measurement in urine is similar to that in blood, although somewhat reduced in precision in terms of detecting short-term changes. On the other hand, there are advantages to the meaurement of excreted hormones which provides a more integrated picture of recent endocrine events, than does the minute-to-minute fluctuations seen in plasma. Quality of sample is particularly important for urine determinations, and is subject to influence from a variety of factors, including time since voiding, presence of contaminants and water content. Faecal measurements are still relatively laborious, but methods (particularly for extraction) have been simplified to some extent, and there is a rapidly increasing number of species for which faecal hormone analysis has provided reliable information on reproductive status.

When measuring hormones in urine or faeces, the delay period from secretory event to time of excretion needs to be taken into account. For urine, this is generally less than 6 hours, whereas metabolism and elimination of faecal steroids usually occurs within the range 24–48 hours, but varies according to species and can be affected by factors such as diet and health status (Wasser *et al.*, 1993, and references in

Heistermann *et al.*, 1995; Schwarzenberger *et al.*, 1996). Thus, faecal analysis should be restricted to situations where retrospective information on reproductive status suffices.

A number of factors can affect the relative value and/or suitability of faecal versus urinary analysis. One of the main considerations is species differences in metabolism and route of excretion (e.g. Heistermann *et al.*, 1995; Palme *et al.*, 1996). For example, both approaches are suitable in primates when considered as a whole, but experience with carnivores (Felidae and Canidae) indicates that the majority of steroids are excreted via the faecal route and that urinary analysis yields little useful information (Shille *et al.*, 1985; Brown *et al.*, 1994; Brown and Wildt, 1997; Monfort *et al.*, 1997). Looking within the primates, however, variation is considerable, with some species excreting steroid metabolites almost exclusively in faeces, others mainly into urine, whilst others use both routes of excretion to more or less similar extents (see Heistermann *et al.*, 1995). Relative abundances of the individual metabolites of the same circulating parent compound also differ considerably between species. The extent of the variation of both oestrogen and progesterone metabolites within the Rhino-ceratidae for example (Hodges, 1992; Heistermann *et al.*, 1998) clearly indicates that the nature of metabolites excreted should not be presupposed on the degree of taxonomic relatedness and emphasizes the importance of careful method validation.

The range of assay methodology available as well as the detailed technical con-siderations relevant to the establishment and validation of immunological detection of hormones in urine and/or faeces has been previously described (e.g. Hodges and Green, 1989; Lasley and Kirkpatrick, 1991; Hodges, 1992; Wasser *et al.*, 1988; Shideler *et al.*, 1993; Palme *et al.*, 1996; Whitten *et al.*, 1998). Very briefly, steroids in urine are usually present as conjugates which can be measured after hydrolysis or by direct assay. Not only are direct assays much simpler to perform, but measurement of conjugates or groups of conjugates can be more suitable for multi species application and sometimes results in improved resolution. As most urine samples represent either single voidings or incomplete 24 collections, hormone measurements are indexed using creatinine to compensate for differences in urine concentration and volume. Peptide hormones, such as LH, follicle-stimulating hormone (FSH) and prolactin (PRL) are measurable in urine (but probably not in faeces) and there are numerous papers describing their application to non-domestic species, most notably non-human primates (e.g. Ziegler *et al.*, 1990, 1993; Rosenbusch *et al.*, 1997; Hodges 1996). Steroids are present in faeces as a mixture of free and conjugated forms. Although free forms usually predominate, this varies between species. Extraction of hormones prior to assay is necessary and samples need to be selected carefully since faecal matter is not homogeneous and hormone distribution varies within faeces. Hormone levels can be expressed per wet weight or, slightly more reliably, in terms of dry weight after extraction of freeze-dried material (see Wasser *et al.*, 1993; Heistermann *et al.*, 1995).

Over the last 10–15 years, a large literature has accumulated describing the successful application of urinary and faecal hormone assays for monitoring reproductive status in most orders of non-domestic mammalian species (for reviews see Hodges, 1985, 1996; Lasley and Kirkpatrick, 1991; Bamberg *et al.*, 1991; Brown *et al.*, 1994; Schwarzenberger *et al.*, 1996; Heistermann *et al.*, 1995; Whitten *et al.*, 1998), with occasional reports also for non-mammalian species (e.g. Bercowitz *et al.*, 1987; Bishop and Hall, 1991; Döbeli *et al.*, 1992).

6.3   MANIPULATION OF REPRODUCTIVE STATUS

6.3.1   Timing of ovulation

Since there is considerable variation in the length of the ovarian cycle and its component phases both within and between species, prediction and timing of ovulation in natural cycles is not easy. There are, therefore, a number of practical advantages to exerting external control over timing of events, particularly in terms of improving efficiency of insemination and/or gamete recovery procedures and in facilitating working with several individuals simultaneously (such as donor and recipient animals for embryo transfer).

Factors necessary for achieving acceptable control over timing of ovulation are well described for laboratory species and domestic livestock (Hunter, 1980; Hodges, 1996; Pope and Loskutoff, 1997), although species differences in reproductive mechanisms, together with difficulties in implementing intensive management practices, has made application to zoo animals a much more challenging prospect. There are two basic approaches: (a) the use of luteolytic agents to terminate the functional lifespan of the corpus luteum, and (b) exogenous progestogen administration, followed by removal. A third possibility is a combination of both methods. In each case the principle is the same: a controlled, abrupt withdrawal of progesterone triggers the final stages of follicular development leading to ovulation at a predetermined time. Prostaglandin (PG or its analogues) is given intramuscularly which simplifies application to non-tractible species and facilitates remote delivery, whereas progesterone administration is reportedly more effective in several seasonally polyoestrous species and can also be used to induce follicular development out of the breeding season or in other anoestrus conditions. In situations where application can be timed to a known stage of the cycle, PG is administered as a single injection or, if cycle stage is not known, two injections separated by an interval of about 10 days are needed. Use of progestin requires continuous delivery either by repeated oral doses of oil-based preparations such as Regumate® or more usually, intravaginal application of progesterone-containing sponges or other devices (PRID®, CIDR®).

CHAPTER 6

Since the shorter the interval from progesterone withdrawal to ovulation the better the degree of control over its timing, the approach is most suitable for species with short natural follicular (interluteal) phases such as ungulates. In these species ovulation will usually occur within 24–60 hours after progesterone withdrawal (Loskutoff *et al.*, 1995; Jabbour *et al.*, 1997). In contrast, PG is not effective in regulating ovarian cycles in most primate species, although the Callitrichidae (marmosets and tamarins) represent an interesting exception and PG application has been widely used to facilitate timing of ovulation for gamete collection and embryo transfer in the common marmoset (see Hodges, 1992). Use of steroid containing contraceptive preparations to exert some control over timing of follicular development has been described in the gorilla and may be applicable to other Old World species (Loskutoff *et al.*, 1991b; Goodrowe *et al.*, 1992). In general, the progesterone withdrawal approach is not suitable for use in rodents, carnivores and other induced ovulators.

Details of the use of progesterone withdrawal for cycle synchronization are best described for the Cervidae (see Jabbour *et al.*, 1997), but the approach has also been successfully used in other Bovid species including non-domestic cattle, diverse antelope species (bongo, eland, blackbuck, suni) and giraffe (Loskutoff *et al.*, 1995; Pope and Loskutoff, 1997). Although undoubtedly useful, one limitation of the method that has been described is the variable and sometimes unpredictable manifestation of behavioural oestrus following treatment in non-domestic species, which can result in difficulties in timing ovulation without the use of alternative monitoring techniques.

6.3.2 Ovarian stimulation

Since breeding in many non-domestic species occurs to a greater or lesser extent in a seasonal manner, the ability to induce ovulation in a quiescent (non-cyclic) ovary offers the potential for extension of breeding season and/or out of season collection/ transfer of gametes. Ovarian stimulation protocols would also enable treatment of certain anovulatory conditions and collection of gametes/embryos from individuals which otherwise are not contributing to the genetic pool.

The two available strategies essentially involve either (a) administration of substances which enhance endogenous gonadotrophin secretion or (b) direct application of exogenous (usually heterologous) gonadotrophins. In the first approach, melatonin can be administered by implant or feeding and is an effective method for inducing and/or extending ovarian activity in a variety of seasonally breeding exotic species, including deer (e.g. Bubenik, 1983) and marsupials (Loudon, 1985). Alternatively, the hypothalamic-releasing hormone GnRH can be applied to induce endogenous gonadotrophin release, although for long-term treatment, a pulsatile mode of delivery is probably required, making this impractical for routine application.

Use of exogenous gonadotrophins to induce ovulation has also been widely applied in domestic livestock, largely for the purposes of stimulating multiple follicular development for the collection of increased numbers of embryos and/or oocytes for IVF (Hunter, 1980; Loskutoff *et al.*, 1995; Pope and Loskutoff, 1997). According to dose and mode of treatment it is, in principle, possible to design protocols for stimulating the natural ovulatory quota or increased follicular development although, since ovarian response is often unpredictable, in practice this is difficult to achieve. A variety of exogenous gonadotrophin preparations are available, including porcine FSH, human menopausal gonadotrophin (hMG) (more recently highly purified hFSH or recFSH) and equine chorionic gonadotrophin (eCG) (formerly PMSG), primarily for their ability to stimulate follicular development, and hCG (human chorionic gonadotrophin) to induce ovulation.

Ovarian stimulation protocols have been successful in generating *in vitro* and/or *in vivo* derived embryos that have resulted in live births of a number of species of non-domestic ungulate, carnivore and non-human primate (Jabbour *et al.*, 1997; Wildt and Roth, 1997; Pope and Loskutoff, 1997). PMSG (eCG) has practical advantages in that usually only one application is necessary and, as such, is particularly suitable for use with non-tractable or wild animals. Its main disadvantages are a higher tendency for inconsistent ovulation rates and the induction of multiple waves of follicular development than with other preparations (Jabbour *et al.*, 1997). FSH generally results in a more controlled response but, with a shorter half-life it requires multiple applications. Other potential problems common to most preparations are variable response, overstimulation and compromised luteal function, effects on gamete transport and (especially with the use of heterologous gonadotrophins in primates) production of neutralizing antibodies (Bavister *et al.*, 1986).

Experience with non-domestic animals has indicated a large degree of species variation in response to different gonadotrophin preparations (Schiewe, 1989). For instance, among ungulates, giraffes respond to eCG and porcine FSH equally well, while eCG is less effective than porcine FSH in several antelope species, and okapis do not appear to be responsive to either (Schiewe *et al.*, 1991; Loskutoff and Betteridge, 1993). Species-specific sensitivity is also well documented for the Felidae, in which exogenous gonadotrophins (usually eCG followed by hCG) have been used extensively to induce ovulation either for AI or oocyte recovery for *in vitro* fertilization (see Wildt and Roth, 1997, for references). The finding, for example, of a lack of relationship between body mass and effective dose of gonadotrophin highlights the dangers of extrapolation of results even between closely related species, and emphasizes the importance of basic research to achieving practical success.

In non-human primates, hMG and more recently purified or recombinant FSH preparations (Meng and Wolf, 1997) have been used in various dose regimens for up to 7–10 days, followed by hCG to induce ovulation. Procedures are routine in several

CHAPTER 6

macaque species, including the lion-tailed macaque (Cranfield *et al.*, 1993), and have also been successful in the gorilla (Lanzendorf *et al.*, 1992; Pope *et al.*, 1997). Individual variation remains a limitation, although use of GnRH analogues to suppress endogenous gonadotrophin secretion prior to and during stimulation has helped to reduce this to some extent (e.g. Zelenski-Wooten *et al.*, 1995; Hataseka *et al.*, 1997). A successful stimulation protocol in the chimpanzee based on the use of clomiphene citrate during the latter part of the follicular phase followed by hCG has been described by Gould (1983). In contrast to experience with Old World monkeys, there has been little success (i.e. resulting in live births) with the use of gonadotrophins to stimulate follicular development in New World monkeys, although fertile ovulation can be induced with hCG in the marmoset (Hodges *et al.*, 1987).

6.4 COLLECTION AND TRANSFER OF GAMETES

6.4.1 Oocyte recovery and follicle aspiration

Techniques for the fertilization of oocytes *in vitro* have led to the the birth of offspring after transfer of *in vitro*-derived embryos from a number of non-domestic ungulates, carnivores and non-human primates (see Loskutoff *et al.*, 1995; Wildt and Roth, 1997). Collection of mature oocytes by follicular aspiration can be performed either surgically or (more commonly) laparoscopically, although the difficulties involved in achieving the necessary precision in timing limit the general applicability of this approach for most non-domestic species. Recent advances in the techniques of maturation of oocytes under *in vitro*-conditions, however, have greatly expanded the potential for IVF by enabling (at least in theory) the use of non-mature eggs which can be recovered independent of the reproductive status of the donor. In recent years, transvaginal ultrasound-guided oocyte retrieval has been shown to be safe and efficient for collecting oocytes from domestic and non-domestic ungulates, both in the pregnant and non-pregnant condition. Prior administration of FSH improves the yield and possibly fertilizability, and *in vitro* production of embryos deriving from transvaginally collected immature oocytes has now been reported for several non-domestic ruminant species (Loskutoff *et al.*, 1995; Meintjes *et al.*, 1997).

The ability to mature and fertilize oocytes *in vitro* also enables the utilization of gametes recovered *post-mortem*, representing an enormous potential source of material for genetic resource banking (e.g. Raphael *et al.*, 1991; Johnston *et al.*, 1994a). A further extension of *post-mortem* gamete rescue is that of the cryopreservation of ovarian tissue pieces or slices. Although subsequent *in vitro* maturation of the oocytes after thawing cannot yet be achieved with reliability, viability of the tissue has been demonstrated by transplantation *in vivo* (e.g. Gosden *et al.*, 1994; Candy *et al.*, 1995).

6.4.2 Semen collection and artificial insemination

The method of semen collection most commonly used is that of rectal probe electroejaculation, although other procedures include penile stimulation, vibro-stimulation, artificial vagina, manual stimulation, donation (masturbation) and post-mortem collection. Details of the various semen collection methods and their relative merits have been described elsewhere in detail (e.g. Watson, 1978; Gould and Martin, 1985; Wildt, 1996; Brown and Loskutoff, 1998) and will not be presented here.

Three main sites of insemination in mammals have been described: vaginal, intracervical and intrauterine. Of these, the vaginal site is the physiologically normal one in most species. In practical terms it is also the simplest to carry out and can usually be performed in unanaesthetized animals. Disadvantages associated with this site of deposition include the requirement for high numbers of sperm (an important factor when using stored semen where ejaculate volumes and/or numbers of viable sperm are limited) and a relatively low fertilization rate. Success rate is generally improved when intracervical or intrauterine insemination is used. In several species (including many non-human primates) in which the anatomy of the cervix makes placement of a catheter into the uterus difficult, intracervical insemination is preferred. The same method has also been employed successfully in deer, although the requirement for higher precision in the timing of ovulation, makes application to species in which physiological events surrounding ovulation are poorly defined somewhat impractical. Thus, intrauterine placement of washed sperm (either surgically or via a catheter passing through the cervix) currently provides the most reliable method for artificial insemination in a wide range of species. Possible effects of anaesthesia should not be overlooked and there is evidence that this may influence the natural motility and activity of the female pelvic organs and interfere with sperm transport to the site of fertilization (Gould and Martin, 1986).

Laparoscopically guided intrauterine insemination, initially developed in sheep, has now been successfully applied to a wide range of non-domestic species, including carnivores (puma, ferret, ocelot, tiger, clouded leopard–see Wildt and Roth, 1997 for references), numerous deer species (see Jabbour et al., 1997; Pope and Loskutoff, 1997), non-domestic bovids, giraffes and camels (Pope and Loskutoff, 1997) as well as non-human primates (e.g. Gould and Martin, 1986; Morrell, 1995). Insemination using frozen semen has also been widely reported, but in general, fertilization rates are lower than those achieved with fresh semen. Even when equivalent numbers of motile cryopreserved spermatozoa are inseminated, results are generally poorer than with fresh samples, an effect most likely attributable to reduced survival and progression through the female tract, rather than to an inherent loss of fertilizing ability.

6.4.3   Embryo recovery and transfer

Most procedures for applying embryo transfer technology to non-domestic species (especially ungulates) are based on methods developed in cattle. Since, however, the principles on which this is based are generally not amenable to extensive management systems involving minimal animal contact, reliable (and therefore successful) procedures have been difficult to establish (Pope and Loskutoff, 1997). From the anatomical perspective, conventional non-surgical embryo recovery can be performed on most large non-domestic ungulate species, exceptions being the okapi and giraffe, in both of which the cervix is extremely difficult to penetrate (Loskutoff *et al.*, 1988). Non-surgical recovery has also been successfully reported for small antelope species (Loskutoff *et al.*, 1991c) and several non-human primates (Pope *et al.*, 1983; Marshall *et al.*, 1997), although rates of recovery are generally lower than with surgical methods. The method appears not to be applicable in many felid species due to physical difficulties in flushing embryos from the uterus (Wildt and Roth, 1997).

It has been reported for deer (and this presumably applies to other species) that the later the recovery in relation to insemination, the greater the degree of variation in embryo stage at the time of collection. Thus, collection early, followed by culture *in vitro* (or *in vivo* culture in an intermediate host, e.g. mouse) may be advantageous in producing a greater degree of developmental homogeneity at the time of transfer and, ultimately, a higher pregnancy rate (e.g. Jabbour *et al.*, 1997).

As in domestic livestock, embryo transfer procedures in non-domestic species are often performed in conjunction with ovarian stimulation protocols to enable the collection of larger number of embryos either for immediate replacement or storage. Whilst this approach has certainly been useful on occasions, as previously mentioned, a major limitation continues to be the variation and unpredictability in ovarian responsiveness to exogenous stimulation (both at an individual and species level) with its associated effects on luteal function and gamete transport. Embryo transfer itself is the procedure of introducing embryos into the uterus of the recipient female at the appropriate stage of the postovulatory or luteal phase of the ovarian cycle. Generally, results are best when donor and recipient cycles are synchronized to within ± one day. Non-surgical methods for reintroducing embryos into the uterus have been established for a number of large antelope, other bovid and camelid species, as well as for some non-human primates. Site of transfer (within the uterus) can be important since, for example, only the right horn is functional in many small antelopes (Loskutoff *et al.*, 1990) whereas pregnancies can only be established in the left uterine horn of alpacas and llamas (Loskutoff and Betteridge, 1993). Birth of live offspring following extra-specific embryo transfer has also been reported for a number of non-domestic ungulate species (Summers, 1986; Pope and Loskutoff, 1997).

6.4.4   Effects of stress and anaesthesia

It has long been recognized that stress can influence reproductive parameters, notably ovarian function and early pregnancy in the female, and likewise, testicular function and semen quality in the male. The physiological mechanisms responsible are complex and incompletely understood, but catecholamines and corticoids are both involved, at least in part through modulatory influences on gonadotrophin secretion. Minimizing stress through the application of low or non-invasive procedures for monitoring reproductive status has been emphasized earlier in this chapter, but is equally important when devising procedures for the collection and transfer of gametes and embryos.

Although stressful situations may be reduced by careful design of management and holding systems, chemical sedation is often necessary for manipulative treatments. Since anaesthesia itself, however, is a form of stress it needs to be applied with an awareness of the potential risks associated. Furthermore, anaesthetic agents may also have a direct effect on physiological processes, such as suppression of pulsatile LH secretion (Peet and Lincoln, 1977) and the inhibition of the LH surge in rodents which occurs with both barbiturate and ether anaesthesia (Kim et al., 1994). Few systematic studies have been carried out in non-domestic species, although evidence exists for delay and/or inhibition of ovulation in connection with AI procedures performed under anaesthesia in several non-domestic species including the gorilla (Lasley et al., 1982), puma (Barone et al., 1994) and tiger (Donoghue et al., 1996). Anaesthesia may also complicate AI attempts by impairing sperm transport in the female tract, possibly by affecting smooth muscle contractility, in domestic cats (Wildt et al., 1992) and chimpanzees (Gould et al., 1985). Potential effects of anaesthesia on semen collection and in particular on the reflex components of the ejaculatory response to electro-stimulation have been reviewed by Watson (1978).

6.5   *IN VITRO* EMBRYO PRODUCTION AND GAMETE MANIPULATION

6.5.1   *In vitro* maturation and *in vitro* fertilization (IVM–IVF)

Although less conventional than other forms of assisted reproduction (AI, embryo transfer), the *in vitro* production of embryos is of enormous potential for supporting the objectives of germplasm banking (e.g. Moore, 1992; Loskutoff et al., 1995). In general terms, these include potential for utilization of non-mature oocytes, treatment of infertility related to anatomical defects and tubal obstructions, production of increased numbers of embryos (compared to flushing), utilization of gametes from pre-pubertal or aged animals, potential for sex determination and reduction in the requirement for large numbers of viable sperm (Figure 6.2). IVF–IVM would also help to overcome certain difficulties in timing ovulation for artificial insemination, and in the recovery of embryos which, for instance in many Felidae, is reported to be extremely difficult (Wildt and Roth, 1997).

Procedures developed for domestic ruminants have been successful in producing IVF offspring from a number of non-domestic ungulates, including sheep, cattle, deer, and *in vitro* generation of embryos has been reported for a variety of African antelope, llamas and some deer species (see Pope and Loskutoff 1997, for references). Most reports on IVM of oocytes from non-domestic ungulates have been based on the use of material collected *post-mortem*, although more recently transvaginal, ultrasound-guided follicle aspiration has been used to recover oocytes from live non-domestic donors (Pope and Loskutoff, 1995), even under free-ranging conditions (e.g. Meintjes *et al.*, 1997).

Amongst the Felidae, IVF-derived offspring have been produced in the Indian desert cat (Pope *et al.*, 1989) and tiger (Donoghue *et al.*, 1990), although important species differences in the requirements for sperm–egg interaction have been identified (Wildt *et al.*, 1992). Immature eggs recovered from the ovaries of a number of felid species are capable of maturing and fertilizing *in vitro*, and some success has also been reported in Ursidae (Johnston *et al.*, 1994a). IVF has resulted in births in a variety of non-human primate species (Loskutoff *et al.*, 1991a), including a Western lowland gorilla (Pope *et al.*,

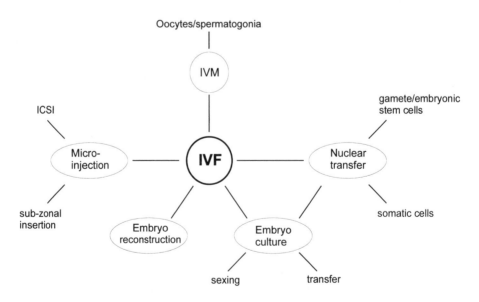

Figure 6.2: IVF and related technologies for *in vitro* production of embryos. Despite technical limitations, IVF presents a number of options with considerable potential practical value such as the utilization of immature gametes.

1997) and reports of *in vitro* embryonic development following the *in vitro* fertilization of IVM oocytes also exist (Lanzendorf *et al.*, 1992; Schramm and Bavister, 1996; Gilchrist *et al.*, 1997).

Although the technology is still at a relatively undeveloped stage, IVF combined with *in vitro* oocyte maturation offers particularly exciting prospects for germplasm banking, since it facilitates the utilization of large numbers of immature oocytes from ovaries of undefined status. In turn, this provides the capability for salvaging genetic material from animals in a wide range of situations, even after the time of death. The potential for cryostorage of ovarian tissue pieces, as has been described for both sheep and the marmoset monkey (Gosden *et al.*, 1994 and Candy *et al.*, 1995, respectively), offers a further extension to the possibilities for post-mortem gamete retrieval. Although rates of IVM–IVF from such cryopreserved tissues can be expected to be low using current techniques, viability of the tissue in both studies was confirmed by *in vivo* development following transplantation.

Inherent in any successful IVM–IVF protocol is an efficient method for embryo culture. Not surprisingly, conditions for supporting (normal) embryonic development under *in vitro* conditions vary considerably between species. The essential requirements for *in vitro* embryo culture are well established in domestic ungulates, many laboratory species and women, and have been comprehensively reviewed (Bavister, 1995; Thompson, 1996). Among non-domestic species, conditions required for the production and culture of embryos *in vitro* are less well defined, but have been referred to (Summers, 1986; Wildt *et al.*, 1992; Berg *et al.*, 1995).

Although developmental competency of *in vitro* derived embryos has been confirmed by live births in a number of species, differences from *in vivo*-derived embryos are to be expected. Even among domestic species there are reports of various abnormalities, including large birth weight, dystocic parturition and perinatal mortality (e.g. Walker *et al.*, 1996; Kruip and den Daas, 1997) and clearly, this should not be overlooked when evaluating the suitability of IVF and related procedures for endangered species.

6.5.2 Gamete/embryo manipulation

In vitro production of embryos also offers the potential for the incorporation of additional techniques useful in germplasm banking, such as sex determination. Segregation of X- and Y-bearing sperm, an elusive research goal for many years, can now be achieved with reasonable reliability using flow cytometry to separate on the basis of DNA content (e.g. Johnson, 1997). Numbers of sperm so recovered would probably restrict application to *in vitro* use and the risk of damage to DNA associated with the fluorescence stains needs to be better defined, particularly before application in highly endangered species. On the other hand, availability of *in vitro*-derived

CHAPTER 6

embryos facilitates the use of preimplantation (i.e. pretransfer) sex determination using DNA-amplification procedures on individual blastomeres.

A further technological possibility arising out of the production of embryos *in vitro* is that of sperm microinjection. Methods for intracytoplasmatic sperm injection (ICSI) have resulted in the generation of live offspring from a number of species including human, cattle and rabbits (see Payne, 1995; Loskutoff *et al.*, 1995, for reviews) although in some species (e.g. felids) other approaches such as subzonal insertion appear more successful (Pope *et al.*, 1995). The primary advantage to either approach is the potential for generating embryos from a number of previously untapped sperm sources such as oligo/terato-spermic donors, testicular sperm and even from dead or damaged sperm fragments. The need for highly developed and continuously practised skills, expensive equipment and the potential risk of facilitating the transmission of sperm-linked genetic defects (Vogt, 1995), however, are likely to mitigate against the widespread introduction of such techniques in the near future.

6.5.3 Other advanced technologies

Reproductive biology is a field in which *in vitro* technologies are developing at a rapid rate. Among the more recent advances which show at least theoretical promise for germplasm banking are nuclear transfer and spermatogonial stem cell transfer. Nuclear transfer as demonstrated in the sheep (Wilmut *et al.*, 1997) and rhesus monkey (Meng and Wolf, 1997) is a form of embryo reconstruction whereby enucleated oocyte cytoplasm serves as host to a nucleus derived from another cell. Although the procedure provides the basis for so-called cloning, its use solely for the creation of large numbers of genetically identical individuals is a misconception. Of considerable advantage to germplasm preservation is the fact that embryos can theoretically be constructed using donor nuclei (or DNA) from a range of cell types, including cultured stem cells or even from fully differentiated adult somatic cells, such as fibroblasts. Spermatogonial stem cell transplantation (Avarbock *et al.*, 1996) enables the cryopreservation of testicular stem cells which are subsequently capable of generating spermatogenesis, and are thus of particular interest in being able to undergo proliferation and genetic recombination after storage. In both approaches cells are easier to freeze by standard methodologies than gametes, for which the development of species-specific freezing protocols is required. A further possibility is the recently demonstrated use of freeze-dried spermatozoa for creating an embryo by ICSI (Wakayama and Yanagimachi, 1998). However, despite their potential, the question of whether these and other highly manipulative techniques will ever make a significant contribution to germplasm resource banking and animal conservation remains debatable. At present, one must conclude that technological difficulties will limit the extent to which such methods can be reliably applied to a wide variety of species.

They nevertheless represent a potential for the future that should be neither over-looked nor underestimated.

REFERENCES

ADAM, C. L. and ARKINSON, T. (1984) 'Effect of feeding melatonin to red deer *(Cervus elaphus)* on the onset of the breeding season', *J. Reprod. Fertil.* **72**, 463–466.

ADAMS, G. P., PLOTKA, E. D., ASA, D. S. and GINTHER, O. J. (1991) 'Feasibility of charac-terizing reproductive events in large non-domestic species by transrectal ultrasonic imaging', *Zoo Biol.* **10**, 247–259.

AVARBOCK, M. R., BRINSTER, C. J. and BRINSTER, R. L. (1996) 'Reconstitution of spermato-genesis from frozen spermatogonial stem cells', *Nature Med.* **2**, 691–696.

BAMBERG, E., MÖSTL, E., PATZL, M. and KING, G. J. (1991) 'Pregnancy diagnosis by enzyme immunoassay of estrogens in feces from nondomestic species'. *J. Zoo Wildlife Med.* **22**, 73–777.

BARONE, M. A., WILDT, D. E., BYERS, A. P., ROELKE, M. E., GLASS, C. M. and HOWARD, J. G. (1994) 'Gonadotrophin dose and timing of anaesthesia for laparoscopic artificial insemination in the puma *(Felis concolor)*', *J. Reprod. Fertil.* **101**, 103–108.

BAVISTER, B. D. (1995) 'Culture of preimplantation embryos: facts and artifacts', *Hum. Reprod. Update* **1**, 91–148.

BAVISTER, B. D., DEES, C. and SHULTZ, R. D. (1986) 'Refractoriness of rhesus monkeys to repeated ovarian stimulation by exogenous gonadotrophins is caused by non-precipitating antibodies', *Am. J. Reprod. Immunol. Microbiol.* **11**, 11–16.

BERCOVITZ, A. B., COLLINS, J,. PRICE, P. and TUTTLE, D. (1982) 'Non-invasive assessment of seasonal hormone profile in captive bald eagles *(Haliaeetus leucocephalus)*', *Zoo Biol.* **1**, 111–117.

BISHOP, C. M. and HALL, M. R. (1991) 'Non-invasive monitoring of avian reproduction by simplified faecal steroid analysis', *J. Zool. (Lond.)* **224**, 649–668.

BRAVO, P. W., FOWLER, M. E., STABENFELDT, G. H. and LASLEY, B. L. (1990) 'Ovarian follicular dynamics in the Llama', *Biol. Reprod.* **43**, 579–585.

BROWN, C. S. AND LOSKUTOFF, N. M. (1998) 'A training program for noninvasive semen collection in captive Western lowland gorillas *(Gorilla gorilla gorilla)*', *Zoo Biol.* **17**, 143–151.

BROWN, J. L. and WILDT, D. E. (1997) 'Assessing reproductive status in wild felids by non-invasive faecal steroid monitoring', *International Zoo Yearbook* **35**, 173–191.

BROWN, J. L., WASSER, S. K., WILDT, D. E., and GRAHAM, L. H. (1994) 'Comparative aspects of steroid hormone metabolism and ovarian activity in felids, measured noninvasively in feces', *Biol. Reprod.* **51**, 776–786.

BUBENIK, G. A. (1983) 'Shift of seasonal cycle in white-tailed deer by oral administration of melatonin', *J. Exp. Zool.* **235**, 155–156.

CANDY, C. J., WOOD, M. J. and WHITTINGHAM, D. G. (1995) 'Follicular development in crypreserved marmoset ovarian tissue after transplantation', *Hum. Reprod.* **10**, 2334–2338.

CASARES, M., RUBEL, A. and HONEGGER, R. E. (1997) 'Observations on the female reproductive cycle of captive giant tortoises (*Geochelone spp.*) using ultrasound scanning', *J. Zoo Wildlife Med.* **28**, 267–273.

CRANFIELD, M. R., BAVISTER, B. D., BOATMAN, D. E., BERGER, N. G., SCHAFFER, N., KEMPSKE, S. E., IALEGGIO, D. M. and SMART, J. (1993) 'Assisted reproduction in the propagation management of the endangered lion-tailed macaque (*Macaca silenus*)', in Wolf, D.P., Stouffer, R. L. and Brenner, R. M. (eds) *In vitro Fertilization and Embryo Transfer in Primates*, New York: Springer Verlag, pp. 331–348.

DÖBELI, M., RÜHLI, M., PFEIFFER, M., RÜBEL, A., HONEGGER, R. and ISENBÜGEL, E. (1992) 'Preliminary results on faecal steroid measurements in tortoises', *Proceedings of the First International Symposium on Faecal Steroid Monitoring in Zoo Animals*, Rotterdam, pp. 73–83.

DONOGHUE, A. M., JOHNSTON, L. A., SEAL, U. S., ARMSTRONG, D. L., TILSON, R. L., WOLF, P., PETRINI, K., SIMMONS, L. G., GROSS, T. and WILDT, D. E. (1990) '*In vitro* fertilization and embryo development *in vitro* and *in vivo* in the tiger (*Panthera tigris*)', *Biol. Reprod.* **43**, 733–744.

DONOGHUE, A. M., BYERS, A. P., JOHNSTON, L. A., ARMSTRONG, D. L. and WILDT, D. E. (1996) 'Timing of ovulation after gonadotrophin induction and its importance to successful intrauterine insemination in the tiger (*Panthera tigris*)', *J. Reprod. Fert.* **107**, 53–58.

DU BOULAY, G. H. and WILSON, O. L. (1988) 'Diagnosis of pregnancy and disease by ultrasound in exotic species', *Symp. Zool. Soc. Lond.* **60**, 135–150.

GERMAN, J. (1968) 'Mongolism, delayed fertilization and human sexual behaviour', *Nature Lond.* **127**, 516–518.

GILCHRIST, R. B., NAYUDU, P. L. and HODGES, J. K. (1977) 'The maturation, fertilization and development of marmoset monkey oocytes in vitro', *Biol. Reprod.* **56**, 238–246.

GOODROWE, K. L., WILDT, D. E. and MONFORT, S. L. (1992) 'Effective suppression of ovarian cyclicity in the lowland gorilla with an oral contraceptive', *Zoo Biol.* **11**, 261–269.

GÖRITZ, F. (1996) 'Sonographie bei Zoo- und Wildtieren', PhD dissertation, University of Berlin.

GÖRITZ, F., HILDEBRANDT, T., STRAUß, G., GÖLTENROTH, R. and PITRA, C. (1996) 'Sonomorphological Sexing in Spotted Hyena (*Crocuta crocuta Erxleben*)', *J. Ultrasound Med.* **15**, 60.

GOSDEN, R. G., BAIRD, D. T., WADE, J. C. and WEBB, R. (1994) 'Restoration of fertility to oophorectomized sheep by ovarian autografts stored at −196°C', *Hum. Reprod.* **9**, 597–603.

GOULD, K. G. (1983) 'Ovum recovery and *in vitro* fertilization in the chimpanzee', *Fertil. Steril.* **40**, 378–383.

GOULD, K. G. and MARTIN, D. E. (1985) 'Artificial insemination of nonhuman primates', in Benirschke, *Primates the Road to Self-sustaining Populations,* Springer Verlag, Berlin, pp. 425–443.

GOULD, K. G., MARTIN, D. E. and WARNER, H. (1985) 'Improved method for artificial insemination in the great apes', *American Journal of Primatology.* 8, 61–67.

HATASAKA, H. H., SCHAFFER, N. E., CHENETTE, P. E., KOWALSKI, W., HECHT, B. R., MEEHAN, T. P., WENTZ, A. C., VALLE, R. F., CHATTERTON, R. T. and JEYENDRAN, R. S. (1997) 'Strategies for ovulation induction and oocyte retrieval in the lowland gorilla', *J. Assist. Reprod. Genet.* **14**, 102–110.

HEISTERMANN, M., AGIL, M., BÜTHE, A. and HODGES, J. K. (1998) 'Metabolism and excretion of oestradiol-17β and progesterone in the Sumatran rhinoceros (*Dicerorhinus sumatrensis*)', *Anim. Reprod. Sci.* **53**, 157–172.

HEISTERMANN, M., MÖSTL, E. and HODGES, J.K. (1995) 'Non-invasive endocrine monitoring of female reproductive status: methods and applications to captive breeding and conservation of exotic species', in Gansloßer, U., Hodges, J.K. and Kaumanns, W. (eds) *Research and Captive Propagation,* Fürth: Filander Verlag, pp. 36–48.

HILDEBRANDT, T. and GÖRITZ, F. (1995) 'Ultrasonography as a tool in zoo animal management', in Gansloßer, U., Hodges, J. K. and Kaumanns, W. (eds) *Research and Captive Propagation,* Fürth: Filander Verlag, pp. 49–58.

HODGES, J. K. (1985) 'The endocrine control of reproduction', *Symp. Zool. Soc. Lond.* **54**, 149–168.

HODGES, J. K. (1992) 'Detection of oestrous cycles and timing of ovulation', in Moore, H. D. M., Holt, W. V. and Mace, G. M. (eds) *Biotechnology and the Conservation of Genetic Diversity, Symp. Zool. Soc. Lond.* **64**, 73–88.

HODGES, J. K. (1996) 'Determining and manipulating female reproductive parameters', in Kleiman, D. G., Allen, M. E., Thompson, K. V. and Lumpkin, S. (eds)

Wild Mammals in Captivity, Chicago and London: The University of Chicago Press. pp. 418–428.

HODGES, J. K. and GREEN, D. G. (1989) 'A simplified enzyme immunoassay for urinary pregnanediol-3–glucuronide: applications to reproductive assessment of exotic species', *J. Zool. (Lond.)* **219**, 89–99.

HUNTER, R. F. H. (1980) *Physiology and Technology of Reproduction in Female Domestic Animals*, London: Academic Press.

JABBOUR, H. N., HAYSSEN, V. and BRUFORD, M. W. (1997) 'Conservation of deer: contributions from molecular biology, evolutionary ecology and reproductive physiology', *J. Zool. (Lond.)* **243**, 461–484.

JAQUISH, C. E., TOAL, R. L., TARDIF, S. D. and CARSON, R. L. (1995) 'Use of ultrasound to monitor prenatal growth and development in the common marmoset (*Callithrix jacchus*)', *Am. J. Primatol.* **36**, 259–275.

JOHNSON, L. A. (1997) 'Advances in gender preselection in swine'. *J. Reprod. Fertil. Suppl.* **52**, 255–66.

JOHNSTON, L. A., DONOGHUE, A. M., IGO, W., SIMMONS, L. G., WILDT, D. E. and RIEFFENBERGER, J. (1994a) 'Oocyte recovery and maturation in the American black bear (*Ursus americanus*): a model for endangered ursids'. *J. Exp. Zool.* **269**: 53–61.

JOHNSTON, L. A., PARRISH, J. J., MONSON, R., LEIBFRIED-RUTLEDGE, L., SUSKO-PARRISH, J. L., NORTHEY, D. L., RUTLEDGE, J. J. and SIMMONS, L. G. (1994b) 'Oocyte maturation, fertilization and embryo development *in vitro* and *in vivo* in the gaur (*Bos gaurus*)', *J. Reprod. Fertil.* **100**, 131–136.

KIM, C. Y., WAKABAYASHI, K. and NOBUNAGA, T. (1994) 'Time-dependent ovulation-blocking effect of ether anesthesia differs from pentobarbital in rats', *Tohoku J. Exp. Med.* **172**, 237–242.

KRUIP, TH. A. M. and DEN DAAS, J. H. G. (1997) '*In vitro* produced and cloned embryos: effects on pregnancy, parturition and offspring', *Theriogenology* **42**, 1257–1262.

LANZENDORF, S. E., HOLMGREN, W. J., SCHAFFER, N., HATASAKA, H. H., WENTZ, A. C. and JEYENDRAN, R. S. (1992) '*In vitro* fertilization and gamete micromanipulation in the lowland gorilla', *J. Assist. Reprod. Genet.* **9**, 358–364.

LASLEY, B. L. and KIRKPATRICK, J. F. (1991) 'Monitoring ovarian function in captive and free-ranging wildlife by means of urinary and faecal steroids', *J. Zoo Wildlife Med.* **22**, 23–31.

LASLEY, B. L., CZEKALA, N. M. and PRESLEY, S. (1982) 'A practical approach to the evaluation of fertility in the female gorilla', *Am. J. Primatol.* Suppl. **1**, 45–50.

LOSKUTOFF, N. M. and BETTERIDGE, K. J. (1993) 'Embryo technology in pets and endangered species', in Lauria, A. and Gandolfi, F. (eds) *Embryonic Development and Manipulation in Animal Production: Trends in Embryo Transfer,* London: Portland Press, pp. 235–248.

LOSKUTOFF, N. M., RAPHAEL, B. L., DORN, C. G., NEMEC, L. A., CALLE, P. P., PETRIC, A. M. and KRAEMER, D. C. (1988) 'Comparative reproductive traits of the okapi and giraffe: Implications for intraspecific and intergeneric embryo transfer', *Acta Zool. Path. Antverpiensia* **80**, 29–42.

LOSKUTOFF, N. M., RAPHAEL, B. L., NEMEC, L. A., WOLFE, B. A., HOWARD, J. G. and KRAEMER, D. C. (1990) 'Reproductive anatomy, manipulation of ovarian activity and non-surgical embryo recovery in suni (Neotragus moschatus zuluensis)', *J. Reprod. Fert.* **88**, 521–532.

LOSKUTOFF, N. M., KRAEMER, D. C., RAPHAEL, B. L., HUNTRESS, S. L. and WILDT, D. E. (1991a) 'Advances in reproduction in captive, female great apes: an emphasis on the value of biotechniques', *Am. J. Primatol.* **24**, 151–166.

LOSKUTOFF, N. M., HUNTRESS, S. L., PUTMAN, J. M., YEE, B., BOWSHER, T. R., CHACON, R. R., CALLE, P. P., CAMBRE, R. C., ROSEN, G. F., KRAEMER, D. C., CZEKALA, N. M. and RAPHAEL, B. L. (1991b) 'Stimulation of ovarian activity for oocyte retrieval in nonreproductive Western lowland gorillas *(Gorilla gorilla gorilla)*', *J. Zoo Wildlife Med.* **22**, 32–41.

LOSKUTOFF, N. M., RAPHAEL, B. L., WOLFE, B. A., FRENCH, L. A. N., BUICE, R. B., HOWARD, J. G., SCHIEWE, M. C. and KRAEMER, D. C. (1991c) 'Embryo transfer in small antelope', *Proc. Soc. Study Theriogenol.* 341–342.

LOSKUTOFF, N. M., BARTELS, P., MEINTJES, M., GODKE, R. A. and SCHIEWE, M. C. (1995) 'Assisted reproductive technology in nondomestic ungulates: a model approach to preserving and managing genetic diversity', *Theriogenology* **43**, 3–12.

LOUDON, A. S. I. (1985) 'Lactation and neonatal survival', *Symp. Zool. Soc. Lond.* **54**, 183–207.

MARSHALL, V. S., KALISHMAN, J. and THOMPSON, J. A. (1997) 'Nonsurgical embryo transfer in the common marmoset monkey', *J. Med. Primatol.* **26**, 241–247.

MEINTJES, M., BEZUIDENHOUT, C., BARTELS, P., VISSER, D. S., MEINTJES, J., LOSKUTOFF, N.M., FOURIE, F. L. R., BARRY, D. M. and GODKE, R. A. (1997) '*In vitro* maturation and fertilization of oocytes recovered from free-ranging Burchell's zebra (*Equus burchelli*) and Hartmann's zebra (*Equus zebra hartmannae*)', *J. Zoo Wildlife Med.* **28**, 251–259.

MENG, L. and WOLF, D. P. (1997) 'Sperm-induced oocyte activation in the rhesus monkey: nuclear and cytoplasmic changes following intracytoplasmic sperm injection', *Hum. Reprod.* **12**, 1062–1068.

MONFORT, S. L., WASSER, S. K., MASHBURN, K. L., BURKE, M., BREWER, B. A. and CREEL, S. R. (1997) 'Steroid metabolism and validation of non-invasive endocrine monitoring in the African wild dog (*Lycaon pictus*)', *Zoo Biol.* **16**, 533–548.

MOORE, H. D. M. (1992) '*In vitro* fertilization and the development of gene banks for wild mammals', *Symp. Zool. Soc. Lond.* **64**, 89–99.

MORRELL, J. M. (1995) 'Artificial insemination in non-human primates', in Gansloßer, U., HODGES, J. K. and KAUMANNS, W. (eds) *Research and Captive Propogation*, Fürth, Filander Verlag. pp. 59–70.

OERKE, A.-K., EINSPANIER, A. and HODGES, J. K. (1995) 'Detection of pregnancy and monitoring patterns of uterine and fetal growth in the marmoset monkey (*Callithrix jacchus*) by real-time ultrasonography', *Am. J. Primatol.* **36**, 1–13.

OERKE, A.-K., EINSPANIER, A. and HODGES, J. K. (1996) 'Noninvasive monitoring of follicle development, ovulation and corpus luteum formation in the marmoset monkey (*Callithrix jacchus*) by ultrasonography', *Am. J. Primatol.* **39**, 99–113.

PALME, R., FISCHER, P., SCHILDORFER, H. and ISMAIL, M. N. (1996) 'Excretion of infused 14C-steroid hormones via faeces and urine in domestic livestock', *Anim. Reprod. Sci.* **43**, 43–63.

PAYNE, D. (1995) 'Micro-assisted fertilization'. *Reprod. Fertil. Dev.* **7**, 831–839.

PEET, M. and LINCOLN, G. (1977) 'Blockade of episodic gonadotropin secretion by Immobilon in ovariectomized ewes', *J. Reprod. Fertil.* **50**, 97–100.

POPE, C. E. and LOSKUTOFF, N. M. (1997) 'Embryo transfer and semen technology from cattle applied to nondomestic artiodactylids', in Fowler, M. E. and Miller, R. E. (eds) *Zoo and Wild Animal Medicine: Current Therapy,* 4th edn, Philadelphia: W.B. Saunders Co., pp. 597–604.

POPE, C. E., POPE, V. Z. and BECK, L. R. (1980) 'Non-surgical recovery of uterine embryos in the baboon', *Biol. Reprod.* **23**, 657–662.

POPE, C. E., POPE, V. Z. and BECK, L. R. (1983) 'Successful non-surgical transfer of a non-surgically recovered four-cell uterine embryo in the baboon', *Theriogenology* **19**, 144.

POPE, C. E., POPE, V. Z. and BECK, L. R. (1986) 'Cryopreservation and transfer of baboon embryos', *J. In Vitro Fertil. Embryo Transf.* **3**, 33–39.

POPE, C. E., GELWICKS, E. J., WACHS, K. B., KELLER, G. L., MARUSKA, E. J. and DRESSER, B. L. (1989) 'Successful interspecies transfer of embryos from the Indian desert cat (*Felis silvestris ornata*) to the domestic art (*Felis catus*) following *in vitro* fertilization (IVF)', *Biol. Reprod.* **40**, 61.

POPE, C. E., JOHNSON, C. A., McRAE, M. A., KELLER, G. L. and DRESSER, B. L. (1995) 'In vitro and in vivo development of cat oocytes following intracytoplasmic sperm injection or subzonal insemination', *Theriogenology* 43, abstr.

POPE, C. E., DRESSER, B. L., CHIN, N. W., LIU, J. H., LOSKUTOFF, N. M., BEHNKE, E. J., BROWN, C., McRAE, M. A., SINOWAY, C. E., CAMPBELL, M. K., CAMERON, K. N., OWENS, O. M., JOHNSON, C. A., EVANS, R. R. and CEDARS, M. I. (1997) 'Birth of a Western lowland gorilla *(Gorilla gorilla gorilla)*, following *in vitro* fertilization and embryo transfer', *Am. J. Primatol.* 41, 247–260.

RADCLIFFE, R. W., CZEKALA, N. M. and OSOFSKY, S. A. (1997) 'Combined serial ultra-sonography and fecal progestin analysis for reproductive evaluation of the female white rhinoceros (*Ceratotherium simum simum*): preliminary results', *Zoo Biol.* 16, 445–456.

RAPHAEL, B. L., LOSKUTOFF, N. M., HUNTRESS, S. L. and KRAEMER, D. C. (1991) 'Postmortem recovery, *in vitro* maturation and fertilization of klipspringer (*Oreotragus oreotragus*) ovarian oocytes', *J. Zoo Wildlife Med.* 22, 115–118.

ROSENBUSCH, J., DIAS, J. A. and HODGES, J. K. (1997) 'Development of an enzyme-immunoassay (EIA) for the measurement of follicle-stimulating-hormone (FSH) in callitrichid primates using a monoclonal antibody against the human-FSH-β-subunit', *Am. J. Primatol.* 41, 179–193.

SCHAFFER, N. E., ZAINAL-ZAHARI, Z., SURI, M. S. M., JAINUDEEN, M. R. and JEYENDRAN, R. S. (1994) 'Ultrasonography of the reproductive anatomy in the Sumatran rhinoceros (*Dicerorhinus sumatrensis*)', *J. Zoo Wildlife Med.* 25, 337–348.

SCHIEWE, M. C. (1989) 'Comparative studies of estrus synchronization, ovulation induction, luteal function and embryo cryopreservation in domestic sheep and application to related investigations to nondomestic ungulate species', PhD Dissertation, Uniformed Services University of the Health Sciences, Bethesda, MD.

SCHRAMM, R. D. and BAVISTER, B. D. (1996) 'Use of purified porcine follicle-stimulating hormone for ovarian stimulation of macaque monkeys', *Theriogenology* 45, 727–732.

SCHWARZENBERGER, F., MÖSTL, E., PALME, R. and BAMBERG, E. (1996) 'Faecal steroids analysis for non-invasive monitoring of reproductive status in farm, wild and zoo animals', *Anim. Reprod. Sci.* 42, 515–526.

SHIDELER, S. E., ORTUNO, A. M., MORAN, F. M., MOORMAN, E. A. and LASLEY, B. L. (1993) 'Simple extraction and enzyme immunoassays for estrogen and progesterone

■ CHAPTER 6 ■

metabolites in the feces of *Macaca fascicularis* during non-conceptive and conceptive ovarian cycles', *Biol. Reprod.* **48**, 1290–1298.

SHILLE, V. M., WING, A. E., LASLEY, B. L. and BANKS, J. A. (1985) 'Excretion of radiolabeled estradiol in the cat (*Felis catus* L): A preliminary report', *Zoo Biol.* **3**, 201–209.

SKIDMORE, J. A., BILLAH, M. and ALLEN, W. R. (1996) 'The ovarian follicular wave pattern and induction of ovulation in the mated and non-mated one-humped camel (*Camelus dromedarius*)', *J. Reprod. Fertil.* **106**, 185–192.

STONE, L. R. (1990) 'Diagnostic ultrasound in marine mammals', in Dierauf, L.A. (ed.), *CRC Handbook of Marine Medicine: Health, Disease and Rehabilitation,* Florida: CRC Press, pp. 235–264.

SUMMERS, P. M. (1986) 'Collection, storage and use of mammalian embryos', *Int. Zool. Yearbook* **24/25**, 131–138.

TARANTAL, A. F. (1992) 'Sonographic assessment of nongravid female macaques (*Macaca mulatta* and *Macaca fascicularis*)', *J. Med. Primatol.* **21**, 308–315.

TARANTAL, A. F. and HENDRICKX, A. G. (1988) 'Use of ultrasound for early pregnancy detection in the rhesus and cynomolgus macaque (*Macaca mulatta* and *Macaca fascicularis*)', *J. Med. Primatol.* **15**, 309–323.

THOMPSON, J. G. (1996) 'Defining the requirements for bovine embryo culture', *Theriogenology* **45**, 27–40.

VOGT, P.H. (1995) 'Genetic aspects of artificial fertilization', *Hum. Reprod.* **10**, 128–137.

WAKAYAMA, T., YANAGIMACHI, R. (1998) 'Development of normal mice from oocytes injected with freeze-dried spermatozoa', *Nature Biotechnol.* **16**, 639–641.

WALKER, S. K., HARTWICH, K. M. and SEAMARK, R. F. (1996) 'The production of unusually large offspring following embryo manipulation: concepts and challenges', *Theriogenology* **45**, 111–120.

WASSER, S. K., RISLER, L. and STEINER, R. A. (1988) 'Excreted steroids in primate feces over the menstrual cycle and pregnancy', *Biol. Reprod.* **39**, 862–872.

WASSER, S. K., THOMAS, R., NAIR, P. P., GUIDRY, C., SOUTHERS, J., LUCAS, J., WILDT, D. E. and MONFORT, S. L. (1993) 'Effects of dietary fibre on faecal steroid measurements in baboons (*Papio cynocephalus cynocephalus*)', *J. Reprod. Fertil.* **93**, 569–574.

WATSON, P. F. (1978) 'A review of techniques of semen collection in mammals', in Watson, P. F. (ed.) *Artificial Breeding of Non-Domestic Animals, Symp. Zool. Soc. Lond.* **43**, 97–126.

WHITTEN, P. L., BROCKMAN, D. K. and STAVISKY, R. C. (1998) 'Recent advances in non-invasive techniques to monitor hormone-behavior interactions', *Yearbook Phys. Anthropol.* **41**, 1–23.

WILDT, D. E. (1980) 'Laparoscopy in the dog and cat', in Harrison, R. M. and Wildt, D. E. (eds), *Animal Laparoscopy,* Baltimore: Williams and Wilkins, pp. 31–72.

WILDT, D. E. (1996) 'Male reproduction: assessment, management, and control of fertility', in Kleiman, D. G., Allen, M. E., Thompson, K. V. and Lumpkin, S. (eds) *Wild Mammals in Captivity,* Chicago: Chicago Press, pp. 429–450.

WILDT, D. E. and ROTH, T. L. (1997) 'Assisted reproduction for managing and conserving threatened felids', *International Zoo Yearbook* **35**, 164–172.

WILDT, D. E., MONFORT, S. L., DONOGHUE, A. M., JOHNSTON, L. A. and HOWARD, J. (1992) 'Embryogenesis in conservation biology–or, how to make an endangered species embryo', *Theriogenology* **37**, 161–182.

WILMUT, I., SCHNIEKE, A. E., MCWHIR, J., KIND, A. J. and CAMPBELL, K. H. S. (1997) 'Viable offspring derived from fetal and adult mammalian cells', *Nature, Lond.* **385**, 810–813.

ZIEGLER, T. E., SNOWDON, C. T., WARNEKE, M. and BRIDSON, W. E. (1990) 'Urinary excretion of oestrone conjugates and gonadotrophins during pregnancy in the Goeldi's monkey *(Callimico goeldii)'*, *J. Reprod. Fertil.* **89**, 163–168.

ZIEGLER, T. E., MATTERI, R. L. and WEGNER, F. H. (1993) 'Detection of urinary gonado-trophins in callitrichid monkeys with a sensitive immunoassay based upon a unique monoclonal antibody', *Am. J. Primatol.* **31**, 181–188.

CHAPTER 6

Organizational Issues Concerning the Establishment of a Genetic Resource Bank

P. F. WATSON[1] **and W. V. HOLT**[2]

[1]Department of Veterinary Basic Sciences, The Royal Veterinary College, London NW1 0TU, UK
[2]The Institute of Zoology, The Zoological Society of London, Regent's Park, London NW1 4RY, UK

Contents

7.1   INTRODUCTION

A GRB must have a long-term future if it is to make more than a brief impact on conservation measures. As was pointed out in Chapter 4, a GRB can make a useful contribution to maintaining a wide genetic base if it is used for extending the generation interval and making the individual genome available to subsequent generations. To do this the GRB must have a continuous existence, in the case of some species, for more than a human lifetime.

Accordingly, certain features must be considered in the establishment of such a bank. Many of these aspects have been mentioned in other chapters, but we consider it important to gather them together here as a unified set of considerations for those contemplating the establishment of a working GRB. They relate to any bank which has as its goal a contribution to biodiversity, and particularly if it is seen as interacting with the wild *in-situ* populations.

Table 7.1 gives a list of the issues to be considered and they are tackled in turn in the rest of this chapter.

7.2   PURPOSE OF THE GENETIC RESOURCE BANK

It is necessary that there is thorough preparation and that the aims and objectives are carefully considered. As has been noted, there are several conflicting possible aims of a GRB. A bank to conserve 'useful' genes for future benefit of humanity will have a strategy different to that for a bank designed to protect biodiversity. Moreover, a bank of frozen spermatozoa stored with the intention that, should it become necessary, it may one day be used to assist reproduction of a single species in a single institution will have a policy different to that of a bank intended to contribute to coordinating the conservation of worldwide captive genetic resources. Such matters need detailed planning to ensure that the strategy adopted makes maximum use of

CHAPTER 7

TABLE 7.1
Topics to be considered in the establishment of a GRB

- Purpose of GRB
- Size
- Location
- Recording
- Security
- Safety
- Management
- Training
- Ownership
- Long-term legal requirements

available resources as efficiently as possible. Thus before any other detailed planning is possible, the type of bank must be decided. What are its goals or what will it aim to achieve?

7.3 SIZE

Next, the scope of the GRB is a major consideration. Will it work solely within a single location or will it coordinate activities within more than one institution? Is it intended to work nationally or internationally? Will it attempt to conserve the genetic basis of a single species or of multiple species?

These questions lead to the setting of objectives or intermediate outcomes. The scope must be planned within the available physical resources. It is no good having a great plan to save the species if the available resources are only a couple of individual animals and a single animal house without laboratory back-up. GRBs need to be established where there is expert support staff and additional expertise to draw on.

Other further questions will then come to the fore. One such query is where to begin. How will the species to be conserved be decided? This simple question disguises a major issue for the planning stage. As has frequently been noted in the volume, this question raises issues about whether one should be motivated by the scarcity of the species in question, its availability, likely future utility or its public appeal. Moreover, the likelihood that the species is ultimately viable if supported in this way should be a major consideration. There is clearly no use in choosing a species in which no individuals are easily available. Moreover, it is doubtful whether one can achieve very much in terms of ensuring the long-term survival of a species if only a few individuals are left on the planet. How small a population is still considered viable will depend on a number of factors, as outlined in Chapter 4. If the project is dependent on public support then work with certain appealing species is likely to attract better support than work with less alluring species. Large mammals, for example, the giant panda or the elephant, are more interesting to the public than, say, insects. Moreover, some types of animals, e.g. snakes or spiders, evoke the opposite response in the public mind and are detrimental to fundraising ventures.

Obviously, an immediate consideration is the financial and physical resources available to devote to the project. This will influence which species and the scale of the programme. However, for GRB work one should also consider the longer term availability of resources. It is important that the efforts invested now should not be wasted in the future because of the inadequacies in the planning stage. Programmes can be planned to grow, but it is more difficult to reduce the scale in the future if resources become limited.

7.4 LOCATION

The geographical location of the operation should be planned with care. Choice of country is important as difficulties are likely to be encountered with transporting germplasm across national borders, whether because of disease transmission risks or to avoid the perception that genetic resources are being stolen from the country of origin. It is also important, if possible, for the laboratory facilities to be sited close to the animal quarters. Where wild animals are being used a small mobile laboratory may be desirable but there will be a need for a more permanent laboratory resource to be available. Frozen storage allows shipment to a permanent storage site some distance away.

Long-term storage of gametes and embryos should be conveniently sited where they can be accessed for use. They also need to be sited in countries where the political climate is sufficiently stable to have a reasonable expectancy of continued stability over many years. It may seem that this argues for storage sites to be located in the developed countries, but this is not necessarily so. There are many potential countries for partnership in a venture such as this.

One consideration about location is the importance of not having all the stored material in a single site. Apart from the need to split stored stocks into more than a single container because of problems of breakdown of vacuum in the nitrogen storage vessels, there are other issues pertinent to divided storage. Natural disasters, e.g. earthquakes, floods and storms, create circumstances in which, even if the storage facility is itself undamaged, supplies of liquid nitrogen may become endangered. The future of a GRB is therefore put at risk.

Moreover, as Kirkwood and Colenbrander (Chapter 5) point out, animal disease epidemics can cause temporary restrictions to be placed on movement of personnel and stocks of stored gametes and embryos into and out of the affected areas. Such restriction orders can be in place for extended periods.

Indeed, given that countries have different importation controls depending on the country of origin, in an international venture it might be argued that one should store material in different countries whose background disease status is very diverse.

7.5 RECORDING

It is essential to draw attention to the importance of recording, for it is one of the most vulnerable aspects of any long-term project. Recording involves both what is recorded and how it is recorded. Clearly, the identity of the samples in storage needs to be carefully documented. The markings on the container that identify its content should be permanent. It is worth stressing the need to use approved marking materials, which do not deteriorate in liquid nitrogen with time. Moreover, details of its location in the storage vessel should be clearly identified.

With this, should go the background information about the manner of its collection and handling in the laboratory. In particular, details of the storage medium in which the cells are suspended are essential, and also a description of the freezing protocol. The disease status of the individual(s) from which the samples were derived should be described and any tests to establish it should be recorded. Veterinary health certificates are often mandatory when international shipment of samples is being undertaken; insufficient attention to such details at the time may undermine the future value of the stored samples. Details of blood and tissue samples collected at the same time should be linked with the gamete sample record. Finally, the genetic identity of individual samples should be recorded, accompanied where possible by data derived from genetic analyses (karyotypes, mitochondrial DNA analyses). In a captive situation, if pedigrees are known they should be linked to the sample record; for wild species the geographic location of collection should be recorded, together with descriptive evidence. Such information could be crucial, as attempts to define a species become entangled in arguments once morphological, ecological and behavioural criteria are all taken into account.

The manner of recording should also be considered. Paper records can be lost or destroyed over time. Duplicate records should be maintained and updated regularly to ensure the long-term continuance of the record. Good laboratory practice (GLP) procedures ensure that laboratory personnel take responsibility for their own recording by signing the record and by adopting standardized procedures to ensure that any corrections are entered in a clearly identifiable manner.

Alternatively, computerized records could be maintained. They should be regularly backed up, preferably with no time lag between modifying and backing up so that nothing is lost if the system fails. The system itself should be regularly updated so that the records do not become tied to outdated software. This is particularly important in this situation when the record has to be kept for many years.

7.6 SECURITY

Security is concerned with ensuring the long-term survival of the material and with protecting the personnel and animals in the handling of material being put in or taken out of storage. The latter is considered under the heading of 'Safety' (see Section 7.7). Nevertheless, apart from the questions of disease status affecting import and export explored in the previous section, there are questions of disease risks to be considered under the topic of security.

Kirkwood and Colenbrander (Chapter 5) urge that whenever gametes or embryos are placed in frozen storage a blood sample taken at the time, and a second sample taken two weeks later, is also stored with the genetic material. This is in order that, as further tests of disease status become available, there will be relevant available material to test. Moreover, Bennett (Chapter 4) recommends that a tissue sample (skin or connective tissue) be stored at the same time in order that genetic typing might be available at a future date. This is to ensure that material is used with the appropriate knowledge of the genetic identity of the individual donor(s). Such considerations also come under the broader concept of security.

However, the term security raises in most people's minds the need to ensure that material is safely stored over long periods. This includes regular inspection and topping up of nitrogen levels and perhaps the use of automated alarm systems triggering emergency procedures to rescue frozen material. It also implies restricted entry and passes for those involved in access to the GRB. After all, the frozen material is the most valuable resource to the whole venture and on which it all depends. It is essential that it be held secure from intruders bent on destruction.

7.7 SAFETY

It is also important to consider the safety of personnel. Apart from the legal requirements of employer legislation there is a moral obligation on those responsible to provide a safe working environment. Safe handling procedures are called for at all times and proper working protocols should be adopted and observed continuously. Such high-quality laboratory work is costly and qualified and trained staff are also expensive. These matters should be included in the resource planning at the outset.

When material from wild animals is being handled, especially if it is from primates, the potential of zoonoses should be borne in mind. The use of proper microbiological safe handling procedures should be adopted to protect staff from harm.

7.8 MANAGEMENT

A store of gametes and embryos, 'a frozen zoo', is not particularly useful as a GRB, but only when it is integrated into an ongoing breeding programme. Thus decisions have to be made regarding who should have access to the frozen genetic resource. It is generally considered wise to make these decisions from a policy agreed before the requests arrive. This avoids accusations of favouritism or bias in decision-making. Ideally, the policy should be determined by a management committee and not left to the responsibility of a single individual. Also, a responsible group should agree the particular decisions on use.

Decisions relating to the use of the resources will involve considerations as to the potential benefits to accrue from the particular use. The expertise and facilities available to the applicant, the particular genetic gains to be enjoyed if successful, and the potential value placed on the stored material will all influence the decision. In many instances, expertise will be evidenced by track record of past achievements, but this will not always be the case and risk of failure needs to be acknowledged. Often, decisions will be related to the wider needs of a conservation programme. In these situations, studbook holders and Taxon Advisory Group (TAG) managers would need to be consulted.

Once a decision about donating materials from the bank has been reached, it is useful to consider the need for a formal contract between the parties involved. The purpose of putting such an agreement on a formal basis is to prevent unauthorized use of the material by a third party, to whom it may be given without the donor's knowledge.

Further to the consideration of use in an international transfer of genetic resources will be the possibility of gaining licences for import of the material into the country of intended use. This will be governed both by the countries involved and by what information is available about the disease status of the animal(s) from which the material was derived.

GRB programmes have to be managed by people who understand their objectives, strengths and limitations. Adequately trained personnel are therefore an essential component of any programme, something which is often overlooked. At present there are no training programmes which relate specifically to this issue, even through a number of GRBs are already in operation (for example, the Rare Breeds Survival Trust in the UK has operated a semen bank for many years). A comprehensive training programme would have to include not only sample collection and management, but also tuition on related topics such as taxonomy, reproductive biology and anaesthesia.

7.9 OWNERSHIP

In any GRB, questions of ownership should be clarified. When material is stored from within a single institution, there is generally little doubt as to ownership. The situation becomes more complex when wild animal material that has been collected on field trips is stored. Does the material belong to the person(s) who collected it, or to the owners of the land on which the animals were trapped? Are there any other organizations that may have a claim on the material, e.g. a national or regional government that directs the wildlife service, a research institution who provided facilities for the collection or processing of the material?

Questions of ownership can become quite complex, especially if international collaboration is involved. This is not least because legal systems differ between countries; in some cases the export of genetic resources of any description is regarded as illegal. Such questions are likely to become more frequent in the future and it would be well to be prepared for disputes.

7.10 LONG-TERM LEGAL RESPONSIBILITIES

Under this heading are questions concerned with management responsibilities to staff and to the security of the stocks. Should aggrieved parties enter into litigation, who is legally responsible and what limits are placed on that responsibility? Such considerations may not be thought about early in the project and may only later become an issue when a problem arises. Alternatively, these matters are included in the initial planning but as time goes on, especially if the responsible personnel change, they can be overlooked or forgotten. It is important they are recorded for the benefit of staff engaged in the management of the project over time.

7.11 UNANSWERED BIOLOGICAL QUESTIONS

As GRB usage becomes more of a reality, one question which will arise will relate to the impact of storage and generation time upon the frequency with which stored samples should be replenished. Given that population management protocols are designed with long time-scales in mind, for example to minimize losses of genetic diversity over 200 years, will the genetic characteristics of originally collected founder material still be suitable for use after that period? At present, population models would suggest that this is unlikely to be a problem. However, if the genetic material is heavily used it will need to be replenished using an optimal strategy which has yet to be evaluated (for further discussion see Chapter 4).

A technical conundrum, which will also arise over a prolonged period, relates to the advancement of cryopreservation technology. A GRB programme may start by imposing a standardized protocol for germplasm cryopreservation, thus avoiding the risk of acquiring samples by ad hoc methods. However, a systematic and periodic review of techniques should be built into the schedule, thus ensuring that improvements in technology are not being ignored.

7.12 CONCLUSION

The issues raised in this chapter are intended to demonstrate that the initiation of a GRB programme is not something to be undertaken lightly. Exploration of apparently simple issues such as species recognition and recording can lead to complex questions which can only be answered by performing research. Similarly, although the GRB itself is often envisaged simply as a repository of frozen germplasm, its future utility will depend heavily upon the development of suitably efficient reproductive technologies. This underlines the need for effective fundamental research projects in reproduction to accompany any GRB programme. Very often, especially in the case of threatened species, such research projects are not easily developed. Inability to accompany a GRB programme with suitable research is likely to act as a major deciding factor when prioritizing species for support.

This coverage, although brief, is intended to provide a checklist of matters to be considered in setting up a GRB. Because of the long-term nature of the venture it is important to anticipate the features likely to impinge on its success. Careful estimation of the cost implications is not a novel concept but is still an essential process. One is reminded of the Biblical parable of the man who wanted to build a tower (Luke 14: 28–30)!

Towards the Development of a Genetic Resource Bank for the Mohor Gazelle: Putting Theory into Practice

TERESA ABAIGAR[1] and W. V. HOLT[2]

[1]Consejo Superior de Investigaciones Científicas, Estación Experimental de Zonas Áridas, c/. General Segura 1, 04001 Almería, Spain
[2]The Institute of Zoology, The Zoological Society of London, Regent's Park, London NW1 4RY, UK

Contents

8.1 INTRODUCTION

Much has been written about the conceptual background to the use of GRBs, but there is still relatively little evidence that these ideas are being used for the practical support of captive breeding programmes. To develop a greater appreciation of the practical problems faced when GRBs are to be put into practice seriously, a collaborative GRB research programme was developed between the Institute of Zoology (IOZ) in London (UK) and the Estación Experimental de Zonas Aridas (EEZA) in Almería, South eastern Spain. IOZ represents the main research component within the Zoological Society of London and EEZA is an Institute of the Consejo Superior de Investigaciones Científicas (CSIC), a national research organization in Spain. The aim of the programme was to support the conservation and breeding of three endangered gazelle species which the EEZA had been successfully breeding since 1971. The species protected and living in Almería are the Mohor gazelle (*Gazella dama mhorr*), Cuvier's gazelle (*Gazella cuvieri*), Dorcas gazelle (*Gazella dorcas neglecta*) and the Saharan barbary sheep (*Ammotragus lervia sahariensis*). The breeding programmes are based within the Parque de Rescate de la Fauna Sahariana (PRFS), a dedicated animal facility, created by the Spanish authorities in 1971 to prevent the complete extinction of certain large ungulates from the Western Sahara. It is a 21–hectare farm ('La Hoya'), situated at the foot of Almería's historic Muslim castle, the Alcazaba.

The PRFS was sited in Almería because the prevailing Mediterranean semi-arid climate, with short mild winters, scant annual rainfall (<200 mm) and extremely dry summers, was well suited to the captive breeding of desert and semi-desert North African species. Moreover, the area is sheltered from the northerly winter winds that would otherwise harm these desert animals. In addition to the favour-able climatic conditions, the support of a public research centre devoted to the ecology of arid zones was fundamental to the success of this venture. Not only does the EEZA provide expertise in all aspects of animal management and care, including a dedicated veterinarian and on-site clinic, it also provides secure, long-term, funding of the captive breeding programme without having to operate as a public amenity.

This chapter provides an overview of the conservation activities carried out in La Hoya, and shows how these have contributed to the maintenance of the gazelle species and their restoration to native habitats. However, our purpose here is also to show how these activities are embracing the use of reproductive technologies and genome banking as additional tools which support the overall programme. We describe how the development of reproductive technologies for these species has presented new practical and theoretical challenges, and also show how the initiation of these studies in the gazelle have, in fact, stimulated exciting fundamental studies of reproduction in these species.

8.2 THE SPECIES

8.2.1 Mohor gazelle (*Gazella (Nanger) dama mhorr,* Bennet 1832), native names: Mohor, Addra

Status: Red Data Book: Endangered (E), CITES: Appendix I

This subspecies of *Gazella dama* once occupied the western strip of the Sahara Desert from the south of the Anti-Atlas Mountains to the desert of Senegal, and from the Atlantic coast to about 250 km inland (Cano, 1991). Overhunting was the principal cause of extinction and no wild animals have been observed since 1968. Small populations were kept in captivity in military quarters in the Western Sahara (previously a Spanish colony), and the main captive population in Almería was founded in 1971 when four males and thirteen females were taken to EEZA. In its natural environment this species likes flat, stony land and dry rivers ('oueds') characterized by the scattered presence of acacias (*Acacia raddiana* and *A. albida*). It is one of the largest gazelles and shows an attractively patterned and coloured coat. At birth, males weigh more than 5 kg and females 4 kg. Adult males can weigh up to 65 kg and females up to 60 kg. The horns are relatively small in comparison with other gazelles and

Figure 8.1: A group of Mohor gazelles in 'La Hoya', Almería. Photograph courtesy of Drs Teresa Abaigar and Mar Cano.

antelopes, with the points characteristically curved forward. At 15 months, females can give birth to a single offspring after a gestation period of 200 days (Cano, 1991). In Almería, births are distributed over the entire year but parturition is more frequent in the spring.

8.2.2 Cuvier's gazelle (*Gazella cuvieri*, Ogilby 1840), native names: Harmusch, Edmi)

Status: Red Data Book: Endangered (E), CITES: Appendix III

The general distribution of Cuvier's gazelle includes the mountain regions of Morocco, Algeria and Tunisia. Although it seems that some small populations survive in these three countries, the population has decreased considerably due to overhunting and increased human pressure. Conservation policies in these three countries during the last decade have allowed several populations to flourish, for example, at Djebel Chambi in Tunisia where a population of 400–500 individuals now exists. The Moroccan population, mainly in the Saharan Atlas Mountains, is fragmented. Recent discoveries have confirmed a range extension southwards between the lower Drâa and the de Aydar massif. In Algeria, the range falls between the Tell Atlas and the Saharan Atlas (Lafontaine *et al.*, 1999). These gazelles live in pine forest of *Pinus halepensis*, *Juniperus phoenica* and *Tetraclinis articulata* with plenty of shrub cover.

At birth the calves weigh approximately 3 kg. Adult males can weigh up to 35 kg and females up to 30 kg. The horns are straight and up to 30 cm long in males and 24 cm in females. Gestation length is 159 days, and sexual maturity is reached during the first year. A high frequency of twinning (38,7%; Escós, 1992) is characteristic of this species and although calves have been born in every season of the year in Almería, most births occur at the end of winter (February), early spring (March) and autumn (Escós, 1992). The captive population in Almería was founded in 1975 with an initial population of four animals, two males and two females.

8.2.3 Dorcas gazelle (*Gazella dorcas neglecta*, Lavauden 1926), native name: Gueslam)

Status: Red Data Book: Vulnerable (V), CITES: Appendix III (species dorcas)

The subspecies *neglecta* is one of five subspecies of *G. dorcas* described by Alados (1987) in one of the last taxonomic reviews of this species. This subspecies occupied the western edge of the Sahara Desert from the south of the Anti-Atlas Mountains to the Mauritanian deserts. The eastern limit of its distribution is uncertain, but must include part of the Algerian and Mauritanian deserts. These gazelles like stony ground ('regs' or 'hamadas') with sparse vegetation (*Aizoon, Nucularia, Salsola, Heliotropum*) in desert and semi-desert areas and 'oueds' with Acacia trees (*Acacia* spp.), which make up the basis of their food. Previously an abundant species, its number has diminished considerably because of the excessive hunting pressure. Its present situation in the wild is unknown although it seems to be recovering. The recent war between Morocco and Frente Polisario, in south-western Sahara, has unexpectedly helped the recovery of the Dorcas gazelle population because the extensive deployment of landmines in the area has rendered hunting activities too dangerous.

The Dorcas is a small gazelle; newborn weight is less than 2 kg. Adult males weigh up to 16 kg and females 13 kg. Sexual dimorphism, apart from the larger size of the males, is mainly evident in the horns. Horns of males are lyre-shaped and up to 30 cm in length, while those of the females are thinner, straighter and no more than 25 cm long. Females reach sexual maturity in the first year of life and, after a gestation period of 168 days, give birth to single offspring. Calves are born in captivity all year-round. The captive founder population in Almería consisted of nine males and nine females.

8.2.4 Saharan Barbary sheep (*Ammotragus lervia sahariensis*, Rothschild 1913), native names: Arruit, Aoudad)

Status: Red Data Book: Vulnerable (V), CITES: not included

The Saharan Barbary sheep is a member of the Caprinae family. This species used to be found throughout the mountainous parts of the Sahara Desert and subdesert, reaching the Mediterranean coast to the north. Six subspecies have been described (Ansell, 1971), this being *A. l. sahariensis,* the western dweller. It lived among the inaccessible rocks of the Djebel, feeding in the foothills on *Nucularia, Panicum, Acacia spp.* and other edible plants, which are denser than on the surrounding desert plains. Despite the intense hunting pressure which this species has experienced, there are still some small populations in protected areas of Morocco, Algeria, Tunisia, Sudan, Mauritania and Egypt. The *sahariensis* subspecies is considered extinct, although some relict populations may still exist between the south of the Western Sahara and the northern Mauritanian desert.

The most characteristic features are its size, the male's large horns, and the long hairs that hang from its chest and front legs. Males weigh up to 130 kg, with horns that can measure up to 65 cm long; females may be up to 60 kg, with horns up to 40 cm long. Females give birth from the first year of life and twin births are frequent; births take place throughout the year, but are more frequent in the spring. The gestation period is 150 days. The captive reproduction programme for this species started in Almería in 1975 with only one male and one female as founders.

8.3   OBJECTIVES OF THE CONSERVATION PROGRAMMES

When the captive breeding programmes were established in the PRFS, the immediate aim was to prevent the gazelles and Barbary sheep from becoming extinct. However, the long-term goal was to reintroduce them to their original areas of distribution. In order to work towards this long-term objective a range of strategic and practical measures were implemented:

1 Studbooks were established for all species and subspecies.
2 Biological, behavioural and veterinary research programmes were initiated to increase knowledge of these poorly documented species. This was regarded as important for assuring the success of the captive programmes.
3 Captive-bred animals were supplied to zoos and breeding centres. This was seen as a practical conservation measure, aimed at assuring survival of the species in the event of natural catastrophe in Almería.

8.4   PRACTICAL MANAGEMENT OF THE CAPTIVE ANIMALS

Within the PFRS the gazelles are maintained under three different types of management: (1) reproductive herds containing an adult male and several females (between 5 and 10, depending upon enclosure size) with their offspring; (2) bachelor groups, created by gathering young males (6–7 months old) from the different reproductive herds, which are kept as future breeding males; and (3) isolated males, which are mainly adult males that have already reproduced. In contrast, the Saharan Barbary sheep are kept in mixed/reproductive herds on the steep hillside of 'La Hoya'.

The gazelle pens are enclosed by flexible wire mesh and metal posts (2 m high). Inside the pens, a small enclosure with two doors is used for the isolation and capture of individuals when required. A sun roof provides shade and also protects both food and animals from rainfall. Inside the enclosures, branches and obstacles provide hiding places for the offspring during the first days of life, and are used by the adults as a means of displaying aggression, playfulness and as marking sites. The diet is based on commercial pellets, barley and fresh alfalfa; water, salts and mineral complex are provided *ad libitum*.

For handling purposes, gazelles are routinely restrained using a flexible net; however, the Saharan Barbary sheep have to be anaesthetized using a rifle and dart.

8.5   GENETIC MANAGEMENT OF THE GAZELLES

One of the problems in captive breeding programmes based on small founder populations is the need to minimize the loss of existing genetic variability. Maintenance of

CHAPTER 8

the most diverse gene pool possible is thought to provide the genetic plasticity that increases the chances of successfully surviving in varying environmental conditions (see Chapter 4). The number of founder individuals in a captive breeding programme sets the limit for the amount of genetic diversity originally available, and ideally this should be as large as possible. This is expressed mathematically by the formula ($H=1-\frac{1}{2}N$) (Seal and Flesness, 1978), where N is the number of unrelated and non-inbred founder individuals, and H is the amount of genetic variability which can be retained from this founder population. Given the small founder population sizes available for the species survival programmes in Almería, their evident success is most encouraging. In fact, the intensive recording and documentation of the history of these populations since they were founded now provides an unusually valuable resource of data suitable for testing much of the theory associated with inbreeding and species fitness.

The number of founder individuals for the expansion of the Mohor and Dorcas gazelle populations appears to have been sufficient. The populations have flourished in the thirty years since they were founded, and little impact of inbreeding depression is evident. For the Cuvier's gazelle and Saharan Barbary sheep the genetic variability within the founding populations was clearly minimal, but even here the captive breeding programmes have been a success. Lack of genetic diversity in these species may not, however, become a problem while the animals are being maintained under ideal conditions and may only manifest itself in an adverse environment. (For further discussion of the effects of inbreeding upon the fitness components of captive populations, see Alados and Escós, 1991; Ralls et al., 1979, 1988; Thornhill, 1993). Alados and Escós (1991) investigated the effects of inbreeding in the gazelles of the PRFS. They found that a high inbreeding coefficient reduced longevity in Cuvier's and Mohor gazelles but not in Dorcas gazelles. Fecundity and juvenile survival of the female Mohor gazelle was severely depressed and evident, although less pronounced, in Dorcas gazelles. The effects of inbreeding upon reproductive function were minimal in Cuvier's gazelle and only evident in the twinning rates. As Alados and Escós (1991) pointed out, this result is surprising in view of the high inbreeding coefficient of this species relative to the other two.

The most common management strategies for avoiding loss of genetic diversity are: (1) mating carefully chosen pairs of animals so as to maintain inbreeding coefficients as low as possible, (2) increasing the effective population size (which from a practical point of view means allowing all the animals to reproduce), and (3) increasing the interval between generations. There are a number of practical problems to be overcome when implementing these breeding programmes, some of which could be solved by the ready availability of reproductive technologies. In territorial species like gazelles, it is nearly impossible to allow to every animal to reproduce. The reproductive groups consist of several adult females with an adult male. Therefore, unless a huge amount of spare space is available, many males will inevitably never have the opportunity to reproduce. Moreover, it is virtually impossible to achieve the ideal situation for genetic management where specific male-female pairs can be set up to produce calves with the lowest inbreeding coefficients. Mortality, particularly of youngsters and mainly of males, interferes with genetic management as some animals are genetically very valuable. These problems are exacerbated because many zoos and breeding centres possess reproductive groups that are severely limited in size and that cannot be augmented by the new wild-caught founders. The risks of inbreeding are therefore ever present, but are difficult to avoid.

The gazelle captive breeding programmes suffer from all of the practical difficulties of genetic management mentioned above. However, various measures are taken to minimize the inbreeding coefficient as far as possible. Dedicated computer programs have been developed by the systems manager of the EEZA specifically to help plan the matings between animals in the PRFS and other zoos participating in the gazelle conservation programmes. Studbook keepers for all four species held at the PRFS are based in Almería. The overarching objectives of the demographic management are to maintain stable populations in terms of sex ratio and age classes, both for the populations in Almería and also for the global captive populations.

8.6 THE INTEGRATION OF GENETIC RESOURCE BANKS AND THE PRFS PROGRAMMES

8.6.1 Why set up a GRB for the Mohor gazelle?

The main aim of a GRB for endangered species is to support the existing genetic management activities. Simply keeping the genetic material as a research resource could be considered an objective in itself, but serves a distinctly different purpose and therefore is not the primary aim.

The genetic resource bank programme in Almería started as a pilot scheme when the PRFS participated in a Biotechnology project funded by the European Union under Framework III. The objective of this project, which involved sixteen different European centres, was the establishment of guidelines for implementing GRBs for conservation purposes (Holt *et al.*, 1996c). At the first meeting held within the framework of this collaboration in 1994 it was felt that undertaking a small number of practical GRB trials would help to evaluate the degree of difficulty involved in putting these ideas into practice. Several vertebrate species were selected for these pilot experiments (a cichlid fish species from Lake Victoria, a New World primate (the common marmoset) and a large carnivore, the cheetah). The Mohor gazelle was selected to represent an endangered ungulate. These species were selected because they fulfilled several important prerequisites for selection, in particular the need for detailed genetic

CHAPTER 8

histories. The Mohor gazelle fitted this requirement admirably because although it is an extinct subspecies in the wild, about 250 animals live in captivity and small reintroduced populations in areas of Morocco, Senegal and Tunisia. As described above, a well-documented captive breeding programme already exists, which is supported by the studbook initiated when the captive herd was set up. Some research into the reproductive biology of the species had already been undertaken and there were enough animals to carry out meaningful experiments. The existence of the reintroduction programmes for this species means that there is an important motive for maintaining maximal genetic diversity in the captive herd.

It could be argued that the criteria applied to the selection of the Mohor gazelle apply equally to the Dorcas or Cuvier's gazelles, and it has to be admitted that various practical issues influenced the choice of species. For example, although semen collection was possible in all three species by the electroejaculation of anaesthetized healthy males, initial trials revealed that Dorcas and Cuvier's gazelles consistently produced smaller volumes of less concentrated semen than the Mohor gazelles. This was considered important in the choice of species because the feasibility of semen freezing required investigation as an important first step. Very little information about semen freezing in gazelles was available (Boever *et al.*, 1980; Merilan *et al.*, 1977), and therefore some preliminary experimentation was necessary. The minimal quantities of semen available from the Cuvier's and Dorcas gazelles severely limited the number of variables, such as egg yolk or glycerol concentration, which could be investigated. A further practical reason for choosing the Mohor gazelle was that this species is calmer than either Dorcas or Cuvier's. Although this reason may seem somewhat surprising, it was nonetheless important in this context because there would be less risk of accidents during capture and management procedures.

8.6.2 Animal handling and semen collection

A major advantage of developing the gazelle GRB programme in an existing collection was the availability of a highly capable and experienced staff, used to handling the animals for various management reasons. Not only did this include staff with expertise in catching and handling the animals, it also included a veterinarian with considerable experience in the anaesthesia of the gazelles in question. The value of such a capable team of individuals cannot be overstated and it meant that the research goals of the project could be addressed immediately. In our view this is a fundamental consideration for anyone who contemplates setting up a GRB programme. The practical procedure used for isolating and catching the gazelles involves coaxing an animal into a net, held vertically like a temporary fence by several keepers. The animal is then manually restrained, its face covered and legs tied together with cords; it is then moved to the on-site veterinary clinic where anaesthesia is administered. Initially, anaesthetics were administered manually using a syringe rather than a dart gun, but recently this technique has been superseded by the use of gaseous halothane. The entire procedure is carried out with remarkable efficiency.

Animal handling is undoubtedly a key determinant of success in the practical application of reproductive technologies with large ungulates; prolonged attempts to catch animals almost undoubtedly cause stress which may impact negatively upon many physiological processes including the reproductive axis. This is especially well recognized by deer farmers in New Zealand who make extensive use of AI and embryo transfer procedures. Zoos and wildlife reserves that wish to develop this aspect of their activities should ensure that they possess the appropriate facilities, manpower and skills.

Semen collection from the Mohor gazelle (electroejaculation; see Chapters 6 and 15) is completed remarkably reliably and rapidly (typically less than 3 minutes) once the animal has been brought to the veterinary clinic. Unfortunately the PRFS does not yet possess suitable equipment on-site, so the semen is transported to the main EEZA laboratories as soon as possible after collection.

The most readily assessed semen parameters are: volume, concentration, viability and motility (wave motion, individual and progressive motility). These parameters are readily measured requiring only micropipettes, counting chamber, slides and stains (for references on semen assessment, see Holt and Medrano, 1997).

8.6.3 Initial experiments on semen cryopreservation

As the objective of this work was to create a semen bank, the first priority was to develop suitable protocols for long-term semen cryopreservation. However, there was very little background information about freezing methods for gazelle semen, and we wished to avoid a long series of preliminary trials. The first important decision was whether semen freezing should be performed using straws or pellets. On the basis of wide-ranging discussions it was considered that straw freezing not only would be better from a technical point of view, but would also be more acceptable in terms of hygiene and disease control, especially if samples of semen were ultimately exported. We therefore reviewed the general literature on semen freezing in ungulates in an effort to identify protocols that showed promising results with similar species. As the TEST-yolk diluents had been used with some success with most species in which they had been tested, a decision was made to use this combination as the basic diluent. The next decisions concerning diluent composition were impossible to evaluate without some practical experimentation; what concentrations of egg yolk and glycerol would be best for gazelle semen? Evidence from other species indicates that glycerol can be damaging if the concentration is either too high (e.g. pigs and mice) or too low (e.g. marsupials). As bovid spermatozoa usually survive best when the concentration is 6–8% v/v, a

CHAPTER 8

decision was taken to use 6% glycerol in initial semen freezing experiments, and investigate the effects of varying the egg yolk concentration. The availability of large quantities of spermatozoa from the Mohor gazelles permitted one more variable to be investigated within the initial experiments, and the effectiveness of including a detergent (Equex) was also tested. This compound had been shown in other studies to enhance the preservation of acrosomal integrity during cryopreservation.

An initial trial to investigate semen freezing in the Mohor gazelles was therefore set up using TEST-yolk with 6% glycerol and three different concentrations of egg yolk (5%, 10% and 20%); these combinations were tested in the presence and absence of detergent (Equex). To evaluate post-thaw sperm survival, variables tested were: percentage motility, acrosomal integrity and sperm motion parameters determined by the Hobson sperm tracker (see Holt *et al.*, 1996a, for definitions and results). In summary, the proportion of motile spermatozoa decreased as the egg yolk concentration increased; moreover the proportion of spermatozoa with damaged acrosomes also increased with egg yolk concentrations. No protective effect of Equex on acrosomal integrity or sperm motility parameters was detected. No significant effects of Equex or egg yolk concentration on the motion parameters of individual spermatozoa were detected.

Significant interanimal variation in semen quality after freezing was found for nearly all semen parameters. To examine some of the factors responsible for such interanimal variation, individual attributes (age, weight, inbreeding coefficient and herd management conditions) were tested. Although significant differences were found only for some motion parameters and herd conditions, we suspected that body condition and inbreeding coefficient might have significant effects on semen quality both before and after freezing. We found some indication that sperm survival after thawing was worse in the more inbred animals, but the relationship was weak and needs further validation. Inbreeding seems to be one of the more important characteristics affecting reproductive success in both males and females in captive populations (Roldan *et al.*, 1998). It is worth noting that some of the reproductive research performed as part of the GRB programme has prompted the initiation of a high-priority research programme in this area which parallels the establishment of genetic resource banks.

8.6.4 Setting up the laboratory

Since commencing the GRB programme, a laboratory has been refurbished and equipped within the EEZA. In contrast to the situation in 1994, the laboratory now possesses a phase-contrast microscope, warm stage and video recorder, enabling later sperm motility analyses by computer-assisted methods (Abaigar *et al.*, 1999). The programme has also required investment in more basic equipment such as centrifuges, incubators, balances for preparing media and containers for storing liquid nitrogen and frozen samples. Besides considering the purchase of essential new equipment, a few practical issues in laboratory organization also had to be addressed. Packaging diluted semen into straws presents a surprisingly complex problem in an under-equipped laboratory. If the packaging is carried out after cooling to 5°C, the procedure must be performed in a cooled area, ideally a thermostatically controlled cold room. The alternative technique of packaging the semen prior to cooling presents an attractive method of avoiding the need for a cold room, but removes the option of adding cryoprotectant solution after completion of the initial slow cooling process. This is a technical step that is both theoretically sensible and which seems to promote sperm survival. In Almería, this problem was solved because a refrigerated cold room was available. Other important, but deceptively trivial issues that had to be considered were the regular availability of liquid nitrogen supplies for sample storage and setting up a routine protocol for filling the storage containers, ensuring that holiday periods were always covered.

One of the major debates in gamete storage technology for human clinical infertility centres has been the prevention of disease transmission between frozen samples within the storage containers. In that context, the main concern has focused upon the risks of HIV and hepatitis transmission. This issue is also relevant to the establishment of GRBs for wildlife conservation, especially if samples of vastly different origin are maintained within the same storage vessel. In this particular instance, however, where all of the stored semen samples originate from animals at the same site, the risks of cross-infection were considered to be much less important. Nevertheless, before semen samples are collected, the males are tested for the more common infectious diseases in bovids: namely, brucellosis, tuberculosis and paratuberculosis. At present, the straws are not protected by additional secondary containment such as plastic outer sleeves, as has been suggested for human samples.

Identification of straws within the liquid nitrogen storage containers is achieved as follows. Each container and each of the canisters within the container are given an identifying number. Although the GRB programme specifically involves the Mohor gazelles, experimental samples from Cuvier's and Dorcas gazelles are also stored within the same containers. To avoid confusion, differently coloured visitubes, which hold sets of straws, are used for each species. Each visitube is labelled with the studbook number of the animal and the date of semen collection. When different experimental treatments are used, they are identified by the use of coloured straws. These details are recorded in a computer database.

8.6.5 Artificial insemination trials

The only sure way to test the viability of frozen–thawed semen is to use it in an AI trial. Therefore, in addition to testing the viability of the semen bank using the sperm quality evaluations indicated above, an AI trial was also set up using thirteen females. The females and males were selected to comply with the principles of genetic management, i.e. calves would have the best inbreeding coefficients. In this case, however, an additional requirement was imposed–a minimum of 30% sperm motility after thawing. The first criterion was based on findings from natural mating where high inbreeding coefficients increased the mortality of calves (Alados and Escós, 1991). If not controlled, this factor itself could affect the outcome of the AI trial.

Oestrous synchronization techniques are widely used in AI so that the optimal insemination timing can be achieved (for details, see Chapter 6). As with other aspects of this work, there was little detailed knowledge of reproduction in the Mohor gazelle and guidance on the best approach was sought by reference to practices with other species. The main questions to be asked within an AI trial thus not only concerned the viability and fertility of the semen, but also the responses of the females to oestrous synchronization procedures. In particular, it was essential to know not only whether or not the females responded to the synchronization procedure at all, and if so, what interval should be allowed between synchronization and insemination.

Previous behavioural data indicated that the oestrous cycle of the Mohor gazelles is around 15 days, with an ovulatory phase of 2–3 days. Until recently, however, no hormonal data existed for this species. Oestrous synchronization was nevertheless undertaken using intravaginal progesterone-releasing devices (CIDRs) following a protocol developed for fallow deer (Holt et al., 1996b; Jabbour et al., 1993). The alternative procedure, administration of two doses of prostaglandin F_2 approximately 12 days apart, could have been chosen, but experience with this approach has shown more interspecies variability in the length of time taken to return to oestrus.

Each female received a single intravaginal CIDR device. This was a simple and rapid manipulation and did not cause any stress to the animals. Precautions were taken to put the tip of the drawstring into the perianal area to avoid breakage during animal contact. No losses of the intravaginal devices were observed. After 12 days, the devices were removed. The females were divided into two treatment groups and inseminated with frozen semen in utero (both uterine horns) by laparoscopy at 48 hours ($n=7$) and 60 hours ($n=6$) after CIDR device removal. Pregnancy was diagnosed on day 52 after insemination by ultrasound transabdominal imaging; females were not anaesthetized for this procedure. Three pregnancies within the 48–hour group were identified, whereas only one pregnancy was identified within the 60–hour group. A single pregnancy within the 48–hour group was carried to term; the other three pregnancies were not carried to term, but no evidence of abortion was observed (for details, see Holt et al., 1996b).

This trial rapidly provided a good deal of useful information. First, it demonstrated that the frozen semen was indeed fertile. It also revealed that CIDR devices could be used for oestrous synchronization, and seemed to indicate that a 48–hour interval between CIDR removal and insemination is likely to be better than 60 hours. This aspect will become clearer as more inseminations are performed. It was useful to know that the laparoscopy could be carried out by an operative whose skills were developed with sheep and deer, rather than with gazelles themselves. This is an important point because interspecies differences in anatomy, for example between carnivores and ungulates, can cause confusion. The reasons for the failures of pregnancy remain undetermined.

This experiment indicated a number of areas where more precise information is required if artificial insemination methods are to be used routinely. Better characterization of the oestrous cycle was one obvious area for future work, preferably using non-invasive procedures such as faecal hormone analysis. Moreover, pregnancy diagnosis by faecal hormone profiles will be preferable to the use of ultrasound imaging because the stress produced during the manipulations is avoided. Any such stress is best minimized in pregnant females. If it proves necessary to use ultrasound, use of transrectal probes in anaesthetized females would be better than using transabdominal probes with manually restrained animals.

8.6.6 Semen exchange

One of the more practical uses of semen banks is the possibility of using them to interchange semen for reproductive purpose between different zoos and breeding centres participating in programmes of captive conservation. Such exchanges have many advantages that have already been mentioned in other parts in this book. In particular, the risk of accidents and death of valuable animals and the risks of disease transmission would be avoided. Routine use of the semen banks requires that the techniques involved should be as simple as possible. Clearly, the development of non-laparoscopic insemination techniques would be a major advantage as they could be performed with relatively simple equipment and without the need for much specialist training. Initial efforts to develop such transcervical insemination methods have shown considerable promise, but have yet to produce any successful results.

8.7 CONCLUDING REMARKS

Working towards the establishment of the GRB programme for the Mohor gazelle has underlined the fact that while the intentions are well focused and apparently simple, the implementation is surprisingly complex. While effective sperm cryopreservation is obviously centrally important within the overall plan and requires investigation, efficient insemination techniques must be developed at the same time. This adds a requirement for detailed endocrinological studies to the research programme. While these could be undertaken easily with domesticated species, where regular blood

CHAPTER 8

sampling is a realistic possibility, only the use of stress-free investigative techniques such as faecal hormone assessments are possible with animals of such a nervous disposition. Pregnancy diagnosis is fraught with difficulty for the same reason. Faecal hormone analyses can now be used to diagnose pregnancy, but because this technique does not allow discrimination between fertilization failure and embryonic loss, it is difficult to pinpoint the reasons for failed inseminations, which may include ovulatory insufficiency as well as sperm problems.

Attempting to address all of these technical problems without sufficient background knowledge of reproductive processes in the Mohor gazelle has highlighted the need for fundamental research. Thus, when any GRB programme is contemplated a suitably detailed research programme that addresses the reproductive biology of the species in question should accompany it. Unfortunately, this type of research is rather difficult to fund through application to the mainstream research agencies, because by its nature it is species specific. We have been lucky in this respect because our research programme has been supported by modest travel grants from the Royal Society, the British Council and the CSIC, while our research costs, also relatively modest, have largely been underwritten by the IOZ and EEZA. .

REFERENCES

Abaigar, T., Holt, W. V., Harrison, R. A. P. and del Barrio, G. (1999) 'Sperm subpopulations in boar (*Sus scrofa*) and gazelle (*Gazella dama mhorr*) semen as revealed by pattern analysis of computer-assisted motility assessments', *Biol. Reprod.* **60**, 32–41.

Alados, C. L. (1987) 'A cladistic approach to the taxonomy of the Dorcas gazelles', *Israel J. Zool.* **34**, 33–49.

Alados, C. L. and Escós, J. (1991) 'Phenotypic and genetic characteristics affecting lifetime reproductive success in female Cuvier's, dama and dorcas gazelles *(Gazella cuvieri, G. dama and G. dorcas)'*, *J. Zool. Lond.* **223**, 307–321.

Ansell, W. F. M. (1971) 'Order artiodactyla', in Meester, J. and Setzer, H.W. (eds) *The Mammals of Africa: an Identification Manual,* Washington: Smithsonian Institution Press, pp. 1–84.

Boever, J., Knox, D., Merilan, C. and Read, B. (1980) 'Estrus induction and artificial insemination with successful pregnancy in Speke's gazelle', in *9th International Congress on Animal Reproduction and Artificial Insemination (Madrid)*, pp. 565–569.

Cano, M. (1991) 'El Antílope Mohor *Gazella (=Nanger) dama mhorr* Bennett, 1832 en cautividad. Taxonomía, biología, ecología, etología, técnicas de salvamento y reintroducción y posibilidades de aprovechamiento económico', PhD thesis, University of Granada (España), Granada.

ESCÓS, J. (1992) '*Gazella cuvieri* studbook. Instituto de estudios almerienses', *Cuadernos monograficos* no. 20, Almería.

HOLT, W. V. and MEDRANO, J. A. (1997) 'Assessment of sperm function in relation to freezing and storage', *J. Reprod. Fertil.* Suppl. **52**, 213–222.

HOLT, C., HOLT, W. V. and MOORE, H. D. M. (1996a) 'Choice of operating conditions to minimize sperm subpopulation sampling bias in the assessment of boar semen by computer-assisted semen analysis', *J. Androl.* **17**, 587–596.

HOLT, W. V., ABAIGAR, T. and JABBOUR, H. N. (1996b) 'Oestrous synchronization, semen preservation and artificial insemination in the Mohor gazelle (*Gazella dama mhorr*) for the establishment of a genome resource bank programme', *Reprod. Fertil. Dev.* **8**, 1215–1222.

HOLT, W. V., BENNETT, P. M., VOLOBOUEV, V. and WATSON, P.F. (1996c) 'Genetic resource banks in wildlife conservation', *J. Zool. Lond.* **238**, 531–544.

JABBOUR, H. N., ARGO, C. M., BRINKLOW, B. R., LOUDON, A. S. I. and HOOTON, J. (1993) 'Conception rates following intrauterine insemination of European (*Dama dama dama*) fallow deer does with fresh or frozen-thawed mesopotamian (*Dama dama mesopotamica*) fallow deer spermatozoa', *J. Zool. Lond.* **230**, 379–384.

LAFONTAINE, R. M., BEUDELS-JAMAR, R. C. and DEVILLERS, P. (1999) 'Report on the status and perspectives of a *species: Gazella cuvieri*', in *Conservation Measures for Sahelo-Saharan Antelopes. Action Plan and Status Reports.* CMS Technical Series Publication No. 4. UNEP–CMS Secretariat, Bonn, Germany.

MERILAN, C. P., SIKES, J. D., READ, B. W., BOEVER, W. J. and KANE, K. K. (1977) 'Comparative characteristics of spermatozoa and semen from Greater Kudu, Speke's gazelle and springbuck antelope', *J. Zoo Anim. Med.* **8**, 16–18.

RALLS, K., BRUGGER, K. and BALLOU, J. (1979) 'Inbreeding and juvenile mortality in small populations of ungulates', *Science* **206**, 1101–1103.

RALLS, K., BALLOU, J. and TEMPLETON, A. (1988) 'Estimates of lethal equivalents and the cost of inbreeding in mammals', *Conserv. Biol.* **2**, 185–193.

ROLDAN, E. R. S., CASSINELLO, J., ABAIGAR, T. and GOMENDIO, M. (1998) 'Inbreeding, fluctuating asymmetry and ejaculate quality in an endangered ungulate', *Proc. R. Soc. Lond. B.* **265**, 243–248.

SEAL, U. and FLESNESS, N. (1978) 'Sex and Survival', Proc. Annual Meeting of the American Association of Zoological Parks and Aquaria. Wheeling, West Virginia, USA.

THORNHILL, N. W. (ed.) (1993) *The Natural History of Inbreeding and Outbreeding*, Chicago: University of Chicago Press.

CHAPTER 8

Part B:

Survey of the Literature on Cryopreservation of Gametes and Embryos

Techniques of Genetic Resource Banking in Fish

R. BILLARD[1] **AND TIANTIAN ZHANG**[2]

[1]Muséum National d'Histoire Naturelle, Laboratoire d'Ichtyologie,
43 rue Cuvier, 75231 Paris Cedex 05, France
[2]Department of Biology, Research Centre, University of Luton, Luton LU1 5DU, UK

Contents

9.1 CRYOPRESERVATION OF FISH SPERMATOZOA
(by Rowland Billard)

Research on technologies for the cryopreservation of fish semen have been carried out extensively in laboratories in order to store spermatozoa for controlling reproduction in fish culture and for *ex-situ* conservation of species. Many reviews have been devoted to this topic, the most significant being: Scott and Baynes (1980), Stoss (1983) and Jamieson (1991) for the older literature and McAndrews *et al.* (1993) and Maisse (1996) for more recent studies. Maisse (1996) has counted about forty publications related to the cryopreservation of fish spermatozoa and Rana and Gilmour (1996) have reported that spermatozoa cryopreservation was attempted on 200 fish species. Major studies were conducted recently by the teams of Lahnsteiner *et al.* (1995, 1996a, 1998a) and Maisse (Ogier de Baulny, 1997; Maisse *et al.*, 1998). The salmonids are the most commonly studied group and a consistent corpus of knowledge is now available with identification of the critical factors limiting the success of cryoconservation. A research effort was also devoted to the cryopreservation of the spermatozoa of other freshwater fish, such as cyprinids and silurids, and several marine species. The parameters usually taken into account are the cryoprotectant, the buffer and pH, the composition of the extender, the dilution ratio and the freezing and thawing procedure.

9.1.1 Evaluation of the viability of thawed spermatozoa

A large variety of criteria are used to test the success of freezing and thawing in fish spermatozoa; they are based on cell damage (alteration of morphology and intra-cellular organelles), on motility and fertilizing capacity. To be informative, the study should be carried out on some key steps of the procedure: on fresh (freshly collected) semen, on semen diluted in the extender (containing cryprotectants and additives), and on thawed spermatozoa.

Alteration of morphology and enzymatic activity

A simple microscopic examination ($\times 400$ or $\times 1000$) allows the counting of damaged cells which reached 80–90% in the grayling (*Thymallus thymallus*) (Lahnsteiner *et al.*, 1992) and the rainbow trout (*Oncorhynchus mykiss*) (Lahnsteiner *et al.*, 1996a,b,c), 40% in the common carp (*Cyprinus carpio*) and 60% in the Siberian sturgeon (*Acipenser baeri*) (Table 9.1). Alteration of chromatin was reported after transmission electron microscopical observation of thawed spermatozoa of the rainbow trout (Billard, 1983), the grayling (Lahnsteiner *et al.*, 1992) and the Atlantic croaker (*Micropogonia undulatus*) (Gwo and Arnold, 1992). In the Siberian sturgeon (Chondrostean) an acrosome reaction is seen in 9% of the thawed spermatozoa

TABLE 9.1

Percentage of intact and abnormal fresh and thawed spermatozoa of *Cyprinus carpio* (Cognie *et al.*, 1989) and *Acipenser baerii* (Fiereville *et al.*, unpublished)

	Cyprinus carpio		*Acipenser baerii* (1)	
	Fresh	Thawed	Fresh	Thawed
Head and flagellum intact	83	61	79	37
Head and flagellum abnormal	7	27	16	28
Head and flagellum separated	10	12	5	29
Acrosome reaction	–	–	0.1	9

(1) Extender: 18 mM saccharose, 0.2 mM KCl, HCl 30 mM Tris, pH 8, 20% egg yolk and 10% methanol. Freezing rate 3.5°C/min from +5 to −15°C, 18.5°C/min from −15 to −70°C.

(Table 9.2). Morphological alteration of the flagellum with coiling of the axoneme was observed under scanning electron microscopy on thawed carp spermatozoa (Cognie *et al.*, 1989). Some of the altered spermatozoa were still motile but the swimming efficiency was reduced. Alteration of the membrane structure and its ion permeability was measured by flow cytometry in salmonid spermatozoa (McNiven *et al.*, 1992). Some alteration of the plasma membrane integrity of rainbow trout spermatozoa was demonstrated by staining with propidium iodide and mitochondrial membranes with rhodamine 123; it was found that less than 18% of thawed spermatozoa had an intact plasma membrane and functional mitochondria (Ogier de Baulny *et al.*, 1997). These percentages were in a range of 26–76% for turbot (*Psetta maxima*), 6–50% for European catfish (*Silurus glanis*), and 12–59% for tilapia. The leaking of proteins from the cell, for example membrane proteins (Yoo *et al.*, 1985), glutamate-oxaloacetate transaminase (GOT) mitochondrial enzyme (Maléjac *et al.*, 1990), is strongly increased after thawing. Also leaking (K$^+$, Mg^{2+}) and retention (Na$^+$, Ca^{2+}) of ions were reported (Kurokura and Hirano, 1980). Lahnsteiner *et al.* (1996b) showed a decrease of some enzymatic activity (adenosine triphosphatase, isocitrate dehydrogenase, lactate dehydrogenase and malate dehydrogenase) in thawed rainbow trout spermatozoa.

Motility

There are several ways to measure motility of fresh and thawed spermatozoa. Basically, the motility is measured under a microscope ($\times$100–200) on slides coated with bovine serum albumin (BSA) 2 mg/ml or polyvinyl alcohol (1%) to prevent attachment of the cells to the glass. In order to see the trajectories of the spermatozoa clearly, the concentration should be less than 100 cells per microscopic field. As the thawed spermatozoa are fragile and sensitive to ionic stress, the double dilution technique of Billard and Cosson (1992) is not appropriate. Instead, a minute amount ($\sim$1 μl) of

TABLE 9.2
Mineral ions, buffers and sugars (mM) of some extenders successfully used for cryopreservation of fish sperm (after Maisse, 1996)

Species	NaCL	KCl	CaCl₂ 2H₂0	MgSO₄ 7H₂O	Buffer (mM)	Sugar (mM)	Authors
Acipenser baerii	0	0.2	0	0	Tris 30	sacch 23.4	Billard et al., unpublished
Acipenser baerii	0	0	0	0	Tris 118	sacch 18	Tsvetkova et al., 1996
Cyprinus carpio	128	2.7	0.9	0	NaHCO₃ 2.4		Kurokura et al., 1984
Cyprinus carpio	100	100	0	0	Tris 20		Cognié et al., 1989
Cyprinus carpio	75	83	2	0.8	NaHCO₃ 2.4		Kurokura et al., 1984
Dicentrarchus labrax	171	0	0	0	Tris 20		Billard 1984
H. hippoglossus	0	0	1.7	7	glyc. 86 Tris 30		Billard et al., 1993
Micropogonias undulatus	172	0	0	0	0		Gwo et al., 1991
Oncorhynchus mykiss	101	23	4.6	6	Tris 20		Büyükhatipoglu and Holtz 1978
Oncorhynchus mykiss	35	18	0	0	Ami-meth. prop. 60		Kurokura and Hirano 1980
Thunnus thynnus	0	100*	0	0		sucr. 125	Doi et al., 1990
Orechromis sp.	111	40	2	0	NaHCO₃ 2.4		Rana and McAndrew 1989
Sparus aurata	150	0	1.7	1	glyc. 83 Tris 20		Chambeyron and Zohar 1990
Aspius aspius						gluc 300, sucr 300/600	Babiak et al., 1998

* KHCO3

sperm suspension is taken on the tip of a micropipette cone and diluted directly in activating solution ($30 \,\mu$l) placed on the coated slide. The global motility measured in the rainbow trout according to a 1–5 arbitrary scale was shown to decrease after thawing to value 1, compared with 4 in fresh spermatozoa (Legendre and Billard, 1980).

More precise parameters are the percentage of motile cells and changes with time after activation, the beat frequency (Hz) of the flagellum and the velocity. In recent studies, measurements were conducted with computer-assisted sperm analysis (CASA). The motility rate (percentage of motile cells) is a good predictor of post-thaw fertilization in salmonids (Lahnsteiner et al., 1995). The energetics of motility (ATP content in the cell, respiration) is also used (Ogier de Baulny, 1997; Dreanno et al., 1997). In rainbow trout spermatozoa a decrease of 50–90% of intracellular ATP was observed during the freezing procedure; this loss is prevented by 5% methanol and is increased with 15% glycerol (Ogier de Baulny, 1997). In turbot spermatozoa, the ATP content was also decreased by 60% during the freezing/thawing procedure but the respiration rate did not change (Dreanno et al., 1997).

Fertilization

The percentage of fertilized eggs usually measured at the eyed stage or at the closure of the blastopore is often completed by the percentages of normal or abnormal embryos or hatched larvae. Sometimes the percentage of fertilized eggs is measured at the two- to four-cell stage which requires a control batch of eggs without added spermatozoa, since in some species, activation results from a simple exposure of ovum to water and leads to an appearance resembling early embryonic development. The measurement of the percentage of fertilization requires some care and a precise protocol is needed to compare fresh and thawed spermatozoa. Very often an excess of spermatozoa is used and does not permit differences to be seen, as the large number of spermatozoa compensates for the poorer quality of the frozen–thawed spermatozoa. The density of spermatozoa around the egg should be known precisely, i.e. the number of spermatozoa per egg and the volume of liquid in which gametes are diluted; the minimum volume of diluent ensuring maximum fertilization should be used. Interpretation of data must take account of the proportion of motile spermatozoa (Tsvekova *et al.*, 1996). In addition, fertilization tests must be carried out at different concentrations of spermatozoa: one with the minimum concentration of fresh spermatozoa ensuring the fertilization of all fertilizable eggs (e.g. 10^{-4}–10^{-5} dilution in the rainbow trout) and others at higher concentration (e.g. 10^{-3}–10^{-2} dilution) to evaluate the true fertilization capacity of thawed spermatozoa (Legendre and Billard, 1980).

The choice of the semen extender must take into account the ionic requirement for the fertilization of the eggs. For instance an extender based on 50 mM KCl yields good motility of spermatozoa but at that K^+ concentration no fertilization occurs (Saad and Billard, 1987). Reported success of fertilization with thawed spermatozoa is usually low (e.g. 30% compared with 73% in control in pike (*Esox masquinongy*) (Lin *et al.*, 1996), and variable (e.g. 30–40% of control in carp (Cognie *et al.*, 1989), or 3–80% in rainbow trout (Büyükhatipoglu and Holtz, 1978).

Abnormalities of embryos and larvae have not often been reported after fertilization with thawed spermatozoa. A high percentage of abnormalities was observed in the European catfish but was not different from the control (Linhart *et al.*, 1993). Similarly the hatching rate, larvae survival and the weight of larvae were the same for fresh and thawed spermatozoa of turbot (*Psetta maxima*) (Suquet *et al.*, 1998) and tilapia (Rana and McAndrew, 1989).

9.1.2 Some critical points in the freezing/thawing procedure

Urine contamination of semen

After collection by stripping, milt is often contaminated by urine which induces activation of a fraction of the spermatozoa and at least a part of their endogenous stores of ATP are exhausted (Perchec-Poupard *et al.*, 1998). Ogier de Baulny (1997) has shown that a lower ATP content results in a lower survival of thawed spermatozoa. The use of a catheter introduced into the sperm duct is one way to avoid urine contamination but it is not always possible due to the morphology of the sperm ducts (e.g. carp, turbot) and when it is feasible (e.g. in salmonids) this results in irritation of the epithelium, bleeding and infection, especially if collection is frequent. In turbot, however, it is possible to insert a catheter in the urethra and eliminate at least a part of the urine from the bladder. The clearing of the bladder may also be done by gentle squeezing (Harvey, 1983a). Another way to prevent the activation of spermatozoa by urine is to sample the semen directly in an immobilizing solution which mimics the osmotic pressure (cyprinids and marine fish) or the K^+ concentration (salmonids, sturgeons) of the seminal fluid and inhibits motility. This is commonly used in salmonids (Ogier de Baulny, 1997) and catfish (Linhart *et al.*, 1993). Maisse *et al.* (1998) advise the collection of the milt directly into an immobilization solution. A more drastic technique is to use intratesticular spermatozoa (which are immotile) after killing the males, especially when the testes are small (gonado-somatic index less than 1%) and the yield of spermiation is low (Padhi and Mandal, 1995; Christensen and Tiersch, 1997). This is also the way to get urine-free semen and is common practice on fish farms for the European catfish, *Silurus glanis*.

Extender composition

Basic solutions made of salts or sugars. The aim of the extender is to dilute the semen, which is highly concentrated in most fish species (10^{10} spermatozoa per ml), so that all individual spermatozoa are exposed to the cryoprotectant. The extender is usually based on a saline solution, which sometimes mimics the mineral composition of the seminal fluid but often the choice of salts is not explained. As pointed out by Maisse (1996) the mineral components of the extenders have little influence on the success of cryopreservation (although Schmidt 1985 quoted by Maisse, 1996, has reported a deleterious effect on the trout spermatozoa due to Ca^{2+} in the extender). Sometimes various sugars are included as additives. For example, of 0.5% sucrose was added for rainbow trout (Lahnsteiner *et al.*, 1995) and 0.4 mM glucose for turbot (Dreanno *et al.*, 1997) spermatozoa. In recent studies only sugars were included in the extender, e.g. 125 mM sucrose for rainbow trout spermatozoa (Legendre and Billard, 1980) or 300 mM glucose for the Atlantic salmon spermatozoa (Stoss and Refstie, 1983), 400 mM glucose for milkfish (*Chanos chanos*) spermatozoa (Hara *et al.*, 1982). Cheriguini *et al.* (1997) have shown better thawing performances of spermatozoa frozen in an extender made of saccharose compared to a saline solution. A comparative study by Maisse (1994) showed that post-thaw fertility was the same using sucrose, maltose, trehalose, galactose, fructose or glucose as extender at 125 or 250 mM (there was no fertilization at 500 mM). Strangely, Babiak et al. (1998) found good post-thaw fertility using 0.6 M sucrose in the extender in pike.

The role of the extender ultimately is to mimic the osmotic pressure found in the seminal fluid which inhibits motility in most species (except salmonids and sturgeons). In the rainbow trout, however, the osmotic pressure seems important, as Lahnsteiner et al. (1996b) have reported that an osmolality of the seminal fluid >330 mOsmol/kg positively influences the fertilizing capacity of thawed spermatozoa. In contrast, Maisse et al. (1988) found that the spermatozoa fitness for cryoconservation was lower when osmolality was higher than 260 mOsmol/kg.

The pH of the proposed extenders varies from 5.2 to 8.5 (Maisse, 1996) and no significant effect of pH and buffer was found. A concentration of Tris of 118 mM was used in sturgeons with recovery of 15–23% motility after thawing (Tsvetkova et al., 1996). Lahnsteiner et al. (1996b) have reported that rainbow trout semen with a pH less than 8.2 showed good post-thaw fertility (more than 50%).

Membrane stabilizers. Lipoproteins, which bind to the plasma membrane and give a better stability during the freezing/thawing procedure, are used in the extenders. Egg yolk (10–20%) is frequently added and sometimes skimmed milk powder (15%), cell culture medium (e.g. Menezo B2 15%), proteins such as BSA (4 mg/ml) or soy bean (Promine D 7.5 mg/ml) (review by Maisse, 1996). They are usually found to be favourable, but only a few comparative studies have been conducted. Maisse et al. (1998) reported significant increase of post-thaw fertilizing capacity of rainbow trout spermatozoa with egg yolk compared with that with skimmed milk, lecithin or BSA. Urea (4%) added to the extender improved the post-thaw motility of carp spermatozoa significantly (Cognie et al., 1989). The use of vitamin E or D as antioxidant has been suggested, but Ogier de Baulny (1997) did not any observe significant effect.

Cryoprotectants. Several extracellular (non-permeating) or intracellular (permeating) cryoprotectants are used for fish spermatozoa (Table 10.3). The most common is dimethyl sulphoxide (DMSO) which is potent in nearly all species and, to a lesser extent, glycerol. The combination of DMSO (5%) + glycerol (1%) improved the motility and fertilizing capacity of thawed spermatozoa of some salmonid species by comparison with 10% DMSO (Lahnsteiner et al., 1996c,d). Methanol, ethylene glycol, propanediol and N-dimethyl acetamide (DMA) are potent in a small number of species. Some interactions with other compounds in the extender have been reported, e.g. the protective effect of DMSO for the membrane liposomes of rainbow trout spermatozoa disappeared when phosphate buffer was present (Labbé et al., 1997). Using DMA as a cryoprotectant, Ogier de Baulny (1997) observed an increase in the ATP content of spermatozoa and has suggested that it serves as a substrate for the synthesis of ATP. Another interaction was reported: when methanol was combined with skimmed milk the post-thaw motility (70%) was higher than with egg yolk (10%) (Harvey, 1983a).

TABLE 9.3

Efficiency of various intracellular cryoprotectants for marine and freshwater fish sperm: (++) good, (+) average, (−) poor, (% volume in cryoprotectant) (after Maisse, 1996)

	DMSO	Glycerol	Methanol	Ethylene glycol	Propane diol	Propylene-glycol	DMA	Authors
Marine Species								
Micropogonias undulatus	++	−	−	+	+			Gwo et al., 1991
Sillago ciliata	++	++	−		−			Young et al., 1992
Epinephelus tauvina	++	−						Withler and Lim 1992
Acanthopagrus australis	+	++						Thorogood and Blackshaw 1992
Acanthopagrus schlegeli	++5	++5						Chao et al., 1986
Dicentrachus labrax	++	+						Billard 1984
Morone saxatilis	++	−		−	−			Kerby 1983
H. hippoglossus	+ 10				++ 10			Billard et al., 1993
Psetta maxima	++ 15	+ 5–10						Dréanno et al., 1997
Pogonias cromis	++ 5–10	++ 5	−	−			−	Wayman et al., 1997
Cynoscion nebulosus	++ 10	−	−				−	Wayman et al.,1997
Psetta maxima	++ 10–15	−	−			++	++	Ogier de Baulny 1997
Freshwater species								
Salmonids	+ 10*		+++ 10					Lahnsteiner et al., 1997
Oncorhynchus mykiss	++ 5–10		± 5–10			−	++ 5–15	Ogier de Baulny 1997
	++ 10							Maisse 1996
Oncorhynchus kisutch	++ 12	−		+	−		−	Ott and Orton 1971
Salmo trutta	++	+		++	−			Erdahl et al., 1984
Salvelinus fontinalis	++	+		++				Erdahl et al., 1984
T. thymallus, H. hucha	+ 10*	± 5	+++ 10	−	−		+ 10	Lahnsteiner et al., 1996c
Cyprinus carpio	++ 10	−						Cognie et al., 1989
Oreochromis mossambicus	+	+	++ 5					Harvey 1983
Oreochromis niloticus		++	++ 15			−	+	Ogier de Baulny 1997
			−					Steyn and Van Vuren 1987
Clarias gariepinus	++	++	+					Mongkonpunya et al., 1995
Piangasius gigas	++ 9		++5–10				−	Christensen and Tierch 1994
Ictalurus puntatus	−							Linhart et al., 1993
Silurus glanis	−	+ 10–15	+			−		Ogier de Baulny 1997
Xyrauchen texanus	−	−	+ 10				++	Tierch et al., 1998
Coregonus muksun	++ 10	++ 20					−	Piironen and Hyvarinen 1983

*++ with 1% glycerol added to DMSO 5%.

The potentiality of the cryoprotectants differs from one species to another, and when working on sperm cryopreservation of a new species the first test to be conducted is a screening of cryoprotectants.

Handling semen before freezing

After collection, the semen should be placed in a thin layer (<5 mm) on ice to allow oxygen diffusion. Storage before freezing should be as short as possible (Maisse, 1996), but Rana (1995) claimed that semen may be stored for hours or days before freezing.

Addition of O$_2$. Improvement of 57% of post-thaw motility was found by Magyary *et al.* (1996a) when spermatozoa of carp was exposed to O$_2$ for 30 min prior to freezing. This may be because of an increase in the intracellular ATP content, which was correlated with the success of cryopreservation in rainbow trout (see above). This direct exposure to O$_2$ is not apparently detrimental to spermatozoa.

Equilibration time. In order to allow the permeant cryoprotectants to penetrate into the cells, some equilibration time (10–20 min) was allowed before freezing. This usually results in a decrease of the motility after thawing (Harvey, 1983a). In addition, Ogier de Baulny (1997) found that a penetration of the cryoprotectant into the cell was not necessary (the protection is made directly on the membrane and no equilibration time is justified).

The ratio of spermatozoa to extender. The sperm extender ratio is usually 1:3 for highly concentrated semen (Legendre and Billard, 1980). In tilapia there was no improvement in thawing motility when the ratio exceeded 5 (Harvey, 1983a). However Magyary *et al.* (1996a) used a 1:9 ratio for carp. In marine fish, equilibration time is detrimental as the high osmotic pressure of the extender tends to activate the spermatozoa (Billard, 1984).

Size of the straws or pellets. For experimental purposes 250-μl or 500-μl straws are quite convenient but larger devices are needed for use in a fish farm. Linhart *et al.* (1993) have used 5-ml aluminium plates and Maisse (1996) used 5-ml straws (IMV-AA303) with some success. The fertilization rate of the thawed semen of the striped trumpeter (*Latris lineata*) was found to be lower in 0.25-ml straws than in 0.5-ml straws or 0.25- and 2.0-ml pellets (Ritar, 1999).

Freezing and thawing

Freezing rate. Programmable freezing devices (e.g. Minicool, Air Liquide, Grenoble) have been used and, in carp, the optimum freezing rate was found to be 5°C/min from +2 to −7°C and 25°C/min from −7 to −70°C (Cognie *et al.*, 1989). Simpler devices are also employed, for instance, a 3-cm-thick polystyrene frame floating on top of liquid nitrogen and holding the straws horizontally in the nitrogen vapour for a period of 20 min. Lahnsteiner *et al.* (1996e) found that a height of 5 cm above the surface of the liquid nitrogen gave better results for salmonids than a height of 1 or 2 cm. Pellets are made by simply placing 100 μl of extended semen on a block of dry ice; after 5 min after the pellets are plunged into liquid nitrogen. The temperature of the straw or pellets should be at least $-80°C$ when they are placed in the liquid nitrogen (Billard, 1984). The freezing rate measured directly inside the straws is highly variable being, 25–41°C/min and 5–13°C/min respectively during the pre-freezing and post-freezing phases (prior and after the initial ice crystal formation), according to Rana and Gilmour (1996), who also observed that the freezing slope was not linear. Rana (1995) recommended a portable cooler with fixed freezing rate which generates reproducible linear cooling rates.

Thawing and post-thaw treatments. Thawing is generally carried out as fast as possible as the motility and fertilizing capacity decrease with time after thawing. Microscopic examination and fertility tests are conducted as soon as possible after thawing (Kurokura *et al.*, 1984). Straws of 500 μl are placed in a water bath at 40°C for 5–10 seconds (30 seconds for 5-ml straws) and the melting semen is poured directly into a dish containing the eggs (1 vol) and the fertilization diluent (1 vol). Tests with increasing concentration of spermatozoa in the diluent should be carried out (see above). Pellets are placed directly on the diluted eggs or they may be thawed before in a test tube in a water bath at 40°C for 10 seconds.

In thawed turbot spermatozoa with glycerol as cryoprotectant, the ATP content was found to be low, and spermatozoa were incubated in a saline solution (which mimics the seminal fluid) allowing a reconstitution of the ATP stores (Ogier de Baulny, 1997). The low ATP concentration in thawed catfish, trout and turbot spermatozoa was related to the high osmolality of the extenders and could be explained by the functioning of ionic pumps; this can be overcome by the removal of the cryoprotectant or a sufficient dilution in isotonic saline solution, allowing the intracellular recovery of ATP.

Another way is to add 5 mM caffeine or other phosphodiesterase inhibitors to the diluent and prevent the degradation of cyclic AMP; this increases the energetic status of the cell and extends the duration of motility and the fertilizing capacity of rainbow trout spermatozoa either fresh (Billard, 1980) or thawed (Scheerer and Thorgaard, 1989; Maisse *et al.*, 1998). The duration of motility of thawed sterlet (*Acipenser ruthenus*) spermatozoa is prolonged after addition of $CaCl_2$ in the activating solution (Jähninchen *et al*, 1999).

A summary of the technical procedure used for rainbow trout

A refined technique for the cryopreservation of rainbow trout semen was proposed by Ogier de Baulny (1997):

1 The semen (2.5 ml) is collected directly in a basin partly filled with 6 ml of the extender (Mounib solution: 125 mM saccharose, 100 mM KHCO$_3$, 6.5 mM reduced glutathione, 0.75 ml DMSO and egg yolk substitute (IMV, L'Aigle, France), 7.28 g per litre of extender.
2 Straws (500 μl) are filled and frozen in the nitrogen vapour, 3 cm above the surface of the liquid for 20 min and then stored in liquid nitrogen.
3 Straws are removed from the liquid nitrogen and thawed in a 40°C water bath for 5 seconds.
4 Ova are washed in a solution that mimics the composition of the ovarian fluid: NaCl 9.08 g/l, MgSO$_4$ 0.84 g/l, KCl 0.23 g/l and Tris 2.42 g/l.
5 Fertilization is achieved in the standard diluent for artificial fertilization: NaCl 5.52 mg/l, Tris 2.42 mg/l, glycine 3.75 mg/l+1 mM caffeine.

9.1.3 Fitness of spermatozoa for cryopreservation and possible improvements

It is commonly reported that spermatozoa of marine fish species are more resistant to the cryoprocedure than those of freshwater species. Few strict comparative studies have been conducted; Maisse *et al.* (1998) showed that sperm survival was less than 20% in rainbow trout and tilapia but greater than 40% in turbot, European catfish and sea bream (*Sparus aurata*). Drokin (1993) has reported that the molar ratio cholesterol:phospholipids was 2–3 times higher in marine fish spermatozoa than in freshwater fish spermatozoa but this is not a satisfactory explanation for the better sperm survival, as Labbé and Maisse (1986) have correlated a low membrane cholesterol:phospholipids ratio with good post-thaw survival in trout spermatozoa. It is possible that the poor motility performances of thawed (and even fresh) spermatozoa of rainbow trout is a result of over a century of domestication, in which sperm motility has never been taken into account as a criteria for selection. It should be pointed out that in wild salmonid species, such as Atlantic salmon, Mounib (1978) has reported a similar motility in both thawed and fresh spermatozoa.

It is also known that the capacity for cryopreservation declines during the spawning season as the spermatozoa undergo ageing phenomenon as seen in the sea bass (Billard *et al.*, 1977). Lahnsteiner *et al.* (1998b) reported that in the pike (*Esox lucius*) the post-thaw fertilizing capacity was better in intratesticular spermatozoa than in stripped milt. Inter-male variability is often reported; an example is seen in halibut (*Hippoglossus hyppoglossus*) (Bolla *et al.*, 1987). Even in a single ejaculate there is a large variability in the cryopreservation fitness of individual spermatozoa. When an ejaculate is frozen without cryoprotectant some spermatozoa still survive and show both an undamaged plasma membrane and mitochondrial envelope as revealed by a rhodamine 123 test (Ogier de Baulny *et al.*, 1997). In general, especially in marine fish, the spermatozoa which survive the freezing/thawing stress still show good motility performances, nearly as good as before freezing. In the calculation of the number of spermatozoa per egg, the number of motile spermatozoa (and not the total initial number) should be used; in that case the fertilizing capacity often appears similar for fresh and thawed spermatozoa. This means that a proportion of spermatozoa (which vary according to the species or the strain, the time in the spawning season, the rearing environment, etc.) are highly resistant. Some attempts have been made to improve this proportion. An approach for rainbow trout is to keep the males at an appropriate rearing temperature (18°C) during spermatogenesis in the summer and 5–13°C in the winter; this improved the sperm cryoresistance (Labbé and Maisse, 1996). Another approach is to supply the males with membrane lipids via feeds during spermatogenesis and the period of sperm maturation as attempted by Labbé *et al.* (1993). It should be pointed out that fresh, as well as thawed, fish spermatozoa show some heterogeneity in their quality; for instance, the initial percentage of motile cells is usually 90–100% but it declines immediately after activation and 50% of the spermatozoa have stopped swimming 15–60 seconds later, depending on the species. In the case of homogeneous quality 90–100% should continue to be motile for some time.

The practical application of fish spermatozoa cryopreservation seems limited. The technology is not yet well established for rainbow trout, which is one of the most widely cultivated fish. The semen of some other species can be easily cryopreserved (European catfish, sea bream, sea bass, grouper, etc.) but their culture is only just starting. Some implementation may be expected in the near future. Extension studies and field operations have been reported in Taiwan (Chao, 1991) and in Sri Lanka and Mexico (Rana, 1995), and the use of a gene bank (spermatozoa) has been proposed to restore the loss of genetic variability in a farmed population of catfish (*Heterobranchus longifilis*) (Otémé and Agnese, 1997).

Some patented material for fish semen cryopreservation is now available, such as programmable freezing equipment and ready made solutions for use as extenders, containing additives and cryoprotectants.

9.1.4 Conclusion

In general, it can be seen that the whole procedure for cryopreservation is detrimental to the motility of a large fraction of spermatozoa in the ejaculate of most species due to alterations in the plasma membrane and the mitochondria. The present technology still needs some improvement, especially in rainbow trout and other salmonids.

The environment of the brood male is of importance in salmonids, and probably in other species. The rearing temperature and the diet determine the lipid composition of the membrane. This is of interest in the case of the mitochondrial membrane because it is difficult to influence its composition via the extender (contrary to the plasma membrane, which is easily stabilized by additives such as the egg yolk). The main role of the extender is to keep the spermatozoa immotile during the cryoprocedure and the first approach was to mimic the composition of the seminal fluid. Strangely, the exact ionic composition of the seminal fluid is not required and simple sugar solutions are sufficient to obtain the right osmotic pressure, with the exception of salmonids and sturgeons which require K^+.

The addition of egg yolk and protein improve the post-thaw survival of spermatozoa. The cryoprotectant is a key component and, when dealing with a new species, a screening of the various cryoprotectants has to be conducted, starting with DMSO which is the best in most species.

After the freezing and thawing procedure, it appears that spermatozoa have exhausted a large part of their endogenous ATP (or have lost the capacity to synthesize it). Removing the cryoprotectant allows the spermatozoa to reconstitute their ATP stores (provided that the mitochondria are still active and that this does not deplete the lipid content of the membranes) and to include inhibitors of phosphodiesterases in the fertilization medium.

9.2 CRYOPRESERVATION OF FISH EGGS AND EMBRYOS (by Tiantian Zhang)

9.2.1 Introduction

Cryopreservation of fish eggs and embryos with successful retention of viability would offer considerable commercial and environmental opportunities. Three main areas of application for the cryopreservation of fish eggs and embryos are in fish culture and farming, conservation of biodiversity of endangered species and ecotoxicological testing on early life stages. In fish culture and farming, the successful cryopreservation of eggs and embryos will offer new commercial possibilities, with the availability of cryopreserved eggs (in combination with cryopreserved semen) or embryos allowing the unlimited production of fry and potentially more robust and better conditioned fish as required. Further advantages include optimal utilization of hatchery facilities and facilitation of transport of stocks between hatcheries. Embryo cryopreservation also provides a secure *ex situ* method for preserving the genomes of endangered species in a diversity high enough to reconstruct stable populations when environmental conditions make it possible. More than 65% of the European fish species are threatened (Kirchofer, 1996) and extremely endangered species may be extinct before recolonization is possible or their genetic variability so reduced that reconstruction of stable population is impossible (Gilpin and Soulé, 1986). Fish eggs and embryos are of particular interest for ecotoxicological testing because of their environmental relevance and sensitivity. Early life stage tests have been favoured to replace acute fish tests which contravene animal protection laws. Successful cryopreservation of fish eggs or embryos would guarantee time-independent availability of qualitatively homogeneous biological material for toxicity testing.

In the last twenty years, attempts to cryopreserve fish eggs and embryos have been conducted on ten species, including herring (*Clupea harengus*) (Whittingham and Rosenthal, 1978; Ben-Amotz and Rosenthal, 1981), rainbow trout (*Salmo mykiss*) (Haga, 1982), brown trout (*Salmo trutta*) (Erdahl and Graham, 1980), brook trout (*Salvelinus fontinalis*) (Zell, 1978), coho salmon (*Onorhynchus kisutch*) (Stoss and Donaldson, 1983), Atlantic salmon (*Salmo salar*) (Zell, 1978; Harvey and Ashwood-Smith, 1982), common carp (*Cyprinus carpio*) (Zhang *et al.*, 1989), medaka (*Oryzias latipes*) (Onizuka *et al.*, 1984), African catfish (*Clarias gariepinus*) (Magyary *et al.*, 1996b) and zebrafish (*Danio rerio*) (Harvey, 1983b; Zhang *et al.*, 1993; Zhang and Rawson, 1996a). Eggs or embryos from all species have shown some tolerance to subzero temperatures but the successful cryopreservation of teleost eggs and embryos has remained elusive. There has been very limited published information on the cryopreservation of ovary or unfertilized fish eggs.

9.2.2 Structure of fish eggs and embryos

Teleost egg membranes

In the teleost egg, two distinct membranes are recognized: the outer chorionic membrane and the inner vitelline membrane. A third layer develops after fertilization and the onset of embryo division by the nucleation of the cytoplasmic layer surrounding the yolk, resulting in the formation of the yolk syncytial layer (Kimmel and Law, 1986). Studies of the fine structure of the chorion (Hart and Donovan, 1983; Kalicharan *et al.*, 1998) of eggs showed the chorion to be a thin envelope, constructed of three distinct zones: an outer, electron-dense zone containing pore canals rich in polysaccharides (Tesoriero, 1977), a middle fibrillar zone, and an inner zone of lower electron density generally believed to be rich in proteins. Such a structure may play a role in diffusive exchange of gases as well as providing physical protection (Grierson and Neville, 1981). It also plays a role as a flexible filter for transport of some materials (Toshimori and Yasuzumi, 1976) and protects against microorganisms (Schoots *et al.*, 1982). Studies on the chorion permeability of the zebrafish eggs (Hisaoka, 1958; Zhang and Rawson, 1996a) demonstrated it to be a porous membrane, freely permeable to water, electrolytes and range of cryoprotectants. The vitelline membrane and the underlying syncytial layer are believed to constitute the main permeability barrier to water and cryoprotectants (Hagedorn *et al.*, 1996; Zhang and Rawson, 1996b).

Perivitelline space

Water activation of teleost eggs results in a small amount of fluid and protein filling the space between the chorion and the vitelline membrane in a process known as 'water hardening' (Potts and Eddy, 1973). The perivitelline fluid of the Atlantic salmon (*Salmo salar*) egg was found to consist of 58% water, 25% protein, 12% lipid, and 1.7% carbohydrate (Eddy, 1974). The perivitelline fluid and its multilamellar envelopes with their varied specialized patterns and filamentous elaborations provide a number of protective, nutritive, floatative, polyspermy preventive and regulatory functions (Laale, 1980).

Yolk

The structural components of fish yolk include yolk platelets and oil globules. Yolk platelets are composed of mucopolysaccharides, lipovitelline and phosvitin or analogous lipoproteins and phosphoproteins (Heming and Buddington, 1988). The yolk, besides providing solute nutrient to the cells of the rapidly developing blastoderm, contributes ribosomes, and possibly membranous material as well, to the embryonic cells for their subsequent differentiation (Kimmel and Law, 1986).

9.2.3 Problems associated with cryopreservation of fish eggs and embryos

Cryopreservation of fish eggs and embryos has posed several problems associated with the injuries induced during the cooling and the thawing processes and four characteristics in particular have been identified as possibly being responsible. (1) The eggs of most species are greater than 1 mm in diameter (previously successfully cryopreserved eggs are all considerably smaller), resulting in a much lower surface area to volume ratio. One consequence of the low ratio is a reduction in the rate at which water and cryoprotectants can move into and out of the embryo during the steps of cryopreservation. (2) Fish eggs have a high yolk content and during the steps of cryopreservation, the yolk probably acts as an independent compartment and responds osmotically in a manner analogous to the cellular cytoplasm. The development of a single effective protocol for cryoprotectant permeation and osmotic dehydration of both the yolk and cells of the embryos may be difficult due to the distinctive volume of the two compartments (Rall, 1993). (3) Fish eggs have a complex membrane system with some membranes having very low permeability (Loeffler and Lovstrup, 1970; Zhang and Rawson, 1996b, 1998; Hagedorn *et al.*, 1997b, c) and an important role in controlling the immediate environment of the embryo. The chorion and membranes surrounding both the embryo and yolk constitute complex barriers that need to be crossed if effective procedures for cryoprotectant permeation and osmotic dehydration are to be achieved. (4) High chilling sensitivities to zero and subzero temperatures have been noted for certain species (Zhang and Rawson, 1995; Hagedorn *et al.*, 1997a). Studies involving mammalian embryos suggest that a high sensitivity to chilling injury is associated with large amounts of intraembryonic lipids (Polge *et al.*, 1974), which are commonly present in fish embryo yolk and cell compartments.

9.2.4   Approaches for cryopreservation of fish eggs and embryos

To date, two approaches have been applied to the cryopreservation of biological materials: controlled slow cooling and vitrification. However, neither approach has yet been successfully employed to cryopreserve fish eggs and embryos. Low-temperature storage has offered an alternative, if short term, solution to practical problems while research into cryopreservation of fish eggs and embryos is still in progress.

Attempts to cryopreserve fish embryos using controlled slow cooling

With controlled slow cooling, the selection and the optimization of the following factors need to be considered:

Embryo developmental stage. Intermediate embryo development stages between postgastrula and heart beat have higher survival rates. For example, tail-bud stage for common carp (Zhang *et al.*, 1989), post eyed stages for rainbow trout (Haga, 1982) and six–somite to heart beat stage for zebrafish (Zhang *et al.*, 1993) embryos showed better survival after cooling to $-30°C$.

Cryoprotectants – type, concentration, treatment time and methods. The most commonly used cryoprotectants in fish egg and embryo preservation are dimethyl sulphoxide, methanol, glycerol, ethanediol and propane-1,2–diol with the typical concentration range of 1–2M (Robertson *et al.*, 1988; Zhang *et al.*, 1993; Adam *et al.*, 1995). Embryos are normally treated with cryoprotectants at room temperature or 0°C for 30 minutes to 1 hour in either one-step or multistep additions. The selection of cryoprotectants and protocols is species related and will very much depend on toxicity and the permeability of the embryos (Rall, 1993).

Cooling rates. Slow cooling rates normally result in higher survival for fish embryos than high cooling rates, with optimum cooling rates being reported in the range of 0.01–0.75°C/min (Harvey and Ashwood-Smith, 1982; Stoss and Donaldson, 1983; Onizuka *et al.*, 1984; Zhang *et al.*, 1993).

Thawing rates and methods. Optimum thawing rates reported for fish embryos vary, although a slow rate (8°C/min) was optimal for common carp embryos (Zhang *et al.*, 1989), an intermediate rate (43°C/min) was preferred for zebrafish blastoderm

(Harvey, 1983b) and a fast rate (300°C/min) resulted in best survival for zebrafish embryos (Zhang et al., 1993).

Removal of cryoprotectant. The use of sucrose in the diluting medium to minimize osmotic damage on removal of cryoprotectant is reported to improve the survival of common carp embryos (Zhang et al., 1989) after cooling, whilst no difference was observed for zebrafish embryos (Zhang et al., 1993).

Cryopreservation studies of fish embryos with controlled slow cooling have indicated that although embryos from all species show a certain degree of survival at subzero temperatures, they do not normally survive after cooling to −35°C. The loss of viability is mainly due to intracellular ice formation as a result of low embryo membrane permeability to water and cryoprotectants and, in the case of some warm water species, embryo chilling sensitivity.

Attempts to cryopreserve fish embryos using vitrification

Cryopreservation of fish embryos using vitrification has so far been performed only with zebrafish embryos as a model system (Zhang and Rawson, 1996a; Liu et al., 1998). Despite differences in the methods used to produce osmotic dehydration, the factors that need to be considered with the vitrification approach are very similar to those for controlled slow cooling:

Embryo developmental stage. Studies of vitrification of zebrafish embryos (Liu et al., 1998) have shown that intermediate embryo developmental stages at 50% epiboly to prim-six stages give best results. There would be advantages for using early stage embryos if their membrane permeabilities were proven to be higher and the problems associated with their chilling sensitivity and cryoprotectants toxicity could be dealt with.

Stability and toxicity of vitrification solutions. The formulation of the vitrification solutions for fish embryo cryopreservation must match the choice of cryoprotectants with the intrinsic permeability and toxicity properties of the embryos in question. Vitrification solutions DPP (2 M DMSO+3 M PrOH+0.5 M PEG 400), BPP (2 M butane-2,3–diol+3 M PrOH+6% PEG 400) and 10 M methanol have been shown to be stable and have relatively low toxicity to zebrafish embryos.

Cooling methods. To achieve the 'glassy solid state' required, cooling rates must be sufficiently high to avoid crystallization of vitrification solution/specimen. Commercially available plastic straws and electron microscope gold grids in combination with liquid nitrogen or nitrogen slush have been applied to zebrafish embryos.

Thawing and removal of cryoprotectants. Rapid warming rates are required during thawing to avoid crystallization. Immersion into embryo medium at the normal culturing temperature has been used for thawing. To increase the thawing rate, the volume of vitrification solution is reduced to a minimum (<0.5 ml if plastic straws are used and <10 μl when grids are used). Immediately after thawing, the embryo is taken through a series of washing steps to remove cryoprotectants and reduce toxicity.

So far, the results obtained with the vitrification approach have shown no embryo survival although approximately 80% of six–somite and prim-six stage zebrafish embryos remained morphologically intact after freezing and thawing (Liu *et al.*, 1998). The low membrane permeability of fish embryos to water and cryoprotectants remains the biggest problem, and approaches to overcoming the problem need to be identified before effective vitrification protocols can be designed.

9.2.5 Low-temperature storage of fish embryos

Whilst long-term cryopreservation of fish embryos at extremely low temperatures (typically −196°C) remains elusive, storage of these embryos at reduced temperatures offers an alternative short-term solution. Earlier studies have shown that both chinook (*Oncorhynchus nerka*) and pink salmon (*Oncorhynchus garbuscha*) eggs could tolerate 1.7°C for long periods if they were initially stored at 5.6°C for a month (Combs and Burrows, 1957). The incubation period of brown trout ova could also be extended for up to four months at a temperature of 1.4°C if ova were initially stored at a temperature of 7.6°C for 13 days (Maddock, 1974). The survival rates of plaice (*Pleuronectes platessa*) eggs at low temperatures increase with increasing development of the eggs (Pullin and Bailey, 1981). More recently, research was carried out on the storage of fish eggs or embryos at zero and subzero temperatures. Harvey *et al.* (1983) reported that unfertilized salmonid ova can be stored at −1°C for up to 20 days in artificial media and in ovarian fluid. Studies of the chilling sensitivity of zebrafish embryos showed that embryos between 27 hours and 40 hours after fertilization were least sensitive to chilling with embryo survival averaging 100±1.5% and 55.6±7.6% respectively after 10 and 18 hours exposure at 0°C (Zhang and Rawson, 1995). The study also showed that methanol was effective as a cryoprotectant for non-freezing storage of embryos at zero and subzero temperatures. Using 1 M methanol (supplemented with 0.1 M sucrose), the best survivals obtained were 88.4±10.7%, 81.8±9.2%, and 30.2±3.5% after storage for 18, 24 and 48 hours respectively at 0°C.

Factors such as oxygen and bacterial infection limit the development and survival of fish eggs during storage. The study of Garside (1966) on the effects of oxygen in relation to temperature on the development of embryos of brook trout (*Salvelinus fontinalis*) and rainbow trout showed that the speed of development was increasingly reduced by progressively lower levels of dissolved oxygen.

9.2.6 Approaches towards successful cryopreservation

There are two main obstacles to the successful cryopreservation of fish embryos: their high sensitivity to chilling as observed with zebrafish embryos (Zhang and Rawson, 1995) and their low membrane permeability to cryoprotectants. The high sensitivity of certain fish embryos to low temperatures is believed to be associated with the presence of large amounts of intraembryonic lipids, suggesting that vitrification will be required. Use of controlled slow cooling may also be possible if embryo chilling sensitivity can be reduced. Recent research has suggested that partial removal of the yolk of zebrafish embryos at the high-pec stage results in a higher embryo survival and reduced chilling sensitivity (Liu *et al.*, 1999). The more difficult problem to overcome is probably that posed by low permeability of the complex membrane systems. Understanding the exact nature of the permeability barriers in fish egg/embryos is seen as vital to progress in their cryopreservation. Further studies are needed to examine the approaches and methods required to tackle these problems before successful cryopreservation of fish embryos can be achieved.

Acknowledgements

Professor Billard's work is part of EC project IC-15CT966–1005. His text was typed by J. Barthélémy and Paul Watson edited the English version of the manuscript.

REFERENCES

ADAM, M. M., RANA, K. J. and McANDREW, B. J. (1995) 'Effect of cryoprotectants on activity of selected enzymes in fish embryos', *Cryobiology* **32**, 92–104.

BABIAK, I., GLOGOWSKI, J., KUJAWA, D., KUCHARCZYK, D. and MAMCARZ A. (1998) 'Cryo-conservation of sperm from Asp *Aspius aspius*', *Progressive Fish Culturist* **60**, 146–148.

BEN-AMOTZ, A. and ROSENTHAL, H. (1981) 'Cryopreservation of marine unicellular algae and early life stage of fish for use in mariculture', *Eur. Maricult. Soc. Special Publication* **6**, 149–162.

BILLARD, R. (1980) 'Prolongation de la durée de motilité et du pouvoir fécondant des spermatozoïdes de truite arc-en-ciel par addition de théophylline au milieu de dilution', *C.R. Acad. Sci. Paris* (Series D) **291**, 649–652.

BILLARD, R. (1983) 'Ultrastructure of trout spermatozoa: changes after dilution and deep freezing', *Cell Tissue Res.* **228**, 205–218.

BILLARD, R. (1984) 'La conservation des gamètes et l'insémination artificielle chez le bar et la daurade', in Barnabé, G. and Billard, R. (eds) *L'Aquaculture du Bar et des Sparidés*, Paris: INRA Publications, pp. 95–116.

BILLARD, R. and COSSON, M. P. (1992) 'Some problems related to the assessment of sperm motility in freshwater fish', *J. Exp. Zool.* **261**, 122–131.

BILLARD, R., DUPONT, J. and BARNABÉ, G. (1977) 'Diminution de la motilité et de la durée de conservation du sperme de *Dicentrarchus labrax* (poisson téléostéen) pendant la période de spermiation', *Aquaculture* **11**, 363–367.

BILLARD, R., COSSON, J. and CRIM, L. W. (1993) 'Motility of fresh and aged halibut sperm', *Aquat. Living Resour.* **6**, 67–75.

BOLLA, S., HOLEFJORD, I. and REFTIE T. (1987) 'Cryogenic preservation of Atlantic halibut sperm', *Aquaculture* **65**, 371–374.

BÜYÜKHATIPOGLU, S. and HOLTZ, W. (1978) 'Preservation of trout sperm in liquid or frozen state', *Aquaculture* **14**, 49–56.

CHAMBEYRON, F. and ZOHAR, Y. (1990) 'A diluent for sperm cryopreservation of gilthead seabream, *Sparus aurata*', *Aquaculture* **90**, 345–352.

CHAO, N. H. (1991) 'Fish sperm cryopreservation in Taiwan: technology advancement and extension efforts', *Bull. Inst. Zool., Acad. Sinica, Monograph* **16**, 263–283.

CHAO, N. H., CHEN, H. P. and LIAO, I. C. (1975) 'Study on cryogenic preservation of grey mullet sperm', *Aquaculture* **5**, 389–406.

CHAO, N. H., CHAO, W. C., LIU, K. C. and LIAO, I. C. (1986) 'The biological properties of black porgy (*Acanthopagrus schlegeli*) sperm and its cryopreservation', *Proc. Natl Sci. Counc. B. ROC* **10**(2), 145–149.

CHEREGUINI, O., CAL, R. M., DREANNO, C., OGIER DE BAULNY, B., SUQUET, M. and MAISSE, G. (1997) 'Short-term storage of turbot (*Scophthalmus maximus*) sperm', *Aquat. Living Resour.* **10**, 251–255.

CHRISTENSEN, J. M. and TIERSCH, T. R. (1997) 'Cryopreservation of channel catfish spermatozoa : effect of cryoprotectant, straw size, and formulation of extender', *Theriogenology* **47**, 639–645.

COGNIE, F., BILLARD, R. and CHAO, N. H. (1989) 'La cryoconservation de la laitance de la carpe, *Cyprinus carpio*', *J. Appl. Ichthyol.* **5**, 165–176.

COMBS, B. D. AND BURROWS, R. E. (1957) 'Threshold temperatures for the normal development of chinook salmon eggs', *Progressive Fish Culturist* **1**, 3–6.

DOI, M., HOSHINO, T., TAKI, Y. and OGASAWARA, Y. (1982) 'Activity of the sperm of the bluefin Tuna *Thunnus thynnus* under fresh and preserved conditions', *Bull. Jap. Soc. Sci. Fish.* **48**, 495–498.

DREANNO, C., SUQUET, M., QUEMENER, L., COSSON, J., FIERVILLE, F., NORMANT, Y. and BILLARD, R. (1997) 'Cryopreservation of turbot (*Scophthalmus maximus*) spermatozoa', *Theriogenology* **48**, 589–603.

DROKIN, S. I. (1993) 'Phospholipid distribution and fatty acid composition of phosphatidylcholine and phosphatidylethanolamine in sperm of some freshwater and marine species of fish', *Aquat. Living Resour.* **6**, 49–56.

EDDY, F. B. (1974) 'Osmotic properties of the perivitelline fluid and some properties of the chorion of Atlantic salmon eggs (*Salmo salar*)', *J. Zool.* **174**, 237–243.

ERDAHL, A. W., ERDAHL, D. A. and GRAHAM, E. F. (1984) 'Some factors affecting the preservation of salmonid spermatozoa', *Aquaculture* **43**, 341–350.

ERDAHL, D. A. and GRAHAM, E. F. (1980) 'Preservation of gametes of freshwater fish', in *Proceedings of the International Congress on Animal Reproduction and Artificial Insemination* (Madrid) vol. 2, pp. 317–326.

GARSIDE, E. T. (1966) 'Effects of oxygen in relation to temperature on the development of embryos of brook trout and rainbow trout', *J. Fish. Res. Bd Can.* **23**, 1121–1134.

GILPIN, M. E. and SOULÉ, M. E. (1986) 'Minimum viable populations: Processes of species extinction', in Soulé, M. E. (ed.) *Conservation Biology: The Science of Scarity and Diversity*, Sunderland: Sinauer Associates, pp. 19–34.

GRIERSON, J. P. and NEVILLE, A. C. (1981) 'Helicoidal architecture of fish egg shell', *Tissue Cell* **13**, 819–830.

GWO, J. C. and ARNOLD, C. R. (1992) 'Cryopreservation of Atlantic croaker spermatozoa: evaluation of morphological changes', *J. Exp. Zool.* **264**, 444–453.

GWO, J. C., STRAWN, K., LONGNECKER, M. T. and ARNOLD, C. R. (1991) 'Cryopreservation of Atlantic croaker spermatozoa', *Aquaculture* **94**, 355–375.

HAGA, Y. (1982) 'On the subzero temperature preservation of fertilised eggs of rainbow trout', *Bull. Jpn. Soc. Sci. Fish.* **48**, 1569–1572.

HAGEDORN, M., HSU, E. W., PILATUS, U., WILDT, D., RALL, W. F. and BLACKBAND, S. J. (1996) 'Magnetic resonance microscopy and spectroscopy reveal kinetics of cryoprotectant permeation in a multicompartmental biological system', *Proc. Natl Acad. Sci. USA* **93**, 7454–7459.

HAGEDORN, M., KLEINHANS, F. W., WILDT, D. E. and RALL, W. F. (1997a) 'Chill sensitivity and cryoprotectant permeability of dechorionated zebrafish embryos, *Brachydanio rerio*', *Cryobiology* **34**, 251–263.

HAGEDORN, M., HSU, E., KLEIHANS, F. W. and WILDT, D. E. (1997b) 'New approaches for studying permeability of fish embryos: toward successful cryopreservation', *Cryobiology* **34**, 335–347.

HAGEDORN, M., KLEINHANS, F. W., FREITAS, R., LIU, J., HSU, E. W., WILDT, D. E. and RALL, W. F. (1997c) 'Water distribution and permeability of zebrafish embryos, *Brachydanio rerio*', *J. Exp. Zool.* **278**, 356–337.

HARA, S., CANTO, J. T. and ALMENDRAS, J. M. E. (1982) 'Comparative study of various extenders for milkfish, *Chanos chanos* (Forsskal), sperm preservation', *Aquaculture* **28**, 339–346.

HART, N. H. and DONOVAN, M. (1983a) 'Fine structure of the chorion and site of sperm entry in the egg of *Brachydanio*', *J. Exp. Zool.* **227**, 277–296.

HARVEY, B. (1983a) 'Cryopreservation of *Sarotherodon mossambicus* spermatozoa', *Aquaculture*, **32**, 313–320.

HARVEY, B. (1983b) 'Cooling of embryonic cells, isolated blastoderm and intact embryos of the zebrafish *Brachydanio rerio* to −196°C', *Cryobiology* **20**, 440–447.

HARVEY, B. and ASHWOOD-SMITH, M. J. (1982) 'Cryoprotectant penetration and supper-cooling in the eggs of samonid fishes', *Cryobiology* **19**, 29–40.

HARVEY, B., STOSS, J. and BUTCHART, W. (1983) 'Supercooled storage of salmonid ova', *Can. Techn. Rep. Fish. Aquatic Sci.* 1222.

HEMING, T. A. and BUDDINGTON, R. K. (1988) 'Yolk absorption in embryonic and larval fishes', in Hoar, W. S. and Randall, D.J. (eds) *Fish Physiology*, New York: Academic Press, pp. 407–445.

HISAOKA, K. K. (1958) 'Microscopic studies of the teleost chorion', *Trans. Am. Microsc. Soc.* **77**, 240–243.

JÄHNINCHEN, H., WARNECKE, D., TRÖLSCH, E., KOHLMANN, K., BERGLER, H. and PLUTA, H. J. (1999) 'Motility and fertilizing capability of cryopreserved *Acipenser ruthenus* L. sperm', *J. Appl. Ichthyol.* **15**, 204–206.

JAMIESON, B. G. M. (1991) *Fish Evolution and Systematics: Evidence from Spermatozoa*. Cambridge: Cambridge University Press.

KALICHARAN, D., JONGEBLOED, W. L., RAWSON, D. M. and ZHANG, T. T. (1998) 'Variation in fixation techniques for field emission SEM and TEM of zebrafish (*Brachydanio rerio*) embryo inner and outer membranes', *J. Electr. Microsc.* **47**, 645–658.

KERBY, J. H. (1983) 'Cryogenic preservation of sperm from striped bass', *Trans. Am. Fish. Soc.* **112**, 86–94.

KIMMEL, C. B. and LAW, R. D. (1986) 'Cell lineage of zebrafish blastomeres', *Dev. Biol.* **108**, 86–93.

KIRCHOFER, A. (1996) *Conservation of Endangered Freshwater Fish in Europe*, Basel: Birkhäuser Verlag.

KUROKURA, H. and HIRANO, R. (1980) 'Cryopreservation of rainbow trout sperm', *Bull. Jpn. Soc. Sci. Fish.* **46**, 1493–1495.

KUROKURA, H., HIRANO, R., TOMITA, M. and IWAHASHI, M. (1984) 'Cryopreservation of carp sperm', *Aquaculture* **37**, 267–273.

LAALE, H. W. (1980) 'The perivitelline space and egg envelopes of bony fishes: a review', *Copeia* **2**, 210–226.

LABBÉ, C. and MAISSE, G. (1996) 'Influence of rainbow trout thermal acclimation on sperm cryopreservation: relation with change in the lipid composition of the plasma membrane', *Aquaculture* **145**, 281–294.

LABBÉ, C., LOIR, M., KAUSHIK, S. and MAISSE, G. (1993) 'The influence of both rearing temperature and dietary lipid origin on fatty acid composition of spermatozoan phospholipids in rainbow trout (*Oncorhynchus mykiss*). Effect on sperm cryo-preservation tolerance', *Fish Nutrition in Practice, Biarritz (France), 24–27 June, 1991*, Paris: INRA, (Les Colloques, no. 61), pp. 49–59.

Labbé, C., Crowe, L. M. and Crowe, J. M. (1997) 'Stability of the lipid component of trout sperm plasma membrane during freeze-thawing', *Cryobiology* **34**, 176–182.

Lahnsteiner, F., Weismann, T. and Patzner, R. A. (1992) 'Fine structural changes in spermatozoa of the grayling, *Thymallus thymallus* (Pisces: Teleostei), during routine cryopreservation', *Aquaculture* **103**, 73–84.

Lahnsteiner, F., Weismann, T. and Patzner, R. A. (1995) 'A uniform method for cryopreservation of semen of salmonid fishes (*Oncorhynchus mykiss, Salmo trutta* f. *fario, Salmo trutta* f. *lacustris, Coregonus* sp.)', *Aquacult. Res.* **26**, 801–807.

Lahnsteiner, F., Berger, B., Weismann, T. and Patzner, R. A. (1996a) 'Changes in morphology, physiology, metabolism, and fertilization capacity of rainbow trout semen following cryopreservation', *Progressive Fish Culturist* **58**, 149–159.

Lahnsteiner, F., Berger, B., Weismann, T. and Patzner, R. A. (1996b) 'Physiological and biochemical determination of rainbow trout, *Oncorhynchus mykiss*, semen quality for cryopreservation', *J. Appl. Aquacult.* **6**, 47–73.

Lahnsteiner, F., Weismann, T. and Patzner, R. A. (1996c) 'Cryopreservation of semen of the grayling (*Thymallus thymallus*) and the Danube salmon (*Hucho hucho*)', *Aquaculture* **144**, 265–274.

Lahnsteiner, F., Berger, B., Weismann, T. and Patzner, R. A. (1996d) 'The influence of various cryoprotectants on semen quality of the rainbow trout (*Oncorhynchus mykiss*) before and after cryopreservation', *J. Appl. Ichthyol.* **12**, 99–106.

Lahnsteiner, F., Patzner, R. A. and Weismann, T. (1996e) 'Semen cryopreservation of salmonid fishes : influence of handling parameters on the postthaw fertilization rate', *Aquacult. Rese.* **27**, 659–671.

Lahnsteiner, F., Weismann, T. and Patzner, R. A. (1997) 'Methanol as cryoprotectant and the suitability of 1.2 ml and 5 ml straws for cryopreservation of semen from salmonid fishes', *Aquacult. Res.* **28**, 471–479.

Lahnsteiner, F., Berger, B., Weismann, T. and Patzner, R. A. (1998a) 'Determination of semen quality of the rainbow trout, *Oncorhynchus mykiss*, by sperm motility, seminal plasma parameters, and spermatozoal metabolism', *Aquaculture* **163**, 163–181.

Lahnsteiner, F., Weismann, T. and Patzner, R. A. (1998b) 'An efficient method for cryopreservation of testicular sperm from the Northern pike, *Esox lucius* L.', *Aquacult. Res.* **29**, 341–347.

Legendre, M. and Billard, R. (1980) 'Cryopreservation of rainbow trout sperm by deep freezing', *Reprod. Nutr. Dévelop.* **20**, 1859–1868.

Lin, F., Ciereszko, A. and Dabrowski, K. (1996) 'Sperm production and cryopreservation in Muskellunge after carp pituitary extract and human chorionic gonadotropin injection', *Progressive Fish Culturist* **58**, 32–37.

Linhart, O., Billard, R. and Proteau, J. P. (1993) 'Cryopreservation of European catfish (*Silurus glanis* L.) spermatozoa', *Aquaculture* **115**, 347–359.

Liu, X. H., Zhang, T. T. and Rawson, D. M. (1998) 'Feasibility of vitrification of zebrafish (*Danio rerio*) embryos using methanol', *Cryo-Letters* **19**, 309–318.

LIU, X. H., ZHANG, T. T. and RAWSON, D. M. (2000) 'The effect of partial removal of yolk on the chilling sensitivity of zebrafish (*Danio rerio*) embryos', *Cryobiology* (in press).

LOEFFLER, C. A. AND LOVSTRUP, S. (1970) 'Water balance in the salmon egg', *J. Exp. Biol.* **52**, 291–298.

MCANDREW, B. J., RANA, K. J. and PENMAN, D. J. (1993) 'Conservation and preservation in aquatic organisms', in Muir, J. F. and Roberts, R. J. (eds) *Recent Advances in Aquaculture*, Vol. IV, Oxford: Blackwell Science, pp. 295–336.

MCNIVEN, M. A., GALLANT, R. K. and RICHARDSON, G. F. (1992) '*In vitro* methods of assessing the viability of rainbow trout spermatozoa', *Theriogenology* **38**, 679–686.

MADDOCK, B. G. (1974) 'A technique to prolong the incubation period of brown trout ova', *Progressive Fish Culturist* **36**, 219–222.

MAGYARY, I., URBANYI, B. and HORVATH, L. (1996a) 'Cryopreservation of common carp (*Cyprinus carpio* L.) sperm. I. The importance of oxygen supply', *J. Appl. Ichthyol.* **12**, 113–115.

MAGYARY, I., DINNYES, A., VARKONYI, E., SZABO, R. and VARADI, L. (1996b) 'Cryopreservation of fish embryos and embryonic cells', *Aquaculture* **137**, 103–108.

MAISSE, G. (1994) 'Comparaison de l'effet cryoprotecteur de différents glucides sur le sperme de truite arc-en-ciel *Oncorhynchus mykiss*', *Aquat. Living Resour.* **7**, 217–219.

MAISSE, G. (1996) 'Cryopreservation of fish semen: a review', *Refrigeration and Aquaculture Conference, Bordeaux, 20–22/03/96*, pp. 443–467.

MAISSE, G., PINSON, A. and LOIR, M. (1998) 'Caractérisation de l'aptitude à la congélation du sperme de truite arc-en-ciel (*Salmo gairdneri*) par des critères physico-chimiques', *Aquat. Living Resour.* **1**, 45–51.

MAISSE, G., LABBÈ, C., OGIER DE BAULNY, B., LEVERONI CALVI, S. and HAFFRAY, P. (1998) 'Cryoconservation du sperme et des embryons de poissons', *INRA Prod. Anim.* **11**, 57–65.

MALÉJAC, M., LOIR, M. and MAISSE, G. (1990) 'Qualité de la membrane des spermatozoïdes de truite arc-en-ciel (*Oncorhynchus mykiss*); relation avec l'aptitude du sperme à la congélation', *Aquat. Living Resour.* **3**, 43–54.

MONGKONPUNYA, K., CHAIRAK, N., PUPITAT, T. and TIERSCH, T. R. (1995) 'Cryopreservation of Mekong giant catfish sperm', *Asian Fish. Sci.* **8**, 211–221.

MOUNIB, M. S. (1978) 'Cryogenic preservation of fish and mammalian spermatozoa', *J. Reprod. Fertil.* **53**, 13–18.

OGIER DE BAULNY, B. (1997) 'Cryoconservation du sperme de poissons. Evaluation des dommages cellulaires, amélioration de la technique de congélation, perméabilité membranaire aux cryoprotecteurs', *Thèse Doctorat Ecole Nationale Supérieure Agronomique de Rennes*, 129 pp.

OGIER DE BAULNY, B., LE VERN, Y., KERBOEUF, D. and MAISSE, G. (1997) 'Flow cytometric evaluation of mitochondrial activity and membrane integrity in fresh and cryopreserved rainbow trout (*Oncorhynchus mykiss*) spermatozoa', *Cryobiology* **34**, 141–149.

ONIZUKA, N., KATOR, K. and EGAMI, N. (1984) 'Mass cooling of embryos and fry of the fish, (*Oryzias latipes*)', *Cryobiology* **21**, 709–710.

OTÉMÉ, Z. S. and AGNÈSE, J. F. (1997) 'Sensitivity to inbreeding and sperm cryopreservation in the catfish *Heterobranchus longifilis* Valenciennes, 1840', *Actes du Colloque Génétique et Aquaculture en Afrique, Abidjan, 1–4 avril 1997*, pp. 257–268.

OTT, A. G. and HORTON, H. F. (1971) 'Fertilization of Chinook and Coho salmon eggs with cryopreserved sperm', *J. Fish. Res. Bd Can.* **28**, 745–748.

PADHI, B. K. and MANDAL, R. K. (1995) 'Cryopreservation of spermatozoa of two asian freshwater catfishes, *Heteropneustes fossilis* and *Clarias batrachus*', *J. Aqua. Trop.* **10**, 23–28.

PERCHEC-POUPARD, G., PAXION, C., COSSON, J., JEULIN, C., FIERVILLE, F. and BILLARD, R. (1998) 'Initiation of carp spermatozoa motility and early ATP reduction after milt contamination by urine', *Aquaculture* **160**, 317–328.

PIIRONEN, J. and HYVÄRINEN, H. (1983) 'Cryopreservation of spermatozoa of the whitefish *Coregonus muksun* Pallas', *J. Fish Biol.* **22**, 159–163.

POLGE, C., SMITH, A. U. and ROWSON, A. S. (1974) 'The low temperature preservation of cow, sheep, and pig embryos', *Cryobiology* **11**, 560.

POTTS, W. T. and EDDY, F. B. (1973) 'The permeability to water of the eggs of certain marine teleost', *J. Comp. Physiol.* **82**, 305–315.

PULLIN, R. S. V. and BAILEY, H. (1981) 'Progress in storing marine flatfish eggs at low temperatures', *Rapp. P. Reun. Cons. Int. Explor. Mer.* **178**, 514–517.

RALL, W.F. (1993) 'Advances in the cryopreservation of embryos and prospects for application to the conservation of samonid fishes', in Cloud, J. G. and Thorgaard, G. H. (eds) *Genetic Conservation of Salmonid Fishes*, New York: Plenum Press, pp. 137–158.

RANA, K. J. (1995) 'Cryopreservation of aquatic gametes and embryos: recent advances and applications', in Goetz, F. W. and Thomas, P. (eds) *Proceedings of the 5th International Symposium on the Reproduction and Physiology of Fish, Austin University, Texas, TX, 2–8/07/95*, pp. 85–89.

RANA, K. J. and GILMOUR, A. (1996) 'Cryopreservation of fish spermatozoa: effect of cooling methods on the reproducibility of cooling rates and viability', in *Refrigeration and Aquaculture Conference, Bordeaux, 20–22/03/96* pp. 3–12.

RANA, K. J. and McANDREW, B. J. (1989) 'The viability of cryopreserved tilapia spermatozoa', *Aquaculture* **76**, 335–345.

RANA, K. J., MUIRURI, R. M., McANDREW, B. J. and GILMOUR, A. (1990) 'The influence of diluents, equilibration time and prefreezing storage time on the viability of cryopreserved *Oreochromis niloticus* (L.) spermatozoa', *Aqua. Fish. Mgmt.* **21**, 25–30.

RITAR, A.J. (1999) 'Artificial insemination with cryopreserved semen from striped trumpeter (*Latris lineata*)', *Aquaculture* **180**, 177–187.

ROBERTSON, S. M., LAWRENCE, A. L., NELL, W. H., ARNOLD, C. R. and McCARTY, G. (1988) 'Toxicity of the cryoprotectants glycerol, dimethyl sulfoxide, ethylene glycol, methanol, sucrose, and sea salt solutions to the embryos of red drum', *Progressive Fish Culturist,* **50**, 148–154.

SAAD, A. and BILLARD, R. (1987) 'Composition et emploi d'un dilueur d'insémination chez la carpe, *Cyprinus carpio'*, *Aquaculture* **66**, 329–345.

SCHEERER, P. D. and THORGAARD, G. H. (1989) 'Improved fertilization by cryopreserved rainbow trout semen treated with theophylline', *Progressive Fish Culturist* **51**, 179–182.

SCHOOTS, A. F. M., STIKKELBROECK, J. J. M., BEKHUIS, J. F. and DENUCE, J. M. (1982) 'Hatching in teleost fishes: fine structure changes in the egg envelope during enzymatic breakdown *in vivo* and *in vitro'*, *J. Ultra. Res.* **80**, 185–196.

SCOTT, A. P. and BAYNES, S. M. (1980) 'A review of the biology, handling and storage of salmonid spermatozoa', *J. Fish Biol.* **17**, 707–739.

STEYN, G. J. and VAN VUREN, J. H. J. (1987) 'The fertilizing capacity of cryopreserved sharptooth catfish (*Clarias gariepinus*) sperm', *Aquaculture* **63**, 187–193.

STOSS, J. (1983) 'Fish gamete preservation and spermatozoa physiology', in Hoar W. S., Randall D. J. and Donaldson E. M. (eds) *Fish Physiology,* Vol. IXB, New York and London: Academic Press, pp. 305–350.

STOSS, J. and DONALDSON, E. M. (1983) 'Studies on cryopreservation of eggs from rainbow trout (*Salmo gairdneri*) and coho salmon (*Oncorhynchus kisutch*)', *Aquaculture* **31**, 51–65.

STOSS, J. and REFSTIE, T. (1983) 'Short-term storage and cryopreservation of milt from Atlantic salmon and sea trout', *Aquaculture* **30**, 229–236.

SUQUET, M., DREANNO, C., PETTON, B., NORMANT, Y., OMNES, M. H. and BILLARD, R. (1998) 'Long term effects of the cryopreservation of turbot (*Psetta maxima*) spermatozoa.' *Aquat. Living Resour.* **11**, 45–48.

TESORIERO, J. (1977) 'Formation of the chorion (zona pellucida) in the teleost, *Oryzias latipes.* II polysaccharide cytochemistry of early oogenesis', *J. Histochem. Cytochem.* **25**, 1376–1380.

THOROGOOD, J. and BLACKSHAW, A. (1992) 'Factors affecting the activation, motility and cryopreservation of the spermatozoa of the yellowfin bream, *Acanthopagrus australis* (Günther)', *Aqua. Fish. Mgmt.* **23**, 337–344.

TIERSCH, T. R., GOUDIE, C. A. and CARMICHAEL, G. J. (1994) 'Cryopreservation of Channel catfish sperm: storage in cryoprotectants, fertilization trials, and growth of channel catfish produced with cryopreserved sperm', *Trans. Am. Fish. Soc.* **123**, 580–586.

TIERSCH, T. R., FIGIEL, C. R., WAYMAN, W. R., WILLIAMSON, J. H., CARMICHAEL, G. J. and GORMAN, O. T. (1998) 'Cryopreservation of sperm of the endangered razorback sucker', *Trans. Am. Fish. Soc.* **127**, 95–104.

TOSHIMORI, K. and YASUZUMI, F. (1976) 'The morphology and the function of the oocyte chorion in the teleost, *Plecoglossus altivelis'*, *J. Electron Microsc.* **25**, 210.

TSVETKOVA, L. I., COSSON, J., LINHART, O. and BILLARD, R. (1996) 'Motility and fertilizing capacity of fresh and frozen-thawed spermatozoa in sturgeons *Acipenser baeri* and *A. ruthenus'*, *J. Appl. Ichthyol.* **12**, 107–112.

WAYMAN, W. R., THOMAS, R. G. and TIERSCH, T. R. (1996) 'Cryopreservation of sperm of spotted seatrout (*Cynoscion nebulosus*)', *Gulf Res. Rep.* **9**, 183–188.

WAYMAN, W. R., THOMAS, R. G. and TIERSCH, T. R. (1997) 'Refrigerated storage and cryopreservation of black drum (*Pogonias cromis*) spermatozoa', *Theriogenology* **47**, 1519–1529.

WHITTINGHAM, D. G. and ROSENTHAL, H. (1978) 'Attempts to preserve herring embryos at subzero temperatures', *Arch. Fish Wiss.* **29**, 75–79.

WITHLER, F. C. and LIM, L. C. (1982) 'Preliminary observations of chilled and deep-frozen storage of Grouper (*Epinephelus tauvina*) sperm', *Aquaculture* **27**, 389–392.

YOO, B. Y., RYAN, M. A. and WIGGS, A. J. (1985) 'Loss of protein from spermatozoa of Atlantic salmon (*Salmo salar* L) because of cryopreservation', *Can. J. Zool.* **65**, 9–13.

YOUNG, J. A., CAPRA, M. F. and BLACKSHAW, A. W. (1992) 'Cryopreservation of summer whiting (*Sillago ciliata*) spermatozoa', *Aquaculture* **102**, 155–160.

ZELL, S. R. (1978) 'Cryopreservation of gametes and embryos of salmonid fishes', *Ann. Biol. Anim. Biochim. Biophys.* **18**, 1089–1099.

ZHANG, T. T. and RAWSON, D. M. (1995) 'Studies on chilling sensitivity of zebrafish (*Brachydanio rerio*) embryos', *Cryobiology* **32**, 239–246.

ZHANG, T. T. and RAWSON, D. M. (1996a) 'Feasibility studies on vitrification of intact zebrafish (*Brachydanio rerio*) embryos', *Cryobiology* **33**, 1–13.

ZHANG, T. T. and RAWSON, D. M. (1996b) 'Permeability of the vitelline membrane of zebrafish (*Brachydanio rerio*) embryos to methanol and propane-1,2–diol', *Cryo-Letters* **17**(6), 273–280.

ZHANG, T. T. and RAWSON, D. M. (1998) 'Permeability of dechorionated 1-cell and 6–somite stage zebrafish (*Brachydanio rerio*) embryos to water and methanol', *Cryobiology* **32**, 239–246.

ZHANG, T. T., RAWSON, D. M. and MORRIS, G. J. (1993) 'Cryopreservation of pre-hatch embryos of zebrafish (*Brachydanio rerio*)', *Aquat. Living Resour.* **6**, 145–153.

ZHANG, X. S., ZHAO, L., HUA, T. C., CHEN, X. H. and ZHU, H. Y. (1989) 'A study on the cryopreservation of common carp (*Cyprinus carpio*) embryos', *Cryo-Letters* **10**, 271–278.

Cryopreservation of Gametes and Embryos in Reptiles and Amphibians

J. D. MILLAR and P. F. WATSON

Department of Veterinary Basic Sciences, The Royal Veterinary College, London NW1 0TU, UK

Contents

10.1 REPTILES

Amongst the Reptilia, there have been few attempts at artificial insemination and even fewer studies of cryopreservation of gametes. No successes from artificial insemination with cryopreserved semen have been recorded.

10.1.1 Spermatozoa

Semen collection

Samples of spermatozoa obtained from snakes by a 'stroking' method (see Watson, 1990) were frequently found to be contaminated (Fitch, 1960). Viable uncontaminated ejaculates from several species were obtained by an improved method (Mengden *et al.*, 1980), and spermatozoa were obtained from pythons, but motility was not mentioned. Weekly collection appeared to be tolerated during the breeding period; electro-ejaculation was less satisfactory than the manual procedure. Samour (1986) reported collections from Sinaloan milk snakes using a similar procedure.

For alligators, attempts using either electroejaculation or chemical stimulants of ejaculation in live animals failed to improve on the numbers of spermatozoa which could be aspirated from the penile groove in untreated males (Larsen *et al.*, 1982). Spermatozoa in sufficient numbers for laboratory studies and AI have been obtained from alligators by this latter method (Larsen *et al.*, 1982). Spermatozoa have also been obtained from lizards but only post-mortem (Depeiges and Dacheux, 1985).

Results with chelonians have been more successful using methods developed by Platz *et al.* (1980). Wood *et al.* (1982) routinely achieved electroejaculation in green sea turtles. Similar methods have been applied to the Galapagos tortoise and the red-eared pond turtle (Platz *et al.*, 1980).

Dilution and storage

Information is limited concerning the dilution and storage of reptile spermatozoa. Depeiges and Dacheux (1985) reported that a 5% egg yolk–Tyrode's solution was most suited for diluting and incubating lizard spermatozoa at 30°C but lower temperatures were not investigated. Several diluents have been investigated for storing snake spermatozoa. The most successful at 5°C was a modified McCoy's tissue culture medium which permitted motility to be continued beyond 96 hours (Mengden *et al.*, 1980). Spermatozoa recovered post-mortem from alligators were stored in an organic buffer–egg yolk diluent at 5°C, with motility values of above 75% maintained for 6 days (Larsen *et al.*, 1982).

■ CHAPTER 10 ■

Cryopreservation

Glycerol is apparently toxic to snake spermatozoa. Snake spermatozoa have been frozen by the pellet method using a commercial diluent (Mengden *et al.*, 1980), but no details were given; a 30% post-thaw motility was observed, but with several other diluents, revivals were poor. Platz *et al.* (1980) attempted to freeze chelonian semen by the pellet method, but without success. No other reports have apparently been published.

Artificial insemination

Artificial insemination has been accomplished in alligators and snakes but only with fresh semen. Details can be found in Watson (1990).

10.1.2 Embryo and oocyte preservation

No reports have been found.

10.2 AMPHIBIANS

10.2.1 Spermatozoa

Semen collection

There appears to be no available information on semen collection from live animals, although amplexus (mating behaviour of the male anuran) and sperm shedding have been induced with pituitary extracts (Rugh, 1934). Spermatozoa have also been collected post-mortem (Rugh, 1934).

Sperm responses to diluent components

Where fertilization is external to the body in a freshwater environment, dilution of the seminal fluid results in activation of the spermatozoa. Thus, spermatozoa are only motile in a hyposmotic solution. Dimethyl sulphoxide (7.5%) was found to be a better tolerated cryoprotectant for toad spermatozoa than either glycerol or ethylene glycol in an investigation of the three agents not involving freezing, but results were different after freezing (see below–Barton and Guttman, 1972); high motility and fertility was retained. Frog spermatozoa seemed to be tolerant to high levels of cryoprotectant up to at least 20%, although Beesley *et al.* (1998) claim less cytotoxicity with 0.5 M DMSO (approximately 4%) than the 1.5–3.0 M used previously (Mugnano *et al.*, 1998).

Cryopreservation

Barton and Guttman (1972) investigated the actions of seven extenders, three cooling rates and three warming rates on the preservation of the spermatozoa of the American toad, *Bufo americanus*. Two particular diluents, a basal tissue culture medium (pH 7) and a modified Cortland medium, each with 10% ethylene glycol and with a slow freeze protocol (0.7°C/min to −20°C), showed some protective ability as judged by sperm motility at 24 hours incubation after thawing, but this was no better than with dechlorinated tapwater containing the same cryoprotectant. The most successful combination was Alsever's medium in conjunction with ethylene glycol at 15%, using a freezing rate of 0.7°C/minute and a fast thaw method (samples placed in a 25°C water bath until all visible ice crystals had melted, and then removed from the water bath and allowed to warm to room temperature). After freeze-thaw to −20°C for one day, this gave 88% motility at 24 hours incubation, reducing to 2% after 15 days incubation. Although initially less protective after one day, 20% ethylene glycol gave better motility from 5 to 15 days of incubation, but no procedure was successful in maintaining motility beyond this duration of storage. Higher freezing rates (45°C/min or 200°C/min) met with no success in preserving motility or viability of the spermatozoa. A preliminary test with fetal calf serum was the only extender to preserve motility for up to 20 days incubation (9% with slow freeze rate and >15% ethylene glycol). Combinations of Alsever's medium and fetal calf serum also showed considerable promise (Barton and Guttman, 1972). However, fertilizing ability of cryopreserved spermatozoa was not examined in this study. Other workers have also claimed that a slow rate of freezing (complex five-part temperature contour) is of benefit to recovery of spermatozoa motility for *Bufo marinus* (Browne *et al.*, 1998).

Mugnano *et al.* (1998) found poor recovery of spermatozoa of the freeze-tolerant wood frog *Rana sylvatica* frozen at a cooling rate of 130°C/min, even in the best case, when the extender contained 1.5 or 3.0 M DMSO. However, using this same rate Beesley *et al.* (1998) reported an 81% recovery of viable spermatozoa relative to unfrozen controls for spermatozoa from *R. sylvatica*. Lower recoveries were obtained from cells of the freeze-intolerant *R. pipiens* and *Bufo americanus* (59% and 48% respectively), but only if the extender contained 0.5 M DMSO and a supplement of fetal bovine serum (Beesley *et al.*, 1998).

Work from a Russian laboratory (Kaurova *et al.*, 1996) on spermatozoa of *R. temporaria* suggested better cryoprotection by 15% DMSO than glycerol. Rapid freezing by directly submerging into liquid nitrogen was used and the samples were suspended in a solution of 0.25% NaCl with 0.01 M HEPES (pH 7); inclusion of 5% glucose in the medium was necessary to prevent DMSO obstructing subsequent fertilization (Kaurova *et al.*, 1996).

Finally, in some cases attempts to cryopreserve whole testes or testicular slices have been carried out but results were not promising (Costanzo *et al.*, 1998; Mugnano *et al.*, 1998).

Semination of eggs with frozen semen

There are no reported attempts to seminate eggs with frozen semen.

10.2.2 Embryo preservation

No reports exist.

10.3 CONCLUSION

It is no doubt apparent that the subject of amphibian and, to a still lesser extent, reptilian gamete preservation has not yet progressed very far. Much more systematic work needs to be done before reliable protocols could be prescribed for use in gamete resource banking. In particular, there must be some evidence of the effects of freezing and thawing on the fertility of samples. Until that is achieved, appropriate protocols will at best be speculative. The recent work on amphibian species, inspired by a conservation motive, may be expected to produce some relevant information in the next few years.

REFERENCES

BARTON, H. L. and GUTTMAN, S. I. (1972) 'Low temperature preservation of toad spermatozoa (Genus *Bufo*)', *Texas J. Sci.* **23**, 363–370.

BEESLEY, S. G., COSTANZO, J. P. and LEE, R. E. (1998) 'Cryopreservation of spermatozoa from freeze-tolerant and intolerant anurans', *Cryobiology* **37**, 155–162.

BROWNE, R. K., CLULOW, J., MAHONY, M. and CLARK, A. (1998) 'Successful recovery of motility and fertility of cryopreserved cane toad (*Bufo marinus*) sperm', *Cryobiology* **37**, 339–345.

COSTANZO, J. P., MUGNANO, J. A., WEHRHEIM, H. M. and LEE, R. E. (1998) 'Osmotic and freezing tolerance in spermatozoa of freeze-tolerant and -intolerant frogs', *Am. J. Physiol.* **275**, R713–R719.

DEPEIGES, A. and DACHEUX, J. L. (1985) 'Acquisition of sperm motility and its maintenance during storage in the lizard (*Lacerta vivipara*)', *J. Reprod. Fertil.* **74**, 23–27.

FITCH, H.S. (1960) 'Criteria for determining sex and breeding maturity in snakes', *Herpetologica* **16**, 49–51.

KAUROVA, S. A., CHEKUROVA, N. R., MELNIKOVA, E. V., UTESHEV, V. K. and GAKHOVA, E. N. (1996) 'Cryopreservation of frog (*Rana temporaria*) sperm without a loss of fertilizing capacity', in *Genetic Resource Conservation. Proceedings of the XIV Working Meeting (Pushchino, 28–30 May, 1996)*, Russian Academy of Sciences Pushchino Scientific Center: Puschino, pp. 106–107.

LARSEN, R. E., DeSENA, R. R., PUCKETT, H. M. and CARDEILHAC, P. T. (1982) 'Collection of semen for artificial insemination', in Cardeilhac, P., Lane, P. and Larsen, R. (eds) *Proceedings of the Second Annual Alligator Production Conference (Gainsville, Florida)*, University of Florida: Gainsville, pp. 42–43.

MENGDEN, G. A., PLATZ, C. C., HUBBARD, R. and QUINN, H. (1980) 'Semen collection, freezing and artificial insemination in snakes', in Murphy, J. B. and Collins, J. T. (eds) *Contributions to Herpetology. No. 1. Reproductive Biology and Diseases of Captive Reptiles*, Society for the Study of Amphibians and Reptiles, St Louis University: St Louis, MO, pp. 71–78.

MUGNANO, J. A., COSTANZO, J. P., BEESLEY, S. G. and LEE, R. E. (1998) 'Evaluation of glycerol and dimethyl sulfoxide for the cryopreservation of spermatozoa from the wood frog (*Rana sylvatica*)', *Cryo-Letters* **19**, 249–254.

PLATZ, C. C., MENGDEN, G., QUINN, H., WOOD, F. and WOOD, J. (1980) 'Semen collection, evaluation and freezing in the green sea turtle, Galapagos tortoise, and red-eared pond turtle', *Proc. Am. Assoc. Zoo Vet.* 47–53.

RUGH, R. (1934) 'Induced ovulation and artificial fertilization in the frog', *Biol. Bull.* **66**, 22–29.

SAMOUR, J. H. (1986) 'Recent advances in artificial breeding techniques in birds and reptiles', *Int. Zoo Yearbook* **24/25**, 143–148.

WATSON, P. F. (1990) 'Artificial insemination and the preservation of semen', in Lamming, G. E. (ed.) *Marshall's Physiology of Reproduction*, 4th edn, Vol. 2. Edinburgh: Churchill Livingstone, pp. 747–769.

WOOD, F., PLATZ, C., CRITCHLEY, K. and WOOD, J. (1982) 'Semen collection by electro-ejaculation of the green turtle (*Chelonia mydas*)', *Br. J. Herpetol.* **6**, 200–202.

CHAPTER 10

The Cryopreservation of Germplasm in Domestic and Non-Domestic Birds

G. J. WISHART

Avian Reproduction Group, University of Abertay Dundee,
Bell Street, Dundee DD1 1HG, Scotland

Contents

11.1 INTRODUCTION

The layout of this chapter has been arranged to reflect the rather uneven distribution of information on the comparatively limited range of cryopreservation technologies which have been applied to avian species. Most work has involved developing methodologies for freezing spermatozoa of the domestic fowl or chicken (*Gallus domesticus*) and, since applications to spermatozoa of other species are based on these systems, the first section on freezing chicken spermatozoa will serve as a general guide to avian sperm cryopreservation technologies. Other sections on freezing spermatozoa will document the particular adaptations and applications of these systems, first to other domestic and then to non-domestic species. Since personal communication is invaluable for planning any programme, examples of reports from most of the major groups involved in (chicken) sperm cryopreservation studies over the past twenty years are given in Table 11.1. Of those mentioned, Haije, Kurbatov, Lake and Sexton are no longer actively working in the field, but the colleagues of the latter three – Tselutin, Wishart and Bakst, respectively – can, along with the others, still be contacted. There are also several reviews on avian sperm cryopreservation which may be consulted (Lake, 1986; Bakst, 1990; Busch *et al.*, 1991; Hammerstedt and Graham, 1992; Bellagamba *et al.*, 1993; Hübner *et al.*, 1994; Hammerstedt, 1995; Gee, 1995; Surai and Wishart, 1996; Wishart and Hartley, 1998; Donoghue and Wishart, 2000) as well as some practical descriptions of methodologies (Wishart, 1995a; Buss, 1997; Hammerstedt, 1997; Sexton, 1997).

Unlike avian sperm freezing technology, which has a history of around fifty years (Polge, 1951), systems for producing progeny from embryonic cells are only a few years old (Naito *et al.*, 1994), limited to chickens, and technically demanding. Thus, it should be realized that these systems, which are described in the last section, are still very much at an embryonic stage of their development and are likely to require a considerable investment of personnel, time and facilities.

It will be noticed that there is no section on freezing avian ova: manipulation of the megalecithal avian ovum (the 'yolk') is physiologically impractical and, anyway, its cryopreservation would be biophysically impossible.

11.2 CHICKEN SPERMATOZOA

11.2.1 Seasonality

Mature commercial poultry are held under stimulatory photoperiods in a controlled environment (>14 hours of light per 24 hours; see Lewis and Perry, 1995), so that seasonality is not a relevant factor. Whether or not sperm quality declines during the life of a breeder male is arguable, but it might be worth using spermatozoa from birds in the first half of their breeding season. It is likely to be more rewarding to select individual birds on the basis of their sperm quality (Lake and Stewart, 1978a; Hübner and Schramm, 1988a) and sperm quality–or perhaps 'freezability'–has been shown to be a selectable trait (Ansah et al., 1985) that varies between strains (Bacon et al., 1986: Tajima et al., 1990; Alexander et al., 1993). Of course, birds held under natural lighting in temperate zones will respond to a variable photoperiod and will only come into production in the 'long-day' season. Naturally, this will vary with latitude, but rather than discuss all variations, it may be assumed that anyone wishing to apply sperm cryopreservation technology will be aware of, or have access to information on, appropriate husbandry systems.

11.2.2 Semen collection

The process of manual semen collection from chickens was introduced by Burrows and Quinn (1937) and is usually referred to as 'abdominal massage', although it mostly involves stroking the back and lifting the tail before squeezing the semen out of the phallus. Semen should be free of urates and faeces, but whether the 'transparent fluid' exuded from the tumescent phallus is detrimental, remains unclear. However, it will dilute the contents of the ductus deferens, so it is probably best to collect semen free of this 'contaminant' (Lake, 1957). Although some publications (Lake and Stewart, 1978b) offer pictures of the technique for semen collection from chickens, it is useful to find someone to demonstrate the technique. Semen is more readily collected from birds housed individually and used to being handled. It may be rather difficult to collect from birds which have been mating naturally with females. Ideally, birds producing semen for freezing should be 'milked' twice weekly.

11.2.3 Diluent composition

There are many different diluents, most of which are glutamate-based. These include Minnesota A diluent (Tajima et al., 1989), also used by Buss, Gill, Hammerstedt and colleagues (Alexander et al., 1993; Gill et al., 1996); Beltsville diluent (Duplaix and Sexton, 1983), Lake's diluent (Lake et al., 1981), also used by Wishart (1985), Seigneurin and Blesbois (1995), Buckland and colleagues (Ansah and Buckland, 1983), Ogasawara (Bacon et al., 1986) and, with some adaptations, as LKS-1, by Kurbatov/Tselutin and colleagues (Tselutin et al., 1995); VIRGJ-2 (Kurbatov et al., 1984); and Blumberg diluent (Schramm and Hübner, 1989). There are plenty of other diluents, not all of which contain glutamate (e.g. Watanabe and Terada, 1980). Some of these have been tabulated elsewhere (Bakst, 1990; Surai and Wishart, 1996), but it would not be of particular value to list them here, since the relative contribution of diluent characteristics to the outcome of sperm cryopreservation is less significant than other factors (Duplaix and Sexton, 1983; Haije, 1990). However, in a Russian trial, LKS-1 maintained better fertility than some other diluents (see Surai and Wishart, 1996).

11.2.4 Cryoprotectants

For penetrating cryoprotectants, glycerol (Gly), dimethyl sulphoxide (DMSO), dimethyl acetamide (DMA), ethylene glycol (EG), dimethyl formamide (DMF) and propylene glycol (PG, also known as propanediol) have been used most frequently (see Hammerstedt and Graham, 1992; Surai and Wishart, 1996; Donoghue and Wishart, 2000). Some examples of publications from the major research groups who have employed these cryoprotectants under different cooling systems are provided in Table 11.1. These do not reflect the volume of work from the different groups, but rather a single example of the 'best' results from any one cryoprotectant/system. All of these methods are capable of producing spermatozoa which, with an appropriate insemination regime, will fertilize more than 50% of eggs laid by inseminated hens. However, since many uncontrolled variables will influence this outcome, details of sperm fertilizing ability is not listed. The relative efficacy of these cryoprotectants, in terms of the fertilizing ability of frozen–thawed spermatozoa, is more meaningful when this has been ascertained within the same experiment, is shown in Table 11.2. The overall ranking of these will undoubtedly be confounded by the different freezing (see, for example, Tselutin et al., 1999) and insemination systems, but a reasonable approximation is DMF/Gly > DMA > EG > DMSO.

Of non-penetrating cryoprotectants, sucrose (see Surai and Wishart, 1996) polyvinyl pyrollidine (Lake et al., 1981); trehalose (Terada et al., 1989), and methyl cellulose (Phillips et al., 1996) have been used, the latter three in combination with glycerol. Of these, only trehalose has been demonstrated to improve the quality of cryopreserved spermatozoa and then this was only measured in vitro (Terada et al., 1989).

11.2.5 Dilution/equilibration

Semen samples may be mixed with diluent (without cryoprotectant) at room temperature before cooling to 5°C (Seigneurin and Blesbois, 1995) or cooled to 5°C before mixing with diluent at the same temperature (Tselutin et al., 1995). These samples are often equilibrated at 5°C for up to 40 minutes before adding cryoprotectant (Seigneurin and Blesbois, 1995; Tselutin et al., 1995). Alternatively, semen may be mixed directly with cryoprotectant solution at 5°C (Lake et al., 1981). The length of time of equilibration with cryoprotectant may vary from between 2 minutes with DMA (Tselutin et al., 1995) and 10 minutes (Lake et al., 1981) or 60 minutes (Alexander et al., 1993) with glycerol .

CHAPTER 11

TABLE 11.1

Examples of systems used for cryopreservation of chicken spermatozoa

Cryoprotectant (Concentration)	Cryopreservation system	Reference(s)
Glycerol (7–10%)	Pelleted at −40°C on solid CO_2	Watanabe and Terada, 1980 (Japan)
Glycerol (13.6%)	−1°C/min to −35°C PF/glass ampoules	Lake et al., 1981 (UK) Wishart, 1985 (UK)
Glycerol (13.6%)	−6°C/min to −35°C PF/ampoules	Ansah and Buckland, 1983 (Canada)
Glycerol (13.6%)	−3°C/min to −35°C PF/ampoules	Bacon et al., 1986; (USA)
Glycerol (9%)	−3°C/min to −45°C PF/straws	Tajima et al., 1989 (USA)
Glycerol (9%)	−6°C/min to −120°C NV/straws	Alexander et al., 1993 (USA) Phillips et al., 1996 (USA)
Glycerol (12–16%)	−5°C/min to −50°C PF/Cryocell	Buss, 1993 (USA) Gill et al., 1996 (USA)
Glycerol (11%)	−7°C/min to −35°C PF/straws	Seigneurin and Blesbois, 1995 (France); Tselutin et al., 1999 (Russia/France)
EG (10%)	Pelleted at −80°C onto plastic plate	Kurbatov et al., 1980 (Russia)
EG (6%)	−1°C/min to −30°C PF/glass ampoules	Hübner and Schramm, 1988b (Germany)
DMA (6%)	Pelleted at −80°C onto plastic plate	Kurbatov et al., 1984 (Russia) Tselutin et al., 1995 (Russia)
DMA (6%)	−1°C/min to −35°C PF/glass ampoules	Hübner and Schramm, 1988a (Germany)
DMA (6%)	Pelleted at −196°C into liquid nitrogen	Tselutin et al., 1995 (Russia) Tselutin et al, 1999 (Russia/France)
DMSO (4%)	−1°C/min to −20°C (40°C to (80°C alcohol-NV/straws	Duplaix and Sexton, 1983 (USA)
DMSO (4.5%)	−1°C/min to −20°C −40°C to −80°C alcohol-NV/straws	Haije, 1990; Van Voorst and Leenstra, 1994 (The Netherlands)
DMF (6%)	−1°C/min to −35°C PF/glass ampoules	Schramm, 1991 (Germany)
DMF (7%)	Approx. −50°C/min to −80°C PF/straws	Tereshchenko et al., 1992 (Ukraine)

EG, ethylene glycol; DMA, dimethyl acetamide; DMSO, dimethyl sulphoxide; DMF, dimethyl formamide; PF, programmable freezer; NV, nitrogen vapour.

11.2.6 Packaging

Some of the systems used are noted in Table 11.1. Two-millilitre glass ampoules (Lake and Lavie, 1984); 2-ml plastic ampoules (Wishart, 1995a); 0.25- and 0.5-ml plastic straws (Duplaix and Sexton, 1984; Seigneurin and Blesbois, 1995); 10-ml glass vials

TABLE 11.2
Comparative fertilizing ability of chicken spermatozoa cryopreserved using different cryoprotectants

Efficacy ranking	Cryopreservation method	Reference
EG > DMSO	Pelleted at −80°C	Kurbatov et al., 1979
DMF > EG > DMSO	Pelleted at −80°C	Otpuschennikov and Krivtsova, 1983
DMA > EG = DMSO	−1°C/min to −35°C PF/glass ampoules	Lake and Ravie, 1984
Gly > DMA	13°C/min to −35°C PF/glass ampoules	Bacon et al.,1986
DMA > EG	−1°C/min to −35°C PF/glass ampoules	Hubner and Schramm, 1988b
Gly > DMSO = DMA	−3°C/min to −45°C PF/straws	Tajima et al., 1990
Gly > DMSO	−1°C/min to −35°C PF/glass ampoules	Haije, 1990
DMF > DMA > EG	−1°C/min to −35°C PF/glass ampoules	Schramm, 1991
Gly > DMA	−7°C/min to −35°C PF/straws	Tselutin et al., 1999
DMA > Gly	Pelleted directly into liquid nitrogen	Tselutin et al., 1999

EG, ethylene glycol; DMA, dimethyl acetamide; DMSO, dimethyl sulphoxide; DMF, dimethyl formamide; PF, programmable freezer.

(Kurbatov *et al.*, 1984) have all been used. At least one comparison between glass vials and plastic straws demonstrated no significant differences in the resultant fertility (Ravie and Lake, 1984); nor did the size of plastic straw (Duplaix and Sexton, 1984). The Cryocell® is a 1–ml cuboidal container in which glycerolated semen samples may be frozen, the advantage being that it may be used to dialyse out the glycerol after freezing (Buss, 1993). Pellets of semen/diluent/cryprotectant suspensions may be made by dropping liquid samples onto solid carbon dioxide (Watanabe and Terada, 1980; Terada *et al.*, 1989) or plastic plates with small depressions held in nitrogen vapour at around 70°C (Kurbatov *et al.*, 1984; Tselutin *et al.*, 1995). More directly, pellets may be made by dropping liquid samples directly into liquid nitrogen (Yerashevich and Sviridova, 1990; Tselutin *et al.*, 1995). These pellets are then transferred to glass vials for storage in liquid nitrogen.

11.2.7 Cooling procedures

These may be summarized as follows:
- *Pellet formation 1.* Semen is dropped in 0.2-ml volumes onto a depression in solid CO_2, then transferred into liquid nitrogen (Watanabe and Terada, 1980; Terada *et al.*, 1989).

- *Pellet formation 2.* Semen (0.2-ml) is dropped onto a fluoroplastic plate held in liquid nitrogen vapour at −70°C then transferred into liquid nitrogen (Kurbatov *et al.*, 1984; Tselutin *et al.*, 1995).
- *Pellet formation 3.* Equilibrated semen (0.2-ml) are dropped directly into liquid nitrogen (Yerashivich and Sviridova, 1990; Tselutin *et al.*, 1995).
- *Rotation method.* One-millilitre volumes within a 10-ml capacity glass vial are rotated in liquid nitrogen vapour at −70°C before plunging into liquid nitrogen (Kurbatov *et al.*, 1984).
- *Nitrogen vapour freezing.* Samples, usually in plastic straws, are placed in nitrogen vapour at a given distance (e.g. 6 cm) above the liquid nitrogen and held for 15 minutes (estimating −6°C/min) before plunging into liquid nitrogen (Alexander *et al.*, 1993; Phillips *et al.*, 1996; Hammerstedt, 1995).
- *Programmable freezer.* Samples within ampoules or straws (see above) are cooled from 5°C to −35°C at between 1 and 10°C/min, before plunging into liquid nitrogen (Lake and Ravie, 1984; Tajima *et al.*, 1989; Wishart, 1995a; Seigneurin and Blesbois, 1996).

There are very few examples of studies in which two of these methods have been compared within the same laboratory. The simplest method of forming pellets by dropping semen/DMA mixtures into liquid nitrogen has compared favourably with the more sophisticated method of freezing spermatozoa in glycerol using a programmable freezer, in terms of both fertility (Tselutin *et al.*, 1999; Chala *et al.*, 1999) and sperm quality (Chala *et al.*, 1999; Hartley, 1999). As for the freezing rates used in program-mable freezing, Seigneurin and Blesbois (1995) found, using glycerol, that a cooling rate of −7°C /min between 5 and −35°C maintained fertility better than rates of −1, −5 and −10°C/min. Examples of different freezing rates and methods are given in Table 11.1.

11.2.8 Thawing

When glycerol is used, it is important that the samples do not rise above 5°C, so that glycerol removal does not invoke osmotic shock in the samples (see below) . Samples of straws or ampoules containing glycerolated semen are removed directly from liquid nitrogen to 5°C in air (Tajima *et al.*, 1989; Alexander *et al.*, 1993), or an alcohol (Lake *et al.*, 1981) or water (Phillips *et al.*, 1996) bath. Samples thaw more quickly in baths, especially with agitation, although water tends to freeze around the samples. Ice baths were also used to thaw samples in straws frozen in DMSO (Sexton, 1997) and DMA (Hübner and Schramm, 1988a).

Semen stored in Cryocells® (or CellStor™) are thawed at a rate of 10°C/min to 4°C in a customized heater (Buss, 1993, 1997). Pellets of glycerolated spermatozoa have been thawed by placing into test tubes and shaking in a waterbath at 37°C until liquid

(Terada *et al.*, 1989). A similar method is used for spermatozoa frozen as pellets in DMA, although Tselutin (1982) found that using a bath up to 75°C had no effect on the resultant fertilizing ability. It is, of course important that the samples are removed from the bath as soon as they have thawed. Novel jacket-heated metal funnels have been developed for thawing sperm pellets with DMA (Narubina *et al.*, 1988; Tselutin *et al.*, 1995).

11.2.9   Post-thaw processing – removal of glycerol

Ironically, whilst its cryoprotective action was first discovered using chicken spermatozoa (Polge, 1951), glycerol, when mixed with spermatozoa at concentrations over 1%, inhibits fertility of intravaginally inseminated spermatozoa (see Hammerstedt and Graham, 1992). Thus, glycerol – although not (necessarily) any of the other cryoprotectants mentioned here – must be removed from samples before insemination. Transfer of spermatozoa from a glycerolated medium to a non-glycerolated medium must be done slowly to avoid osmotic shock (see Hammerstedt and Graham, 1992) and is usually performed at around 5°C when transmembrane fluxes are less rapid. Removal of glycerol by dialysis was used in the earliest work (Polge, 1951) and continues to be employed with current systems (Buss, 1993). Dialysis with the Cryocells® (or CellStor™) takes around 90 minutes at 4–6°C (Hammerstedt, 1997). The more common alternative is to add diluent to the thawed samples in a stepwise fashion, diluting the sample by around ten-fold, before centrifugation and resuspension of the spermatozoa (Lake *et al.*, 1981; Wishart, 1995a). Once again it is difficult to recommend either method: centrifugation undoubtedly harms spermatozoa (Steele and Wishart, 1996), but dialysis involves a longer post-thaw treatment.

11.2.10   Assessment of effectiveness of systems

The success of any system for chicken sperm cryopreservation is usually measured in terms of the proportion of fertile eggs laid by inseminated hens. Except when two systems are compared concurrently on the same strain of birds, this is a poor measure for assessing different sperm cryopreservation methods, since it varies with: the innate fecundity of the strain of birds used (never really quantified in absolute terms); the depth of intravaginal insemination (details often omitted); the insemination dose; and the numbers of inseminations (not always clear). As examples, 53% of fertile eggs were laid during one week after a 'deep' intravaginal insemination of 600 million spermatozoa (Lake and Stewart, 1978b) and 80–94% fertility was achieved following insemination of 400 million spermatozoa 3–4 cm into the vagina every 3 days for 'several' weeks (Kurbatov *et al.*, 1984). Both seem acceptable methods, but are incomplete in detail, so that a proper comparison is difficult. Comparison made by relating the fertilizing ability of frozen–thawed to control, unfrozen spermatozoa, as was done in each of these studies, is not particularly helpful, since the relationship between the proportion of fertile eggs produced by inseminated hens is non-linear. This is best demonstrated by the results shown in Figure 11.1. These show the inadequacy of using single insemination doses for comparing the fertilizing ability of cryopreserved and control spermatozoa and also that around 60 times more cryopreserved than control spermatozoa are required to enable fertilization of 50% of fertile eggs (Wishart, 1985). That this truly reflects the differences in the functional status of these spermatozoa was confirmed by demonstration that the numbers of cryopreserved spermatozoa which reach the perivitelline layer of the egg *in vivo* was only 1% of control, unfrozen spermatozoa (Alexander *et al.*, 1993).

The reason that this outcome is so poor, in comparison to mammalian systems, is likely to be the more stringent processes of vaginal transport of chicken spermatozoa and the fact that they are required to survive for several days within the oviducal sperm storage tubules, so that the hen can produce several fertile eggs (see Bakst *et al.*, 1994). Most functions or characteristics of chicken spermatozoa measured *in vitro* are only reduced to 20–50% of prefreeze levels by cryopreservation (Wishart, 1989; Donoghue and Wishart, 2000), so that the spermatozoa do not seem to be particularly susceptible to freezing damage. This discrepancy between the proportional loss of sperm function measurable *in vitro* and *in vivo* after insemination should be borne in mind when making preliminary assessments of any methodology by testing sperm function *in vitro*. Furthermore, it is recommended that sperm function before and after cryopreservation is best quantified as the numbers of spermatozoa able to reach the egg at fertilization (see Wishart, 1995b, 1996). These can be readily measured in laid eggs as trapped spermatozoa within the outer perivitelline layer (Wishart, 1997), or the holes left by their penetration through the inner perivitelline layer (Howarth and Donoghue, 1997).

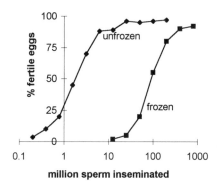

Figure 11.1: Effect of insemination dose on the fertility of fresh and cryopreserved chicken spermatozoa. Each point represents the mean proportion of fertile eggs laid by groups of hens during days 2–8 following intravaginal insemination. After Wishart (1985).

In general, avian sperm cryopreservation technology should be approached with a quantitative understanding of how avian fertility works, in terms of oviducal sperm transport and storage and sperm:egg interaction, so that the likely outcome of any procedure may be predicted. A brief outline of this is presented here and further detail may be found in several reviews (Bakst *et al.*, 1994; Wishart, 1995b, 1996).

In practice, all the protocols listed in Table 11.1 enable production of 50% or more fertile eggs in the week following an intravaginal insemination and the actual fertility figures may be obtained from the original work and from lists in other reviews (Busch *et al.*, 1991; Hammerstedt and Graham, 1992). However, even with normal spermatozoa, around 99% of spermatozoa are lost in the few centimetres between the site of insemination and the sperm storage tubules at the uterovaginal junction (see Bakst *et al.*, 1994) and, additionally, the intravaginal migration of spermatozoa varies greatly between different inseminations (Wishart *et al.*, 1992). With frozen–thawed spermatozoa these problems are even more exaggerated and one option for increasing the proportion of fertile eggs is to utilize deeper inseminations through the vagina into the uterus (Allen and Bobr, 1955) or to inseminate into the peritoneum (Brown *et al.*, 1963) or the infundibulum (Van Krey *et al.*, 1966). These techniques were developed to obtain fertility with glycerolated spermatozoa, which is negligible if inseminated into the vagina (see Hammerstedt and Graham, 1992). However, it remains unclear whether the poor fertility of glycerolated spermatozoa inseminated into the vagina involves a specific vagina–spermatozoa–glycerol interaction, or whether bypassing the vagina non-specifically increases the numbers of spermatozoa which reach the upper oviduct (see Bakst *et al.*, 1994). Breaching the uterovaginal junction, or subjecting the birds to minor surgery, is liable to interrupt the hen's laying cycle, but continues to find application (Bacon *et al.*, 1986; see Wishart, 1995a)

11.3 SPERMATOZOA FROM OTHER DOMESTIC SPECIES

11.3.1 Semen collection/preparation

Turkey spermatozoa are collected by the massage method, whilst semen from drakes and ganders may be collected by manual extrusion/manipulation of the phallus or by intercepting mating with a 'teaser' female (see Lake and Stewart, 1978a). Semen is prepared and diluted 1:1 or 1:2 in diluent/cryoprotectant solutions as for chicken semen.

11.3.2 Turkey spermatozoa

A system that produced good fertility from chicken spermatozoa, cryopreserved using glycerol (Lake *et al.*, 1981) or DMSO (Bakst and Sexton, 1979) and a programmable freezer, was not successful with turkey spermatozoa (P.E. Lake, personal communication; Bakst and Sexton, 1979). However, Sexton (1981) later reported some success with DMSO and others also found limited success with DMSO (Graham *et al.*, 1982; Zavos and Graham, 1983). Whilst this could be due to differences in the freezing/ thawing process, it could also result from the fact that more spermatozoa require to be inseminated to obtain fertile eggs with turkey spermatozoa (Wishart, 1996).

Schramm and Hübner (1988) obtained better fertility with 6–8% EG than with DMA (56 versus 33% fertile eggs) and found that sperm frozen in glass ampoules at −1°C/min down to −30°C had equivalent fertilizing ability to similar samples frozen in an alcohol bath at−40°C but better fertility than samples pelleted on solid carbon dioxide (72 versus 56 versus 19% fertile eggs). Kurbatov *et al.* (1985) used 8% DMA and the rotation method to obtain over 70% fertility and sperm frozen in pellets formed in liquid nitrogen produced similar fertility (Tur and Mavrodina, 1987) .

11.3.3 Drake spermatozoa

Kasyanenko and Kurbatov (1986) obtained 75% fertility from drake spermatozoa frozen with DMA in pellets on a plastic tray held in liquid nitrogen vapour whilst Kurbatov *et al.* (1988) used the rotation method and 4–5% DMA to obtain >90% fertility. Schramm and Hübner (1989) employed EG at 6–8% with programmable freezing at −1°C/min for Muscovy drake spermatozoa.

11.3.4 Gander spermatozoa

Andreev *et al.* (1984) cooled gander spermatozoa in a programmable freezer at −50°C/min and found that 15% EG and 10% DMF gave similar fertilities and Sakhatsky (1990) used a similar procedure with DMA. Mavrodina and Kurbatov (1983) froze gander spermatozoa as pellets formed at −185°C and found that 4% DMA was better than 5% EG which was, in turn, better than 3% DMSO.

11.4 SPERMATOZOA FROM NON-DOMESTICATED SPECIES

11.4.1 Semen collection

These birds are more likely to be held under 'natural' environment conditions and will respond to the photoperiod or other environmental signals by circannually entering breeding condition. The methods for semen collection from non-domestic birds include: massage (for pheasant: Durrant *et al.*, 1995; greater sandhill crane: Gee *et al.*, 1985; American kestrel: Brock *et al.*, 1983; budgerigar: Samour *et al.*, 1988); interruption of mating with a dummy female (Houbara bustard: Hartley *et al.*, 1999);

electroejaculation (Aleutian Canada goose: Gee and Sexton 1990); and semen deposition onto an imprinted person or object (peregrine falcon: Parkes *et al.*, 1986). A good review of these techniques is provided by Gee (1995).

11.4.2 Cryopreservation

A (hopefully) comprehensive list of avian species which have been bred using cryopreserved semen is shown in Table 11.3. The majority of these use the methods of Sexton (DMSO: Sexton, 1997) or Lake (glycerol: Lake *et al.*, 1981), presumably because of collaborative links with these researchers. With the American kestrel, however, several methods have been attempted and results with DMSO have been more

TABLE 11.3
Systems used successfully for production of progeny from non-domesticated avian species with cryopreserved spermatozoa

Species	Cryoprotectant	Cooling system	Reference
Sandhill crane	6% DMSO	0.5-ml plastic straws −1°C/min to −20°C then −50°C/min to −80°C in programmable freezer	Gee et al., 1985
Aleutian Canada goose	6% DMSO	0.5-ml plastic straws −1°C/min to −20°C then −50°C/min to −80°C in programmable freezer	Gee and Sexton, 1990
Impeyan Pheasant	4% DMSO	0.5-ml plastic straws −1°C/min to −20°C then −50°C/min to −80°C in programmable freezer	Durrant and Burch, 1991
American kestrel	6–10% DMSO	0.5-ml plastic straws −1°C/min to −20°C then −50°C/min to −80°C in programmable freezer	Gee et al., 1993
Peregrine falcon	13.6% glycerol	0.25-ml plastic straws −6°C/min in nitrogen vapour	Parks et al., 1996
Budgerigar	13.6% glycerol	polythene tubes −6°C/min to −70°C in programmabe freezer	Samour et al., 1988
American kestrel	12.3% DMA	0.5-ml plastic straws −6°C/min in nitrogen vapour	Brock and Bird, 1991
Silver pheasant	6% DMSO	0.5-ml plastic straws	Rose, 1996
Edward's pheasant	13% glycerol	−1°C/min to −20°C then −50°C/min to −80°C in programmable freezer	
Houbara bustard	8% DMA	Pellets formed directly in liquid nitrogen	Hartley et al., 1999

successful (14 fertile eggs out of 34: Gee *et al.*, 1993) than with DMA (7/23: Brock and Bird, 1991) and glycerol (2/6: Parks *et al.*, 1996). For all the reasons outlined earlier in this review, proper comparisons between these systems are inappropriate, but they do show a degree of success with the three cryoprotectants. The decision on which system to recommend for cryopreservation of spermatozoa from non-domesticated species may therefore be made on more practical criteria. The volumes and total sperm content of ejaculates are often low (see Gee, 1995) and post-thaw manipulation to remove glycerol by centrifugation (Samour *et al.*, 1988) or dialysis (Parks *et al.*, 1996) is likely to involve loss of a greater proportion of spermatozoa. More sophisticated programmable freezers will be expensive and less adaptable to field conditions. Thus, of the systems outlined in Table 11.3, the methods with DMA best satisfy these criteria, although other systems, especially those with DMSO, have more demonstrable effectiveness.

11.5 CRYOPRESERVATION OF EARLY CHICK EMBRYO CELLS

By the time the egg is laid, embryonic development in the chicken has progressed to produce a blastoderm of around 50 000 cells (Eyal-Giladi and Kochav, 1976). Earlier developmental stages take place *in utero* and it is technically complex to return cells from prelaid eggs to an equivalent developmental stage (Perry, 1988), so the cells that are available for cryopreservation are from laid or incubated eggs.

Cryopreservation of these cells *in situ* is impractical, since by the time the egg is laid the embryo already has a defined organizational structure which would be disarranged. So the principle for production of progeny from cryopreserved embryonic cells is to remove these from embryos and return them, after processing as single cell suspensions, to a host embryo. If the resultant embryo proves to be a germline chimaera, then the cells from an individual bird will have been preserved to form either spermatozoa or eggs. If germline chimaeras of both sexes can be produced from embryonic cells from different individuals of the same strain, then a strain will have been reconstituted completely from cryopreserved cells. The cells which have been successfully used for this technology are blastodermal cells from laid, unincubated eggs and primordial germ cells (PGCs). PGCs are the somatic precursors of oocytes and spermatozoa which first appear in the germinal crescent of primitive streak embryos. At around 50 hours of incubation, they migrate to the germinal ridge via the embryonic circulation, from which they can, by skilled manipulation, be removed, processed and replaced. A simplified outline of the two methods is provided below.

11.5.1 Blastodermal cells

Cells from the blastoderm of laid, unincubated eggs were collected and dissociated enzymatically. These were then suspended in a tissue culture medium at 4°C, to which

DMSO was added to a final concentration of 10% and transferred into plastic ampoules. They were then placed at −7°C in an alcohol bath, ice crystallization was seeded, and the samples were then cooled to −35°C at −1°C/min before plunging into liquid nitrogen. Thawing took place at 37°C. After removing dead cells and debris by density gradient centrifugation, approximately 500 frozen–thawed cells were injected into host embryos which had been γ-irradiated. Germline chimaeras were formed at a rate of around 10% and, the proportion of donor-derived progeny from mating these birds on maturity was approximately 14% (Kino et al., 1997; Etches et al., 1997).

11.5.2 Primordial germ cells

At around 50 hours of incubation, blood containing around 50 PGCs was removed from the dorsal aorta by micropipette. The PGCs were purified by density gradient centrifugation and suspended, at 4°C, in culture medium containing 10% DMSO. Samples in plastic cryovials were then cooled to −80°C at −1°C/min, before plunging into liquid nitrogen. Thawing took place in a waterbath at 4°C. Approximately 100 frozen–thawed PGCs were injected into the dorsal aorta of prepared host embryos, which were then transferred to a 'surrogate' eggshell for subsequent development. Approximately 10% of manipulated embryos survived to hatch and of those, 90% were germline chimaeras. Matings of the male and female germline chimaeras produced, on average, 11.5% donor-derived progeny (Naito et al., 1994).

REFERENCES

ALEXANDER, A., GRAHAM, J., HAMMERSTEDT, R. H. and BARBATO, G. F. (1993) 'Effects of genotype and cryopreservation of avian semen on fertility and number of perivitelline spermatozoa', Br. Poultry Sci. 34, 757–764.

ALLEN, T. E. and BOBR, L. W. (1955) 'The fertility of fowl spermatozoa in glycerol diluents after intrauterine insemination', Poultry Sci. 342, 1167–1169.

ANDREEV, V. I., SAKHATSKY, N. I. and OSTASHKO, F. I. (1984) 'Use of ethylene glycol and dimethylformamide as cryoprotectants for deep freezing of goose sperm', Ptitsevodstvo (Kiev) 37, 53–55.

ANSAH, G. A. and BUCKLAND, R. B. (1983) 'Eight generations of selection for duration of fertility of frozen-thawed semen in the chicken', Poultry Sci. 62, 1529–1538.

ANSAH, G. A., SEGURA, J. C. and BUCKLAND, R. B. (1985) 'Semen production, sperm quality, and their heritabilities as influenced by selection of fertility of frozen-thawed semen in the chicken', Poultry Sci. 64, 1801–1803.

BACON, L. D., SALTER, D. W., MOTTA, J. B., CRITTENDEN, L. B. and OGASAWARA, F. X. (1986) 'Cryopreservation of chicken semen of inbred or specialized strains', *Poultry Sci.* **65**, 1965–1971.

BAKST, M. R. (1990) 'Preservation of avian cells', in Crawford R.D. (ed.) *Poultry Breeding and Genetics*, Amsterdam: Elsevier. pp. 91–108

BAKST, M. R. and SEXTON, T. J. (1979) 'Fertilising capacity and ultrastructure of fowl and turkey spermatozoa before and after freezing', *J. Reprod. Fertil.* **28**, 108–120.

BAKST, M. R., WISHART, G. J. and BRILLARD, J.-P. (1994) 'Oviductal sperm selection, transport and storage in poultry', *Poultry Sci. Rev.* **5**, 117–143

BELLAGAMBA, F., CEROLINI, S. and CAVALCHINI, L. G. (1993) 'Cryopreservation of poultry semen: a review', *World's Poultry Sci. J.* **49**, 157–166.

BROCK, M. K. and BIRD, D. M. (1991) 'Prefreeze and postthaw effects of glycerol and dimethylacetamide on motility and fertilizing ability of American kestrel (*Falco sparverius*) spermatozoa', *J. Zoo Wildlife Med.* **22**, 453–459.

BROCK, M. K., BIRD, D. M. and ANSAH, G. A. (1983) 'Cryogenic preservation of spermatozoa of the American Kestrel', *Int. Zoo Yearbook* **23**, 15–20.

BROWN, J. E., HARRIS, G. C. and HOBBS, T. D. (1963) 'Effect of intraperitoneal insemination on egg production and fertilizing capacity of fresh and frozen chicken sperm', *Poultry Sci.* **52**, 810–815.

BURROWS, W. H. and QUINN, J. P. (1937) 'The collection of spermatozoa from the domestic fowl and turkey', *Poultry Sci.* **16**, 19–24.

BUSCH, W., LOHLE, K. and PETER, W. (1991) 'Spermaverdunnung und –konservierung', in *Kunstliche Besamung bei Nutztieren*, Stuttgart: Gustav Fischer Verlag Jena, pp. 614–632

BUSS, E. G. (1993) 'Cryopreservation of rooster sperm', *Poultry Sci.* **72**, 944–954.

BUSS, E. G. (1997) 'Cryopreservation of rooster sperm using glycerol and novel packaging technologies', in Bakst M. R. and Cecil H. C. (eds.) *Techniques for Semen Evaluation, Semen Storage and Fertility Determination*, Savoy, IL: The Poultry Science Association, pp. 78–79.

CHALA, T., SEIGNEURIN, F., BLESBOIS, E. and BRILLARD, J.-P. (1999) '*In vitro* comparison of fowl sperm viability in ejaculates frozen by three different techniques and relationship with subsequent fertility *in vivo*', *Cryobiology* **39**, 185–191.

DONOGHUE, A. M. and WISHART, G. J. (2000) 'Preservation of poultry semen', *Anim. Reprod. Sci.* **62**, 213–232.

DUPLAIX, M. and SEXTON, T. J. (1983) 'Effects of prefreeze treatment on the fertilizing capacity of unfrozen and frozen chicken semen: extender characteristics and dilution method', *Poultry Sci.* **62**, 2255–2260.

DUPLAIX, M. and SEXTON, T. J. (1984) 'Effects of type of freeze straw and thaw temperature on the fertilizing capacity of frozen chicken semen', *Poultry Sci.* **63**, 775–780.

DURRANT, B. S. and BURCH, C. (1991) 'Successful artificial insemination of cryopreserved pheasant semen', *J. Androl.* **12**, 56.

DURRANT, B. S., BURCH, C. D., YAMADA, J. K. and GOOD, J. (1995) 'Seminal characteristics and artificial insemination of Chinese pheasants, *Tragopan temminckii, Lophophorus impeyanus* and *Lophophorus ihuysii', Zoo Biology* **14**, 523–532.

ETCHES, R. J., LOBIN, S., STUNDEN, C. and GAVORA, J. S. (1997) 'Cryopreservation and future reconstitution of genetically defined stocks of chickens', *Poultry Sci. (Suppl.)* **38**, S50.

EYAL-GILADI, H. and KOCHAV, S. (1976) 'From cleavage to primitive streak formation: a complementary normal table and a new look at the first stage of the development of the chick I. General morphology', *Dev. Biol.* **49**, 321–337.

GEE, G. F. (1995) 'Artificial insemination and cryopreservation of semen from non-domestic birds', in Bakst, M.R and Wishart, G.J. (eds) *Proceedings of the First International Symposium on the Artificial Insemination of Poultry,* Savoy, IL: The Poultry Science Association, pp. 262–279.

GEE, G. F. and SEXTON, T. J. (1990) 'Cryopreservation of semen from the Aleutian Canada Goose', *Zoo Biol.* **9**, 361–371.

GEE, G. F., BAKST, M. R. and SEXTON, T. J. (1985) 'Cryogenic preservation of semen from the Greater Sandhill Crane', *Jo. Wildlife Mgmt.* **49**, 480–484.

GEE, G. F., MORRELL, C. A., FRANSON, J. C., PATTEE, O. H. (1993) 'Cryopreservation of American kestrel semen with dimethylsulfoxide', *J. Raptor Res.* **27**, 21–25.

GILL, S. P. S., BUSS, E. G. and MALLIS, R. J. (1996) 'Cryopreservation of rooster semen in thirteen and sixteen percent glycerol', *Poultry Sci.* **75**, 254–256.

GRAHAM, E. F., NELSON, D. S. and SCHMEL, M. K. L. (1982) 'Development of an extender for frozen turkey semen 2. Fertility trials', *Poultry Sci.* **61**, 558–563.

HAIJE, U. (1990) 'Evaluation and cryopreservation of fowl semen (*Gallus domesticus*)', Doctoral thesis, University of Utrecht.

HAMMERSTEDT, R. H. (1995) 'Cryopreservation of poultry semen–current status and economics', in Bakst M. R. and Wishart G. J. (eds) *Proceedings of the First International Symposium on the Artificial Insemination of Poultry,* Savoy, IL: The Poultry Science Association, pp. 229–250,

HAMMERSTEDT, R. H. (1997) 'Cryopreservation of rooster sperm using glycerol', in Bakst M. R.and Cecil, H. C. (eds) *Techniques for Semen Evaluation, Semen Storage and Fertility Determination,* Savoy, IL: The Poultry Science Association, pp. 75–77.

HAMMERSTEDT, R. H. and GRAHAM, J. K. (1992) 'Cryopreservation of poultry sperm: the enigma of glycerol', *Cryobiology* **29**, 26–38.

HARTLEY, P. S. (1999) 'The cryopreservation of semen from non-domestic avian species'. MPhil thesis, University of Abertay Dundee.

HARTLEY, P. S., DAWSON, B., LINDSAY, C., McCORMICK, P. and WISHART, G. (1998) 'Cryopreservation of Houbara semen: a pilot study', *Zoo Biol.* **18**, 147–152.

HOWARTH, B. and DONOGHUE, A. M. (1997) 'Determination of holes made by sperm in the perivitelline layer of laid eggs', in Bakst M. R.and Cecil H. C. (eds) *Techniques for Semen Evaluation, Semen Storage and Fertility Determination*, Savoy, IL: The Poultry Science Association, pp. 93–97.

HÜBNER, V. R. and SCHRAMM, G.-P. (1988a) 'Studies into the influence of genotype and individual bird differences on the cryoconservation of cock spermatozoa', *Monatsh. Veterinarmed.* **43**, 647–649.

HÜBNER, V. R. and SCHRAMM, G.-P. (1988b) 'Studies into cryoprotective potentials of ethylene glycol and dimethylacetamide for deep-freeze preservation of cock sperm', *Monatsh. Veterinarmed.* **43**, 279–282.

HÜBNER, V. R., LOHLE, K. and SCHRAMM, G.-P. (1994) 'The artificial insemination of poultry in retrospect , Long-term storage of poultry sperm', *Arch. Tierzucht.* **37**, 77–87.

KASYANENKO, S. V. and KURBATOV, A. D. (1986) 'Drake sperm cryopreservation', *Ptitsevodstvo (Moscow)* **6**, 27–28.

KINO, K., PAIN, B., LIEBO, S. P., COCHRAN, M., CLARK, M. E. and ETCHES, R. J. (1997) 'Production of chicken chimeras from injection of frozen-thawed blastodermal cells', *Poultry Sci.* **76**, 753–760.

KURBATOV, A. D., NARUBINA, L., BUBLIAEVA, G. B. and MOSKALENKO, L. I. (1979) 'Testing diluents used for cock sperm dilution, storage and deep freezing', *Sbornik Nauchnich Trudov VNIRGJ* **24**, 150–154.

KURBATOV, A. D., NARUBINA, L., IVANOV, B. G., BUBLIAEVA, G. B. and MOSKALENKO, L. I. (1980) 'Effect of ETG on cock sperm at temperatures above and below 0°C', *Bull. VNIRGJ* **43**, 15–20.

KURBATOV, A. D., NARUBINA, L., BUBLIAEVA, G. and TSELUTIN, K. V. (1984) 'Cryopreservation of cock semen', *Pitsevodstvo* **11**, 28–29.

KURBATOV, A., MAVRODINA, T. and TUR, B. (1985) 'Artificial insemination of turkeys with frozen sperm', *Ptitsevodstvo (Moscow)* **2**, 19–20.

KURBATOV, A. D., PLATOV, E. M., KORBAN, N. V. and TSELUTIN, K. (1988) 'Cryopreservation of farm animal sperm', *Agropromizdat, Leningrad*, pp. 195–245.

LAKE, P. E. (1957) 'Fowl semen as collected by the massage method', *J. Agricult. Sci., Cambridge* **49**, 120–126.

LAKE, P. E. (1986) 'The history and future of the cryopreservation of avian germ plasm', *Poultry Sci.* **65**, 1–15.

LAKE, P. E. and RAVIE, O. (1984) 'An exploration of cryoprotective compounds for fowl spermatozoa', *Br. Poultry Sci.* **25**, 145–150.

LAKE P. E. and STEWART, J. M. (1978a) *Artificial Insemination in Poultry, Ministry of Agriculture, Fisheries and Food, Bulletin 213*, London: HMSO.

LAKE, P. E. and STEWART, J. M. (1978b) 'Preservation of fowl semen in liquid nitrogen – an improved method', *Br. Poultry Sci.* **19**, 187–194.

LAKE, P. E., RAVIE, O. and MCADAM, J. (1981) 'Preservation of fowl semen in liquid nitrogen : application to breeding programmes', *British Poultry Science*, **22**, 71–77.

LEWIS, P. D. and PERRY, G. C. (1995) 'Effects of lighting on reproduction in poultry', in Hunton, P. (ed.) *Poultry Production*, Amsterdam: Elsevier, pp. 359–388.

MAEDA, T., TERADA, T. and TSUTSUMI, Y. (1984) 'Comparative study of the effects of various cryoprotectants in preserving the morphology of frozen and thawed fowl spermatozoa', *Br. Poultry Sci.* **25**, 547–553.

MAVRODINA, T. G. and KURBATOV, A. D. (1983) 'Cryopreservation of gander sperm', *Sbornik Nauchnikh Trudov VNIRGJ, Leningrad*, pp. 10–17.

NAITO, M., TAJIMA, A., TAGAMI, T., YASUDA, Y. and KUWANA, T. (1994) 'Preservation of chick primordial germ cells in liquid nitrogen and subsequent production of viable offspring', *J. Reprod. Fertil.* **102**, 321–325.

NARUBINA, L. E., KURBATOV, A. D., BUBLIAYEVA, G. V. and TSELUTIN, K. V. (1988) 'Improvement of the method of cock sperm thawing', in *Proceedings of Conference of National Branch of WPSA, Riga*, pp. 46–47.

OTPUSCHENNIKOV, V. F. and KRIVTSOVA, E. B. (1983) 'Diluents for cock sperm cryopreservation and thawing', in *Sbornik Nauchnich Trudov VNITIP, Zagorsk*, pp. 34–40.

PARKS, J. E., HECK, W. R. and HARDASWICK, V. (1996) 'Cryopreservation of peregrine falcon semen and postthaw dialysis to remove glycerol', *Raptor Res.* **20**, 15–20.

PERRY, M. M. (1988) 'A complete culture system for the chick embryo', *Nature, Lond.* **331**, 70–72.

PHILLIPS, J. J., BRAMWELL, R. K. and GRAHAM, J. K. (1996) 'Cryopreservation of rooster sperm using methyl cellulose', *Poultry Sci.* **75**, 915–923.

POLGE, C. (1951) 'Functional survival of fowl spermatozoa after freezing at $-70°C$', *Nature, Lond.*, **167**, 949–950.

CHAPTER 11

RAVIE, O. and LAKE, P. E. (1984) 'A comparison of glass ampoules and plastic straws as receptacles for freezing fowl semen', *Cryo-Letters* **5**, 201–208.

ROSE, K. A. (1996) 'Evaluation, liquid storage and cryopreservation of silver pheasant (*Lophura nycthemera*) and Edwards pheasant (*Lophura edwards*) Semen', D.V.Sc. thesis, University of Guelph.

SAKHATSKY, N. I. (1990) 'Preservation of poultry germplasm', Doctoral thesis, Ukrainian Poultry Research Institute, Borky.

SAMOUR, J. H., MARKHAM, J. A., MOORE, H. D. M. and WATSON, P. F. (1988) 'Semen cryopreservation and artificial insemination in budgerigars (*Melopsittacus undulatus*)', *J. Zool, Lond.* **216**, 169–176.

SCHRAMM, G.-P. (1991) 'Suitability of different antifreeze agents for cryoprotection of cock sperm', *Monatsh. Veterinarmed.* **46**, 438–440.

SCHRAMM, G.-P. and HÜBNER, R. (1988) 'Effects of different cryoprotectives and deep freeze techniques on the reproductive potential of turkey sperm after prolonged storage', *Monatsh. Veterinarmed.* **43**, 426–427.

SCHRAMM, G.-P. and HÜBNER, R. (1989) 'Konservierung von Geflügelsperma', *Arch. Tierz* **32**, 51–61.

SEIGNEURIN, F. and BLESBOIS, E. (1995) 'Effects of the freezing rate on viability and fertility of frozen-thawed fowl spermatozoa', *Theriogenology* **43**, 1351–1358.

SEXTON, T. J. (1981) 'Development of a commercial method for freezing turkey semen 1. Effect of prefreeze techniques on the fertility of frozen and frozen-thawed semen', *Poultry Sci.* **60**, 1567–1572.

SEXTON, T. J. (1997) 'Semen cryopreservation with dimethylsulfoxide', in Bakst M. R. and Cecil H. C. (eds) *Techniques for Semen Evaluation, Semen Storage and Fertility Determination*, Savoy, IL: The Poultry Science Association, pp. 72–74.

STEELE, M. G. and WISHART, G. J. (1996) 'The effect of removing surface-associated proteins from viable chicken spermatozoa on sperm function *in vitro* and *in vivo*', *Anim. Reprod. Sci.* **45**, 139–147.

SURAI, P. F. and WISHART, G. J. (1996) 'Poultry artificial insemination technology in the countries of the former USSR', *World's Poultry Sci. J.* **52**, 227–243.

TAJIMA, A., GRAHAM, E. F., and HAWKINS, D. M. (1989) 'Estimation of the relative fertilizing ability of frozen chicken spermatozoa using a heterospermic competition method', *J. Reprod. Fertil.* **85**, 1–5.

TAJIMA, A., GRAHAM, E. F., SHOFFNER, R. N., OTIS, J. S. and HAWKINS, D. M. (1990) 'Research note: cryopreservation of semen from unique lines of chicken germ plasm', *Poultry Sci.* **69**, 999–1002.

TERADA T, ASHIZAWA K, MAEDA T. and TSUTSUMI Y. (1989) 'Efficacy of trehalose in cryopreservation of chicken spermatozoa', *Jpn J. Anim. Reprod.* **35**, 20–25.

TERESCHENKO, A. V., ARTEMENKO, A. B. and SOKHATSKY, N. I. (1992) 'Cryopreservation of chicken semen', *Proc. 12th Int. Congr. Anim. Reprod.* (The Hague) Vol. 3, 1602–1604.

TSELUTIN, K. (1982) 'Effect of thawing method on activity, viability and fertilizing capacity of frozen cock sperm', *Bull. VNIRGJ* **57**, 20–26.

TSELUTIN, K., NARUBINA, L., MAVRODINA, T. and TUR, B. (1995) 'Cryopreservation of poultry semen', *Br. Poultry Sci.* **36**, 805–811.

TSELUTIN, K., SEIGNEURIN, F. and BLESBOIS, E. (1999) 'Comparison of cryoprotectants amd methods of cryopreservation of fowl spermatozoa', *Poultry Sci.* **78**, 586–590.

TUR, B. and MAVRODINA, T. (1987) 'Turkey sperm cryopreservation', *Ptitsevodstvo (Moscow)* **8**, 28–29.

VAN KREY, H. P., OGASAWARA, F. X. and LORENZ, F. W. (1966) 'Distribution of spermatozoa in the oviduct and fertility in domestic birds IV. Fertility of spermatozoa from infundibular and uterovaginal glands', *J. Reprod. Fertil.* **11**, 257–262.

VAN VOORST, A. V. and LEENSTRA, F. R. (1994) 'Fertility rate of daily collected and cryopreserved fowl semen', *Poultry Sci.* **74**, 136–140.

WATANABE, M. and TERADA, T. (1980) 'Studies on the deep freezing of fowl semen in pellet form,' in *Proceedings of the 9th International Congress on Animal Reproduction and AI (Madrid)*, Vol. 5, pp. 477–479.

WATANABE, M., TERADA, T. and SHIRAKAWA, Y. (1977) 'A diluent for deep freezing preservation of fowl spermatozoa', *J. Faculty of Fisheries and Animal Husbandry of Hiroshima University* **16**, 59–64.

WISHART, G. J. (1985) 'Quantitation of the fertilizing ability of fresh compared with frozen and thawed fowl spermatozoa', *Br. Poultry Sci.* **26**, 375–380.

WISHART, G. J. (1989) 'Physiological changes in fowl and turkey spermatozoa during in vitro storage', *Br. Poultry Sci.* **30**, 443–454.

WISHART, G. J. (1995a) 'Cryopreservation of Avian Spermatozoa', in Day, J. G. and McLellan, M. R. (eds) *Cryopreservation and Freeze-Drying Protocols. Methods in Molecular Biology*, Vol. 38, Totowa, NJ: Humana Press, pp. 167–177.

WISHART, G. J. (1995b) 'New approaches to evaluating male and female fertility', in Bakst, M. R. and Wishart, G. J. (eds) *Proceedings of the First International Symposium on the Artificial Insemination of Poultry*, Savoy, IL: The Poultry Science Association, pp. 207–223.

WISHART, G. J. (1996) 'How fertility works', *Poultry Int.* **35**, 54–58.

WISHART, G. J. (1997) 'Predicting the duration of fertility by counting sperm in the perivitelline layer of laid eggs', in Bakst, M. R. and Cecil, H. C. (eds) *Techniques for Semen Evaluation, Semen Storage and Fertility Determination*, Savoy, IL: The Poultry Science Association, pp. 89–92.

WISHART, G. J. and HARTLEY, P. S. (1998) 'Cryoconservation of avian species', *Cryo-Letters Suppl. 1*, 39–46.

WISHART, G. J., STAINES, H. J. and STEELE, M. G. (1992) 'A method for predicting impending infertility in naturally-mated chickens and demonstration of gross variation in sperm transfer efficiency', in *Proceedings of the XIX World's Poultry Science Congress, Amsterdam*, Ponsen and Looijen, Wageningen, pp. 631–634.

YERASHEVICH, V. S. and SVIRIDOVA, S. (1990) 'Use of cryopreserved sperm', *Ptitsevodstvo (Moscow)* **3**, 23–25.

ZAVOS, P. M. and GRAHAM, E. F. (1983) 'Effects of various degrees of supercooling and nucleation temperatures on fertility of frozen turkey spermatozoa', *Cryobiology* **20**, 553–559.

Germplasm Conservation in Marsupials

S. D. JOHNSTON[1] AND W. V. HOLT[2]

[1]School of Veterinary Science and Animal Production,
University of Queensland, Brisbane, Queensland 4072, Australia
[2]The Institute of Zoology, The Zoological Society of London,
Regent's Park, London NW1 4RY, UK

Contents

12.1   INTRODUCTION

Artificial breeding of marsupials has been reviewed by Rodger (1990), Tribe *et al.* (1994), Taggart *et al.* (1997), Mate *et al.* (1998) and Johnston (1994, 1999). All authors reflect on the advantages of reproductive technologies to both the captive management (George, 1988) and conservation of this taxon, presenting similar arguments to those proposed for eutherian species (Wildt *et al.*, 1997). Although such arguments are very persuasive, the tangible benefits of this technology have yet to materialize, the koala being the only marsupial that has been produced by means of artificial insemination so far (Johnston, 1999)

   Lack of progress in the use of assisted reproductive technology (ART) in the marsupials may be partly attributed to the relative immaturity of this discipline and the absence of financial incentives with respect to the commercial applications of the research (Johnston, 1994). It would also be fair to say that many conservation managers still tend to view artificial breeding with a degree of warranted suspicion (Soulé, 1992), their reluctance making it difficult to access populations of captive marsupials, particularly endangered species. However, by far the most significant limitation to the widespread use of ART in marsupials is an inadequate comprehension of the reproductive processes that underpin this diverse fauna. Although there have been significant advances in our knowledge of marsupial reproduction in the past ten years, the majority of this information is limited to two or three common or laboratory-based species, the brush-tail possum (*Trichosurus vulpecula*), Tammar wallaby (*Macropus eugenii*) and fat-tailed dunnart (*Sminthopsis crassicaudata*). However, even in these species, there is still only partial understanding regarding hormonal control of the oestrous cycle or knowledge of the events of fertilization, information critical for advanced breeding techniques such as AI and IVF. In addition, marsupial AI presents a series of technical challenges with respect to the placement of semen, as females have lateral vaginae and cul-de-sac compartments of varying degrees of complexity (Tyndale-Biscoe and Renfree, 1987); these structures make deposition of semen into or close to the cervix via the urogenital canal virtually impossible.

   Currently there are five marsupial species listed as critically endangered and a further seventeen considered endangered (Schedule 1, Endangered Species Act, Australian Nature Conservation Agency, Canberra, July 1994). While the use of ART and the establishment of genetic resource banks are agenda issues for Australian conservation agencies (Maxwell *et al.*, 1996), there is currently no species of marsupial, endangered or otherwise, consistently being produced by means of artificial breeding programmes. Nevertheless, interest in the potential use of reproductive technology in marsupial populations continues to gain acceptance and credibility as the information base expands. This chapter presents a brief introduction into some general features of marsupial reproduction that might represent challenges to its progress and future application as well as an overview of the use and development of marsupial ART as it stands at the start of the new millennium.

12.2 MARSUPIAL REPRODUCTION: CHALLENGES IN THE USE OF ASSISTED REPRODUCTION TECHNOLOGY

Having evolved from common origins about 60 million years ago, eutherian and metatherian species now exhibit a variety of anatomical and physiological differences, none more striking than those associated with reproduction. A detailed knowledge of these reproductive idiosyncrasies is extremely important in order to develop specific protocols for marsupial ART. Those not familiar with the diversity of reproductive form and function in this taxa may mistakenly develop a blanket approach to ART based upon the application of similar technology in eutherian species. The quoll and the kangaroo, for example, are as diverse in their respective modes of reproduction as are domestic cats and cattle.

12.2.1 Male marsupial reproduction

While the reproductive tract of the male marsupial differs from the eutherian counterpart in lacking seminal vesicles, coagulating glands and ampullae, they do possess a comparatively enlarged prostate and a well-developed series of bulbo-urethral glands (Figure 12.1). Only the prostate gland shows evidence of diverse morphology (Rodger and Hughes, 1973), the functional significance of which may be important to the processes involved with electroejaculation. In all the macropodids so far examined, the accessory glands produce a viscous seminal fluid that coagulates postejaculation into a dense rubbery consistency (Rodger and White, 1975). This phenomenon makes assessment of standard seminal characteristics extremely difficult. Other species such as the koala (*Phascolarctos cinereus*) and brush-tail possum produce an ejaculum that does not normally coagulate and can be assessed in the normal manner. The seminal biochemistry of marsupials is also different to that found in eutherian species in that fructose is only found in low concentrations and *N*-acetylglucosamine or glyogen are the major sugars (Tyndale-Biscoe and Renfree, 1987). These differences, apart from perhaps influencing the osmotic potential of the seminal plasma, should play little role in the preservation of the sperm *ex situ* as *M. eugenii* spermatozoa are capable of utilizing endogenous substrates for prolonged metabolism (Murdoch and Jones, 1994). Such variety in the form and function of male marsupials means that procedures such as semen collection, manipulation and preservation may require species-specific protocols.

Marsupial spermatozoa are also fundamentally different to those of eutherian spermatozoa with respect to their mode of production, morphology and physiology.

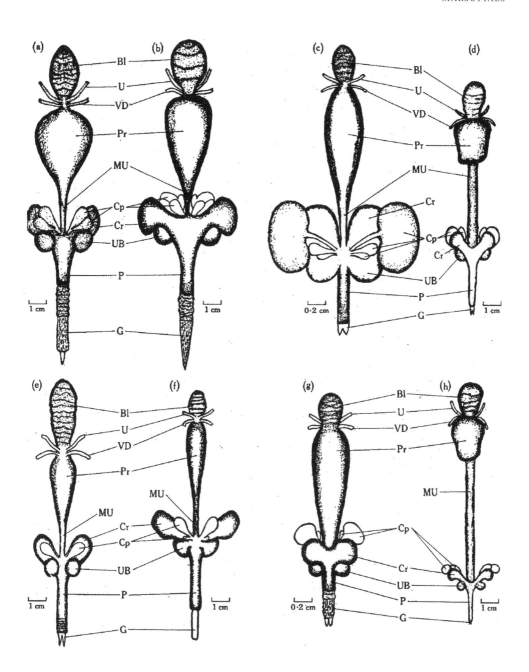

Figure 12.1: Male reproductive tracts of (a) *Trichosurus vulpecula* (dorsal view); (b) *Macropus eugenii* (ventral view); (c) *Antechinus stuartii* (dorsal view); (d) *Perameles nasuta* (ventral view); (e) *Pseudocheirus peregrinus* (dorsal view); (f) *Potorous tridactylus* (dorsal view); (g) *Sminthopsis crassicaudata* (ventral view); (h) *Isoodon macrourus* (ventral view). Bl, bladder; Cp, Cowper's gland; Cr, crus penis; G, glans penis; MU, membranous urethra; P, penis; Pr, prostate; U, ureter; UB, urethral bulb; VD, vas deferens.

Reproduced from Rodger and Hughes (1973) with permission of the publisher.

During spermiogenesis, condensation of nuclear contents occurs in a dorsoventral plane so that the spermatozoa take on a 'thumb-tack or T-shaped' appearance. Depending on the species, the sperm head rotates parallel to the longitudinal axis of the flagellum during either the remaining stages of spermiogenesis or following epididymidal transit (Taggart *et al.*, 1995). Marsupial sperm also exhibit other morphological changes during epididymal transit associated with maturation of the acrosome and midpiece region, much of which is taxon dependent; hence, sperm morphology is a major means of investigating phylogenetic relationships (Temple-Smith *et. al.* 1996). The complexity of the marsupial sperm cytoskeleton as described by transmission electron microscope may be one of the factors contributing to the difficulty of cryopreservation. Sperm membrane composition remains to be characterized for any marsupial.

In addition, the marsupial sperm nucleus has no disulphide linkages to stabilize its chromatin and as such the spermatozoa may be susceptible to decondensation under certain environmental conditions (Cummins, 1980). For example, post-thaw cryopreserved koala spermatozoa show a tendency to decondense within 2 hours of incubation at 35°C (Johnston, unpublished observations).

This phenomenon is in direct contrast to the marsupial acrosome, which shows remarkable resilience to repeated freeze–thaw procedures (Sistena *et al.*, 1993c) that would typically render cryo-damage to the acrosomes of eutherian spermatozoa (Watson, 1979). Studies by Mate and Rodger (1991) and Sistena *et al.* (1993a,b) have also revealed fundamental differences in acrosome function; substances traditionally used to induce the acrosome reaction in eutherian spermatozoa do not have the same effect on marsupial spermatozoa (Mate and Rodger, 1991).

Sperm from species within the Thylacomyidae and Peramelidae possess a flagellum that completely dissociates from the original implantation fossa of the sperm head and migrates cranially into a secondary implantation fossa (Taggart *et al.*, 1995; Johnston *et al.*, 1995). The spermatozoa of the honey possum (*Tarsipes rostratus*) (Cummins and Woodall, 1985) are the largest sperm cells so far described, and along with members of the Dasyuridae show unusual features in the size and displacement of coarse fibres of the axoneme. One could imagine that spermatozoa from all these species might represent a significant challenge to cryopreserve successfully, although Johnston *et al.* (1994b) have reported successful cryopreservation of greater bilby (*Macrotis lagotis*) spermatoozoa after epididymal recovery.

12.2.2 Female marsupial reproduction

Perhaps the most demanding of all the unique aspects of marsupial reproduction with respect to artificial breeding is the reproductive anatomy of the female (Figure 12.2). The caudal region of the female reproductive tract typically possesses two lateral

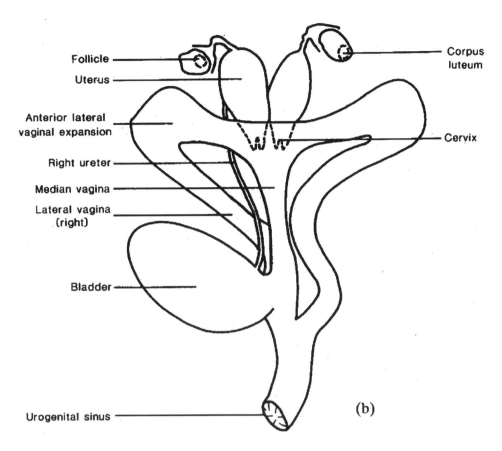

Follicle

Uterus

Anterior lateral
vaginal expansion

Right ureter

Median vagina

Lateral vagina
(right)

Bladder

Corpus
luteum

Cervix

Urogenital sinus

(b)

Figure 12.2: Line drawing of the female reproductive tract of the Tammar wallaby showing the double cervix, separate right and left uterine horns, and the lateral vaginal canals. The drawing was made from an oestrous parturient animal. Reproduced from Renfree (1983) with the permission of the publisher.

vaginae, each of which opens into a urogenital sinus that also receives the urethra. Semen is presumably deposited during copulation into the cranial portion of the urogenital sinus, from where it moves through the lateral vaginae towards the uterus and oviducts via the cervices. Unlike the reproductive anatomy of male marsupials, there is great diversity in the form of the female reproductive tract, both between (Tyndale-Biscoe and Renfree, 1987) and even within the same species (e.g. koala; Johnston, 1999). Such anatomical specializations have to be taken into account when considering the development and routes of artificial insemination procedures.

The diversity of female reproductive form and function in the Marsupialia is often underestimated by those not familiar with this group. Other popular misconceptions regarding marsupial reproduction include the notion that all marsupials possess a well-defined pouch, lack a placenta and/or are able to breed continuously throughout the year. The fact is that some dasyurid species do not possess a pouch at all; the Peramelidae have a well-developed invasive chorioallantoic placenta, and the majority of species so far studied are seasonal breeders. It also needs to be emphasized that metatherian reproduction is no less efficient or evolved than that of eutherian reproduction, but they are end points of two evolutionary lines with different trajectories from similar beginnings (Tyndale-Biscoe and Renfree, 1987).

To illustrate the scarcity of information surrounding the basic reproductive physiology of female marsupials we currently only have combined data on progestagen and oestrogen profiles from four species (*M. eugenii* summarized by Tyndale-Biscoe and Renfree, 1987; *Didelphis virginiana*, Harder and Fleming, 1981; *T. vulpecula*, Curlewis *et al.*, 1985; *P. cinereus*, Johnston *et al.*, 2000b). Oestrous detection and synchronization remains a major limitation to the development of assisted breeding programmes in marsupials (Mate *et al.*, 1998).

Another major difference in the gamete biology of marsupials and eutherian mammals is that the oocyte continues throughout folliculogenesis (Rodger *et al.*, 1992), so that marsupial oocytes are generally two- to three-fold greater in size than those of eutherian species. In addition, the zonae pellucidae of the majority of marsupial species (the koala being the exception, Johnston, 1999) are significantly thinner than those of eutherian species (Tyndale-Biscoe and Renfree, 1987). After fertilization, the developing embryo becomes coated with oviductal glycoproteins that give rise to a mucoid layer that prevents entry of excess spermatozoa and later becomes surrounded by the shell membrane. Early embryonic division results in the extrusion of a yolk body and, in some species, the blastocysts exhibit a degree of polarity reminiscent of amphibian development (Selwood, 1994). All these factors will undoubtedly influence the method and success of oocyte and embryo cryopreservation procedures.

Although the reproductive biology of many individual species still remains uncharacterized, there is at least now sufficient knowledge of the essential differences in the mode of reproductive function within the Metatheria. In an effort to classify the various reproductive patterns found in marsupials, Tyndale-Biscoe and Renfree (1987) proposed four categories, which are helpful in making sense of the complex reproductive diversity in this group:

Group 1. Polyovular, polyoestrous species in which the gestation period is considerably shorter than the oestrous cycle and that coincides with the luteal phase; postpartum oestrus and ovulation are suppressed during lactation. This pattern is representative of the *Didelphidae, Dasyuridae, Petauridae, Phalangeridae* and a single member of the Burramyidae, *Burramys parvus*. This group also contains the monoestrous species such as *Antechinus* spp. that presumably evolved from a polyoestrous condition and the koala, the luteal phase of which is induced following coital stimulation (Johnston *et al.*, 2000b). Group 1 is the most diverse of the reproductive categories and undoubtedly requires further sub-division.

Group 2. Polyoestrous, polyovular species with an ultrashort gestation period (12–14 days), shorter than the luteal phase and which is unusually prolonged into lactation. Species in this group include the Peramelidae and Thlyacomyidae. The Peramelidae also possess a well-developed chorioallantoic placenta, the function of which requires further investigation.

Group 3. Monovular, polyoestrous species in which the gestation period is almost the same length as the oestrous cycle and extends into the subsequent follicular phase so that postpartum oestrus and ovulation occurs. During lactation ovarian activity is arrested and, if fertilization does occur, the embryo remains arrested as a blastocyst in diapause. The majority of the Macropodidae and Potoroidae share this reproductive pattern, although some exceptions do occur, notably eastern grey kangaroo (*M. giganteus*), western grey kangaroo (*M. fuliginosus*) and the whiptail wallaby, *M. parryi*. These species have a prolonged gestation resulting from an extended luteal phase so that postpartum ovulation rarely occurs. *Wallabia bicolor* is unique in possessing a gestation period substantially longer than its oestrous cycle length; endocrinological studies are currently underway to investigate this unusual mode of reproduction (Johnston, unpublished).

Group 4. Polyoestrous, polyovular species, with a prolonged preluteal phase and gestation that includes a long period of embryonic diapause. Whether diapause is controlled by lactation or is obligatory is unclear. Species in this group include members of the Burramyidae (except *Burramys parvus*) and the Tarsipedidae.

In the majority of marsupials, a short period of embryonic differentiation *in utero,* less than the duration of an oestrous cycle, is followed by the birth of an altricial fetus so that their primary reproductive investment is placed in lactation rather than in gestation and placentation. In the Macropodidae, the lactation system is so well refined that they exhibit concurrent asynchronous lactation (Tyndale-Biscoe and Renfree, 1987). This unique form of development lends itself to manipulative procedures such as pouch young transfer (Merchant and Sharman, 1966) that potentially have similar outcomes to that of embryo transfer technology in domestic farm species.

Understanding the reproductive biology of marsupials is crucially important for programmes designed to prevent population growth or the total extinction of highly endangered populations. However, the degree of evolutionary divergence within the Marsupialia suggests that the development of generic reproductive technologies is unlikely and that a species – or at least a family – specific approach is required (Johnston, 1999).

CHAPTER 12

12.3 ASSISTED BREEDING TECHNOLOGY IN MARSUPIALS – SUMMARY

12.3.1 Semen collection

Johnston (1994) has recently reviewed and tabulated the use of electroejaculation in marsupials as a means of obtaining semen for research and for conservation purposes. The technique has been successfully extended to at least twelve marsupial species representing five families (Phalangeridae, Peramelidae, Phascolarctidae, Vombatidae and Macropodidae; Johnston *et al.*, 1997b); however, many successful one-off attempts have not been reported in the scientific literature. For example, Johnston *et al.*, (unpublished data) have recently collected semen from the Tasmanian devil *(Sarcophilus harrisii)*. Semen collection in other species (Tammar wallaby, brush-tail possum, eastern grey kangaroo and koala) is now considered routine and commonly used in studies of spermatology and/or AI.

The technique of electroejaculation differs very little from that used with other taxa and needs no detailed description, although Rodger and Pollitt (1981) have indicated that stimulation of the prostatic urethra was an important determinant of successful semen collection. All electroejaculation procedures in marsupials require the animal to be placed under general anaesthesia but this is generally not an impediment for field applicability (Taggart *et al.*, 1996b; Johnston *et al.*, 1997a). Ejaculate coagulation is a consistent feature of kangaroo and wallaby ejaculates (Rodger and White, 1975), and occasionally has also been reported to occur in koala electroejaculates (Johnston *et al.*, 1994a). There is no consistent method of avoiding this problem in the macropodidae, but sperm recovery can be achieved by swim-up methods detailed by Sistena *et al.* (1993a). Johnston (1999) has suggested that the kangaroo sperm coagulum may be worth investigating as a storage or deposition medium for sperm encapsulation experiments.

It is worth noting that electroejaculation is still not a routine procedure for most species of marsupials (12 of 249), particularly the smaller dasyurid species. This may be related to the highly seasonal nature of reproduction in some of these species, their peculiar mating strategies and/or the low number of spermatozoa found in the ejaculate of these species. Perhaps methods of pharmaceutical ejaculation currently being developed in muridae (Dr Ian Gunn, Monash University, Melbourne, Australia, personal communication) will be suitable for dasyurid species. It is particularly important to develop successful ART in these species, as while some do breed reasonably well in captivity, the majority have a short generation length and therefore are ecologically vulnerable.

Semen has been successfully collected by means of an artificial vagina (AV) from the koala (Biery, 1991; Johnston *et al.*, 1997a). In the technique reported by Johnston *et al.*

(1997a) a standard ovine AV was modified for use by reducing its length to 85 mm to accommodate the length of the erect koala penis. Semen collection involved identifying a female in oestrus, putting her on a vertical tree pole approximately 1.5 m above the ground, then placing a male immediately underneath her. Once the male secured a copulatory position, he was allowed to achieve intromission and thrust his penis several times into the female's urogenital sinus before the penis was manually diverted into the AV. In marked contrast to the situation with most species, the koala required little if any training prior to service. While the technique offers a reliable and non-invasive method of collecting semen from captive koalas, it is unlikely to replace electroejaculation for small captive or free-range populations. The success of the AV collection procedure can be directly related to the unique reproductive behaviour and physiology of this species; it will be interesting to see whether semen from other marsupials can be collected in a similar manner.

Spermatozoa can also be salvaged opportunistically directly from the caudae epididymides of necropsied marsupials. Under these circumstances it is useful to know that sperm viability in some species can be retained for several days, provided the epididymides are left undisturbed in the scrotum and refrigerated at 4°C. Taggart et al. (1996a) specifically investigated the maintenance of sperm viability in stored caudae epididymides of the fat-tailed dunnart. By examining epididymal spermatozoa that had been stored in situ for up to 8 days at 4°C, they were able to determine that motile spermatozoa (15–39%) could still be obtained after a week of storage. However, these authors also made the point that very few spermatozoa could be obtained from the epididymis of a single fat-tailed dunnart, a consequence of the mating strategy adopted by this species. This limitation caused considerable difficulty in obtaining sufficient spermatozoa for an investigation, and may seriously prejudice the practicality of genetic resource bank technology for the smaller dasyurid marsupials. Arguably, as small numbers of frozen/thawed mouse spermatozoa are used for in vitro fertilization and, moreover, single human spermatozoa are now being cryopreserved for use with intracytoplasmic sperm injection (Cohen et al., 1997), there should be no reason for this to be a serious disadvantage. However, it has to be recognized that these are medical or biotechnological procedures. It is unlikely that such intensive approaches would be practical enough for the purpose of serious wildlife conservation, unless a species were on the verge of extinction. Even then, this type of technology may not be a sensible conservation option.

12.3.2 Semen manipulation

If sperm are to remain viable for manipulation or preservation, their metabolic activity must be reduced by chemical inhibition or by lowering the temperature; either approach requires dilution (Watson, 1990). As diluent requirements for the preservation of spermatozoa vary between individual species (Watson, 1979; Mann and Lutwak-Mann, 1981; Holt, 1997), studies which investigate the tolerance of diluted spermatozoa to a range of physico-chemical environments are helpful in the selection of media for semen extension, the most significant of the physical and chemical influences on diluted spermatozoa in vitro being variations in ionic strength (pH and osmolality), dilution rate and temperature (Mann, 1964).

Apart from a specific study on the collection, handling and properties of *T. vulpecula* semen by Rodger and White (1978), details of the manipulation of marsupial semen can mostly be found in passing references to methodologies of studies dealing with motility patterns, short-term sperm preservation, cryopreservation, *in vitro* fertilization and acrosomal function (reviewed by Johnston, 1999).

While it appears that marsupial spermatozoa are generally more tolerant of 'cold shock' (Rodger and White, 1978; Taggart *et al.*, 1996a, Molinia and Rodger, 1996), than the spermatozoa of domestic eutherian species (Watson, 1979) recent studies by Johnston *et al.* (2000a) found a small but significant decrease in the motility of koala spermatozoa if the semen was cooled rapidly from 35°C to 5°C; however, no detrimental effect was observed when semen was cooled rapidly to either 15°C or 25°C. These findings need to be incorporated into the protocols and procedures for chilled and frozen storage of marsupial semen and suggest that a more thorough evaluation of temperature shock tolerance might be warranted.

Similarly, while Rodger and White (1978) noted *T. vulpecula* spermatozoa were tolerant of frequent washing and dilution, no quantitative data were given. However, a dilution-like effect (Watson, 1990) has been reported by Rodger *et al.* (1991) and Taggart *et al.* (1996b) for *T. vulpecula* and the southern hairy-nosed wombat (*Lasiorhinus latifrons*) respectively; both studies found that if the concentration of spermatozoa fell below 4×10^6 per ml, cryopreservation was not optimal.

The relationship between ejaculated sperm motility and diluent pH and/or osmolality has only been determined for koala spermatozoa (Johnston *et al.*, 2000a). Under differing pH and osmolality conditions, koala spermatozoa behave in a manner similar to that of eutherian spermatozoa. Most studies of marsupial semen have used buffer systems and additives which maintain the diluent pH and osmolality in the range of 6.8–7.4 and 280–320 mmol/kg respectively. Jones and Clulow (1994) have noted that *M. eugenii* epididymidal spermatozoa were irreversibly immobilized by dilution in media of low pH and which contained lactate; regulation of intracellular pH might provide a mechanism for manipulating sperm motility and be useful for short-term preservation.

12.3.3 Semen bacteriology

Before developing a practicable AI programme for captive wildlife, it is necessary to develop methods of treating semen so that it can be stored and transported without significant decrease in viability. The use of selected antibiotics reduces the potential transmission of pathogenic bacteria and prolongs survival of stored spermatozoa by controlling the growth of bacterial contaminants; most of which originate from the urethra, prepuce and penis (Watson, 1990). Although antibiotics have been used routinely as additives to diluents in the course of studies of marsupial sperm function and preservation (e.g. Mate and Rodger, 1991; Sistena *et al.*, 1993a), there has been only one systematic investigation of the effects of antibiotics on marsupial sperm survival or of the ability of antibiotics to control bacterial contamination in diluted semen during liquid storage. In a study of koala semen, Johnston *et al.* (1998) described the microbial fauna cultured from the prepuce and ejaculates collected by means of either electroejaculation or artificial vagina. Based on the antibacterial sensitivity patterns of isolates from the prepuce and semen, Johnston *et al.* (1998) chose an antibiotic treatment that reduced bacterial growth but that was not detrimental to koala sperm survival. In the case of male koalas infected with *Chamydia* spp. the ability to eradicate potential pathogens via antibiotic cleansing is particularly appealing and currently under investigation. Similar studies are required on the semen of other marsupial species in preparation for cryopreservation and AI programmes in order to reduce the accidental transfer of pathogens during insemination.

12.3.4 Short-term preservation

There have been few studies of short-term preservation of marsupial semen. First, Rodger and White (1978) showed that washed *T. vulpecula* spermatozoa could maintain motility for 6 hours if incubated in Krebs-Ringer-phosphate at 37°C. This study was followed by that of Johnston *et al.* (1992) which examined koala semen diluted 1:1 in 'Kiev' diluent and stored at 16°C; sperm motility was maintained for up to 48 hours. Electroejaculated eastern grey kangaroo (*Macropus giganteus*) spermatozoa have also been stored at 5°C for 48 hours in PBS containing combinations of egg yolk and D-glucose (Johnston *et al.*, 1997b). The limited storage time of spermatozoa in both these studies may have been related to the lack of antibiotics in the semen diluent. Recently, Johnston *et al.* (2000a) reported that koala spermatozoa could remain motile for up to 42 days if stored in a Tris–citrate–glucose extender at 5°C; the fertility of these spermatozoa remains to be validated. Penfold *et al.* (unpublished observations) have also reported survival of various macropod spermatozoa for upwards of 5 days in simple PBS or MEM media with or without fetal calf serum and using antibiotics.

12.3.5 Cryopreservation

Unlike eutherian species, *T. vulpecula* and *P. cinereus* spermatozoa require high levels of glycerol (up to 17.5%) for cryopreservation (Rodger *et al.*, 1991; Johnston *et al.*, 1993;

Molinia and Rodger, 1996). While *T. vulpecula* spermatozoa appear to tolerate these high levels of glycerol for 15 minutes prior to freezing, Johnston *et al.* (1993) showed that glycerol exerted a negative effect on the motility of *P. cinereus* spermatozoa if the semen was incubated at 35°C for 1 hour prior to cryopreservation. Therefore, the effectiveness of glycerol as a cryoprotectant for marsupial spermatozoa is somewhat paradoxical, being necessary at high concentrations for adequate cryopreservation, but at the same time 'cytotoxic'. Molinia and Rodger (1996) have recently investigated the use of other cryoprotectants on *M. eugenii* spermatozoa, including glycerol, DMSO, EG and PrOH in PBS. This study found that the motility of *M. eugenii* spermatozoa was reduced by 20–85% when incubated for 30 minutes in the cryoprotectants described above. Cooper *et al.* (1996) also described a similar cytotoxic effect of glycerol on the motility of *M. giganteus* epididymidal spermatozoa. Despite its known cytotoxic properties (Fahy, 1986), glycerol currently remains the cryoprotectant of choice for marsupial spermatozoa.

Since the original success of freezing *T. vulpecula* spermatozoa (Rodger *et al.*, 1991), cryopreservation of marsupial semen has been reported in a further seven species including the koala, long-footed potoroo (*Potorus longipes*), northern brown bandicoot (*Isoodon macrourus*), common ringtail possum (*Pseudocheirus peregrinus*), *Lasiorhinus latifrons*, *Vombatus ursinus* and *M. eugenii* (Johnston *et al.*, 1993; Taggart *et al.*, 1996b; Molinia and Rodger, 1996).

With regard to cryopreservation protocols, Rodger *et al.* (1991) and Taggart *et al.* (1996a) have both frozen marsupial semen in straws suspended in liquid nitrogen vapour using relatively rapid cooling rates. In a preliminary study to investigate the cryopreservation of koala spermatozoa, Johnston *et al.* (1993) used a programmable freezer to cool spermatozoa at a slow rate of only −6°C per min. Molinia and Rodger (1996) have also reported a successful pellet method of freezing spermatozoa from *T. vulpecula*. Interestingly, Molinia and Rodger (1996) also found that the same pelleting technique used for *T. vulpecula*, but with different combinations of cryoprotectants and equilibration periods, was only moderately successful for the cryopreservation of *M. eugenii* spermatozoa. The successful cryopreservation of macropod semen remains a substantial challenge.

In contrast to the findings of Rodger *et al.* (1991) and Johnston *et al.* (1993), Taggart and his colleagues (Taggart *et al.*, 1996a,b) showed that more conventional concentrations of glycerol (4–8%) could also result in successful post-thaw recovery of sperm motility of *Lasiorhinus krefftii*, *Vombatus ursinus*, *Isoodon macrourus* and *Petauroides volans*, although only 12% and 3% motility recovery was obtained with spermatozoa from *P. cinereus* and *S. crassicaudata* respectively. Particularly fascinating was the comparative success of freezing wombat and koala spermatozoa; both species have spermatozoa of similar size and morphology, yet koala spermatozoa require glycerol concentrations two- to three-fold higher than wombat spermatozoa. Such data point to the need for species-specific cryopreservation protocols.

The similarities and differences between the experimental approaches indicated above make direct comparisons difficult, especially the inconsistent use of egg yolk in diluents. Egg yolk lipoproteins appear to protect spermatozoa during cryopreservation by binding to the sperm surface (Watson, 1976), thereby protecting it from the unfrozen and hyperosmotic salt solutions to which it is exposed during freezing. The benefits to be gained after thawing, if egg yolk is present during freezing, were analysed by Holt *et al.* (1992). In a study of ram spermatozoa, performed using cryomicroscopy so that sperm viability could be monitored continuously during rewarming, a buffered glycerol solution (2% v/v) was only capable of supporting plasma membrane integrity into the range 10–14°C after thawing; this, however, was significantly better than freezing in the absence of glycerol. Membrane stability could be maintained during the entire rewarming phase (to 30°C) when egg yolk was added to the glycerol, thus demonstrating that the two components are complementary. There is therefore a case for investigating the interactions of egg yolk and glycerol with respect to marsupial sperm cryopreservation. As egg yolk and glycerol are both lipophilic substances, there is every likelihood that if they are mixed in excessive concentrations they might interact and destabilize the sperm plasma membrane. It is surprising that no formal experiments have been undertaken to test these interactive effects upon marsupial spermatozoa.

Molinia and Rodger (1996) investigated the cryopreservation of Tammar wallaby spermatozoa; using a pellet freezing method they found a combination of 7.5% glycerol + 10% DMSO allowed approximately 10% recovery of motile spermatozoa. To date, this result has not been surpassed, though recent cryomicroscopic studies of *M. rufogriseus* and *M. giganteus* spermatozoa showed up to 70% of spermatozoa were motile immediately after thawing and provided that the temperature remained below 20°C (Holt *et al.*, 1999). Continued warming to 35°C resulted in almost complete loss of sperm motility and plasma membrane integrity.

The factors responsible for the unexpected behaviour of marsupial spermatozoa in response to cryopreservation treatments, i.e. requirement for high glycerol concentration and inability to maintain cell integrity during rewarming, are unknown at present. However, some inferences may be drawn from the differences between these and eutherian spermatozoa. Ultrastructural studies have revealed that marsupial spermatozoa typically possess an elaborate cytoskeletal network beneath the plasma membrane; this appears to be especially well organized in the mid-piece (Temple-Smith, 1994) and develops during epididymal maturation. On the principle that the analogous cytoskeleton detected in mouse spermatozoa (Noiles *et al.*, 1997) prevents the cells from swelling and shrinking in response to anisosmotic conditions, the marsupial spermatozoa may be unable to respond to the changes in osmolarity which accompany freeze–thawing. If the addition of glycerol in high concentration helps to destabilize the cytoskeleton, cryopreservation should be facilitated. Evidence to support the hypothesis that osmotic responses are improved if the cytoskeletal network is disrupted was obtained by Holt and Johnston (1999), who showed that koala spermatozoa exposed to hypotonic solutions were able to swell, and therefore retain membrane integrity, if the cytoskeletal network was disrupted by the addition of cytochalasin B.

12.3.6 Oestrus synchronization and induction of ovulation

Another reason for the relative lack of advance in artificial breeding of marsupials with respect to eutherian species, is our inadequate knowledge of the timing of ovulation and fertilization (Hinds *et al.*, 1996). Reproductive technologies such as superovulation and AI require the ability to manipulate and control precisely the occurrence of oestrus and ovulation. Until recently, the major technique of experimentally synchronizing and inducing oestrus in marsupials has been the removal of pouch young (Renfree and Tyndale-Biscoe, 1978; Rodger and Bedford, 1982; Tyndale-Biscoe, 1984; Tyndale-Biscoe and Renfree, 1987). The removal of pouch young eliminates lactational inhibition of ovarian activity, the mother returning to oestrus some days later. While this method is suitable for experimental studies it is obviously not appropriate for endangered species. In addition, the synchrony of oestrus achieved via pouch young removal is quite variable and therefore not appropriate for fixed time insemination.

Induction of oestrus and ovulation in marsupials can also be achieved pharmaceutically. Since the original studies of Nelson and Maxwell (1942) and Nelson and White (1941) on *D. virginiana*, and Smith and Godfrey (1970) on *Sminthopsis crassicaudata*, considerable progress towards the development of methods for the induction of oestrus and ovulation in marsupials have been made (see Hinds *et al.*, 1996 for a tabulated summary of the majority of these studies). Hinds *et al.* (1996) noted that while follicular growth in marsupials was consistently stimulated by administration of PMSG, the optimal dose rate was typically lower than that used for eutherian species, and except for *S. crassicaudata*, successful ovulation also required a single or multiple injection of GnRH some 2–3 days after initial PMSG administration. More recently, a protocol utilizing either porcine FSH or PMSG and LH has been used successfully to induce multiple ovulation in *M. eugenii* and *T. vulpecula* (Fletcher *et al.*, 1998; Molinia *et al.*, 1998a,b; Molinia and Myers, 1999).

As mentioned early in this chapter the koala is the only marsupial described where the luteal phase (ovulation) is induced by coitus. Animals that show this type of ovulatory pattern typically present less difficulty in inducing ovulation. For example, Johnston (1999) and Johnston *et al.* (2000c) have shown that it is possible to induce ovulation in the koala using either a method of interrupted coitus or following administration of 250 IU of hCG. Further studies are necessary to examine whether ovulation in the koala can also be induced by mechanical stimulation of the urogenital sinus or whether porcine LH rather than hCG might improve pharmaceutical induction of ovulation.

12.3.7 Artificial insemination

The use of AI for the conservation and management of marsupial populations was originally proposed by Rodger (1990). In the ten years which have passed since then there have been eight published studies which have systematically investigated the use of AI in marsupials as exemplified by the *T. vulpecula* and *M. eugenii* (Molinia *et al.*, 1997, 1998a; Molinia and Rodger, 1996; Nickel *et al.*, 1996; 1997). These pioneering studies resulted in the successful production of fertilized embryos in both species following induction of oestrus, multiple ovulation and laparoscopic insemination. More recently, Molinia and Myers (1999) described the successful fertilization of *T. vulpecula* oocytes following the laparoscopic insemination of frozen–thawed spermatozoa. Despite these very encouraging results there are still no published reports of possum pouch young conceived and born by means of AI. Once fertilized, these embryos apparently fail to develop beyond the four-cell stage, perhaps due to an inappropriate hormonal environment in the superovulated female (Molinia *et al.*, 1998b).

In 1994, Johnston reported five unsuccessful preliminary attempts at koala AI, in which 2 ml of diluted electroejaculated semen was inseminated directly into each female's urogenital sinus. However, at that stage it was not known that ovulation in the koala was coitally induced (Johnston *et al.*, 2000b). Given new information on the reproductive physiology, behaviour and anatomy of the koala it became possible to commence a more targeted attempt at AI in this species (Johnston, 1999). In May 1998, the University of Queensland and Lone Pine Koala Sanctuary (Brisbane, Australia), announced the birth of six koala pouch young born and conceived by means of AI. Five pouch young were produced following urogenital insemination of semen collected by means of an artificial vagina and following induction of ovulation by interrupted coitus; a further pouch young was also produced following urogenital insemination and induction of ovulation with hCG (Johnston, 1999). Studies are currently underway to refine the AI procedure using either extended or frozen semen.

12.3.8 Embryo transfer and cryopreservation

Successful embryo transfer in macropods was achieved several decades ago (Tyndale-Biscoe, 1963, 1970; Renfree and Tyndale-Biscoe, 1978) and more recently has been carried out in the fat-tailed dunnart (Breed and Leigh, 1996). The procedure for transferring these embryos was relatively straightforward and involved injecting the embryo through the uterine wall. Performing these procedures for the purposes of species conservation, however, will undoubtedly require further refinement of the methodology used with both donors and recipients. The use of laparoscopic procedures for embryo collection has been suggested (Taggart *et al.*, 1997; Mate *et al.*, 1998) to ensure minimal trauma to the donor.

Only one study of embryo cryopreservation has been performed in any marsupial, the fat-tailed dunnart (Breed *et al.*, 1994). Three methods were examined, one slow and two rapid freezing protocols. After freezing and thawing, a relatively small proportion of embryos (17%) went on to divide in culture. The large size and relatively yolk-filled composition of the marsupial embryo make this result particularly encouraging.

12.3.9 Pouch young transfer

One novel but ingenious use of artificial breeding technology in marsupials which is completely non-invasive, is the technique of interspecies pouch young transfer (Taggart *et al.*, 1997). Akin to embryo transfer, the individual pouch young produced by one species can be transferred to the pouch of a recipient conspecific or congeneric female that is at a similar stage of the donor's reproductive cycle. Following removal of her pouch young, the donor female will soon return to oestrus and be mated again. Even if the donor species has a relatively short breeding season it may be possible to increase the reproductive rate of the population during the season by up to 600%. This technique is elegant in its simplicity and makes use of the unique mode of reproduction in marsupials. Taggart *et al.* (1997) have recently reviewed studies of cross-fostering in marsupials, noting that this technique was originally pioneered by Sharman and Calaby in 1966 but is currently being used to transfer and rear black-footed rock wallabies (*Petrogale lateralis*) to Tammar wallabies (*M. eugenii*) and northern bettongs (*Bettongia tropica*) to brush-tail bettongs (*B. penicillata*).

12.4 CONCLUSION

Reproductive studies in marsupials, having been of somewhat limited and specialized interest for many years, have recently been subject to an upsurge of interest. This is at a time when the applications of GRB techniques are receiving serious consideration as a way of supporting conservation activities. The physiological and anatomical specializations of marsupial reproduction dictate, however, that many of the accepted ancillary techniques used with GRB programmes would be substantially deficient if applied thoughtlessly. For this reason, we have used the current chapter to present a brief overview of marsupial reproduction as it applies to GRBs and the development of technologies. The field has experienced rapid growth over the past few years, culminating in the recent birth of several koalas after AI. Concentrated efforts are likely to provide more of these successes in the future because the willingness exists to exploit every means possible for the conservation of the marsupial fauna in Australia.

REFERENCES

BIERY, K. S. (1991) 'Sex and the single koala', *Zoonooz* pp. 12–13.

BREED, W. G. and LEIGH, C. M. (1996) 'Successful embryo transfer in a small dasyurid marsupial, *Sminthopsis crassicaudata*', *Theriogenology* **45**, 1075–1080.

BREED, W. G., TAGGART, D. A., BRADTKE, V., LEIGH, C. M., GAMEAU, L. and CARROLL, J. (1994) 'Effect of cryopreservation on development and ultrastructure of preimplantation embryos from the dasyurid marsupial *Sminthopsis crassicaudata*', *J. Reprod. Fertil.* **100**, 429–438.

COHEN, J., GARRISI, G. J., CONGEDOFERRARA, T. A., KIECK, K. A., SCHIMMEL, T. W. and SCOTT, R. T. (1997) 'Cryopreservation of single human spermatozoa', *Hum. Reprod.* **12**, 994–1001.

COOPER, J. W., JOHNSTON, S. D., BLYDE, D., KUIPER, Y., McGOWAN, M. R. and BOOTH, R. (1996) 'Effect of glycerol and egg yolk on the motility of *Macropus giganteus cauda* epididymal spermatozoa stored at 5°C', *Proc. 13th Intern. Congr. Anim. Reprod. (Sydney)*, Vol. 2, 2–4.

CUMMINS, J. M. (1980) 'Decondensation of sperm nuclei of Australian marsupials: effects of air drying and of calcium and magnesium'. *Gamete Res.* **3**, 351–367.

CUMMINS, J. M. and WOODALL, P. F. (1985). 'On mammalian sperm dimensions, *J. Reprod. Fertil.* **75**, 153–175.

CURLEWIS, J. D., AXELSON, M. and STONE, G. M. (1985) 'Identification of the major steroids in ovarian and adrenal venous plasma of the Brush-tail Possum (*Trichosurus vulpecula*) and changes in the peripheral level of oestradiol and progesterone during the reproductive cycle', *J. Endocrinol.* **105**, 53–62.

FAHY, F. G. (1986) 'The relevance of cryoprotectant toxicity to cryobiology'. *Cryobiology* **23**, 1–13.

FLETCHER, T. P. (1983) 'Endocrinology of reproduction in the dasyurid marsupial, *Dasyuroides byrnei* (Spencer)', PhD thesis, La Trobe University, Melbourne.

FLETCHER, T. P., MOLINIA, F. C., GLAZIER, A. M. and RODGER, J. C. (1998) 'Comparison of exogenous hormone treatments for inducing superovulation during seasonal anoestrus in the Brushtail Possum', in *Proceedings of the 29th Annual Conference of Australian Society of Reproductive Biology*, University of Western Australia, Perth, p. 28.

GEORGE, G. G. (1988) 'Conservation genetics and the management of species in captivity', in *Australian Wildlife, Proceedings Number 104*, Sydney: University of Sydney Post-Graduate Committee in Veterinary Science, pp. 945–952.

HARDER, J. D. and FLEMING, M. W. (1981) 'Estradiol and progesterone profiles indicate a lack of endocrine recognition of pregnancy in the Opossum' *Science* **212**, 1400–1402.

HINDS, L. A., FLETCHER, T. P. and RODGER, J. C. (1996) 'Hormones of oestrus and ovulation and their manipulation in marsupials', *Reprod. Fertil. Dev.* **8**, 661–672.

HOLT, W. V. (1997) 'Alternative strategies for the long-term preservation of spermatozoa', *Reprod. Fertil. Dev.* **9**, 309–319.

HOLT, W. V. and JOHNSTON, S. D. (1999) 'Enhanced osmotic tolerance of koala spermatozoa following treatment with the cytoskeletal disrupting agent, cytochalasin B', in *Proceedings of the Australian Society of Reproductive Biology, Annual Conference, Melbourne* (in press).

HOLT, W. V., HEAD, M. F. and NORTH, R. D. (1992) 'Freeze-induced membrane damage in ram spermatozoa is manifested after thawing–observations with experimental cryomicroscopy', *Biol. Reprod.* **46**, 1086–1094.

HOLT, W. V., PENFOLD, L. M., JOHNSTON, S. D., TEMPLE-SMITH, P., McCALLUM, C., SHAW, J., LINDEMANS, W. and BLYDE, D. (1999) 'Cryopreservation of macropodid spermatozoa: new insights from the cryomicroscope', *Reprod. Fert. Dev.* **11**, 345–353.

JOHNSTON, S. D. (1994) 'Reproductive biology of the Queensland koala *(Phascolarctos cinereus adustus: Goldfuss)*', honours thesis, University of Queensland, Brisbane.

JOHNSTON, S. D. (1999) 'Studies towards the development of an artificial insemination protocol in the koala *(Phascolarctos cinereus)*', PhD thesis, University of Queensland, Brisbane.

JOHNSTON, S. D., McGOWAN, M. R., CARRICK, F. N. and CAMERON, R. D. A. (1992) 'Towards the development of an artificial insemination programme for koalas', *Proceedings of the 12th International Congress of Animal Reproduction (Urbana-Champaign)*, pp. 1954–1957.

JOHNSTON, S. D., McGOWAN, M. R., CARRICK, F. N. and TRIBE, A. (1993) 'Preliminary investigations into the feasibility of freezing koala *(Phascolarctos cinereus)* semen'. *Austr. Vet. J.* **70**, 424–425. (Correction published in the *Austr. Vet. J.* **72**, 473).

JOHNSTON, S. D., McGOWAN, M. R., CARRICK, F. N., CAMERON, R. D. A. and TRIBE, A. (1994a) 'Seminal characteristics and spermatozoal morphology of captive Queensland koalas *(Phascolarctos cinereus adustus)*', *Theriogenology* **42**, 501–511.

JOHNSTON, S. D., TRIBE, A., PERKINS, N., BLYDE, D. and McGOWAN, M. R. (1994b) 'Collaborative studies in marsupial theriogenology', in *Proceedings of the Australian*

Association of Veterinary Conservation Biologists, Annual Australian Veterinary Association Conference, Canberra, Australia.

JOHNSTON, S. D., DADDOW, L. and CARRICK, F. N. (1995) 'Ultrastructural and light observations of mature spermatozoa and sperm maturation in the Greater Bilby (*Macrotis lagotis*)', in Jamieson, B. G. M., Ausio, J. and Justine, J. L. (eds). *Advances in spermatozoal taxonomy and phylogeny*, Memoires du Museum National d'Histoire Naturelle, Paris, pp. 397–408.

JOHNSTON, S. D., BLYDE, D., GAMBLE, J., HIGGINS, D., FIELD, H. and COOPER, J. (1997a) 'Collection and short-term preservation of semen from free-ranging eastern grey kangaroos (*Macropus giganteus;* Macropodidae)', *Austr. Vet. J.* **75**, 648–651.

JOHNSTON, S. D., O'CALLAGHAN, P., McGOWAN, M. R. and PHILLIPS, N. J. (1997b) 'Characteristics of koala (*Phascolarctos cinereus adustus*) semen collected by artificial vagina', *J. Reprod. Fertil.* **109**, 319–323.

JOHNSTON, S. D., O'BOYLE, D., FROST, A. J., McGOWAN, M. R., TRIBE, A. and HIGGINS, D. (1998) 'Antibiotics for the preservation of Koala (*Phascolarctos cinereus*) semen', *Austr. Vet. J.* **76**, 335–338.

JOHNSTON, S. D., McGOWAN, M. R., PHILLIPS, N. J. and O'CALLAGHAN, P. (2000a) 'Optimal physicochemical conditions for the manipulation and short-term preservation of Koala (*Phascolarctos cinereus*) spermatozoa', *J. Reprod. Fertil.* **118**, 273–281.

JOHNSTON, S. D., McGOWAN, M. R., O'CALLAGHAN, P., COX, R. and NICOLSON, V. (2000b) 'Studies of the oestrous cycle, oestrus and pregnancy in the Koala (*Phascolarctos cinereus*)', *J. Reprod. Fertil.* **120**, 49–57.

JOHNSTON, S. D., McGOWAN, M. R., O'CALLAGHAN, P., COX, R. and NICOLSON, V. (2000c) 'Natural and artificial methods of inducing the luteal phase in the koala (*Phascolarctos cinereus*)', *J. Reprod. Fertil.* **120**, 59–64.

JONES, R. C. AND CLULOW, J. (1994) 'Interactions of sperm and the reproductive tracts of the male Tammar Wallaby (Macropididae-marsupialia)', *Reprod. Fert. Dev.* **6**, 540–553.

MANN, T. (1964) *The Biochemistry of Semen and of the Male Reproductive Tract*, London: Methuen.

MANN, T. and LUTWAK-MANN, C. (1981) *Male Reproductive Function and Semen*, New York: Springer-Verlag.

MATE, K. E. and RODGER, J. C. (1991) 'Stability of the acrosome of the brush-tailed possum (*Trichosurus vulpecula*) and Tammar wallaby (*Macropus eugenii*) *in vitro* and after exposure to conditions and agents known to cause capacitation or acrosome reaction of eutherian spermatozoa', *J. Reprod. Fertil.* **91**, 41–48.

■ CHAPTER 12 ■

MATE, K. E., MOLINIA, F. C. and RODGER, J. C. (1998) 'Manipulation and fertility of marsupials for conservation of endangered species and control of over-abundant populations', *Anim. Reprod. Sci.* **53**, 65–76.

MAXWELL, S., BURBIDGE, A. A. and MORRIS, K. D. (1996) *The 1996 Action Plan for Australian Marsupials and Monotremes,* Canberra: National Parks and Wildlife Publishing.

MERCHANT, J. C. and SHARMAN, G. B. (1966) 'Observations on the attachment of marsupial pouch young to the teats and on the rearing of pouch young by foster-mothers of the same or different species', *Australian Journal of Zoology* **14**, 593–609.

MOLINIA, F. C. and MYERS, J. V. (1999) 'Fertility of frozen-thawed possom spermatozoa after laparoscopic artificial insemination', *Proc. 13th Ann. Conf. Austr. Soc. Reprod. Biol.* p.134.

MOLINIA, F. C. and RODGER, J. C. (1996) 'Pellet-freezing spermatozoa of 2 marsupials–the tammar wallaby, *Macropus eugenii,* and the brushtail possum, *Trichosurus vulpecula',* *Reprod. Fertil. Dev.* **8**, 681–684.

MOLINIA, F. C., NICKEL, M. K., GLAZIER, A. M. and RODGER, J. C. (1997) 'Intrauterine and intravaginal artificial insemination of PMSG/LH treated brushtail possums', *Proc. 28th Ann. Conf. Aust. Soc. Reprod. Biol.,* p. 91.

MOLINIA, F. C., GIBSON, R. J., BROWN, A. M., GLAZIER, A. M. and RODGER, J. C. (1998a) 'Successful fertilization after superovulation and laparoscopic intrauterine insemination of the brushtail possum, *Trichosurus vulpecula,* and tammar wallaby, *Macropus eugenii',* *J. Reprod. Fertil.* **113**, 9–17.

MOLINIA, F. C., GIBSON, R. J., SMEDLEY, M. A. and RODGER, J. C. (1998b) 'Further observations of the ovarian response of the tammar wallaby (*Macropus eugenii*) to exogenous gonadotrophins: an improved method for superovulation using FSH/LH', *Anim. Reprod. Sci.* **53**, 251–263.

MURDOCH, R.N. and JONES, R.C. (1994) 'Glucose and acetate utilisation by marsupial epididymidal spermatozoa is inhibited by a prostatic secretion', in *Proceedings of the 26th Annual Conference of the Australian Society of Reproductive Biology,* Vol. 26, p. 189.

NELSON, O. E. and WHITE, E. T. (1941) 'A method of inducing ovulation in the anoestrous Opossum *Didelphis virginiana',* *Anat. Rec.* **81**, 529–535.

NELSON, O. E. and MAXWELL, N. (1942) 'The structure and function of the urogenital region in male Opossum compared with the same region in other marsupials', *J. Morphol.* **71**, 463–492.

NICKEL, M. K., MOLINIA, F. C., HINDS, L. A. and RODGER, J. C. (1996) 'Attempts to refine a superovulation protocol for the tammar Wallaby (*Macropus eugenii*)', in *Proceedings of the 13th International Congress on Animal Reproduction (The Hague),* pp. 4–27.

NICKEL, M. K., MOLINIA, F. C., LIN, M. and RODGER, J. C. (1997) 'Sperm transport in the female reproductive tract of the brushtail possum, *Trichosurus vulpecula*', *Proc. 28th Ann. Conf. Aust. Soc. Reprod. Biol.* p. 68.

NOILES, E. E., THOMPSON, K. A. and STOREY, B. T. (1997) 'Water permeability, L_p, of the mouse sperm plasma membrane and its activation energy are strongly dependent on interaction of the plasma membrane with the sperm cytoskeleton'. *Cryobiology* **35**, 79–92.

RENFREE, M. B. (1983) 'Marsupial reproduction: the choice between placentation and lactation', *Oxford Rev. Reprod. Biol.* **5**, 1–29.

RENFREE, M. B. and TYNDALE-BISCOE, C. H. (1978) 'Manipulation of marsupial embryos and pouch young', in Daniel, J. C. (ed.) *Methods in Mammalian Reproduction*, New York: Academic Press, pp. 307–331.

RODGER, J. C. (1990) 'Prospects for the artificial manipulation of marsupial reproduction and its application in research and conservation', *Austr. J. Zool.* **37**, 249–258.

RODGER, J. C. and BEDFORD, J. M. (1982) 'Induction of oestrus, recovery of gametes, and the timing of fertilization events in the Opossum, *Didelphis virginiana*', *J. Reprod. Fertil.* **64**, 159–169.

RODGER, J. C. and HUGHES, R. L. (1973) 'Studies of the accessory glands of male marsupials', *Austr. J. Zool.* **21**, 303–320.

RODGER, J. C and MATE, K. E. (1988) 'A PMSG/GnRH method for the superovulation of the monovulatory brush-tailed possum (*Trichosurus vulpecula*)', *J. Reprod. Fertil.* **83**, 885–891.

RODGER, J. C. and MATE, K. E. (1993) 'Marsupial gametes and fertilization', *Today's Life Science*, 28–33.

RODGER, J. C. and POLLITT, C. C. (1981) 'Radiographic examination of electroejaculation in marsupials'. *Biol. Reprod.* **24**, 1125–1134.

RODGER, J. C. and WHITE, I. G. (1975) 'Electro-ejaculation of Australian marsupials and analyses of the sugars in the seminal plasma from three macropod species'. *J. Reprod. Fertil.* **43**, 233–239.

RODGER, J. C. and WHITE, I. G. (1978) 'The collection, handling and some properties of marsupial semen', in Watson, P. F. (ed.) *Artificial Breeding of Non-Domestic Animals, Symposia of the Zoological Society of London*, vol. 43, London: Academic Press, pp. 289–301.

RODGER, J. C., COUSINS, S. J. and MATE, K. E. (1991) 'A simple glycerol-based freezing protocol for the semen of a marsupial *Trichosurus vulpecula*, the common brushtail possum'. *Reprod. Fertil. Dev.* **3**, 119–125.

RODGER, J. C., BREED, W. G. and BENNETT, J. H. (1992) 'Gonadotrophin-induced oestrus and ovulation in the polyovulatory marsupial *Sminthopsis crassicaudata*', *Reprod. Fertil. Dev.* **4**, 145–152.

SISTENA, Y., LIN, M., MATE, K., ROBINSON, E. S. and RODGER, J. C. (1993a) 'The unique stability of the marsupial sperm acrosomal membranes examined by unprotected freeze-thawing and treatment with detergent Triton X-100'. *Reprod. Fertil. Dev.* **5**, 1–14.

SISTENA, Y., LIN, M. and RODGER, J. C. (1993b) 'Lysophosphatidylcholine disrupts the acrosome of Tammar wallaby (*Macropus eugenii*) spermatozoa', *Mol. Reprod. Dev.* **35**, 277–284.

SISTENA, Y., LIN, M., MATE, K. E. and RODGER, J. C. (1993c) 'Induction of the marsupial acrosome reaction *in vitro* by treatment with diacylglycerols', *J. Reprod. Fertil.* **99**, 335–341.

SMITH, M. J. and GODFREY, G. K. (1970) 'Ovulation induced by gonadotrophins in the marsupial, *Sminthopsis crassicaudata* (Gould)', *J. Reprod. Fertil.* **22**, 41–47.

SOULÉ, M. E. (1992) 'Ten years ago, ten years from now: summary remarks for the symposium', in *Symposia of the Zoological Society of London,* Vol. 64, London: Academic Press, pp. 225–234.

TAGGART, D. A., LEIGH, C. M., SCHULTZ, D. and BREED, W. G. (1995) 'Ultrastructure and motility of spermatozoa in the male reproductive tract of parameloid marsupials', *Reprod. Fertil. Dev.* **7**, 1141–1156.

TAGGART, D. A., LEIGH, C. M., STEELE, V. R., BREED, W. G., TEMPLESMITH, P. D. and PHELAN, J. (1996a) 'Effect of cooling and cryopreservation on sperm motility and morphology of several species of marsupial'. *Reprod. Fertil. Dev.* **8**, 673–679.

TAGGART, D. A., STEELE, V. R., SCHULTZ, D. and TEMPLE-SMITH, P. D. (1996b) 'Semen collection and cryopreservation in the southern hairy-nosed wombat (*Lasiorhinus latifrons*): implications for conservation of the northern hairy-nosed wombat (*Lasiorhinus krefftii*)', in Wells, R. (ed.) *Wombats in Australia: Biology, History, Art and Literature,* Sydney: Surrey, Beatty and Sons.

TAGGART, D. A., SCHULTZ, D. and TEMPLE-SMITH, P. D. (1997) 'Development and application of assisted reproductive technologies in marsupials; their value for conservation of rock wallabies'. *Austr. Mammal.* **19**, 183–190.

TEMPLE-SMITH, P. (1994) 'Comparative structure and function of marsupial spermatozoa', *Reprod. Fertil. Dev.* **6**, 1–16.

TEMPLE-SMITH, P., SELWOOD, L., HARRISON, R. A. P., BEDFORD, J. M., MOORE, H. D. M., HUGHES, R. L., RODGER, J. C., EPPIG, J. J., TAGGART, D. A., MATE, K. E., BREED, W. G., JOHNSON, M. H.,

TYNDALE-BISCOE, C. H. and COOPER, T. G. (1996) 'Gamete interaction, fertilization and post-fertilization events'. *Reprod. Fertil. Dev.* **8**, 649–654.

TRIBE, A., JOHNSTON, S. D. and CARRICK, F. N. (1994) 'Artificial reproduction in marsupials', in *Proceedings of the 110th Postgraduate Committee in Veterinary Sciences, Sydney.*

TYNDALE-BISCOE, C. H. (1963) 'Blastocyst transfer in the marsupial, *Setonix brachyurus*', *J. Reprod. Fertil.* **6**, 41–48.

TYNDALE-BISCOE, C. H. (1970) 'Resumption of development by quiescent blastocysts transferred to primed, ovariectomised recipients in the marsupial, *Macropus eugenii*', *J. Reprod. Fertil.* **23**, 25–32.

TYNDALE-BISCOE, C. H. (1984) 'Mammals – Marsupials', in Lamming, G.E. (ed.) *Marshall's Physiology of Reproduction*, 4th edn, Vol. 1, Edinburgh: Churchill Livingstone, pp. 386–454.

TYNDALE-BISCOE, C. H. and RENFREE, M. B. (1987) *Reproductive Physiology of Marsupials*, Cambridge: Cambridge University Press.

WATSON, P. F. (1976) 'The protection of ram and bull spermatozoa by the low density lipoprotein fraction of egg yolk during storage at 5°C, and deep freezing', *J. Thermal Biol.* **1**, 137–141.

WATSON, P. F. (1979) 'The preservation of semen in mammals'. *Oxford Rev. Reprod. Biol.* **1**, 283–350.

WATSON, P. F. (1990) 'Artificial insemination and the preservation of semen', in Lamming, G. E. (ed.) *Marshall's Physiology of Reproduction*, 4th edn, Vol. 2, Edinburgh: Churchill Livingstone, pp. 747–869.

WILDT, D. E., RALL, W. F., CRITSER, J. K., MONFORT, S. L. and SEAL, U. S. (1997) 'Genome resource banks : Living collections for biodiversity conservation', *Bioscience* **47**, 689–698.

Gamete and Embryo Cryopreservation in Rodents

M. J. WOOD,[1] **C. J. CANDY**[1] **AND W. V. HOLT**[2]

[1]Department of Anatomy, St George's Hospital Medical School,
Cranmer Terrace, London SW17 0RE, UK
[2]The Institute of Zoology, The Zoological Society of London,
Regent's Park, London NW1 4RY, UK

Contents

13.1 INTRODUCTION

To date the overwhelming justification for germplasm cryopreservation in rodents has come from the biomedical sector, which makes extensive use of mutant mouse genetic models in research. The numerous new mutant lines arising from transgenesis and gene targeting far outstrip the resources available for maintaining each as a live population, and embryo cryopreservation has become a practical alternative. Interest in sperm cryopreservation has developed recently, partly because it is potentially more cost effective than embryo preservation, but also because a significant number of the mutant lines exhibit defective male reproductive function which can nevertheless be overcome by fertilization *in vitro* and embryo transfer. Using *in vitro* techniques and embryo transfer, live young have also been obtained from cryopreserved mature oocytes, and from immature oocytes cryopreserved in pieces of ovarian tissue, in isolated ovarian follicles or after isolation from the follicles. These approaches to germplasm storage are not yet used routinely.

The cryopreservation of germplasm is more advanced in the laboratory mouse than in any other rodent. Comparatively little attention has focused on other rodent species for two main reasons: (1) Techniques for the manipulation of gametes and embryos *in vitro* are less well developed than in the mouse. (2) There was little economic or scientific pressure to develop cryopreservation procedures because few genetically important stocks were available. Recently, the increasing use of transgenic rats in biomedical research has renewed interest in the possibility of banking rat embryos. Cryopreservation has not yet been used to conserve endangered rodent species.

13.2 MOUSE

13.2.1 SPERMATOZOA

The cryopreservation of mouse spermatozoa is a relatively novel technique that requires further refinement. With the exception of chinchilla (Ponce *et al.*, 1998), it appears that virtually nothing has been done to develop cryopreservation protocols for spermatozoa of other rodent species; consequently this review is almost exclusively concerned with laboratory mice.

IVF and embryo transfer are established procedures in the mouse, and have recently been extended by the development of techniques for the direct injection of spermatozoa into the oocyte (ICSI). In consequence, experimental work with preserved mouse spermatozoa has progressed beyond that seen with other vertebrate species. Successful ICSI is feasible with uncryoprotected, and therefore membrane-damaged and immotile, frozen spermatozoa.

Collection

The most practical option for collecting mouse spermatozoa is to kill the animals and remove the caudae epididymides. These are put into small volumes (400–2000 μl) of tissue culture medium or the cryopreservation medium, and several small incisions are made into the epididymal duct. After incubating the preparation at 37°C for 10–15 minutes, the tissue is removed from the sperm suspension. Mouse spermatozoa are relatively fragile and should be handled gently thereafter, avoiding unnecessary centrifugation. Interestingly, viable and fertile spermatozoa can be recovered from the cauda epididymidis up to 24 hours *post-mortem* if the tissues are kept in a refrigerator before dissection (Songsasen *et al.*, 1998). This observation has wider relevance to the practice of genetic resource banking for animal conservation, where tissues are frequently unavailable until several hours after death.

The recovery of ejaculated spermatozoa from the female reproductive tract after mating is a feasible alternative to epididymal collection. This method, used in the 1960s for the development of IVF methods (e.g. Whittingham, 1968), has recently undergone a revival because it avoids the euthanasia of valuable males and allows spermatozoa to be collected repeatedly from the same animals. Songsasen and Leibo (1998) demonstrated that the spermatozoa obtained are suitable for cryopreservation.

Cryopreservation

The first reports of live mice born after IVF with cryopreserved spermatozoa appeared in 1990 (Okuyama *et al.*, 1990; Tada *et al.*, 1990; Yokoyama *et al.*, 1990). Tada *et al.* (1990) assessed the performance of various cryoprotectants (sucrose, raffinose, DMSO, glycerol), at different concentrations in a basal sodium chloride (0.86%) solution. The greatest protection was afforded by a mixture of 18% raffinose and 1.75% glycerol in combination with either pellet (50 μl) freezing on dry ice or slower cooling in a programmable freezer. The better freezing technique was not clearly specified in the original paper, although it was apparently pellet freezing. Post-thaw sperm motility varied from 30% to 60%, and fertilizing ability varied significantly amongst the seven mouse strains in the study. The rate of fertilization (i.e. oocytes fertilized/oocytes mixed with spermatozoa) was lowest (13%) with C57BL/6N spermatozoa and highest (64%) with DBA/2N spermatozoa. This strain difference was also evident in the subsequent rate of development to the blastocyst stage. When eggs that had been fertilized by frozen–thawed C57BL/6N spermatozoa were transferred to pseudopregnant recipients, some developed into viable fetuses (11/57). Post-thaw motility was not a reliable indicator of fertilizing ability (Tada *et al.*, 1990). Yokoyama *et al.* (1990) reported that ~50% of spermatozoa were recovered after freezing in 10% raffinose with 5% glycerol and the mean rate of fertilization was 37%. When 28 embryos were transferred to recipients, 21 (75%) developed to term. The freezing method differed markedly from that described by Tada *et al.* (1990): Aliquots (200 μl) of diluted spermatozoa in plastic cryotubes were cooled to 4°C at 1°C/min and then to −70°C at 10°C/min before storage in liquid nitrogen. Tada *et al.* (1990) thawed the frozen pellets very rapidly in culture medium at 37°C. In contrast, Yokoyama *et al.* (1990) controlled the rate of warming at 10°C/min to 0°C, then removed the cryoprotective medium and introduced the spermatozoa into a modified Tyrode's medium. Yet another approach was described by Okuyama *et al.* (1990): the spermatozoa were collected at 37°C directly into a cryoprotective diluent containing 3% skim milk and 18% raffinose and frozen rapidly. The rate of fertilization was 50%, tested by artificial insemination.

Some difficulties were experienced when other research workers began to replicate these freezing techniques, and various modifications evolved. One variation was the use of a TES-Tris-based egg yolk diluent containing 0.1% sodium lauryl sulphate, 1.25% (v/v) glycerol and 25% (v/v) egg yolk (Penfold and Moore, 1993). Approximately 25% of spermatozoa were motile after thawing and the rate of fertilization *in vitro* was about 50%. This method has not been developed further, although the beneficial effects of including egg yolk in diluents for mouse spermatozoa have been confirmed (Songsasen *et al.*, 1997; Songsasen and Leibo, 1997a,b). Currently two generically different approaches for freezing mouse spermatozoa can be discerned; these involve the use of diluents containing either raffinose and skim milk, or raffinose and glycerol. In some studies the raffinose–glycerol media have been supplemented with egg yolk. The basic approaches have been subjected to slight modifications and improvements. To avoid confusion, the methods will be grouped according to the thematic differences outlined above.

Raffinose–skim milk diluents without glycerol

Takeshima *et al.* (1991) tested various concentrations of raffinose in combination with 3% skim milk in distilled water as a cryoprotective diluent, and found that post-thaw motility was highest when the diluent contained 18% raffinose. Samples (100 μl) of sperm suspension in plastic tubes were allowed to freeze in liquid nitrogen vapour before storage in the liquid phase. For thawing, the tubes were warmed rapidly in water at ambient temperature. The cryoprotectant was removed by an ingenious filtration method which allowed the freezing solution to be exchanged for tissue culture medium. The rate of fertilization *in vitro* was 74% with frozen spermatozoa, compared with 93% with unfrozen spermatozoa. Thirty-four per cent of the fertilized oocytes developed to the two-cell stage, and 45% of the embryos transferred to foster mothers developed into live young. The same procedure was used by Nakagata (1993) to preserve spermatozoa from strains DBA/2N and Jcl:CR, that were then mixed with cryopreserved oocytes of strains C57BL/6N and C3H/He for IVF. Post-thaw motility varied from 42 to 58%, being higher for DBA/2N spermatozoa, and the rate of fertilization was higher using DBA/2N spermatozoa (36–45% versus 22–27%). Between 23% and 35% of the embryos transferred to foster mothers were born alive.

Sztein et al. (1997) also used a diluent containing 18% raffinose and 3% skim milk in distilled water, but the solution was first centrifuged at 10 000g for 15 minutes. The spermatozoa were harvested from the epididymis at different temperatures (3°C, 23°C and 37°C) and the frozen samples were thawed by different methods. They concluded that sperm harvesting was more effective at 37°C, and that post-thaw sperm motility was significantly better if thawing was carried out at 37°C in water rather than at 23°C in air. The cryoprotectant was removed by centrifugation at 735g for 4 minutes, followed by replacement of the supernatant by 50 μl of minimum essential medium supplemented with BSA (3 mg/ml). The spermatozoa swam up into the medium, allowing collection of a highly motile fraction. The rate of fertilization in vitro with these spermatozoa was as high as that with fresh spermatozoa (91% versus 89%). A precise protocol for freezing spermatozoa in a raffinose-skim milk diluent can be found in Glenister and Rall (1999).

In the only report of the cryopreservation of spermatozoa from wild mice (Nakagata et al., 1995), spermatozoa from mice caught in China, Czechoslovakia, Denmark, India, Japan and Switzerland were frozen in 18% raffinose and 3% skim milk. Aliquots (100 μl) of sperm suspension were loaded into 0.25-ml plastic straws for freezing. The straws were cooled in the vapour in the neck of a liquid nitrogen container for 10 minutes, then immersed in the liquid nitrogen. For recovery, the straws were warmed in water at 20–24°C for 5 minutes, and the cryoprotectant was removed by filtration. Post-thaw motility was high for the Czechoslovakian, Danish and Indian mouse spermatozoa, which were mixed with intact oocytes for IVF. By contrast, the post-thaw motility of the Chinese, Japanese and Swiss mouse spermatozoa was 'low' (although not specified), and these spermatozoa were used to inseminate oocytes which had undergone partial dissection of the zona pellucida (PZD). Fertilization rates of 48–67% were obtained with the frozen–thawed spermatozoa and the incidence of polyspermy was not significantly higher after PZD. The incidence of live young born from the Indian and Danish mice (44–51% of embryos transferred) was, however, significantly higher than for the other strains (17–24%). A more detailed evaluation of PZD for the improvement of fertilization rates with cryopreserved spermatozoa from transgenic strains was presented by Nakagata et al. (1997).

Raffinose–glycerol diluents

The addition of glycerol to the raffinose-based cryopreservation medium was first reported by Tada et al. (1990) who used 1.75% glycerol as a supplementary cryoprotectant. In contrast to the samples frozen in raffinose–skim milk diluents, the sperm suspensions were frozen as 50-μl pellets on dry ice. Fertilization rates were increased from 35% to 85% when the cryoprotectant was removed by centrifugation (Tada *et al.*, 1993). The thawed sperm suspension (400 μl) was washed twice at 2000g for 1 minute, and resuspended in 400 μl of fresh IVF medium.

In extensive studies aimed at optimizing sperm survival and viability (Songsasen *et al.*, 1997; Songsasen and Leibo, 1997a,b), the diluent combined glycerol (200 mM; 1.84% w/v) and raffinose (300 mM), and also included the detergent-treated egg yolk fraction, introduced earlier by Penfold and Moore (1993). Initially the diluted egg yolk (4 ml yolk plus 12 ml Dulbecco's phosphate-buffered saline; D-PBS) was mixed with 16 mg of sodium lauryl sulphate (SDS). After allowing 30 minutes for solubilization, this mixture was centrifuged at 8800g for 30 minutes, and the supernatant used for subsequent diluent preparation by the addition of glycerol and raffinose. Aliquots (50 μl) of diluted sperm suspension were loaded into 0.25-ml plastic straws, and cooled at 5°C/min from ambient temperature to 4°C. Cooling continued either at at 20°C/min to −70°C before cooling to −196°C in liquid nitrogen, or at 10°C/min to −4°C for ice nucleation (seeding) and then at 20°C/min to −70°C before cooling to −196°C. The straws were thawed in water at 37°C for 10 seconds. The sperm suspensions were washed twice with D-PBS (400 μl) containing BSA (4.5 mg/ml) and centrifuged at 300g for 3 minutes. Finally, the spermatozoa were resuspended in D-PBS (200 μl) and incubated at 37°C.

The inclusion of egg yolk considerably improved sperm motility and fertilization rates after cryopreservation (Songsasen *et al.*, 1997), and seeding the straws produced a small but significant improvement in the rate of embryonic cleavage after IVF (Songsasen and Leibo, 1997a). Fertilization rates were similar when a one-step dilution method was tested against a stepwise method, but the pregnancy rates after embryo transfer were significantly better following stepwise dilution. The authors considered that one major benefit of this method is the ability to perform IVF using the sperm concentration normally used for mouse IVF (approximately 2×10^5 spermatozoa/ml). Some earlier authors used sperm concentrations which were 5–10 times higher.

As with earlier techniques, this cryopreservation method was not equally effective with all the strains of mice tested. In one report for example (Songsasen and Leibo, 1997b), it was shown that simply exposing spermatozoa to the cryoprotective additive (CPA), without freezing, reduced fertilization rates at IVF in two strains of mice (CPA treated versus untreated spermatozoa: strain 129/J, 40% versus 75%; strain C57BL/6J, 16% versus 82%). Spermatozoa from a third strain (B6D2Fl) were unaffected by exposure to CPA. After freezing and IVF, the rate of fertilization was 61% for strain B6D2Fl but fertility was severely depressed in the other strains (17% versus 3% for strains 129/J and C57BL/6J respectively). Further experiments showed that these differences were probably attributable to differential sensitivity to the osmotic shocks associated with the addition and removal of the cryoprotectant. Whilst strain variations are inconvenient for practical purposes, they offer an important opportunity to unravel the factors which govern sperm sensitivity to cryopreservation. Songsasen and Leibo (1997b) demonstrated that spermatozoa from the three strains tested would only tolerate exposure to osmolalities between 200 and 400 mOsm, but the presence of egg yolk extended the range up to 800 mOsm. Clearly this effect must be advantageous once ice formation has occurred, when the osmolarity of the unfrozen liquid fraction increases several fold. Responses to anisosmotic conditions were nevertheless unable to explain the interstrain differences between 129/J and B6D2F1 in susceptibility to cryoprotectants and freezing.

Investigations of the osmotic responses of the sperm plasma membrane in relation to sperm cryopreservation have been undertaken in a number of species, and mouse spermatozoa were recently added to the list (Noiles *et al.*, 1995; Willoughby *et al.*, 1996). Although this approach has its limitations, Noiles *et al.* (1997) raised the interesting possibility that the mouse sperm plasma membrane is unable to respond as expected to hyposmotic conditions because it is stabilized by cytoskeletal proteins. These authors showed that destabilization of the cytoskeletal network with cytochalasin D changed the cellular osmotic response, allowing the cells to swell as expected. This type of study might go some way towards explaining the interstrain differences, and clearly there is now a need to compare membrane stabilities across strains. This could also be an instructive exercise if carried out between species.

Timing of IVF with cryopreserved spermatozoa

Cooling to 4°C induces changes in the plasma membrane of mouse epididymal spermatozoa that resemble the changes that occur during capacitation. When cooled spermatozoa were mixed with oocytes immediately after warming their fertility was similar to that of freshly collected spermatozoa capacitated by culture *in vitro* for 90 minutes (Fuller and Whittingham, 1997). Thus it may be possible to increase the fertility of cryopreserved spermatozoa by treating them as capacitated cells and minimizing the time that elapses between thawing and IVF.

Freezing without cryoprotection

The extensive biological background surrounding the use of mice in biomedical research has led some researchers to question the need for maintaining the physiological viability of mouse spermatozoa. Based on earlier observations that isolated sperm nuclei can support embryonic development in cattle, human and hamster (Goto *et al.*, 1990; Katayose *et al.*, 1992), it was suggested that ICSI would be a practical method for fertilization if only 'dead' spermatozoa were available. This was tested using mouse spermatozoa frozen without cryoprotection (Wakayama *et al.*, 1998; Wakayama and Yanagimachi, 1998) and shown to be feasible. Spermatozoa were suspended in culture medium, with and without the inclusion of raffinose as a dehydrating agent. Aliquots (50 μl) of sperm suspension in 1-ml cryotubes were placed in a freezer (at $-20°C$ or $-50°C$) or directly into liquid nitrogen. After thawing, viability assays confirmed that the plasma membranes of these spermatozoa were damaged and thus the spermatozoa were immotile. When the heads of spermatozoa frozen without cryoproection were injected into oocytes, >95% were activated and fertilized normally. The authors noted some differences between the various modifications of the sperm freezing procedure, but qualified their remarks by saying that all of the treatments were successful, and that females produced litters of normal size with no apparent abnormalities.

These observations are obviously very significant since they offer the prospect of a simple, but highly effective, method of sperm storage. Clearly, the spermatozoa cannot be used without ICSI but, given the technical sophistication required for mouse IVF and embryo transfer, only a small increment in laboratory facilities and skills would be required to make this a viable option. Serious consideration should also be given to this approach as a way of using cryopreserved spermatozoa from other rodent species, given that there is virtually no information in the literature about the more traditional methods.

13.2.2   MATURE OOCYTES

For conservation purposes, the scarcity of mature, metaphase II oocytes will be a major stumbling block, unless the donors can be induced to superovulate or techniques for the *in vitro* growth and maturation of immature oocytes are perfected. Oocytes are cryopreserved using methods similar to those developed for embryos.

Origin and recovery

Mature oocytes of several common laboratory stocks have been cryopreserved successfully. Oocytes are recovered from 3- to 4-week-old or adult mice induced to superovulate by injection of eCG and hCG given 48–52 hours apart (Gates, 1971). The oocytes, surrounded by cumulus cells, are released from the oviducts 13–16 hours post-hCG into phosphate-buffered PB1 (Whittingham, 1974) or HEPES-buffered M2 (Wood *et al.*, 1987). The influence of the buffer on oocyte survival has not been tested, but under certain circumstances the macromolecular supplement (BSA, FBS, PVA) in the freezing medium, has a profound effect on subsequent rates of fertilization (Carroll *et al.*, 1993). Stacheki *et al.* (1998) found that substituting choline for sodium in the handling and freezing media increased the survival of oocytes (94% versus 71%) and the rate of fertilization *in vitro* (77% versus 50%). Removal of the cumulus cells with hyaluronidase had no effect on the proportion of normal oocytes recovered after thawing or on the subsequent rate of fertilization *in vitro* (Whittingham, 1977b).

Equilibrium rate freezing

Cryoprotectant and method of introduction

Oocytes are usually frozen in DMSO introduced in a single step at 0°C. Exposure to DMSO at higher temperatures in medium containing BSA 'hardened' the zona pellucida and decreased the subsequent rate of fertilization *in vitro* (Johnson, 1989). Stacheki *et al.* (1998) froze oocytes in PrOH and sucrose introduced in two steps at ambient temperature.

Freezing and thawing rates

After induction of ice in the freezing medium at temperatures between −5°C and −7°C, oocytes were cooled at slow rates between 0.25°C and 0.6°C/min to −33°C (Stacheki *et al.*, 1998), −40°C (Carroll *et al.*, 1993) or −80°C (Whittingham, 1977b; Glenister *et al.*, 1987; Schroeder *et al*, 1990; Carroll *et al.*, 1993), before rapid cooling in liquid nitrogen.

Warming and dilution of the cryoprotectant

After slow cooling to −80°C before transfer into liquid nitrogen, oocytes were warmed slowly at rates between −8°C and 20°C/min. Oocytes cooled slowly to −33°C or −40°C before rapid cooling were warmed rapidly by holding the straw in air for 30 seconds and then in water at 30°C until the ice melted. DMSO was diluted from the oocytes in a single step at ambient temperature (Glenister *et al.*, 1987; Carroll *et al.*, 1993) or stepwise at 0°C (Schroeder *et al.*, 1990) or ambient temperature (Stacheki *et al.*, 1998). Contemporary comparisons of the alternative methods have not been made.

More than 80% of oocytes survived freezing by the most successful and widely used methods reported to date (Schroeder *et al.*, 1990; Carroll *et al.*, 1993), and the proportion of these fertilized *in vitro* (~85%) was similar to unfrozen control oocytes. A precise protocol for the procedure of Carroll *et al.* (1993) may be found in Glenister and Rall (1999). Survival and fertilization were also high (94% and 77% respectively) in oocytes frozen in low-sodium medium (Stacheki *et al.*, 1998). Unfortunately, all of these procedures have the disadvantage of relying on the inclusion of FBS in the medium to prevent hardening of the zona pellucida, a practice that may be prohibited if oocytes are to be transported internationally. Zona hardening, measured by the time taken to digest the zona pellucida with α-chymotrypsin, was less marked in oocytes in which DMSO was added and removed at 4°C than in those where one or other of the procedures was carried out at 37°C (Johnson, 1989). Whittingham (1977b) probably achieved high rates of fertilization after freezing oocytes in medium containing BSA because the cryoprotectant was added and removed at 0°C.

The viability of embryos obtained by fertilization *in vitro* of frozen and unfrozen oocytes is similar, irrespective of the freezing method or the macromolecular supplement in the freezing medium. When embryos were transferred at the two-cell stage to the oviducts of pseudopregnant recipients, 67–78% implanted and 50–58% had formed normal fetuses at autopsy in late gestation (Glenister *et al.*, 1987; Carroll *et al.*, 1993). Previously, Whittingham (1977b) reported rather lower rates of development when the embryos were transferred at the two-cell stage (16–38%) or allowed to develop to blastocysts before transfer to the uterus of recipients (36%). The rates did not differ from controls and may reflect strain differences or the small sample sizes. A few live fetuses were recovered when oocytes were transferred immediately after thawing to the oviduct of recipients mated 2 hours previously, but the procedure was less efficient than fertilization *in vitro* (Whittingham, 1977b).

Ultra-rapid freezing and vitrification

Oocytes have been frozen rapidly after dehydration at ambient temperature in DMSO and sucrose (Van der Elst *et al.*, 1993a) or EG and sucrose or trehalose (Rayos *et al.*, 1994). About 78% of oocytes survived freezing and thawing, and 60–70% of these were fertilized normally. The freezing and diluting media in both studies contained FBS. Development *in vitro* and *in vivo* was reduced compared with controls, but Rayos *et al.* (1994) reported an overall survival (fetuses/oocytes frozen) of ~20%.

Overall rates of survival comparable with those obtained after slow cooling in DMSO (~37%: Carroll *et al.*, 1993) have been achieved for oocytes vitrified in VS1 (33%: Nakagata, 1989). (For the formula of VS1 a vitrification solution containing a high concentrations of cryoprotectives, see Rall and Fahy, 1985.) Others reported variability in survival and viability between samples (Shaw *et al.*, 1992) and high rates of embryonic loss after transfer (Kola *et al.*, 1988). Survival was high (>70%) after vitrification in 6.0 M DMSO but there was considerable variation between straws. When the surviving oocytes were fertilized *in vitro* and then transferred to foster mothers, the incidence of post-implantation loss was high, with only 40% developing to normal fetuses compared with 61% of control embryos (Wood *et al.*, 1993). The addition of PEG to the vitrification solution (O'Neill *et al.*, 1997) reduced the incidence of samples that crystallized during warming and also the variability between samples. Overall, 63% of vitrified oocytes developed to blastocysts after fertilization *in vitro* (O'Neill *et al.*, 1997).

Evaluation

Cryopreserved oocytes are usually assessed by fertilization *in vitro* and subsequent development, either *in vitro* or after embryo transfer. Cell number was reduced in blastocysts developed from frozen oocytes (Van der Elst *et al.*, 1993a). The occurrence of polyploidy, but not aneuploidy, was increased in cryopreserved oocytes fertilized *in vitro* (Glenister *et al.*, 1987; Van der Elst *et al.*, 1993a). Cytoskeletal aberrations seen immediately after thawing were partially (spindle morphology) or fully (microfilaments and microtubules) restored to normal after 1 hour incubation *in vitro* (Eroglu *et al.*, 1998a).

13.2.3 IMMATURE OOCYTES

The use of cryopreserved immature oocytes is limited mainly by the inadequacy of techniques for their growth and maturation *in vitro* after thawing.

Origin and recovery

Immature oocytes at the germinal vesicle (GV) stage have been recovered from the ovaries of 3 to 6-week-old F1 hybrid or outbred mice, by puncturing the antral follicles 40–52 hours after injection of eCG (Schroeder *et al.*, 1990; Van der Elst *et al.*, 1992, 1993b; Candy *et al.*, 1994; Eroglu *et al.*, 1998b; Isachenko and Nayudu, 1999). In most cases they were cryopreserved surrounded by layers of cumulus cells. Immature oocytes recovered from unstimulated donors were cryopreserved after removal of the cumulus cells by mechanical pipetting (Van Blerkom, 1989; Van Blerkom and Davis, 1994; Frydman *et al.*, 1997). There has been no comparative study but results suggest that denuding GV oocytes does not compromise their survival after freezing and thawing, although denuded oocytes matured *in vitro* may have a lower developmental capacity than cumulus-enclosed oocytes (Schroeder *et al.*, 1990). The inclusion of a meiotic inhibitor in media used for handling and freezing, maintains oocytes at the GV stage and may be important during cryopreservation to avoid spontaneous resumption of meiosis in suboptimal conditions, such as cold or osmotic stress. The addition of egg yolk to media used during vitrification and dilution had a beneficial effect on survival and subsequent maturation *in vitro* (Isachenko and Nayudu, 1999).

Cryopreservation

Cryoprotectant and method of introduction

Oocytes have usually been cooled slowly in DMSO added at 0–4°C, and Van der Elst *et al.* (1993b) found that DMSO offers more protection during slow cooling than PrOH and sucrose. Oocytes have been cooled rapidly in VS1 (Van Blerkom, 1989), EG and sucrose (Isachenko and Nayudu, 1999), and DMSO and PrOH with or without sucrose (Van der Elst *et al.*, 1992, 1993b; Van Blerkom and Davis, 1994). In general, the oocytes were exposed to increasing concentrations of cryoprotectants at ambient temperature or 37°C. Exposure to EG and sucrose at 37°C compared with 25°C improved survival and subsequent maturation of vitrified immature oocytes (Isachenko and Nayudu, 1999).

Freezing method and cooling rates

Oocytes in low concentrations of cryoprotectant (<2.0 M) contained in plastic straws and cryovials were cooled slowly (0.3–0.5°C/min) to −40°C (Candy *et al.*, 1994; Frydman *et al.*, 1997) or below −70°C (Schroeder *et al.*, 1990; Van der Elst *et al.*, 1993b; Cooper *et al.*, 1998; Eroglu *et al.*, 1998b) before immersion in liquid nitrogen. Oocytes in more concentrated cryoprotective solutions were cooled rapidly in liquid nitrogen.

Thawing rates

Rapidly cooled oocytes and oocytes in which slow cooling was terminated at –40°C were warmed rapidly (−500°C/min). When slow cooling was terminated below −70°C, oocytes were warmed slowly (<10°C/min).

Diluent composition and method of dilution of cryoprotectant

Cryoprotectants have been removed in a single step with isotonic medium or medium containing sucrose, or stepwise by transferring the oocytes through gradually decreasing concentrations of the cryopreservation solution. Survival after ultrarapid freezing in 3 M DMSO was better after single-step dilution compared with stepwise dilution (78% versus 58%: Van der Elst *et al.*, 1993b).

Evaluation

The highest survival rates (around 90%) have been achieved after slow cooling to −40°C in 1.5 M DMSO, immersion in liquid nitrogen then rapid warming and dilution of the cryoprotectant in a single step with isotonic medium (Candy *et al.*, 1994; Frydman *et al.*, 1997). Oocytes were cultured *in vitro* in most studies and, typically, >75% matured. Similar proportions of fresh and frozen GV oocytes matured *in vitro* were penetrated by spermatozoa (88%: Isachenko and Nayudu, 1999), and developed to the two-cell (70–80%: Candy *et al.*, 1994; Cooper *et al.*, 1998) and the blastocyst (40%: Van der Elst *et al.*, 1993b) stages *in vitro*. Late-stage fetuses (42%) developed after two-cell embryos derived from frozen–thawed GV oocytes were transferred into pseudopregnant recipients (Candy *et al.*, 1994); and pups (21/37) were born to recipients allowed to carry their litters to term.

13.2.4 OVARY

Origin and recovery

Ovaries have been recovered from laboratory strains at autopsy or during surgical ovariectomy, then frozen intact or cut into pieces no bigger than 1 mm³ before freezing. The donors were usually adult (Harp *et al.*, 1994; Gunasena *et al.*, 1997a) but ovaries from neonates (10 days old: Candy *et al.*, 1997, 2000) and fetuses (day 16 of gestation: Cox *et al.*, 1996) have also been frozen. Phosphate-, HEPES- or bicarbonate-buffered media have been used for recovery and during cryopreservation, but comparisons have not been made.

Cryopreservation

Cryoprotectant and method of introduction

In a comparison of DMSO, PrOH, EG and glycerol introduced in a single step at ambient temperature or 4°C, DMSO offered the best protection against freezing damage. Ovaries frozen in glycerol had the highest proportion of damaged primordial follicles and fewest follicles remaining 15 days after grafting (Candy *et al.*, 1997).

Freezing method and cooling rates

Ovarian tissue has been frozen by cooling slowly (0.3–0.5°C/min) to −40°C (Cox *et al.*, 1996; Shaw *et al.*, 1996; Candy *et al.*, 1997, 2000), −55°C (Harp *et al.*, 1994; Gunasena *et al.*, 1997a,b) or −80°C (Sztein *et al.*, 1998) before rapid cooling in liquid nitrogen.

Warming rates

Slow warming rates (~15°C/min) have generally been used when ovarian tissue was cooled slowly to −55°C and below, whereas rapid warming rates (~85°C/min) have been used when slow cooling was terminated at −40°C. A comparison of warming rates after slow cooling to −40°C suggested that more recipients of rapidly warmed ovaries became pregnant (Cox *et al.*, 1996).

Diluent composition and method of dilution of cryoprotectant

Cryoprotectants have been diluted at ambient temperature in a single step with handling medium or stepwise with medium containing sucrose. No comparisons have been made.

Post-thaw handling

Gunasena *et al.* (1997b) cut the ovaries after thawing and dilution to enable them to fit within the ovarian bursa.

Evaluation

Estimates of the survival of follicles in cryopreserved ovaries were based on histological counts of morphologically normal follicles in ovaries before and after grafting (Candy *et al.*, 1997). Fertility was fully restored with the birth of pups to 57–73% of recipients of orthotopic grafts of cryopreserved ovarian tissue (Gunasena *et al.*, 1997a,b; Sztein *et al.*, 1998; Candy *et al.*, 2000). Recipients of grafts of cryopreserved ovaries had a normal reproductive lifespan with normal fertility (Candy *et al.*, 2000). It is important to include a genetic marker to distinguish pups derived from grafted ovaries because of the risk of incomplete removal of native ovary during surgical ovariectomy (Gunasena *et al.*, 1997b; Sztein *et al.*, 1998; Candy *et al.*, 2000). Tissue rejection is easily avoided in laboratory mice by grafting into histocompatible or immunologically compromised (nude or SCID) recipients, but in other species it will be a major problem. The growth and maturation *in vitro* of oocytes recovered from frozen ovary is perhaps a more promising approach for conservation.

13.2.5 ISOLATED OVARIAN FOLLICLES

There have been few attempts to cryopreserve ovarian follicles, largely because of the difficulties associated with subsequent development *in vitro*.

Origin and recovery

Primordial and primary follicles were isolated from the ovaries of 4- to10-day-old B6CBF1 hybrid mice by digestion with collagenase followed by mechanical disaggregation (Carroll *et al.*, 1990; Carroll and Gosden, 1993). Early pre-antral follicles were dissected from the ovaries of 14-day-old mice (Cortvrindt *et al.*, 1996). The follicles were handled and frozen in M2 or Leibovitz medium containing FBS (5–10 %).

Cryopreservation method

Follicles were exposed to DMSO (1.5 M) in a single step at 0–4°C then loaded into plastic straws (Carroll *et al.*, 1990; Carroll and Gosden, 1993) or plastic cryovials (Cortvrindt *et al.*, 1996). After seeding at −7°C they were cooled slowly (0.3°C/min) to −40°C then stored in liquid nitrogen. After rapid warming in water at 37°C, the cryoprotectant was diluted at ambient temperature either in a single step with handling medium (Carroll *et al.*, 1990; Carroll and Gosden, 1993) or stepwise, through decreasing concentrations of DMSO (Cortvrindt *et al.*, 1996).

Post-thaw handling

Primordial follicles were reaggregated in a fibrin clot to facilitate orthotopic grafting (Carroll and Gosden, 1993). Primary follicles were embedded in collagen gels for culture *in vitro* and subsequently the gels were inserted beneath the renal capsules of ovariectomized recipients (Carroll *et al.*, 1990).

Evaluation

A trypan blue exclusion assay showed that 80% of primordial follicles survived cryopreservation (Carroll and Gosden, 1993) and 78% of primary follicles appeared morphologically normal immediately after thawing (Carroll *et al.*, 1990). Frozen primordial follicles in fibrin clots were grafted into the ovarian bursae of ovari-ectomized mice that were then mated, and 44% of recipients gave birth to pups (Carroll and Gosden, 1993). The development of primary follicles in collagen gels was limited. The recipients of gels were injected with gonadotrophins, but only 7% of oocytes (19) subsequently recovered from the gels had undergone nuclear maturation and extruded the first polar body. These oocytes were inseminated *in vitro* and three pups were born after transfer of the resultant two-cell embryos to pseudopregnant recipients (Carroll *et al.*, 1990). Irreversible damage, assessed histologically, was seen in 24% of cryopreserved pre-antral follicles (Cortvrindt *et al.*, 1996). After culture *in vitro*, oocytes were recovered from similar proportions (~85%) of fresh and frozen pre-antral follicles. Between 20% and 50% of oocytes were fertilized and continued embryonic development *in vitro* to the hatched blastocyst stage (Cortvrindt *et al.*, 1996).

13.2.6 EMBRYOS

Mouse embryos are cryopreserved in laboratories worldwide and inevitably this has resulted in the development of many cryopreservation protocols of varying efficiency, some of which differ in minor details only. No attempt will be made to provide a comprehensive review of them. Instead attention will focus mainly on robust methods that are used successfully in more than one laboratory.

Strains

Embryos of inbred, outbred, random-bred, mutant, congenic, transgenic, knockin and knockout laboratory mice are routinely cryopreserved for embryo banking. The overall rate of survival (i.e. the proportion of the embryos frozen that subsequently develop to form normal late-stage fetuses or live mice after thawing and transfer to foster mothers) varies between strains (Dinnyés *et al.* 1995). This should be taken into account when deciding how many embryos are needed to conserve a particular genotype.

Developmental stage and recovery

Embryos at all stages of preimplantation development from the pronucleate zygote to the expanded blastocyst can be cryopreserved, although the eight-cell stage is considered optimal for routine banking (Wood *et al.*, 1987). Embryos are recovered by flushing the excised reproductive tract on days 1–5 of pregnancy (when day 1 is the day on which the copulation plug is seen), with medium M2, medium PB1 or a simple PBS. The donors are mated in a natural oestrous cycle or after intra-peritoneal injection of eCG and hCG given 44–52 hours apart (Gates, 1971). The response of strains to exogenous gonadotrophins varies from total refractoriness, through synchronization of oestrus to reliable superovulation. Embryos produced by IVF and cryopreserved at the two-cell stage, subsequently developed to expanded blastocysts *in vitro* at a rate similar to embryos from fertilization *in vivo* (Bernard and Fuller, 1983). Blastocysts derived from IVF embryos were cryopreserved and subsequently developed normally after embryo transfer, albeit at a low rate (Massip *et al.*, 1984). There have been insufficient studies to conclude whether fertilization or development *in vitro* renders embryos more susceptible to cryopreservation injury than their counterparts fertilized and developed *in vivo*.

Handling *in vitro*

After recovery, embryos are pipetted through several changes of the flushing medium at ambient temperature and then held at ambient temperature or at 0°C before freezing. There has been no controlled study to examine the effect of the holding temperature and the time between collection and freezing. For routine embryo banking either temperature seems to be suitable and the period of delay before freezing may be >1 hour. PB1 and M2 contain pyruvate and glucose and are usually supplemented with BSA. M2 also contains lactate. These energy sources may help to avoid depletion of metabolic pools in the embryos during preparation for freezing, particularly in embryos held at ambient temperature for long periods. Pronucleate-stage embryos may be treated briefly with hyaluronidase to remove any adhering cumulus cells and then washed through several changes of flushing medium.

Cryopreservation

Mouse embryos are cryopreserved by 'slow' equilibrium rate freezing, non-equilibrium rate 'ultra-rapid' freezing, and vitrification. In contemporary comparisons similar rates of success were achieved with these alternative approaches. Between 63% and 76% of eight-cell embryos vitrified or frozen in glycerol developed to form normal late-stage fetuses and pups after transfer to recipients (Rall and Wood, 1994). When eight-cell embryos were frozen slowly in DMSO or ultra-rapidly in DMSO and sucrose, overall survival was estimated at about 40% (Wood et al., 1992). The novice may find slow cooling procedures more manageable. Similarly, when first trying to cryopreserve embryos from a new species, the greater range of conditions over which at least some survival is achieved may make slow cooling the method of choice. The major disadvantage is that slow cooling usually requires a programmable freezing machine, although a simple homemade apparatus will suffice (Wood et al., 1987). Vitrification is a useful approach when storing small samples of embryos but slow cooling in a programmed freezer is far more efficient for the preservation of a large batch of embryos. It is noteworthy that the world's major embryo banking facilities prefer slow cooling procedures although some occasionally vitrify embryos when the sample is small.

Slow (equilibrium rate) freezing

Slow, equilibrium rate freezing depends on the gradual dehydration of the embryo during slow cooling after ice is formed in the suspending medium. Detailed protocols for the most commonly used slow freezing methods are found in Wood et al. (1987) and Glenister and Rall (1999).

> *Cryoprotectant.* Mouse embryos are usually frozen slowly in low concentrations (1–2 M) of DMSO (Whittingham et al., 1972, 1979), PrOH (Renard and Babinet, 1984) or glycerol (Rall and Wood, 1994). DMSO and PrOH are used for embryos at any stage of preimplantation development. Early embryonic stages have a low permeability for glycerol which is usually used only for the eight-cell to blastocyst stages. Rall et al. (1984b) obtained viable offspring after the transfer of morulae and early blastocysts frozen in 3.0 M methanol. More recently, using development *in vitro* to assess survival, EG was shown to protect mouse zygotes, eight-cell stage embryos and blastocysts (Leibo and Oda, 1993; Shaw et al., 1994a,b). The cryoprotectant is usually introduced in a single step at ambient temperature, except DMSO which is introduced at 0°C in a single step or, particularly for blastocysts, in three incremental steps. Embryo cryopreservation solutions usually contain BSA but Leibo and Oda (1993) substituted PVP and reported high rates of survival *in vitro*. There is no evidence that antifreeze proteins afford any protection to mouse embryos and they may even be deleterious (Shaw et al., 1994a,b).

> *Container.* Embryos have been frozen slowly in glass test tubes (Whittingham et al., 1972, 1979), glass (Wood et al., 1987) or plastic ampoules (Whittingham et al.,

1977) and plastic insemination straws (Renard and Babinet, 1984; Rall, 1992). The loss of viability reported for embryos warmed rapidly in plastic ampoules probably reflects the poor rate of heat conduction compared with glass containers (Whittingham *et al.*, 1977).

Cooling rate and method. After inducing ice formation in the freezing medium, embryos are cooled: (1) in DMSO at rates between 0.3 and 0.5°C/min to −40°C or −80°C before immersion in liquid nitrogen (Whittingham *et al.*, 1972, 1979); (2) in PrOH at 0.3°C/min to −30°C, then at >10°C/min to −150°C before immersion in liquid nitrogen (Renard and Babinet, 1984); (3) in glycerol at 0.4–0.5°C/min to −40°C, held at −40°C for 10 minutes, then immersed in liquid nitrogen (Rall, 1992; Rall and Wood, 1994).

Warming and dilution of the cryoprotectant. The rate of warming for optimal survival is determined by the choice of cryoprotectant and the temperature at which slow cooling is terminated. Irrespective of the cryoprotectant, when slow cooling is terminated at higher subzero temperatures (above about −55°C), rapid warming (>200°C/min) is essential. After slow cooling to temperatures below −55°C, embryos in DMSO require slow warming (~8–25°C/min: Whittingham *et al.*, 1979) but embryos in glycerol and PrOH are insensitive to the rate of warming (Rall and Polge, 1984).

The more rapidly permeating cryoprotectants (DMSO and PrOH) are diluted approximately ten-fold using PB1 or M2, stepwise at 0°C or ambient temperature, or in a single step at ambient temperature, before returning the embryos to isotonic conditions. Alternatively, dilution is done in a single step using medium containing sucrose (0.8–1.0 M) to buffer the movement of water into the blastomeres during cryoprotectant removal, before they are finally transferred to isotonic medium. For eight-cell embryos in 1.5 M PrOH warmed at ~300°C/min, the inclusion of sucrose in the diluent did not influence embryo survival and subsequent development *in vitro* (~90% of embryos diluted with or without sucrose developed normally; Renard and Babinet, 1984). Nonetheless, it has become common practice to use sucrose to remove PrOH and this may have the advantage of improving survival if embryos have been cooled suboptimally. Similar rates of survival and development *in vitro* (50–60%) were obtained after stepwise dilution of DMSO at 0°C and ambient temperature, and single-step dilution at ambient temperature (Whittingham *et al.*, 1979). Sucrose has rarely been used to remove the DMSO from slowly frozen embryos. Glycerol is diluted stepwise at ambient temperature with isotonic medium (Rall and Polge, 1984) or in a single step with medium containing sucrose at 35°C (Rall, 1992).

When developing a freezing method, it may be advantageous to observe the embryos in a Petri dish or embryological watchglass immediately after thawing and during dilution, so that changes in the volume of the embryos can be recorded. Subsequently, for dilution with medium containing sucrose, it is convenient to freeze the diluent in the straw separated by an air bubble from the column of freezing medium containing the embryos. The volume of the air bubble determines whether it moves and allows mixing of the fractions during thawing, or whether the fractions remain separate until the straw is shaken or the contents are expelled into a petri dish (for details of loading the straws, see, for example, Renard and Babinet, 1984; Rall, 1992; Rall and Wood, 1994). Incubation of the straws at 35°C during dilution may further assist the removal of glycerol. After cryopreservation in glycerol, warming at ~2000°C min and dilution immediately after thawing within the straw, the majority (155/159) of eight-cell embryos resumed development *in vitro*, and of these, 76% developed normally after transfer to foster mothers (Rall and Wood, 1994). Renard and Babinet (1984) found that dilution of PrOH within the straw as the ice melted was essential to maintain a high rate of survival of embryos warmed at ~2500°C/min.

It is not always essential to remove rapidly permeating cryoprotectants before embryo transfer. Rall *et al.* (1984b) compared the survival of mouse embryos frozen in methanol and then transferred to pseudopregnant recipients either immediately after thawing without dilution, or after dilution of the methanol and culture for 12–15 hours. Irrespective of the procedure, 25% of the embryos recovered after thawing subsequently developed to late stage fetuses. Similarly embryos frozen in DMSO may be transferred to foster mothers without first removing the DMSO (Rall *et al.*, 1984a).

Ultra-rapid (non-equilibrium rate) freezing and vitrification

These approaches to cryopreservation depend on exposing the embryos to concentrated cryoprotective solutions to dehydrate and concentrate the cytoplasm before cooling. The time and temperature of exposure to the solutions is critical to achieve optimal dehydration with minimal toxic damage. For vitrification, the solution solidifies without crystallization during cooling to −196°C and remains free from ice crystals during rapid warming (>200°C/min). Under some circumstances, high rates of embryo survival are achieved even though crystallization occurs during rapid cooling or warming. These procedures are commonly called ultra-rapid freezing.

Acceptable rates of survival have been achieved with ultra-rapid freezing procedures using a variety of cryoprotectant solutions. For example, overall survival was 30–40% for eight-cell embryos cooled in nitrogen vapour or liquid nitrogen in 4.0 M glycerol and 0.5 M sucrose or in 3.0–3.5 M DMSO and 0.25 M sucrose (Széll and Shelton, 1987; Trounson *et al.*, 1988; Wood *et al.*, 1992). Chromosome rearrangements occurred in two-cell embryos frozen rapidly in 3.0 M DMSO and 0.25 M sucrose, but no anomalies were seen and overall survival was estimated at ~71% when the concentration of DMSO was increased to 4.5 M (Shaw *et al.*, 1991b). Similar high rates of overall survival (>60%) were obtained for all embryonic stages from pronucleate zygote to blastocyst (Shaw *et al.*, 1991a). To the best of our knowledge, ultra-rapid freezing procedures have not been adopted for large-scale embryo banking.

Embryos were vitrified successfully for the first time in a solution of DMSO, PrOH, acetamide and PEG (VS1; Rall and Fahy, 1985). VS1 is highly toxic even when added and removed at ~4°C (Rall, 1987; Rall *et al.*, 1987). Less toxic alternative solutions were soon developed in which embryos can be equilibrated at ambient temperature. These included 25% PROH and 25% glycerol (Scheffen *et al.*, 1986), 40% ethylene glycol, 30% Ficoll and 0.5 M sucrose (EFS, Kasai *et al.*, 1990), 6.5 M glycerol and 6% BSA (VS3a; Rall and Wood, 1994). Embryos are transferred from isotonic medium directly into solution EFS but for vitrification in the glycerol-based solutions, embryos are equilibrated in low concentrations of the cryoprotectants and then, immediately before cooling, loaded into straws containing the vitrification solution. The time of exposure to the vitrification solution before cooling is critical for survival (Kasai *et al.*, 1992; Glenister and Rall, 1999). The straws are cooled at >200°C/min in nitrogen vapour or liquid nitrogen. After rapid warming (>2500°C/min), the vitrification solution is diluted with sucrose (0.5–1.0 M). Detailed protocols for vitrification using EFS and VS3a can be found in Kasai (1995) and Glenister and Rall (1999). Kasai (1995) includes modifications for vitrification of embryos at all stages of development in EFS, but VS3a is not used for embryos before the eight-cell stage.

Overall survival was 31% for compacted morulae vitrified in solution EFS (Kasai *et al.*, 1990) and 63% for eight to twelve-cell embryos vitrified in solution VS3a (Rall and Wood, 1994). These differences may reflect true differences in the cryopreservation procedures but other factors may be implicated. The higher rate of pregnancy failure in the recipients of embryos vitrified in EFS (5/16) compared with those receiving embryos vitrified in VS3a (1/28) may be due to strain variation in the recipients. The degree of asynchrony between the embryo and endometrium was only about 12 hours for the embryos vitrified in EFS but between 24 and 48 hours for those vitrified in VS3a. Thus the embryos vitrified in VS3a had longer for the resumption of normal development before synchronization with the endometrium for implantation. Also, most of the embryos vitrified in VS3a were recovered before parturition, whereas, by allowing all of the recipients to litter, Kasai *et al.* (1990) used a more stringent evaluation of embryo viability, and may have lost normal pups by cannibalization or neglect.

It is noteworthy that for embryos in VS3a, a wide range of cooling and warming rates are consistent with high rates of survival (assessed by development *in vitro*). When ice formation was avoided (i.e. true vitrification) by cooling and warming at rates >200°C/min, 86–97% of embryos subsequently developed *in vitro*. Similarly 75–93% of

■
CHAPTER 13
■

embryos developed normally after slow cooling at 5°C/min, or slow warming at 20°C/min, or both, even though the solution crystallized (Rall and Wood, 1994).

Post-thaw handling

Thawed embryos are cultured *in vitro* to morula or blastocyst stages then transferred to the uterine horns of recipients on day 3 of pseudopregnancy. Alternatively, embryos at any stage of development may be transferred immediately after thawing or after culture, to the oviducts of recipients on day 1 of pseudopregnancy (Renard and Babinet, 1984; Wood *et al.*, 1987).

Evaluation

Frozen embryos have been evaluated using a variety of assays, e.g. the uptake of albumin and leucine and fluorescein diacetate accumulation (Onohara *et al.*, 1994), distribution of cell surface antigens (Wood *et al.*, 1992). The most frequently used assay of new cryopreservation procedures is the ability of the thawed embryos to resume development during culture *in vitro*. This correlates highly with the ultimate assay of viability, i.e. live births after transfer to pseudopregnant recipients (Wood *et al.*, 1987). Comparison of the cell numbers of fresh and frozen eight-cell embryos showed that, after 24 hours culture *in vitro*, frozen embryos were approximately one mitotic division behind their fresh counterparts, suggesting that development is delayed by freezing (Whittingham, 1977a).

13.3   RAT

13.3.1   OOCYTES

Origin and recovery

Oocytes were recovered in phosphate- or bicarbonate-buffered medium from 21- to 27-day-old Wistar and Sprague-Dawley rats injected with eCG and hCG 48 hours apart. Mature oocytes were flushed from the oviducts ~14–16 hours post hCG and the cumulus cells removed with hyaluronidase (Niwa *et al.*, 1979; Nakagata, 1992). Immature oocytes were pricked from the ovary ~48 hours after injection of eCG without hCG or between 3 and 9 hours after injection of hCG (Kasai *et al.*, 1979; Pellicer *et al.*, 1988). Post-thaw survival increased with time post-hCG (Kasai *et al.*, 1979). Immature oocytes with more than five layers of cumulus cells survived better than denuded oocytes (Pellicer *et al.*, 1988). Neither Kasai *et al.* (1979) nor Pellicer *et al.* (1988) used a meiotic inhibitor to arrest GV breakdown during collection and freezing.

Cryopreservation

Cryoprotectant and method of introduction

Oocytes were frozen slowly in DMSO introduced stepwise at 0–37°C (Kasai *et al.*, 1979; Niwa *et al.*, 1979) or in a single step at 0°C (Pellicer *et al.*, 1988). Survival was highest when DMSO was added at ambient temperature (Kasai *et al.*, 1979). Nakagata (1992) froze mature oocytes ultrarapidly in a mixture of DMSO, acetamide and PrOH.

Freezing method and cooling rates

Oocytes in glass ampoules or test tubes were cooled slowly (0.3–1.0°C/min) to temperatures between −36°C and −80°C before rapid cooling in liquid nitrogen. For ultra-rapid freezing, the oocytes were loaded into straws and immersed in liquid nitrogen.

Thawing rates

Oocytes cooled slowly to −80°C before storage in liquid nitrogen were warmed at 25°C/min (Kasai *et al.*, 1979; Niwa *et al.*, 1979). After slow cooling terminated at −36°C and after ultrarapid freezing, oocytes were warmed rapidly in water at 37°C (Pellicer *et al.*, 1988; Nakagata, 1992).

Diluent composition and method of dilution of cryoprotectant

Oocytes were diluted with isotonic medium stepwise or in a single step at ambient temperature (Kasai *et al.*, 1979; Niwa *et al.*, 1979; Pellicer *et al.*, 1988). Compared with dilution at 0°C, dilution at ambient temperature or 37°C increased the survival of immature oocytes (29% versus ~50%) and the proportion penetrated by spermatozoa after maturation *in vitro* (12% versus ~33%: Kasai *et al.*, 1979).

Evaluation

Up to 73% of immature oocytes survived cryopreservation (Pellicer *et al.*, 1988). Subsequently GV breakdown occurred at a slower rate than in unfrozen oocytes (Pellicer *et al.*, 1988) and fewer frozen than control oocytes were penetrated by spermatozoa (Kasai *et al.*, 1979). Examination of uridine uptake showed that freezing and thawing caused a reduction in the metabolic coupling between the cumulus cells and the oocyte (Pellicer *et al.*, 1988). Only ~20% of mature oocytes survived after slow cooling, ~80% of the survivors were penetrated by spermatozoa *in vitro* but only 4/13 cleaved (Niwa *et al.*, 1979). In contrast, 65% of mature oocytes survived vitrification; 60% of these were penetrated by spermatozoa after IVF but only 16% cleaved normally. After transfer to foster mothers at the pronucleate stage, 18% of eggs (28/150) developed to form normal pups (Nakagata, 1992).

13.3.2 Ovary

Origin and recovery

Ovaries were removed surgically from adult donors to facilitate autografting after cryopreservation (Aubard *et al.*, 1998) or at autopsy from 7-day-old donors (Sugimoto *et al.*, 1996). The ovaries, in PBS or Leibovitz medium, were freed from surrounding fat and mesentery, then frozen intact (Sugimoto *et al.*, 1996) or bisected before freezing (Aubard *et al.*, 1998).

Freezing

After incubation in DMSO or EG at ~4°C, bisected ovaries were cooled slowly at 0.3°C/min to −40°C and stored in liquid nitrogen. They were warmed rapidly in water at 20°C and diluted rapidly in a single step in physiological saline. Similar numbers of follicles survived freezing in DMSO or EG (Aubard *et al.*, 1998).

Vitrification

Whole ovaries were exposed to solution VS1 stepwise for 40 minutes, initially at ambient temperature and then at 4°C, before rapid cooling in liquid nitrogen. They were warmed slowly in water at 0°C. The survival of follicles was similar after stepwise dilution and dilution using sucrose as an osmotic buffer (Sugimoto *et al.*, 1996).

Evaluation

The apparently viable follicles in cryopreserved ovaries were counted after 4 days in culture (Sugimoto *et al.*, 1996) or 18 days after orthotopic grafting (Aubard *et al.*, 1998). Vitrified ovaries contained only 26–28% viable follicles compared with fresh ovaries. Grafts of ovaries frozen in EG and DMSO contained 23 and 31% respectively of the follicle population of ungrafted ovaries. Seventy-two per cent of the recipients of autografts of cryopreserved ovaries became pregnant but, in the absence of a genetic marker, fertility could not be attributed with certainty to the grafted ovary.

13.3.3 Embryos

Origin, developmental stage and recovery

Random-bred, inbred, F1 hybrid and transgenic rat embryos have been cryopreserved successfully but the influence of strain on survival has not been examined. Embryos are usually collected by flushing from the reproductive tract of adult rats in a natural cycle because fertilization may be disrupted after stimulation with gonadotrophins. Also, gonadotrophin stimulation does not reliably increase the number of normal embryos recovered. Efficiency is increased by selecting females in pro-oestrus for mating. Alternatively, Rall *et al.* (1996) collected embryos for freezing from 64% of donors after synchronization of their oestrous cycles with a single injection of an analogue of GnRH.

Embryos have been collected and frozen in phosphate-, HEPES- and bicarbonate-buffered media with or without protein supplements (e.g. BSA, steer serum, human serum, FBS). The overall survival of rat blastocysts collected and then frozen in phosphate-buffered PB1 or HEPES-buffered Tyrode's medium was similar (Wood and Whittingham, 1981).

Live offspring have been recovered from embryos cryopreserved at the 2-cell to blastocyst stages of development (Whittingham, 1975; Wood and Whittingham, 1981; Kasai *et al.*, 1982; Kono *et al.*, 1988; Stein *et al.*, 1993). The overall survival of eight-cell embryos collected on day 4 of pregnancy was lower than that of morulae and blastocysts collected on day 5 (<7% versus 30%; Wood and Whittingham, 1981).

Cryopreservation

Embryos have been preserved by slow, equilibrium rate freezing, ultrarapid, non-equilibrium rate freezing and vitrification. With one exception (Kasai *et al.*, 1982) there have been no comparisons of alternative approaches.

Slow equilibrium rate freezing

Successful cryopreservation, with live offspring or late-stage fetuses recovered after the transfer of frozen embryos, has been achieved using the following cryoprotectants, DMSO (Whittingham, 1975; Wood and Whittingham, 1981; Stein *et al.*, 1993), PrOH and sucrose (Stein *et al.*, 1993), EG (Kasai *et al.*, 1982) and glycerol (Kasai *et al.*, 1982; Stein *et al.*, 1993). Embryos recovered after slow freezing in erythritol (morulae; Kasai *et al.*, 1982), diethylene glycol, triethylene glycol, PrOH and PEG (eight-cell; Miyamoto and Ishibashi, 1978) developed to the blastocyst stage *in vitro* but their viability after embryo transfer was not assessed.

DMSO and glycols have been added in a single step at 0°C or in stepwise increments at ambient temperature. Stein *et al.* (1993) added PrOH in a single step at ambient temperature and after 15 minutes transferred the embryos to PrOH and sucrose for freezing. The survival of blastocysts was increased significantly by adding PrOH at ambient temperature in three increments at 5-minute intervals, compared with addition in a single step (81% versus 63%; Wood, Tucker and Vernon, unpublished). Kasai *et al.* (1982) added glycerol in a single step at 0°C, whilst Stein *et al.* (1993) increased the concentration in two increments at ambient temperature.

With regard to containers, embryos have been frozen slowly in glass test tubes, plastic ampoules and plastic insemination straws but there have been no comparisons of relative rates of survival using the different containers.

Samples were seeded at temperatures between −4°C and −9°C before cooling at rates between 0.3°C and 1.0°C/min. Slow cooling was terminated and the embryos transferred into liquid nitrogen at relatively high subzero temperatures (−30°C: Stein *et al.*, 1993; −40°C: Wood and Whittingham, 1981; −50°C: Kasai *et al.*, 1982) or at temperatures below −70°C (Wood and Whittingham, 1981; Kasai *et al.*, 1982; Stein *et al.*, 1993). The rate of warming (8–65°C/min or >350°C/min) was determined by the temperature at which slow cooling was terminated. Wood and Whittingham (1981) compared morulae and blastocysts in DMSO cooled slowly to −40°C or −80°C before transfer into liquid nitrogen and then warmed at rates of ~500°C/min and ~20°C/min respectively. Survival was increased significantly from 12% to 30% when slow cooling was continued to −80°C and the embryos were warmed slowly. Using the method developed for mouse embryos by Renard and Babinet (1984), 75% of 448 frozen and thawed rat morulae and blastocysts developed as normal fetuses after embryo transfer (Wood, Tucker and Vernon, unpublished). In a comparison of embryos cooled slowly and rapidly, Kasai *et al.* (1982) demonstrated an interraction between cryoprotectant, cooling and warming rates.

There have been no significant comparisons of the dilution procedures used to remove the cryoprotectant after slow cooling. Morulae and blastocysts are returned to isotonic conditions stepwise at room temperature using medium alone or medium containing sucrose.

Non-equilibrium rate freezing and vitrification

Chupin and De Reviers (1986) and Isachenko *et al.* (1997) avoided the requirement for slow cooling by dehydrating morulae and blastocysts in solutions containing glycerol and sucrose before ultra-rapid freezing. A high proportion of embryos (70–90%) resumed development *in vitro*. The outcome of embryo transfer was not reported.

A high proportion (79%) of early blastocysts in solution VS1 survived vitrification by immersion in liquid nitrogen and rapid warming. All of the 48 embryos cultured *in vitro* developed to expanded or hatched blastocysts and 41% of 69 embryos transferred to pseudopregnant foster mothers immediately after warming, developed to term (Kono *et al.*, 1988). Rall (personal communication) used the protocol developed for mouse embryos (Rall, 1992; Glenister and Rall, 1999) to vitrify rat blastocysts in solution VS3a. Blastocysts vitrified in a solution of 40% EG, 5% PEG and 0.5 M sucrose were able to re-expand in culture and 7/24 embryos transferred to recipients developed to normal late-stage fetuses (Ohboshi *et al.*, 1993).

13.4 HAMSTER

13.4.1 Oocyte

Hamster oocyte cryopreservation was developed as a convenient method of transporting oocytes and ensuring the availability of material for use in a diagnostic test of the function of spermatozoa from subfertile men. For the test, zona-free oocytes are incubated with human spermatozoa. There have been few attempts to inseminate zona intact oocytes with homologous spermatozoa.

Origin and recovery

Oocyte donors were 3- to 4-week-old and adult golden hamsters induced to superovulate by injection of eCG and hCG. Mature oocytes were recovered from the oviducts 14–18 hours post-hCG using phosphate or HEPES-buffered media. Removal of the cumulus cells with hyaluronidase did not affect oocyte survival (Mandelbaum *et al.*, 1988). The survival of immature oocytes recovered 48–52 hours post-eCG and frozen with intact layers of cumulus cells was reduced compared with mature oocytes (63% versus 81%; Mandelbaum *et al.*, 1988).

Cryopreservation

Cryoprotectant and method of introduction

Oocytes have been frozen slowly in DMSO (1–2 M) and PrOH (1.5 M) with or without the addition of sucrose (0.1–0.25 M), or a combination of DMSO and PrOH with sucrose. The cryoprotectant was added stepwise or in a single step and the embryos held at 0–4°C or at ambient temperature for 5–20 minutes before further cooling. Higher concentrations of DMSO (3–6 M: Lewin *et al.*, 1990; Wood *et al.*, 1993) and solution VS1 (Critser *et al.*, 1986) were used for ultra-rapid freezing and vitrification. The cryoprotectants were added stepwise and the embryos exposed to the final concentration of the solution for no more than 5 minutes at 0°C or ambient temperature.

Freezing method and cooling rates

High proportions (75–90%) of oocytes survived freezing by cooling at rates between 0.3°C and 1.0°C/min to −40°C or about −80°C before storage in liquid nitrogen (Quinn *et al.*, 1982; Leibo *et al.*, 1990; Tateno *et al.*, 1992). Similarly, ~83% of oocytes appeared normal after ultra-rapid freezing and after vitrification (Lewin *et al.*, 1990; Wood *et al.*, 1993). Survival was similar (~75%) after slow cooling to −80°C and vitrification, but more frozen than vitrified oocytes (45% versus 15–37%) were subsequently penetrated by human spermatozoa (Critser *et al.*, 1986).

Thawing rates

Oocytes cooled slowly to about −80°C before rapid cooling in liquid nitrogen were warmed slowly (~8°C/min). When slow cooling was terminated at −40°C, and after ultrarapid freezing and vitrification, the rate of warming was increased to >300°C/min.

Diluent composition and method of dilution of cryoprotectant

There was no difference in survival when the cryoprotectant was removed stepwise or in a single step at ambient temperature with isotonic medium (Quinn *et al.*, 1982). Very high rates of survival were achieved using sucrose as an osmotic buffer during dilution (Leibo *et al.*, 1990) but comparisons with other methods have not been made.

Post-thaw handling

Oocytes used for interspecific fertilization were treated with trypsin to remove the zona pellucida before incubation with spermatozoa.

Evaluation

Survival was generally assessed morphologically, but the trypan blue exclusion test and fluorescein diacetate uptake have also been used (Chunong and Coulam, 1986; Lewin *et al.*, 1990). Morphological survival was generally high (75–90%) irrespective of the method of cryopreservation. Fewer frozen than fresh immature oocytes matured during culture *in vitro* (22% versus 58%: Mandelbaum *et al.*, 1988). After removal of the zona pellucida, similar proportions of slowly frozen and freshly collected oocytes (Quinn *et al.*, 1982; Tateno *et al.*, 1992), but fewer vitrified and ultra-rapidly frozen than fresh oocytes (Lewin *et al.*, 1990; Wood *et al.*, 1993) were penetrated by mouse and human spermatozoa. Fewer zona-intact vitrified oocytes were penetrated by hamster spermatozoa compared with fresh oocytes (73% versus 87%) but the rates of fertilization (>90%) did not differ after removal of the zona (Wood *et al.*, 1993).

13.4.2 Embryo

Few attempts have been made to cryopreserve hamster embryos, probably because of their extreme sensitivity to manipulation *in vitro*.

Origin and recovery

Embryos are flushed from the oviducts and uterine horns of superovulated or naturally mated golden and Chinese hamsters using phosphate- and HEPES-buffered media.

Cryopreservation

Cryoprotectant and method of introduction

Zygotes and cleavage-stage embryos have been frozen slowly in DMSO, PrOH or a mixture of the two (Ridha and Dukelow, 1985; Todorow *et al.*, 1989). Survival was similar when the cryoprotectant was added in a single step or stepwise at 0°C, ambient temperature or 37°C (Todorow *et al.*, 1989). For vitrification, embryos were exposed in two steps to a solution of EG and DMSO (Lane *et al.*, 1999).

Freezing method and cooling rates

Embryos in glass ampoules and plastic straws were cooled slowly (0.3–1°C/min) to around −35°C or −80°C before storage in liquid nitrogen. For vitrification, embryos in a drop of vitrification solution on a small nylon loop were cooled very rapidly (~3000°C/min) by immersion in liquid nitrogen (Lane *et al.*, 1999)

Warming rate

Generally embryos cooled slowly to about −35°C before rapid cooling in liquid nitrogen were warmed rapidly (>300°C/min) and those cooled slowly to −80°C were warmed slowly (1.5–8°C/min). Vitrified embryos were warmed 'instantaneously' by placing the cryoloop in warm culture medium.

Diluent composition and method of dilution of cryoprotectant

The cryoprotectant was usually diluted stepwise by transferring the embryos through decreasing concentrations of cryoprotectant. Todorow *et al.* (1989) and Lane *et al.* (1999) added sucrose to the diluent.

Evaluation

Microscopic assessment of morphology correlated well with the outcome of a trypan blue exclusion assay, showing that up to 95% of embryos were normal immediately after thawing (Ridha and Dukelow, 1985). More than 50% of vitrified one- and two-cell stage embryos and 85% of frozen eight-cell embryos reached the morula and blastocyst stages *in vitro* (Iida, 1992; Lane *et al.*, 1999). Cell number was reduced in morulae and blastocysts developing from cryopreserved embryos (Iida, 1992; Lane *et al.*, 1999). There was no significant increase in chromosomal abnormalities after freezing (Iida, 1992). When frozen embryos from the one-cell to morula stages were transferred into synchronous recipients (Ridha and Dukelow, 1985), implantation was similar for all stages (~78% of embryos transferred), but a higher proportion of embryos at the 4-cell to morula stages developed to fetuses (70–78%) compared with those at the one- and two-cell stages (22–41%). Vitrified embryos cultured to the morula and blastocyst stages before transfer to asynchronous recipients developed to live young at rates similar to those of controls (one-cell 29%, two-cell 50%; Lane *et al.*, 1999).

13.5 MONGOLIAN GERBIL

There is one brief report of the cryopreservation of four-cell to blastocyst stage gerbil embryos collected from superovulated females and vitrified in a mixture of EG, Ficoll and sucrose (Mochida *et al.*, 1999). More than 90% of 257 embryos appeared normal after warming. A total of 155 blastocysts derived from vitrified embryos were transferred asynchronously to ten recipients, of which three delivered fifteen pups. There are no control data but it seems likely that some of the embryonic loss was due to problems associated with embryo transfer rather than cryopreservation.

13.6 CONCLUSION

Plainly, the methods developed for the storage of mouse germplasm, perhaps with the exception of spermatozoa, have translated with acceptable levels of survival for other laboratory species; and there is no reason to think that this will not be true for wild rodent species. Nevertheless, there is scope for the improvement of survival rates and subsequent viability of the germplasm; and some of the improvements may stem from changes in the cryopreservation protocols. Our detailed examination of the literature has revealed a lack of contemporary comparisons of procedures and also a failure to acknowledge that the various steps of a cryopreservation protocol are inter-related; changing one step may require changes in other steps to maintain cellular integrity. There are three critical requirements for the conservation of endangered rodents, and for increased efficiency in the storage of laboratory species. (1) The development of *in vitro* techniques for the growth and maturation of immature oocytes is needed, whether those oocytes are cryopreserved within pieces of ovarian tissue, in isolated follicles or after isolation from the follicle. This will eliminate the need for collection of embryos or mature oocytes at precise stages of the reproductive cycle. (2) Improved methods must be developed for sperm cryopreservation that reliably maintain the functional integrity of a high proportion of spermatozoa in each sample. (3) The further development of ICSI procedures in rodent species is necessary.

REFERENCES

AUBARD, Y., NEWTON, H., SCHEFFER, G. and GOSDEN, R. (1998) 'Conservation of the follicular population in irradiated rats by the cryopreservation and orthotopic autografting of ovarian tissue', *Eur. J. Obstetr. Gynecol. Reprod. Biol.* **79**, 83–87.

BERNARD, A. and FULLER, B. J. (1983) 'Cryopreservation of *in vitro* fertilized 2 cell mouse embryos using a low glycerol concentration and normothermic cryoprotectant equilibration: a comparison with *in vivo* fertilized ova', *Cryo-Letters* **4**, 171–178.

CANDY, C. J., WOOD, M. J., WHITTINGHAM, D. G., MERRIMAN, J. A. and CHOUDHURY, N. (1994) 'Cryopreservation of immature oocytes', *Hum. Reprod.* **9**, 1738–1742.

CANDY, C. J., WOOD, M. J. and WHITTINGHAM, D. G. (1997) 'Effects of cryoprotectants on the survival of follicles in frozen mouse ovaries', *J. Reprod. Fertil.* **110**, 11–19.

CANDY, C. J., WOOD, M. J. and WHITTINGHAM, D. G. (2000) 'Restoration of a normal reproductive lifespan after transplantation of cryopreserved mouse ovaries', *Hum. Reprod.* **15**, 1300–1304.

CARROLL, J. and GOSDEN, R. G. (1993) 'Transplantation of frozen-thawed primordial follicles', *Human Reproduction* **8**, 1163–1167.

CARROLL, J., WHITTINGHAM, D. G., WOOD, M. J., TELFER, E. and GOSDEN, R. G. (1990) 'Extra-ovarian production of mature viable mouse oocytes from frozen primary follicles', *J. Reprod. Fertil.* **90**, 321–327.

CARROLL, J., WOOD, M. J. and WHITTINGHAM, D. G. (1993) 'Normal fertilization and development of frozen-thawed mouse oocytes: protective action of certain macromolecules', *Biol. Reprod.* **48**, 606–612.

CHUNONG, C. J. and COULAM, C. B. (1986) 'Effects of cryopreservation on the viability and fertilizability of unfertilized hamster oocytes', *Am. J. Obstetr. Gynaecol.* **155**, 1240–1245.

CHUPIN, D. and DE REVIERS, M. M. (1986) 'Quick freezing of rat embryos', *Theriogenology* **26**, 157–166.

CHAPTER 13

COOPER, A., PAYNTER, S. J., FULLER, B. J. and SHAW, R. W. (1998) 'Differential effects of cryopreservation on nuclear or cytoplasmic maturation *in vitro* in immature mouse oocytes from stimulated ovaries', *Hum. Reprod.* **13**, 971–978.

CORTVRINDT, R., SMITZ, J. and VAN STEIRTEGHEM, A. C. (1996) 'A morphological and functional study of the effect of slow freezing followed by complete in-vitro maturation of primary mouse ovarian follicles', *Hum. Reprod.* **11**, 2648–2655.

COX, S.-L., SHAW, J. and JENKIN, G. (1996) 'Transplantation of cryopreserved fetal ovarian tissue to adult recipients in mice', *J. Reprod. Fertil.* **107**, 315–322.

CRITSER, J. K., ARNESON, B. W., AAKER, D. V. and BALL G. D. (1986) 'Cryopreservation of hamster oocytes: effects of vitrification or freezing on human sperm penetration of zona-free hamster oocytes', *Fertil. Steril.* **46**, 277–284.

DINNYÉS, A., WALLACE, G. A. and RALL, W. F. (1995) 'Effect of genotype on the efficiency of mouse embryo cryopreservation by vitrification or slow freezing methods', *Mol. Reprod. Dev.* **40**, 429–435.

EROGLU, A., TOTH, T. L. and TONER, M. (1998a) 'Alterations of the cytoskeleton and polyploidy induced by cryopreservation of metaphase II mouse oocytes', *Fertil. Steril.* **69**, 944–957.

EROGLU, A., TONER, M., LEYKIN, L. and TOTH, T. L. (1998b) 'Cytoskeleton and polyploidy after maturation and fertilization of cryopreserved germinal vesicle-stage mouse oocytes', *J. Assist. Reprod. Genet.* **15**, 447–454.

FULLER, S. J. and WHITTINGHAM, D. G. (1997) 'Capacitation-like changes occur in mouse spermatozoa cooled to low temperatures', *Mol. Reprod. Dev.* **46**, 318–324.

FRYDMAN, N., SELVE, J., BERGERE, M., AUROUX, M. and MARO, B. (1997) 'Cryopreserved immature mouse oocytes: a chromosomal and spindle study', *J. Assist. Reprod. Genet.* **14**, 617–623.

GATES, A. H. (1971) 'Maximizing yield and developmental uniformity of eggs', in Daniel, J. C. Jr. (Ed.) *Methods in Mammalian Embryology*, San Francisco: W.H. Freeman, pp. 64–75.

GLENISTER, P. H. and RALL, W. F. (1999) 'Cryopreservation and rederivation of embryos and gametes', in Jackson, I. and Abbott, C. (eds) *Mouse Genetics and Transgenics: A Practical Approach*, 2nd edn, Oxford: Oxford University Press, pp. 27–59

GLENISTER, P. H., WOOD, M. J., KIRBY, C. and WHITTINGHAM, D. G. (1987) 'Incidence of chromosome anomalies in first cleavage mouse embryos obtained from frozen-thawed oocytes fertilized *in vitro*', *Gamete Res.* **16**, 205–216.

GOTO, K., KINOSHITA, A. and TAKUMA, Y. (1990) 'Fertilization of bovine oocytes by the injection of immobilized, killed, spermatozoa', *Vet. Rec.* **127**, 517–520.

GUNASENA, K. T., VILLINES, P. M., CRITSER, E. S. and CRITSER, J. K. (1997a) 'Live births after autologous transplant of cryopreserved mouse ovaries', *Hum. Reprod.* **12**, 101–106.

GUNASENA, K. T., LAKEY, J. R. T., VILLINES, P. M., CRITSER, E. S. and CRITSER, J. K. (1997b) 'Allogeneic and xenogeneic transplantation of cryopreserved ovarian tissue to athymic mice', *Biol. Reprod.* **57**, 226–231.

HARP, R., LEIBACH, J., BLACK, J., KELDAHL, C. and KAROW, A. (1994) 'Cryopreservation of murine ovarian tissue', *Cryobiology* **31**, 336–343.

IIDA, T. (1992) 'The effects of cryopreservation on early development and chromosome constitution in Chinese hamster embryos', *Asia-Oceania J. Obstetr. Gynaecol.* **18**, 407–412.

ISACHENKO, E. F. and NAYUDU, P. L. (1999) 'Vitrification of mouse germinal vesicle oocytes: effect of treatment temperature and egg yolk on chromatin and spindle normality and cumulus integrity', *Hum. Reprod.* **14**, 400–408.

ISACHENKO, V. V., ISACHENKO, E. F., OSTASHKO, F. I. and GRISHCHENKO, V. I. (1997) 'Ultrarapid freezing of rat embryos with rapid dilution of permeable cryoprotectants', *Cryobiology* **34**, 157–164.

JOHNSON, M. H. (1989) 'The effect on fertilization of exposure of mouse oocytes to dimethyl sulfoxide: an optimal protocol', *J. in vitro Fertil. Embryo Transfer* **6**, 168–175.

KASAI, M. (1995) 'Cryopreservation of mammalian embryos. Vitrification', in Day, J. G. and McLellan, M. R. (eds) *Cryopreservation and Freeze-Drying Protocols (Methods in Molecular Biology, Vol. 38)*, Totowa, NJ: Humana Press Inc., pp. 211–219.

KASAI, M., IRITANI, A. and CHANG, M. C. (1979) 'Fertilization in vitro of rat ovarian oocytes after freezing and thawing', *Biol. Reprod.* **21**, 839–844.

KASAI, M., NIWA, K. and IRITANI, A. (1982) 'Survival of rat embryos after freezing', *J. Reprod. Fertil.* **66**, 367–370.

KASAI, M., KOMI, J. H., TAKAKAMO, A., TSUDERA, H., SAKURAI, T. and MACHIDA, T. (1990) 'A simple method for mouse embryo cryopreservation in a low toxicity vitrification solution, without appreciable loss of viability', *J. Reprod. Fertil.* **89**, 91–97.

KASAI, M., NISHIMORI, M., ZHU, S. E., SAKURAI, T. and MACHIDA, T. (1992) 'Survival of mouse morulae vitrified in an ethylene glycol-based solution after exposure to the solution at various temperatures', *Biol. Reprod.* **47**, 1134–1139.

KATAYOSE, H., MATSUDA, J. and YANAGIMACHI, R. (1992) 'The ability of dehydrated hamster and human sperm nuclei to develop into pronuclei', *Biol. Reprod.* **47**, 277–284.

KOLA, I., KIRBY, C., SHAW, J., DAVEY, A. and TROUNSON, A. (1988) 'Vitrification of mouse oocytes results in aneuploid zygotes and malformed fetuses', *Teratology* **38**, 467–474.

KONO, T., SUZUKI, O. and TSUNODA, Y. (1988) 'Cryopreservation of rat blastocysts by vitrification', *Cryobiology* **25**, 170–173.

LANE, M., BAVISTER, B. D., LYONS, E. A., and FOREST, K. T. (1999) 'Containerless vitrification of mammalian oocytes and embryos. Adapting a proven method for flash-cooling protein crystals to the cryopreservation of live cells', *Nature Biotechnol.* **17**, 1234–1236.

LEIBO, S. P. and ODA, K. (1993) 'High survival of mouse zygotes and embryos cooled rapidly or slowly in ethylene glycol plus polyvinylpyrrolidone', *Cryo-Letters* **14**, 133–144.

LEIBO, S. P., GIAMBERNARDI, T. A., MEYER, T. K., BASTIAS, M. C. and ROGERS, B. J. (1990) 'The efficacy of cryopreserved hamster ova in the sperm penetration assay', *Fertil. Steril.* **53**, 906–912.

LEWIN, A., TAL, Z., ZOHAV, E. and SCHENKER, J. G. (1990) 'Ultrarapid freezing and thawing of hamster oocytes', *J. Reprod. Med.* **35**, 136–140.

MANDELBAUM, J., JUNCA, A. M., TIBI, C., PLACHOT, M., ALNOT, M. O., RIM, H., SALAT-BAROUX, J. and COHEN, J. (1988) 'Cryopreservation of immature and mature hamster and human oocytes', *Ann. NY Acad. Sci.* **541**, 550–561.

MASSIP, A., VAN DER ZWALMEN, P., PUISSANT, F., CAMUS, M. and LEROY, F. (1984) 'Effects of in-vitro fertilization, culture, freezing and transfer on the ability of mouse embryos to implant and survive', *J. Reprod. Fertil.* **71**, 199–204.

MIYAMOTO, H. and ISHIBASHI, T. (1978) 'The protective action of glycols against freezing damage of mouse and rat embryos', *J. Reprod. Fertil.* **54**, 427–432.

MOCHIDA, K., WAKAYAMA, T., TAKANO, K., NOGUCHI, Y., YAMAMOTO, Y., SUZUKI, O., OGURA, A., and MATSUDA, J. (1999) 'Successful cryopreservation of Mongolian gerbil embryos by vitrification', *Theriogenology* **51**, 171.

NAKAGATA, N. (1989) 'High survival rate of unfertilized mouse oocytes after vitrification', *J. Reprod. Fertil.* **87**, 479–483.

NAKAGATA, N. (1992) 'Cryopreservation of unfertilized rat oocytes by ultrarapid freezing', *Exp. Anim.* **41**, 443–447.

NAKAGATA, N. (1993) 'Production of normal young following transfer of mouse embryos obtained by in vitro fertilization between cryopreserved gametes', *J. Reprod. Fertil.* **99**, 77–80.

NAKAGATA, N., UEDA, S., YAMANOUCHI, K., OKAMOTO, M., MATSUDA, Y., TSUCHIYA, K., NISHIMURA, M., ODA, S., KOYASU, K., AZUMA, S. and TOYODA, Y. (1995) 'Cryopreservation of wild mouse spermatozoa', *Theriogenology* **43**, 635–643.

NAKAGATA, N., OKAMOTO, M., UEDA, O. and SUZUKI, H. (1997) 'The positive effect of partial zona-pellucida dissection on the in vitro fertilizing capacity of cryopreserved C57BL/6J transgenic mouse spermatozoa of low motility', *Biol. Reprod.* **57**, 1050–1055.

NIWA, K., KASAI, M. and IRITANI, A. (1979) 'Fertilization *in vitro* of rat eggs after freezing and thawing', *Jpn J. Zootechn. Sci.* **50**, 747–752.

NOILES, E. E., BAILEY, J. L. and STOREY, B. T. (1995) 'The temperature dependence in the hydraulic conductivity, $L_{(p)}$, of the mouse sperm plasma membrane shows a discontinuity between 4 and 0°C', *Cryobiology* **32**, 220–238.

NOILES, E. E., THOMPSON, K. A. and STOREY, B. T. (1997) 'Water permeability, $L_{(p)}$, of the mouse sperm plasma membrane and its activation energy are strongly dependent on interaction of the plasma membrane with the sperm cytoskeleton', *Cryobiology* **35**, 79–92.

OHBOSHI, S., NAKAMICHI, R. and FUJIHARA, N. (1993) 'Cryopreservation of rat blastocysts by vitrification using ethylene glycol, polyethylene glycol and sucrose', *J. Mammal. Ova Res.* **10**, 185–193.

OKUYAMA, M., ISOGAI, S., SAGA, M., HAMADA, H. and OGAWA, S. (1990) '*In vitro* fertilization (IVF) and artificial insemination (AI) by cryopreserved spermatozoa in mouse', *J. Fertil. Implant.* **7**, 116–119.

O'NEILL, L., PAYNTER, S. J., FULLER, B. J. and SHAW, R. W. (1997) 'Vitrification of mature mouse oocytes: improved results following addition of polyethylene glycol to a dimethyl sulfoxide solution', *Cryobiology* **34**, 295–301.

ONOHARA, Y., HARADA, T., TANIKAWA, M., MIO, Y. and TERAKAWA, N. (1994) 'Assessment of functional integrity of frozen-thawed mouse embryos by albumin and leucine uptake', *Hum. Reprod.* **9**, 122–127.

PELLICER, A., LIGHTMAN, A., PARMER, T. G., BEHRMAN, H. R. and DE CHERNEY, A. H. (1988) 'Morphologic and functional studies of immature rat oocyte-cumulus complexes after cryopreservation', *Fertil. Steril.* **50**, 805–810.

PENFOLD, L. M. and MOORE, H. D. M. (1993) 'A new method for cryopreservation of mouse spermatozoa', *J. Reprod. Fertil.* **99**, 131–134.

PONCE, A. A., AIRES, V. A., CARRASCOSA, R., DECUNEO, M. F., RUIZ, R. D. and LACUARA, J. L. (1998) 'Functional activity of epididymal *Chinchilla laniger* spermatozoa cryopreserved in different extenders', *Res. Vet. Sci.* **64**, 239–243.

QUINN, P., BARROS, C. and WHITTINGHAM, D. G. (1982) 'Preservation of hamster oocytes to assay the fertilizing capacity of human spermatozoa', *J. Reprod. Fertil.* **66**, 161–168.

RALL, W. F. (1987) 'Factors affecting survival of mouse embryos cryopreserved by vitrification', *Cryobiology* **24**, 387–402.

CHAPTER 13

RALL, W. F. (1992) 'Cryopreservation of oocytes and embryos: methods and applications', *Animal Reprod. Sci.* **28**, 237–245.

RALL, W. F. and FAHY, G. M. (1985) 'Ice-free cryopreservation of mouse embryos at −196°C by vitrification', *Nature, Lond.* **313**, 573–575.

RALL, W. F. and POLGE, C. (1984) 'Effect of warming rate on mouse embryos frozen and thawed in glycerol', *J. Reprod. Fertil.* **70**, 285–289.

RALL, W. F. and WOOD, M. J. (1994) 'High *in vitro* and *in vivo* survival of day 3 mouse embryos vitrified or frozen in a non-toxic solution of glycerol and albumin', *J. Reprod. Fertil.* **101**, 681–688.

RALL, W. F., WOOD, M. J. and KIRBY, C. (1984a) 'The transfer of frozen-thawed mouse embryos in dimethyl sulfoxide: effect of dilution and short-term culture', *Cryobiology* **21**, 710–711.

RALL, W. F., CZLONKOWSKA, M., BARTON, S. C. and POLGE, C. (1984b) 'Cryoprotection of Day-4 mouse embryos by methanol', *J. Reprod. Fertil.* **70**, 293–300.

RALL, W. F., WOOD, M. J., KIRBY, C., and WHITTINGHAM. (1987) 'Development of mouse embryos cryopreserved by vitrification', *J. Reprod. Fertil.* **80**, 499–504.

RALL, W. F., LIN, X., SCHMIDT, P. M., BROWN, S. S., HOLLIFIELD, V. M. and HANSEN, C. T. (1996) 'The effect of genotype on the synchronization of estrous cycles of laboratory rats by an analog of gonadotropin releasing hormone', *Theriogenology* **45**, 319.

RAYOS, A. A., TAKAHASHI, Y., HISHINUMA, M. and KANAGAWA, H. (1994) 'Quick freezing of unfertilized mouse oocytes using ethylene glycol with sucrose or trehalose', *J. Reprod. Fertil.* **100**, 123–129.

RENARD, J. P. and BABINET, C. (1984) 'High survival of mouse embryos after rapid freezing and thawing inside plastic straws with 1,2–propanediol as cryoprotectant', *J. Exp. Zool.* **230**, 443–448.

RIDHA, M. T. and DUKELOW, W. R. (1985) 'The developmental potential of frozen-thawed hamster preimplantation embryos following embryo transfer: viability of slowly frozen embryos following slow and rapid thawing', *Anim. Reprod. Sci.* **9**, 253–259.

SCHEFFEN, B., VAN DER ZWALMEN, P. and MASSIP, A. (1986) 'A simple and efficient procedure for preservation of mouse embryos by vitrification', *Cryo-Letters* **7**, 260–269.

SCHROEDER, A. C., CHAMPLIN, A. K., MOBRAATEN, L. E. and EPPIG, J. J. (1990) 'Developmental capacity of mouse oocytes cryopreserved before and after maturation *in vitro*', *J. Reprod. Fertil.* **89**, 43–50.

SHAW, J. M., DIOTALLEVI, L. and TROUNSON, A. O. (1991a) 'A simple 4.5 M dimethyl-sulfoxide freezing technique for the cryopreservation of one-cell to blastocyst stage preimplantation mouse embryos', *Reprod. Fertil. Dev.* **3**, 621–626.

SHAW, J. M., KOLA, I., MACFARLANE, D. R. and TROUNSON, A. O. (1991b) 'An association between chromosomal abnormalities in rapidly frozen 2-cell mouse embryos and the ice-forming properties of the cryoprotective solution', *J. Reprod. Fertil.* **91**, 9–18.

SHAW, J. M., WARD, C. and TROUNSON, A. O. (1995a) 'Evaluation of propanediol, ethylene glycol, sucrose and antifreeze proteins on the survival of slow-cooled mouse pronuclear and 4-cell embryos', *Hum. Reprod.* **10**, 396–402.

SHAW, J. M., WARD, C. and TROUNSON, A. O. (1995b) 'Survival of mouse blastocysts slow cooled in propanediol or ethylene glycol is influenced by thawing procedure, sucrose and antifreeze proteins', *Theriogenology* **43**, 1289–1300.

SHAW, J. M., BOWLES, J., KOOPMAN, P., WOOD, E. C. and TROUNSON, A. O. (1996) 'Fresh and cryopreserved ovarian tissue samples from donors with lymphoma transmit the cancer to graft recipients', *Hum. Reprod.* **11**, 1668–1673.

SHAW, P. W., BERNARD, A. G., FULLER, B. J., HUNTER, J. H. and SHAW, R. W. (1992) 'Vitrification of mouse oocytes using short cryoprotectant exposure: effects of varying exposure times on survival', *Mol. Reprod. Dev.* **33**, 210–214.

SONGSASEN, N. and LEIBO, S. P. (1997a) 'Cryopreservation of mouse spermatozoa. 1. Effect of seeding on fertilizing ability of cryopreserved spermatozoa', *Cryobiology* **35**, 240–254.

SONGSASEN, N. and LEIBO, S. P. (1997b) 'Cryopreservation of mouse spermatozoa. 2. Relationship between survival after cryopreservation and osmotic tolerance of spermatozoa from three strains of mice', *Cryobiology* **35**, 255–269.

SONGSASEN, N. and LEIBO, S. P. (1998) 'Live mice from cryopreserved embryos derived in vitro with cryopreserved ejaculated spermatozoa', *Lab. Anim. Scie.* **48**, 275–281.

SONGSASEN, N., BETTERIDGE, K. J. and LEIBO, S. P. (1997) 'Birth of live mice resulting from oocytes fertilized in vitro with cryopreserved spermatozoa', *Biol. Reprod.* **56**, 143–152.

SONGSASEN, N., TONG, J. and LEIBO, S. P. (1998) 'Birth of live mice derived by in vitro fertilization with spermatozoa retrieved up to twenty four hours after death', *J. Exp. Zool.* **280**, 189–196.

STACHEKI, J. J., COHEN, J. and WILLADSEN, S. M. (1998) 'Cryopreservation of unfertilized mouse oocytes: the effect of replacing sodium with choline in the freezing medium', *Cryobiology* **37**, 346–354.

STEIN, A., FISCH, B., TADIR, Y., OVADIA, J. and KRAICER, P. F. (1993) 'Cryopreservation of rat blastocysts: a comparative study of different cryoprotectants and freezing/thawing methods', *Cryobiology* **30**, 128–134.

SUGIMOTO, M., MIYAMOTO, H., KABASAWA, T. and MANABE, N. (1996) 'Follicle survival in neonatal rat ovaries cryopreserved by vitrification', *Cryo-Letters* **17**, 93–98.

■ CHAPTER 13 ■

SZÉLL, A. and SHELTON, J. N. (1987) 'Osmotic and cryoprotective effects of glycerol-sucrose solutions on Day-3 mouse embryos', *J. Reprod. Fertil.* **80**, 309–316.

SZTEIN, J. M., FARLEY, J. S., YOUNG, A. F. and MOBRAATEN, L. E. (1997) 'Motility of cryo-preserved mouse spermatozoa affected by temperature of collection and rate of thawing', *Cryobiology* **35**, 46–52.

SZTEIN, J., SWEET, H., FARLEY, J. and MOBRAATEN, L. (1998) 'Cryopreservation and orthotopic transplantation of mouse ovaries: new approach in gamete banking', *Biol. Reprod.* **58**, 1071–1074.

TADA, N., SATO, M., YAMANOI, J., MIZOROGI, T., KASAI, K. and OGAWA, S. (1990) 'Cryopreservation of mouse spermatozoa in the presence of raffinose and glycerol', *J. Reprod. Fertil.* **89**, 511–516.

TADA, N., SATO, M., AMANN, E. and OGAWA, S. (1993) 'Effect of pre-freezing equilibration and post-thawing centrifugation on the fertilizing capacity of frozen mouse epididymal spermatozoa', *Cryo-Letters* **14**, 195–206.

TAKESHIMA, T., NAKAGATA, N. and OGAWA, S. (1991) 'Cryopreservation of mouse spermatozoa', *Exp. Anim.* **40**, 493–497.

TATENO, H., KAMIGUCHI, Y. and MIKAMO, K. (1992) 'A freezing and thawing method of hamster oocytes designed for both the penetration test and chromosome assay of human spermatozoa', *Mol. Reprod. Dev.* **33**, 202–209.

TODOROW, S. J., SIEBZEHNRÜBL, E. R., KOCH, R., WILDT, L. and LANG, N. (1989) 'Comparative results on survival of human and animal eggs using different cryoprotectants and freeze-thawing regimens. I. Mouse and hamster', *Hum. Reprod.* **4**, 805–811.

TROUNSON, A., PEURA, A., FREEMANN, L. and KIRBY, C. (1988) 'Ultrarapid freezing of early cleavage stage human embryos and eight-cell mouse embryos', *Fertil. Steril.* **49**, 822–826.

VAN BLERKOM, J. (1989) 'Maturation at high frequency of germinal-vesicle-stage mouse oocytes after cryopreservation: alterations in cytoplasmic, nuclear, nucleolar and chromosomal structure and organization associated with vitrification', *Hum. Reprod.* **4**, 883–898.

VAN BLERKOM, J. and DAVIS, P. W. (1994) 'Cytogenetic, cellular, and developmental consequences of cryopreservation of immature and mature mouse and human oocytes', *Microsc. Res. Techn.* **27**, 165–193.

VAN DER ELST, J., NERINCKX, S. and VAN STEIRTEGHEM, A.C. (1992) '*In vitro* maturation of mouse germinal vesicle-stage oocytes following cooling, exposure to cryoprotectants and ultrarapid freezing: limited effect on the morphology of the second meiotic spindle', *Hum. Reprod.* **7**, 1440–1446.

Van der Elst, J., Nerinckx, S. and Van Steirteghem, A. C. (1993a) 'Association of ultrarapid freezing of mouse oocytes with increased polyploidy at the pronucleate stage, reduced cell numbers in blastocysts and impaired fetal development', *J. Reprod. Fertil.* **99**, 25–32.

Van der Elst, J., Nerinckx, S. and Van Steirteghem, A.C. (1993b) 'Slow and ultrarapid freezing of fully grown germinal vesicle-stage mouse oocytes: optimization of survival rate outweighed by defective blastocyst formation', *J. Assist. Reprod. Genet.* **10**, 202–212.

Wakayama, T. and Yanagimachi, R. (1998) 'Development of normal mice from oocytes injected with freeze-dried spermatozoa', *Nature Biotechnol.* **16**, 639–641.

Wakayama, T., Whittingham, D. G. and Yanagimachi, R. (1998) 'Production of normal offspring from mouse oocytes injected with spermatozoa cryopreserved with or without cryoprotection', *J. Reprod. Fertil.* **112**, 11–17.

Whittingham, D. G. (1968) 'Fertilization of mouse eggs *in vitro*', *Nature, Lond.* **220**, 592–593.

Whittingham, D. G. (1974) 'Embryo banks in the future of developmental genetics', *Genetics, Suppl.* **78**, 395–402.

Whittingham, D. G. (1975) 'Survival of rat embryos after freezing and thawing', *J. Reprod. Fertil.* **43**, 575–578.

Whittingham, D. G. (1977a) 'Some factors affecting embryo storage in laboratory animals', in Elliott, K and Whelan, J. (eds) *The Freezing of Mammalian Embryos*, Amsterdam: Elsevier, pp. 97–127.

Whittingham, D. G. (1977b) 'Fertilization *in vitro* and development to term of unfertilized mouse oocytes previously stored at −196°C', *J. Reprod. Fertil.* **49**, 89–94.

Whittingham, D. G., Leibo, S. P. and Mazur, P. (1972) 'Survival of mouse embryos frozen to −196° and −269°C', *Science* **178**, 411–414.

Whittingham, D. G., Lyon, M. F. and Glenister, P. H. (1977) 'Long-term storage of mouse embryos at –196°C: the effect of background radiation', *Genet. Res. Cambridge* **29**, 171–181.

Whittingham, D. G., Wood, M. J., Farrant, J, Lee, H. and Halsey, J. A. (1979) 'Survival of frozen mouse embryos after rapid thawing from −196°C', *J. Reprod. Fertil.* **56**, 11–21.

Willoughby, C. E., Mazur, P., Peter, A. T. and Critser, J. K. (1996) 'Osmotic tolerance limits and properties of murine spermatozoa', *Biol. Reprod.* **55**, 715–727.

Wood, M. J. and Whittingham, D. G. (1981) 'Low temperature storage of rat embryos', in Zeilmaker, G. H. (ed.) *Frozen Storage of Laboratory Animals*, Stuttgart: Gustav Fischer Verlag, pp. 119–128.

CHAPTER 13

WOOD, M. J., WHITTINGHAM, D. G. and RALL, W. F. (1987) 'The low temperature preservation of mouse oocytes and embryos', in Monk, M. J. (ed.) *Mammalian Development: A Practical Approach*, Oxford: IRL Press, pp. 255–280.

WOOD, M. J., SJÖBLOM, P., LINDENBERG, S. and KIMBER, S. J. (1992) 'Effect of slow and ultra-rapid freezing on cell surface antigens of 8-cell mouse embryos', *J. Exp. Zool.* **262**, 330–339.

WOOD, M. J., BARROS, C., CANDY, C. J., CARROLL, J., MELENDEZ, J. and WHITTINGHAM, D. G. (1993) 'High rates of survival and fertilization of mouse and hamster oocytes after vitrification in dimethylsulphoxide', *Biol. Reprod.* **49**, 489–495.

YOKOYAMA, M., AKIBA, H., KATSUKI, M. and NOMURA, T. (1990) 'Production of normal young following transfer of mouse embryos obtained in *in vitro* fertilization using cryopreserved spermatozoa', *Exp. Anim.* **39**, 125–128.

Cryopreservation of Lagomorph Gametes and Embryos

W. V. HOLT,[1] L. M. PENFOLD[2] AND P. F. WATSON[3]

[1]The institute of Zoology, The Zoological Society of London, Regent's Park, London NW1 4RY. UK
[2]White Oaks Conservation Center, 3823 Owens Road, Yulee, FL 32097, USA
[3]Department of Veterinary Basic Sciences, The Royal Veterinary College, London NW1 0TU, UK

Contents

14.1 INTRODUCTION

Semen cryopreservation in lagomorphs is almost exclusively concerned with a single species, the domestic rabbit. However, it should be recognized that there are significant benefits to be obtained from the application of genetic resource banking to the variously threatened rabbit and hare species of the world, for example, the riverine rabbit (*Bunolagus monticularis*) of southern Africa.

14.2 SPERMATOZOA

14.2.1 Cryopreservation

The lagomorph semen cryopreservation literature is completely dominated by the domestic rabbit. Semen cryopreservation procedures are sufficiently reliable that the establishment of genetic resource bank programmes for rabbits has been accomplished, and semen samples exchanged between centres. Furthermore, rabbit breeding by the use of artificial insemination and semen cryopreservation is carried out on an agricultural scale in countries such as France, Spain and Italy, There is, however, very little in the literature about the collection and cryopreservation of spermatozoa from non-domestic lagomorphs such as hares. Basic biological studies with the species of interest will therefore be needed before sensible recommendations about semen collection and freezing can be made.

14.2.2 Seasonality

Weitze *et al.* (1983a) observed clear seasonal effects with the use of frozen semen, inseminations in the summer months giving a lower fertility. While seasonality may be highly modified or artificially controlled by photoperiod management in domestic rabbits, wild lagomorphs exhibit marked breeding seasonality (Bronson, 1989). Specific details of seasonality would have to be investigated, however, for any given species of interest.

An essential consideration for the use of artificial insemination with rabbits is that ovulation is normally induced by the mating process. In the absence of mating, follicle development and ovulation has to be achieved by the use of exogenous hormones. The industrial scale of rabbit breeding by artificial insemination has led to the development of reliable techniques for this purpose, which typically involve the injection of females with 20 IU of PMSG 48 hours before insemination, and the induction of ovulation by the use of GnRH immediately before or after insemination (Battaglini *et al.*, 1988).

CHAPTER 14

14.2.3 Semen collection

Semen is normally collected from bucks by the use of an artificial vagina, and can be obtained on a regular schedule of 2–3 times per week if required, with two ejaculates collected on any given day (Bredderman *et al.*, 1964). As artificial insemination is widely used in intensive rabbitries there has been concern about the microbial contamination rate in semen collected by artificial vagina. A number of studies have characterized the sources of contamination, which include the sheath of the artificial vagina, the orifice of the tube used for semen collection, the buck's perineal zone and the collector's hands. Efforts to design more hygienic systems of semen collection have been reported (for example, Dal Bosco *et al.*, 1996).

14.2.4 Cryopreservation procedure

Typical cryopreservation protocols involve gradual dilution of semen with extender at 35–37°C, followed by a slow cooling procedure to 5°C and addition of cryoprotectant. However, variants of this procedure have been adopted, especially when using DMSO or acetamide. Battaglini *et al.* (1988), who used glycerol, left the spermatozoa for 8 hours at 5°C prior to adding glycerol by further dilution with the glycerol-containing extender. Packaging in 0.5-ml plastic straws and freezing in the vapour phase of liquid nitrogen is normal practice. Thawing is usually by immersion of the straws in a waterbath at 35–37°C for 15–30 seconds; however, higher thawing rates have been achieved by using a waterbath at 45°C and immersing the straws for 20 seconds (Chen *et al.*, 1989).

DMSO has been regarded as an effective cryoprotectant for rabbit spermatozoa (Weitze *et al.*, 1983b), although this has been disputed (Dalimata and Graham, 1997). A concentration of 12% v/v DMSO in BF5 diluent (see Table 16.2) gave the highest percentages of post-thaw motile spermatozoa and normal acrosomes (Bamba and Adams, 1990). A combination of DMSO (1.75 M) and sucrose (0.5 M) proved optimal (42% motile) in a study conducted by Vicente and Viudes-de-Castro (1996) and resulted in no significant differences compared with fresh spermatozoa in number of embryos recovered (8.9 per donor dose) and their survival after vitrification (52% live fetuses at 29 days gestation).

If glycerol is used as a cryoprotectant, semen is generally diluted in extender and cooled to 5°C before its addition (Chen *et al.*, 1988). The inclusion of sodium lauryl sulphate (0.1% w/v, SDS) has been shown to have a beneficial effect on motility and acrosome integrity, but may result in lower pregnancy rates and litter sizes (Wales and O'Shea, 1968; Helleman and Gigoux, 1988). Rabbit spermatozoa cryopreserved in an acetamide–yolk diluent had a reduced fertility compared with fresh spermatozoa. This was apparently due to failure of sperm transport (Parrish and Foote, 1986).

Weitze *et al.* (1982) achieved pregnancy rates of 59–71% with artificial insemination of semen frozen–thawed in straws in a DMSO diluent, and this did not differ from the fertility obtained with fresh semen.

A large study of rabbit semen storage in relation to AI success was reported by Battaglini *et al.* (1988). They inseminated a total of 1627 does in different seasons of the year, but using fresh, cooled and stored, or frozen–thawed spermatozoa. When fertility rates were compared, the control fertility rate with fresh spermatozoa (22×10^6 live sperm/ml) was 65%, but this dropped to 45.6% if the spermatozoa were cooled in an egg yolk-containing, Tris-buffered medium and kept at 5°C for 48 hours before use. Spermatozoa frozen and thawed in the same extender containing 1% glycerol resulted in almost exactly the same fertility rate (45.3%) as the stored samples. Significantly, however, their reduced fertility data after storage and freezing was associated with approximately halved numbers of live spermatozoa in the inseminates (12.37 and 10.74×10^6 sperm/ml for stored and frozen–thawed samples respectively). These results are of considerable interest because they show that the fertility of the surviving cooled or frozen/thawed spermatozoa was equivalent to that of those in the fresh samples. By implication, if the stored or cryopreserved spermatozoa are used at higher concentration the fertility results would be restored to control values. In addition to this conclusion, the authors also suggested that if used correctly, glycerol was better than DMSO as a cryoprotectant for rabbit spermatozoa.

The unsatisfactory performance of DMSO was confirmed by Dalimata and Graham, (1997) who, however, also regarded glycerol as unsuitable. In a novel approach to semen cryopreservation these authors tested a variety of permeating (acetamide, ethylene glycol, DMSO and glycerol) and non-permeating cryoprotectants, alone and in combination. They concluded that addition of methyl cellulose and trehalose to media containing acetamide provided the better results (53% live, acrosome-intact spermatozoa) than acetamide-containing diluent alone (37% live, acrosome-intact spermatozoa).

14.3 OOCYTES

14.3.1 Source of oocytes

Postovulatory oocytes have been collected from the oviducts of rabbits 13 hours after an injection of hCG (al-Hasani *et al.*, 1989). Superovulation with FSH followed by LH to cause oocyte maturation resulted in oocytes which could be collected by puncturing the preovulatory follicles; alternatively they were collected by flushing the oviducts 12 hours after LH injection (al-Hasani *et al.*, 1986).

Vincent *et al.* (1989) induced superovulation in New Zealand white rabbit females with FSH and LH (Kennelly and Foote, 1965) and then mated them with a vasectomized male; postovulatory oocytes were obtained by flushing of the oviducts *post-mortem*.

14.3.2 Cryopreservation

In a study of these cryoprotectants on cellular cytoskeletal structures during cooling, PrOH altered the appearance of filamentous actin and caused the development of cytoplasmic microtubules and the dissassembly of the spindle (Vincent *et al.*, 1989). After cryopreservation and removal of the cryoprotectant, microtubules were still present but resolved after incubation in culture and the spindle reformed. Microtubules were also associated with DMSO, although it was subsequently shown that DMSO does not depolymerize actin (Vincent *et al.*, 1990). These authors conclude that PrOH is a better cryoprotectant for pronuclear (one-cell) embryos than DMSO.

Rabbit oocytes survived best (89%) when PrOH was added in single step and freezing was controlled down to −110°C before plunging into liquid nitrogen; the best survival with DMSO was seen with multi-step addition and controlled cooling down to only −70°C (Siebzehnruebl *et al.*, 1989). Subsequent development showed DMSO to be superior to PrOH (51% versus 37%) when oocytes were cooled slowly to −110°C. Using 1.5M DMSO and cooling oocytes slowly in plastic straws to −30°C before transferring them to liquid nitrogen, al-Hasani *et al.* (1986) found that best results were obtained by thawing rapidly and diluting out the DMSO stepwise. In their results, 29% had acceptable morphology after 4 hours in culture, but this declined to 5% after 14 hours in culture. In a later study (al-Hasani *et al.*, 1989), a 32% survival rate was obtained, of which 74% fertilized *in vitro*; 4 of 53 transferred embryos resulted in births.

Thus, there is little clear indication of which cryoprotectant or cryopreservation protocol is favoured. The overall conclusion is that survival is possible with a variety of methods but the process needs to be optimized in each situation.

14.3.3 Assessment

Thirty-nine per cent of frozen oocytes could be fertilized *in vitro* but only 9% went on to develop normal fetuses (Vincent *et al.*, 1989). This is a success rate very similar to that quoted above (al-Hasani *et al.*, 1989). The survival of pronuclear stage embryos frozen in a mixture of PrOH and sucrose was found to be 71% morphologically but only 10% reached blastocyst stage after 5 days in culture; this compared with 59% of fresh collected pronuclear stage embryos (al-Hasani *et al.*, 1992). A 24% implantation rate was observed compared with a 52% rate for fresh pronuclear stage embryos.

14.4 EMBRYOS

As previously stated, rabbits are induced ovulators, requiring copulation to stimulate the release of LH to cause ovulation. Rabbit embryos have been successfully cryopreserved, with the greatest survivals generally being associated with the the later stages of preimplantation embryonic development, i.e. morula and blastocyst. Cryoprotectants commonly in use include DMSO and PrOH. Most of the research has been as a model for human embryo cryopreservation. Strain differences have been observed.

14.4.1   Source

Work on pronuclear stage one-cell embryos (al-Hasani *et al.*, 1992) is summarized in Section 14.3. Morulae have been recovered 63–66 hours postcoitally from large numbers of adult does by routine uterine flushing (Kasai *et al.*, 1992; Vicente and Garcia-Ximénez, 1993a,b). These authors used 25 IU hCG in addition to copulation to ensure oocyte maturation and ovulation. Morulae can apparently be collected readily by a non-surgical route from the vagina of rabbits treated with prostaglandin at 65 hours post-coitum; the embryos showed the same responses to cryopreservation as those collected from the uterus (Garnier *et al.*, 1988).

When a two-step cooling protocol was adopted to compare the survival potential of embryos cryopreserved at different stages of development, Lopez-Bejar *et al.* (1994) found that compacted morulae and early blastocysts showed a developmental capacity *in vitro* not significantly different from that of control unfrozen blastocysts; two- to sixteen-cell stages showed a poorer developmental capacity.

14.4.2   Standard slow freezing with ice formation

Diluent and cryoprotectant

There appear to be no studies comparing cryoprotectants. For a rapid freezing method involving either one step or two steps, a combination of DMSO (3.5 M) and sucrose (0.25 M) was used (Lopez-Bejar *et al.*, 1994). In this diluent, the one-step method was inferior to the two-step method, regardless of stage of development of the embryos. A cryoprotectant suitable for morulae is 1.5 M DMSO (Vicente and Garcia-Ximénez, 1993a).

Protocol

A standard protocol using slow freezing was employed by Vicente and Garcia-Ximénez (1993a,b).

14.4.3   Vitrification

Most studies have focused on rapid or ultra-rapid cooling methods in the presence of high concentrations of cryoprotectants, which results in vitrification rather than

CHAPTER 14

freezing. For these studies, a range of cryoprotectant solutions have been used. Lopez-Bejar *et al.* (1994), in a protocol which probably resulted in a non-equilibrium freezing regime rather than vitrification, used a diluent containing DMSO and sucrose (see above), but for true vitrification a mixture of 1.36 M glycerol, 2.72 M PrOH and 1 M sucrose has been employed (Papis *et al.*, 1993). Kasai *et al.* (1992) used a modified PBS containing 40% EG, 18% Ficoll (an inert high molecular weight substance) and 0.3% sucrose, and found good results, especially if the mucin coat around the embryos was left intact.

A comparative study of the effect of a serum or BSA supplement on rabbit embryos vitrified in the presence of a mixture of DMSO and EG showed the advantage of the presence of protein during cryopreservation, although the authors concluded that moderate success was possible without the supplement (Vicente *et al.*, 1999).

14.4.4 Thawing

There appear to be no studies of thawing procedures but methods used in other species are employed, including sucrose to osmotically buffer the effects of the high concentrations of cryoprotectant. Rapid thawing is employed, especially when rapid cooling has occurred to avoid the possibility of growth of intracellular ice crystals (see Chapter 3).

14.4.5 Assessment

Cryopreservation success is commonly assessed morphologically, survival being judged successful if the zona pellucida is intact and and there are evenly sized blastomeres without cell debris or fragmentation. However, the most valuable assessments are those relating to the subsequent development of frozen–thawed embryos. Approximately 90% of cryopreserved embryos resumed development *in vitro* (Papis *et al.*, 1993) an observation echoed by Lopez-Bejar *et al.* (1994).

In some cases, the results are reported in two stages: the proportion of embryos that survive freezing and thawing as judged morphologically or with limited development *in vitro*, and of those judged acceptable, the proportion that implant and undergo subsequent development. For example, Kasai *et al.* (1992) reported that 87% of morulae survived vitrification and were capable of forming expanded blastocysts; of 131 embryos cryopreserved using their optimal method, 120 were suitable for transfer of which 78 (65%) resulted in a full-term fetus or young born live. A similar success rate with the most successful treatments was reported by Vicente *et al.* (1999). Compacted morulae vitrified in a solution of 20% EG/20% DMSO were rewarmed and transferred directly to recipients without prior dilution of the vitification solution; 94% of does delivered live young and the survival rate of transferred embryos was 40% compared with 55% for fresh embryos (Vicente and Garcia-Ximénez, 1996).

Strain differences were apparent in post-thawing percentages of normal embryos (Vicente and Garcia-Ximénez, 1993a), but their subsequent survival *in vivo* was related to the strain of the recipient and not the embryo (Vicente and Garcia-Ximénez, 1993a).

REFERENCES

AL-HASANI, S., TOLKSDORF, A., DIEDRICH, K., VAN DER VEN, H. and KREBS, D. (1986) 'Successful in-vitro fertilization of frozen-thawed rabbit oocytes', *Hum. Reprod.* **1**, 309–312.

AL-HASANI, S., KIRSCH, J., DIEDRICH, K., BLANKE, S., VAN DER VEN, H. and KREBS, D. (1989) 'Successful embryo transfer of cryopreserved and in-vitro fertilized rabbit oocytes'. *Hum. Reprod.* **4**, 77–79.

AL-HASANI, S., HEPNAR, C., DIEDRICH, K., VAN DER VEN, H. and KREBS, D. (1992) 'Cryopreservation of rabbit zygotes', *Hum. Reprod.* **7** (Suppl. 1), 81–83.

BAMBA, K. and ADAMS, C. E. (1990) 'Freezing rabbit semen by the use of BF5 diluent', *Lab. Anim.* **24**, 172–175.

BATTAGLINI, M., COSTANTINI, F. and CASTELLINI, C. (1988). 'Fecondazione artificiale del coniglio con sperma refrigerato e congelato', *Zootecn. nutrizione anim.* **14**, 267–272.

BREDDERMAN, P. J., FOOTE, R. H. and YASSEN, A. M. (1964) 'Improved artificial vagina for collecting rabbit semen', *J. Reprod. Fertil.* **7**, 401–404.

BRONSON, F. H. (1989) *Mammalian Reproductive Biology,* Chicago and London: University of Chicago Press.

CHEN, Y., YANG, X. and FOOTE, R. H. (1988). 'Timed breeding in rabbits with fresh and frozen semen and evidence of acrosome alteration following freezing and thawing', *Proceedings of the International Congress on Animal Reproduction and Artificial Insemination (Dublin)* vol. 1, p. 392.

CHEN, Y., LI, J., SIMKIN, M. E., YANG, X. and FOOTE, R. H. (1989). 'Fertility of fresh and frozen rabbit semen inseminated at different times is indicative of male differences in capacitation time', *Biol. Reprod.* **41**, 848–853.

DAL BOSCO, A., SCUOTA, S., CASTELLINI, C. and CENCI, T. (1996). 'Study of an artificial vagina to reduce the microbial contamination of rabbit semen', *World Rabbit Sci.* **4**, 201–204.

DALIMATA, A. M. and GRAHAM, J. K. (1997). 'Cryopreservation of rabbit spermatozoa using acetamide in combination with trehalose and methyl cellulose', *Theriogenology* **48**, 831–841.

GARNIER, V., RENARD, J. P. and MENEZO, Y. (1988) 'Viability and freezing ability of rabbit embryos collected in the vagina after prostaglandin treatment'. *Jpn J Physiol.* **38**, 585–589.

HELLEMAN, C. and GIGOUX, E. (1988). 'Freezing of rabbit semen. Effect of a surfactant on fertilizing ability', *Zuchthygiene* **23**, 33–37.

KASAI, M., HAMAGUCHI, Y., ZHU, S. E.,, MIYAKE, T., SAKURAI, T. and MACHIDA, T. (1992) 'High survival of rabbit morulae after vitrification in an ethylene glycol-based solution by a simple method', *Biol. Reprod.* **46**, 1042–1046.

KENNELLY, J. J. and FOOTE, R. H. (1965) 'Superovulatory response of pre- and post-pubertal rabbits to commercially available gonadotrophins', *J. Reprod. Fertil.* **9**, 177–188.

LOPEZ-BEJAR, M., LOPEZ-GATIUS, F., CAMON, J., RUTLLANT, J. and LABERNIA, J. (1994) 'Development in vitro of rabbit embryos after freezing by two-step or ultra-rapid cooling methods', *Zentralbl. Veterinarmed. A* **41**, 780–790.

PAPIS, K., FUJIKAWA, S., KOJIMA, T. and OGURI, N. (1993) 'Effect of the composition of vitrification media on survival of rabbit embryos', *Cryobiology* **30**, 98–105.

PARRISH, J. J. and FOOTE, R. H. (1986) 'Fertility of cooled and frozen rabbit sperm measured by competitive fertilization', *Biol. Reprod.* **35**, 253–257.

SIEBZEHNRUEBL, E. R., TODOROW, S., VAN UEM, J., KOCH, R., WILDT, L. and LANG N. (1989) 'Cryopreservation of human and rabbit oocytes and one-cell embryos: a comparison of DMSO and propanediol', *Hum. Reprod.* **4**, 312–317.

VICENTE, J. S. and GARCIA-XIMÉNEZ, F. (1993a) 'Effect of recipient doe genotype on survival rate at birth of frozen rabbit embryos', *Reprod. Nutr. Dev.* **33**, 229–234.

VICENTE, J. S. and GARCIA-XIMÉNEZ, F. (1993b) 'Effects of strain and embryo transfer model (embryos from one versus two donor does/recipient) on results of cryopreservation in rabbit', *Reprod. Nutr. Dev.* **33**, 5–13.

VICENTE, J. S. and GARCIA-XIMÉNEZ, F. (1996) 'Direct transfer of vitrified rabbit embryos', *Theriogenology* **45**, 811–815.

VICENTE, J. S. and VIUDES-DE-CASTRO, M. P. (1996) 'A sucrose-DMSO extender for freezing rabbit semen', *Reprod. Nutr. Dev.* **36**, 485–492.

VICENTE, J. S. and VIUDES-DE-CASTRO, M. P. and GARCIA, M. L. (1999) '*In vivo* survival rate of rabbit morulae after vitrification in a medium without serum protein', *Reprod. Nutr. Dev.* **39**, 657–662.

VINCENT, C., GARNIER, V., HEYMAN, Y. and RENARD, J. P. (1989) 'Solvent effects on cytoskeletal organization and in-vivo survival after freezing of rabbit oocytes', *J. Reprod. Fertil.* **87**, 809–820.

VINCENT, C., PRULIERE, G., PAJOT-AUGY, E., CAMPION, E., GARNIER, V. and RENARD. J.-P. (1990) 'Effects of cryoprotectants on actin filaments during the cryopreservation of one-cell rabbit embryos', *Cryobiology* **27**, 9–23. (Published erratum appears in *Cryobiology* (1990) **27**, 343–344.)

WALES, R. G. and O'SHEA, T. (1968) 'The deep freezing of rabbit sperm', *Aust. J. Biol. Sci.* **21**, 831–833.

WEITZE, K. F., SCHARNHÖLZ, A. and BADER, H. (1982) 'Tiefgefrierkonservierung von Kaninchensperma. II. Einfluss der Langzeitlagerung auf die Befruchtungsfähigkeit', *Zuchthygiene* **17**, 172–177.

WEITZE, K. F., RATH, D. and KRAUSE, D. (1983a) 'Tiefgefrierkonservierung von Kaninchensperma. III. Jahreszeitliche Schwankungen der Besamungsergebnisse', *Zuchthygiene* **18**, 63–66.

WEITZE, K. F., SCHARNHÖLZ, A. and HELLEMANN, C. (1983b) 'Tiefgefrierkonservierung von Kaninchensperma. IV. Eidfluss von Glycerin auf des Befruchttungsvermögen', *Zuchthygiene* **18**, 67–70.

CHAPTER 14

The Cryopreservation of Gametes and Embryos of Cattle, Sheep, Goats and Pigs

L. M. PENFOLD[1] AND P. F. WATSON[2]

[2]White Oaks Conservation Center, 3823 Owens Road, Yulee, FL 32097, USA
[3]Department of Veterinary Basic Sciences, The Royal Veterinary College,
London NW1 0TU, UK

Contents

15.1 INTRODUCTION

The literature on the preservation of gametes and embryos of domestic animals is immense. Many reviews can be found covering these topics in much detail. For example, for spermatozoa, general reviews include those of Watson (1979, 1990) and Curry (2000), and species-based reviews can be found for several of the species, such as sheep (Maxwell and Salamon 1995a,b), goat (Chemineau *et al.*, 1999) and pigs (Bwanga, 1991). For embryos, there are a number of reviews which cover the subject in general (e.g. Fahning and Garcia, 1992), or more specifically for sheep (Loi *et al.*, 1998), goats (Amoah and Gelaye, 1997) or pigs (Niemann and Reichelt, 1993), and the International Embryo Transfer Society proceedings provide a regular update of knowledge in this area. Less is published concerning oocyte cryopreservation because oocyte maturation and fertilization has yet to find a commercial application. Because these reviews cover the ground quite thoroughly, this chapter contains either selected key findings that are regarded as founding dogma of the subject, or less accessible material which may have a contribution to make to the subject.

15.2 CATTLE

15.2.1 Spermatozoa

Cryopreservation is used extensively in the cattle AI industry as a means of storing spermatozoa. Empirical studies have resulted in the development of an adequate protocol for bull sperm cryopreservation but a large percentage of bull spermatozoa fail to survive the freeze–thaw process, requiring five-fold sperm insemination doses to reach fertility rates comparable with those of a natural mating. The basic diluent, composed of egg yolk, a buffer system and glycerol, has not changed dramatically in over forty years, and inclusion of a range of additives has not increased post-thaw fertility rates. In spite of this, bull sperm cryopreservation continues to lead the way as the most effective method for mammalian sperm cryopreservation, and the basic technique has been adapted for a range of other species.

Semen collection and processing

Semen is usually collected using an artificial vagina (AV). Domestic cattle are not considered to be highly seasonal, but in red-and-white and Swedish Friesian bulls several parameters (i.e. libido, ejaculate volume, number of spermatozoa per ejaculate, sperm motility before and after freezing, and number of semen doses per collection) have all been shown to be affected by season of collection and age (Stalhammer *et al.*, 1988). In Holstein-Friesian and Friesian bulls, the percentage of abnormal spermatozoa was highest during the summer months and the ability to survive freezing was lowest during the summer (Parkinson, 1987). Cryogenic changes, manifested as a considerable loss of glutamic oxalacetic transaminase and hyaluronidase into the extracellular medium, as well as easier access to acrosin, are greatest in April–June and are correlated with high activity of acrosin inhibitors in seminal plasma (Swidowiez and Strzezek, 1986). Cauda epididymal spermatozoa also have been collected and frozen, with percentages of motile caudal epididymal spermatozoa ranging from 5 to 45% before freezing and increasing to 45–60% after thawing (Soderquist *et al.*, 1988), presumably due to membrane changes induced by the freeze–thaw process.

Cryopreservation diluents and additives

Dialysis of diluted bull semen before cryopreservation has been shown to be beneficial because it removes low molecular weight seminal plasma components that are deleterious to sperm survival (Garcia and Graham, 1989a). Dialysis of bull semen against various zwitterion buffers during a 2-hour cooling period identified highest sperm survival in extenders containing PIPES buffer (Garcia and Graham, 1989a). Motility of bull spermatozoa dialysed against buffer solutions containing 30% isosmotic solutions of glucose, galactose, ribose, xylose, arabinose or their corresponding sugar alcohols, was higher than in extenders without sugar (Garcia and Graham, 1989b). Filtration of bovine semen through a Sephadex ion-exchange column prior to freezing resulted in an increased ($P<0.005$) proportion of spermatozoa surviving the freeze–thaw process by harvesting spermatozoa with stronger plasma membranes (Anzar *et al.*, 1997). Also, after thawing there were higher ($P<0.005$) numbers of normal acrosomes in filtered versus non-filtered, and a higher ($P<0.005$) incidence of zona-free hamster egg penetration (Anzar *et al.*, 1997).

The cryoprotection offered by egg yolk could not be matched by dioleoyl-phosphatidylcholine (DOPC) vesicles or DOPC/phosphatidic acid/cholesterol vesicles in concentrations of up to 29 or 9 mM, respectively (De Leeuw *et al.*, 1993). Similarly, phosphatidylserine was less effective than egg yolk in protecting spermatozoa during freezing. But addition of cholesterol, or phosphatidylcholine and cholesterol to phosphatidylserine produced post-thaw motilities similar to that of egg yolk-treated spermatozoa (Graham and Foote, 1987). Diluents made with egg yolk modified by feeding hens diets supplemented with sunflower oil or beef tallow did not produce differences in post-thaw sperm motility compared with diluents made with egg yolk from non-treated hens (Foulkes *et al.*, 1980). The effects of sucrose and trehalose on bull sperm motility following cryopreservation were small (55% and 61% respectively for 0.05 and 0.1 M sucrose, 62% and 57% for 0.01 M and 0.1 M trehalose versus 62% for controls; Chen *et al.*, 1993). Post-thaw bull sperm motility was 10% higher in whole milk diluent containing 0.5 mM and 0.75 mM butylated hydroxytoluene, than in samples with no additive (Killian *et al.*, 1989). However, 0.5 mM butylated hydroxytoluene has been shown to have no effect on bull non-return rates (73.9%, butylated hydroxytoluene; 74.1%, control; Anderson *et al.*, 1994). Significantly higher post-thaw motilities were obtained following freezing in whole egg–Tris diluent containing 0.125% sodium triethanolamine lauryl sulphate (STLS), than diluent without STLS (Arriola and Foote, 1987). Fertility of spermatozoa frozen in an egg yolk–Tris detergent diluent has been found to be equivalent to that of spermatozoa frozen in whole milk (Arriola and Foote, 1987). Combinations of extenders revealed higher numbers of membrane-intact spermatozoa were obtained in extenders containing egg yolk–citrate, but lower post-thaw motilities were obtained when both extender fractions were egg yolk–citrate (Karabinus *et al.*, 1991). Bull spermatozoa tolerate relatively high concentrations of glycerol (6–9%), which is the preferred cryoprotectant. Substitution of glycerol by polyvinyl alcohol resulted in all spermatozoa dying (Okolski and Jamer, 1986). Vitamin D (ergocalciferol) has been reported to have some beneficial effects on post-thaw sperm motility (al-Khanak *et al.*, 1989).

Packaging, freezing and thawing

Bull spermatozoa are traditionally frozen in 0.25-ml ministraws but also have been cryopreserved in minitubes, medium sized straws and in glass ampoules, resulting in post-thaw motilities of $62\pm5.2\%$, $53\pm2.5\%$ and $52\pm2.5\%$ respectively (Hube *et al.*, 1983). Survival ranged from 24.6% for spermatozoa frozen at 129.2°C/min to 58.9% for semen frozen at 28.3°C/min (Jansen, 1988). Fertility trials have shown that semen cryopreserved over liquid nitrogen vapour has marginally better fertility results than that frozen in a programmable freezer (Almquist *et al.*, 1982). However, post-thaw motilities have been reported to be higher when frozen in a programmable cell freezer than in liquid nitrogen vapour (Dunskii *et al.*, 1986). Also, programmable cell freezers have the advantage of allowing optimization of sperm freezing for bulls whose semen showed poor survival when conventional methods are used (Parkinson and Whitfield, 1987). Seeding before significant supercooling was found to improve sperm survival when freezing in a programmable freezer (Parkinson and Whitfield, 1987).

Straws are normally thawed by immersion in a waterbath at 37°C. Fast thawing rates (60°C versus 4°C and 30°C/min) gave higher motilities and acrosome integrity for frozen spermatozoa (Arriola and Foote, 1987). A comparison of thawing rates and processing temperatures showed that thawing 0.25ml straws in a waterbath at 37°C for 10–15 seconds followed by transfer to a waterbath at 21°C for 2 minutes to complete thawing, resulted in similar percentages (77%) of motile spermatozoa as for straws thawed and processed at 37°C. However, a higher response to a hyposmotic swelling test was observed for spermatozoa thawed by the former method (Correa *et al.*, 1996).

Post-thaw assessment

Computer-assisted sperm analysis (CASA) allows accurate, objective assessments (Tuli *et al.*, 1992) and the competitive fertility index for nine bulls has been correlated with percentage of motile spermatozoa, linear velocity and straight line velocity (Budworth *et al.*, 1988). Fluorescent staining in combination with flow cytometry has been shown to be useful in assessing post-thaw sperm viability (Garner *et al.*, 1988; Karabinus *et al.*, 1991; Penfold *et al.*, 1997). Rhodamine 123 has also been used to determine post-thaw sperm mitochondrial activity (Karabinus *et al.*, 1991). Three ATPase enzymes were found to be affected by the cryopreservation process: Mg^{2+}-ATPase was found to have a reduced activity following freezing and thawing. Cryopreservation caused a greater reduction of Na^+/K^+-ATPase activity in the head of cryopreserved spermatozoa than for any other ATPase (Zhao and Buhr, 1996), which in turn may be linked with the acrosome reaction. Ca^{2+}-ATPase activity has been shown to be localized in the tail, and was found to be decreased in activity following freezing and thawing (Zhao and Buhr, 1996) and probably associated with a post-thaw reduction in motility.

15.2.2 Oocytes and embryos

Embryo cryopreservation is a well established technique in the bovine embryo transfer industry. Embryos survive cryopreservation more readily than oocytes, which continue to be difficult to freeze. Cryopreservation success is stage dependent for both oocytes and embryos, with the GV stage more sensitive to freeze–thaw damage than other more mature oocyte stages. Similarly, morula and blastocyst stage embryos survive the freeze–thaw process better than earlier stage embryos. Large surface area:volume ratio, high lipid content and the cytoskeleton remain limiting factors in cryopreservation success. Both slow freezing and vitrification are effective methods of freezing oocytes and embryos, but require high concentrations of cryoprotectant, that in turn can have toxic effects. For the oocyte, post-thaw effects can still be manifested up to 7 days later by embryo cleavage failure following IVF. Lastly, limited numbers of both oocytes and embryos can preclude large-scale fertility studies.

Collection and processing

Oocytes have been recovered from slaughterhouse ovaries and cryopreserved at the GV stage (Fuku *et al.*, 1992; Schellender *et al.*, 1994; Im *et al.*, 1997) or matured *in vitro* and cryopreserved at a later stage (Fuku *et al.*, 1992; Lim *et al.*, 1992; Im *et al.*, 1997; Otoi *et al.*, 1998). GV stage oocytes are more sensitive to the freeze–thaw process, and following cryopreservation less than 5% underwent GV breakdown (Fuku *et al.*, 1992). Of those that underwent GV breakdown, only 1.5% of the zygotes cleaved, and none developed to morulae. Matured MII oocytes survived the freezing process better than GV stage oocytes with glycerol as the cryoprotectant (Lim *et al.*, 1992; Schellender *et al.*, 1994). However, MII oocytes also are sensitive to cooling; after chilling for 80 seconds at 0°C, only 10% developed to the blastocyst stage (Martino *et al.*, 1996). If immature follicular oocytes are to be frozen, selecting those with dense cumulus cells results in highest post-thaw viability (Im *et al.*, 1997). Twin calves have been produced from frozen–thawed oocytes that were matured, fertilized and cultured *in vitro* to the morulae/blastocyst stage (Lim *et al.*, 1992; Fuku *et al.*, 1992).

After fertilization, the stage of the embryonic development continues to affect success of cryopreservation with later stages being more resistant to damage. Cryopreservation of eight-cell stage embryos following centrifugation and lipid removal at the zygote stage failed to improve embryo freezing tolerance (Murakami *et al.*, 1998). Blastocyst stage embryos for freezing have been produced from IVF of oocytes recovered from cow ovaries (Fuku *et al.*, 1992; Kuwayama *et al.*, 1992; Mermillod *et al.*, 1992; Massip *et al.*, 1993; Suzuki *et al.*, 1993), or recovered transcervically from cows (Pickard *et al.*, 1985; Seike *et al.*, 1991). Cryopreservation of *in vitro* produced zygotes cultured for 7 days under different oxygen concentrations (20% O_2, 5% CO_2 in air or 5% O_2, 5% CO_2, 90% N_2) resulted in post-thaw survival rates of 53% and 67%, respectively (Voelkel and Hu, 1992a). Morulae and blastocysts survive the freeze–thaw process better than earlier stage embryos, but even the day of blastocyst development can affect post-thaw survival. Pregnancy rate following transfer of IVF blastocysts frozen on day 7 was 42%, but dropped to 20% for blastocysts frozen on day 8 with a higher than normal incidence of early abortions and dystocias (Hasler *et al.*, 1995). Embryos have also been produced following IVF of previously frozen MII oocytes. The developmental capacity of these frozen–thawed embryos was not different from those of thawed embryos derived from mature oocytes (Otoi *et al.*, 1992).

The quality of embryos selected for cryopreservation has a significant impact on post-thaw survival, with high-grade embryos surviving better than low-grade embryos (de Leeuw *et al.*, 1991). Higher pregnancy rates were achieved after transfer of thawed dark versus light embryos (49% versus 40%; Hill and Kuehner, 1998) at the blastocyst stage, but higher pregnancy rates were obtained after transferring thawed light versus dark or very light embryos at the morula stage (51% versus 27% and 42% respectively; Hill and Kuehner, 1998). These appearances are given by the degree of refractoriness of the cytoplasm, and reflect embryonic cell quality.

Donor serum cholesterol levels also have an effect on post-thaw embryo viability with a 48% pregnancy rate after transfer of thawed morulae from donors with cholesterol levels of 3–5 mmol/l versus <3 mmol/l and >5 mmol/l. Highest pregnancy rates were obtained after transfer of thawed blastocyst stage embryos from donors with >5 mmol/l cholesterol (Hill and Kuehner, 1998).

Embryos cultured in the absence of serum survived cryopreservation significantly better than those produced with serum at 48 hours post insemination (86 versus 61%; $P<0.01$; Dinnyes et al., 1996). Similar or higher embryo survival rates were obtained after vitrification than freezing (72% versus 57%) for bovine embryos produced in synthetic oviductal fluid (Dinnyes et al., 1996). Hatched blastocysts survived freezing or vitrification well (80–100%; Dinnyes et al., 1996). It has been suggested that a greater number of male fetuses may result from transfer of frozen–thawed in vitro produced expanded blastocysts (fully expanded 68%, hatched 100%), presenting a potential problem for cattle breeders Carvalho et al., 1996).

Cryoprotectant and additives

Oocytes at different stages of maturation have been cryopreserved in PrOH (Fuku et al., 1992; Otoi et al., 1994), EG (Otoi et al., 1998) and glycerol, PrOH, or DMSO (Schellender et al., 1994). DMSO was less suitable as a cryoprotectant than glycerol or PROH for GV stage oocyte cryopreservation. DMSO was better than glycerol for MII oocytes and equally effective as a cryoprotectant compared with glycerol and PROH (Schellender et al., 1994). The addition of sugars (sucrose, lactose or trehalose) did not improve post-thaw oocyte cleavage and omission of sugars increased the cleavage rate for GV stage oocytes (Schellender et al., 1994). In contrast, exposure of oocytes to 0.35 M sucrose for five minutes before vitrification in 40% EG resulted in highest developmental rates (10%) compared at 1- and 10-minute exposure times (Otoi et al., 1998).

A range of cryoprotectants have been used for bovine embryo cryopreservation, including DMSO, glycerol, PrOH, diethylene glycol (DEG), EG and 1,3–butylene glycol (Maltseva, 1990; Goto et al., 1992; Dinnyes et al., 1996; Hochi and Leibo, 1996). For day 7–8 embryos cryopreserved in 1.3 M methyl cellosolve (MC, a soluble methyl cellulose), 1.1 M DEG, 1.8 M EG, 1.6 M PrOH or 1.1 M BG survival rate was 50, 53.6, 56.9, 58 and 11.5% respectively, with subsequent pregnancy rates of 48, 30, 74, and 40% for MC, DEG, EG and PrOH respectively (Suzuki et al., 1993). For 135 and 399 embryos cryopreserved in glycerol concentrations of 1 M and 1.4 M, the percentages judged suitable for transfer were 94.1% and 92.2% respectively, with pregnancy rates of 46.5 and 49.6% (Maltseva, 1990). Higher embryo survival rates were obtained after equilibration of embryos in 0.5 M PrOH for 5 minutes, 1 M PrOH for 5 minute and 1.6 M PrOH for 10–15 minutes in PBS and 20% cow serum (Goto et al., 1992). The presence of 25 mg/ml of heat-stable plant proteins in a 40% EG/sucrose solution did not improve post-thaw viability of IVM/IVF vitrified blastocysts (Larssen and Mapletoft, 1997).

Packaging, freezing and thawing

Bovine oocytes are generally packaged in straws for freezing, often part-filled with a thawing diluent, separated by air bubbles. Oocytes are cryopreserved by slow cooling

(Otoi *et al.*, 1994), ultra-rapid cooling (Martino *et al.*, 1996) or vitrification (Yang *et al.*, 1994). Cooling rate (0.3°C/min, 0.6°C/min and 0.9°C/min) did not affect developmental competence of frozen–thawed oocytes, with post-thaw cleavage rates of 15.2%, 14.9% and 10.8%, respectively (Otoi *et al.*, 1994). Vitrification may be a better process than slow freezing for GV stage oocytes, which seem to be more sensitive to freeze–thaw damage, but low fertilization rates (12.1%) are still obtained (Yang *et al.*, 1994). Ultra-rapid freezing of oocytes in ~1 µl of 4 or 5.5 M EG solution resulted in 30% cleaving following IVF and 50% of these developing to the blastocyst stage (Martino *et al.*, 1996).

Embryos have been cryopreserved using a programmable cell freezer to control the slow rates (0.3°C/min to −25 to −29°C; Touati *et al.*, 1990) before plunging into liquid nitrogen. Vitrification has been used successfully to freeze bovine embryos (Van der Zwalmen *et al.*, 1989) with 7/14 pregnancies after 90 days. In a large-scale comparative study, freezing by vitrification and thawing using a modified one-step dilution method of Rall resulted in higher embryo survival than by conventional controlled slow freezing, by conventional controlled freezing followed by a modified one-step dilution procedure using sucrose (de Leeuw *et al.*, 1991). The 'open pulled straw' method of Vajta *et al.* (1998) was claimed to yield cooling and warming rates of over 20000°C/min, reducing the amount of time the embryos are in contact with the cryoprotectant. Using this method, cryopreserved embryos (days 3–7) developed to blastocysts at rates comparable with those of controls (Vajta *et al.*, 1998).

Straws have been thawed in air for 5 seconds before transferring to a waterbath at 32–37°C for both oocytes (Otoi *et al.*, 1994; Schellender *et al.*, 1994) and embryos (Suzuki *et al.*, 1993). Embryos also have been thawed by direct transfer to a waterbath at 37°C (Lehn-Jensen and Greve, 1981). Irrespective of cooling rate (0.3, 0.6, 0.9, 1.2 or 1.5°C/min) slow warming (in air) was detrimental to cryopreserved morulae and blastocysts (Hochi and Leibo, 1996). Cryoprotectant was removed in a three-step procedure (5 minutes in 0.7 M cryoprotectant plus carbohydrate, 5 minutes in 0.3 M cryoprotectant and carbohydrate and 5 minutes in carbohydrate only) using the sugars sucrose, trehalose and lactose. Sucrose had the most beneficial effect on thawing of mature oocytes (Hochi and Leibo, 1996), but omission of the carbohydrates resulted in more two-cell embryos developing from GV oocytes (Schellender *et al.*, 1994). Including a thawing diluent in the straw with the embryo allows direct embryo transfer after thawing, with the cryoprotectant diluted out in the straw prior to transfer (Leibo, 1984; Massip and VanderZwalmen, 1987). Direct transfer of cryopreserved embryos to recipient females has had similar results in terms of pregnancy when compared with conventional methods (Voelkel and Hu, 1992b) eliminating the need for post-thaw processing. Co-culture of frozen/thawed blastocyst stage embryos with oviduct epithelial cells resulted in optimum post-thaw survival of embryos where 55–82% re-expanded and 41–54% hatched (Massip *et al.*, 1993).

Post-thaw assessment

The most effective method of testing the post-thaw viability of oocytes and embryos is ultimately the production of offspring. But large-scale embryo transfer trials are not always possible. Alternate methods include IVM/IVF of oocytes (Schellender *et al.*, 1994; Yang *et al.*, 1994; Martino *et al.*, 1996) and embryo blastocoele expansion (Dinnyes *et al.*, 1996). Morphological studies have revealed ultrastructural damage of the oocyte after freezing, such as decrease or disappearance of microvilli, rupture of zona or plasma membrane, disappearance of mitochondrial cristae and premature exocytosis of cortical granules (Yang *et al.*, 1994).

Embryos that were 7 days old were frozen and thawed ($n=412$) and 96.5% were transferred to recipient females on day 6 or day 8 of the cycle; pregnancy rates of 45.7% for day 8 and 65.8% for day 6 were obtained while control transfers of fresh embryos resulted in a pregnancy rate of 65.4% (Falge *et al.*, 1990). In two trials in which one or two frozen–thawed embryos were transferred to recipients, pregnancy rates of 57% and 44% were obtained for females receiving one embryo, and 54% and 55% were obtained for females receiving two embryos (Refsdal *et al.*, 1988). This suggests that in contrast to results from human embryo transfer, viable frozen–thawed bovine embryos are more likely to establish a pregnancy.

15.2.3 Conclusion

Improved cryopreservation protocols are warranted as more breeding units per ejaculate would be preferred for commercial reasons, and it is more practical to use cryopreserved spermatozoa than to maintain and house a stud bull. Further investigation into bull sperm cryopreservation might also yield important information as to why certain populations of spermatozoa survive cryopreservation and others do not.

Cryopreservation of GV stage oocytes avoids the problem of cytoskeleton disruption associated with freezing mature oocytes. However, GV stage oocytes also can be difficult to cryopreserve. In spite of the many variables associated with cryopreservation, embryo transfer using frozen–thawed embryos can result in fertility rates approaching that using fresh embryos. A large-scale field trial by Wagtendonk-de Leeuw and colleagues (1997) has revealed vitrification to be a more effective method of cryopreservation than slow freezing. The ability to include a thawing diluent in the straw, allowing direct transfer of the embryo after thawing, simplified the procedure.

15.3 SHEEP

15.3.1 Spermatozoa

Ram semen is comparatively easily cryopreserved in pellet form, and glycerol (4–6%) is the cryoprotectant of choice. For commercial reasons, straws and minitubes are preferred over pellets. Standard straw freezing rates (10–100°C/min) and thawing methods (immersion in a waterbath) are employed and straw contents are usually directly inseminated into ewes using either surgical or non-surgical techniques. Although glycerol has a slight negative impact on fertility, removal by dialysis does not reverse the effect.

Semen collection and processing

Ram semen collection is usually by artificial vagina. Although rams produce semen all year round, higher percentages of post-thaw motile spermatozoa have been obtained when semen was collected during a decreasing photoperiod than during an increasing photoperiod (Fiser and Fairfull, 1983, 1986a). Ejaculates have been diluted in cryo-preservation buffer before (Fiser and Fairfull, 1986b; Lopez et al., 1988) and after (Abdelhakeam et al., 1991b) cooling. Studies have shown that higher ($P<0.05$) post-thaw motilities are obtained when semen is diluted after cooling (Fiser and Fairfull, 1989; Abdelhakeam et al., 1991b).

Cryopreservation diluents and additives

Cryopreservation diluents are usually egg yolk-based. Glycerol has been shown to affect fertility negatively, and post-thaw removal by dialysis does not remove the effect (Abdelhakeam et al., 1991a). However, it remains the preferred cryoprotectant and has been used at concentrations ranging from 3 to 9% (Lopez et al., 1988). Replacing glycerol with polyvinyl alcohol did not result in any spermatozoa regaining post-thaw motility (Okolski and Jamer, 1986), although glycerol can be omitted from the diluent if the egg concentration is increased to 30% and sugars such as erythritol, inositol, sorbitol, fructose, glucose, mannose, lactose, maltose, sucrose and raffinose are used (Abdelhakeam et al., 1991a). In this case, highest post-thaw motilities (60%) were obtained with maltose. The addition of proline and glycine/betaine to diluents has been shown to improve sperm survival with post-thaw motility values of greater than 60% (Sanchez-Partida et al., 1992). The inclusion of liposomes containing preparations of phosphatidylcholine and cholesterol increased percentages of motile and acrosome intact spermatozoa when stored at 5°C, but the inclusion of a proprietary membrane fluidizing agent A_2C did not improve post-thaw sperm survival, and had slight deleterious effects (Holt and North, 1988). However, incubation of sperm plasma membranes with dipalmitoylphosphatidylcholine or the lactose diluent of Nagase and Niwa before freezing increased membrane rigidity and prevented a decrease in phospholipase A_2 that is normally observed after freezing (Hinkovska-Galcheva et al., 1988).

Packaging, freezing and thawing

Highest fertility rates are obtained when spermatozoa are frozen as pellets (Petruijkic *et al.*, 1987; Maxwell *et al.*, 1995), but for ease of handling, disease control and identification, packaging in 0.25-ml straws (Maxwell *et al.*, 1995), 0.5-ml straws (Abdelhakeam *et al.*, 1991a; Maxwell *et al.*, 1995) or minitubes is preferred (Maxwell *et al.*, 1995). Fertility rates comparable with those obtained with pellet freezing have been achieved using minitubes (Maxwell *et al.*, 1995), which allow improved labelling and storage. Ejaculates have been diluted up to 1:4 either as a single dilution at 5°C (Fiser *et al.*, 1987; Abdelhakeam *et al.*, 1991a,b) or divided before and after cooling to 5°C (Fiser and Fairfull, 1986b). Ram spermatozoa frozen as pellets have been thawed 'dry' at 40°C, with post-thaw motilities of >50%. Following AI in the months of June, July, August and September, percentage lambing rates were 37.5, 27.3, 39.5 and 20 % respectively (Petruijkic *et al.*, 1987). Pellets also have been thawed in 1 ml of medium containing different prostaglandins (PG). At 5, 10 and 15 μg per pellet, prostaglandin resulted in higher sperm survival than controls without prostaglandin; no significant effects were seen on the acrosome (Anel *et al.*, 1988). Straws are usually thawed with a conventional straw thawing method, by immersion in a waterbath at 37–39°C for 20–30 seconds.

Post-thaw assessment

Percentage progressive sperm motility and subsequent fertility rates are the most important measures of post-thaw sperm viability. Fluorescent stains such as propidium iodide or ethidium homodimer together with carboxyfluorescein diacetate or SYBR-14 stain have been useful in assessing plasma membrane integrity and in combination with cryomicroscopy have been used to pinpoint precise temperatures at which plasma membrane integrity has been lost (Holt *et al.*, 1992). An alternative, non-fluorescent supravital dye, amaranth, stains the nuclei of non-viable spermatozoa pink. The dye has no effect on motility of viable spermatozoa and insemination of ewes with fresh semen containing amaranth or semen frozen in the presence of amaranth resulted in pregnancy in 7 of 10 ewes in each group versus 6 of 9 ewes inseminated with fresh, unstained semen (Fiser and Marcus, 1989). Transmission electron microscopy has been used to examine ultrastructural changes after freezing and thawing and has revealed the acrosome to be the most damaged structure during cryopreservation, followed by the cell membrane (Zibrin *et al.*, 1987). Further studies of spermatozoa that had been treated with an actin monoclonal antibody have revealed a subpopulation that exhibits postacrosomal actin immunoreactivity after cooling (Holt *et al.*, 1992).

15.3.2 Oocytes

Oocytes are readily derived from slaughterhouse material, and can be cultured *in vitro*.

Sheep oocytes demonstrated a typical Boyle Van t'Hoff relationship with increases in osmolality and revealed a non-osmotic volume by extrapolation of approximately 19% of their isotonic volume (Songsasen *et al.*, 1995). Newton *et al.* (1999) derived oocyte–granulosa cell complexes for studies of IVM in fresh and frozen–thawed ovine ovarian tissue. They found that fresh or frozen oocyte–granulosa cell complexes of >190 μm went on in culture to form antral cavities in 25±9% and 18±6% of cases (mean±SEM), respectively. Antrum formation was more likely in the presence of gonadotrophins and the incidence did not differ between fresh or frozen material. Oocytes survived 30 days in culture, demonstrating the ability of frozen oocyte–granulosa cell complexes to survive cryopreservation and subsequently to resume development.

15.3.3 Embryos

Embryos are successfully cryopreserved by slow freezing or vitrification using standard embryo freezing and thawing techniques. Post-thaw survival ranges from 50 to 69%.

Embryo collection

Embryos are recovered using a surgical technique 5–6 days after natural mating (Czllonkowska *et al.*, 1991) or 6–7 days after superovulation with FSH (Sakul *et al.*, 1993). Higher post-thaw embryo survival rates were obtained when late stage morula and early blastocysts are selected for vitrification; inferior results were achieved with early morula (de Paz *et al.*, 1994). Attempts to bisect and cryopreserve demi-embryos resulted in lower post-thaw fertility rates (8 of 142 [5.6%]) than those with whole embryos (14 of 31 [45.2%]; Shelton, 1992).

Packaging, freezing and thawing

Sheep embryos have been cryopreserved by slow freezing (Cocero *et al.*, 1996; Schiewe *et al.*, 1991; De Paz *et al.*, 1994) and by vitrification (Schiewe *et al.*, 1991; De Paz *et al.*, 1994; Naitana *et al.*, 1996). Higher percentages of embryos survived slow freezing (31% morulae, 67% blastocyst) than vitrification (12% morulae, 19% blastocyst; De Paz *et al.*, 1994). In contrast, embryos vitrified after exposure to 3.5 M glycerol plus 3.5 M PrOH for 30 or 60 seconds, resulted in 22/42 thawed embryos developing into lambs after embryo transfer (Szell and Windsor, 1994).

Embryos are often cryopreserved in straws, allowing better labelling. However, post-thaw embryo viability was found to be improved in glass ampoules after slow cooling to below −30°C (1°C/min to −5°C, seeding and cooling at 0.3°C/min) before rapid cooling in liquid nitrogen (Schiewe *et al.*, 1991). Sheep embryos have been successfully cryopreserved by a one-step method using 1.5 M EG and a two-step method using an intermediate step of 0.75 M EG (McGinnis *et al.*, 1993). No difference in embryo survival was seen between the two dilution techniques. Embryos at the morula/blastocyst stage were equilibrated in 3 M methanol or in 1.5 M DMSO at −10°C then cooled at a rate of 0.3°C/min to −30°C or at 0.5°C/min to −35°C. Pregnancies obtained after embryo transfer of frozen–thawed embryos was 7/12 for methanol frozen embryos and 14/21 for DMSO frozen embryos (Czllonkowska *et al.*, 1991). Less damage to the zona pellucida was seen in embryos cryopreserved in PrOH (4%) rather than glycerol (40%; Schiewe *et al.*, 1991). Comparative studies of cryoprotectants revealed a relative permeability of EG>PrOH>DMSO=glycerol, and survival after freezing with these cryoprotectants was in the same order; EG appeared to be superior for sheep embryos, giving 77% developing into hatched blastocysts (Songsasen *et al.*, 1995). Ten lambs born from a total of 47 embryos transferred showed the potential of these techniques.

No difference in embryo survival was seen using either a one- or two-step method of thawing, involving 1.0 M sucrose or 0.25 M sucrose and 1 M sucrose, giving an overall survival of 69% (McGinnis *et al.*, 1993).

Post-thaw assessment

Post-thaw embryo survival is usually assessed as the percentage of embryos that expand *in vitro* to the blastocoele stage (De Paz *et al.*, 1994) or the number of transferred embryos that develop into live born lambs. Embryos have been transferred to ligated rabbit oviducts, recovered, assessed for normal appearance and then transferred to recipient ewes (Willadsen *et al.*, 1976); of eleven embryos transferred to seven ewes, four ewes lambed, producing five lambs. Also, eight frozen/thawed embryos were transferred directly to four ewes and three ewes produced three lambs (Willadsen *et al.*, 1976). The normal appearance of embryos after thawing can determine the pregnancy rate after transfer. For embryos classified either as good or fair after freezing and thawing, the survival rates following transfer were 61% and 48%, respectively (Sakul *et al.*, 1993).

15.3.4 Conclusions

Unlike bull spermatozoa, those of the ram do not tolerate higher concentrations (>6%) of glycerol well. Glycerol also depresses fertility if semen is introduced intracervically. The presence of various sugars and additives allows the glycerol concentration to be decreased, but optimal levels remain at 4–6%. Future work investigating methods of reducing or eliminating glycerol from diluents whilst maintaining viability would probably enhance fertility rates. There is a need for oocyte cryopreservation protocols to be developed and tested, but protocols for embryo cryopreservation are well established.

15.4 GOAT

15.4.1 Spermatozoa

Semen collection and processing

Collection of semen twice weekly in a series of 15 ejaculates per male has been achieved using an AV; ejaculates of <0.2 ml and with a sperm concentration of <1.0× 10^9/ml were discarded (Corteel *et al.*, 1987). The fertilizing capacity of frozen–thawed spermatozoa collected in the spring is lower than that collected in the fall °Corteel, 1973). Seasonal effects outside the breeding season have been observed as a larger ejaculate volume, containing lower numbers of spermatozoa, but other semen traits, such as pH and osmolarity, were not found to differ between seasons (Strohmeyer, 1988). Optimum semen output and quality is obtained throughout the breeding season for Saanen, Alpine and Damascus bucks (Karatzas *et al.*, 1997). The presence of phospholipase A, an enzyme found in seminal plasma, varies between individuals and seasons and has been suggested to account for fertility differences in cryopreserved spermatozoa (Corteel, 1974).

Goat semen is normally washed before freezing to remove phospholipase A, an enzyme that causes egg yolk coagulation (Corteel, 1974; Corteel *et al.*, 1987). However, washing spermatozoa can have a detrimental effect. Alternatively, a skimmed milk diluent instead of egg yolk has been used to freeze goat spermatozoa, to circumvent the problem of coagulation by phospholipase A (Oszar *et al.*, 1988). Insemination with either washed or unwashed spermatozoa frozen in a skim milk diluent gave conception rates of 8/15 and 7/11 does, respectively (Oszar *et al.*, 1988).

Cryopreservation, diluents and additives

Diluents containing concentrations of egg yolk higher than 1.5% result in reduced post-thaw motility if semen is not washed prior to dilution (Salamon and Ritar, 1982). However, washing the semen twice allowed goat spermatozoa to be cryopreserved in a Tris–glucose or fructose diluent containing 5% glycerol and 12% egg yolk (Salamon and Ritar, 1982). In one study, 15 ejaculates from five native goats were diluted in four diluents, frozen and stored for 0–4 hours; sperm motility was highest (52.2±3.3%) and acrosome damage lowest (17.7±2.15%) for semen diluted in a Tris–egg yolk, citric acid, fructose–glycerol diluent (Deka and Rao, 1987a). However, in another study, no difference in sperm motility was observed when native goat semen was frozen in Tris–citric acid, egg yolk or skim milk diluents (Mukherjee and Nelson, 1987). Differences between diluents and breeds were not significant for semen volume, sperm motility or number (Mukherjee and Nelson, 1987). The inclusion of Orvus ES (sodium triethanolamine lauryl sulphate, OES) paste in the freezing diluent resulted in higher percentages of motile (29.42%±15%) and acrosome-intact (38.53%±14.3%) spermatozoa (Strohmeyer, 1988).

Cooling and warming protocols

Studies on fresh and frozen Korean goat semen revealed the best freezing regime to be 12°C/min with 9% glycerol (Park *et al.*, 1989). Twelve females were inseminated with semen frozen this way and three animals produced three live young. Split ejaculates were diluted 1:5 with Tris–citric acid egg yolk–fructose, cooled from 35°C to 5°C over 0.5, 1.5 or 2.5 hours before stepwise glycerol addition, equilibration for 5 hours, and frozen in liquid nitrogen. Acrosomal damage was found to be less in the sample that was cooled over 2.5 hours (Deka and Rao, 1987b).

Highest post-thaw motilities were obtained after rapid thawing (52.5±3.3%) when compared to slow thawing (13.0±4.0%). Lowest numbers of acrosome-damaged spermatozoa were also obtained after rapid thawing (16.1±2.1%) when compared with slow thawing (17.7±2.15%) after 4 hours storage in liquid nitrogen (Deka and Rao, 1987a).

Packaging

Spermatozoa have been successfully frozen in straws and pellets. In one study, straw freezing was compared with conventional pellet freezing: both 0.25-ml and 0.5-ml straws were held in liquid nitrogen vapour for 30 seconds before plunging into liquid nitrogen. However, superior results were obtained with pellet freezing (Ritar *et al.*, 1990a).

Post-thaw assessment

Computer-assisted sperm analysis (CASA) and subjective assessment of fresh and frozen–thawed goat spermatozoa yielded comparable results. However, CASA consistently gave more accurate results (Tuli *et al.*, 1992). Higher pregnancy rates were obtained when 1833 Cashmere does were inseminated with frozen–thawed spermatozoa by laparoscopy (two trials; 63.6% and 52.1%) than cervical inseminations (39.1%; Ritar *et al.*, 1990b). Fertility was higher when does were inseminated before ovulation and laparoscopic results were similar using semen frozen as straws or as pellets (Ritar *et al.*, 1990b). Using samples showing good post-thaw survival and/or intrauterine insemination, inseminations with frozen–thawed spermatozoa have been found to be similar to those with fresh spermatozoa (Corteel, 1976; Ritar and Salamon, 1983). Breed differences revealed higher kidding rates following AI of frozen–thawed spermatozoa from Damascus rather than Alpine or Saanen breeds of goat (Karatzas *et al.*, 1997).

15.4.2   Oocytes and embryos

Oocyte collection and processing

Oocytes have been collected from superovulated Alpine and Saanen goats by oviductal flushing with phosphate-buffered saline, 40 hours after the onset of oestrus. Mature oocytes were kept at 38°C before use (Le Gal *et al.*, 1995). One superovulation regime involved 6 intramuscular injections at 12-hour intervals of FSH with increasing doses of LH (4/0.5, 4/0.5, 2/2, 2/2, 2/5 and 2/5 in mg). Females were checked for oestrus at 4-hour intervals using a teaser buck (Baril *et al.*, 1989). Oocytes also have been collected by ovary dissection after stimulating follicular development by three intramuscular injections of FSH (3, 2 and 2 mg, 12 hours apart) on days 14–15 of the oestrous cycle. Does were slaughtered 26 hours after the last injection (Le Gal, 1996).

Embryos have been collected by laparotomy (Nowshari and Holtz, 1993) and laparoscopically (Le Gal *et al.*, 1993), 6–8 days after the onset of oestrus using PBS as a flushing media and keeping the embryos at 28°C. When collected at day 5, 6 and 7, embryos survived freezing best at the hatched blastocyst stage of development (Li *et al.*, 1990). After collection, embryos have been kept at 28°C, and washed 10 times in PBS before transferring to cryoprotectant prior to freezing (Le Gal *et al.*, 1993). Embryos with good or fair morphology have been bisected and half blastocysts incubated for 2 hours and half morulae for 24 hours, before freezing (Nowshari and Holtz, 1993).

Cryoprotectant, diluent composition and dilution

Permeability studies on goat oocytes suggest that the optimum cryoprotectant may be a combination of a high-permeability cryoprotectant such as PrOH, with a lower permeability cryoprotectant such as EG or glycerol. Oocytes would be exposed to the PrOH at 20°C during the first 2 minutes, followed by the same concentration of PrOH supplemented with EG or glycerol at 0°C (Le Gal *et al.*, 1995). Oocytes have also been cryopreserved in 1.5 M PrOH in TCM 199–HEPES supplemented with 10% FCS (Le Gal, 1996).

Goat embryos were first frozen successfully by Bilton and Moore (1976), using glycerol as a cryoprotectant. Goat embryos have survived freezing in a 1 M glycerol solution (Rong *et al.*, 1989) and in Menezo medium containing 1.4 M glycerol (Tsunoda *et al.*, 1984). The survival rate of embryos frozen in DMSO has been shown to be higher than that of embryos frozen in glycerol ($P<0.05$; Li *et al.*, 1990). Freezing with EG rather than glycerol has been shown to result in a better embryo development rate for both morula and blastocyst stage embryos (Le Gal *et al.*, 1993).

Packaging, freezing and thawing

A rapid freezing procedure has been suggested for oocytes, using the above mentioned cryoprotectants (Le Gal et al., 1995).

Goat embryos have been effectively cryopreserved in glycerol at a rate of 0.3°C/min to −35°C after seeding and then 30°C/min to −150°C before plunging into liquid nitrogen. Embryos have also been successfully cryopreserved in 0.25-ml straws at a rate of 2.5°C/min to −7°C, seeded, further cooled at a rate of 0.3°C/min to −30°C, held for 15 minutes at this temperature before plunging into liquid nitrogen (Le Gal et al., 1993). Straws containing embryos at the morula and blastocyst stage of development have been frozen at a rate of 1°C/min to −7°C, seeded, cooled at 0.3–0.8°C/min to −30°C before plunging into liquid nitrogen (Rui et al., 1990). Half embryos have been frozen after seeding at −7°C by cooling at 0.05°C/min for 15 minutes and then at 0.3°C/min to −35°C before plunging into liquid nitrogen (Zhang et al., 1991).

GV oocytes have been thawed by immersion of 0.25-ml straws in a 37°C waterbath for 20 seconds. Cryoprotectant was removed by a one–step method in 0.25 M sucrose solution in TCM 199–HEPES for 15 minutes, followed by three washes with TCM 199–HEPES containing 10% FCS (Le Gal, 1996).

Goat embryos cryopreserved in EG or glycerol were thawed using three cryoprotectant removal procedures: progressive dilution in 1.0, 0.5, 0.3 and 0 M cryoprotectant in PBS; similar progressive dilution with PBS containing 0.25 M sucrose; or one-step transfer to PBS containing 0.25 M sucrose (Le Gal et al., 1993). Cryoprotectant removal significantly affected embryo survival. Successive dilution of glycerol with sucrose from thawed morulae resulted in a kidding rate of 8/10 does, whereas removal of the cryoprotectant by sucrose in a one-step procedure or by successive dilution without sucrose resulted in a low kidding rate (2/11 and 2/17 does, respectively; Le Gal et al., 1993).

Post-thaw assessment

Post-thaw viability of GV oocytes has been assessed by in vitro maturation and in vitro fertilization. Of those that developed to MII (23.7%), 28.8% fertilized, of which 19.2% were assessed as diploid (Le Gal, 1996). One assessment of embryo survival is the ability of the embryo to re-expand in culture after freezing and thawing. In a study by Li et al. (1990), hatched blastocysts re-expanded in vitro irrespective of the cryoprotectant used. Differences in the criteria used to assess post-thaw embryo viability can make data interpretation difficult. In one study, the pregnancy rate of transferred embryos after 7 weeks was 60% for 111 fresh embryos and 64% for 109 cryopreserved embryos (Li et al., 1990). Other post-thaw embryo assessments have included investigating morphological criteria such as increase in cell number, homogeneity, size and shape of blastomeres (Le Gal et al., 1993).

15.5 PIG

15.5.1 Spermatozoa

Unlike the bull, artificial insemination with frozen–thawed boar spermatozoa has not yet achieved fertility rates comparable with those of fresh spermatozoa, and lower farrowing rates and littersizes are obtained following AI with frozen spermatozoa. Short-term liquid storage is currently the preferred preservation technique for pig AI. Boar spermatozoa are acutely susceptible to cold shock, and even slow cooling below 15°C results in a decrease in sperm survival. Glycerol is less tolerated as a cryo-protectant by boar spermatozoa than bull spermatozoa, and lower concentrations of 2–3% are usually used. To compound the problem, acrosome integrity and sperm motility benefit from different glycerol concentrations.

Semen collection and processing

Boar semen is usually collected by the 'gloved-hand' method (in which the spiral tip of the erect penis is grasped in the fingers and squeezed, simulating the cervical lock), and strained into a thermos flask to remove the gel fraction and avoid temperature changes. The sperm-rich fraction is separated visually and allowed slowly to reach room temperature before extending for freezing (Pursel and Johnson, 1975). In Ontario, highest post-thaw sperm motility was obtained when semen was cryo-preserved following collection between March and May (Joyal et al., 1986). Prefreeze processing revealed that centrifugation, dilution and adjusting concentration to 1200×10^6/ml before freezing resulted in higher (20.3%; $P<0.01$) percentages of post-thaw motile spermatozoa compared to dilution, centrifugation, and adjusting concentration to 900×10^6/ml (18.3%; Paquignon et al., 1986).

Cryoprotectants

The most commonly used freezing diluents for boar spermatozoa are BF5F, a Tes/Tris-buffered egg yolk diluent (Johnson, 1985) and LEY, a lactose–egg yolk diluent (Westendorf et al., 1975). Both diluents contain glycerol and Orvus ES paste (OES; sodium tri-ethanolamine lauryl sulphate, also known as Equex STM or STLS). Higher percentages of spermatozoa with normal apical ridges were obtained after cryo-preservation in the lactose–detergent rather than glucose diluent (38.3% and 10% respectively, $P<0.01$) even though post-thaw motilities (22%) were similar (Paquignon et al., 1986). Glycerol concentration has a significant effect on boar spermatozoa post-thaw motility and acrosome integrity (Paquignon, 1985), but remains the most effective cryoprotectant. Ejaculates ($n=13$) from two boars were frozen in straws in cryoprotectant containing 2 or 4% glycerol. Sperm motility and plasma membrane integrity were higher in 4% glycerol ($P<0.05$), whereas the percentage of spermatozoa with a normal apical ridge was higher for 2% glycerol (Almlid *et al.*, 1989). The authors concluded that 4% glycerol may be optimal for straw freezing of boar semen.

Replacing glycerol with 6% PrOH resulted in reduced sperm survival. Polyvinyl alcohol has been shown to be ineffective as a replacement to glycerol as a cryoprotectant, with no spermatozoa surviving the cryopreservation process (Okolski and Jamer, 1986). An investigation of the effects of fourteen hydrophobic and two hydrophilic aromatic compounds on cold shock injury in boar spermatozoa revealed that the majority of the hydrophobic compounds provided protection, but the hydrophilic compounds were ineffective (Bamba and Miyagawa, 1992). Of the aromatic compounds tested, naphthalene was most effective in reducing cold shock effects on boar sperm motility and acrosomal integrity (Bamba and Miyagawa, 1992).

Packaging

The Beltsville pellet method (Pursel and Johnson, 1975) or the Hulsenberg straw method (Westendorf *et al.*, 1975) are commonly used for freezing boar spermatozoa, and no difference has been shown in the fertilizing capacity of either method (~55% farrowing rate; Johnson, 1985). Better results (post-thaw motility and acrosome integrity) were obtained by freezing boar semen in plastic bags than in maxi-straws (5 ml), and the results were similar to those of 0.25-ml mini-straws (Bwanga *et al.*, 1991). Higher rates of fertilized ova were recovered from oviducts of gilts inseminated with semen in bags (73%) from those inseminated with semen than in maxi-straws (63%; Bwanga *et al.*, 1991). Split ejaculates from four boars were frozen in a programmable cell freezer in mini-straws and maxi-straws. Significantly more normal apical ridges were present in mini-straws than in maxi-straws (Bwanga *et al.*, 1990). It is clear that the smaller packaging of the mini-straw allows better control of the freezing curve profile, but the use of flat-pack bags may circumvent the problem.

Cooling procedure

Following cooling to 5°C, equilibration in glycerolated diluent for 0.5–75 minutes had no effect on post-thaw sperm viability (Almlid and Johnson, 1988). Addition of glycerol to boar semen at 5°C resulted in higher post-thaw survival rates than addition at 0°C ($P<0.05$; Almlid *et al.*, 1988). Interactions of glycerol concentration (0–10%) and cooling rates from 1 to 1500°C/min with sperm motility and acrosome integrity, were studied in semen frozen in 0.5-ml straws and thawed at a constant rate (Fiser and Fairfall, 1990). Highest numbers of spermatozoa with normal apical ridges were obtained with 0–1% glycerol and cooling at 30°C/min. However, at these glycerol concentrations, motility was low. Optimal survival for boar spermatozoa frozen in 0.5-

ml straws was obtained with 3% glycerol, cooling at a rate of 30°C/min. Direct plunging of straws into liquid nitrogen (1500°C/min) resulted in all spermatozoa losing motility and acrosome integrity (Fiser and Fairfall, 1990).

Thawing procedure

The influence of thawing on boar spermatozoa survival depends on the rate at which it was frozen (Fiser *et al.*, 1993). Thawing velocities ranging between 10°C/min to 1800°C/min were investigated and for semen frozen at the optimal rate of 30°C/min, increases in thawing rate above 200°C/min substantially improved motility (Fiser *et al.*, 1993). Sperm motility and acrosome integrity after cryopreservation in flat straws and maxi-straws was significantly lower after thawing using microwaves compared with using a waterbath (Ewert, 1988). Rapid dilution of boar spermatozoa at low temperatures of 15°C caused visible acrosome damage when the sample contained 7.5% glycerol, but damage could be reduced by raising the temperature to 25°C before dilution (Bamba and Cran, 1988).

Post-thaw assessment

Boar spermatozoa were incubated at 42.5°C for 45 minutes in a heat stress test, instead of the routinely used 180 minutes at 37°C. The shorter procedure was found to have the same ability in assessing freeze damage and had a greater ability to distinguish the effects of different glycerol concentrations (Fiser *et al.*, 1991). The hamster egg penetration test can be used to assess the potential fertilizing capacity of boar spermatozoa (Clarke and Johnson, 1987). Three hundred and thirty ejaculates from Norwegian Landrace boars were frozen in 5 ml straws, thawed, and motility and acrosome integrity assessed. Two hundred and fifty gilts or sows were inseminated once or twice with frozen semen. Litter sizes averaged 11.8±2.8 and 10.3±3.2 for fresh and frozen spermatozoa respectively ($P<0.05$; Almlid *et al.*, 1989). Sperm plasma membrane integrity following cryopreservation in 5-ml (6-mm diameter) maxi-straws has been determined by flow cytometric analysis of spermatozoa treated with carboxyfluorescein diacetate and propidium iodide (Almlid and Johnson, 1988). Subjective and computer-assisted (HTM-2000 motility analyser) assessment of sperm motility in fresh and frozen–thawed semen of boars yielded comparable results (Tuli *et al.*, 1992).

15.5.2 Oocytes

Oocyte collection and processing

Recently, oocytes have been recovered, cultured and fertilized *in vitro*, with successful development as far as the blastocyst stage (Abeydeera *et al.*, 1998). IVM oocytes have been fertilized, cultured and returned to gilts to establish pregnancy (Coy *et al.*, 1999). The failures in this study were attributed to polyspermy in the IVF system rather than inadequacy of the IVM system. Cumulus–intact oocytes recovered at the germinal vesicle stage from slaughterhouse ovaries were subjected to cooling but, at the germinal vesicle stage, did not survive cooling below 15°C (Didion *et al.*, 1990; Arav *et al.*, 1991). However, cumulus–oocyte complexes have recently been vitrified with EG as cryoprotectant and have shown the ability subsequently to progress in culture to MII; cytochalasin B, a cytoskeletal inhibitor, was shown to be beneficial to the survival of the oocyte complexes (Isachenko *et al.*, 1998)

Cryoprotectant, diluent composition and dilution

Pig oocytes were rapidly cooled in vitrifying solutions with and without antifreeze proteins. Four types of antifreeze polypeptides and glycoproteins were tested. All protein types were found to have a beneficial effect on the plasma membrane during freezing and thawing (Arav *et al.*, 1993).

Post-thaw assessment

The effects of antifreeze proteins on the oolemma during freezing and thawing were assessed using fluorescein diacetate stain. The oolemma is a primary site of damage during exposure to low temperatures (Arav *et al.*, 1993). Survivability of oocytes following cryopreservation has been assessed using trypan blue staining. Oocytes surviving the freezing process were determined to be those that excluded trypan blue and stained with fluorescein diacetate (Arav *et al.*, 1991). Using cryomicroscopy, the process of oocyte freezing has been monitored determining freezing and thawing rates which avoid ice crystal formation (Arav *et al.*, 1991).

15.5.3 Embryo

Slow cooling and conventional freezing has resulted in the successful cryopreservation of porcine embryos with the subsequent production of live offspring. Porcine embryos are extremely sensitive to chilling injury when cooled to temperatures below 15°C. The high lipid content is thought to affect the embryo's ability to survive the cryopreservation procedure. Vitrification offers an alternative to conventional freezing, which can have variable results, but much work is still required to optimize the embryo cryopreservation technique for this species.

Embryo collection and processing

Embryos have been recovered following AI by flushing tracts after slaughter (Dobrinsky and Johnson, 1994) and by laparotomy on days 5 and 6, flushing uterine horns with PBS containing 2% FCS (Hayaski *et al.*, 1989). Embryo recovery from groups of sows and gilts treated with 1000 or 1500 IU of PMSG averaged 13, 15 and 10.4, respectively (Jung *et al.*, 1990). Stage and embryo size have been shown to influence post-thaw survival, with hatched blastocysts showing higher survival rates than early blastocysts or advanced stage (>300 μm) hatched blastocysts (Nagashima *et al.*, 1992).

In vitro handling

Prefreeze culture of hatched blastocyst stage embryos in medium supplemented with 12% BSA resulted in higher post-thaw survival rates (32/39) than embryos cultured in 15% FCS (0/14; Nagashima *et al.*, 1992). There is evidence that porcine embryo freezing sensitivity is related to lipid content. After removal of some of the cytoplasmic lipid, 68% of one-cell embryos survived cooling to 4°C, and 44% developed to the eight-cell stage. Of frozen embryos, 41% survived freezing by the slow cooling method and 12% developed to the eight-cell stage (Nagashima *et al.*, 1994). To displace intracellular lipid, early cleavage stage embryos have been centrifuged at 12 500g for 9 minutes in modified PBS with 10% FCS and 7.5 μg/ml cytochalasin B (Nagashima *et al.*, 1996). After lipid removal using a bevelled suction pipette, vitrification and thawing in a 37°C waterbath, 50% versus 0% of control embryos developed to the blastocyst stage. Vitrification pretreatment with cytochalasin B improved post-thaw development rates of expanded blastocysts (22% versus 60%; $P<0.01$) and hatched blastocysts (28% versus 90%; $P<0.01$) compared with controls and resulted in four developmentally normal fetuses at day 25 of pregnancy (Dobrinsky *et al.*, 1997). Day 6 expanded blastocysts treated similarly resulted in the birth of five normal offspring (Dobrinsky *et al.*, 1998).

Cryoprotectant, diluent composition and dilution

Embryos at the blastocyst stage have been frozen in 1.5 M DMSO (Nagashima *et al.*, 1988). Day 6 and 7 embryos have been vitrified in a glycerol/BSA solution (VS3a) containing 6.5 M glycerol and 6% BSA (Dobrinsky and Johnson, 1994).

Packaging, freezing and thawing

Cooling rates of 1°C/min to −5°C, seeding and cooling at 0.3°C/min resulted in post-thaw survival rate of 48.5% for expanded blastocysts and 47.3% for hatched blastocysts, as assessed by blastocoele expansion (Nagashima *et al.*, 1988). Day 6 and 7 embryos have been vitrified with post-thaw viabilities of 27% and 39%, respectively (Dobrinsky and Johnson, 1994); no day 5 embryos survived the vitrification process.

CHAPTER 15

Post-expanded stage blastocysts have been cooled at a rate of 1°C/min from 35°C to −6.8°C, held for 10 minutes while seeding occurred and cooled at 0.3°C/min to −35°C; after thawing and transfer, 5/11 developed to live piglets (Hayaski *et al.*, 1989).

Vitrified embryos have been thawed by immersing 0.25-ml straws in a waterbath at 25°C for 10 seconds and emptying the contents into a Petri dish (Dobrinsky and Johnson, 1994).

Post-thaw assessment

Blastocysts which expanded or maintained a blastocoele after vitrification or freezing and thawing have been assessed as viable (Nagashima *et al.*, 1988; Kashiwazaki *et al.*, 1991; Dobrinsky and Johnson, 1994). Frozen/thawed peri-hatching blastocyst stage embryos were assessed by examining post-thaw morphology. Those containing a distinct inner cell mass and well-developed trophectoderm were assessed as good. Following transfer of 32 surviving hatched blastocysts to the uterine horn of a recipient female, four normal piglets were produced (Kashiwazaki *et al.*, 1991). Differential fluorochrome staining has been used to assess the cells of the inner cell mass and the trophectoderm after freezing (Iwasaki *et al.*, 1994). Using this technique it was observed that the shape of inner cell mass cells was distorted and cell-to-cell contact was loose or scattered after freezing.

15.5.4 Conclusion

The synergistic effect of egg yolk and OES paste has provided the basis of most boar sperm cryopreservation diluents. Though the exact mechanism by which they work is unknown, it is likely that the detergent is solubilizing egg yolk lipids. The discrepancy in glycerol concentrations required for maximal acrosome integrity (2%) and sperm motility (3–4%) indicate that further work to maintain acrosomal integrity may improve post-thaw sperm fertility. The use of cryopreserved boar spermatozoa in AI work will remain limited until fertility rates approach those of liquid semen.

Considering the challenges associated with boar sperm cryopreservation, it is not surprising that pig oocytes also are extremely difficult to cryopreserve and little information is yet available on pig oocyte cryopreservation. Embryo cryopreservation still has not been perfected; dependent on stage and size, conventional cooling produces low percentages of surviving embryos. Vitrification provides an alternative to conventional freezing, but the high concentrations of cryoprotectant required often prove toxic to the embryo. The sensitivity of both boar spermatozoa and the embryo to temperatures below 15°C indicate that there is likely to be a species sensitivity to this temperature.

REFERENCES

ABDELHAKEAM, A. A., GRAHAM, E. F. and VAZQUEZ, I. A. (1991a) 'Studies on the presence and absence of glycerol in unfrozen and frozen ram semen: Fertility trials and the effect of dilution methods on freezing ram semen in the absence of glycerol', *Cryobiology* **28**, 36–42.

ABDELHAKEAM, A. A., GRAHAM, E. F., VAZQUEZ, I. A. and CHALONER, K. M. (1991b) 'Studies on the absence of glycerol in unfrozen and frozen ram semen. Development of an extender for freezing: Effects of osmotic pressure, egg yolk levels, type of sugars, and the method of dilution', *Cryobiology* **28**, 43–49.

ABEYDEERA, L. R., WANG, W. H., CANTLEY, T. C., PRATHER, R. S. and DAY, B. N. (1998) 'Presence of beta-mercaptoethanol can increase the glutathione content of pig oocytes matured in vitro and the rate of blastocyst development after in vitro fertilization', *Theriogenology* **50**, 747–756.

AL-KHANEK, H., ZAKHARIEV, Z., GRUDOVA, C. H., IOTOVE, M., YOTOVA, M. and AL-HANEK, H. (1989) 'Effect of adding vitamin D to bull semen on some biological properties of spermatozoa and their response to freezing', *Veterinana-Sbirka* **87**, 49–51.

ALMLID, T. and JOHNSON, L. A. (1988) 'Effects of glycerol concentration, equilibrium time and temperature of glycerol addition on post-thaw viability of boar spermatozoa frozen in straws', *J. Anim. Sci.* **66**, 2899–2905.

ALMLID, T., STAVNE, S. E. and JOHNSON, L. A. (1987) 'Fertility evaluation of the straw freezing technique for boar semen under practical artificial insemination conditions', *Zuchthygiene* **22**, 193–202.

ALMLID, T., JOHNSON, L. A., CLARKE, R. N. and PURSEL, V. G. (1988) 'Cryopreservation of boar semen: studies to determine optimum glycerol levels and the relationship of *in vitro* evaluation to *in vivo* fertility', in *11th International Congress on Animal Reproduction and Artificial Insemination (Dublin)* Vol. 3, No. 220.

ALMLID, T., CLARKE, R. N., PURSEL, V. G. and JOHNSON, L. A. (1989) 'Effectiveness of *in vitro* methods for predicting *in vivo* fertilizing capacity of boar semen cryopreserved with 2–percent or 4–percent glycerol', *Zuchthygiene* **24**, 8–15.

ALMQUIST, J. O., ALLEN, C. H. and BRANAS, R. J. (1982) 'Effect on fertility of freezing large numbers of straws of bovine spermatozoa in a mechanical freezer', *J. Anim. Sci.* **55**, 232–235.

AMOAH, E. A. and GELAYE, S. (1997) 'Biotechnological advances in goat reproduction', *J. Anim. Sci.* **75**, 578–85.

ANDERSON, S., HARKNESS, W., AKIN, Y., KAPROTH, M. and KILLIAN, G. (1994) 'Categorical data analysis of the effect on bull fertility of butylated hydroxytoluene addition to semen extenders prior to freezing', *J. Dairy Sci.* **77**, 2302–2307.

CHAPTER 15

ANEL, L., DOMINGUEZ, J. C. and ABAD, M. (1988) 'Prostaglandin supplementation of frozen–thawed ram semen. II. In vitro effects on sperm survival and acrosome integrity', in *11th International Congress on Animal Reproduction and Artificial Insemination (Dublin)*, Vol. 3, No. 223.

ANZAR, M., GRAHAM, E. F. and IQBAL, N. (1997) 'Post-thaw plasma membrane integrity of bull spermatozoa separated with a Sephadex ion-exchange column', *Theriogenology* **47**, 845–856.

ARAV, A., RUBINSKY, B., BACCI, M. L. and SEREN, E. (1991) 'Cryopreservation of sow immature oocytes by vitrification', *Selezione Veterinaria* **32** (Suppl. 1), 315–319.

ARAV, A., RUBINSKY, B., FLETCHER, G. and SEREN, E. (1993) 'Cryogenic protection of oocytes with antifreeze proteins', *Mol. Reprod. Dev.* **36**, 488–493.

ARRIOLA, J. and FOOTE, R. H. (1987) 'Glycerolation and thawing effects on bull spermatozoa frozen in detergent-treated egg yolk and whole egg extenders', *J. Dairy Sci.* **70**, 1664–1670.

BAMBA, K. and CRAN, D. G. (1988) 'Further studies on rapid dilution and warming of boar semen', *J. Reprod. Fertil.* **82**, 509–518.

BAMBA, K. and MIYAGAWA, N. (1992) 'Protective action of aromatic compounds against cold shock injuries in boar spermatozoa', *Cryobiology* **29**, 533–536.

BARIL, G., CASAMIJANA, P., PERRIN, J. and VALLET, J. C. (1989) 'Embryo production, freezing and transfer in Angora alpine and Saanen goats', *Zuchthygiene* **24**, 101–115.

BILTON, R. J. and MOORE, N. W. (1976) '*In vitro* culture, storage and transfer of goat embryos', *Austr. J. Biol. Sci.* **29**, 125–146.

BUDWORTH, P. R., AMANN, R. P. and CHAPMAN, P. L. (1988) 'Relationships between computerized measurements of motion of frozen–thawed bull spermatozoa and fertility', *J. Androl.* **9**, 41–54.

BWANGA, C. O. (1991) 'Cryopreservation of boar semen. I. A literature review', *Acta vet. Scand.* **32**, 431–453.

BWANGA, C. O., DE BRAGANCA, M. M., EINARSSON, S. and RODRIGUEZ-MARTINEZ, H. (1990) 'Cryopreservation of boar semen in mini- and maxi-straws', *Zentralbl-Veterinarmed-A* **37**, 651–658.

BWANGA, C. O., HOFMO, P. O., GREVLE, I. S., EINARSSON, S. and RODRIGUEZ-MARTINEZ, H. (1991) '*In vivo* fertilizing capacity of deep frozen boar semen packaged in plastic bags and maxi-straws', *Zentralbl-Veterinarmed* **38**, 281–286.

CARVALHO, R. V., DEL CAMPO, M. R., PALASZ, A. T., PLANTE, Y. and MAPLETOFT, R. J. (1996) 'Survival rates and sex ratio of bovine IVF embryos frozen at different developmental stages on day 7', *Theriogenology* **45**, 489–498.

CHEMINEAU, P., BARIL, G., LEBOEUF, B., MAUREL, M. C., ROY, F., PELLICER-RUBIO M., MALPAUX, B. and COGNIE, Y. (1999) 'Implications of recent advances in reproductive physiology for reproductive management of goats', *J. Reprod. Fertil. Suppl.* **54**, 129–142.

CHEN, Y., FOOTE, R. H. and BROCKETT, C. C. (1993) 'Effect of sucrose, trehalose, hypotaurine, taurine and blood serum on survival of frozen bull sperm', *Cryobiology* **30**, 423–431.

CLARKE, R. N. and JOHNSON, L. A. (1987) 'Effect of liquid storage and cryopreservation of boar spermatozoa on acrosomal integrity and the penetration of zona free hamster ova *in vitro*', *Gamete Res.* **16**, 193–204.

COCERO, M. J., LOPEZ SEBASTION, A., BARRAGAN, M. L. and PICAZO, R. A. (1996) 'Differences on post-thawing survival between ovine morulae and blastocysts cryopreserved with ethylene glycol or glycerol', *Cryobiology* **33**, 502–507.

CORTEEL, J.-M. (1973) 'L'insémination artificielle caprine: bases physiologiques, état actuel et perspectives d'avenir', *World Rev. Anim. Prod.* **9**(1), 73–99.

CORTEEL, J. M. (1974) 'Viabilité des spermatozoides de bouc conservé et congelé avec ou sans leur plasma seminal: effet de glucose', *Ann. biol. anim. biochim. biophys.* **14**, 741–745.

CORTEEL, J. M., BARIL, G. and LEBOEUF, B. (1987) 'Development and application of artificial insemination with deep frozen semen and out-of-season breeding of goats in France', *Proceedings of the IV International Conference on Goats (Brasilia). Vol. 1 Plenary sessions.* Symposia, 523–547.

COY, P., RUIZ, S., ROMAR, R., CAMPOS, I. and GADEA, J. (1999) 'Maturation, fertilization and complete development of porcine oocytes matured under different systems', *Theriogenology* **51**, 799–812.

CURRY, M. R. (2000) 'Cryopreservation of semen from domestic livestock', *Rev. Reprod.* **5**, 46–52.

CZLLONKOWSKA, M., PAPIS, K., GUSZKIEWICZ, A., KOSSAKOWSKI, M. and EYSYMONT, U. (1991) 'Freezing of sheep embryos in 3M methanol', *Cryo-Letters* **12**, 11–16.

DE LEEUW, A. M. (1992) 'Number and viability of embryos collected in vivo or from the excised uteri of slaughtered donor cows', *Theriogenology* **37**, 907 -913.

DE LEEUW, A. M., RALL, W. F., DEN DAAS, J. H. G. and KRUIP, A. M. T. (1991) 'Comparative studies of the efficiency of rapid cryopreservation methods for bovine embryos', in *European Embryo Transfer Association: 7th Scientific Meeting, Cambridge, UK*, pp. 77–86.

DE LEEUW, F. E., DE LEEUW, A. M., DEN DAAS, J. H., COLENBRANDER, B. and VERKLEIJ, A. J. (1993) ''Effects of various cryoprotective agents and membrane stabilizing compounds on bull sperm membrane integrity after cooling and freezing', *Cryobiology* **30**, 32–44.

CHAPTER 15

DE PAZ, P., SANCHEZ, A. J., FERNANDEZ, J. G., CARBAJO, M., DOMINGUEZ, J. C., CHAMORRO, C. A. and ANEL, L. (1994) 'Sheep embryo cryopreservation by vitrification and conventional freezing', *Theriogenology* **42**, 327–338.

DEKA, B. C. and RAO, A. R. (1987a) 'Effect of extenders and thawing methods on post-thawing preservation of goat semen', *Ind. Vet. J.* **64**, 591–594.

DEKA, B. C. and RAO, A. R. (1987b) 'Effect of cooling time on quality of frozen goat semen', *Ind. J. Anim. Reprod.* **8**, 25–27.

DIDION, B. A., POMP, D., MARTIN, M. J., HOMANICS, G. E. and MARKERT, C. L. (1990) 'Observations on the cooling and cryopreservation of pig oocytes at the germinal vesicle stage', *J. Anim. Sci.* **68**, 2803–2810.

DINNYES, A., CAROLAN, C., LONERGRAN, P., MASSIP, A. and MERMILLOD, P. (1996) 'Survival of frozen or vitrified bovine blastocysts produced *in vitro* in synthetic oviduct fluid', *Theriogenology* **46**, 1425–1439.

DOBRINSKY, J. R. and JOHNSON, L. A. (1994) 'Cryopreservation of porcine embryos by vitrification: a study of *in vitro* development', *Theriogenology* **42**, 25–35.

DOBRINSKY, J. R., PURSEL, V. G., LONG, C. R. and JOHNSON, L. A. (1997) 'Cryopreservation of swine embryos: *In vitro* and *in vivo* developmental competence', *J. Anim. Sci.* **75** (Abstract), 328, 219.

DOBRINSKY, J. R., PURSEL, V. G., LONG, C. R. and JOHNSON, L. A. (1998) 'Birth of normal piglets after cytoskeletal stabilization of embryos and cryopreservation by vitrification', *Theriogenology* **49**, Abstract 166.

DUNSKII, S. A., ZHURAVEL, M. P. and YATSYK, P. A. (1986) 'An investigation of programmed freezing of gametes in cattle', *Razvedeie i Vosprizvodstvo sel'-khoz*, 34–37.

EWERT, L. (1988) 'Experiments on the preparation of pig semen for freezing in straws, and biological and physical aspects of thawing using microwaves', thesis, Tierarztliche Hochschule, Hannover, German Federal Republic.

FAHNING, M.L. and GARCIA, M.A. (1992) 'Status of cryopreserved embryos from domestic animals', *Cryoobiology* **29**, 1–18.

FALGE, R., ROMMEL, P., OESTERREICH, D., SEIFERT, F., MULLER, H., FREYMANN, U. and DRAHEIM, B. (1990) 'Freezing of cattle embryos', *Arch. exp. Veterinarmed.* **44**, 127–134.

FISER, P. S. and FAIRFULL, R. W. (1983) 'Effects of change in photoperiod on freezability of ram spermatozoa', *Cryobiology* **20**, 684–689.

FISER, P. S. and FAIRFULL, R. W. (1986a) 'The effects of rapid cooling (Cold shock) of ram semen, photoperiod and egg yolk in diluents on the survival of spermatozoa before and after freezing', *Cryobiology* **23**, 518–524.

FISER, P. S. and FAIRFULL, R. W. (1986b) 'Combined effects of glycerol concentration, cooling velocity, and osmolarity of skim milk diluents on cryopreservation of ram spermatozoa', *Theriogenology* 25, 473–484.

FISER, P. S. and FAIRFULL, R. W. (1989) 'The effect of glycerol-related osmotic changes on post-thaw motility and acrosomal integrity of ram spermatozoa', *Cryobiology* 26, 64–69.

FISER, P. S., and FAIRFULL, R. W. (1990) 'Combined effect of glycerol concentration and cooling velocity on motility and acrosomal integrity of boar spermatozoa frozen in 0.5 ml straws', *Mol. Reprod. Dev.* 25, 123–129.

FISER, P. S. and MARCUS, G. J. (1989) 'Continuous live-dead discrimination of ram sperm during freezing', *Gamete Res.* 22, 301–305.

FISER, P. S., AINSWORTH, L. and FAIRFULL, R. W. (1987) 'Evaluation of a new diluent and different processing procedures for cryopreservation of ram', *Theriogenology* 28, 599–607.

FISER, P. S., HANSEN, C., UNDERHILL, L. and MARCUS, G. J. (1991) 'New thermal stress test to assess the viability of cryopreserved boar sperm', *Cryobiology* 28, 454–459.

FISER, P. S., FAIRFULL, R. W., HANSEN, C., PANICH, P. L., SHRESTHA, J. N. and UNDERHILL, L. (1993) 'The effect of warming velocity on motility and acrosomal integrity of boar sperm as influenced by the rate of freezing and glycerol level', *Mol. Reprod. Dev.* 3, 190–195.

FOULKES, J. A., SWEASEY, D. and GOODEY, R. G. (1980) 'Fertility of bull spermatozoa in egg yolk diluents of varied lipid fatty acid composition', *J. Reprod. Fertil.* 60, 165–169.

FUKU, E., KOJIMA, Y., SHJOIJA, Y., MARCUS, J. and DOWNEY, B. (1992) '*In vitro* fertilization and development of frozen–thawed bovine oocytes', *Cryobiology* 29, 485–492.

GARCIA, M. A. and GRAHAM, E. F. (1989a) 'Development of a buffer system for dialysis of bovine spermatozoa before freezing. I. Effect of zwitterion buffers', *Theriogenology* 31, 1021–1028.

GARCIA, M. A. and GRAHAM, E. F. (1989b) 'Development of a buffer system for dialysis of bovine spermatozoa before freezing. II. Effect of sugars on post-thaw motility', *Theriogenology* 31, 1029–1037.

GARNER, D. L., JOHNSON, L. A. and ALLEN, C. H. (1988) 'Fluorometric evaluation of cryopreserved bovine spermatozoa extended in egg yolk and milk', *Theriogenology* 30, 369–378.

GRAHAM, J. K. and FOOTE R. H. (1987) 'Effect of several lipids, fatty acyl chain length and the degree of unsaturation on the motility of bull sperm after cold shock and freezing', *Cryobiology* 24, 42–52

GOTO, K., TAKUMA, Y., MATSUURA, S., NAKANISHI, Y., YANAGIDA, K., KATAHIRA, K., TOGUCHI, M. and NONAKA, K. (1992) 'The viability of thawed cattle blastocysts produced by *in vitro* fertilization using two methods adapted for practical conditions', *J. Reprod. Dev.* **38**, 15–19.

HASLER, J. F., HENDERSON, W. B., HURTGEN, P. J., JIN, Z. Q., McCAULEY, A. D., MOWER, S. A., NEELY, B., SHUEY, L. S., STOKES, J. E. and TRIMMER, S. A. (1995) 'Production, freezing and transfer of bovine IVF embryos and subsequent calving results', *Theriogenology* **43**, 141–152.

HAYASKI, S., KOBAYASKI, K., MIZUMO, J., SAITON, K. and HIRANO, S. (1989) 'Birth of piglets from frozen–thawed embryos', *Vet. Record.* **125**, 43–44.

HILL, B. R. and KUEHNER, L. F. (1998) 'Donor blood cholesterol, embryo colour and embryo freezibility', *Theriogenology* **49**, 168 Abstract.

HINKOVSKA-GALCHEVA, V., PEEVA, D., MOMCHILOVA-PANKOVA, A., PETKOVA, D. and KOUMANOV, K. (1988) 'Phosphatidylcholine and phosphatidylethanolamine derivatives, membrane fluidity and changes in the lipolytic activity of ram spermatozoa plasma membranes during cryoconservation', *Int. J. Biochem.* **20**, 867–871.

HOCHI, S. and LEIBO, S. P. (1996) 'Effect of cooling and warming rates during cryopreservation on survival of in vitro produced bovine embryos', *Theriogenology* **46**, 837–847.

HOLT, W. V. and NORTH, R. D. (1988) 'The role of membrane lipids in the protection of ram spermatozoa during cooling and storage', *Gamete Res.* **19**, 77–89.

HOLT, W. V., HEAD, M. and NORTH, R. D. (1992) 'Freeze-induced membrane damage in ram spermatozoa is manifested after thawing: observations with experimental cryomicroscopy', *Biol. Reprod.* **46**, 1086–1094.

HUBE, A., OLTRA, J., JARA, C. and BARRIO, N. (1983) 'Effect of different storage methods on the quality of frozen bull sperm', in *9th Meeting of the Associacion Latin Americana de Produccion Animal*, Vol. 18, 148–149 Abstract.

IM, K. S., KANG, J. K. and KIM, H. S. (1997) 'Effects of cumulus cells, different cryo-protectants, various maturation stages and pre-incubation before insemination on developmental capacity of frozen–thawed oocytes', *Theriogenology* **47**, 881–891.

ISACHENKO, V., SOLER, C., ISACHENKO, E., PEREZ-SANCHEZ, F. and GRISHCHENKO, V. (1998) 'Vitrification of immature porcine oocytes: effects of lipid droplets, temperature, cytoskeleton, and addition and removal of cryoprotectant', *Cryobiology* **36**, 250–253.

IWASAKI, S. J., MIZUNO, K., KOBAYASHI, Y., YOSHIKANE and HAYASHI, T. (1994) 'Changes in morphology and cell number of inner cell mass of porcine blastocysts during freezing', *Theriogenology* **42**, 841–848.

JANSEN, H. B. (1988) 'The influence of cooling rates practised in the Netherlands on the survival of bovine spermatozoa', in *11th International Congress on Animal Reproduction and Artificial Insemination (Dublin)*, Vol. 3, No. 258.

JOHNSON, L. A. (1985) 'Fertility results using frozen boar spermatozoa: 1970–1985', in Johnson, L.A. and Larssen, K. (eds) *Deep Freezing of Boar Semen*, Uppsala: Swedish University of Agricultural Sciences, pp. 199–222.

JOYAL, S. M., KENNEDY, B. W. and WILKINS, J. N. (1986) 'Boar breed and environmental effects on motility of frozen–thawed spermatozoa', Annual report, Centre for Genetic Improvement of Livestock, Department of Animal and Poultry Science, Ontario Agricultural College, University of Guelph, Canada.

JUNG, J. K., CHANG, W. K. and YOO S. H. (1990) 'Studies on pig embryo freezing', *Korean J. Anim. Sci.* **32**, 445–449.

KARABINUS, D. S., EVENSON, D. P. and KAPROTH, M. T. (1991) 'Effects of egg yolk-citrate and milk extenders on chromatin structure and viability of cryopreserved bull sperm', *J. Dairy Sci.* **74**, 3836–3848.

KARATZAS, G., KARAGIAUNIDIO, A., VARSAKELI, S. and BRIKAS, P. (1997) 'Fertility of fresh and frozen–thawed goat semen during the non-breeding season', *Theriogenology* **48**, 1049–1059.

KASHIWAZAKI, H., OHTANI, H. S., MIYAMOTO, K. and OGAWA, S. (1991) 'Production of normal piglets from hatched blastocysts frozen at −196°C', *Vet. Rec.* **128**, 356–357.

KILLIAN, G., HONADEL, T., McNUTT, T., HENAULT, M., WEGNER, C. and DUNLAP, D. (1989) 'Evaluation of butylated hydroxytoluene as a cryopreservative added to whole or skim milk diluent for bull semen', *J. Dairy Sci.* **72**, 1291–1295.

KUWAYAMA, M., HAMANO, S., NAGAI T. (1992) 'Vitrification of bovine blastocysts obtained by *in vitro* culture of oocytes matured and fertilised *in vitro*', *J. Reprod. Fertil.* **96**, 187–193.

LARSSEN, B. and MAPLETOFT, R. J. (1997) 'Vitrification of bovine IVF blastocysts in an ethylene glycol/sucrose solution and heat stable plant extracted proteins', *Theriogenology* **47**, 865–879.

LE GAL, F. (1996) '*In vitro* maturation and fertilization of goat oocytes frozen at the GV stage', *Theriogenology* **45**, 1177–1185.

LE GAL, F., BARIL, G., VALLET, J. C. and LEBOEUF, B. (1993) '*In vivo* and *in vitro* survival of goat embryos after freezing with ethylene glycol or glycerol', *Theriogenology* **40**, 771–777.

LE GAL, F., GASQUI, P. and RENARD, J. P. (1995) 'Evaluation of intracellular cryoprotectant concentration before freezing of goat mature oocyte', *Cryo-Letters* **16**, 3–12.

LEHN-JENSEN, H. and GREVE, T. (1981) 'Survival of cow blastocysts utilizing short freezing curves', *Nordisk Veterinaermedicin* **33**, 523–529.

LEIBO, S. P. (1984) 'A one-step method for direct non-surgical transfer of frozen–thawed bovine embryos', *Theriogenology* **21**, 767–790.

LI, R., CAMERON, A. W. N., BATT, P. A. and TROUNSON, A. O. (1990) 'Maximum survival of frozen goat embryos is attained at the expanded, hatching and hatched blastocyst stages of development', *Reprod. Fertil. Dev.* **2**, 345–350.

LIM, J. M., FUKAI, Y., and ONO, H. (1992) 'Developmental competence of bovine oocytes frozen at various maturation stages followed by in vitro maturation and fertilization', *Theriogenology* **37**, 351–361.

LOI, P., PTAK, G., DATTENA, M., LEDDA, S., NAITANA, S. and CAPPAI, P. (1998) 'Embryo transfer and related technologies in sheep reproduction', *Reprod. Nutr. Dev.* **38**, 615–628.

LOPEZ, G. A. P., SOSA, C. F. and GONZALEZ, E. P. (1988) 'Evaluation of different techniques of freezing ram sperm', in *11th International Congress on Animal Reproduction and AI (Dublin)*, Vol. 3, No. 272.

McGINNIS, L. K., DUPLANTIS, JR. S. C. and YOUNGS, C. R. (1993) 'Cryopreservation of sheep embryos using ethylene glycol', *Anim. Reprod. Sci.* **30**, 272–280.

MAFFEO, G., VIGO, D. and GOTTARDI, L. (1989) 'Artificial insemination of pigs with frozen semen: preliminary field tests', *Selezione-Veterinaria* **30**, 307–310.

MALTSEVA, M. (1990) 'Factors affecting viability and survival of frozen–thawed embryos', *Molochnoe i Myasonoe Skotovodstvo* **1**, 25–26.

MARTINO, A, SONGSASEN N. and LEIBO S. P. (1996) 'Development into blastocysts of bovine oocytes cryopreserved by ultra-rapid cooling', *Biol. Reprod.* **54**, 1059–1069.

MASSIP, A. and VAN DER ZWALMEN, P. (1987) 'Direct transfer of frozen cow embryos in glycerol-sucrose', *Vet. Rec.* **115**, 327–328.

MASSIP, A, MERMILLOD, P., WILS, C. and DESSY, F. (1993) 'Effects of dilution procedure and culture conditions after thawing on survival of frozen bovine blastocysts produced *in vitro*', *J. Reprod. Fertil.* **97**, 65–69.

MAXWELL, W. M. C. and SALAMON, S. (1995a) 'Frozen storage of ram semen I. Processing, freezing, thawing and fertility after cervical insemination', *Anim. Reprod. Sci.* **37**, 185–249.

MAXWELL, W. M. C. and SALAMON, S. (1995b) 'Frozen storage of ram semen II. Causes of low fertility after cervical insemination and methods of improvement', *Anim. Reprod. Sci.* **38**, 1–36.

MAXWELL, W. M. C., LANDERS, A. J. and EVANS, G. (1995) 'Survival and fertility of ram spermatozoa frozen in pellets, straws and minitubes', *Theriogenology* **43**, 1201–1210.

MERMILLOD, P., MASSIP, A. and DESSY, F. (1992) '*In vitro* production of cattle embryos: review and Belgian results', *Int. J. Dev. Biol.* **36**, 185–195.

MUKHERJEE, T. K. and NELSON, E. A. (1987) 'Comparison of two diluents for freezing semen of local and F1 goats', *Pertanika* **10**, 113–116.

MURAKAMI, M., OTOI, T., SUMANTRI, C. and SUZUKI, T. (1998) 'Effects of centrifugation and lipid removal on the cryopreservation of *in vitro* produced bovine embryos at the eight cell stage', *Cryobiology* **36**, 206–212.

NAGASHIMA, H., KATO, Y., YAMAKAWA, H. and OGAWA, S. (1988) 'Survival of pig hatched blastocysts exposed below 15°C', *Theriogenology* **29**, 280.

NAGASHIMA, H., YAMAKAWA, H. and NIEMANN, H. (1992) 'Freezability of porcine blastocysts at different peri-hatching stages', *Theriogenology* **37**, 839–850.

NAGASHIMA, H., KASHIWAZAKI, H., ASHMAN, R., GRUPEN, C., SEAMARK, R. F. and NOTTLE, M. (1994) 'Recent advances in cryopreservation of porcine embryos', *Theriogenology* **41**, 113–118.

NAGASHIMA, N., KUWAYAMA, N., GRUPEN, C. G., ASHMAN, R. J. and NOTTLE, M. B. (1996) 'Vitrification of procine early cleavage stage embryos and oocytes after removal of cytoplasmic lipid droplets', *Theriogenology* **45**, 180.

NAITANA, S., LOI, P., LEDDA, S., CAPPAI, P., DATTENA, M. and BOGLIOLO, L. (1996) 'Effect of biopsy and vitrification on *in vitro* survival of ovine embryos at different stages of development', *Theriogenology* **46**, 813–824.

NEWTON, H., PICTON, H. and GOSDEN, R. G. (1999) '*In vitro* growth of oocyte-granulosa cell complexes isolated from cryopreserved ovine tissue', *J. Reprod. Fertil.* **115**, 141–150.

NIEMANN, H. and REICHELT, B. (1993) 'Manipulating early pig embryos', *J. Reprod. Fertil. Suppl.* **48**, 75–94.

NOWSHARI, M. A. and HOLTZ, W. (1993) 'Transfer of split goat embryos without zonae pellucidae either fresh or after freezing', *J. Anim. Sci.* **71**, 3403–3408.

OKOLSKI, A. and JAMER, B. (1986) 'Substitution of glycerol by polyvinyl-alcohol in freezing bull ram and boar semen', *Acta Agraria et Silvestri, Zootechn.* **25**, 83–90.

OSZAR, S., GUVEN, B., EKICI, A. and ARIF, S. (1988) 'Controlled breeding and artificial insemination of Angora goats in Turkey', in *Isotope-aided Studies on Livestock Productivity in Mediterranean and North African Countries. Proceedings of the Final Research co-ordination Meeting*, International Atomic Energy Agency, Vienna, pp. 117–129.

OTOI, T., TACHIKAWA, S., KONDO, S. and SUSUKI, T. (1992) 'Developmental capacity of bovine oocytes cryopreserved after maturation in vitro and of frozen–thawed

CHAPTER 15

bovine embryos derived from frozen mature oocytes', *Theriogenology* **38**, 711–719.

OTOI, T. S., TACHIKAWA, S., KONDO, S., TAKAGI, M. and SUZUKI, T. (1994) 'Developmental competence of bovine oocytes frozen at different cooling rates', *Cryobiology* **31**, 344–348.

OTOI, T. S. YAMAMOTO K., KOYAMA N., TACHIKAWA S. and SUZUKI, T. (1998) 'Cryopreservation of mature bovine oocytes by vitrification in straws', *Cryobiology* **37**, 77–85.

PAQUIGNON, M. (1985) 'Freezing and thawing extenders for boar spermatozoa', in Johnson, L. A. and Larsson, K. (eds) *Deep Freezing of Boar Semen*, Uppsala: Swedish University Agricultural Science, pp. 129–146.

PAQUIGNON, M., QUELLIER, P. and DACHEUX, J. L. (1986) 'Deep-freezing of boar semen: comparison between different diluents, processing and deep-freezing methods, and thawing temperature', *Ann. Zootechn.* **35**, 173–184.

PARK, C. S., YANG, M. H., HWANG, D. S., LEE, K. S. and SEO, K. W. (1989) 'Study on fresh and deep frozen storage of Korean native goat spermatozoa', *Korean J. Anim. Sci.* **31**, 412–417.

PARKINSON, T. J. (1987) 'Seasonal variations in semen quality of bulls: Correlations with environmental temperature', *Vet. Rec.* **120**, 479–482

PARKINSON, T. J. and WHITFIELD, C. H. (1987) 'Optimization of freezing conditions for bovine spermatozoa', *Theriogenology* **27**, 781–797.

PENFOLD, L. M., GARNER D. L., DONOGHUE A. M. and JOHNSON L. A. (1997) 'Comparative viability of bovine sperm frozen on a cryomicroscope or in straws', *Theriogenology* **47**, 521–530.

PETRUIJKIC, T., MRVOS, G., MILJKOVIC, V., MARKOVIC, B. and JAKSIE, Z. (1987) 'Preserving ram semen using deep freezing in minitubes', *Veterinarski Glasnik* **41**, 934–937.

PICARD, L., KING, W. A. and BETTERIDGE, K. J. (1985) 'Production of sexed calves from frozen–thawed embryos', *Vet. Rec.* **117**, 603–608.

PURSEL, V. G. and JOHNSON, L. A. (1975) 'Freezing of boar spermatozoa: fertilizing capacity with concentrated semen and a new thawing procedure', *J. Anim. Sci.* **40**, 99–102.

REFSDAL, A. O., VATN, T., LANDSVERK, K. and KOMMISRUD, E. (1988) 'Embryo transfer in cattle under Norwegian conditions', *Norsk Veterinaertidsskrift* **100**, 11–19.

RITAR, A. J. and SALAMON, S. (1983) 'Fertility of fresh and frozen–thawed semen of the Angora goat', *Austr. J. Biol. Sci.* **36**, 49–59.

RITAR, A. J., BALL, P. D. and O'MAY, P. J. (1990a) 'Examination of methods for the deep freezing of goat semen', *Reprod. Fertil. Dev.* **2**, 27–34.

RITAR, A. J., BALL, P. D. and O'MAY, P. J. (1990b) 'Artificial insemination of Cashmere goats: effects on fertility and fecundity of intravaginal treatment, method and time of insemination, semen freezing process, number of motile spermatozoa and age of females', *Reprod. Fertil. Dev.* **2**, 377–384.

RONG, R., GUANGYA, W., JUFEN, Q. and JIANCHEN, W. (1989) 'Simplified quick freezing of goat embryos', *Theriogenology* **29**, 295.

RUI, R., WANG, J. C., WANG, G. G., QIAN, J. F., ZHU, B. and HAO, Z. M. (1990) 'A simple technique for rapidly freezing goat embryos', *Acta Vet. Zootechn. Sinica* **12**, 127–131.

SAKUL, H., BRADFORD, G. E., BONDURANT, R. H., ANDERSON, G. B. and DONAHUE, S. E. (1993) 'Cryopreservation of embryos as a means of germ plasm conservation in sheep', *Theriogenology* **39**, 401–409.

SALAMON, S. and RITAR, A. J. (1982) 'Deep-freezing of Angora goat semen: effects of diluent composition and method and rate of dilution on survival of spermatozoa', *Austr. J. Biol. Sci.* **35**, 295–303.

SANCHEZ-PARTIDA, L. G., MAXWELL, W. M., PALEG, L. G. and SETCHELL, B. P. (1992) 'Proline and glycine betaine in cryoprotective diluents for ram spermatozoa', *Reprod. Fertil. Dev.* **4**, 113–118.

SCHELLENDER, K., PELI J., SCHMOLL, F. and BREM, G. (1994) 'Effects of different cryoprotectants and carbohydrates on freezing of matured and unmatured bovine oocytes', *Theriogenology* **42**, 909–915.

SCHIEWE, M. C., RALL, W. F., STUART, L. D. and WILDT, D. E. (1991) 'Analysis of cryo-protectant, cooling rate, and in situ dilution using conventional freezing or vitrification for cryopreserving sheep embryos', *Theriogenology* **36**, 279–294.

SEIKE, N., SAKAI, M. and KANAGAWA, H. (1991) 'Development of frozen–thawed demi-embryos and production of identical twin calves of different ages', *J. Vet. Med. Sci.* **53**, 37–42.

SHELTON, J. N. (1992) 'Factors affecting viability of fresh and frozen–thawed sheep demi-embryos', *Theriogenology* **37**, 713–721.

SODERQUIST, L., LARSSON, K. and DREJARE, L. (1988) 'Ejaculate and sperm cell characteristics in bulls with low post-thaw motility', in *11th Congress on Animal Reproduction and Artificial Insemination (Dublin)*, Vol. 3, No. 384.

SONGSASEN, N., BUCKRELL, B. C., PLANTE, C. and LEIBO, S. P. (1995) '*In vitro* and *in vivo* survival of cryopreserved sheep embryos', *Cryobiology* **32**, 78–91.

STALHAMMER, E. H., JANSEN, L. and PHILIPSSON, J. (1988) 'Genetic and environmental studies on semen characteristics and fertility in young AI bulls', in *Proceedings VI*

CHAPTER 15

World Conference on Animal Production 576, Helsinki, Finland: Finnish Animal Breeding Association.

STROHMEYER, M. (1988) 'Freezing of goat semen with regard to season, centrifugation and use of detergent', thesis, Tierarztliche Hochschule Hannover, German Federal Republic.

SUZUKI, T., TAKAGI, M., YAMAMOTO, M., BOEDIONO, A., SAHA, S., SAKAKIBARA, H. and OOE, M. (1993) 'Pregnancy rate and survival in culture of *in vitro* fertilized bovine embryos frozen in various cryoprotectants and thawed using a one-step system', *Theriogenology* **40**, 651–659.

SWIDOWIEZ, K. and STRZEZEK, J. (1986) 'Effects of age of bull and season on cryogenic changes in the biochemistry of semen', *Zuchthygiene* **21**, 247–256.

SZELL, A. Z. and WINDSOR, D. P. (1994) 'Survival of vitrified embryos *in vitro* and *in vivo*', *Theriogenology* **42**, 881–889.

TOUATI, K., BORMANS, M., ECTORS, F. and MASSIP, A. (1990) 'Freezing of cattle embryos in glycerol-sucrose for direct transfer', *Ann. Med. Vet.* **134**, 249–251.

TSUNODA, Y., WAKASU, M. and SUGIE, T. (1984) 'Micromanipulation and freezing of goat embryos', in *10th International Congress of Animal Reproduction and Artificial Insemination (Urbana-Champaign)*, Vol. 2, 249–250.

TULI, R. K., SCHMIDT-BAULAIN, R. and HOLTZ, W. (1992) 'Computer-assisted motility assessment of spermatozoa from fresh and frozen–thawed semen of the bull, boar and goat', *Theriogenology* **38**, 487–490.

VAJTA, G., HOLM, P., KUWAYAMA, M., BOOTH, P. J., JACOBSEN , H., GREVE, T. and CALLESEN, H. (1998) 'Open pulled straw (OPS) vitrification: A new way to reduce cryoinjuries of bovine ova and embryos', *Mol. Reprod. Dev.* **51**, 53–58.

VAN DE ZWALMEN, P., TOUATI, K., ECTORS, F. J., MASSIP, A., BECKERS, J. F. and ECTORS, F. (1989) 'Vitrification of bovine blastocysts', *Theriogenology* **31**, 270.

VOELKEL, S. A. and HU, Y. X. (1992a) 'Effect of gas atmosphere on the development of one-cell bovine embryos in two culture systems', *Theriogenology* **37**, 1117–1131.

VOELKEL, S. A. and HU, Y. X. (1992b) 'Direct transfer of frozen–thawed bovine embryos', Proceedings of the Annual Conference of the International Embryo Transfer Society. *Theriogenology* **37**, 23–37.

WAGTENDONK-DE LEEUW, A. M. VAN, DAAS, J. H. G. DEN AND RALL, W. F. (1997) 'Field trial to compare pregnancy of bovine embryo cryopreservation methods: vitrification and one-step dilution versus slow freezing and three-step dilution', *Theriogenology* **48**, 1071–1084.

WATSON, P. F. (1979) 'The preservation of semen in mammals', *Oxford Rev. Reprod. Biol.* **1**, 283–350.

Watson, P. F. (1990) 'Artificial insemination and the preservation of semen', in Lamming, G. E. (ed.) *Marshall's Physiology of Reproduction,* 4th edn., Vol. 2, Edinburgh: Churchill Livingstone, pp. 747–869.

Westendorf, P., Richter, L. and Treu, H. (1975) 'Zur tiefgefrierung von ebersperma Labor-und Besamungsergebnisse mit dem Hulsenberger Pailletten-Verfahren', *Deutsche Tierarztl. Wochenschr.* **82**, 261–300.

Willadsen, S. M., Polge, C., Rowson, L. E. and Moor, R. M. (1976) 'Deep freezing of sheep embryos', *J. Reprod. Fertil.* **46**, 151–154.

Yang, Q. Z., Sun, Q. Y., Lui, G. Y., Qin, P. C. and Feng, H. L. (1994) 'Developmental competence and ultrastructure damage of cryopreserved GV-stage bovine oocytes', *Theriogenology* **41**, 342.

Zhang, Y., Wang, J. C., Xu, J. and Qian, J. F. (1991) 'Freezing of goat half embryos', *Sci. Agricult. Sinica* **24**, 11–15.

Zhao, Y. and Buhr, M. M. (1996) 'Localization of various ATPases in fresh and cryopreserved bovine spermatozoa', *Anim. Reprod. Sci.* **44**, 139–148.

Zibrin, M., Belak, M., Mesaros, P., Gamcik, P. and Tomajkova, E. (1987) 'The ultrastructure of frozen–thawed ram spermatozoa', *Z. Mikrosk. Anat. Forsch.* **101**, 904–912.

CHAPTER 15

Germplasm Cryopreservation in Elephants and Wild Ungulates

W. V. HOLT

The Institute of Zoology, The Zoological Society of London,
Regent's Park, London NW1 4RY, UK

Contents

16.1 INTRODUCTION

This chapter deals mainly with artiodactyls, the large even-toed ungulates. The group contains 171 species (Bronson, 1989) and includes domestic livestock, their wild ancestors, deer and antelope-like species, and other species such as the giraffe and hippopotamus. For ease of writing and reference the small number of reports dealing with odd-toed ungulates, wild equids, tapirs and rhinoceros have been included in this section.

Reports dealing with reproductive technologies in these species show considerable heterogeneity in the objectives and sizes of studies; some authors report results from studies with only one or two animals, while others have undertaken detailed studies with designed experiments. This property of the scientific literature in this area makes reviewing extremely difficult. The main objective of this review will therefore be to attempt to identify useful guiding principles that emerge from the literature, rather than to include every relevant study ever undertaken.

16.2 SPERMATOZOA

16.2.1 Seasonality

Artiodactyls are found in most regions of the globe and this is reflected in their varied patterns of seasonal breeding. Those inhabiting the higher latitudes of the temperate zone are rigidly seasonal in their reproduction. Lactation normally occurs during spring and early summer, and the breeding season is therefore determined by the length of gestation. Tropical artiodactyls exhibit both seasonal and continuous breeding patterns. Photoperiod is the main proximal cue for seasonality in temperate species, and here it must be remembered that when captive animals are in unnatural environments such as zoos and wildlife reserves, their normal seasonality may be disrupted. This has an important implication for those wishing to undertake reproductive technologies, who should understand the specific details of any species of interest. However, it also has an implication for the reviewer because most of the reports deal with animals studied outside their normal ranges.

Many deer species are highly seasonal, showing annual cycles of testicular regression, quiescence and resumption of spermatogenesis (e.g. Gosch et al., 1989). These effects are correlated with dramatic fluctuations in circulating serum testosterone (Lincoln, 1971; Haigh et al., 1984a). Attempts to collect semen at the beginning and end of the breeding season may be unsuccessful. However, even when spermatogenesis is in decline, spermatozoa of epididymal origin may still appear within the ejaculate; the fertility status of such spermatozoa is uncertain.

Photoperiod may not be the primary cue for seasonality in tropical ungulates. While some tropical artiodactyls such as the pigmy antelope (*Neotragus batesi*) and nyala (*Tragelaphus angasi*) exhibit continuous or asynchronous patterns of reproduction, the wildebeest (*Connochaetes taurinus*) demonstrates a three-week synchrony of births on the equatorial plains of Tanzania. Consequently their mating behaviour and ovulations must also be highly synchronous. The factors controlling this exceptional type of seasonality may involve food type and availability rather than photoperiod. Animals in zoos and wildlife reserves outside their natural habitats are unlikely to receive these specific seasonality cues.

In some seasonally reproducing species spermatogenesis continues throughout the year, and indeed semen collection is possible throughout the year. Domestic sheep, which normally breed during decreasing photoperiods, i.e. autumn, exhibit this physiological pattern. A number of studies have demonstrated, however, that photoperiod affects semen quality and the success of semen cryopreservation methods (Colas, 1984; Fiser and Batra, 1984), with best results being obtained during the equivalent of the breeding season. Such findings indicate that where possible, semen collection and storage is likely to be most successful if matched to known seasonality patterns, even when sperm production continues unabated throughout the year.

16.2.2 Semen collection

With a few exceptions, semen collection from wild ungulates can only be undertaken by the electroejaculation of anaesthetized animals. At present this tends to exclude the equidae as a group because anaesthetic protocols are considered unreliable and best avoided. The exceptions occur with species in which some individuals can be trained to the use of an artificial vagina (e.g. zebras; Crump and Crump, 1994) and a few deer species for which novel artificial vagina systems have been developed. These systems involve insertion or attachment of the AV to an oestrous female; once the male has mounted and ejaculated naturally it is then possible to recover the semen from the devices. Electroejaculation itself is a somewhat unpredictable technique with large ungulates. It sometimes fails for no apparent reason, and the results do not necessarily represent the quality and quantity of semen produced by natural ejaculation. The technique itself is based upon the electrical stimulation of the nerve supply to the accessory sex glands; the stimuli are normally delivered using rectal electrodes built into a rigid plastic rod. In practice it is beneficial to remove faeces before insertion of the rectal probe. The accessory glands, whose secretions contribute to seminal plasma, may or may not be stimulated by electroejaculation, and there is no way to assess this response during stimulation. The technique has remained essentially unchanged for several decades, and urgently requires greater understanding and development. The advent of computer-assisted electrical stimulation, whereby all aspects of the applied stimulus can be controlled with precision, should help in this respect. Furthermore, the application of ultrasound probes to assess the anatomical positions of the accessory sexual glands *in situ*, and in relation to probe positioning, will be beneficial. Very little anatomical information on wild ungulates exists, even in the older scientific literature. New insights of this type might result in improved probes designed to target their electrical stimuli precisely over the appropriate nerve complexes. The type and depth of anaesthesia may interact with the success of electroejaculation; some hold the opinion that light anaesthesia is best, while others take the opposite view. Thus there is a need for detailed veterinary studies in this area. Methods of semen collection have been reviewed previously by Watson (1978) and Howard *et al.* (1986b).

In a few cases, a rectal massage technique can be used for semen collection; this method involves manual massage of the ampullae of the vas deferens via the rectum. This technique has been applied to red deer and sable antelope in London Zoo and in some cases was highly successful.

Table 16.1 shows a summary of various reports of semen collection in the published literature, most having been achieved using electroejaculation. In some cases where the same species has been studied by different authors, the results are completely different. Thus the table can only be used as a very rough guide. Dott and Skinner (1989) published a similar table, documenting their own experiences with semen collection, by electroejaculation and post-mortem epididymal recovery, in various African mammals. A number of ungulate species were included in this table (elephant, Burchell's zebra, bontebok, blesbok, tsessebe, impala, sable antelope, nyala and mountain reedbuck). Sperm concentrations were given in their table, but not semen volumes. Their data are very detailed in many respects, concentrating on sperm head and tail dimensions and morphology. This information has, however, been omitted from Table 16.1 in this chapter as it can readily be consulted if required. Their electroejaculation technique involved the use of two alternative probes, the Ruakura ram semen collection probe and a 70-mm-diameter probe with two circular electrodes and a maximum output of 30 V (60 Hz sine wave).

The successful development of deer farming, especially in New Zealand, has generated a large body of research literature about reproductive technologies for the cervid species and a number of detailed reviews covering reproductive technologies in deer as a group (Jabbour and Asher, 1992; Mylrea *et al.*, 1992) have already been published. Much of this information is useful for understanding reproductive mechanisms and developing technologies of value in the threatened deer species, which are widespread throughout Europe and Asia. For this reason the data on deer presented in Table 16.1 should be regarded as representative, rather than exhaustive.

16.2.3 Semen preparation, dilution and freezing procedures

In many cases it is necessary to recover spermatozoa from the male reproductive tract after the death of a genetically important animal. When a male is healthy, and dies

TABLE 16.1

Summary of semen collection in non-domestic mammals

Common name	Species	N (males)	Anaesthesia	Procedure	Mean volume (ml) Mean concentration (millions/ml)	Reference
Antelopes and gazelles						
Addax	*Addax nasomaculatus*	2	Etorphine+ xylazine	Electroejaculation; details not given	Not reported	Densmore *et al.*, 1987
Blackbuck	*Antelope cervicapra*	8	Etorphine+ xylazine	Rectal probe 2.5 cm diam. Inserted to approx. 10 cm 5 V max (50 Hz)	1.9 ml 338×10^6/ml (34 ejaculates)	Holt *et al.*, 1996
Blesbok	*Damaliscus dorcas phillipsi*	2	Etorphine+ Xylazine	Rectal probe 2.2 cm diam., 15.2 cm long. 4–14V	1–10 ml 20–270×10^6/ml	Merilan *et al.*, 1982
Impala	*Aepyceros melampus*	1	Etorphine+ Xylazine	Rectal probe 2.2 cm diam., 15.2 cm long. 12V max	1 ml 580×10^6/ml	Merilan *et al.*, 1982
Brindled gnu	*Connochaetes taurinus*	1	Xylazine	Finger ring probes. 5-s pulses; sine wave 10–30Hz; 15 V max	11.25 ml 352×10^6/ml (2 ejaculates)	Watson, 1976
White-bearded wildebeest	*Connochaetes taurinus*	8	Carfentanyl+ xylazine	Rectal probe 5cm. diam. Longitudinal electrodes. 60 Hz sine wave. 7V max	11.7 ml 854×10^6/ml	Schiewe *et al.*, 1991
White-tailed gnu	*Connochaetes gnou*	2	Etorphine+ Xylazine	Rectal probe 3.2 cm diam. 15.2 cm long. 16–20V	0.5–1.2 ml $<10 \times 10^6$/ml	Merilan *et al.* (1982)
Gazelle (Cuvier's)	*Gazella cuvieri*	11	Ketamine+ xylazine	Rectal probe 2.5 cm diam. Longitudinal electrodes. 50 Hz. 9V max	0.64 ml 419×10^6/ml	Roldan *et al.*, 1998

Common name	Species	n	Anaesthetic	Method	Volume / concentration	Reference
Gazelle (Dorcas)	*Gazella dorcas neglecta*	7	Ketamine+ xylazine	Rectal probe; 1.95 cm diam., 6 cm long. 1–5 V (50Hz)	0.53 ml 922×10^6/ml	Cassinello *et al.*, 1998
Gazelle (Mohor)	*Gazella dama mhorr*	12	Ketamine+ xylazine	Rectal probe; 2.5 cm diam. Longitudinal electrodes. 50 Hz. 9 V max	0.98 ml (median) 1160×10^6/ml (median)	Holt *et al.*, 1996
Gazelle (Speke's)	*Gazella spekei*	6	Etorphine+ Xylazine	Rectal probe 2.2 cm diam., 7.6 cm. long 5–7 V	0.25 – 3ml 120–504×10^6/ml	Merilan *et al.*, 1982
Greater kudu	*Tragelaphus strepsiceros*	6	Carfentanyl+ xylazine	Rectal probe 5cm diam. Longitudinal electrodes. 60 Hz sine wave. 7 V max	4.4 ml 375.2×10^6/ml	Schiewe *et al.*, 1991
Lesser kudu	*Tragelaphus imberbis*	2	Etorphine+ Xylazine	Rectal probe 3.2 cm diam., 22.9 cm long. 6–21 V	0.75 -4 ml 80 – 135×10^6/ml	Merilan *et al.*, 1982
Sable antelope	*Hippotragus niger*	2	Etorphine+ Xylazine	Rectal probe 3.5 cm diam. 15.2 cm long. 12–14 V	1–4.2 ml 10–5700×10^6/ml	Merilan *et al.*, 1982
Springbok	*Antidorcas marsupialis*	3	Etorphine+ Xylazine	Rectal probe 2.2 cm diam. 7.6 cm long. 7–11 V	1.5 – 3ml 640 – 815×10^6/ml	Merilan *et al.*, 1982
Scimitar-horned oryx	*Oryx dammah*	1	Ketamine+ xylazine	Pulsator III electroejaculator (Lane manufacturing, Denver, Colorado, USA). Details not given	1.7 – 10ml 60–765×10^6/ml	Garland, 1989
Scimitar-horned oryx	*Oryx dammah*	4	Etorphine or carfentanyl	3–4 series of 30 stimulations; 2.5–6.5 V	3.3 ml 360×10^6/ml	Loskutoff *et al.*, 1989
Elephants						
African elephant	*Loxodonta africana*	13	Etorphine or arfentanyl	Rectal probe	90.5 ml 2283×10^6/ml	Howard *et al.*, 1986a

TABLE 16.1 (continued)

Common name	Species	N (males)	Anaesthesia	Procedure	Mean volume (ml) Mean concentration (millions/ml)	Reference
Elephants (continued)						
African elephant	Loxodonta africana	2	Immobilon	Rectal probe, 13 cm diam., 66 cm long. 30 Hz, 6–10 V	260 ml (from one bull) 4.8×10^6/ml	Jones, 1973
Camelids						
Bactrian camel	Camelus bactrianus	1	Etorphine+ xylazine	Rectal probe 4.5 cm diam., 25.4 cm long. 30 V max	30 ml 80×0^6/ml	Merilan et al., 1982
Bactrian camel	Camelus bactrianus	10	Not applicable	Artificial vagina	4.35 ml 5600×10^6/ml (158 ejaculates)	Zhao et al., 1994
Bactrian camel	Camelus bactrianus	8	Not applicable	Artificial vagina	15.6 ml (55 ejaculates) $100–176\times10^6$/ml	Rakhimzhanov, 1971 cited by Sipko et al., 1997
Dromedary	Camelus dromedarius	1	Etorphine+ xylazine	Rectal probe 4.5 cm diam., 25.4 cm long. 27 V max	3.5 ml 250×10^6/ml	Merilan et al., 1982
Llama	Llama glama	1	Etorphine+ xylazine	Rectal probe 4.5 cm diam., 25.4 cm long. 24 V max	4.5 ml 20×10^6/ml	Merilan et al., 1982
Bovids						
Banteng	Bos javanicus	1	Etorphine+ Xylazine	Rectal probe 4.5 cm diam. 25.4 cm long. 15–16V max.	8–11 ml $600–700\times10^6$/ml	Merilan et al. (1982)
Gaur	Bos gaurus	1	Xylazine+ carfentanyl	Probe size not given. Series of 2–3 s with 1-s. rests. 10 V max	Semen collection 'unsatisfactory'	Hopkins et al. (1988)

Common name	Species	n	Anaesthetic	Method	Volume/concentration	Reference
Gaur	*Bos gaurus*	8	Xylazine+ carfentanyl	Probe size not given. 45 stimuli, 2–9-V in 0.5-V increments	21.7 ml 689×10^6/ml	Schiewe *et al.*, 1989
Yak	*Bos mutus*	1	Not applicable	Collection during natural copulation	3.25 ml 1500×10^6/ml	Usupov, 1981 cited by Sipko *et al.*, 1997
Equids						
Grant's zebra	*Equus burchellii boehmii*	1	Not applicable	Trained animal; use of artificial vagina	34 ml (range 10–70) 74.8×10^6/ml (0–332× 10^6/ml) (200 ejaculates)	Crump and Crump, 1994
Grevy's zebra	*Equus grevyi*	1	Not applicable	Trained animal; use of artificial vagina	Total sperm in ejaculate 13,000– 21,000×10^6 sperm. (550 ejaculates)	Crump and Crump, 1994
Black rhinoceros	*Diceros bicornis*	1		Foil electrodes around penis. 10–29 V	44.6 and 18.8 ml 440 and 140×10^6/ml (2 ejaculates)	Platz *et al.*, 1979
Deer species						
Reindeer	*Rangifer tarandus*	6	Not applicable	Artificial vagina method.	0.5 ml 467×10^6/ml (16 ejaculates). Use of electroejaculation unsuccessful.	Dott and Utsi, 1973
Caribou	*Rangifer tarandus*	3	Stag tethered.	Rectal probe 2.5 cm diam with brass rings 7mm wide. Probe inserted to 17–20 cm. 5-s pulses (4–6 V, 30– 40 Hz) at 5-s intervals	0.97 ml 1753×10^6/ml	Sipko *et al.*, 1997
Eld's	*Cervus eldi thamin*	3	Ketamine + xylazine	Sine wave stimulator (60Hz), series of stimulations between 4 and 8 V	High semen quality; used for freezing and inseminations	Montfort *et al.*, 1993

TABLE 16.1 (continued)

Common name	Species	N (males)	Anaesthesia	Procedure	Mean volume (ml) Mean concentration (millions/ml)	Reference
Deer species (continued)						
Fallow	*Dama dama*	7	Not specified	Ruakura ram probe	0.6–1.5 ml 2900×10^6/ml (7 ejaculates)	Mulley et al., 1988
Red deer	*Cervus elaphus*	>13	Fentanyl citrate/ azaperone/ xylazine	Rectal probe 50 mm diam., 240 mm long.	Variable response; some urine contamination. Samples of 1 to 2.5 ml used for freezing.	Fennessy et al., 1990
Red deer (Siberian Maral)	*Cervus elaphus sibiricus*	3	Diacetylcholine + displacin	Electroejaculation 3–4 stimulations (5 s each at 10-s intervals; 8 V max	2.6 ml 464×10^6/ml	Sankevich, 1979 cited by Sipko et al., 1997
Wapiti	*Cervus elaphus nelsoni*	5	June and July, Carfentanil + xylazine used. August onwards animals restrained	Rectal probe.5.5 cm diam., 29 cm long. 3 longitudinal electrodes on ventral surface	No sperm collected in June and July. Subsequent collections contained sperm	Haigh et al., 1984b
White-tailed deer	*Odocoileus virginianus*	13	Xylazine	Rectal probe 2.2 cm diam. 32 cm long, longitudinal electrodes 7cm long×0.6 cm diam. Inserted 15 cm. 60 Hz. Max voltage not given	1.02 ml 1121×10^6/ml	Platz et al., 1982
White-tailed deer	*Odocoileus virginianus*	4 (Controls)	At least one animal not anaesthetized died within 12 hour. Other animals anaesthetized by an unspecified method	Commercial electroejaculator; ovine/porcine probe	Control group 0.84 ml (0.5–1.5 ml)	Bierschwal et al., 1970
		11 (dieldrin-treated)		Dieldrin group.	2.16×10^6/ml Data may be abnormal; no sperm from 2 animals	

during the breeding season, spermatozoa can readily be expressed from the caudae epididymides. The easiest approach is to make a few small incisions into the epididymal tubules, then allow the sperm masses to extrude into culture medium or sperm diluent. As contamination of the resultant sample by blood components can be deleterious, it is advisable to clean the epididymal tissues as thoroughly as possible before attempting sperm recovery; removal of epididymal blood vessels is also recommended at this stage for the same reason. The choice of sperm recovery medium for this purpose is somewhat problematic. Recovery into excessive amounts of a tissue culture medium will mean that a sperm concentration step will be needed before the spermatozoa can be transferred into a cryopreservation medium. The culture medium itself may also initiate cellular processes such as capacitation and activation of motility. For this reason, there is some merit in using a simple medium, such as a calcium-free buffered saline, rather than a complex mixture whose effects may be unpredictable. Post-mortem sperm recovery is often attempted as a last resort in cases where individual males are genetically important. These cases are often difficult, as animals have sometimes been debilitated for a period before death.

Once semen has been successfully obtained by electroejaculation or an alternative technique the next steps involve dilution and slow cooling to 4–5°C. In some species the concentration of spermatozoa in semen is sufficiently high that the dilution steps will result in a final sperm concentration which is suitable for freezing and storage (typically 50–100 million viable sperm per 0.25- or 0.5-ml straw; for a detailed practical protocol, see Marshall, 1984). Table 16.1 shows that this approach, which is used with ram and bull semen, could be used with species such as Grevy's zebra, fallow deer and possibly sable antelope. However, for many species in Table 16.1, where the sperm concentrations are approximately 500×10^6 sperm/ml or less, omission of a sperm concentration step followed by dilution with glycerolated medium results in excessively low sperm concentration in the final frozen semen samples. Coincidentally, efforts to minimize this dilution effect also result in the retention of high seminal plasma concentrations in the frozen semen samples, something that may also be undesirable. Gentle centrifugation is probably the only practical option for achieving suitable sperm concentration.

A cryoprotective medium is often added to semen in a stepwise manner. An initial dilution at 30–35°C to half the final volume can be carried out with media lacking cryoprotectant. The samples are then cooled slowly to 4–5°C, whereupon the next portion of diluent, containing double the final concentration of cryoprotectant, is added slowly, over a period of about 30 minutes. Diluent composition, as reported in methods sections of publications, is usually described in its undiluted form; it is important to note that final concentrations of individual diluent components are often two- or fourfold lower than they seem. The stepwise addition and removal of cryoprotectant has been advocated as a way of minimizing osmotic shock effects associated with sudden changes in the osmolarity of the external environment (Gao *et al.*, 1993, 1995). Furthermore, exposure to cryoprotectants at body temperature seems to produce more toxic injury than exposure at around 5°C. Some protocols include a prolonged equilibration period at this point; the justification for this in terms of cryoprotectant permeation into the cells is unclear, as glycerol would probably be fully equilibrated within a few seconds. At this stage, the diluted samples are typically either loaded into straws, sealed and frozen in cold nitrogen vapour (−80°C), or frozen as pellets within small depressions in dry ice. These techniques provide non-linear cooling curves. Typical initial cooling rates obtained by these methods range between 30°C and 80°C per minute. Very few authors have reported using controlled-rate freezing machines for the cryopreservation of wild ungulate spermatozoa.

16.2.4   Diluent composition

Few authors have reported studies aimed at establishing optimal protocols for given species, and it is therefore difficult to discern general principles influencing the success of cryopreservation methods. Furthermore, the criteria used for judging the post-thaw quality of spermatozoa have sometimes been poorly defined. Examination of the literature shows that a small number of diluent recipes are repeatedly tested with various species. Unfortunately, many of these are known by short codes, which fail to convey information about their composition. To help with the following discussion, some of the common diluent compositions are listed in Table 16.2).

Choice of cryoprotectant

Glycerol is the most widely used cryoprotectant for spermatozoa. The concentration range 4–8% (v/v) is most commonly used but this choice is based, not upon experimental data, but on experience with bovine and ovine semen. Two exceptions to this are studies on wildebeest and greater kudu (Schiewe *et al.*, 1991) and African elephant (Howard *et al.*, 1986a), in which the diluents were mainly based on methods used with boar semen, and therefore resulted in a final glycerol concentration of 2–2.5%. Where techniques are under further development for commercial purposes, efforts to optimize glycerol concentrations have been continued. For example, Kumar *et al.* (1993b), who studied Murrah buffalo, examined the effect of varying glycerol concentration upon spermatozoa frozen in the presence of milk instead of egg yolk, and concluded that 6% glycerol produced best post-thaw motility. No similar reports exist for non-domestic ungulates, although Jones (1973) commented that for African elephant semen a mixture of cryoprotectants (7% DMSO and 1% glycerol) was superior to one cryoprotectant alone (8% DMSO). Subtleties of this nature are unpredictable and indicate the pressing need for experimentation where possible. Some caution is

TABLE 16.2
Composition of some common cryopreservation diluents

Component	Common names for diluents								
	BF5F	TEST	TRIS	HEPT	PDV-62	EQ	SG-1	SYG-2	Yolk-citrate
Egg yolk	20%	20%	20%	20%	20%	20%	18%	20%	20%
TES[a]	1.2%	4.83%	–	–	–	–	–	–	–
Tris[b]	0.2%	1.15%	2.82%	1.09%	–	–	–	–	–
HEPES	–	–	–	5.54%	–	–	–	–	–
Lactose	–	–	–	–	11%	50 ml of 11% lactose solution.	11%	–	–
Sucrose	–	–	–	–	–	–	–	8.8%	–
Glucose	1.6%	0.4%	1.4%	0.4%	–	Glucose+EDTA	–	–	3.0
Fructose	1.6%	–	–	–	–	–	–	–	–
Equex (STLS)	0.5%	–	–	–	–	0.5%	1.5%	–	–
Citric acid	–	–	1.3%	–	–	–	–	–	–
Sodium citrate	–	–	–	–	–	–	–	–	2.32
Glycerol	4%	5%	5%	5%	4%	5%	6.6%	7%	6–8%

[a]N–Tris(hydroxymethyl)methyl–2aminoethanesulphonic acid.
[b]Tris(hydroxymethyl)aminomethane.

also needed, however, in the assessment of such experiments; while high cryopro-tectant concentrations benefit some aspects of sperm survival, they can also induce acrosomal damage. Boar spermatozoa are classic examples of this problem; motility (flagellar function) is better preserved when the glycerol concentration exceeds 3%, but the increase in acrosomal damage simultaneously depresses fertilizing ability. Investigators should therefore aim to find the minimum possible cryoprotectant concentration compatible with the preservation of cell structure and function.

Choice of buffer

Several alternative buffer systems have been used as the basis of sperm cryopreserv-ation diluents; these include TES, Tris, HEPES and mixtures of all three. Other diluents are based on compounds such as sodium citrate and lactose, and omit the buffer salts completely. It seems apparent that the diluents which include TES and Tris (the so-called TEST buffers) can be successfully used with a wide variety of species. Use of such buffers was recently reviewed and advocated for human use by Jeyendran et al. (1995), and there are many reports of their use with exotic ungulates. The Beltsville Farm diluents (BF5 and BF5F), originally developed for boar semen preservation, which contain these buffer components have proved beneficial for a number of wild ungulate species, including kudu, wildebeest (Schiewe et al., 1991), elephant (Howard et al., 1986a) and Mohor gazelle (Holt et al., 1996).

Semen cryopreservation has been followed by successful insemination in only a few wild ungulate species, and there is insufficient evidence to link these successes with any particular choice of buffer system in the diluent. Egg yolk–citrate media have, however, been used in a number of successful trials, although this is likely to have been coincidental rather than meaningful (red deer, European and Mesopotamian fallow deer, Pere David deer and moose semen: Krzywinski and Jaczewski, 1978; Asher et al., 1988; Fennessy et al., 1990; Jabbour et al., 1993; Blackbuck: Holt et al., 1996). Citrate diluents have also been used for artificial insemination in Speke's gazelle (Boever et al., 1980), but in this case a calf was born after insemination with fresh, rather than cryopreserved, semen.

Some diluents do not contain any system of pH buffering but are based on media with high sugar content. Diluents PDV-62 and EQ, which were developed for carnivore and equine semen respectively (Loomis et al., 1983; Platz et al., 1982), are based on 11% lactose solution, and contain different combinations of egg yolk, glycerol and glucose; EQ also contains surfactant and EDTA. These have been tested with a number of ungulates, and seem particularly well suited to pellet freezing on dry ice. Two alternative sugar-based diluents (SG-1 and SYG-2), originally developed for pig sperm freezing, are based either on 11% lactose (SG-1) or 12% sucrose, and also contain egg yolk and glycerol. SYG-2 was successfully used for the cryopreservation of Bactrian camel spermatozoa in ampoules (Zhao *et al.*, 1994) in a large artificial insemination study. One hundred and two out of 106 (96%) animals inseminated with frozen semen became pregnant, confirming that this cryopreservation technique was highly effective in this species. The authors commented that this combination of SYG-2 diluent and ampoule freezing was superior to cryopreservation with six other extenders developed for bull, stallion, boar, ram and buck semen. Unfortunately their description of the dilution method does not permit calculation of the final glycerol or sucrose concentrations, and moreover they did not specify the volumes contained within ampoules or the cooling and freezing protocols.

The use of surfactants

Several investigators have concluded that the addition of detergent to egg yolk diluents improves the post-thaw motility, acrosomal integrity and survival of ungulate spermatozoa. The surfactant used is usually sodium triethanolamine lauryl sulphate (STLS; also known as Orvus ES paste or Equex), which is added to diluents (at 0.5–1.5% v/v) ostensibly to disperse the egg yolk components and allow better interaction with the sperm plasma membrane surface. Diluents for boar semen freezing (e.g. BF5 and BF5F) routinely contain this detergent, and evidence from studies in the ram (Pontbriand *et al.*, 1989) confirmed its value for this species. More exotic species where surfactant appears to be advantageous include zebra °Crump and Crump, 1994), elephant (Howard *et al.*, 1986a), simitar-horned oryx (Foxworth *et al.*, 1989), Eld's deer (Montfort *et al.*, 1993), wildebeest and kudu (Schiewe *et al.*, 1991). A study in the Mohor gazelle failed to confirm the benefits of this surfactant (Holt *et al.*, 1996). However, with the notable exceptions of the elephant, kudu, wildebeest and gazelle studies (Holt *et al.*, 1996; Howard *et al.*, 1986a; Schiewe *et al.*, 1991) experiments aimed at testing the effects of STLS in exotic species have not been systematically designed to compare treatments with and without surfactant. As STLS can be difficult to obtain, other detergent compounds are sometimes used. For example, in a mouse sperm study, sodium dodecyl sulphate was successfully substituted for STLS (Penfold and Moore, 1993).

Egg yolk lipoprotein and milk proteins

Egg yolk components seem to provide an important degree of membrane protection to spermatozoa during cryopreservation; it cannot, however, be adequately explained by current biophysical models of freezing and thawing. Thus, while the action of glycerol and other cryoprotectants is explained by alteration of the colligative properties of salt-water solutions, and non-penetrating cryoprotectants are thought to reduce the likelihood of intracellular ice formation by causing cell dehydration, there is no firm evidence that egg yolk affects these processes or even changes membrane lipid composition and thermal behaviour. Protocols for some other groups of species, such as rodents, often omit egg yolk and in some cases it seems positively harmful (for example, in the kangaroo; unpublished observation). Thus, ungulates as a group may have some particular sperm plasma membrane property that responds to egg yolk. A possible clue was afforded by Okamura *et al.* (1991) who showed that a water-insoluble egg yolk fraction was capable of stimulating pig sperm adenylate cyclase, thus stimulating motility.

The egg yolk concentrations used in various protocols normally vary between 5% (v/v) and 20% (v/v). Few authors have assessed the effects of varying the egg yolk concentration; this is partly through lack of opportunity but also because other, arguably more important, variables such as freezing rate, have been studied instead. Where such evaluations have been performed the results have been surprising. Watson (1976), who studied brindled gnu semen cryopreservation, found that 6.25% (v/v) egg yolk produced better post-thaw motility and acrosomal integrity than 12.5% or 25%. Similar results have been reported for the Mohor gazelle (Holt *et al.*, 1996) and Murrah buffalo (Kumar *et al.*, 1993a).

There is some evidence that the effects of egg yolk are modulated by the choice of buffer system used. For example, experiments with brindled gnu semen Watson (1976) indicated that while 5% egg yolk was best with a citrate-based buffer, 10% egg yolk was better when a phosphate-based buffer was used. The problem of complex interactions between egg yolk and other diluent components, including additives such as various sugars, means that the comparisons of trials and results are difficult to interpret, even within a single species.

In some sperm cryopreservation protocols the egg yolk is either replaced or supplemented by milk proteins. The successful scimitar-horned oryx inseminations performed in New Zealand (Garland, 1989) used this methodology. Comparison of a lactose–yolk glycerol mixture containing Equex with a milk–yolk–glycerol mixture, also with Equex, for Grevy's zebra sperm cryopreservation showed that the milk supplement produced 5–10% higher post-thaw motility (Crump and Crump, 1994). Despite such findings, milk proteins have rarely been included within diluents.

16.2.5 Methods of packaging

Two alternative sample packaging and freezing methods are commonly used; these involve freezing in pellets on depressions in dry ice or in plastic straws. Balancing the merits of these two approaches requires more than a cursory consideration. For genome banking to be effective the preserved semen clearly must maintain its optimal viability and fertility; however, certain health standards must also be met if future international transport is contemplated. These two requirements are not always compatible, however. Ungulate semen is viewed with special caution by national and international veterinary health authorities concerned about the risks of disease transmission, so the use of straws for semen packaging is undoubtedly the method of choice. Straws can be sealed, thus preventing contact between the semen and the outside environment. Furthermore, if required the straws can be frozen using controlled-rate freezing machines and subsequently loaded directly into insemination equipment for either transcervical or laparoscopic use. Aseptic isolation is more difficult to maintain with pellets, which must be frozen in direct contact with dry ice. Although pellets may be less satisfactory in terms of hygiene, a number of studies have shown that for particular species they are technically superior to straws. For example, in studies of the African elephant, Howard *et al.* (1986a) reported that pellet freezing gave better post-thaw sperm motility and survival than straws. In this study best results were obtained using the boar semen diluents BF5F and SG1 (final concentrations of glycerol, 1.3% and 2.2% respectively). Here, the success of pellet freezing, in combination with relatively low glycerol concentrations, may be attributable to the rapid initial cooling rate achieved with pellet formation on dry ice. Furthermore, as the pellet size used in this study (30 μl) was much smaller than that used by many routine laboratories (200–300 μl), the freezing rates would have been correspondingly faster. It is also noteworthy that the diluents used in this study were developed specifically for boar semen where a low glycerol concentration is needed for the avoidance of acrosomal damage; faster freezing rates are known to produce better results under such circumstances.

Somewhat similar comparisons were reported for scimitar horned oryx semen by Foxworth *et al.* (1989). These authors used two different semen extenders; the boar sperm diluent BF5F and PDB-62 (based on 11% lactose–20% yolk–4% glycerol; probably the same as PDV-62 quoted in other reports); freezing was performed by four different methods, and then two thawing techniques were used. Interestingly, the PDB-62 diluent was reported as providing the best post-thaw sperm quality when pellet freezing was used. As the semen was diluted 1:4 with extender prior to freezing, the final glycerol concentration was 1% in both cases. This seems to suggest that the lactose formulation confers an advantage when pellet freezing is used. The final outcome of this study was that BF5F, used in conjunction with 0.25-ml straws and cooling 6 cm above the surface of liquid nitrogen, produced the highest post-thaw motility (37.8%), and kinetic rating.

16.2.6 Thawing procedure

The packaging method greatly influences the practical requirements for thawing. Straws can be thawed by plunging them directly into warm water; however, opinion varies about the most effective time–temperature combination. Quarter-millilitre straws of cattle semen are taken from the liquid nitrogen container and thawed for 10 seconds at 34°C. This is said to bring the temperature rapidly to about 5°C. This procedure is designed to avoid any cold-shock effects that might be caused if semen is warmed to body temperature, then handled in the open air on a cold winter's day. Others advocate thawing straws in water at higher temperatures, up to 80°C, but for a necessarily brief period. Thawing procedures for pellets involve placing them into thin-walled glass tubes in a waterbath. The tubes can either be empty, in which case the semen simply thaws, or they can contain warm media which rapidly reduce the glycerol concentration during the thawing process. In the latter case the type of media used and the thawing temperature are likely to affect post-thaw sperm quality.

Very few studies of wild ungulates have investigated the influence of thawing on sperm quality. Two detailed practical studies of semen cryopreservation in the African elephant (Howard et al., 1986a) and wildebeest and kudu (Schiewe et al., 1991) investigated the procedure in detail. Both included comparisons of pellet thawing into either normal saline or a tissue culture medium (Tyrode's), but Schiewe et al. (1991) carried out the comparison at two different temperatures (24°C and 37°C). Interestingly, both the wildebeest and kudu spermatozoa showed significantly better duration of post-thaw motility when thawing was performed at 24°C. Furthermore, the saline thawing solution produced more prolonged duration of sperm motility, although this might be explained if the Tyrode's medium supported a higher metabolic rate. This difference between Tyrode's medium and saline was detectable, although less obvious, in the elephant study. The scimitar-horned oryx study (Foxworth et al., 1989) mentioned that two thawing methods were compared but did not comment on the outcomes.

16.2.7 Aspects of semen cryopreservation and artificial insemination procedures in individual species

Semen assessment

Most studies of semen cryopreservation in ungulates have used indirect measures of sperm quality to assess the success of the protocols used. Such measures usually involve the examination of sperm motility, viability and acrosomal integrity. These measures are typically expressed as percentages, although motility estimates sometimes include a kinetic score. More modern approaches to semen assessment include (1) the use of computer-assisted semen analysis (CASA) to measure sperm motion objectively, (2) the use fluorescence probes to measure sperm viability or acrosomal integrity, and/or (3) assessment of capacitation status or zona pellucida penetration ability. There are virtually no reports of such techniques being used to assess semen from wild ungulates; fluorescein-labelled *Pisum sativum* lectin was, however, used for post-thaw acrosomal assessment in the Mohor gazelle (Holt et al., 1996).

In a detailed study of scimitar-horned oryx semen cryopreservation, Roth *et al.* (1999) tested sperm function using a heterologous IVF system, where the spermatozoa were mixed with domestic cow oocytes. The EQ diluent was used; freezing was achieved by (a) placing straws on dry ice for 10 minutes then, plunging them into liquid nitrogen, (b) lowering straws into a fully charged but empty dry shipper, in one or two steps, or (c) laying straws horizontally in the vapour phase above liquid nitrogen. All methods resulted in good acrosomal preservation (>60% intact), and high levels of oocyte penetration. The penetrated oocytes were monitored for fertilization and cleavage, but there were no differences attributable to the freezing methodologies. These results indicate that the control of freezing rate is rather less important than has been suggested in the past.

The ultimate test of sperm quality is, of course, its ability to effect fertilization *in vivo*, but relatively few reports include insemination results. Rott (1995) presented a table of species for which progeny had been obtained after semen cryopreservation and artificial insemination. The table included fourteen artiodactyl species, of which eight were cervidae, three were bovine and one ovine species (snow sheep). Only three types of antelope or gazelle species were represented (addax, blackbuck and scimitar-horned oryx). At least one gazelle species, Mohor gazelle, has since been added to this list (Holt *et al.*, 1996), while other groups have repeated the successful insemination of scimitar-horned oryx. Orana Park Zoo in New Zealand successfully obtained scimitar-horned oryx calves using frozen semen imported from Metro-Toronto Zoo in Canada (Garland, 1989), and calves were also recently born at the National Zoo in Washington, USA. It is noteworthy that this list represents a series of species for which more is known than simply how to cryopreserve semen. The success of artificial insemination with frozen semen depends upon knowing the characteristics of the female reproductive cycle and its responses to hormonal oestrus synchronization treatment. Other factors that appear deceptively simple, such as knowing whether the cervix is longitudinally separated into canals which serve each uterine horn independently, as in the scimitar-horned oryx, can also confound artificial insemination attempts with the best quality semen. If semen is placed into the non-ovulating horn, it is unlikely to reach the oocyte. Anatomical descriptions that encompass this degree of detail are remarkably difficult to find. Recently, however, interest in the application of reproductive technologies to rhinoceroses and elephants has stimulated anatomical studies in these species (Balke *et al.*, 1988a,b, Godfrey *et al.*, 1991). Similarly, Loskutoff *et al.* (1990) described the female reproductive tract anatomy of the suni antelope (*Neotragus moschatus zuluensis*).

Insemination timing

As cryopreservation shortens the expected duration of sperm survival within the female reproductive tract, it is important to perform artificial insemination close to the time of ovulation. The required degree of synchrony can be achieved in a number of ways. e.g. by using behavioural observations to identify the natural oestrous period, by using regular hormonal measurements to track several reproductive cycles accurately, then predict the most likely timing for the next oestrous cycle, or by actively modifying and resetting the oestrous cycle by administering exogenous hormones. All approaches have been reported, but the latter approach (commonly known as synchronization) has probably been the most widely used, especially for deer species. Camelids, being induced ovulators, represent a physiologically exceptional group within the large herbivorous mammals. Ovulation can be induced by the administration of exogenous gonadotrophins or, as described by Zhao *et al.* (1994) in a study of Bactrian camels, by the intramuscular injection of seminal plasma. The active substance in seminal plasma induces ovulation 30–48 hours after injection, and was described as trypsin-labile, stable to heating, acid and alkali treatments, but so far has not been identified.

Behavioural detection of oestrus is helped by the fact that many ungulates display characteristic sexual behaviour at this time. The male typically picks out the oestrous female and follows her, while showing the behaviour known as 'flehmen' (in which the upper lip is curled back); the behaviour is also accompanied by neck stretching, tongue flicking and attempting to mount. Eventually, the female will stand still and allow the male to mount. If a vasectomized male is available, his behaviour will indicate the presence of oestrous females. In a study of blackbuck artificial insemination this approach was used with some success (Holt *et al.*, 1988), when inseminations were timed for 24 hours after the oestrus observation. Similarly, Magyar *et al.* (1989) successfully used behavioural observations to determine insemination timing in white-tailed deer. In our hands there were some significant disadvantages to this approach, however. For example, it was found that oestrus was detected in only about half of the blackbuck females tested, even though parallel hormonal measurements showed that they were cycling regularly. This low success rate was probably attributable to difficulties of monitoring the animal behaviour continuously. Agricultural techniques (whereby the male places a coloured mark on the rump of the female during mounting; i.e. harnesses, raddles, use of paint itself (see Dott and Utsi, 1973)) were unsuitable for blackbuck. For practical purposes this approach is too unreliable to be a sole option for oestrous detection. However, when a vasectomized male is available the behavioural approach significantly enhances the use of the other techniques.

Regular analysis of reproductive hormones offers a means of monitoring the reproductive cycle in wild ungulates. However, in contrast to the agricultural species, which in this case include domesticated deer, where regular blood samples can be obtained for analysis, this option is impractical for wild species. In general, they are too intractable and nervous to be handled without anaesthesia. Some researchers have alleviated the problem of animal-handling by the use of special animal handling equipment, i.e. drop-floor and adjustable sidewall crushes, together with races for shepherding the animals in the required direction. Such installations are used successfully for scimitar-horned oryx and blackbuck in some New Zealand zoos, such as at Christchurch and Hamilton, with designs based on deer farming practice. Assuming that such equipment is not available, alternative methods of tracking reproductive hormones are needed; fortunately, it is possible to use urinary, and more recently faecal, analysis for this purpose (for review, see Schwarzenberger *et al.*, 1996; see also Chapter 6).

Possessing information about previous reproductive cycles of a particular animal is clearly insufficient, *per se*, to enable insemination timings to be identified. To do this the required analyses must be performed each day, with results being produced as rapidly as possible. For most purposes this is impractical. Furthermore, there is a significant time lag between the real occurrence of physiological events, such as ovulation, and the manifestation of appropriate hormonal changes in urine (approximately 24 hours) and faeces (up to 4 days; Shaw *et al.*, 1995).

The most satisfactory and practical methods of achieving synchrony between inseminations and oestrus/ovulation are based on manipulation of the reproductive cycle. In ungulates this is mainly achieved using one of two approaches. One method involves prostaglandin $F_{2\alpha}$ injections to curtail the lifespan of the corpus luteum, thereby inducing a new follicular phase within 24–48 hours, and the other mimics a prolonged luteal phase by the exogenous administration of progesterone over a period of about two weeks. In the latter case the progesterone is administered by placing a progesterone source (sponge or other releasing device) in the vagina; removal of the source usually induces ovulation within 48–72 hours. Manipulation of the oestrous cycle is described more fully in Chapter 6.

The most comprehensive studies of oestrous synchronization in wild ungulates have been carried out with deer species, and using the second strategy outlined above. The main objective of such studies is finding the optimal interval between removal of the progesterone source and the insemination time. The results depend upon two factors: the time from progesterone withdrawal to ovulation, and the dynamics of sperm transport and capacitation. The latter is likely to differ depending whether the spermatozoa are fresh or frozen. There is a growing belief that cryopreservation accelerates capacitation (Watson, 1995), and therefore that a shorter interval is required between insemination and ovulation when using frozen–thawed semen.

Fennessy *et al.* (1990) tested the effects of inseminating red deer with frozen semen at various intervals after removal of the progesterone source. In this experiment the withdrawal of progesterone was accompanied by administration of 225 IU pregnant mare's serum gonadotrophin (PMSG, eCG) as a further stimulus to follicle development. Pregnancy rates did not vary (38–44%) when vaginal inseminations were performed at 36, 44, 52 and 60 hours, although extending the interval to 68 hours substantially

CHAPTER 16

reduced the conception rate (6%). When they performed a similar experiment using intrauterine laparoscopic insemination, although the overall pregnancy rate was higher (56% versus 34%), there was no effect of varying the interval between 48, 52 and 55 hours. Longer intervals were not tested for effectiveness using the intrauterine route. The average interval to ovulation in red deer is approximately 72 hours, although the authors suggested that there would have been considerable variation. This means that the fertilizing spermatozoa may have survived for 24 hours and possibly longer in the female tract, irrespective of the insemination route.

A more stringent test of sperm survival and insemination timing was undertaken by Mylrea *et al.* (1991) when European fallow deer were inseminated with spermatozoa from the larger Mesopotamian fallow deer. In this case, a significant time effect was detected when 56- and 66-hour intervals were compared (20.7% versus 58.8% conception rates respectively). As the authors believed that ovulation would occur about 72 hours after progesterone withdrawal, there is good reason to suppose that while the spermatozoa could survive adequately for at least 6 hours, they could not easily remain fertile for an additional 10 hours. Very similar results were obtained by Jabbour *et al.* (1993) who inseminated European fallow deer with Mesopotamian fallow deer semen 65 hours after progesterone withdrawal. Using similar protocols, Montfort *et al.* (1993) achieved 9/20 pregnancies in Eld's deer when frozen–thawed semen was inseminated laparoscopically 70 hours after withdrawal of progesterone.

These and other studies in deer indicate that the use of progesterone-releasing devices provides a reliable method for insemination timing. Although extensive controlled studies are more difficult to perform in other ungulates, it is evident that the technique can also be used successfully with gazelles (Holt *et al.*, 1996), scimitar-horned oryx (Garland, 1989) and Suni antelope *(Neotragus moschatus zuluensis;* Raphael *et al.,* 1988). Two intervals between progesterone withdrawal and intrauterine insemination, 48 hours and 60 hours, were tested in Mohor gazelles (Holt *et al.,* 1996): 3/7 and 1/6 conceptions occurred respectively with the two regimens, possibly indicating that the interval to ovulation may be shorter than in cervids; however, this needs to be confirmed with further studies. The Suni antelope study demonstrated that progesterone-impregnated vaginal sponges could be used for oestrous synchronization and confirmed the occurrence of ovulation in treated females. However, as the main aim of this study was the development of embryo transfer techniques, no artificial inseminations were performed. A similar study in the giraffe (Gilbert *et al.,* 1988) indicated that progesterone-releasing devices may be less effective in suppressing ovulation in this species, thereby making oestrous synchronization unreliable. However, the unreliability could simply be due to the larger body size of these animals and a different dose requirement.

Although oestrous synchronization with prostaglandins is widely used for domestic cattle, mixed results have been obtained with wild ungulates. For example, administration of prostaglandin to female blackbuck about 9 days into the luteal phase reliably induced luteolysis and return to oestrus within 3 days (Hodges, 1992). However, when a similar regimen was used on a series of scimitar-horned oryx at Marwell Zoo in the UK, the period for return to oestrus ranged from 3 to 9 days (Holt and Bircher, unpublished data). Durrant (1983) undertook a small-scale study of responses to prostaglandin in three oryx species, scimitar-horned, fringe-eared and Arabian oryx. The scimitar-horned oryx and Arabian oryx responded to prostaglandin by returning to oestrus within 48–72 hours, but the fringe-eared oryx took 4 days. Densmore *et al.* (1987) obtained similar results when prostaglandin was administered to a female addax during the luteal phase of the cycle. This treatment was followed by artificial insemination with frozen–thawed semen on 4 successive days (days 2–6 post-prostaglandin) and resulted in a pregnancy. Urinary hormone analysis for preg-nanediol glucuronide (PdG) indicated that the single prostaglandin dose must have provoked luteolysis immediately.

In theory at least, prostaglandin has a major practical advantage over the use of progesterone-releasing devices for the manipulation of the oestrous cycle in wild species. It can be administered by injection using a blowpipe and dart, and thus avoids any need for animal capture, handling and possibly anaesthesia. However, experience to date suggests that the results can be less reliable; this is partly because it is more difficult to confirm that the full dose has been received.

16.3 OOCYTES

There are no investigations of oocyte freezing in exotic ungulates and similarly no investigations of freezing immature oocytes or ovarian tissues for future *in vitro* maturation protocols.

Oocyte recovery, *in vitro* maturation and *in vitro* fertilization have been reported for the gaur (*Bos gaurus*) (Johnston *et al.*, 1994), klipspringer (*Oreotragus oreotragus*) (Raphael *et al.*, 1991), bongo (*Tragelaphus euryceros*) (Pope *et al.*, 1998) and addax (*Addax nasomasculatus*) (Asa *et al.*, 1998). In the gaur and klipspringer studies the oocytes were collected post-mortem from antral follicles, and then matured under laboratory conditions by incubation in tissue culture media supplemented with fetal calf serum (FCS). Four gaur blastocysts were transferred individually to Holstein cow recipients after 7 days in culture; one subsequently developed to term. Twelve klipspringer oocytes were prepared for *in vitro* fertilization using fresh semen, but only one embryo resulted. The authors reported that this embryo developed to the sixteen-cell stage and was then cryopreserved using a standard bovine protocol. In the addax and bongo studies (Asa *et al.*, 1998; Pope *et al.*, 1998) the oocytes were aspirated from preovulatory follicles by a transvaginal route, as routinely used in human clinical practice. The oocytes were matured *in vitro* for 24 hours by incubation in culture medium (TCM 199) supplemented with 10% FCS and 0.01 units/ml FSH and LH for the addax, or 5% FCS with 1 unit/ml hCG and eCG for the bongo. Fertilization was achieved using fresh and frozen spermatozoa; embryo cleavage occurred with both species but none of the addax embryos developed to blastocyst and only one bongo embryo (out of 11) reached this stage.

Although domestic buffalo may not be considered prime candidates for conservation, embryo transfer technology has met with limited success in this species. To some extent this mirrors the attempts to develop embryo technology with the more exotic ungulates mentioned above. There is a very large specialist literature on buffalo embryo technology and no attempt will be made to cover it here. However, it is worth pointing out that some progress has been made with the post-mortem retrieval and maturation of small antral follicles (2 to 6-mm diameter), using protocols very similar to those described above for the addax (see, for example, Totey et al., 1992). These authors obtained 30–50% and 17–30% in vitro fertilization rates with fresh and frozen semen respectively, and found that 20–30% of the fertilized eggs went on to the cleavage stage and subsequently formed blastocysts. The use of a rabbit oviduct coculture system considerably improved the success rate of in vitro embryonic development.

16.4 EMBRYOS

Although embryo collection and transfer is now successfully used with cattle, and has also been applied to a number of deer species (Berg et al., 1995; Dixon et al., 1991; Fennessy et al., 1994, 1989; Krzywinsky, 1987; Magyar et al., 1988; Waldhalm et al., 1989), there are limited examples of its use with wild ungulate species. Where successful embryo transfers have been performed they have tended to occur in isolation and without much follow-up. Dresser and her colleagues have demonstrated the feasibility of embryo collection and transfer both within and between species, having concentrated especially upon the larger ungulates such as eland, bongo and gaur (Dresser et al., 1984; Pope et al., 1988, 1991). Summers et al. (1987) carried out interspecies transfer of a zebra embryo into domestic horses and obtained live offspring.

Embryo recovery following attempts to generate multiple ovulations has not proved particularly successful in wild ungulate species. The types of problems encountered include poor fertilization rate after ovarian stimulation, possibly caused by difficulties with the timing of oocyte maturation and inadequate sperm transport in the female reproductive tract. Schiewe et al. (1988) tested various regimes for synchronizing the ovarian cycle and inducing multiple follicular development in seventeen oryx, five eland, four bongo and one kudu. While 91% of oryx oocytes were fertilized after treatment and natural mating, fertilized oocytes were found in only one of the ten animals from the other species groups. These authors suggested that stress effects may adversely affect fertilization and embryonic survival in these wild species. Generation of neutralizing antibodies against the hormonal preparations used for ovarian stimulation is another potential problem.

There do not appear to be any studies involving embryo cryopreservation in exotic ungulates. This presumably reflects the fact that to date such embryo technology has not become sufficiently successful with non-domestic ungulates to make embryo cryopreservation worthwhile. There is, however, one report of pregnancies in red deer following embryo cryopreservation (Dixon *et al.*, 1991). This concerns the importation of red deer embryos from Australia into New Zealand in which 250 embryos were thawed, 247 implanted into recipients of which 153 became pregnant (61% pregnancy rate). The embryos were frozen using 1.4 M glycerol as a cryoprotectant, into which they were introduced in three steps. They were then loaded into 0.25-ml straws, cooled to −6°C at 2°C/min, seeded, then cooled further to −30°C at 0.5°C per minute. The straws were then plunged into liquid nitrogen. Thawing was carried out in water at 30°C, the glycerol removed in two steps using 0.5 M sucrose and the embryos were washed in culture medium prior to transfer.

Wildt *et al.* (1992), in a general review of embryo technology for endangered species, stressed the need for fundamental studies into the biology of embryo development in different species. Until this basic background is available this will remain a difficult area to study and especially to apply in a practical sense.

REFERENCES

ASA, C. S., BAUMAN, K. L., HOUSTON, E. W., FISCHER, M. T., JUNGE, R. E. and KRISHER, R. L. (1998) 'Transvaginal oocyte retrieval and in vitro maturation, fertilization and embryo culture in Addax (*Addax nasomaculatus*)', *Theriogenology* **49**, 261.

ASHER, G. W., ADAM, J. L., JAMES, R. W. and BARNES, D. (1988) 'Artificial-insemination of farmed fallow deer (*Dama dama*)–fixed-time insemination at a synchronized estrus', *Anim. Prod.* **47**, 487–492.

BALKE, J. M. E., BARKER, I. K., HACKENBERGER, M. K., McMANAMON, R. and BOEVER, W. J. (1988a) 'Reproductive anatomy of three nulliparous female Asian elephants: the development of artificial breeding techniques', *Zoo Biol.* **7**, 99–113.

BALKE, J. M. E., BOEVER, W. J., ELLERSIECK, M. R., SEAL, U. S. and SMITH, D. A. (1988b) 'Anatomy of the reproductive tract of the female African elephant (*Loxodonta africana*) with reference to development of techniques for artificial breeding', *J. Reprod. Fertil.* **84**, 485–492.

BERG, D. K., THOMPSON, J. G., PUGH, P. A., TERVIT, H. R. and ASHER, G. W. (1995) 'Successful in vitro culture of early cleavage stage embryos recovered from superovulated Red deer (*Cervus elaphus*)', *Theriogenology* **44**, 247–254.

CHAPTER 16

BIERSCHWAL, C. J., MATHER, E. C., MARTIN, C. E., MURPHY, D. A. and KORSHGEN, L. J. (1970) 'Some characteristics of deer semen collected by electroejaculation', *J. Am. Vet. Med. Assoc.* **157**, 627–632.

BOEVER, J., KNOX, D., MERILAN, C. and READ, B. (1980) 'Estrus induction and artificial insemination with successful pregnancy in Speke's gazelle', in Procceedings of the *9th International Congress on Animal Reproduction and Artificial Insemination (Madrid)*, Vol. 2, 565–570.

BRONSON, F. H. (1989) *Mammalian Reproductive Biology*, Chicago and London: University of Chicago Press.

CASSINELLO, J., ABAIGAR, T., GOMENDIO, M., and ROLDAN, E. R. (1998) 'Characteristics of the semen of three endangered species of gazelles (*Gazella dama mhorr, G. dorcas neglecta* and *G. cuvieri*)', *J. Reprod. Fertil.* **113**, 35–45.

COLAS, G. (1984) 'Semen technology in the ram', in Courot, M. (ed.) *The Male in Farm Animal Reproduction*, Boston: Martinus Nijhoff, pp. 219–234.

CRUMP, J. P. and CRUMP, J. W. (1994) 'Manual semen collection from a Grevy's zebra stallion (*Equus grevyi*), onset of sperm production, semen characteristics, and cryopreservation of semen, with a comparison to the sperm production from a Grant's zebra stallion (*Equus burchelli boehmi*)', *Theriogenology* **41**, 1011–1021.

DENSMORE, M. A., BOWEN, M. J., MAGYAR, S. J., AMOSS, M. S., JR., ROBINSON, R. M., HARMS, P. G. and KRAEMER, D. C. (1987) 'Artificial insemination with frozen, thawed semen and pregnancy diagnosis in addax (*Addax nasomaculatus*)', *Zoo Biol.* **6**, 21–29.

DIXON, T. E., HUNTER, J. W. and BEATSON, N. S. (1991) 'Pregnancies following the export of frozen red deer embryos from New Zealand to Australia', *Theriogenology* **35**, 193.

DOTT, H. M. and SKINNER, J. D. (1989) 'Collection, examination and storage of spermatozoa from some South African mammals', *South African J. Zool.* **24**, 151–160.

DOTT, H. M. and UTSI, M. N. P. (1973) 'Artificial insemination of reindeer, *Rangifer tarandus*', *J. Zool. (Lond.)* **170**, 505–508.

DRESSER, B. L., POPE, C. E., KRAMER, L., KUEHN, G., DAHLHAUSEN, R. D., MARUSKA, E. J., REECE, B. and THOMAS, W. D. (1984) 'Nonsurgical embryo recovery and successful interspecies embryo transfer from bongo (*Tragelaphus euryceros*) to eland (*Tragelaphus oryx*)', *Proc. Am. Assoc. Zoo Vets* 180.

DURRANT, B. S. (1983) 'Reproductive studies of the oryx', *Zoo Biol.* **2**, 191–197.

FENNESSY, P. F., FISHER, M. W., SHACKELL, G. H. and MACKINTOSH, C. G. (1989) 'Superovulation and embryo recovery in red deer (*Cervus elaphus*) hinds', *Theriogenology* **32**, 877–883.

FENNESSY, P. F., MACKINTOSH, C. G. and SHACKELL, G. H. (1990) 'Artificial insemination of farmed red deer (*Cervus elaphus*)', *Anim. Prod.* **51**, 613–621.

FENNESSY, P. F., ASHER, G. W., BEATSON, N. S., DIXON, T. E., HUNTER, J. W. and BRINGANS, M. J. (1994) 'Embryo-transfer in deer', *Theriogenology* **41**, 133–138.

FISER, P. S. and BATRA, T. R. (1984) 'Effect of equilibration time at 5°C and photoperiod on survival of ram spermatozoa frozen in straws', *Can. J. Anim. Sci.* **64**, 777–780.

FOXWORTH, W. B., WOLFE, B. A., LOSKUTOFF, N. M., NEMEC, L. A., HUNTRESS, S. L., RAPHAEL, B. L., JENSEN, J. M., WILLIAMS, B. W., HOWARD, J. G. and KRAEMER, D. C. (1989) 'Post-thaw motility parameters of frozen semen from scimitar-horned oryx (*Oryx dammah*): effects of freezing method, extender and rate of thawing', *Theriogenology* **31**, 193.

GAO, D. Y., ASHWORTH, E., WATSON, P. F., KLEINHANS, F. W., MAZUR, P. and CRITSER, J. K. (1993) 'Hyperosmotic tolerance of human spermatozoa–separate effects of glycerol, sodium-chloride, and sucrose on spermolysis', *Biol. Reprod.* **49**, 112–123.

GAO, D. Y., LIU, J., LIU, C., McGANN, L. E., WATSON, P. F., KLEINHANS, F. W., MAZUR, P., CRITSER, E. S. and CRITSER, J. K. (1995) 'Prevention of osmotic injury to human spermatozoa during addition and removal of glycerol', *Hum. Reprod.* **10**, 1109–1122.

GARLAND, P. (1989) 'Artificial insemination of scimitar-horned oryx (*Oryx dammah*)', *Bull. Zoo Mgmt.* **27**, 29–30.

GILBERT, D. E., LOSKUTOFF, N. M., DORN, C. G., NEMEC, L. A., CALLE, P. P., KRAEMER, D. C., THRELFALL, W. R. and RAPHAEL, B. L. (1988) 'Hormonal manipulation and ultrasonographic monitoring of ovarian activity in the giraffe', *Theriogenology* **29**, 248.

GODFREY, R. W., POPE, C. E., DRESSER, B. L. and OLSEN, J. H. (1991) 'Gross anatomy of the reproductive tract of female black (*Diceros bicornis michaeli*) and white rhinoceros (*Ceratotherium simum simum*)', *Zoo Biol.* **10**, 165–175.

GOSCH, B., BARTOLOMAEUS, T. and FISCHER, K. (1989) 'Light and scanning electronmicroscopy of fallow deer (*Dama dama*) spermatozoa', *J. Reprod. Fertil.* **87**, 187–192.

HAIGH, J. C., CATES, W. F., GLOVER, G. J. and RAWLINGS, N. C. (1984a) 'Relationships between seasonal changes in serum testosterone concentrations, scrotal circumference and sperm morphology of male wapiti (*Cervus elaphus*)', *J. Reprod. Fertil.* **70**, 413–418.

HAIGH, J. C., SHADBOLT, M. P. and GLOVER, G. J. (1984b) 'Artificial insemination of wapiti', *Proc. Am. Assoc. Zoo Vets*, Abstract 174.

HODGES, J. K. (1992) 'Detection of oestrous cycles and timing of ovulation', *Symp. Zool. Soc. Lond.* **54**, 149–168.

HOLT, W. V., ABAIGAR, T. and JABBOUR, H. N. (1996) 'Oestrous synchronization, semen preservation and artificial insemination in the Mohor gazelle (*Gazella dama mhorr*) for the establishment of a genome resource bank programme', *Reprod. Fertil. Dev.* **8**, 1215–1222.

HOLT, W. V., MOORE, H. D. M., NORTH, R. D., HARTMAN, T. D. and HODGES, J. K. (1988) 'Hormonal and behavioural detection of oestrus in blackbuck, *Antilope cervicapra*, and successful artificial insemination with fresh and frozen semen', *J. Reprod. Fertil.* **82**, 717–725.

HOPKINS, S. M., ARMSTRONG, D. L., HUMMEL, S. and JUNIOR, S. (1988) 'Successful cryo-preservation of gaur (*Bos gaurus*) epididymal spermatozoa', *J. Zoo Animal Medicine* **19**, 195–201.

HOWARD, J. G., BUSH, M., DEVOS, V., SCHIEWE, M. C., PURSEL, V. G. and WILDT, D. E. (1986a) 'Influence of cryoprotective diluent on post-thaw viability and acrosomal integrity of spermatozoa of the African elephant (*Loxodonta africana*)', *J. Reprod. Fertil.* **78**, 295–306.

HOWARD, J. G., BUSH, M. and WILDT, D. E. (1986b) 'Semen collection, analysis and cryopreservation in nondomestic mammals', in Morrow, D. A. (ed.) *Current Therapy in Theriogenology*, Philadelphia and London: W.B. Saunders and Co, pp. 1047–1053.

JABBOUR, H. N. and ASHER, G. W. (1992) 'Artificial breeding of farmed fallow deer (*Dama dama*)', in Renecker, L. A. and Hudson, R. J. (eds) *Wildlife Production: Conservation and Sustainable Development*, Alaska: AFES, pp. 91–96.

JABBOUR, H. N., ARGO, C. M., BRINKLOW, B. R., LOUDON, A. S. I. and HOOTON, J. (1993) 'Conception rates following intrauterine insemination of European (*Dama dama dama*) fallow deer does with fresh or frozen–thawed Mesopotamian (*Dama dama mesopotamica*) fallow deer spermatozoa', *J. Zool. (Lond.)* **230**, 379–384.

JEYENDRAN, R. S., GUNAWARDANA, V. K., BARISIC, D. and WENTZ, A. C. (1995) 'Test-yolk media and sperm quality', *Hum. Reprod. Update* **1**, 73–79.

JOHNSTON, L. A., PARRISH, J. J., MONSON, R., LEIBFRIED-RUTLEDGE, L., SUSKO-PARRISH, J. L., NORTHEY, D. L., RUTLEDGE, J. J. and SIMMONS, L. G. (1994) 'Oocyte maturation, fertilization and embryo development *in vitro* and *in vivo* in the gaur (*Bos gaurus*)', *J. Reprod. Fertil.* **100**, 131–136.

JONES, R. C. (1973) 'Collection, motility and storage of spermatozoa from the African elephant, *Loxodonta africana*', *Nature, Lond.* **243**, 38–39.

KRZYWINSKY, A. (1987) 'Artificial insemination and embryo transfer in deer: applying these methods for propagating endangered species', in Wemmer, C. M. (ed.) *Biology and Management of the Cervidae*, Washington DC and London: Smithsonian Institution Press, pp. 1–577.

KRZYWINSKI, A. and JACZEWSKI, Z. (1978) 'Observations on the artificial breeding of red deer', in Watson, P. F. (ed.) *Artificial Breeding of Non-Domestic Animals, Symp. Zool. Soc. Lond.* No. 43, London: Academic Press, pp. 271–287.

KUMAR, S., SAHNI, K. L. and MOHAN, G. (1993a) 'Effect of different extender formulations on acrosomal maintenance of buffalo spermatozoa frozen in milk, tris and sodium-citrate dilutors', *Ind. J. Anim. Sci.* **63**, 1233–1239.

KUMAR, S., SAHNI, K. L., MOHAN, G. and BENJAMIN, B. R. (1993b) 'Effect of different levels of glycerol on survival rate of freeze thawed spermatozoa of buffalo semen in diluents without yolk', *Ind. J. Anim. Sci.* **63**, 836–838.

LINCOLN, G. A. (1971) 'The seasonal reproductive changes in the red deer stag (*Cervus elaphus)', J. Zool. (Lond.)* **163**, 105–123.

LOOMIS, P. R., AMANN, R. P., SQUIRES, E. L. and PICKETT, B. W. (1983) 'Fertility of unfrozen and frozen stallion spermatozoa extended in EDTA-lactose-egg yolk and packaged in straws', *J. Anim. Sci.* **56**, 687–693.

LOSKUTOFF, N. M., NEMEC, L. A., FOXWORTH, W. B., WOLFE, B. A., RAPHAEL, B. L., HUNTRESS, S. L., JENSEN, J. M., WILLIAMS, B. W., HOWARD, J. G. and KRAEMER, D. C. (1989) 'Effects of different extenders and holding temperatures on viability of spermatozoa from the scimitar-horned oryx (*Oryx dammah)', Theriogenology* **31**, 220.

LOSKUTOFF, N. M., RAPHAEL, B. L., NEMEC, L. A., WOLFE, B. A., HOWARD, J. G. and KRAEMER, D. C. (1990) 'Reproductive anatomy, manipulation of ovarian activity and non-surgical embryo recovery in suni (*Neotragus moschatus zuluensis)', J. Reprod. Fertil.* **88**, 521–532.

MAGYAR, S. J., HODGES, C., SEAGER, S. and KRAEMER, D. C. (1988) 'Successful nonsurgical embryo collection with surgical transfer in captive white-tailed deer', *Theriogenology* **29**, 273.

MAGYAR, S. J., BIEDIGER, T., HODGES, C., KRAEMER, D. C. and SEAGER, S. W. J. (1989) 'A method of artificial insemination in captive white-tailed deer (*Odocoileus virginianus)', Theriogenology* **31**, 1075–1080.

MARSHALL, C. E. (1984) 'Considerations for cryopreservation of semen', *Zoo Biol.* **3**, 343–356.

MERILAN, C. P., READ, B. W. and BOEVERS, W. J. (1982) 'Semen collection procedures for captive wild animals' *Int. Zoo Yearbook* **22**, 241–244.

MONTFORT, S. L., ASHER, G. W., WILDT, D. E., WOOD, T. C., SCHIEWE, M. C., WILLIAMSON, L. R., BUSH, M. and RALL, W. F. (1993) 'Successful intrauterine insemination of Eld's deer (*Cervus eldi thiamin*) with frozen–thawed spermatozoa', *J. Reprod. Fertil.* **99**, 459–465.

MULLEY, R. C., MOORE, N. W. and ENGLISH, A. W. (1988) 'Successful uterine insemination of fallow deer with fresh and frozen semen', *Theriogenology* **29**, 1149–1153.

MYLREA, G. E., EVANS, G. and ENGLISH, A. W. (1991) 'Conception rates in European fallow does (*Dama dama dama*) following intrauterine insemination with frozen–thawed semen from mesopotamian fallow *(Dama dama mesopotamica)* and crossbred *(Dama dama dama x Dama dama mesopotamica)* bucks', *Austr. Vet. J.* **68**, 294–295.

■ CHAPTER 16 ■

MYLREA, G. E., ENGLISH, A. W., MULLEY, R. C. and EVANS, G. (1992) 'Artificial insemination of farmed chital deer', in Brown, R. D. (ed.) *The Biology of Deer*, New York: Springer-Verlag, pp. 334–337.

OKAMURA, N., ONOE, S., SUGITA, Y., PAQUINON, M., DACHEUX, F. and DACHEUX, J.-L. (1991) 'Water insoluble fraction of egg yolk maintains porcine sperm motility by activating adenylate cyclase', *Mol. Reprod. Dev.* **28**, 136–142.

PENFOLD, L. M. and MOORE, H. D. M. (1993) 'A new method for cryopreservation of mouse spermatozoa', *J. Reprod. Fertil.* **99**, 131–134.

PLATZ, C. C., JR., SEAGER, S. W. J. and BUSH, M. (1979) 'Collection and analysis of semen from a black rhinoceros', *J. Am. Vet. Med. Assoc.* **175**, 1002–1004.

PLATZ, C. C., JR., MAGYAR, S., CRIDER, N., DENSMORE, M., WILEY, G., BOWEN, M. J., TEMPLETON, J. W. and KRAMER, D. C. (1982) 'Cryopreservation of electroejaculated and epididymal spermatozoa in white tail deer (*Odocoileus virginianus*)', *Proc. Am. Assoc. Zoo Vets Annual Meeting* 127–129.

PONTBRIAND, D., HOWARD, J. G., SCHIEWE, M. C., STUART, L. D. and WILDT, D. E. (1989) ''Effect of cryoprotective diluent and method of freeze-thawing on survival and acrosomal integrity of ram sperm', *Cryobiology* **26**, 341–354.

POPE, C. E., DRESSER, B. L., KUEHN, G. and GILLESPIE, D. (1988) 'Live birth of a gaur (*Bos gaurus*) calf following nonsurgical embryo transfer to a Holstein (*Bos taurus*) recipient', *Theriogenology* **29**, 289.

POPE, C. E., GELWICKS, E. J., BURTON, M., REECE, R. and DRESSER, B. L. (1991) 'Nonsurgical embryo transfer in the scimitar-horned oryx (*Oryx dammah*). Birth of a live offspring', *Zoo Biology* **10**, 43–51.

POPE, C., LIM, J., MIKOTA, S., COCHRAN, R., CARTER, J., GODKE, R. and DRESSER, B. (1998) 'Transvaginal oocyte retrieval and in vitro maturation fertilization and culture in Bongo antelope (*Tragelaphus euryceros*)', *Biol. Reprod.* **58** (Suppl. 1), 102.

RAPHAEL, B. L., LOSKUTOFF, N. M., HUNTRESS, S. L. and KRAEMER, D. C. (1991) 'Postmortem recovery, invitro maturation, and fertilization of klipspringer (*Oreotragus oreotragus*) ovarian oocytes', *J. Zoo Wildlife Med.* **22**, 115–118.

RAPHAEL, B. L., LOSKUTOFF, N. M., NEMEC, L. A., WOLFE, B. A., HOWARD, J. G. and KRAEMER, D. C. (1988) 'Hormonal characterization and manipulation of the estrous-cycle and nonsurgical embryo recovery in suni antelope', *Theriogenology* **29**, 292.

ROLDAN, E. R. S., CASSINELLO, J., ABAIGAR, T. and GOMENDIO, M. (1998) 'Inbreeding, fluctuating asymmetry and ejaculate quality in an endangered ungulate', *Proc. Roy. Soc. Lond. B* **265**, 243–248.

ROTH, T. L., BUSH, L. M., WILDT, D. E. and WEISS, R. B. (1999) 'Scimitar horned oryx (*Oryx *dammah*) spermatozoa are functionally competent in a heterologous bovine in vitro fertilization system after cryopreservation on dry ice, in a dry shipper, or over liquid nitrogen', *Biol. Reprod.* **60**, 493–498.

Rott, N. N. (1995) 'Organization of genetic cryobanks and use of developmental biology methods for conservation of rare animals. 1. Cryoconservation of sperm of wild animals', *J. Dev. Biol.* **26**, 227–237.

Schiewe, M. C., Bush, M., Phillips, L. G. and Wildt, D. E. (1988) 'Variables influencing the collection and cryopreservation of embryos from nondomestic ungulate species', *in Proceedings of the 11th International Congress on Animal Reproduction and Artificial Insemination (Dublin),* Vol. 1, p. 190.

Schiewe, M. C., Junior, S., Armstrong, D. L., Simmons, L. G., Gross, T. S., Hopkins, S. M. and Wildt, D. E. (1989) 'Post-thaw viability and acrosomal integrity of Gaur *(Bos gaurus)* sperm following comparative cryopreservation', *Proc. Am. Assoc. Zoological Parks Aquaria* 62–65.

Schiewe, M. C., Bush, M., de-Vos, V., Brown, J. L. and Wildt, D. E. (1991) 'Semen characteristics, sperm freezing, and endocrine profiles in free-living wildebeest (*Connochaetes taurinus*) and greater kudu (*Tragelaphus strepsiceros)*', *J. Zoo Wildlife Med.* **22**, 58–72.

Schwarzenberger, F., Mostl, E., Palme, E. and Bamberg, E. (1996) 'Faecal steroid analysis for non-invasive monitoring of reproductive status in farm, wild and zoo animals', *Anim. Reprod. Sci.* **42**, 515–526.

Shaw, H. J., Sainsbury, A. W. and Holt, W. V. (1995) 'Monitoring ovarian function in Scimitar-horned oryx (*Oryx dammah*) by measurement of fecal 20α-progestogen metabolites', *Zoo Biol.* **14**, 239–250.

Sipko, T. P., Rautian, G. S., Udina, I. G. and Strelchenko, N. S. (1997) 'Conservation of genetic material from endangered and economically important ungulate species in establishment of cryobanks', *Physiol. Gen. Biol. Rev.* **13**, 35–98.

Summers, P. M., Shephard, A. M., Hodges, J. K., Kydd, J., Boyle, M. S. and Allen, W. R. (1987) 'Successful transfer of the embryo of Przewalski's horse (*Equus przewalskii*) and Grant's zebra *(E. burchelli)* to domestic mares (*E. caballus)*', *J. Reprod. Fertil.* **80**, 13–20.

Totey, S. M., Singh, G., Taneja, M., Pawshe, C. H. and Talwar, G. P. (1992) '*In vitro* maturation, fertilization and development of follicular oocytes from buffalo *(Bubalus bubalis)*', *J. Reprod. Fertil.* **95**, 597–607.

Waldhalm, S. J., Jacobson, H. A., Dhungel, S. K. and Bearden, H. J. (1989) 'Embryo transfer in the white-tailed deer–a reproductive model for endangered deer species of the world', *Theriogenology* **31**, 437–450.

CHAPTER 16

WATSON, P. F. (1976) 'Electroejaculation, semen characteristics and semen preservation of the brindled gnu', *J. Reprod. Fertil.* **47**, 123–126.

WATSON, P. F. (1978) 'A review of techniques of semen collection in mammals', in Watson P. F. (ed.) *Artificial Breeding of Non-Domestic Animals. Symp. Zool. Soc. Lond., No. 43*, London: Academic Press, pp. 97–126.

WATSON, P. F. (1995) 'Recent developments and concepts in the cryopreservation of spermatozoa and the assessment of their post-thawing function', *Reprod. Fertil. Dev.* **7**, 871–891.

WILDT, D. E., MONTFORT, S. L., DONOGHUE, A. M., JOHNSTON, L. A. and HOWARD, J. G. (1992) 'Embryogenesis in conservation biology–or, how to make an endangered species embryo', *Theriogenology* **37**, 161–184.

ZHAO, X. X., HUANG, Y. M. and CHEN, B. X. (1994) 'Artificial-insemination and pregnancy diagnosis in the bactrian camel (*Camelus bactrianus*)', *J. Arid Environ.* **26**, 61–65.

Genetic Resource Banking in the Equidae

JOYCE M. PARLEVLIET AND BEN COLENBRANDER

Department of Herd Health and Reproduction, University of Utrecht,
PO Box 151, 3508 Utrecht, The Netherlands

Contents

17.1 SPERMATOZOA

17.1.1 Seasonality

In general, horse spermatozoa are frozen during the non-breeding season (fall and winter time), when the ejaculate is of small volume (20–50-ml) and contains a highly concentrated number of spermatozoa, which is preferable for freezing. Also, during the breeding season most stallions are used in an AI programme and no semen is available for freezing. There is no information related to this point for the donkey. Sperm production is seasonal in some zebra species (e.g. *Equus burchelli boehmi*) with a high production during winter; this is in contrast to the sperm production of the domestic horse (Crump and Crump, 1994).

17.1.2 Semen collection

Horse semen is collected two or three times per week using an artificial vagina (AV). Occasionally only the sperm-rich fraction is collected (Tischner, 1979). An ovariectomized mare (treated with oestrogens) or a phantom is used as a mounting object; it is rarely manually collected (McDonnell *et al.*, 1991). Donkey semen is collected using an AV (Henry *et al.*, 1991). Crump and Crump (1994) have also developed a method for collecting semen manually from a zebra stallion and using a donkey jenny as a mount animal.

17.1.3 Semen preparation

Normal semen characteristics during the non-breeding season (mean of two ejaculates, taken 1 hour apart) of the Warmblood stallion (mean±SEM) are: volume 65±26 ml; sperm concentration $0.2±0.2×10^9$/ml; progressive motility 68±9%; live spermatozoa with normal morphology 66±15% (Parlevliet *et al.*, 1994). The ejaculate is filtered through a gauze cloth to remove the gel. The gel-free semen is diluted with an extender (1:1). Each freezing protocol in horses includes a washing procedure to remove the seminal plasma before freezing. Seminal characteristics in donkeys (mean±SEM) are: $15.5±7.7×10^9$ spermatozoa/ejaculate; progressive motility 75.7±9.3%; total number of abnormal spermatozoa 18.4±7.8% (Costa *et al.*, 1992).

17.1.4 Dilution procedure

In general, the semen is diluted 1:1 with an extender before washing (centrifugation). The extenders used are based on egg yolk, skim milk, a combination of egg yolk and skim milk or a citrate/glucose-EDTA medium. The final concentration after centrifugation, removal of supernatant and resuspension of the pellet before packaging varies from 50×10^6/ml (Palmer, 1984) to 400×10^6/ml (Parlevliet *et al.*, 1992; Heitland *et al.*, 1996). Zebra semen is frozen in a concentration 600×10^6 motile spermatozoa per straw in either a lactose–yolk–glycerol extender or a milk–yolk–glycerol extender (Crump *et al.*, 1994).

17.1.5 Diluent

Various extenders are used for washing and freezing. In general, there are three types of extenders: one based on egg yolk (2–5%: Klug *et al.*, 1977; Cochran *et al.*, 1984; Amann and Pickett, 1987; Volkmann and van Zyl, 1987; Samper *et al.*, 1991; Bruin *et al.*, 1994; Crump and Crump *et al.*, 1994) another based on skim milk (Kenney *et al.*, 1975) and the third containing both egg yolk and skim milk (Palmer, 1984; Crump and Crump, 1994, Heitland *et al.*, 1996). Glycerol is used as a cryoprotectant by most researchers, the final concentration in the freezing extender varying from 2.5 to 5%. Another ingredient used in the freezing extender is sodium triethanolamine lauryl sulphate (Equex-Paste®, 0.5%), a surfactant which emulsifies the egg yolk particles of the extender.

Antibiotics like penicillin, polymyxin B sulphate, ticarcillin, gentamycin or amikacin are added to preserve the extender and to suppress the growth of pathogenic organisms.

17.1.6 Packaging

Stallion spermatozoa are frozen in various packaging systems such as 2.5-ml tubes (Samper *et al.*, 1991), 4-ml tubes (Klug *et al.*, 1977) or 0.5-ml straws (Palmer, 1984; Cochran *et al.*, 1984; Amann and Pickett, 1987; Volkmann and Van Zyl, 1987; Bruin *et al.*, 1994, Heitland *et al.*, 1996). Zebra spermatozoa are frozen in 0.5-ml straws (Crump and Crump, 1994). The identification of straws can be achieved by printing on the straws.

17.1.7 Freezing procedure

The starting temperature for freezing is generally 20°C, however Palmer (1984), Cochran *et al.* (1984) and Amann and Pickett (1987) describe procedures where the semen is already cooled down to 5°C before the freezing procedure starts. In one of the studies, the motion characteristics of frozen–thawed semen were better if the semen was cooled down to 5°C prior to freezing (Heitland *et al.*, 1996).

Both slow and fast cooling rates or a combination have been used (Palmer, 1984; Cochran *et al.*, 1984; Amann and Pickett, 1987; Parlevliet *et al.*, 1992). Programmable controlled freezers, which can regulate the liquid nitrogen flow, have been used to freeze the semen at between −120°C and −150°C, after which the straws were stored in a liquid nitrogen container (−196°C).

17.1.8 Thawing procedure

There is a wide variation in thawing procedures: 0.5-ml straws are thawed at 37°C for 30 seconds (Palmer, 1984; Amann and Pickett, 1987; Bruin *et al.*, 1994; Heitland *et al.*, 1996) or at 75°C for 6–7 seconds (Cochran *et al.*, 1984; Volkmann and Van Zyl, *et al.*, 1987; Crump *et al.*,1994) after which the straws were placed in a waterbath of 37°C; 2.5 ml and 4 or 5 ml tubes are thawed at 50–52°C for 40–52 seconds (Klug *et al.*, 1977; Samper *et al.*, 1991; Kenney *et al.*, 1975). Care must be taken not to overheat the sperm contents.

17.1.9 Post-thaw treatment and assessment

Several treatments for the evaluation of the frozen–thawed semen are described. The semen is either diluted with an extender containing egg yolk, skim milk, glucose-EDTA or electrolyte solution in a dilution 1:4 to 1:200 or used after thawing without treatment (Volkmann and Van Zyl, 1987; Samper *et al.*, 1991; Bruin *et al.*, 1994).

The evaluation of the frozen–thawed semen is performed with motility check either by eye or by computerized systems like the Hamilton Thorn Motility Analyzer. Motility varied from 30% to 70%. Crump and Crump (1994) observed better post-thaw motility using the milk–yolk–glycerol extender. Parlevliet *et al.* (1992) also assessed morphology by judging the acrosomal status of spermatozoa using different staining techniques. In that study, the extender based on egg yolk was superior to the extender based on skim milk. Fertility results from inseminations with frozen–thawed sperm have shown 10% lower first cycle pregnancy rates (35%) compared to those with fresh semen (45%). First cycle pregnancy rate may vary from 8 to 61% (Volkmann *et al.*, 1987; Samper *et al.*, 1991; Bruin *et al.*, 1994).

Crump and Crump (1994) reported offspring from insemination with frozen zebra semen.

17.2 OOCYTES

17.2.1 Origin

Oocytes have been collected from ovaries of slaughtered mares (Hinrichs and Kenney, 1987; Okolski *et al.*, 1991; Choi *et al.*, 1994; Grøndahl, 1994) or *in vivo* by puncturing the follicles from ovaries by different techniques. *In vivo* puncture techniques are performed by puncturing through the flank (Palmer *et al.*, 1987) or by copoltomy

(Hinrichs and Kenney, 1987). Those techniques are highly invasive for the donor mare. A more gentle technique to obtain horse oocytes is the transvaginal ultrasound-guided follicle aspiration technique (McKinnon and Squires, 1988; Brück *et al.*, 1992; Cook *et al.*, 1992; Bracher *et al.*, 1993). Most researchers have punctured the dominant follicle, except Bracher *et al.* (1993), who punctured every follicle larger than 10 mm. Follicles have also been flushed with PBS after removing the follicular fluid. Oocytes are collected during the breeding season, but collection (without using gonadotrophins) is also possible during the non-breeding season (Parlevliet, 1997).

Before puncturing, the preovulatory follicle on the ovary of the mare can be stimulated with hCG. The follicular growth can be determined by ultrasound monitoring of the mare's ovaries (Bracher *et al.*, 1993).

17.2.2 *In vitro* maturation

Oocyte culture and maturation have been studied (Palmer *et al.*, 1987; Hinrichs and Kenney, 1987; Parlevliet *et al.*, 1993; Grøndahl, 1994). Several culture protocols have been used, and some are based on the *in vitro* culture of cattle oocytes. The morphologies of oocytes before and after culture are judged by light microscopy or after staining using a DNA-staining dye. The maturation steps from GV stage to metaphase II (MII) take 42–48 hours, which is longer than in cattle.

17.2.3 *In vitro* fertilization

In vitro fertilization in the horse has only once been successful and has resulted in a live foal (Palmer *et al.*, 1987). Choi *et al.* (1994) found only 1–3% of zona-intact oocytes were penetrated by spermatozoa, whereas in zona-free oocytes there is a high penetration rate (83%). Grøndahl (1994) observed a fertilization rate with or without cleavage of 15–26%.

17.2.4 Intracytoplasmic sperm injection (ICSI)

A recently developed technique is the injection of one spermatozoon in the ooplasm of an *in vitro*- or *in vivo*-matured oocyte. In future this may become a valuable method of producing embryos (Squires *et al.*, 1996, Grøndahl *et al.*, 1997, McKinnon *et al.*, 1998).

17.2.5 Freezing procedure

The only reported case of oocyte cryopreservation used oocytes recovered from ovaries obtained at an abattoir and they were frozen without cryoprotectant ($-10°F$). A sperm-binding test was performed and the results were compared with the binding results of spermatozoa to salt-stored oocytes. No significant difference between the binding results using these two techniques were found (Malchowand Arns, 1994). Further freezing methods are not yet available.

17.2.6 Cooling rate and thawing rate/post-thaw handling

No reports on the cryopreservation of horse oocytes were found. Also no studies in this field were found relating to donkey and zebra oocytes.

17.3 EMBRYOS

17.3.1 Origin and recovery

The anatomy of the equine ovary is completely different from that of other species and has a special ovulation area, which prevents multiple ovulations. In the horse, superovulation is not successful because hormonal treatment does not result in multiple preovulatory follicles (Squires et al., 1985). Prior to insemination, mares are pretreated with hCG, GnRH or eCG to ensure ovulation, which is important when embryos are transferred immediately after collection and recipients have to be synchronized.

Embryos have been collected non-surgically by flushing the mare's uterus, using PBS as a flushing medium. The optimal time to collect embryos that are to be frozen is at day 6 after ovulation, when the embryos are in the early blastocyst stage. The recovery rate is lower at day 6 after ovulation than at day 7, but the survival rate after freezing and thawing is higher at that time (Allen et al., 1985; Squires et al., 1985). Day 7–8 embryos selected as those of high quality (grade 1 and 2) have been frozen (see below–Young et al., 1997).

17.3.2 Cryopreservation

In vitro *handling, choice of cryoprotectant, diluent and dilution*

After collection, embryos are generally kept at 32°C; the morphology and the stage of development of the embryo are determined prior to freezing. The embryos are exposed into two steps to a medium containing cryoprotectant (Allen et al., 1985; Squires et al., 1985, Young et al., 1997). Japanese researchers reported the birth of a foal from the first frozen–thawed day-6 embryo in 1982 (Squires et al., 1985). They froze the embryo in modified PBS containing either DMSO or glycerol and the embryo was stored in liquid nitrogen ($-196°C$). In general, glycerol is used as a cryoprotectant to freeze horse embryos (Allen *et al.*, 1985; Squires *et al.*, 1985; Boyle *et al.*, 1985; Slade *et al.*, 1985; Young *et al.*, 1997). PrOH seems to be a very poor cryoprotectant for freezing horse embryos (Bruyas *et al.*, 1997).

Cryopreservation method

The embryos can be packed in either glass ampoules or 0.5-ml straws (Boyle *et al.*, 1985; Squires *et al.*, 1985).

Two main approaches to cryopreservation of embryos have been described. In the first, embryos were placed in Dulbecco's PBS with 5% FCS containing glycerol in two stages of 5% and then 10% (1.38 M), with a 10-minute equilibration time for each step (Allen *et al.*, 1985; Squires *et al.*, 1985). A programmable automatic freezing procedure was used: 4°C/min from room temperature to −6°C, seeded at −6°C and held for 15 minutes, then cooled at 0.3°C/min to either −30°C or −35°C and 0.1°C/min to −33°C or to −38°C, and finally plunged into liquid nitrogen (Boyle *et al.*, 1985; Slade *et al.*, 1985; Squires *et al.*, 1985). Plunging into liquid nitrogen at −33°C appeared to be a better method because the embryos were of better quality after freezing and thawing (Slade *et al.*, 1985; Squires *et al.*, 1985). The cryoprotectant was removed in a 4–6 step dilution procedure (Boyle *et al.*, 1985; Slade *et al.*, 1985; Squires *et al.*, 1985). In these studies, frozen–thawed embryos were cultured for 24 hours at 37°C in Ham's F-10 plus 5% FCS. Morphology and stage of development were determined, progression in development being considered as a measure of viability (Boyle *et al.*, 1985; Slade *et al.*, 1985; Squires *et al.*, 1985).

The second approach employed a step-down equilibration of glycerol in two steps, 4.0 M and then 2.0 M, prior to freezing, with galactose (0.3 M) present in the final step, to freeze day 7–8 embryos (Young *et al.*, 1997). The embryos in 0.25 ml straws were cooled to a seeding temperature of −6°C at a rate of 4°C/min. After 5 minutes of equilibration, the straws were seeded and kept for another 5 minutes at −6°C, and then cooled to −35°C at a rate of 0.5°C/min. The embryos then were held at this temperature for 3 minutes before plunging into liquid nitrogen (Young *et al.*, 1997). For thawing, straws containing frozen embryos were exposed in air for 12 seconds followed by 12 seconds in a 37°C waterbath. The released embryos were washed in PBS supplemented with 10% FCS (v/v) containing 1.5 M glycerol and 0.3 M galactose for 5 minutes. Three more washing steps, each of 5 minutes, with PBS media with 0.3 M galactose containing, respectively 0.8, 0.3 and 0 M glycerol, were performed (Young *et al.*, 1997).

17.3.3 Evaluation

Viability and quality are assessed by judging morphology and stage of development after freezing and thawing or culturing of the frozen–thawed embryo. Generally a graded system ranging from 1 (excellent) to 4 (degenerated or dead) is used to evaluate the quality (morphology and size) of the embryos (McKinnon and Squires, 1988).

17.3.4 Embryo transfer

Recipients with a healthy uterus are synchronized and they should ovulate 1–2 days after the donor if embryos are transferred directly after collection. Embryos are transferred surgically via midline or flank laparotomy (Allen *et al.*, 1985; Davies *et al.*, 1985; Kydd *et al.*, 1985, Young *et al.*, 1997) or non-surgically to the uterine body using a plastic cattle insemination pipette (Bennett and Foster, 1985; Kydd *et al.*, 1985). After transfer, pregnancy is diagnosed and monitored by ultrasound examination of the uterus at several stages during pregnancy, also blood samples can be taken for hormone profiles (Kydd *et al.*, 1985). The pregnancy rate in mares with transferred embryos is 30% higher if fresh embryos are used compared with frozen–thawed embryos (Squires *et al.*, 1985).

Extraspecies pregnancies after embryo transfer have been reported (Allen *et al.*, 1985; Davies *et al.*, 1985; Kydd *et al.*, 1985; Bennett *et al.*, 1985). This may provide a useful tool for conserving endangered species.

REFERENCES

ALLEN, W. R., KYDD, J., BOYLE, M. S. and ANTCZAK, D. F. (1985) 'Between-species transfer of horse and donkey embryos: a valuable research tool', *Equine Vet. J. Suppl.* **3**, 53–62.

AMANN, R. P. and PICKETT, B. W. (1987) 'Principles of cryopreservation and a review of cryopreservation of stallion spermatozoa'. *Equine Vet. Sci.* **7**, No. 3.

BENNETT, S. D. and FOSTER, W. R. (1985) 'Succesful transfer of a zebra embryo to a domestic horse.' *Equine Vet. J. Suppl.* **3**, 78–79.

BOYLE, M. S., ALLEN, W. R., TISCHNER, M. and CZLONIKOWSKA, M. (1985) 'Storage and international transport of horse embryos in liquid nitrogen', *Equine Vet. J. Suppl.* **3**, 36–39.

BRACHER, V., PARLEVLIET, J., FAZELI, A. R., PIETERSE, M. C., VOS, P. L. A. M., DIELEMAN, S. J., TAVERNE, M. A. M. and COLENBRANDER, B. (1993) 'Repeated transvaginal ultrasound-guided follicle aspiration in the mare'. *Embryo Transfer III, Equine Vet. J. Suppl.* **15**, 75–78.

BRÜCK, I., RAUN, K., SYNNESTVEDT, B. and GREVE, T. (1992) 'Follicle aspiration in the mare using a transvaginal ultrasound-guided technique'. *Equine Vet. J.* **24**, 58–59.

BRUIN, G., COLENBRANDER, B., FONTIJNE, P., PARLEVLIET, J. M., CREEMERS, J. J. M. and VAN DER SPEK, M. (1994) 'Management en vruchtbaarheid van het paard.' Poster *Voortplantings Symposium Proefstation voor de Rundvee, Schapen en Paardenhouderij, Lelystad,* September 1994.

BRUYAS, J. F., MARTINS-FERREIRA, C., FIENI, F. and TAINTURIER, D. (1997) 'The effect of propanediol on the morphology of fresh and frozen equine embryos', *Embryotransfer IV, Equine Vet. J. Suppl.* **25**, 80–84.

CHOI, Y. H., OKADA, Y., HOCHI, S., BRAUN, J., SATO, K. and OGURI, N. (1994) '*In vitro* fertilization rate of horse oocytes with partially removed zonae', *Theriogenology* **42**, 795–802.

COCHRAN, J. D., AMANN, R. P., FROMAN, D. P. and PICKETT, B. W. (1984) 'Effects of centrifugation, glycerol level, cooling to 5°C, freezing rate and thawing rate on the post-thaw motility of equine sperm', *Theriogenology* **22**, 25–38.

COOK, N. L., SQUIRES, E. L., RAY, B. S., COOK, V. M. and JASKO, D. J. (1992) 'Transvaginal ultrasonically guided follicular aspiration of equine oocytes: preliminary results'. *J. Equine Vet. Sci.* **12**, 204–207.

COSTA, A. J. S. A., VALE FILHO, V. R., SOUTO, N. B. and RIBEIRO, E. A. (1992) 'Andrologic evaluation, testicular biometrics and semen characteristics of *Equus asinus* of the Pega breed, raised in Brazil', in *Proceedings of the 12th International Congress on Animal Reproduction (the Hague)* Vol. 4, 1701–1703.

CRUMP, J. P. JR. and CRUMP, J. W. (1994) 'Manual semen collection from a Grevy's zebra stallion (*Equus grevyi*), onset of sperm production, semen characteristics, and cryopreservation of semen, with a comparison to the sperm production from a Grant's zebra stallion (*Equus burchelli boehmi*)', *Theriogenology* **41**, 1011–1021.

DAVIES, C. J., ANTCZAK, D. F. and ALLEN, W. R. (1985) 'Reproduction in mules: embryo transfer using sterile recipients', *Equine Vet. J. Suppl.* **3**, 63–72.

GRØNDAHL, C. (1994) 'In vitro production of equine embryos. Fertilization in the equine (Oocyte maturation, fertilization and initial embryonic development in the horse)', PhD thesis, Copenhagen, Denmark, pp. 1–25.

GRØNDAHL, C., HØST HANSEN, T., HOSSAINI, A., HEINZE, I. and GREVE, T. (1997) 'Intracytoplasmatic sperm injection of *in vitro*-matured equine oocytes', *Biol. Reprod.* **57**, 1495–1501.

HEITLAND, A. V., JASKO, D. J., SQUIRES, E. L., GRAHAM, J. K., PICKETT, B. W. and HAMILTON, C. (1996) 'Factors affecting motion characteristics of frozen–thawed stallion spermatozoa', *Equine Vet. J.* **28**, 1, 47–53.

HENRY, M., MCDONNELL, S. M., LODI, L. D. and GASTAL, E. L. (1991) 'Pasture mating behaviour of donkeys (*Equus asinus*) at natural and induced oestrus'. *J. Reprod. Fertil. Suppl.* **44**, 77–86.

HINRICHS, K. and KENNEY, R. M. (1987) 'A colpotomy procedure to increase oocyte recovery rates on aspiration of preovulatory follicles', *Theriogenology* **27**, 237.

KENNEY, R. M., BERGMAN, R. V., COOPER, W. L. and MORSE, G. W. (1975) 'Minimal contamination techniques for breeding mares: technique and preliminary findings', *Proc. 22nd AAEP,* Lexington, Kentucky, pp. 327–336.

KLUG E., GÜNZEL, A. R., MERKT, H. and KRAUSE, D. (1977) 'Untersuchungen von Hengste zum Einsatz in der instrumentellen Samenübertragung mit Tiefgefriersperma', *Deutsche Tierärtzl. Wschr.* **84**, 236–238.

KYDD, J., BOYLE, M. S., ALLEN, W. R., SHEPHARD, A. and SUMMERS, P. M. (1985) 'Transfer of exotic equine embryos to domestic horses and donkeys', *Equine Vet. J. Suppl.* **3**, 80–83.

MCDONNELL, S. M., HENRY, M., and BRISTOL, F. (1991) 'Spontaneous erection and masturbation in equids', *J. Reprod. Fertil.* **44**, 664–665.

MCKINNON, A. O. and SQUIRES, E. L. (1988) 'Morphological assessment of the equine embryo'. *J. Am. Vet. Med. Assoc.* **192**, 406–416.

MCKINNON, A. O., CARNEVALE, E. M., SQUIRES, E. L., VOSS, J. L. and SEIDEL, G. E. (1987) 'Heterogenous and xenogenous fertilization of in-vivo matured equine oocytes.' *Equine Vet. Sci.* **8**, 143–147.

MCKINNON, A. O., LACHAM-KAPLAN, O. and TROUNSON, A. O. (2000) 'Pregnancies produced from fertile and infertile stallions by intracytoplasmatic sperm injection of single frozen–thawed spermatozoa into *in vivo* matured oocytes', *J. Reprod. Fert. Suppl.* **56** (in press).

MALCHOW, N. M. and ARNS, M. J. (1994) 'Comparison of salt-stored and frozen equine oocytes as a bioassay for determining sperm maturation', *Theriogenology* **41**, 245.

OKOLSKI, A., BEZARD, J., MAGISTRINI, M. and PALMER, E. (1991) 'Maturation of oocytes from normal and atretic equine ovarian follicles as affected by steroid concentration.' *J. Reprod. Fertil. Suppl.* **44**, 385–392.

PALMER, E. (1984) 'Factors affecting stallion semen survival and fertility.' *Proceedings of the 10th International Congress on Animal Reproduction and AI (Urbana-Champaign)*, Vol. 3, p. 377.

PALMER, E., DUCHAMPS, G., BEZARD, J., MAGISTRINI, M., KING, W. A., BOUSQUET, D. and BETTERIDGE, K. J. (1987) 'Non-surgical recovery of follicular fluid and oocytes of mares', *J. Reprod. Fertil. Suppl.* **35**, 689–690.

PARLEVLIET, J. M. (1997) 'Clinical aspects of stallion fertility', PhD thesis, Utrecht, the Netherlands, pp. 41–53.

PARLEVLIET, J., MALMGREN, L., BOYLE, M., WÖCKENER, A., BADER, H. and COLENBRANDER, B. (1992) 'Influence of conservation method on the motility and morphology of stallion semen (an international project)'. *Acta Vet. Scand. Suppl.* **88**, 153–162.

PARLEVLIET, J. M., DE LOOS, F. A. M., FAZELI, A. R., BEVERS, M. M., VOS, P. L. A. M., PIETERSE, M., TAVERNE, M. A. M. and COLENBRANDER, B. (1993) 'Transvaginal ultrasound-guided ovum pick up in the horse. Recovery rate and oocyte quality'. *J. Reprod. Fertil. Abs. Ser.* **12**, 40.

PARLEVLIET, J. M., KEMP, B. and COLENBRANDER, B. (1994) 'Reproductive characteristics and semen quality in maiden Dutch Warmblood stallions'. *J. Reprod. Fertil.* **101**, 183–187.

SAMPER J. C., HELLANDER J. C. and CRABO B. G. (1991) 'Relationship between the fertility of fresh and frozen stallion semen and semen quality', *J. Reprod. Fertil. Suppl.* **44**, 107–114.

SLADE, N. P., TAKEDA, T. and SQUIRES, E. L. (1985) 'Cryopreservation of the equine embryo', *Equine Vet. J. Suppl.* **3**, 40.

SQUIRES, E. L., COOK, V. M. and VOSS, J. L. (1985) 'Collection and transfer of equine embryos', Colorado State University, Animal Reproduction Laboratory, Bulletin No. 01.

SQUIRES, E. L., WILSON, J. M., KATO, H. and BLASZEZYK A. (1996) 'A pregnancy after intracytoplasmatic sperm injection into equine oocytes matured in vitro', *Theriogenology* **45**(1), 306.

TISCHNER, M. (1979) 'Evaluation of deep-frozen semen in stallions', *J. Reprod. Fertil. Suppl.* **27**, 53.

VOLKMANN, D. H. and VAN ZYL, D. (1987) 'Fertility of stallion semen frozen in 0.5 ml straws', *J. Reprod. Fertil. Suppl.* **35**, 143–148.

YOUNG, C. A., SQUIRES, E. L., SEIDEL, G. E., KATO, H. and McCUE, P. M. (1997) 'Cryopreservation procedures for Day 7–8 equine embryos.' *Embryo transfer IV. Equine Vet. J. Suppl.* **25**, 98–102.

18

Cryopreservation of Gametes and Embryos of Canidae and Felidae

DENISE A. HEWITT,[1] **GARY C. W. ENGLAND**[1] **AND SYLVIE P. A. BEEKMAN**[2]

[1]Department of Farm Animal and Equine Medicine and Surgery, Royal Veterinary College, Hawshead Lane, North Mimms, Hatfield, Herts AL9 7TA, UK
[2]Department of Herd Health and Reproduction, University of Utrecht, PO Box 151, 3508 Utrecht, The Netherlands

Contents

18.1 CANIDAE (by D.A. Hewitt and G.C.W. England)

18.1.1 Spermatozoa

Successful freezing of dog spermatozoa was first achieved by Rowson (1954). Seager (1969) reported the first pregnancy achieved in a bitch using frozen–thawed semen. The technique of cryopreservation of dog semen has been reviewed by England (1993).

Seasonality

A study by Taha *et al.* (1981) has shown that there is some influence of season upon seminal characteristics of dogs but a more detailed study by Taha and Noakes (1982) failed to confirm this.

Semen collection

Dog semen is ejaculated in three distinct fractions, and it has been demonstrated that diluting the sperm-rich second fraction with the first and third fractions is detrimental to the quality of spermatozoa (England and Allen, 1992). Despite this, Nothling and Volkmann (1992) and Nothling *et al.* (1997) achieved good pregnancy rates when frozen–thawed semen was mixed with autologous third fraction and inseminated into the vagina of the bitch. This effect may, however, have simply been the result of an increased volume of inseminate, and therefore requires further investigation.

Some workers have collected the whole ejaculate using an artificial vagina (Harrop, 1954; Bartlett, 1958; James *et al.*, 1979) but for an accurate assessment of semen quality, Harrop (1955) proposed that separation of the fractions was necessary. To achieve this, semen is collected by digital manipulation of the penis in the presence of an oestrous bitch (Seager and Fletcher, 1972). The three fractions of the ejaculate are collected into separate test tubes via glass funnels and only the sperm-rich second fraction used. Semen can be collected from dogs with poor libido under general anaesthesia by electrical stimulation but a small volume of ejaculate may be obtained, and this may be contaminated with urine (Harrop, 1954; Christiansen and Dougherty, 1955).

Semen preparation

The diluent is generally added directly to the sample (England, 1993). Spermatozoa are diluted to a known concentration prior to freezing in most species. The dilution procedure varies according to the concentrations of constituents used in the extender. The dilution procedure is an important consideration as it may affect the longevity of the sample. To date only a few workers have used standard dilutions in the dog

(Martin, 1963b; Davies, 1982). Yubi (1984) used dilutions between 1:5 and 1:10 for optimal longevity with higher dilutions. Davies (1982) found that although post-thaw motility of frozen–thawed dog spermatozoa was highest when a 1:9 dilution was used rather than a 1:5 or a 1:2 dilution, it produced the poorest post-thaw longevity.

Semen packaging

Seager and Fletcher (1973) suggested that the recovery quality of spermatozoa following freezing was the same in 0.25-ml straws, in 0.5-ml straws and in pellets, but later showed that recovery from pellets was better than that from straws (Seager et al., 1975). Davies (1982) compared the two methods and found neither method to be more favourable. Straw and pellet freezing imply distinctly different freezing rates.

Diluent composition

Initial studies using skim milk-based extenders (Martin, 1963b; Takeishi et al., 1976) were less successful than those adapted from the egg yolk–lactose–glycerol and Tris–egg yolk–glycerol diluents (Davis et al., 1963). More recent studies have attempted to improve diluents and freezing methods by modification of those used in cattle (Davies, 1982; Smith, 1984; Olar, 1984; Yubi, 1984). Concentrations of glycerol in the extender range from 4% to 11% (v/v). In an egg yolk–Tris-based diluent, optimal post-thaw motility was achieved with 3–4% glycerol (Olar, 1984) whereas with an egg yolk–PIPES extender the best results were obtained using 9% glycerol (Smith, 1984). Many studies describe the glycerol concentration of the diluent but not the dilution rate (Yubi, 1984; Farstad and Andersen Berg, 1989) resulting in the final concentration remaining unknown. Glycerol has been shown to have toxic effects at high concentrations, possibly affecting the fertilizing capacity of spermatozoa so the optimal glycerol concentration forms a compromise between protective and toxic effects (Watson, 1979). A study by Hay et al. (1997) showed the presence of glycerol to have a detrimental effect upon the binding of dog spermatozoa to homologous oocytes despite having no effect upon acrosomal integrity.

Martin (1963a) used a Krebs Ringer–phosphate buffer, but this has been reported to have toxic effects on spermatozoa (Watson, 1990). Zwitterionic (dipolar ion) buffers have also been used (Crabo et al., 1972; Graham et al., 1972). Egg yolk has a buffering capacity and so has been incorporated in some extenders. A range of egg yolk concentrations have been described, with a 20% concentration being popular (Andersen, 1972; Davies, 1982; Ferguson et al., 1989; Linde-Forsberg and Forsberg, 1989).

Many studies have used lactose with glycerol and egg yolk or a modified form of this diluent (van Gemert 1970; Andersen 1972,; Seager and Fletcher, 1973; Seager et al., 1975; Seager and Platz, 1977). Tris–citrate buffer was found to be the more appropriate solution for the freezing of dog semen in straws (Yubi, 1984), and a Tris–yolk–citrate buffer has been used by many workers (Foote, 1964b; Gill *et al.*, 1970; Andersen, 1972; Christiansen and Schmidt, 1980; Olar, 1984; Yubi, 1984). Smith (1984) found an improved post-thaw motility of dog spermatozoa using a PIPES buffer compared to BES, TES or Tris.

The mean pH of the dog ejaculate second fraction is 6.27 ± 0.3 (mean$\pm$SD, $n=20$). Wales and White (1958) claimed that maximum motility was maintained in the pH range 7.0–8.5, but optimal post-thaw motility of dog spermatozoa frozen in PIPES buffer was found at pH 7 (Smith, 1984). Dog spermatozoal longevity varies considerably with pH so is an important consideration during cryopreservation.

Cooling procedure

Despite freezing semen in pellets after a 3-hour equilibration time, Olar (1984) suggested that this period was unimportant. Prior to freezing semen in straws, Seager (1969) proposed either a 1-hour cooling and 1-hour equilibration or 2 hours cooling and 2 hours equilibration period. Hay *et al.* (1997) compared spermatozoal parameters after slow (0.5 hours) and quick cooling to 0°C and showed that the fast cooling procedure resulted in poorer acrosomal integrity, motility and oocyte penetration than a fresh and slow cooled group.

Freezing procedure

Early dog semen cryopreservation experiments involved rapid freezing rates that were later replaced by slow controlled freezing rates. Methods used include pellets of semen placed on a solid carbon dioxide (dry ice) block (van Gemert, 1970), samples frozen in ampoules (Foote 1964a; Gill *et al.*, 1970; Seager *et al.*, 1975), straws frozen in liquid nitrogen vapour (Andersen, 1972, 1975; Takeishi *et al.*, 1976; Oettle, 1986; Christiansen, 1984; Smith, 1984), and the use of forced vapour freezers (Olar, 1984; Olar *et al.*, 1989; Yubi, 1984; Yubi *et al.*, 1987).

Foote (1964a) compared several freezing rates, but despite the greater survival of spermatozoa with the slower freezing rate, direct comparisons could not be made as different diluents and glycerol concentrations were used. Olar (1984) discovered that a moderate rate (5°C/min from 5 to −15°C, followed by 20°C/min from −15 to (100°C) was preferable to either a fast rate (75°C/min) or a slow rate (2°C/min from 5°C to −15°C, followed by 10°C/min from −15°C to −100°C). With a different extender, Smith (1984) found optimal post-thaw motility with straws held 8 inches (20.5 cm) above the liquid nitrogen surface compared with $1\frac{1}{2}$ or 4 inches (4 or 10 cm). Freezing rates were said to be 8.3°C/min through the critical temperature range (−10°C to −30°C) but measurements were only performed once on one straw.

The optimal freezing rate for dog spermatozoa in a TEST extender at pH 7.3 with 20% glycerol was −20°C/min through the 5°C to −50°C range; faster and slower rates produced post-thaw results similar to each other but were significantly poorer than the intermediate rate (England, 1993).

Thawing procedure

Dog semen frozen in 0.5-ml straws has been thawed successfully at 75°C (in a waterbath) for 6.5 seconds (Andersen, 1975). Yubi (1984) found that a rapid thawing rate (75°C for 6 seconds) caused a decline in percentage motility and percentage live spermatozoa compared with slower thawing (37°C for 2 minutes). Smith (1984) produced similar results, but Olar (1984) demonstrated that there was a higher post-thaw motility when samples are thawed at 75°C compared with 35°C. Davies (1982) also found higher post-thaw motility following thawing at 70°C compared with 37°C. Since there is a significant interaction between extender composition, freezing rates and thawing rates, it is clear that different thawing rates will suit different freezing regimes. The addition of pentoxifylline during thawing enhanced the motility of frozen–thawed dog spermatozoa (Koutsarova et al., 1997), and may be a tool that can be used routinely with poorer quality spermatozoa known to show poor post-thaw recovery.

Post-thawing treatment and assessment

Martin (1963a) found that post-thaw motility was poor until the spermatozoa were suspended in a glycerol-free medium, but Olar (1984) showed that this was not necessary. Despite the fact that dog spermatozoa may live for a long time in the uterus (Doak et al., 1967) fresh semen does not survive well in the vagina of the bitch (G.C.W. England, unpublished observations). Fertility with frozen–thawed semen is therefore dependent upon establishing a viable population in the uterus (Davies, 1982). Andersen (1972, 1975) noted that insemination of frozen–thawed semen into the uterus was preferable to vaginal insemination, although good pregnancy rates have been achieved following vaginal insemination of pelleted frozen semen (Seager et al., 1975), but not semen frozen in straws (Gill et al., 1970; Olar, 1984). Andersen (1975) achieved acceptable pregnancy rates with transcervical intrauterine insemination and Takeishi et al. (1976) developed an intracervical technique. Endoscopic catheterization of the cervix of the bitch in conjunction with insemination of frozen–thawed semen has achieved excellent pregnancy rates (Wilson, 1993). The deposition of the semen directly into the uterus has been shown to improve pregnancy rates when using frozen semen from approximately 40% to 80% (Andersen, 1980), whereas the vaginal technique which is easier to perform can be used with good quality fresh semen (Linde, 1978). In addition, Linde-Forsberg and Forsberg (1989) showed that an increased number of inseminations improved the pregnancy rate.

A variation in survival of spermatozoa after the freeze–thaw process has been observed between dogs (Davies, 1982), so optimization of freezing conditions may be required on an individual basis. Breed influences have not been observed to date.

The most significant factors include the timing of the insemination in relation to ovulation, the quality of the semen, the number of inseminations performed and the site in which the semen is placed. Monitoring of vaginal smears and peripheral plasma progesterone concentrations provide useful information about the timing of ovulation, and therefore the correct timing for insemination in the bitch °Concannon *et al.*, 1975; Linde and Karlsson, 1984). The vaginal smear technique may be sufficient when used with fresh semen of high quality which has a good survival rate in the female reproductive tract, but the more accurate method of monitoring the cycle using observations of plasma progesterone concentrations should be used with frozen semen due to its reduced survival potential.

Seager *et al.* (1975) proposed insemination of 50 million frozen–thawed spermatozoa to achieve an 85% conception rate. Farstad and Andersen Berg (1989) suggested that a total number of 100×10^6 live spermatozoa is required. Intrauterine insemination requires fewer spermatozoa than intravaginal insemination.

Goodrowe *et al.* (1998) have performed work on the endangered red wolf (*Canis rufus*). Their study showed that ejaculates could be frozen and thawed successfully with a protocol similar to that used in the domestic dog; however, some species-specific modifications need to be developed in future studies because significant acrosomal damage was caused by the procedure.

18.1.2 Oocytes

In the majority of mammalian species, meiotic maturation of the oocyte occurs in the preovulatory follicle. In contrast, canine oocytes are immature at ovulation and complete maturation a few days later in the oviduct (Holst and Phemister, 1971). Oocytes have been flushed from reproductive tracts of the bitch and the blue fox (*Alopex lagopus*) after surgical removal (Phemister *et al.*, 1973; Farstad *et al.*, 1989, 1991, 1993a,b; Tsutsui, 1989; Renton *et al.*, 1991), and have been released from follicles of ovaries at routine ovariohysterectomy. For the domestic bitch, ovaries are repeatedly sliced and antral follicles punctured (Mahi and Yanagimachi, 1976, 1978; Shimazu *et al.*, 1992; Yamada *et al.*, 1992, 1993; Nickson *et al.*, 1993; Hewitt, 1997; Hewitt and England, 1997a,b, 1998b,c, 1999b,c; Hewitt *et al.*, 1998). In the blue fox, ovarian follicles are flushed to obtain oocytes (Hyttel *et al.*, 1990).

Hormonal stimulation

The induction of oestrus followed by successful mating and whelping can be achieved by a variety of hormonal regimes, although success rates vary enormously. Examples include the use of oestrogens with or without subsequent exogenous gonadotrophin administration (Shille *et al.*, 1989), exogenous gonadotrophins alone (Thun *et al.*, 1977; Archbald *et al.*, 1980; England and Allen, 1991), gonadotrophin-releasing hormone agonists (Concannon, 1989; Shille *et al.*, 1984) or prolactin inhibitors (van Haaften *et al.*, 1989; Jeukenne and Verstegen, 1977). Yamada *et al.* (1992) described the induction of follicular development using oestrogens with exogenous gonadotrophins to obtain oocytes for *in vitro* maturation and fertilization. Archbald *et al.* (1980) used PMSG and hCG to induce oestrus and ovulation in bitches, later flushing embryos from the uterus. Pregnancy rates are highest following the induction of oestrus using prolactin inhibitors such as cabergoline.

Oocyte maturation

Ovulation occurs approximately 2 days after the LH surge. Two to three days later, oocytes reach metaphase of the first meiotic division, with metaphase of the second meiotic division completed after a further 2 days when the first polar body is extruded and the oocyte is ready for fertilization. Culture media with added serum or protein have been used for *in vitro* maturation in the bitch (Mahi and Yanagimachi, 1976; Nickson *et al.*, 1993; Yamada *et al.*, 1992, 1993; Hewitt, 1997; Hewitt and England, 1997a, 1998b; Hewitt *et al.*, 1998). In the blue fox, oocytes for *in vitro* fertilization were matured *in vivo* (Farstad *et al.* 1989, 1991, 1993a,b; Hyttel *et al.*, 1990).

Mahi and Yanagimachi (1976) matured 25.4% of immature canine oocytes to metaphase I or II after 72 hours, and with a similar population of oocytes, Hewitt *et al.* (1998) matured 25% to metaphase I or II after 96 hours. No improvement was made by sampling oocytes during oestrus or proestrus (Hewitt and England, 1997a) compared with sampling anoestrus oocytes (Hewitt *et al.*, 1998), although Yamada *et al.* (1992) matured 31.9% of oocytes to metaphase II in 72 hours of culture using preovulatory oocytes from superovulated bitches. Fulton *et al.* (1998a) showed that a large proportion of oocytes from preantral and antral follicles matured to metaphase II with the extrusion of the second polar body. Cinone *et al.* (1992) performed *in vitro* maturation using canine oocytes taken at different stages of the oestrous cycle and showed that a low percentage of canine oocytes could mature *in vitro* in several different culture media. They also found that the stage of the oestrous cycle at the time of oocyte collection had no effect upon subsequent maturation *in vitro*, suggesting that preovulatory development of oocytes did not increase their ability to mature *in vitro*. In contrast, in a study in which oocytes were categorized according to their size, Hewitt and England (1998b) showed that the selection of oocytes that had acquired meiotic competence through adequate intrafollicular growth, was important for *in vitro* maturation. In addition, they showed that oocytes obtained from younger bitches had a greater potential to mature than those collected from older animals.

Oocytes collected from anoestrous vixens, both of the blue (Krogenaes *et al.*, 1993) and silver (Wen *et al.*, 1994) fox produced a low rate of oocyte maturation *in vitro*. Results from more detailed work in the blue fox (Kalab *et al.*, 1997) indicated that these oocytes may require the presence of granulosa cells for successful maturation, involving an FSH-dependent pathway.

Durrant *et al.* (1998) and Bolamba *et al.* (1997, 1998) developed a method for isolation and characterization of canine preantral and antral follicles and showed that nuclear maturation of oocytes could occur when they were cultured within their follicles. Both the size and type of follicle had an effect upon the degree of oocyte maturation. This group also investigated the use of synthetic oviductal fluid (SOF) for follicular culture and showed that supplementing SOF with FCS or BSA had a detrimental effect upon the proportion of oocytes maturing to metaphase I (Bolamba *et al.*, 1997). They also cultured follicles in a mixture of Hams F10 and Dulbecco's modified Eagle's medium and showed that although only a small proportion of oocytes cultured in advanced preantral follicles were able to resume meiosis, they did so more quickly and in larger numbers than oocytes which were cultured in early antral follicles (Bolamba *et al.*, 1998).

A sophisticated method involving grafting of canine ovarian tissue to SCID (immunodeficient) mouse ovaries has been developed for salvaging ovarian tissue from valuable bitches (Metcalfe, 1999). The work performed so far has shown that some follicular recruitment is possible, although no antral follicle formation occurred, but with further work, this technique should be another useful tool for manipulating canine fertility *in vitro*.

In vitro fertilization

Canine spermatozoa can capacitate spontaneously *in vitro* in a defined culture medium (Mahi and Yanagimachi, 1978; Kawakami *et al.*, 1991, 1998a,b; Hewitt and England, 1998a, 1999a). Some immature canine oocytes have been penetrated by homologous spermatozoa (Mahi and Yanagimachi, 1976; Hewitt, DA, Fletcher S and England GCW, unpublished observation). Hay (1996), Hay *et al.* (1994, 1997), Hewitt (1997), Hewitt and England (1997b) and Mayenco-Aguirre and Peres-Cortez (1998) have all used penetration of oocytes *in vitro* as an assay of spermatozoal function in the dog.

In vitro fertilization of IVM oocytes in the bitch has been achieved by several workers, but with poor success rates compared with other species (Mahi and Yanagimachi, 1978; Nickson *et al.*, 1993; Yamada *et al.*, 1992, 1993; Shimazu and Naito,

CHAPTER 18

1996; Hewitt, 1997; Hewitt and England, 1997b). In the blue fox, IVF has only been achieved using *in vivo* matured oocytes (Farstad *et al.*, 1989, 1991, 1993a,b; Hyttel *et al.*, 1990).

The most sophisticated study to date has adopted intracytoplasmic sperm injection (ICSI), a technique currently used successfully for human and other mammalian species. The procedure involves injecting a spermatozoon into the ooplasm of the oocyte, thus in theory maximizing the chance of fertilization. The use of this technique in the bitch was described by Fulton *et al.* (1998b) in a study using oocytes taken from the ovarian tissue of bitches ovariohysterectomized at various stages of the oestrous cycle. Oocytes were matured for 48 hours in a commercially available tissue culture medium supplemented with LH and FSH and those that had matured were detected by the presence of a polar body. A spermatozoon was injected into the ooplasm and after incubation for a further 12 hours, oocytes were fixed and stained to allow the determination of fertilization status. It was found that 8% of oocytes had both male and female pronuclei, and 42% had a female pronucleus and decondensed spermatozoon chromatin. These results are encouraging as the first study of its kind in this species, but further work is needed to achieve the level of success found in the human and other mammals.

Cryopreservation

No significant studies could be found relating to the use of cryoprotectants, freezing or thawing.

18.1.3   Embryos

Origin and recovery

Information about canine embryos has mostly been gained from *in vivo* studies (Holst and Phemister, 1971; Tsutsui, 1975a,b; Renton *et al.*, 1991). Catheterization and flushing of the canine oviduct at surgery is a complex procedure, and early embryos are difficult to retrieve. The process is easier between days 9 and 11, when blastocysts are in the uterus (Concannon, 1986). Embryos have been flushed from the oviduct and uterus of the domestic bitch (Phemister *et al.*, 1973; Farstad and Andersen Berg, 1989; Farstad *et al.*, 1989; Harvey *et al.*, 1989; Renton *et al.*, 1991), blue fox (Farstad *et al.*, 1989, 1991, 1993a; Hyttel *et al.*, 1990) and silver fox (Jalkanen and Lindeberg, 1998) after surgical removal of the reproductive tract. This is only practical during experimental work or salvage of embryos from sick or aged animals. Archbald *et al.* (1980) described a surgical method for flushing embryos from mated bitches following the use of gonadotrophins to induce oestrus and ovulation. Embryo transfer of *in vivo* produced embryos has resulted in the birth of live young in the silver fox, although the success rate was low (Jalkanen and Lindberg, 1998). IVF of *in vivo* matured blue fox oocytes (Farstad *et al.*, 1993b) resulted in the development of embryos.

In vitro handling

Many IVM/IVF fertilization studies in the bitch failed to achieve embryonic development, but Yamada *et al.* (1992) used oocytes from 'superovulated' animals and 2% developed to the eight-cell stage 96 hours after insemination. *In vitro* studies performed in the blue fox have enabled oocytes matured *in vivo* to be inseminated *in vitro* with homologous spermatozoa; despite a low fertilization rate, embryos were produced that went on to cleave *in vitro,* with one surviving to the morula stage (Farstad *et al.* 1993a,b).

Cryopreservation

As with oocytes, no studies have been reported concerning the use of cryoprotectants, cooling conditions or thawing rates for canine embryos.

18.1.4   Conclusion

The work reported here shows that there have been a number of attempts to examine the use of gametes and embryos for assisted reproduction in Canidae, but success so far has been sporadic rather than regular. At present, there are methods of preserving spermatozoa with apparently quite good recovery, but non-surgical AI meets with limited results. This suggests that there are still aspects of cellular function post-cryopreservation which need to be improved. The early success with *in vitro* maturation of oocytes is promising. There is still a need to examine systematically details of oocyte and embryo cryopreservation in order for these techniques to make a contribution towards GRBs in these and related species.

18.2   FELIDAE (by S.P.A. Beekman)

18.2.1   Genera

The genera of Felidae consist of *Felis* (small cats) and *Panthera* (large cats). Two other species, namely, the clouded leopard (*Neofelis nebulosa*) and the cheetah (*Acinonyx jubatus*), cannot be assigned to either genera. The domestic cat (*Felis catus*) is often used as a model for both its small and large relatives. For all cats it is assumed that they are induced ovulators like the domestic cat. Therefore the females are treated to induce ovulation before insemination. However, Schmidt *et al.* (1979) found spontaneous ovulations in several oestrous cycles of three African lionesses (*Panthera leo*).

18.2.2 Spermatozoa

Seasonality

Byers *et al.* (1990) found no seasonal influences on any of the semen traits in captive male Siberian tigers (*Panthera tigris altaica*). These males were housed in Minnesota. Male cats held under controlled illumination are capable of copulating, producing spermic ejaculates and siring litters throughout the year (Goodrowe *et al.*, 1989). Seasonal differences in reproductive traits were recorded in a bimonthly study over 20 months in one male Pallas' cat (*Felis manul*) housed under natural lighting conditions (Swanson *et al.*, 1996a). During the breeding season they found increased sperm concentration, total sperm per ejaculate, sperm quality, sperm motility and serum LH levels compared to the non-breeding season.

Semen collection

The methods reported for semen collection in the domestic cat are the use of an artificial vagina and electroejaculation. Some studies use spermatozoa collected directly from the epididymis (Goodrowe and Hay, 1993) and from the ductus deferens (Bowen, 1977; Hay and Goodrowe, 1993) after castration. Platz *et al.* (1978) found a significant difference in volume, total number of spermatozoa and motility between semen collected with an artificial vagina and that collected by electroejaculation. In several non-domestic felidae species electroejaculation has been used almost exclusively (Dresser *et al.*, 1982; Wildt *et al.*, 1986, 1988; Miller *et al.*, 1990; Andrews *et al.*, 1992; Howard *et al.*, 1992; Donoghue *et al.*, 1993; Roth *et al.*, 1994). The electroejaculation regime used consists of three series of stimuli with increasing voltage. Howard (1993) gives information on procedure, starting voltage and ejaculate characteristics for electro-ejaculation for many non-domestic felids. After fasting for 12–24 hours, all males were anaesthetized with either ketamine hydrochloride (with possibly a low dose of xylazine) or tiletamine-zolazepam administered intramuscularly. Anaesthetics like diazepam, phenothiazine derivatives and inhalation anaesthetics including halothane and isoflurane relax the musculature surrounding the bladder, possibly resulting in urine contamination of the semen. Contamination is particularly problematic in canids, ursids and felids (Howard, 1993).

Semen preparation

Directly after collection, domestic cat semen was diluted with saline and a cryo-protective diluent at room temperature (Platz *et al.*, 1978). This was equilibrated at 5°C for 20 minutes, then more diluent was added and a further 10 minutes allowed for equilibration. Then the diluted semen was frozen in pellets. In total six litters were sired with this semen. The seminal plasma of tiger semen was removed after 8 minutes centrifugation at 300*g* (Donoghue *et al.*, 1992b). Then a cryodiluent was added and this mixture was equilibrated at 5°C for 30 minutes, before freezing in pellets. Semen from Siberian tigers was centrifuged for 10 minutes at approximately 110*g*. The seminal plasma was removed and a cryodiluent added. The mixture was slowly cooled (2.5–3 hours) from room temperature to 4°C and then loaded into 0.25-ml French straws before freezing (Byers *et al.*, 1989). In another study of domestic cat spermatozoa, semen was collected in cryodiluent by maceration of the caudal portion of the epididymides. This semen mixture was diluted 1:1 and cooled over a 2-hour period from room temperature to 5°C. After a further dilution to increase the glycerol percentage and 30 minutes equilibration the semen mixture was loaded into 0.5 ml French straws to be frozen (Hay and Goodrowe, 1993).

As described above, the semen was either diluted directly after collection or after centrifugation. No significant studies on preference of dilution procedure are available.

Semen was frozen in 0.25-ml (Byers *et al.*, 1989) or 0.5-ml French straws (Hay and Goodrowe, 1993), or as pellets (Platz *et al.*, 1978; Donoghue *et al.*, 1992b). Pope *et al.* (1991) report a lower post-thaw motility (11% versus 44%) and percentage of intact acrosomes (26% versus 62%) with pellet storage than with straw storage.

Diluent

Several diluents have been used in freezing experiments. One study in domestic cats (Hay and Goodrowe, 1993) compared the influence of three different diluents on spermatozoal characteristics. All three diluents consisted of 20% egg yolk, penicillin (1000 IU/ml) and streptomycin (1000 µg/ml); this was combined with a solution of Tris, citric acid and fructose (TE); Tris, citric acid and glucose (TC); or lactose °CP). Yolk particles were removed by 30 minutes centrifugation at 2000*g*. For freezing, a diluent with 9% glycerol was added to a final concentration of 3%. No differences between the diluents were found, except for a slightly lower result in progressive status found with diluent CP. Other studies used diluents consisting of 20% egg yolk, glycerol (up to 7.5%, Byers *et al.*, 1989) and lactose (Donoghue *et al.*, 1992b) for tiger spermatozoa.

Freezing and thawing procedure

The diluted semen was cooled to 5°C. For pellet freezing the semen was put on dry ice in small droplets to freeze, plunged into liquid nitrogen and stored in labelled vials in liquid nitrogen (Platz *et al.*, 1978; Donoghue *et al.*, 1992b). Alternatively, diluted semen was transferred to straws, which were held in the vapour phase of liquid nitrogen for a period of 15 minutes, before being plunged into liquid nitrogen (Hay and Goodrowe, 1993). In another investigation using a programmable freezer, straws were cooled from 5°C to −40°C at a speed of 3°C/min, followed by a cooling rate of −20°C/min to −100°C; finally the straws were stored in liquid nitrogen (Byers *et al.*, 1989).

Semen is thawed rapidly to obtain high sperm recovery rate. Pellets were thawed in 0.1 ml saline (Platz *et al.*, 1978) or in 500 μl Ham's F10 (Donoghue *et al.*, 1992b) in a water bath of 37–38°C. Straws were thawed by immersing them in water of 37–38°C for 15–30 seconds (Byers *et al.*, 1989; Hay and Goodrowe, 1993).

Post-thawing treatment

After thawing of pellets, domestic cat semen was centrifuged for 5 minutes at 1500*g*; most supernatant was removed and spermatozoa were inseminated within 20 minutes of thawing and 5 minutes of centrifugation into the anterior vaginal area of ovulation-induced females (Platz *et al.*, 1978). In the case of straws, domestic cat semen was taken from the straws and diluted (Hay and Goodrowe, 1993). The semen was then centrifuged at 400*g* for 15 minutes, the supernatant discarded, and the pellet resuspended in 250 μl modified Kreb's Ringer bicarbonate medium. After washing (400*g*, 5 minutes), the penetration rate of tiger spermatozoa into zona-free hamster oocytes increased considerable (Byers *et al.*, 1989).

One study proved the fertility of previously frozen semen with several litters born after AI (Platz *et al.*, 1978). Goodrowe (1992) suggests high acrosomal damage as a result of freezing. Post-thaw pregnancy rates of only about 10% were achieved.

18.2.3 Oocytes

Source of oocytes

For *in vitro* fertilization, Bowen (1977) used oocytes collected through flushing the oviducts after superovulation treatment and ovariohysterectomy of female domestic cats. Oocyte collection by laparoscopic aspiration of follicles has been described by Goodrowe *et al.* (1988b). This technique has been commonly used as a source for oocytes in domestic cats (Johnston *et al.*, 1991b; Donoghue *et al.*, 1992a), puma (*Felis concolor*) (Miller *et al.*, 1990) and tiger (Donoghue *et al.*, 1992b). Oocytes have been collected from the Indian desert cat (*Felis silvestris ornata*), jungle cat (*Felis chaus*), fishing cat (*Felis viverrinus*) and black-footed cat (*Felis nigripes*) by laparotomy and follicle aspiration, after FSH and hCG treatment (Pope *et al.*, 1993). Other sources of oocytes have been from ovaries after ovariectomy (Johnston *et al.*, 1991a; Byers *et al.*,

1992) or after the death of an animal (Johnston *et al.*, 1991a; Goodrowe, 1992). These last two sources will mainly produce immature oocytes, thus *in vitro* maturation is essential.

Immature oocytes recovered from ovaries kept at 4°C for up to 72 hours still reached nuclear maturation. Domestic cat oocytes kept in the ovaries for 24 hours at 4°C did produce blastocysts, but not after storage for 48 hours (Wolfe and Wildt, 1996). However, storage of ovaries in cold saline (4°C) for up to 48 hours did not seem to increase atresia of follicle–oocyte complexes (Wood *et al.* 1997). In granulosa cells, DNA degradation had already begun at 12 hours cold storage, while at 24 hours the results were similar to the results after DNAase treatment (Jewgenow *et al.*, 1997). Oocytes from tiger, lion, leopard, puma, serval, Geoffroy's cat and leopard cat ovaries kept at 4°C for up to 36 hours were successfully fertilized *in vitro* with either homologous or heterologous semen after *in vitro* maturation (Johnston *et al.*, 1991a).

Female domestic cats were superovulated with repeated subcutaneous injections of FSH 24 hours apart, followed by one or two intramuscular injections of hCG (Dresser *et al.*, 1987; Pope *et al.*, 1993). Stimulation of ovarian activity and final maturation followed by ovulation or aspiration has also been achieved with a single intramuscular injection of eCG, followed after 3–4 days with an intramuscular injection of hCG (Niwa *et al.*, 1985). This combination was used to stimulate ovarian activity and ovulation in the domestic cat (Niwa *et al.*, 1985; Johnston *et al.*, 1991b; Donoghue *et al.*, 1992a), puma (Miller *et al.*, 1990; Barone *et al.*, 1994), tiger (Donoghue *et al.*, 1990), ocelot (*Felis pardalis*) (Swanson *et al.*, 1996b), clouded leopard (Howard *et al.*, 1996), caracal (*Felis caracal*) and cheetah (Goodrowe *et al.*, 1991).

In vitro maturation and culture

In vivo matured oocytes have been collected after treatment with eCG and hCG (Niwa *et al.*, 1985; Pope *et al.*, 1993). Immature domestic cat oocytes have been matured successfully *in vitro* in Eagle's Minimum Essential Medium (MEM) with added proteins and gonadotrophins at 38°C under 5% CO_2 (Johnston *et al.*, 1989; 1991a; 1993; Wood *et al.*, 1995; Wolfe and Wildt, 1996) generally for 48–52 hours. Up to 62.5% of immature oocytes recovered per donor of thirteen non-domestic felid species were successfully matured in Eagle's MEM with bovine serum albumin (BSA), ovine FSH and ovine LH for 48 hours at 38°C under 5% CO_2, 5% O_2 and 90% N_2 (Johnston *et al.*, 1991a).

After maturation, oocytes were co-cultured with spermatozoa for 12–18 hours and generally evaluated for cleavage around 30 hours post-insemination (Goodrowe *et al.*, 1988b; Donoghue *et al.*, 1990, 1992a, Miller *et al.*, 1990; Johnston *et al.*, 1991a; Wood *et al.*, 1995; Wolfe and Wildt, 1996). One third of *in vitro* matured puma oocytes were fertilized, compared with half of the *in vivo* matured oocytes (Miller *et al.*, 1990). In 11

CHAPTER 18

of 16 donors, *in vivo* matured tiger oocytes achieved a cleavage rate well over 60% (Donoghue *et al.*, 1990). Salvaged oocytes from healthy donors of different felid species achieved good fertilization rates (33–100%) after *in vitro* maturation (Johnston *et al.*, 1991a). Niwa *et al.* (1985) reported that the male and female pronuclei were first observed in domestic cat oocytes 4 hours after insemination.

Cryopreservation

In a toxicity study, preantral follicles of cat ovaries were exposed to DMSO, glycerol, PrOH and EG (Jewgenow *et al.*, 1998). Follicles exposed to DMSO and EG showed similar percentages of intact oocytes and granulosa cells at all times. Nineteen per cent of the follicles survived cryopreservation using DMSO or EG, while cell activity was sustained for one week in 10% of the follicles.

The cryoprotectant was introduced to a suspension of follicles after a 10–minute incubation in ice water. An equal volume of cryoprotectant was added, resulting in a final concentration of cryoprotectant of 1.5 mol/l with 10% FCS and the mixture was equilibrated for 15 minutes at 0°C. Then the mixture was loaded into 0.25 ml plastic straws. The straws were cooled 0.5°C per minute from 0°C to −7°C. After seeding, at −7°C the straws were cooled further at 0.5°C per minute to −70°C and then plunged into liquid nitrogen. The straws were thawed rapidly in a 37°C waterbath for 1 minute. The follicle suspension was flushed from the straw with 200 μl HEPES-buffered MEM (HMEM). After a 5-minute incubation, the cryoprotectant was removed by adding 400 μl HMEM per two straws. This was incubated for 5 minutes and centrifuged at 300g for 5 minutes. The follicles were then washed with 1 ml HMEM and resuspended in 100 μl culture medium (Jewgenow *et al.*, 1998).

From a single cat ovary approximately 1500 preantral follicles can be recovered, 10% of these remain structurally intact and metabolically active after freeze–thawing (Jewgenow *et al.*, 1998). Thus, approximately 150 preantral follicles with a viable germ cell can be rescued from a cat ovary stored at 4°C for less than 12 hours after excision. If results in other felids are similar the development of oocyte banks can be a serious tool for helping retain genetic diversity in rare species.

18.2.4 Embryos

Origin and recovery

In vivo fertilization

The first embryos from domestic cats were surgically recovered and transferred successfully in 1978 (Kraemer *et al.*, 1979). Dresser *et al.* (1987) compared different superovulation treatments in the domestic cat. The best results were obtained with five daily injections of 0.75 mg FSH, followed by an injection of 0.25 mg FSH on day 6 and two injections of 375 IU of hCG 24 hours apart, starting on day 6. Using laparotomy in domestic cats under full anaesthesia, Goodrowe *et al.* (1988a) collected embryos in supplemented Ham's F-10. Embryo quality was significantly better in females displaying natural oestrus than in females with induced oestrus (Goodrowe *et al.*, 1988a).

In vitro fertilization

Fertilization rates of laparoscopically aspirated oocytes in the domestic cat varied with treatment and trial, from 33.6–65.0% (Donoghue *et al.*, 1992a) to 67.3–85.2% (Johnston *et al.*, 1991b). In the puma, a fertilization rate of 43.5% was obtained (Miller *et al.*, 1990) and for the tiger around 70% of the oocytes were cleaved, for both fresh and frozen–thawed semen. After IVF of aspirated oocytes, embryos were obtained from the Indian desert cat, jungle cat and fishing cat (Pope *et al.*, 1993). Embryos resulting from intracytoplasmic sperm injection were obtained from domestic cats and a jaguarundi (*Herpailurus yaguarondi*) (Pope *et al.*, 1998).

In vitro handling

Embryos produced *in vitro* were monitored for quality during 7 days of culture; after 120 hours over 50% of the embryos had developed into early blastocysts (Johnston *et al.*, 1991b). Surgically collected embryos were washed three times (Roth *et al.*, 1994), transferred into fresh medium, evaluated and classified by developmental stage under stereo inverted microscopes (Dresser *et al.*, 1987, 1988; Goodrowe *et al.*, 1988a). The media were supplemented Ham's F10 containing 5% FCS (Goodrowe *et al.*, 1988a; Rothe *et al.*, 1994) or Dulbecco's PBS supplemented with 15% NCS (Dresser *et al.*, 1987, 1988). Developmental rates of *in vitro*- and *in vivo*-produced embryos were compared during 10 days of culture, and more than 60% of all embryos reached morula stage. However, only *in vivo*-produced embryos underwent compaction and developed into blastocysts (Roth *et al.*, 1994).

Cryoprotection

Domestic cat embryos produced *in vitro* were serially exposed to 0.45 M, 0.90 M and 1.35 M glycerol in Dulbecco's PBS with NCS and allowed to equilibrate for 8, 8 and 20–40 minutes, respectively (Dresser *et al.*, 1988). *In vitro*-produced two- to four-cell embryos were incubated in 1.4 M PrOH in HEPES-buffered Tyrode's solution (HeTy) at room temperature, then incubated in PrOH and sucrose in HeTy, before loading into straws (Pope *et al.*, 1993).

Two- to four-cell domestic cat embryos derived from *in vitro* fertilization were cooled from room temperature to −6°C at 2°C/minute, seeded and held for 15 minutes and then cooled to (30°C at 0.3°C/minute. At −30°C the straws were plunged into liquid nitrogen. Embryos at morula or blastocyst stage were frozen by conventional embryo-freezing methods used in the domestic cattle industry (Dresser *et al.*, 1988). They were seeded at −6°C and incubated for 6 minutes. From −6°C to −32°C the straws were cooled at 0.5°C/minute, held for 15 minutes and further cooled to −34°C. After 30 minutes equilibration the straws were stored in liquid nitrogen (Dresser *et al.*, 1988).

Straws with *in vitro*-produced embryos at two- to four-cell stage were thawed in air for 5 seconds, followed by 10 seconds at 37°C (Pope *et al.*, 1993). *In vivo*-produced embryos were thawed in waterbaths at either 28°C or 37°C for 10 seconds (Dresser *et al.*, 1988). The cryoprotectants were stepwise removed in four to six 5-minute rinses from the *in vitro*-produced embryos (Pope *et al.*, 1993). From the *in vivo*-produced embryos, glycerol was removed in a single step (Dresser *et al.*, 1988). After removal of the cryoprotectant, the embryos were cultured at 37°C in 5% CO_2 and 98% humidity (Dresser *et al.*, 1988).

Post-thaw, *in vitro*-produced two- to four-cell embryos were cultured for 144 hours and classified according to developmental stage. Development into morulas or blastocysts was obtained for 65% of both frozen–thawed and control embryos (Pope *et al.*, 1993). frozen–thawed embryos cultured up to 72 hours appeared dormant for the first 24 hours (Dresser *et al.*, 1988). Transfer of thawed embryos after 18 hours of culture resulted in five pregnancies (Dresser *et al.*, 1988).

18.2.5 Conclusion

In summary, in the domestic cat, young have been born from previously frozen spermatozoa (Platz *et al.*, 1978) and embryos (Dresser *et al.*, 1988). Furthermore, Jewgenow *et al.* (1998) showed that preantral follicles can survive freezing and thawing. Once preantral follicles can be matured and fertilized *in vitro* and all these techniques are adapted for other felids, banks will be extremely useful in the preservation of these species.

REFERENCES

ANDERSEN, A. C. (1980) 'Artificial insemination and storage of canine semen', in Morrow D. A. (ed.) *Current Therapy in Theriogenology*, Philadelphia: W.B. Saunders, pp. 661–665.

ANDERSEN, K. (1972) 'Fertility of frozen dog semen', *Acta Vet. Scand.* **13**, 128–134.

ANDERSEN, K. (1975) 'Insemination with frozen dog semen based on a new insemination technique', *Zuchthygiene* **10**, 1–4.

ANDREWS, J. C., HOWARD, J. G., BAVISTER and WILDT, D. E. (1992) 'Sperm capacitation in the domestic cat (*Felis catus*) and leopard cat (*Felis bengalensis*) as studied with a salt-stored zona pellucida penetration assay', *Mol. Reprod. Dev.* **31**, 200–207.

ARCHBALD, L. F., BAKER, B. A., CLOONEY, L. L. and GODKE, R. A. (1980) 'A surgical method for collecting canine embryos after induction of oestrus and ovulation with exogenous gonadotrophins', *Vet. Med. Small Anim. Clinician February*, 228–238.

BARONE, M. A., WILDT, D. E., BYERS, A. P., ROELKE, M. E., GLASS, C. M. and HOWARD, J. G. (1994) 'Gonadotrophin dose and timing of anaesthesia for laparoscopic artificial insemination in the puma (*Felis concolor*)', *J. Reprod. Fertil.* **101**, 103–108.

BARTLETT, D. J. (1958) 'Biochemical characteristics of dog semen', *Nature, Lond.* **182**, 1605–1606.

BOLAMBA, D., BORDEN-RUSS, K. D. and DURRANT, B. S. (1997) '*In vitro* maturation of dog oocytes derived from advanced preantral follicles in synthetic oviduct fluid: bovine serum albumin and fetal bovine serum are not essentials', *Biol. Reprod.* **56** (Suppl. 1), 96.

BOLAMBA, D., BORDEN-RUSS, K. D. and DURRANT, B. S. (1998) '*In vitro* maturation of domestic dog oocytes cultured in advanced preantral and early antral follicles', *Theriogenology* **49**, 933–942.

BOWEN, R. A. (1977) 'Fertilization *in vitro* of feline ova by spermatozoa from the ductus deferens', *Biol. Reprod.* **17**, 144–147.

BYERS, A. P., HUNTER, A. G., SEAL, U. S., BINCZIK, G. A., GRAHAM, E. F., REINDL, N. J. and TILSON, R. L. (1989) '*In-vitro* induction of capacitation of fresh and frozen spermatozoa of the siberian tiger (*Panthera tigris*)', *J. Reprod. Fertil.* **86**, 599–607.

BYERS, A. P., HUNTER, A. G., SEAL, U. S., GRAHAM, E. F. and TILSON, R. L. (1990) 'Effect of season on seminal traits and serum hormone concentrations in captive male Siberian tigers (*Panthera tigris*)', *J. Reprod. Fertil.* **90**, 119–125.

BYERS, A. P., BARONE, M. A., DONOGHUE, A. M. and WILDT, D. E. (1992) 'Mature domestic cat oocyte does not express a cortical granule-free domain', *Biol. Reprod.* **47**, 709–715.

CHRISTIANSEN, I. J. (1984) *Reproduction in the Dog and Cat,* London: Baillière Tindall, pp. 115–123.

CHRISTIENSEN, G. C. and DOUGHERTY, R. W. (1955) 'A simplified apparatus for obtaining semen from dogs by electrical stimulation', *J. Am. Vet. Assoc.* **127**, 50–52.

CHRISTIANSEN, I. J. and SCHMIDT, M. (1980) 'Freezing of dog semen', *Institute for Sterilitetesforskning, Kongelige Veterinae-og Landbohojskole* **23**, 67–74.

CINONE, M., GHNEIM, A., CAIRA, M., DELL'AQUILA, M. E. and MINOIA, P. (1992) 'Collection and maturation of oocytes in the bitch', in *Proceedings of the 12th International Congress of Animal Reproduction (The Hague)*, Vol. 4, pp. 1767–1769.

CONCANNON, P. W. (1986) 'Canine physiology of reproduction', in Burke, T.J. (ed.) *Small Animal Reproduction and Fertility. A Clinical Approach to Diagnosis and Treatment*, Philadelphia: Lea and Febiger, pp. 23–77.

CONCANNON, P. W. (1989) 'Induction of fertile oestrus in anoestrous dogs by constant infusion of GnRH agonist', *J. Reprod. Fertil. Suppl.* **39**, 149–160.

CONCANNON, P. W., HANSEL, W. and VISEK, W. J. (1975) 'The ovarian cycle of the bitch: Plasma oestrogen, LH and progesterone', *Biol. Reprod.* **13**, 112–121.

CRABO, B. G., BROWN, K. L. and GRAHAM, E. F. (1972) 'Effect of some buffers on storage and freezing of boar spermatozoa', *J. Anim. Sci.* **35**, 377–382.

DAVIES, P. R. (1982) 'A study of spermatogenesis, rates of sperm production, and methods of preserving the semen of dogs', PhD thesis, University of Sydney, Australia.

DAVIS, I. S., BRATTON, R. W. and FOOTE, R. H. (1963) 'Liveability of bovine spermatozoa at 5°, −25° and −85°C in tris-buffered and citrate buffered yolk-glycerol extenders', *J. Dairy Sci.* **46**, 333–336.

DOAK, R. L., HALL, A. and DALE, H. E. (1967) 'Longevity of spermatozoa in the reproductive tract of the bitch', *J. Reprod. Fertil.* **13**, 51–58.

DONOGHUE, A. M., JOHNSTON, L. A., SEAL., U. S., ARMSTRONG, D. L., TILSON, R. L., WOLF, P., PETRINI, K., SIMMONS, L. G., GROSS, T. and WILDT, D. E. (1990) '*In vitro* fertilization and embryo development *in vitro* and *in vivo* in the tiger (*Panthera tigris*)', *Biol. Reprod.* **43**, 733–744.

DONOGHUE, A. M., JOHNSTON, L. A., MUNSON, L., BROWN, J. L. and WILDT, D. E. (1992a) 'Influence of gonadotropin treatment interval on follicular maturation, *in vitro* fertilization, circulating steroid concentrations, and subsequent luteal function in the domestic cat', *Biol. Reprod.* **46**, 972–980.

DONOGHUE, A. M., JOHNSTON, L. A., SEAL., U. S., ARMSTRONG, D. L., SIMMONS, L. G., GROSS, T., TILSON, R. L. and WILDT, D. E. (1992b) 'Ability of thawed tiger (*Panthera tigris*) spermatozoa to fertilize conspecific eggs and bind and penetrate domestic cat eggs *in vitro*', *J. Reprod. Fertil.* **96**, 555–564.

DONOGHUE, A. M., JOHNSTON, L. A., ARMSTRONG, D. L., SIMMONS, L. G. and WILDT, D. E. (1993) 'Birth of a Siberian tiger cub (*Panthera tigris altaica*) following laparoscopic intrauterine artificial insemination', *J. Zoo Wildlife Med.* **24**, 185–189.

DRESSER, B. L., KRAMER, L., REECE, B., and RUSSEL, P. T. (1982) 'Induction of ovulation and successful artificial insemination in a persian leopard (*Panthera pardus saxicolor*)', *Zoo Biol.* **1**, 55–57.

DRESSER, B. L., SEHLHORST, C. S., WACHS, K. B., KELLER, G. L., GELWICKS, E. J. and TURNER, J. L. (1987) 'Hormonal stimulation and embryo collection in the domestic cat (*Felis catus*)', *Theriogenology* **28**, 915–927.

DRESSER, B. L., GELWICKS, E. J., WACHS, K. B. and KELLER, G. L. (1988) 'First successful transfer of cryopreserved feline (*Felis catus*) embryos resulting in live offspring', *J. Exp. Zool.* **246**, 180–186.

DURRANT, B. S., PRATT, N. C., RUSS, K. D. and BOLAMBA, D. (1998) 'Isolation and characterisation of canine advanced preantral and early antral follicles', *Theriogenology* **49**, 917–932.

ENGLAND, G. C. W. (1993) 'Cryopreservation of dog semen: a review', *J. Reprod. Fertil. Suppl.* **47**, 243–255.

ENGLAND, G. C. W. and ALLEN, W. E. (1991) 'Repeatability of events during spontaneous and gonadotrophin-induced oestrus in bitches', *J. Reprod. Fertil.* **93**, 443– 448.

ENGLAND. G. C. W. and ALLEN, W. E. (1992) 'Factors affecting the viability of canine spermatozoa. II. Effects of seminal plasma and blood', *Theriogenology* **37**, 373–381.

FARSTAD, W. and ANDERSEN BERG, K. (1989) 'Factors influencing the success rate of artificial insemination with frozen semen in the dog', *J. Reprod. Fertil. Suppl.* **39**, 289–292.

FARSTAD, W., MONDAIN-MONVAL, M., HYTTEL, P., SMITH, A. J. and MARKENG, D. (1989) 'Periovulatory endocrinology and oocyte maturation in unmated mature blue fox vixens', *Acta Vet. Scand.* **30**, 313–319.

FARSTAD, W., HYTTEL, P., MONDAIN-MONVAL, M. and SMITH, A. J. (1991) 'Oocyte maturation and fertilization in the blue fox', *Assisted Reprod. Technol. Androl.* **11**, 132–133.

FARSTAD, W., HYTTEL, P., GRONDAHL, C., MONDAIN-MONVAL, M. and SMITH, A. J. (1993a) 'Fertilization and early embryonic development in the blue fox (*Alopex lagopus*)', *Mol. Reprod. Dev.* **36**, 331–337.

FARSTAD, W., HYTTEL, P., GRONDAHL, C., KROGENAES, A., MONDAIN-MONVAL, M. and HAFNE, A. L. (1993b) 'Fertilization *in vitro* of oocytes matured *in vivo* in the blue fox (*Alopex lagopus*)', *J. Reprod. Fertil. Suppl.* **47**, 219–226.

FERGUSON, J. M., RENTON, J. P., FARSTAD, J. P. and DOUGLAS, T. A. (1989) 'Insemination of beagle bitches with frozen semen', *J. Reprod. Fertil. Suppl.* **39**, 293–298.

FOOTE, R. H. (1964a) 'Extenders for freezing dog semen', *Am. J. Vet. Res.* **25**, 37–39.

FOOTE, R. H. (1964b) 'The effects of electrolytes, sugars, glycerol and catalase on survival of dog sperm in buffered yolk mediums', *J. Vet. Res.* **25**, 32–36.

FULTON, R. M., DURRANT, B. S., KESKINTEPE, L., BRANDON, C. and FAYRER-HOSKEN, R. A. (1998a) 'Assisted reproductive techniques for the treatment of canine infertility', *Soc. Theriogenol. Newslett.* **21** (2), 7.

FULTON, R. M., KESKINTEPE, L., DURRANT, B. S. and FAYRER-HOSKEN, R. A. (1998b) 'Intracyto-plasmic sperm injection (ICSI) for the treatment of canine infertility', *Theriogenology* **48**, 366.

GILL, H. P., KAUFMAN, C. F., FOOTE, R. H. and KIRK, R. W. (1970) 'Artificial insemination of beagle bitches with freshly collected, liquid-stored and frozen – stored semen', *Am. J. Vet. Res.* **31**, 1807–1813.

GOODROWE, K. L. (1992) 'Feline reproduction and artificial breeding technologies', *Anim. Reprod. Sci.* **28**, 389–397.

GOODROWE, K. L. and HAY, M. (1993) 'Characteristics and zona binding ability of fresh and cooled domestic cat epididymal spermatozoa', *Theriogenology* **40**, 967–975.

GOODROWE, K. L. HOWARD, J. G. and WILDT, D. E. (1988a) 'Comparison of embryo recovery, embryo quality, oestradiol-17β and progesterone profiles in domestic cats (*Felis catus*) at natural or induced oestrus', *J. Reprod. Fertil.* **82**, 553–561.

GOODROWE, K. L., WALL, R. J., O'BRIEN, S. J., SCHMIDT, P. M. and WILDT, D. E. (1988b) 'Developmental competence of domestic cat follicular oocytes after fertilization *in vitro*', *Biol. Reprod.* **39**, 355–372.

GOODROWE, K. L., HOWARD, J. G., SCHMIDT, P. M. and WILDT, D. E. (1989) 'Reproductive biology of the domestic cat with special reference to endocrinology, sperm function and *in vitro* fertilization', *J. Reprod. Fertil. Suppl.* **39**, 73–90.

GOODROWE, K. L., CRAWSHAW, G. J. and MEHREN, K. G. (1991) 'Stimulation of ovarian activity and oocyte recovery in the caracal (*Felis caracal*) and the cheetah (*Acinonyx jubatus*)', *J. Zoo Wildlife Med.* **22**, 42–48.

GOODROWE, K. L, HAY, M. A., PLATZ, C. C., BEHRNS, S. K., JONES, M. H. and WADDELL, W. T. (1998) 'Characteristics of fresh and frozen–thawed red wolf (*Canis rufus*) spermatozoa', *Anim. Reprod. Sci.* **53**, 299–308.

GRAHAM, E. F., CRABO, B. G. and BROWN, K. I. (1972) 'Effect of some zwitter ion buffers on storage of spermatozoa. I. Bull', *J. Dairy Sci.* **55**, 1–7.

HARROP, A. E. (1954) 'Artificial insemination of a bitch with preserved semen', *Br. Vet. J.* **110**, 424–425.

HARROP, A. E. (1955) ' Some observations on canine semen', *Vet. Rec.* **67**, 494–498.

HARVEY, M. J., BOYD, J. S., FERGUSON, J. M. and RENTON, J. P. (1989) 'Stages of ovum maturation and early embryonic development in the bitch', *J. Reprod. Fertil. Abstract Series 3,* **34**, No. 58.

HAY, M. A. (1996) 'Canine gametes–Evaluation of oocyte maturation and penetrating potential of spermatozoa pre-freeze and post-thaw', PhD thesis, University of Guelph, pp. 49–50.

HAY, M. A. and GOODROWE, K. L. (1993) 'Comparative cryopreservation and capacitation of spermatozoa from epididymides and vasa deferentia of the domestic cat', *J. Reprod. Fertil. Suppl.* **47**, 297–305.

HAY, M. A., KING, W. A., GARTLEY, C. J. and GOODROWE, K. L. (1994) 'Influence of spermatozoa on *in vitro* nuclear maturation of canine ova', *Biol. Reprod.* **50** (Suppl. 1), 145.

HAY, M. A., KING, W. A., GARTLEY, C. J., LEIBO, S. P. and GOODROWE, K. L. (1997) 'Effects of cooling, freezing and glycerol on penetration of oocytes by spermatozoa in dogs', *J. Reprod. Fertil. Suppl.* **51**, 99–108.

HEWITT, D. A. (1997) 'Oocyte maturation and fertilization in the bitch: the use of *in vitro* culture', PhD thesis, University of London.

HEWITT, D. A. and ENGLAND, G. C. W. (1997a) 'Effect of pre-ovulatory endocrine events upon maturation of oocytes of the domestic bitch', *J. Reprod. Fertil. Suppl.* **51**, 83–91.

HEWITT, D. A. and ENGLAND, G. C. W. (1997b) 'The canine oocyte penetration assay; Its use as an indicator of dog spermatozoal performance *in vitro*', *Anim. Reprod. Sci.* **50**, 123–139.

HEWITT, D. A. and ENGLAND, G. C. W. (1998a) 'An investigation of capacitation and the acrosome reaction in dog spermatozoa using a dual fluorescent staining technique', *Anim. Reprod. Sci.* **51**, 321–332.

HEWITT, D. A. and ENGLAND, G. C. W. (1998b) 'Incidence of oocyte nuclear maturation within the ovarian follicle of the bitch', *Vet. Rec.* **143**, 590–591.

HEWITT, D. A. and ENGLAND, G. C. W. (1998c) 'The effect of oocyte size and bitch age upon oocyte nuclear maturation', *Theriogenology* **49**, 957–966.

HEWITT, D. A. and ENGLAND, G. C. W. (1999a) 'Culture conditions required to induce capacitation and the acrosome reaction of canine sperm *in vitro*', *Vet. Rec.* **144**, 22–23.

HEWITT, D. A. and ENGLAND, G. C. W. (1999b) 'Influence of gonadotrophin supplementation upon *in vitro* maturation of domestic bitch oocytes', *Vet. Rec.* **144**, 237–239.

HEWITT, D. A. and ENGLAND, G. C. W. (1999c) 'Synthetic oviductal fluid and oviductal cell coculture for canine oocyte maturation *in vitro*', *Anim. Reprod. Sci.* **55**, 63–75.

HEWITT, D. A., WATSON, P. F. and ENGLAND, G. C. W. (1998) 'Nuclear staining and culture requirements for *in vitro* maturation of domestic bitch oocytes', *Theriogenology* **49**, 1083– 1101.

HOLST, P. A. and PHEMISTER, R. D. (1971) 'The prenatal development of the dog: pre-implantation events', *Biol. Reprod.* **5**, 194–206.

HOWARD, J. G. (1993) 'Semen collection and analysis in carnivores', in Fowler, M.E. (ed.) *Zoo and Wild Animal Medicine*, Philadelphia: W.B. Saunders, pp. 390–399.

HOWARD, J. G., DONOGHUE, A. M., BARONE, M. A. GOODROWE, K. L., BLUMER, E. A., SNODGRASS, K., STARNES, D., TUCKER, M., BUSH, M. and WILDT, D. E. (1992) 'Successful induction of ovarian activity and laporoscopic intrauterine artificial insemination in the cheetah (*Acinonyx jubatus*)', *J. Zoo Wildlife Med.* **23**, 288–300.

HOWARD, J. G., BYERS, A. P., BROWN, J. L., BARRETT, S. J., EVANS, M. Z., SCHWARTZ, R. J. and WILDT, D. E. (1996) 'Successful ovulation induction and laparoscopic intrauterine artificial insemination in the clouded leopard (*Neofelis nebulosa*)', *Zoo Biol.* **15**, 55–69.

HYTTEL, P., FARSTAD, W., MONDAIN-MONVAL, M., BAKKE LAJORD, K. and SMITH, A. J. (1990) 'Structural aspects of oocyte maturation in the blue fox (*Alopex lagopus*)', *Anat. Embryol.* **181**, 325–331.

JALKANEN, L. and LINDEBERG, H. (1998) 'Successful embryo transfer in the silver fox (*Vulpes vulpes*)', *Anim. Reprod. Sci.* **54**, 139–147.

JAMES, R. W., HEYWOOD, R. and STREET, A. F. (1979) 'Biochemical observations of beagle dog semen', *Vet. Rec.* **104**, 480–482.

JEUKENNE, P. and VERSTEGEN, J. (1977) 'Termination of dioestrus and induction of oestrus in dioestrous nonpregnant bitches by the prolactin antagonist cabergoline', *J. Reprod. Fertil. Suppl.* **51**, 59–66.

JEWGENOW, K., WOOD, T. C. and WILDT, D. E. (1997) 'DNA degeneration in mural granulosa cells of non- and sligtly atretic follicles of fresh and cold-stored domestic cat ovaries', *Mol. Reprod. Dev.* **48**, 350–355.

JEWGENOW, K., PENFOLD, L. M., MEYER, H. H. D. and WILDT, D. E. (1998) 'Viability of small preantral ovarian follicles from domestic cats after cryoprotectant exposure and cryopreservation', *J. Reprod. Fertil.* **112**, 39–47.

JOHNSTON, L. A., O'BRIEN, S. J. and WILDT, D. E. (1989) '*In vitro* maturation and fertilization of domestic cat follicular oocytes', *Gamete Res.* **24**, 343–356.

JOHNSTON, L. A., DONOGHUE, A. M. O'BRIEN, S. J. and WILDT, D. E. (1991a) 'Rescue and Maturation *in vitro* of follicular oocytes collected from nondomestic felid species', *Biol. Reprod.* **45**, 898–906.

JOHNSTON, L. A., DONOGHUE, A. M. O'BRIEN, S. J. and WILDT, D. E. (1991b) 'Culture medium and protein supplementation influence *in vitro* fertilization and embryo development in the domestic cat', *J. Exp. Zool.* **257**, 350–359.

JOHNSTON, L. A., DONOGHUE, A. M. O'BRIEN, S. J. and WILDT, D. E. (1993) 'Influence of culture medium and protein supplement on *in vitro* oocyte maturation and fertilization in the domestic cat', *Theriogenology* **40**, 829–839.

KALAB, P., SRSEN, V., FARSTAD, W., KROGENAES, A., MOTLIK, J. and HAFNE, A. L. (1997) 'MAP kinase activation and RAF-1 synthesis in blue fox oocytes is controlled by cumulus granulosa cells', *Theriogenology* **47**, 400 (abstract).

KAWAKAMI, E., NAITOH, H., OGASAWARA, M., TAMURA, M., HASEGAWA, J., TSUTSUI, T. and OGASA, A. (1991) 'Hyperactivation and acrosome reaction *in vitro* in spermatozoa ejaculated by cryptorchid dogs after orchiopexy', *J. Vet. Med. Sci.* **53**, 447–450.

KAWAKAMI, E., HORI, T. and TSUTSUI, T. (1998a) 'Changes in semen quality and *in vitro* sperm capacitation during various frequencies of semen collection in dogs with both asthenozoospermia and teratozoospermia', *J. Vet. Med. Sci.* **60**, 607– 614.

KAWAKAMI, E., HORI, T. and TSUTSUI, T. (1998b) 'Induction of dog sperm capacitation by oviductal fluid', *J. Vet. Med. Sci.* **60**, 197–202.

KOUTSAROVA, N., TODOROV, P., and KOUTSAROV, G. (1997) 'Effect of pentoxyfylline on motility and longevity of fresh and thawed dog spermatozoa', *J. Reprod. Fertil. Suppl.* **51**, 117–121.

KRAEMER, D. C., FLOW, B. L., SCHRIVER, M. D., KINNEY, G. M. and PENNYCOCK, J. W. (1979) 'Embryo transfer in the nonhuman primate, feline and canine', *Theriogenology* **11**, 51–62.

KROGENAES, A. K., NAGYOVA, E., FARSTAD, W., and HAFNE, A. L. (1993) '*In vitro* maturation of blue fox oocytes and cAMP production in oocyte-cumulus cell complexes', *Theriogenology* **39**, 250 (abstract).

LINDE, C. (1978) 'Transport of radiopaque fluid into the uterus after vaginal deposition in the oestrous bitch', *Acta Vet. Scand.* **19**, 463–465.

LINDE, C. and KARLSSON, I. (1984) 'The correlation between the cytology of the vaginal smear and the time of ovulation in the bitch', *J. Small Anim. Pract.* **25**, 77–82.

LINDE-FORSBERG, C. and FORSBERG, M. (1989) 'Fertility in dogs in relation to semen quality and the time and site of insemination with fresh and frozen semen', *J. Reprod. Fertil. Suppl.* **39**, 299–310.

MAHI, C. A. and YANAGAMACHI, R. (1976) 'Maturation and sperm penetration of canine ovarian oocytes *in vitro*', *J. Exp. Zool.* **196**, 189–196.

MAHI, C. A. and YANAGAMACHI, R. (1978) 'Capacitation, acrosome reaction and egg penetration by canine spermatozoa in a simple defined medium', *Gamete Res.* **1**, 101–109.

MARTIN, I. C. A. (1963a) 'The freezing of dog spermatozoa to −79°C', *Res. Vet. Sci.* **4**, 304–314.

MARTIN, I. C. A. (1963b) 'The deep freezing of dog spermatozoa in diluents containing skim- milk', *Res. Vet. Sci.* **4**, 315–325.

CHAPTER 18

MAYENCO-AGUIRRE, A. M. and PERES-CORTEZ, A. B. (1998) 'Preliminary results of hemizona assay (HZA) as a fertility test for canine spermatozoa', *Theriogenology* **50**, 195–204.

METCALFE, S. S. (1999) 'Assisted reproduction in the bitch', MSc thesis, Monash University, pp. 109–129.

MILLER, A. M., ROELKE, M. E., GOODROWE, K. L., HOWARD, J. G. and WILDT, D. E. (1990) 'Oocyte recovery, maturation and fertilization in vitro in the puma (*Felis concolor*)', *J. Reprod. Fertil.* **88**, 249–258.

NICKSON, D. A., BOYD, J., ECKERSALL, P. D., FERGUSON, J. M., HARVEY, M. J. A. and RENTON, J. P. (1993) 'Molecular biological methods for monitoring oocyte maturation and *in vitro* fertilization in bitches', *J. Reprod. Fertil. Suppl.* **47**, 231–240.

NIWA, K., OHARA, K., HOSOI, Y. and IRITANI, A. (1985) 'Early events of *in-vitro* fertilization of cat eggs by epididymal spermatozoa', *J. Reprod. Fertil.* **74**, 657–660.

NOTHLING, J. O. and VOLKMANN, D. H. (1992) 'Effect of autologous prostatic fluid on the fertility of frozen–thawed dog semen after intravaginal insemination', *J. Reprod. Fertil. Suppl.* **47**, 329–333.

NOTHLING, J. O., GERSTENBERG, C. and VOLKMANN, D. H. (1997) 'Semen quality after thawing: correlation with fertility and fresh semen quality in dogs', *J. Reprod. Fertil. Suppl.* **51**, 109–116.

OETTLE, E. E. (1986) 'Changes in acrosome morphology during cooling and freezing of dog semen', *Anim. Reprod. Sci.* **12**, 145–150.

OLAR, T. T. (1984) 'Cryopreservation of dog spermatozoa', PhD thesis, Colorado State University.

OLAR, T. T., BOWEN, R. A. and PICKETT, B. W. (1989) 'Influence of extender, cryopreservative and seminal processing procedures on post-thaw motility of canine spermatozoa frozen in straws', *Theriogenology* **31**, 451–461.

PHEMISTER, R. D., HOLST, P. A., SPANO, J. S. and HOPWOOD, M. L. (1973) 'Time of ovulation in the beagle bitch', *Biol. Reprod.* **8**, 74–82.

PLATZ, C. C., WILDT, D. E. and SEAGER, S. W. J. (1978) 'Pregnancy in the domestic cat after artificial insemination with previously frozen spermatozoa', *J. Reprod. Fertil.* **52**, 279–282.

POPE, C. E., JOHNSON, C. A., McRAE, M. A., KELLER, G. L. and DRESSER, B. L. (1998) 'Development of embryos produced by intracytoplasmic sperm injection of cat oocytes', *Anim. Reprod. Sci.* **53**, 221–236.

POPE, C. E., TURNER, J. L., QUATMAN, S. P. and DRESSER, B. L. (1991) 'Semen storage in the domestic felid: a comparison of cryopreservation methods and storage temperatures', *Biol. Reprod.* **44** (Suppl. 1), abstract no. 257, p. 117.

POPE, C. E., KELLER, G. L. and DRESSER, B. L. (1993) '*In vitro* fertilization in domestic and non-domestic cats including sequences of early nuclear events, development in vitro, cryopreservation and successful intra- and interspecies embryo transfer', *J. Reprod. Fertil. Suppl.* **47**, 189–210.

RENTON, J. P., BOYD, J. S., ECKERSALL, P. D., FERGUSON, J. M., HARVEY, M. J. A., MULLANEY, J. and PERRY, B. (1991) 'Ovulation, fertilization and early embryonic development in the bitch (*Canis familiaris*)', *J. Reprod. Fertil.* **93**, 1–10.

ROTH, T. L., HOWARD, J. G., DONOGHUE, A. M., SWANSON, W. F. and WILDT, D. E. (1994) 'Function and culture requirements of snow leopard (*Panthera unica*) spermatozoa *in vitro*', *J. Reprod. Fertil.* **101**, 563–569.

ROWSON, L. E. A. (1954) 'Infertility in cow, sow and bitch', *Irish Vet. J.* **8**, 216– 221.

SCHMIDT, A. M., NADAL, L. A., SCHMIDT, M. J., and BEAMER, N. B. (1979) 'Serum concentrations of oestradiol and progesterone during the normal cycle and early pregnancy in the lion (*Panthera leo*)', *J. Reprod. Fertil.* **57**, 267–272.

SEAGER, S. W. J. (1969) 'Successful pregnancies utilising frozen dog semen', *A.I. Digest* **17**, 6–7.

SEAGER, S. W. J. and FLETCHER, W. S. (1972) 'Collection, storage and insemination of canine semen', *Lab. Anim. Sci.* **22**, 177–182.

SEAGER, S. W. J. and FLETCHER, W. S. (1973) 'Progress on the use of frozen semen in the dog', *Vet. Rec.* **92**, 6–10.

SEAGER, S. W. J. and PLATZ, C. (1977) 'Artificial insemination and frozen semen in the dog', *Vet. Clin. North Am.* **7**, 757–764.

SEAGER, S. W. J., PLATZ, C and FLETCHER, W. S. (1975) 'Conception rates and related data using frozen dog semen', *J. Reprod. Fertil.* **45**, 189–192.

SHILLE, V. M., THATCHER, M. J. and SIMMONS, K. J. (1984) 'Efforts to induce estrus in the bitch, using pituitary gonadotrophins', *J. Am. Vet. Med. Assoc.* **184**, 1469–1473.

SHILLE, V. M., THATCHER, M. J., LLOYD, M. L., MILLER, D. D., SEYFERT, D. F. and SHERROD, J. D. (1989) 'Gonadotrophic control of follicular development and the use of exogenous gonadtrophins for induction of oestrus and ovulation in the bitch', *J. Reprod. Fertil. Suppl.* **39**, 103–113.

SHIMAZU, Y. and NAITO, K. (1996) 'Both male and female pronuclei formation in canine oocytes inseminated at germinal vesicle stage', *J. Mammalian Ovarian Res.* **13**, 122–124.

SHIMAZU, Y., YAMADA, S., KAWANO, Y., KAWAYI, H., NAKAZAWA, M., NAITO, K. and TOYODA, Y. (1992) '*In vitro* capacitation of canine spermatozoa', *J. Reprod. Dev.* **38**, 67–71.

SMITH, F. O. (1984) 'Cryopreservation of canine semen: technique and performance', PhD thesis, University of Minnesota.

SWANSON, W. F., BROWN, J. L. and WILDT, D. E. (1996a) 'Influence of seasonality on reproductive traits of the male pallas cat (*Felis manul*) and implications for captive management', *J. Zoo Wildlife Med.* **27**, 234–240.

SWANSON, W. F., HOWARD, J. G., ROTH, T. L., BROWN, J. L., ALVARADO, T., BURTON, M., STARNES, D. and WILDT, D. E. (1996b) 'Responsiveness of ovaries to exogenous gonadotrophins and laparoscopic artificial insemination with frozen–thawed spermatozoa in ocelots (*Felis pardalis*)', *J. Reprod. Fertil.* **106**, 87–94.

TAHA, M. B. and NOAKES, D. E. (1982) 'The effect of age and season of the year on testicular function in the dog, as determined by histological examination of the seminiferous tubules and the estimation of peripheral plasma testosterone concentrations', *J. Small Anim. Pract.* **23**, 351–357.

TAHA, M. B., NOAKES, D. E. and ALLEN, W. E. (1981) 'The effect of season of the year on the characteristics and composition of dog semen', *J. Small Anim. Prac.* **22**, 177– 184.

TAKEISHI, M., MIKAMI, T., KODAMA, Y., TSUNEKANE, T. and IWAKI, T. (1976) 'Studies on reproduction in the dog. VIII artificial insemination using frozen semen', *Jpn J. Anim. Reprod.* **22**, 28–33.

THUN, R., WATSON, P. and JACKSON, A. M. (1977) 'Induction of oestrus and ovulation in the bitch using exogenous gonadotrophins', *Am. J. Vet. Res.* **38**, 483–486.

TSUTSUI, T. (1975a) 'Studies on the reproduction in the dog. V. On cleavage and transport of fertilised ova in the oviduct', *Jpn J. Anim. Reprod.* **21**, 70–75. (Japanese with English abstract).

TSUTSUI, T. (1975b) 'Studies on the reproduction in the dog. VI. Ovulation rate and transuterine migration of the fertilised ova', *Jpn J. Anim. Reprod.* **28**, 98–101 (Japanese with English abstract).

TSUTSUI, T. (1989) 'Gamete physiology and timing of ovulation and fertilization in dogs', *J. Reprod. Fertil. Suppl.* **39**, 269–275.

VAN GEMERT, W. (1970) 'Puppies from deep frozen semen', *Netherlands J. Vet. Sci.* **4**, 55–58.

VAN HAAFTEN, B., DIELEMAN, S. J., OKKENS, A. C., BEVERS, M. M. and WILLEMSE, A. H. (1989) 'Induction of oestrus and ovulation in dogs by treatment with PMSG and/or bromocriptine', *J. Reprod. Fertil. Suppl.* **39**, 330–331.

WALES, R. G. and WHITE, I. G. (1958) 'The interaction of pH, tonicity and electrolyte concentration on the motility of dog spermatozoa', *J. Physiol.* **141**, 273–280.

WATSON, P. F. (1979) 'The preservation of semen in mammals', *Oxford Rev. Reprod. Biol.* **1**, 283–350.

WATSON, P. F. (1990) 'Artificial insemination and the preservation of semen', in *Marshall's Physiology of Reproduction,* Vol. 2, 4th edn. Edinburgh: Churchill Livingstone, pp. 798–800.

WEN, X. H., FENG, H. L. and SUN, Q. Y. (1994) *In vitro* maturation of follicular oocytes of the silver fox (*Vulpes fulva desm*)', *Theriogenology* **41**, 333 (abstract).

WILDT, D. E., HOWARD, J. G., HALL, L. L. and BUSH, M. (1986) 'Reproductive physiology of the clouded leopard: I. Electroejaculates contain high proportions of pleiomorphic spermatozoa throughout the year', *Biol. Reprod.* **34**, 937–947.

WILDT, D. E., PHILLIPS, L. G. SIMMONS, L. G., CHAKRABORTY, P. K., BROWN, J. L., HOWARD, J. G., TREARE, A. and BUSH, M. (1988) 'A comparative analysis of ejaculate and hormonal characteristics of the captive male cheetah, tiger, leopard and puma', *Biol. Reprod.* **38**, 245–255.

WILSON, M. S. (1993) 'Non-surgical intrauterine artificial insemination in bitches using frozen semen', *J. Reprod. Fertil. Suppl.* **47**, 307–311.

WOLFE, B. A. and WILDT, D. E. (1996) 'Development to blastocysts of domestic cat oocytes matured and fertilized in vitro after prolonged cold storage', *J. Reprod. Fertil.* **106**, 135–141.

WOOD, T. C., BYERS, A. P., JENNETTE, B. E. and WILDT, D. E. (1995) 'Influence of protein and hormone supplement on *in vitro* maturation and fertilization of domestic cat eggs', *J. Reprod. Fertil.* **104**, 315–323.

WOOD, T. C., MONTALI, R. J. and WILDT, D. E. (1997) 'Follicle-oocyte atresia and temporal taphonomy in cold-stored domestic cat ovaries', *Mol. Reprod. Dev.* **46**, 190–200.

YAMADA, S., SHIMAZU, Y., KAWAJI, H., NAKAZAWA, M., NAITO, K. and TOYODA, Y. (1992) 'Maturation, fertilization and development of dog oocytes *in vitro*', *Biol. Reprod.* **46**, 853–858.

YAMADA, S., SHIMAZU, Y., KAWAO, Y., NAKAZAWA, M., NAITO, K. and TOYODA, Y. (1993) 'In vitro maturation and fertilization of pre-ovulatory canine oocytes', *J. Reprod. Fertil. Suppl.* **47**, 227–229.

YUBI, A. C. (1984) 'Investigations of dog semen with particular reference to freezing techniques', MVM thesis, Faculty of Veterinary Medicine, University of Glasgow.

YUBI, A. C., FERGUSON, J. M., RENTON, J. P., HARKER, S., HARVEY, M. J. A., BAGYENJI, B. and DOUGLAS, T. A. (1987) 'Some observations on the dilution, cooling and freezing of canine semen', *J. Small Anim. Pract.* **28**, 753–761.

CHAPTER 18

19

Gamete Cryopreservation and Reproductive Technologies in Miscellaneous Mammals

W. V. HOLT[1] AND P. F. WATSON[2]

[1]The Institute of Zoology, The Zoological Society of London, Regent's Park, London NW1 4RY, UK
[2]Department of Veterinary Basic Sciences, The Royal Veterinary College, London NW1 0TU, UK

Contents

19.1 INTRODUCTION

Several mammalian families in which reproductive technologies have been developed to some level of sophistication are not logically classified with other species groups. This chapter therefore gathers these species together in what may appear to be a haphazard collection; we include one of the notable success stories of reproductive technology, the black-footed ferret, and one of the most charismatic and symbolic species in conservation biology, the giant panda. The aquatic mammals have also been included within this chapter and relevant studies in closely related species are also covered.

19.2 GIANT PANDA

19.2.1 Seasonality and behaviour

The rarity of the giant panda (*Ailuropoda melanoleuca*) has been both a stimulus to conservation research in this species and an important limiting factor. There are considerable gaps in our knowledge of giant panda reproduction. Furthermore, because much of the research has been undertaken outside their natural habitats in southeast China, environmental effects on reproduction, particularly those mediated by seasonality and diet, are unclear. The natural habitats of pandas are heavily wooded bamboo forests at an elevation of 2000–3500 m. For ten months of the year the animals feed on 'arrow bamboo' then in the spring they descend below 2600 m to feed on new shoots of the 'walking stick bamboo' (Knight *et al.*, 1985). Whether these dietary changes have an impact on reproductive activity is unclear; diets in zoos, however, may differ significantly and do not necessarily reflect the seasonal changes that evidently occur. Habitat fragmentation due to road-building, logging and agriculture is a significant cause of isolation among wild giant pandas. Not only does it impede their ability to interact with each other, but probably also limits the range of bamboo species available to them.

In the wild, oestrus normally occurs between April and May and, with some slight variation of timing, this pattern has also been observed in captivity. The species is widely considered to be monoestrous, each year exhibiting an oestrous period lasting 2–3 days. However, Knight *et al.* (1985) pointed out that some authorities in China have reported two periods of oestrus in the spring and also signs of oestrus in the autumn. Oestrus is detected behaviourally by observing male–female interactions. As discussed by Moore *et al.* (1984), signs of overt oestrous behaviour are readily observed, i.e. female displaying lordosis and bleating; however, the behavioural signs are often equivocal and oestrus identification is often problematic. Kleiman (1983) and Knight *et al.* (1985) have described oestrous behaviours in considerable detail.

19.2.2 Spermatozoa

Semen collection

In tandem with seasonal changes in the females, the males appear to undergo seasonal cycles of testicular function. Moore *et al.* (1984) reported that semen samples collected in January and early February contained less than 10% of the sperm concentration found in March. This was correlated with a sustained increase in sperm numbers and sperm motility throughout the early spring; Semen collections attempted in July and August failed despite repeated stimulations (Moore *et al.*, 1984). These experiences support the notion that the testes undergo seasonal changes in spermatogenic activity. In contrast, Platz *et al.* (1983) reported that semen was obtained by electroejaculation in June and July, although only after many stimulations (120–150), and that although an ejaculate was obtained in November, the spermatozoa had low motility. Seasonal fluctuations of spermatogenesis have also been discussed by Masui *et al.* (1985).

Semen collection is typically accomplished by electroejaculation using probes 4.5– 5 cm in diameter, and with either ring or parallel plate electrodes (Platz *et al.*, 1983; Moore *et al.*, 1984). In a later report, Masui *et al.* (1989) described the successful use of a considerably thinner probe (2 cm), commenting that it was based on a design used at Beijing Zoo in China. During the breeding season, 2–6 V stimulatory pulses are normally sufficient for efficient semen collection. Knight *et al.* (1985) observed that once penile erection has been elicited by the electroejaculatory procedure it is possible to massage the ventral floor of the rectum and obtain a flow of semen without further stimulations.

In London Zoo, the males were anaesthetized for semen collection using a mixture of ketamine and xylazine (Moore *et al.*, 1984). During the breeding season, 1–2 ml of semen were typically obtained by electroejaculation, the sperm concentration often exceeding 2000×10^6 cells/ml (Moore *et al.*, 1984).

Semen handling, assessment and short-term storage

Giant panda spermatozoa are surprisingly robust in that they can be stored for up to 5 days in a modified Tyrode's medium (BWW; Biggers *et al.*, 1971) at 30°C or 37°C in the presence or absence of 5% carbon dioxide but containing 4 mg/ml bovine serum albumin. Moore *et al.* (1984) showed that after dilution 85% and 70% motility was retained after storage for 24 hours and 72 hours respectively. Shortly after dilution in BWW medium, spermatozoa display head–head agglutination of the highly motile sperm population; Moore *et al.* (1984) remarked that these aggregates could be dispersed by gentle aspiration, whereupon they displayed progressive motility again until they reaggregated.

Semen assessment in the giant panda has been performed using the range of techniques applied to other species. Sperm motility assessment has not only been performed subjectively, but computerized methods of measuring sperm velocity have also been applied. Moore *et al.* (1984) compared the velocity of spermatozoa diluted in BWW both before and after freezing and thawing, and found no difference (39.0±1.8 μm/s). These authors also demonstrated that preincubation of giant panda sperm in BWW rendered them capable of fusing with zona-free hamster oocytes. As this technique can only succeed with spermatozoa that have undergone the acrosome reaction, it is apparent that BWW induces sperm capacitation in this species and that an alternative medium which lacks this property might be preferable for sperm storage. IVT medium, a buffer designed for the short-term storage of bovine spermatozoa (Van Demark and Sharma, 1957) is one alternative likely to meet this criterion. Moore *et al.* (1984) reported that IVT saturated with carbon dioxide depressed sperm motility and the spermatozoa failed to agglutinate; nevertheless, they remained viable for up to four days and regained motility when exposed to air.

More recently, Sun *et al.* (1996) investigated the cell biology of capacitation and the acrosome reaction in giant panda spermatozoa and have shown that mechanisms found in other eutherian mammals also apply in this species. The protein kinase C activator phorbol 12–myristate 13–acetate stimulated acrosome reaction in a dose-dependent manner and its effect could be overcome by the protein kinase C inhibitor staurosporine. These authors used a fluorescein-labelled lectin, *Lens culinaris* agglutinin, to determine the acrosomal status of the spermatozoa. An alternative fluorescent-labelled lectin, *Pisum sativum* agglutinin, can also be used for this purpose (Holt and Moore, unpublished observations).

Semen cryopreservation

Semen cryopreservation technology in the giant panda has not been investigated in any detail, but considerable success has been obtained with the direct application of standard techniques. Platz *et al.* (1983) diluted the semen with a commercial extender (Life Forces Inc., College Station, Texas) and froze 30 μl pellets on dry ice. Thawing was achieved by adding three pellets to 0.5 ml of 0.85% saline at 37°C. Post-thaw motility was 40–55%. The authors commented that they did not observe any structural damage caused by the freezing technique.

Moore *et al.* (1984) used a cryopreservation medium containing 11% lactose, 47% glycerol and 20% yolk. The semen samples, diluted to a concentration of 100×10^6 sperm/ml were cooled to 5ºC over a 30-minute period, loaded into 0.5-ml straws and frozen in the vapour 4-cm above the surface of liquid nitrogen. Rapid thawing was achieved by placing straws in a small plastic bag in a waterbath at 50°C for 20–30 seconds after which the samples were diluted in BWW medium for motility assessment. This technique resulted in approximately 50% motility after thawing, a value identical to that reported by Platz *et al.* (1983).

In a more recent short report, Yang (1987) compared glycerol and DMSO as cryoprotectants for giant panda semen, including evaluations of concentration ranges (4.7–15% glycerol and 5–15% DMSO) for both. By varying the freezing and rewarming rates, post-thaw sperm recovery rates of 89–95% motility were obtained when the lowest glycerol concentration was used in combination with sample freezing at 105°C/min and rewarming at 40°C/min.

Although there are so few reports of semen freezing in the giant panda, they all agree that good post-thaw recovery of the spermatozoa can be achieved. This encourages the view that semen storage for this species is worthwhile, although no proof has yet been obtained that the cryopreserved semen is fertile. Moore *et al.* (1984) successfully inseminated a female in 1982, but used consecutive doses of fresh and frozen semen.

Insemination timing and procedure

Attempts at artificial insemination have mainly relied upon behavioural observations of oestrous behaviour to determine the correct timing. Endocrine confirmation of oestrus can be obtained by monitoring urinary oestrogens on a daily basis (Bonney *et al.*, 1982), but unless this procedure is performed rapidly the results can only be used retrospectively. Although uncertain, there is some reason to believe that ovulation in the female giant panda is induced by mating, and that oestrous behaviour therefore ceases once ovulation has occurred. This is another useful indicator of insemination timing, although once again it only provides retrospective, rather than prospective, confirmation.

The insemination procedure itself has been described in considerable detail by Knight *et al.* (1985), who also illustrated their paper with anatomical drawings of the female reproductive tract. The technique described by Knight *et al.* (1985), Moore *et al.* (1984) and Masui *et al.* (1989) involved examining the internal structures of the female reproductive tract by the use of a bright light source and speculum. As the urethra is easily mistaken for the opening of the cervix, it is necessary to catheterize the urethra to prevent misdirection of the insemination pipette.

The successful insemination reported by Moore *et al.* (1984) was achieved using 200 million spermatozoa in a total volume of 2 ml BWW medium. Masui *et al.* (1989) reported two successful inseminations in consecutive years, using the total volumes of semen which they collected (0.53 ml and 1 ml respectively).

19.2.3 Oocyte and embryo technology in the giant panda

Very few reports in the literature have dealt with any aspect of oocyte or embryo technology, although studies aimed at developing cloning techniques for the giant panda are reportedly in progress in Chinese laboratories. Two reports of relevance to this work are summarized here.

Zhang *et al.* (1998) obtained ovaries from a giant panda that died of hepatic cirrhosis during the non-breeding season. Oocytes were harvested within 4 hours of death by dissecting the ovarian cortex and collecting the cumulus–oocyte complexes. Cumulus–oocyte complexes were classified as large (>125 μm) and small (100–124 μm) follicular oocytes and placed in culture media (TCM-199) supplemented with FSH (10 μg/ml) and LH (20 μg/ml). After culture for 22 hours at 37°C in air with 5% CO_2, responses were evaluated by examining the growth of oocytes and determining the presence of the first polar body. Of the 26 large follicular oocytes that were harvested, 12 were considered suitable for IVM, and 14 were degenerate, had a broken zona pellucida or had lost some cytoplasm. Of the 12 cultured oocytes, all grew to a mean diameter (±SD) of 141.1±6.7 μm, and four released the first polar body. None of the small follicular oocytes showed growth or other signs of maturation. The authors concluded from their preliminary results that it is possible to obtain functional giant panda oocytes from ovaries obtained post-mortem during the non-breeding season. This work is encouraging, and suggests that harvesting oocytes from genetically valuable females would be a worthwhile option for gamete rescue in this species.

Chen *et al.* (1999) took giant panda skeletal muscle cells, uterus epithelial cells and mammary gland cells from an adult female. These were cultured and used as nucleus donors for the construction of interspecies embryos by transferring them into enucleated rabbit eggs. All three types of somatic cells were reportedly able to reprogramme in rabbit ooplasm and supported early embryonic development. The authors considered that their experiments showed that direct injection of a mammary gland cell into the enucleated rabbit ooplasm, combined with *in vivo* development in ligated rabbit oviducts, achieved higher blastocyst development than *in vitro* culture after a somatic cell was injected into the perivitelline space and fused with the enucleated egg by electrical stimulation. Giant panda mitochondrial DNA (mtDNA) was shown to exist in the interspecies reconstructed blastocyst. The authors concluded that (a) the ability of ooplasm to dedifferentiate somatic cells is not species-specific, and (b) there is compatibility between interspecies somatic nucleus and ooplasm during early development of the reconstructed egg.

It is worth pointing out that for conservation purposes, the cloning approach is probably a measure of last resort. Strategies involving the use of surrogate species as vehicles for embryonic development have been proposed, but these depart even further from practical realities and attempts to use such methods are likely to involve many unforeseen difficulties.

19.3 BEARS

Phylogenetic analyses based on mitochondrial RNA sequence analysis and two-dimensional analyses of fibroblast proteins indicate that the giant panda evolved through lineages close to the Ursidae or bears (Slattery and O'Brien, 1995). Some of these species are under severe threat at present; the brown bear (*Ursus arctos*) population of western Spain is thought to number approximately fifty individuals (Wiegand *et al.*, 1998), and a population of brown bears (*Ursus arctos yesoensis*), restricted to Hokkaido Island, Japan, is fragmented and under pressure from human activities. A few attempts to begin developing reproductive techniques for these species have either been reported, or have been attempted but not published.

Ishikawa *et al.* (1998) collected semen from ten Hokkaido brown bears during the mating season, which extends from early May to early July. The electroejaculation procedure was as reported previously for the giant panda by Masui *et al.* (1989). On some occasions ejaculate volumes were as high as 7–8 ml, although most of the ejaculate volumes were in the range 1–2 ml. Sperm concentration was mostly considerably lower (100–500 sperm/ml) than reported for the giant panda; one of the 21 ejaculates which these authors reported had a concentration of 1570 million cells/ml, but the volume was small (0.2 ml).

As with the giant panda studies there are few reports concerning embryo technology in bears. However, one study (Boone *et al.*, 1999) described embryo transfer in the non-endangered American black bear (*Ursus americanus*) as a model for developing appropriate embryo transfer procedures. The donor bear mated numerous times between late May and early June. In late July a series of telescoping sheaths was used to gain access to the uterus. A catheter was passed through the largest sheath, inflated the balloon, and phosphate-buffered saline was repeatedly infused into and then aspirated from the uterus. Two embryos were collected from these flushings, washed and placed in HEPES-buffered human tubal fluid plus human serum albumin. The recipient bear had mated during mid-June, but in late July an embryo was transferred into the cranial portion of the uterine horn ipsilateral to the ovary containing a corpus luteum. The recipient delivered two cubs in January. DNA from hair samples belonging to the neonates indicated that the male cub belonged to the donor and the female cub to the recipient. The delayed implantation mechanism in bears was thought to allow for the successful development of the embryo despite substantial asynchrony between the donor and the recipient (13 days).

19.4 MUSTELIDAE

The family Mustelidae includes approximately sixty-four widely diverse species, the best known of which are ferrets, badgers, otters and sea otters, weasels, mink and martens. The species are native to many areas of the world, from the Arctic tundra to the tropical rainforests. They are not, however, found in Australia, Madagascar or the Oceanic islands. The phylogeny and systematics of the mustelids was described in detail by Anderson (1989). Reproductive studies have been performed for relatively few of these species, although some have been investigated in detail. Mead (1989) published a comprehensive table of information about mustelid reproduction, giving distribution, seasonality, type of oestrus (i.e. monoestrus or polyoestrus), litter size and gestation length. Many of these species show periods of delayed implantation, and where known, the table includes the duration of the postimplantation phase. Few studies have, however, been performed on semen cryopreservation in this group of species. Detailed studies of the domestic ferret (Howard et al., 1991) have been of considerable importance in the conservation of the endangered Black-footed ferret (*Mustela nigripes*), and there have also been studies of semen cryopreservation in the skunk.

Knowledge of reproductive activity patterns in male mustelids is clearly essential prior to undertaking any exercise involving semen collection (for review, see Mead, 1989). Spermatogenesis in many species is restricted to a period of 3–4 months, commencing before the onset of the female breeding season so that the epididymides contain spermatozoa at the appropriate time for mating. Testicular regression begins before the end of the breeding season; consequently, if females lose their litters and exhibit a second oestrus, few males may be capable of breeding for a second time. Seasonal spermatogenic changes in the European badger (*Meles meles*) are not so marked, spermatozoa being present in the testes and epididymides throughout the breeding season. However, it should be recognized that those spermatozoa found outside the breeding season may not be fertile.

19.4.1 Semen collection

Semen can be collected from domestic ferrets by electroejaculation (Atherton et al., 1989; Wildt et al., 1989) using techniques which differ little from others reported in these chapters; however, Atherton et al. (1989) reported using low voltage ranges (6.3–12.6 mV). Semen volume is small; Howard et al. (1991) reported a mean volume of 50.1 μl from a total of 52 ejaculates, although Atherton et al. (1989) had previously given figures of 5–20 μl.

Electroejaculation of four male badgers was attempted in August 1998 using a 2-cm diameter probe with three longitudinal electrodes, inserted rectally to a depth of 11 cm. The stimulating voltage did not exceed 2.5 V. Poorly motile spermatozoa were obtained from one of the animals (Holt and Pickard, unpublished observations).

19.4.2 Semen cryopreservation

Three detailed studies of semen cryopreservation in the domestic ferret have been reported (Atherton et al., 1989; Budworth et al., 1989; Howard et al., 1991). These are all of interest for the slightly different approaches used.

Atherton *et al.* (1989) initially maintained semen samples at 37°C for up to 90 minutes until all semen collections had been completed. Samples were then cooled to 4°C, whereupon the desired precooled extender, containing double the final concentration of glycerol, was added dropwise over a 1-hour period. The samples were loaded into 0.25-ml straws, equilibrated for 1-hour at 4°C, and frozen for 1–2 hours in the vapour phase 7 cm above the surface of liquid nitrogen. The cryopreservation extenders tested in this study were egg yolk–citrate, TES–Tris yolk, medium TCM199+egg yolk, TCM199+10% FCS, with and without egg yolk, and a commercial glucose–dried skimmed milk horse semen extender. Egg yolk concentration was 20% in each buffer; glycerol concentrations were varied between 0 and 6%. An interesting variable tested in these experiments was the inclusion of 2 mM ATP. The authors cited the work of Lindemann *et al.* (1981), who showed that exogenous ATP increased the proportion of motile bovine spermatozoa that recovered motility after cryopreservation.

Atherton *et al.* (1989) found that the highest recovery of motility (range 35–45%) was obtained with extenders containing 3–4.5% glycerol. Interestingly when the spermatozoa were cryopreserved using the commercial horse extender, 27% motility recovery was noted even in the absence of glycerol. Using this extender in combination with 3–4.5% glycerol did not apparently increase the recovery of sperm motility (15–21% recovery); however, by including ATP within the diluent, the recovery of sperm motility was more than doubled (to 45–48% motility). This effect was attributed to direct stimulation of the sperm axoneme by ATP; however, this effect almost certainly involves a more complex mechanism. Exogenous ATP is normally unable to enter the cell, so one possibility is that the increased motility is attributable to influx of ATP through damaged sperm membranes. More recent evidence has shown, however, that extracellular ATP stimulates human sperm fertilization rates by directly activating motility and the acrosome reaction through a signal transduction pathway (Rossato *et al.*, 1999). ATP-binding induced rapid plasma membrane depolarization and the stimulation of a protein tyrosine kinase.

Budworth *et al.* (1989), who used both pellet freezing and 0.25-ml straw freezing techniques, compared egg yolk–lactose, egg yolk–Tris, and egg yolk–TEST extenders with 2% or 4% glycerol as the cryoprotectant. They found that egg yolk–TEST extender gave significantly better post-thaw recovery (15–35%) than egg yolk–Tris (10–20%). These authors used frozen–thawed spermatozoa to inseminate two females by direct inoculation into the uterus; one female became pregnant and produced at least two offspring.

Howard *et al.* (1991) diluted semen into a variety of media to see which provided the best post-thaw survival. Immediately after collection, semen was transferred into 120 µl TEST diluent (20% egg yolk, 4% glycerol), PDV (20% egg yolk, 4% glycerol, 11% lactose) or BF5F (20% egg yolk, 4% glycerol, 0.5% Equex surfactant). The diluted samples were were cooled at 4°C for 30 minutes, then frozen on dry ice as 30 μl drops, or in 0.25-ml straws at 20°C/min to −100°C in a Planer programmable freezer.

The use of PDV diluent combined with pellet freezing and thawing at 37°C gave the best cryoprotection, yielding 60% motility post-thaw and 50% motility after 1 hour *in vitro*. BF5F provided the least cryoprotection, suggesting that the inclusion of surfactant may be inappropriate for this species. Retention of acrosomal integrity was also best after cryopreservation with PDV medium (40% intact acrosomes). The effectiveness of the cryopreservation procedure was tested by the laparoscopic insemination of spermatozoa.

Howard *et al.* (1991) inseminated ten females with spermatozoa frozen with the PDV method using a laparoscopic technique directly into the uterus; they obtained 7/10 conceptions. Subsequent work with the black-footed ferret has also been based around the use of this procedure. In an effort to simplify the insemination methodology, Kidder *et al.* (1998) devised a non-surgical method of transcervical insemination. The use of a fibreoptic endoscope together with a specially designed speculum and catheter permitted cervical catheterization and intrauterine insemination. Intrauterine inseminations resulted in a conception rate of 17% (4/24) when hCG administration was coincident with insemination, and 79% (19/24) conception rate when inseminations were performed 24 hours after hCG administration.

The cryopreservation of spermatozoa from the western spotted skunk (*Spilogale gracilis latifrons*), a model for the threatened eastern subspecies (*Spilogale putorius interrupta*), has also been studied in some detail (Kaplan and Mead, 1992). A series of semen samples were collected by electroejaculation between January and November; these were immediately diluted 1 part semen + 2 parts extender. The extenders tested were TEST, Tris–citrate and BF5F; the BF5F was prepared using sodium dodecyl sulphate (0.5% w/v) instead of Equex. Another series of samples were collected between July and November; these were diluted in TEST medium containing 3, 5, 10% DMSO and 3, 5, 10% glycerol. The diluted samples were cooled to 4°C over 1–2 hours, loaded into 0.25-ml straws and placed on dry ice (41°C/min cooling rate); then plunged into liquid nitrogen. Samples were thawed in water at 37°C for 20–35 seconds. Four semen samples in TEST+5% DMSO were frozen as 50 μl pellets on dry ice. These were thawed in 50 μl TEST medium at 37°C. Two hours after cooling, samples in BF5F showed lower motility (15%) than spermatozoa than in the other extenders (>25%). Samples frozen with TEST + 5 or 10% DMSO showed better post-thaw motility than any treatment with glycerol. TEST was regarded as the best extender. Straw freezing (mean motility 14%) was better than pellet freezing (1.3% motility).

19.4.3 Embryo and oocyte technology

We are not aware of any published material on this subject.

19.5 SEA MAMMALS

Not a great deal of attention has been directed towards researching the cryobiology of gametes and embryos of any of the sea mammals. What exists in published form arises because of the potential of these animals to benefit humankind, and has less to do with conservation and biodiversity concepts than to do with exploiting these animals for human gain.

19.5.1 Whales

What limited research that has been carried out on whales has been accomplished as a by-product of the Japanese whaling endeavours and has therefore been focused on the Minke whale (*Balaenoptera acutorostrata*). One research laboratory has made a commitment to explore assisted reproductive technology in whales. Spermatozoa were recovered from the vas deferens of dead animals and diluted in a standard Tris-based diluent for cryopreservation (Fukui *et al.*, 1996). After storage at −80°C for between 1.5 and 4 months and subsequent transfer to liquid nitrogen (−196°C), the samples were thawed at 37°C and only about half of the samples had motile spermatozoa (range 2–40%) but all samples had a proportion of 'live' spermatozoa (range 3–44%). The authors claim that this indicates the possibility of cryopreservation. Sperm motility and viability correlated with serum oestradiol concentrations.

Oocytes were recovered *post-mortem* from follicles of immature and mature female Minke whales. Follicular size did not affect the success of recovery, and approximately 60–70% were at germinal vesicle stage (Fukui *et al.*, 1997a); TCM 199 supplemented with fetal whale serum, reproductive hormones and and cumulus cells gave the best *in vitro* maturation (IVM) (21.6%) after 96 hours in culture. In a later experiment (Fukui *et al.*, 1997b), culture for 120 hours yielded better results than culture for 96 hours (34% versus 26% reaching at least MII stage) and the matured oocytes were more successfully penetrated by frozen–thawed spermatozoa (55% versus 32%) and developed to pronuclear (PN) stage (40% versus 20%). However, only approximately 5% of the inseminated oocytes showed any further development, and this was not influenced by the presence of cumulus cells in co-culture.

When oocytes from mature or immature female Minke whales were cryopreserved using EG as a cryoprotectant, approximately 40% were morphologically normal post-thaw, and maturity or cumulus cell presence had no effect (Asada *et al.*, 2000). During IVM, the presence of surrounding cumulus cells significantly enhanced the proportion of oocytes progressing beyond MI (29%), but only four oocytes of 194 in culture matured to MII. Obvious ultrastructural damage was observed resulting from cryopreservation.

19.5.2 Dolphin

Robeck *et al.* (1994) discussed the desirability of assisted reproduction techniques to aid the cooperation between zoos committed to maintaining dolphins in captivity. They wisely observed that much more information about the basic physiology of these animals was required before techniques of assisted reproduction could be instituted. They proposed that the bottle-nosed dolphin would be a suitable species to develop techniques because of its tractable nature and successful breeding in captivity.

19.5.3 Seal

Adult wild grey seals (*Halichoerus grypus*) were anaesthetized with tiletamine-zolazepam, and electroejaculated using a rectal probe and standard voltage range of 1–9 V; ejaculation was induced after 15–29 minutes, yielding semen volumes of 4–17 ml containing vigorously motile spermatozoa (Lawson *et al.*, 1996). Spermatozoa could be kept motile in insulated boxes for up to 4 hours.

REFERENCES

ANDERSON, E. (1989) 'The phylogeny of mustelids and the systematics of ferrets', in Seal, U. S., Thorne, E. T., Bogan, M. A. and Anderson S. H. (eds) *Conservation Biology and the Black-Footed Ferret*, New Haven: Yale University Press, pp. 10–20.

ASADA, M., HORII, M, MOGOE, T., FUKUI, Y., ISHJIKAWA, H AND OHSUMI, S. (2000) 'In vitro maturation and ultrastructural observation of cryopreserved Minke whale (*Balaenoptera acutorostrata*) follicular oocytes', *Biol. Reprod.* **62**, 253–259.

ATHERTON, R. W., STRALEY, M., CURRY, P., SLAUGHTER, R., BURGESS, W. AND KITCHIN, R. M. (1989) 'Electroejaculation and cryopreservation of domestic ferret sperm', in Seal, U. S., Thorne, E. T., Bogan, M. A., and Anderson S. H. (eds) *Conservation Biology and the Black-Footed Ferret*, New Haven: Yale University Press, pp. 177–187.

BIGGERS, J. D., WHITTEN, W. K. AND WHITTINGHAM, D. G. (1971) 'The culture of mouse embryos *in vitro*', in Daniel, J. C. (ed.) *Methods in Mammalian Embryology*, San Francisco: Freeman and Co., pp. 86–116.

BONNEY, R. C., WOOD, D. J. AND KLEIMAN, D. G. (1982) 'Endocrine correlates of behavioural oestrus in the female Giant panda (*Ailuropoda melanoleuca*) and associated hormonal changes in the male', *J. Reprod. Fertil.* **64**, 209–215.

BOONE, W. R., CATLIN, J. C., CASEY, K. J., DYE, P. S., BOONE, E. T. AND SCHUETT, R. J. (1999) 'Live birth of a bear cub following nonsurgical embryo collection', *Theriogenology* **51**, 519–529.

BUDWORTH, P., AMANN, R. P. AND BOWEN, R. A. (1989) 'Cryopreservation of semen from domestic ferrets', in Seal, U. S., Thorne, E. T., Bogan, M. A. and Anderson S. H. (eds) *Conservation Biology and the Black-Footed Ferret*, New Haven: Yale University Press, pp. 187–189.

CHEN, D. Y., SUN, Q. Y., LIU, J. L., LI, G. P., LIAN, L., WANG, M. K., HAN, Z. M., SONG, X. F., LI, J. S., SUN, Q., CHEN, Y. C., ZHANG, Y. P. AND DING, B. (1999) 'The Giant panda (*Ailurapoda melanoleuca*) somatic nucleus can dedifferentiate in rabbit ooplasm and support early development of the reconstructed egg', *Science in China, Series C–Life Sciences* **42**, 346–353.

FUKUI, Y., MOGOE, T, JUNG, Y. G., TERAWAKI, Y., MIYAMOTO, A., ISHIKAWA, H., FUJISE, Y. AND OHSUMI, S. (1996) 'Relationshiops among morphological status, steroid hormones, and post-thawing viability of frozen spermatozoa of male Minke whales (*Balaenoptera acutorostrata*)', *Marine Mammal Sci.* **12**, 28–37.

FUKUI, Y., MOGOE, T, ISHIKAWA, H. AND OHSUMI, S. (1997a) 'Factors affect in vitro maturation of Minke whale (*Balaenoptera acutorostrata*) follicular oocytes', *Biol. Reprod.* **56**, 523–528.

FUKUI, Y., MOGOE, T, ISHIKAWA, H. AND OHSUMI, S. (1997b) 'In vitro fertilization of in vitro matured Minke whale (*Balaenoptera acutorostrata*) follicular oocytes', *Marine Mammal Sci.* **13**, 395–404.

HOWARD, J. G., BUSH, M., MORTON, C., MORTON, F., WENTZEL, K. AND WILDT, D. E. (1991) 'Comparative semen cryopreservation in ferrets (*Mustela putorius furo*) and pregnancies after laparoscopic intrauterine insemination with frozen thawed spermatozoa', *J. Reprod. Fertil.* **92**, 109–118.

ISHIKAWA, A., MATSUI, M., TSURUGA, H., SAKAMOTO, H., TAKAHASHI, Y. AND KANAGAWA, H. (1998) 'Electroejaculation and semen characteristics of the captive Hokkaido brown bear (*Ursus arctos yesoensis*)', *J. Vet. Med. Sci.* **60**, 965–968.

KAPLAN, J. B. AND MEAD, R. A. (1992) 'Evaluation of extenders and cryopreservatives for cooling and cryopreservation of spermatozoa from the western spotted skunk (*Spilogale gracilis*)', *Zoo Biol.* **11**, 397–404.

KIDDER, J. D., FOOTE, R. H, AND RICHMOND, M. E. (1998) 'Transcervical artificial insemination in the domestic ferret (*Mustela putorius furo*)', *Zoo Biol.* **17**, 393–404.

KLEIMAN, D. G. (1983) 'Ethology and reproduction of captive Giant panda (*Ailuropoda melanoleuca*)', *Z. Tierpsychol.* **62**, 1–46.

KNIGHT, J. A., BUSH, M., CELMA, M., GARCIA DEL CAMPO, A. L., GOLTENBOTH, R., HEARN, J. P., HODGES, J. K., JONES, D. M., KLOS, H. G., MONSALVE, L., MONTALI, R. AND MOORE, H. D. M. (1985) 'Veterinary aspects of reproduction in the Giant panda (*Ailuropoda melanoleuca*)', *Bongo, Berlin* **10**, 93–126.

LAWSON, J. W., PARSONS, J. L., CRAIG, S. J., EDDINGTON, J. D. AND KIMMINS, W. C. (1996) 'Use of electroejaculation to collect semen samples from wild seals' *J. Am. Vet. Med. Assoc.* **209**, 1615–1617.

LINDEMANN, C. B., FISHER, M. AND LIPTON, M. (1981) 'A comparative study of the effects of freezing and frozen storage on intact and demembranated bull spermatozoa', *Cryobiology* **19**, 20–28.

MASUI, M., HIRAMATSU, H., SAITO, K., NOSE, N., NAKAZATO, R., SAGAWA, Y., TAJIMA, H., KASAI, N., TANABE, K. AND KAWASAKI, I. (1985) 'Seasonal fluctuations of spermatozoa in urine of Giant panda (*Ailuropoda melanoleuca*)', *Proceedings of the International Symposium on the Giant Panda. Bongo* **10**, 43–44.

MASUI, M., HIRAMATSU, H., NOSE, N., NAKAZATO, R., SAGAWA, Y., TAJIMA, H. AND SAITO, K. (1989) 'Successful artificial insemination in the Giant panda (*Ailuropoda melanoleuca*) at Ueno Zoo', *Zoo Biol.* **8**, 17–26.

MEAD, R. A. (1989) 'Reproduction in mustelids', in Seal, U. S., Thorne, E. T., Bogan, M. A., and Anderson S. H. (eds) *Conservation Biology and the Black-Footed Ferret*, New Haven: Yale University Press, pp. 124–137.

MOORE, H. D. M., BUSH, M., CELMA, M., GARCIA, A.-L., HARTMAN, T. D., HEARN, J. P., HODGES, J. K., JONES, D. M., KNIGHT, J. A., MONSALVE, L. AND WILDT, D. E. (1984) 'Artificial insemination in the Giant panda (*Ailuropoda melanoleuca*)', *J. Zool.* **203**, 269–278.

PLATZ, C. C., WILDT, D. E., HOWARD, J. G. AND BUSH, M. (1983) 'Electroejaculation and semen analysis and freezing in the Giant panda (*Ailuropoda melanoleuca*)', *J. Reprod. Fertil.* **67**, 9–12.

ROBECK, T. R., CURRY, B. E., McBAIN, J. F. AND KRAEMER, D. C. (1994) 'Reproductive biology of the bottle-nosed dolphin (*Tursiops truncatus*) and the potential application of advanced reproductive technologies', *J. Zoo Wildlife Med.* **25**, 321–336.

ROSSATO, M., LA SALA, G. B., BALASINO, M., TARICCO, F., GALEAZZI, C., FERLIN, A. AND FORESTA, C. (1999) 'Sperm treatment with extracellular ATP increases fertilization rates in in-vitro fertilization for male factor infertility', *Hum. Reprod.* **14**, 694–697.

SLATTERY, J. P. AND O'BRIEN, S. J. (1995) 'Molecular phylogeny of the red panda (*Ailurus fulgens*)', *J. Hered.* **86**, 413–422.

SUN, O. Y., LIU, H., LI, X. B., SONG, X. F., YU, J. Q., LI, G. H. AND CHEN, D. Y. (1996) 'The role of Ca^{2+} and protein kinase C in the acrosome reaction of Giant panda (*Ailuropoda melanoleuca*) spermatozoa', *Theriogenology* **46**, 359–367.

VAN DEMARK, N. K. AND SHARMA, U. D. (1957) 'Preliminary results from the preservation of bovine semen at room temperature', *J. Dairy Sci.* **40**, 438–439.

CHAPTER 19

WIEGAND, T., NAVES, J., STEPHAN, T. AND FERNANDEZ, A. (1998) 'Assessing the risk of extinction for the brown bear (*Ursus arctos*) in the Cordillera Cantabrica, Spain', *Ecol. Monogr.* **68**, 539–570.

WILDT, D. E., BUSH, M., MORTON, C., MORTON, F. AND HOWARD, J. G. (1989) 'Semen characteristics and testosterone profiles in ferrets kept in a long-day photoperiod, and the influence of hCG timing and sperm dilution medium on pregnancy rate after laparoscopic insemination', *J. Reprod. Fertil.* **86**, 349–358.

YANG, J. (1987) 'Cryopreservation and cryobiological study of the spermatozoa of the Giant panda (*Ailuropoda melanoleuca*)', *Cryobiology* **24**, 585–586.

ZHANG, M. J., HOU, R., ZHANG, A. J., ZHANG, Z. H., HE, G. X., LI, G. H., WANG, J. S., LI, S. C., SONG, Y. F., FEI, L. S. AND CHEN, H. W. (1998) '*In vitro* maturation of follicular oocytes of the giant panda (*Ailuropoda melanoleuca*): a case report', *Theriogenology* **49**, 1251–1255.

Germplasm Cryopreservation of Non-Human Primates

J. M. MORRELL[1] AND J. K. HODGES[2]

[1]German Primate Centre, Kellnerweg 4, 37077 Göttingen, Germany
[2]Department of Reproductive Biology, German Primate Centre,
Kellnerweg 4, 37077 Göttingen, Germany

Contents

20.1 SPERMATOZOA

Although sporadic attempts at freezing spermatozoa from the more frequently encountered captive non-human primate species have occurred during the last thirty years, reliable information on the most appropriate methodologies is limited. Semen collection methods, choice of extender and sperm handling procedures vary widely between studies, thus complicating comparisons of effectiveness and results. In some studies the functional integrity of the thawed spermatozoa was not tested. Moreover, advances in automated cell freezing, computerized sperm motility assessment and, in some species, AI during this period make comparisons between earlier and more recent sperm cryopreservation studies difficult. In addition, although considerable differences in ejaculate characteristics exist between primate species, few comparative studies have been performed.

The evaluation of a sperm cryopreservation method can only be achieved properly by assessing the functional ability of the thawed spermatozoa. However, reliable techniques for AI or IVF do not exist for many non-human primates, which creates a problem when trying to assess the effectiveness of a sperm cryopreservation technique. Information on the functional integrity of spermatozoa after thawing is lacking for a third of the reports discussed in this chapter.

20.1.1 The influence of season

No studies have examined the influence of season of collection on survival of spermatozoa during cryopreservation; few reports include details of the season in which ejaculates were obtained although seasonality of semen production and ejaculate quality has been reported in several species (e.g. Valerio and Dalgard, 1975; Denis *et al.*, 1976, Brun and Rumpler, 1990; Sankai *et al.*, 1997) but not in others (e.g. Mahone and Dukelow, 1979). Results within a species may be conflicting: seasonal variation in ejaculate quality was observed in rhesus monkeys (*Macaca mulatta*) by some authors (e.g. Zamboni *et al.*, 1974; Wickings *et al.*, 1981) but was not detected by others (Harrison, 1980; Okamoto, 1994).

20.1.2 Collection method

Several methods have been used to obtain spermatozoa:

- *Natural ejaculates.* Chimpanzees were trained to ejaculate into an artificial vagina (Gould and Styperek, 1989) and a lowland gorilla (*Gorilla gorilla gorilla*) was conditioned to ejaculate into a hand-held plastic bag (Pope *et al.*, 1997). Semen could be obtained opportunistically from one bonobo (*Pan paniscus*) which ejaculated on to the floor during natural mating attempts (Matern, 1983).

- *Ejaculates collected from the vagina after mating.* Cynomolgus ejaculates were obtained by aspiration from the vagina (Cho and Honjo, 1973); a combination of aspiration and vaginal washing was used to collect marmoset ejaculates (Morrell, 1997).
- *Electrostimulation* by means of a rectal probe was used to collect semen from baboons (Kraemer and Cruz, 1969), rhesus macaques (Leverage *et al.*, 1972), squirrel monkeys (Denis *et al.*, 1976), cynomolgus macaques (Mahone and Dukelow, 1978; Sankai *et al.*, 1994), and vervet monkeys (Seier *et al.*, 1993; Conradie *et al.*, 1994). Penile electroejaculation was used in the cynomolgus monkey (Tollner *et al.*, 1990) and squirrel monkey (Yeoman *et al.*, 1997).
- *Epididymal spermatozoa* from gorillas have been collected for cryopreservation after the death of a male or elective castration (Beehler *et al.*, 1982; Lanzendorf *et al.*, 1992), marmosets (*Callithrix jacchus*) (Holt *et al.*, 1994) and a Japanese monkey (*M. fuscata*) (Sankai *et al.*, 1997).

Two studies have examined the effect of collection method on survival of spermatozoa during cryopreservation. The recovery of motile baboon (*Papio* spp.) spermatozoa after cryopreservation was similar from natural and electroejaculates (Kraemer and Cruz, 1969) but, in contrast, cynomolgus spermatozoa from vaginal aspirates showed improved survival during freezing and thawing compared with spermatozoa collected by electrostimulation (Cho and Honjo, 1973).

20.1.3 Dilution

Tollner *et al.* (1990) reported no correlation between the extent of dilution and post-thaw survival of cynomolgus monkey spermatozoa cryopreserved at a concentration of 60 million spermatozoa per ml. Likewise, there was no effect of concentration on post-thaw survival of marmoset spermatozoa cryopreserved at concentrations ranging from 10 to 225 million spermatozoa per ml (Morrell, 1997).

20.1.4 Semen handling

Procedures performed before reducing the temperature below 0°C fall into four categories: enzymatic treatment, equilibration of neat ejaculate, equilibration with non-glycerolated extender, and equilibration with glycerolated extender. The inclusion of equilibration stages in cryopreservation protocols varies widely between methods; they are probably included as an aid to the stabilization of sperm membranes, although few comparisons have been made to determine whether such treatments are necessary.

Enzymatic treatment

The semen of most primates, except the gorilla (Gould, 1990), is emitted as a coagulum which later partially liquefies. Trypsin was used to liquefy ejaculates from rhesus and stumptail macaques, patas and African green monkeys (Roussel and Austin, 1967), baboons (Kraemer and Cruz, 1969) and chimpanzees (Roussel and Austin, 1967; Bader, 1983; Matern, 1983) before cryopreservation. However, Denis *et al.* (1976) observed that trypsin adversely affected spermatozoa survival during freezing and thawing. In more recent cryopreservation studies, enzymatic treatment of the coagulum has been excluded from the protocol (e.g. Gould and Styperek, 1989) because of growing evidence that it caused damage to spermatozoa.

Equilibration of neat ejaculate

Three different handling protocols have been described for cynomolgus ejaculates: (a) incubation at 37°C for 10 minutes before adding glycerolated extender at 37°C and cooling to 4°C in 30 minutes (Cho and Honjo, 1973); (b) equilibration at room temperature before adding glycerolated medium at 4°C (Mahone and Dukelow; 1978); (c) maintenance at 37°C before adding non-glycerolated medium at 5°C and, after equilibration, addition of glycerolated medium at 5°C.

Denis *et al.* (1976) incubated squirrel monkey ejaculates at 37°C for 45 minutes before adding glycerolated medium at 5°C, whereas Yeoman *et al.* (1997) added diluent at room temperature after liquefaction of the ejaculate at 37°C.

Equilibration with non-glycerolated extender

Chimpanzee ejaculates were diluted immediately with non-glycerolated medium and cooled slowly to 4°C before adding glycerolated medium (Sadleir, 1966) whereas gorilla ejaculates were equilibrated in non-glycerolated medium at 4°C for 2 hours before adding glycerolated medium at 4°C and equilibrating for a further 2 hour period (Pope *et al.*, 1997). Marmoset ejaculates were equilibrated in non-glycerolated medium for 75 minutes at room temperature before adding glycerolated medium at room temperature (Morrell, 1997).

Leverage *et al.* (1972) compared the effect of adding non-glycerolated medium at 37°C and at 4°C on the recovery of rhesus monkey spermatozoa after cryopreservation. Adding non-glycerolated medium at 37°C and equilibrating for 30 minutes before adding glycerolated medium and cooling to 4°C at 1.3°C/minute produced a higher proportion of motile spermatozoa on thawing than did cooling the ejaculate to 4°C before adding non-glycerolated medium, equilibrating for 4 hours, adding glycerolated medium and holding for 18 hours before freezing. An AI study with thawed spermatozoa frozen using the former method resulted in a conception in one out of 48 inseminated females, but unfortunately this pregnancy aborted.

Equilibration with glycerolated extender

Roussel and Austin (1967) added glycerolated extender directly to ejaculates from rhesus and stumptail macaques, patas and African green monkeys and chimpanzees, which were then equilibrated at room temperature for 30 minutes. Glycerolated extender was added to vervet monkey (Conradie *et al.*, 1994) and lowland gorilla (Lanzendorf *et al.*, 1992) ejaculates before cooling to 5°C.

Gould and Styperek (1989) extended chimpanzee semen slowly with glycerolated medium, adding a volume equivalent to 10% of the original ejaculate volume every 5 minutes. Lowland gorilla semen was extended with glycerolated medium dropwise and was cooled to 4°C at a rate of 5°C/min (Lambert *et al.*, 1991). Similarly, cynomolgus monkey ejaculates were extended by adding glycerolated medium slowly over a 20-minute period, before cooling to 5°C in 2 hours.

Seier *et al.* (1993) compared the effect of cooling vervet monkey ejaculates to 32°C or 5°C before adding glycerolated medium at the same temperature. They concluded that the recovery of motile spermatozoa was greater if the glycerolated medium was added at 32°C, probably because the permeability of glycerol shows temperature dependency, at least over the range 0–20°C (McGann, 1978).

20.1.5 Diluent composition

Extenders for cryopreserving non-human primate spermatozoa typically contain egg yolk and buffers such as TES, Tris or sodium citrate. Some extenders may contain sugars in various proportions. The existence of interspecies differences in the suitability of sperm extenders is not known, since the few comparative studies performed have concentrated on interdiluent differences for one species rather than investigating the possibility of using one extender for several species. The composition of the extenders used for different species are described below, grouped according to the taxonomic classification of species.

Great apes

Diluent containing egg yolk in Tris buffer with 7% glycerol was used to cryopreserve gorilla spermatozoa (Beehler *et al.*, 1982), whereas Pope *et al.* (1997) diluted gorilla ejaculates 1:1 with TALP-HEPES medium, before further dilution 1:1 with TEST-egg yolk extender. Glycerolated TEST-egg yolk extender was then added to give a final concentration of 4% glycerol.

Chimpanzee spermatozoa were extended in egg yolk (20%) in Tris buffer with 4% glycerol (Bader, 1983), or in egg yolk (20%) with glucose (11%) and 5% glycerol (Matern, 1983). In contrast, Ham´s F10 with 15% human cord serum added was used by Gould and Styperek (1989). Sadleir (1966) compared three types of extender for chimpanzee spermatozoa: (a) egg yolk (20%) and sodium citrate (2.2%), (b) egg yolk (20%) and glucose (6%), (c) egg yolk (5%) with reconstituted skim milk (10% w/v). Cryoprotectants were added to give final concentrations of 4%, 5% or 10% glycerol with 1.5% fructose, or 7% DMSO with 1% glycine. The best motilities after 1–3 days storage were obtained from semen extended in egg–yolk–citrate with 10% glycerol, milk–egg yolk with 10% glycerol, or glucose–egg yolk with 7% glycerol.

Old World primates

Cynomolgus monkey spermatozoa have been cryopreserved in a diluents containing egg yolk (20%) and lactose (11%) with 4% glycerol (Mahone and Dukelow, 1978), egg yolk (10%), glucose, lactose, raffinose in ratio 3:4:3 (Cho and Honjo, 1973), and egg yolk (20%) with glucose 20 g/l, lactose 20 g/l, raffinose 2 g/l, TES 12 g/l and Tris 2 g/l (Sankai *et al.*, 1994). In a comparison of three types of extender, the one containing 30% egg yolk, skim milk (20%), TES 4.325 g, Tris 1.0269 g in 80 ml HPLC-grade water resulted in the highest proportion of motile cynomolgus spermatozoa on thawing (Tollner *et al.*, 1990).

The effect of adding different buffers to egg yolk (20%) and glycerol (7%) on rhesus sperm survival during cryopreservation was examined by Leverage *et al.* (1972). A combination of sodium bicarbonate (2.1%), sodium citrate (2.1%) and potassium phosphate (0.32%) solution gave a higher recovery of motile spermatozoa on thawing than was achieved with either sodium bicarbonate or sodium citrate alone.

A diluent containing egg yolk (20%) and sodium glutamate solution with 14% glycerol was used for ejaculates from various Old World primate species and baboons (Roussel and Austin, 1967; Kraemer and Cruz, 1969). Vervet monkey spermatozoa were cryopreserved in an extender containing 30% egg yolk, 1 g dextrose, 4.325 g TES and 1.027 g Tris in 100 ml double distilled deionized water, with 3 or 5% glycerol (Seier *et al.*, 1993; Conradie *et al.*, 1994). TEST–yolk buffer was used to extend drill baboon semen for cryopreservation (Durrant *et al.*, 1999).

New World primates

Squirrel monkey spermatozoa were cryopreserved in either an extender containing egg yolk (20%) and lactose (11%) with 4% glycerol (Denis *et al.*, 1976) or a TEST-based buffer with egg yolk and 8% glycerol (Yeoman *et al.*, 1997). An extender containing egg yolk (20%), glucose 40 mg, TES 483 mg, Tris 115 mg and 5% glycerol was used for marmoset spermatozoa (Holt *et al.*, 1994; Morrell, 1997).

20.1.6 Cryopreservative

Although several compounds possess cryoprotective properties, only glycerol has been used extensively for non-human primate spermatozoa. In four studies with cynomolgus monkey spermatozoa, different conclusions were reached concerning the proportion of glycerol which was optimal for sperm survival, possibly because of variation in the collection methods and cooling rates used.

The potential toxicity of glycerol during pre-freezing equilibration has been observed for rhesus (Leverage *et al.*, 1972), cynomolgus macaque (Mahone and Dukelow, 1978) and marmoset spermatozoa (Morrell, 1997). Greater viability of thawed rhesus spermatozoa was observed when equilibration in glycerolated medium before cooling was restricted to 1 minute, compared with that observed after 25 or 45 minutes (Leverage *et al.*, 1972). Similarly, a prefreezing incubation period with glycerolated medium of 1 minute resulted in significantly greater post-thaw progressive motility of cynomolgus macaque spermatozoa than did incubation periods of 25 or 35 minutes in glycerolated medium (Mahone and Dukelow, 1978). Furthermore, the recovery of motile marmoset spermatozoa declined noticeably when a 15-minute equilibration period preceded cooling compared with a 0, 5 or 10-minute equilibration period (Morrell, 1997). In contrast, Durrant *et al.* (1999) did not observe any difference in sperm motility or viability when glycerol was added to extended drill baboon semen before or after cooling to 4°C.

The cryoprotective ability of DMSO was found to be inferior to that of glycerol for chimpanzee spermatozoa (Sadleir, 1966), while Gould and Styperek (1989) reported that chimpanzee spermatozoa exposed to DMSO failed to penetrate oocytes *in vitro*. The survival of marmoset epididymal spermatozoa was not enhanced by the inclusion of dodecyl sulphate in the cryopreservation medium, compared to glycerol alone (Holt *et al.*, 1994).

20.1.7 Packaging

Three types of packaging have been used for non-human primate spermatozoa: glass ampoules (Roussel and Austin, 1967); plastic cryopreservation vials (Gould and Styperek, 1989; Lambert *et al.*, 1991; Morrell, 1997); and plastic straws (Beehler *et al.*, 1982; Bader, 1983; Tollner *et al.*, 1990; Sankai *et al.*, 1994; Morrell, 1997; Pope *et al.*, 1997; Sankai *et al.*, 1997). However, a comparison of types of packaging has been performed in only one study, where a significantly higher proportion of motile spermatozoa was recovered from straws than from vials cooled in liquid nitrogen vapour (Morrell, 1997).

20.1.8   Cooling procedure

Three cooling techniques have been used for non-human primate spermatozoa, rapid freezing in liquid nitrogen vapour or on a dry ice block and slow freezing using a programmable automated cell freezer. No clear advantage has yet been demonstrated for one method over another.

- *Immersion in liquid nitrogen vapour* (with or without an equilibration period near 4°C), is estimated to cool the spermatozoa at a rate of 10–25°C per minute (Wolf and Patton, 1989), depending on the type of packaging used and the height above the surface of the liquid nitrogen. Examples of the use of this technique are for lowland gorillas (Beehler *et al.*, 1982), chimpanzee (Bader, 1983), cynomolgus macaque (Tollner *et al.*, 1990; Sankai *et al.* 1994), vervet monkey (Seier *et al.*, 1993; Conradie *et al.*, 1994), marmoset (Morrell, 1997), Japanese monkey spermatozoa (Sankai *et al.*, 1997) and drill baboon spermatozoa (Durrant *et al.*, 1999).
- *Pellet freezing* on the surface of a dry ice block is reported to cool at a rate of 8–27°C/min for pellets of 0.03 ml (Denis *et al.*, 1976). Examples are chimpanzee (Sadleir, 1966; Gould and Styperek, 1989), cynomolgus macaque (Cho and Honjo, 1973; Mahone and Dukelow, 1978), squirrel monkey (Denis *et al.*, 1976), bonobo (Matern, 1983), lion-tailed macaque (*M. silenus*) (Cranfield *et al.*, 1988) and lowland gorilla spermatozoa (Lanzendorf *et al.*, 1992). Plastic straws filled with the sperm suspension may also be cooled on the surface of a dry ice block, for example, marmoset (Morrell, 1997) and gorilla (Pope *et al.*, 1997).
- *Programmed freezing* using a computerized automatic cell freezer allows various cooling rates to be used in a controlled manner. Chimpanzee (Gould and Styperek, 1989), marmoset spermatozoa (Holt *et al.*, 1994; Morrell, 1997) and squirrel monkey spermatozoa (Yeoman *et al.*, 1997) have been frozen using controlled freezing. Using an automated cell freezer, a slow temperature reduction of 0.25–1.0°C/min down to approximately 5°C can be achieved. Further cooling can take place more rapidly; for example, epididymal marmoset sperm were cooled from 5°C down to −80°C in 2 minutes (Holt *et al.*, 1994).

The effect of various rates of cooling in programmable cell freezers on the recovery of viable spermatozoa was examined using chimpanzee (Gould and Styperek, 1989) and marmoset spermatozoa (Morrell, 1997). In the first study, chimpanzee spermatozoa cooled from 20°C to 4°C at 1°C/min, followed by a holding period of 25 minutes, a further cooling to −30°C at 5°C/min and finally cooling to −100°C at 25°C/min, showed the highest penetration of hamster oocytes in a sperm penetration assay compared with protocols involving different cooling rates and holding periods, including a pellet freezing method (Gould and Styperek, 1989). Two pregnancies were achieved when eleven chimpanzee females were inseminated with the thawed spermatozoa.

Morrell (1997) compared the effects of three cooling rates in a cell freezer on the recovery of motile marmoset spermatozoa: of the three protocols, cooling from 15°C to 5°C at 0.5°C/min, followed by cooling to −25°C at 6°C/min and finally to −100°C at 15°C/min produced the greatest recovery of motile spermatozoa. However, when this controlled method of freezing was compared with faster freezing in liquid nitrogen vapour and on a dry ice block, the recovery of motile marmoset spermatozoa was similar for all methods. Pregnancies occurred in three out of six females inseminated with thawed spermatozoa.

20.1.9 Thawing procedure

No investigation of possible interactions between rate of thawing and recovery of motile non-human primate spermatozoa has been reported. In the majority of studies thawing has occurred either in the range 36–40°C or at room temperature. However, Pope et al. (1997) thawed gorilla sperm for 4 seconds at room temperature before plunging the straws into a 70°C waterbath for 6 seconds, whereas in a study with chimpanzee, rhesus macaque, stumptail macaque, patas monkey and vervet monkey spermatozoa, Roussel and Austin (1967) used a thawing temperature of 5°C.

20.1.10 Evaluation

The evaluation of a sperm cryopreservation method can only be achieved properly by assessing the functional ability of the thawed spermatozoa. However, reliable techniques for AI or IVF do not exist for many non-human primates, which creates a problem when trying to assess the effectiveness of a sperm cryopreservation technique. Information on the functional integrity of spermatozoa after thawing is lacking for a third of the reports discussed in this chapter.

Sperm fertilizing ability may be indicated by hypo-osmotic swelling of spermatozoa (HOS) and various sperm penetration assays using either homologous or heterologous oocytes. HOS was used to study the effect of diluent composition on survival of lion-tailed macaque spermatozoa during cryopreservation (Cranfield et al., 1988). Hyperactivated spermatozoa from both pig-tailed and lion-tailed macaques were found to penetrate and fertilize pig-tailed macaque oocytes (Cranfield et al., 1988). However, access to oocytes for most non-human primate species is very limited and the culture requirements for these oocytes are poorly understood. Heterologous sperm penetration tests have also been used: for example, the ability of cryopreserved gorilla spermatozoa to penetrate zona-free hamster oocytes varied between 25.3 and 43% compared with >80% for human spermatozoa controls prepared in a similar manner (Lambert et al., 1991). Similarly, zona penetration of salt-stored oocytes provided a useful indication of the potential fertilizing ability of cryopreserved cynomolgus spermatozoa (Sankai *et al.*, 1994); thawed cynomolgus spermatozoa capacitated faster than fresh spermatozoa as shown by penetration of 70.6% salt-stored oocytes after a 2-hour incubation period, in contrast to fresh spermatozoa which penetrated 29.4% after 2 hours but 100% after incubation for 6 or 8 hours.

Six methods of sperm cryopreservation have been evaluated directly by IVF or AI. In IVF with thawed cynomolgus spermatozoa (Sankai *et al.*, 1994), 57% oocytes were fertilized after for 2 hours incubation. When 67 eggs fertilized by frozen–thawed spermatozoa were co-cultured with cumulus cells, 57 cleaved, of which 12 developed into expanded blastocysts and one hatched. Thawed gorilla spermatozoa fertilized 8 out of 11 oocytes in IVF; a term infant resulted from the transfer of three embryos to a recipient (Pope *et al.*, 1997). Holt *et al.* (1994) achieved a 31% fertilization rate in IVF with thawed epididymal marmoset spermatozoa compared with 82% for fresh spermatozoa (Wilton *et al.*, 1993); three offspring resulted from embryo transfer with thawed spermatozoa. Similarly, a fertilization rate of 43% was obtained in IVF with thawed epididymal Japanese monkey spermatozoa but only 4 of the 29 fertilized oocytes developed further (Sankai *et al.*, 1997).

Cryopreservation methods that have been effectively evaluated using AI include those used for chimpanzee spermatozoa (Gould and Styperek, 1989), where two pregnancies followed AI in eleven females; cynomolgus macaque spermatozoa (Tollner *et al.*, 1990), where one out of three inseminated females conceived and gave birth; and marmoset ejaculated spermatozoa (Morrell, 1997) where three out of six females conceived and two gave birth, compared to six out of six females inseminated with fresh spermatozoa. Furthermore, one pregnancy was achieved when six females were inseminated with cryopreserved epididymal marmoset sperm (Morrell *et al.*, 1998).

Other attempts to evaluate cryopreservation procedures by AI may have failed because of the inadequacy of the AI procedure, although poor motility of the thawed spermatozoa (Bader, 1983; Beehler *et al.*, 1983) or excessive sperm damage was also reported (Leverage *et al.*, 1972).

20.2 EMBRYOS

The cryopreservation of embryos from five species of non-human primate has been reported, using embryos derived from both *in vivo* and *in vitro* techniques. Two attempts to freeze gorilla embryos have been included in this chapter although evaluation of the techniques is difficult since the embryos have not been thawed.

20.2.1 Species and stage of development

The following species and stages of embryos have been cryopreserved: baboon (*Papio* sp.) embryos at the six-cell to blastocyst stage (Pope *et al.*, 1984, 1986), cynomolgus monkey (*M. fascicularis*) embryos at the four- and eight-cell stages (Balmaceda *et al.*, 1986), marmoset embryos (*C. jacchus*) at day 4 and day 7 stages (Summers *et al.*, 1987), rhesus monkey (*M. mulatta*) embryos at the three- to six-cell stages (Wolf *et al.*, 1989) and pronuclear stage (Lanzendorf *et al.*, 1990), one pronuclear embryo (Lanzendorf *et al.*, 1992) and two-cell stage embryos of the lowland gorilla (Pope *et al.*, 1997), and hybrid embryos derived from *M. nemestrina* oocytes fertilized *in vitro* by *M. silenus* spermatozoa (Cranfield *et al.*, 1992).

20.2.2   Collection method

Ovarian stimulation protocols vary slightly between species but generally involve the administration of FSH, either alone or in combination with LH, followed by hCG. The exception to this protocol was in the case of the lowland gorilla where a gonadotrophin releasing hormone agonist was used to suppress endogenous gonadotrophins, followed by human menopausal gonadotrophin to stimulate follicular growth (Lanzendorf *et al.*, 1992).

In vivo fertilized embryos were flushed from the uterus of baboons (Pope *et al.*, 1984, 1986) and marmosets (Summers *et al.*, 1987). Preovulatory oocytes were recovered for IVF by follicular aspiration from cynomolgus macaques (Balmaceda *et al.*, 1986), rhesus macaques (Wolf *et al.*, 1989; Lanzendorf *et al.*, 1990), pig-tailed macaques (Cranfield *et al.*, 1992) and lowland gorilla (Lanzendorf *et al.*, 1992; Pope *et al.*, 1997).

20.2.3   Diluent composition

Two types of medium, supplemented with serum, have been used: phosphate-buffered saline for baboon, marmoset, rhesus and gorilla embryos (Pope *et al.*, 1986; Summers *et al.*, 1987; Wolf *et al.*, 1989; Lanzendorf *et al.*, 1990; Pope *et al.*, 1997), and buffers such as TALP or HEPES for cynomolgus, baboon, hybrid macaque and lowland gorilla embryos (Balmaceda *et al.*, 1986; Pope *et al.*, 1984; Cranfield *et al.*, 1992; Lanzendorf *et al.*, 1992).

20.2.4   Cryopreservative

Several cryopreservatives have been utilized: 1.4 M glycerol (Pope *et al.*,1984, 1986) 1.5 M DMSO (Balmaceda *et al.*, 1986), 1.5 M propanediol (Lanzendorf *et al.*, 1990, 1992; Wolf *et al.*, 1989), and propanediol combined with sucrose (Cranfield *et al.*, 1992; Pope *et al.*, 1997). However, Younis *et al.* (1996) demonstrated a glycerol-mediated disruption of the F-actin organization in rhesus monkey oocytes which was temperature-dependent.

In a comparison of 1 M glycerol with 1.5 M DMSO as cryoprotectant for marmoset embryos, glycerol was found to cause excessive cell shrinkage and swelling during dehydration and subsequent rehydration, which damaged the cells (Summers *et al.*,

1987). Morphological changes were observed more often in day 4 embryos where DMSO was used as the cryoprotectant than in day 7 morulae (61% and 33% respectively); however, embryos frozen in 1.5 M DMSO gave a better pregnancy rate than those frozen in 1 M glycerol (70% versus 37.5%) (Summers *et al.*, 1987).

20.2.5 Handling

Embryos were incubated in increasing concentrations of cryoprotectant at room temperature.

20.2.6 Packaging

Plastic straws (Pope *et al.*, 1984, 1997; Balmaceda *et al.*, 1986, 1997), glass ampoules (Pope *et al.*, 1986; Summers *et al.*, 1987), and cryovials (Lanzendorf *et al.*, 1990, 1992) have been used as packaging.

20.2.7 Cooling rate

Embryos were cooled to −6°C or 7°C before inducing seeding. After holding at this temperature for 5–20 minutes they were cooled slowly at 0.3–0.5°C/min to temperatures ranging from −30°C to −80°C before plunging into liquid nitrogen. The plunge temperature was variable: −30°C for baboon embryos (Pope *et al.*, 1984, 1986) and rhesus embryos (Wolf *et al.*, 1989; Lanzendorf *et al.*, 1990), −36°C for gorilla embryos (Pope *et al.*, 1997), −39°C for cynomolgus embryos (Balmaceda *et al.*, 1986), −60°C for marmoset embryos (Summers *et al.*, 1987) and −80° for one lowland gorilla embryo (Lanzendorf *et al.*, 1992).

20.2.8 Thawing rate

Most protocols use a rapid thawing procedure, either at room temperature for 2 minutes (Balmaceda *et al.*, 1986), in a waterbath at 20°C for 10–15 seconds (Pope *et al.*, 1984, 1986) or at 37°C (Wolf *et al.*, 1989; Lanzendorf *et al.*, 1990). However, a programmable cell freezer was used to thaw marmoset embryos slowly (Summers *et al.*, 1987). They were transferred from liquid nitrogen to the cell freezer at −80°C, then warmed to 4°C at a rate of 10°C/min.

20.2.9 Post-thaw handling

The embryos were passed through decreasing concentrations of cryoprotectant, followed by a culture period of approximately 2 hours before evaluation and transfer to recipients (Pope *et al.*, 1984, 1986; Balmaceda *et al.*, 1986; Summers *et al.*, 1987; Wolf *et al.*, 1989; Lanzendorf *et al.*, 1990; Cranfield *et al.*, 1992).

20.2.10 Evaluation

Apart from the two protocols for lowland gorilla embryos (Lanzendorf *et al.*, 1992; Pope *et al.*, 1987), evaluation of the success of each method was based on embryo morphology on thawing and on the outcome of embryo transfer. The results are as follows:

- *Cynomolgus.* Seventy per cent (39 out of 56) of embryos were considered viable after thawing and 11 out of 12 embryos cleaved at least once in overnight culture; 25 embryos were transferred to nine recipients resulting in three pregnancies and the birth of two singletons (Balmaceda *et al.*, 1986).
- *Baboon.* Thirty-two thawed embryos were transferred non-surgically to fourteen females, resulting in four pregnancies with the birth of singletons (Pope *et al.*, 1984, 1986).
- *Marmoset.* Twenty-eight day 4 thawed embryos were transferred to eighteen day 4 recipients, resulting in ten pregnancies, of which six continued to term, producing seven young. Fifteen day 7 embryos were transferred to nine day 6 recipients, resulting in five pregnancies, four term births and six young (Summers *et al.*, 1987). A lower pregnancy rate was achieved after transfer of frozen-thawed morulae and day 4 embryos compared with unfrozen controls (morulae: frozen 55.6%, fresh 85.7%; day 4 embryos: frozen 48%, fresh 100%).
- *Rhesus.* In the first study, post-thaw embryo survival was 11/11; six embryos were transferred to three recipients, resulting in one pregnancy and the birth of one offspring (Wolf *et al.*, 1989). In the second study, post-thaw embryo survival was reported to be 10/15. Eight frozen–thawed embryos were transferred to four unstimulated recipients at the two- to six-cell stage, resulting in three twin pregnancies (Lanzendorf *et al.*, 1990).
- *Hybrid macaque.* Numbers of embryos frozen and surviving were not given. Nine embryos were transferred into one female; one offspring was born (Cranfield *et al.*, 1992).

20.3 OOCYTES

The technology for non-human primate oocyte cryopreservation is much less well developed than that for embryos. Recent fundamental studies on human oocytes, as reviewed by Bernard and Fuller (1996), may facilitate understanding of how the biophysical changes during a cryopreservation regimen affect oocyte function, which in turn could aid the development of protocols for non-human primate oocytes.

There are two published attempts of cryopreservation of non-human primate oocytes, one with squirrel monkey ova (DeMayo *et al.*, 1986) and the other with gorilla oocytes (Lanzendorf *et al.*, 1992).

20.3.1 Collection method

Oocytes were collected by follicular aspiration following ovarian stimulation. Gorilla oocytes were categorized as germinal vesicle, metaphase I (no germinal vesicle or polar body) or metaphase II (with polar body). Squirrel monkey oocytes were not categorized.

20.3.2 Medium composition

Squirrel monkey oocytes were cultured in tissue culture medium 199, with 20% fetal bovine serum, pyruvate and gentamycin or penicillin-streptomycin using DMSO, at 1.5 or 2.0 M as cryoprotectant, whereas TALP with 1.5 M propanediol was used for the lowland gorilla oocytes.

20.3.3 Handling

Squirrel monkey oocytes in 0.1 ml medium were loaded into ampoules and held in an ice bath; DMSO was added prior to freezing. Gorilla oocytes were incubated for 30–60 minutes at room temperature in cryoprotectant.

20.3.4 Packaging

Glass ampoules were used for squirrel monkey oocytes, whereas plastic cryovials were used for lowland gorilla oocytes.

20.3.5 Cooling rate

Squirrel monkey oocytes in ampoules were placed in a 95% ethanol bath at −7°C, and were seeded by touching the ampoules with forceps cooled in liquid nitrogen. Further cooling took place at 0.24°C/min to −80°C, before the ampoules were plunged into liquid nitrogen. The lowland gorilla oocytes were cooled at 1.0°C/min, seeded at −6°C, held for 10 minutes before cooling at 0.5°C/min to −80°C and finally plunged into liquid nitrogen for storage.

20.3.6 Thawing rate

The squirrel monkey oocytes were thawed either slowly by placing the ampoule in 95% ethanol at −110°C and allowing it equilibrate to 20°C, a rate of approximately

1–2°C/min, or rapidly by transferring the ampoule directly into an ice bath, at a rate of approximately 100°C/min. The lowland gorilla oocytes were warmed in a Planer freezer from −100°C to room temperature at a rate of 8°C/min.

20.3.7 Post-thaw handling

Stepwise dilution of cryoprotectant at room temperature was performed for the lowland gorilla oocytes which were then cultured in TALP medium for 72 hours. Dilution of the cryoprotectant for the squirrel monkey oocytes was achieved by adding 0.2 ml, 0.2 ml, 0.4 ml and 1 ml of medium at one-minute intervals. The oocytes were then cultured for 3 hours in modified TCM 199 at 37°C.

20.3.8 Evaluation

The squirrel monkey oocytes were cultured and then fixed. Increasing the concentration of DMSO to 2.0 M resulted in increased survival of frozen–thawed ova in culture (55% survival in 2.0 M DMSO versus 37.5% in 1.5 M DMSO). The lowland gorilla oocytes were evaluated twice daily for nuclear maturity. Of six mature oocytes frozen and thawed, four showed cytoplasmic degeneration, whereas two were healthy in appearance with intact germinal vesicles. After 72 hours in culture, one oocyte matured to MI and then arrested while the remaining oocyte remained at the GV stage.

20.4 OVARIAN TISSUE

There is one report on the cryopreservation of marmoset ovarian tissue (Candy *et al.*, 1995).

- *Collection method.* The ovaries from young adult marmosets were cut into pieces of approximately 1 mm³ in size.
- *Medium composition.* The tissue was incubated in 1.5 M DMSO in medium M2 supplemented with 10% fetal bovine serum (FBS).
- *Handling.* Incubation took place at 4°C for 12–20 minutes.
- *Packaging.* The tissue was aspirated into 0.25-ml plastic straws.
- *Cooling rate.* The straws were cooled at 2°C/min to −8°C and, after 5 minutes, ice crystal formation was induced. After a further 5 minutes, the straws were cooled at 0.3°C/min to −40°C and then at 10°C/min to −150°C before storage in liquid nitrogen.
- *Thawing rate.* The ovarian tissue was thawed rapidly in air at room temperature for 40 seconds and then immersed in water at 30°C for approximately 6 seconds, until the ice melted.

- *Post-thaw handling.* DMSO was diluted in a single step at room temperature with 1–2 ml M2+FBS. The ovarian tissue was washed through three changes of M2 medium+FBS (1–2 ml per wash) before either transplantation or placing in fixative for histology.
- *Evaluation.* Histological examination revealed that 33% of follicles in frozen–thawed tissue appeared normal, compared with 51% of follicles in fresh samples. Some follicles at all stages up to the small antral state of folliculogenesis appeared normal after freezing and thawing. Fresh and frozen tissue pieces were transferred under the kidney capsules of immunologically incompetent female mice (MFI-nu nu). Transfers were made to one kidney capsule per female; the mice were bilaterally ovariectomized in the same operation. The recipients were autopsied 7–60 days later for recovery of the ovarian tissue, which was dissected out and fixed for histology. All grafts contained follicles at all stages of folliculogenesis.

REFERENCES

BADER, H. (1983) 'Electroejaculation in chimpanzees and gorillas and artificial insemination in chimpanzees', *Zoo Biol.* **2**, 307–314.

BALMACEDA, J. P., HEITMAN, T. O., GARCIA, M. R., PAUERSTEIN, C. J. and POOL, T. B. (1986) 'Embryo cryopreservation in cynomolgus monkeys', *Fertil. Steril.* **45**, 403–406.

BEEHLER, B. A., PIPER, A., JACOBS, S. C. and CLOWRY L. J. (1982) 'Post mortem collection of sperm from a lowland gorilla', *Am. Assoc. Zoo Vet. Annu. Proc.* 56–57.

BERNARD, A. and FULLER, B. J. (1996) 'Cryopreservation of human oocytes: a review of current problems and perspectives', *Hum. Reprod.* **2**, 193–207.

BRUN, B. and RUMPLER, Y. (1990) 'Seasonal variation of sperm morphology in the Mayotte Brown Lemur (*Eulemur fulvis mayottensis*)', *Folia Primatologia* **55**, 51–56.

CANDY, C. J., WOOD, M. J. and WHITTINGHAM, D. G. (1995) 'Follicular development in cryopreserved marmoset ovarian tissue after cryopreservation', *Human Reproduction* **10**, 2334–2338.

CHO, F. and HONJO, S. (1973) 'A simplified method for collecting and preserving cynomolgus macaque semen', *Jpn J. Med. Sci. Biol.* **26**, 261–268.

CONRADIE, E., OETTLE, E. E. and SEIER, J. V. (1994) 'Assessment of acrosomal integrity of vervet monkey spermatozoa after cryopreservation', *J. Med. Primatol.* **23**, 315–316.

CRANFIELD, M. R., KEMPSKE, S. E. and SCHAFFER, N. (1988) 'The use of *in vitro* fertilization and embryo transfer techniques for the enhancement of genetic diversity in the captive population of the lion-tailed macaque *Macaca silenius*', *Int. Zoo Yearbook* **27**, 149–159.

CRANFIELD, M. R., BERGER, N. G., KEMPSKE, S., BAVISTER, B. D., BOATMAN, D. E. and LALEGGIO, D. M. (1992) 'Macaque monkey birth following transfer of in vitro fertilized, frozen–thawed embryos to a surrogate mother', *Theriogenology* **37**, 197.

DEMAYO, F. J., HUTZ, R. J. and DUKELOW, W. R. (1986) 'Cryopreservation of squirrel monkey ova', in Taub, D. M. and King, F. A. (eds) *Current Perspectives in Primate Biology*, New York: Van Nostrand Reinhold, pp. 63–70.

DENIS, L. T., POINDEXTER, A. N., RITTER, M. B., SEAGER, S. W. J. and DETER, R. L. (1976) 'Freeze preservation of squirrel monkey sperm for use in timed fertilization studies', *Fertil. Steril.* **27**, 723–729.

DURRANT, B., CAMMIDGE, L., WILEY, S., CARLSSON, I., WESCHE, P. and RUSS, K. (1999) 'Cryopreservation of semen from the drill baboon (*Mandrillus leucophaeus*)', *Biol. Reprod.* **60** (Suppl.), 103.

GOULD, K. G. (1990) 'Techniques and significance of gamete collection and storage in great apes', *J. Med. Primatol.* **19**, 537–551.

GOULD, K. G. and STYPEREK, R. P. (1989) 'Improved methods for freeze preservation of chimpanzee sperm', *Am. J. Primatol.* **18**, 275–284.

HARRISON, R. M. (1980) 'Semen parameters in *Macaca mulatta*: ejaculates from random and selected monkeys', *J. Med. Primatol.* **9**, 265–273.

HOLT, W. V., WILTON, L. J. and MARSHALL, V. S. (1994) 'Cryopreservation of spermatozoa from the marmoset monkey (*Callithrix jacchus*)', in Bradley, M. and Cummins, J. (eds) *Proceedings of the 7th Symposium on Spermatology (Cairns)*, no. 9.17.

KRAEMER, D. C. and CRUZ, N. C. V. (1969) 'Collection, gross characteristics and freezing of baboon semen', *J. Reprod. Fertil.* **20**, 345–348.

LAMBERT, H., CITINO, S., COLLAZO, I. and JEYENDRAN, R. S. (1991) 'Penetration of zona-free hamster oocytes by ejaculated cryopreserved gorilla spermatozoa', *Fertil. Steril.* **56**, 1201–1203.

LANZENDORF, S. E., ZELINSKI-WOOTEN, M. B., STOUFFER, R. L. and WOLF, D. P. (1990) 'Maturity at collection and the developmental potential of rhesus monkey oocytes', *Biol. Reprod.* **42**, 703–711.

LANZENDORF, S. E., HOLMGREN, W. J., SCHAFFER, N., HATASAKA, H., WENTZ A. C. and JEYENDRAN, R. S. (1992) 'In vitro fertilization and gamete micromanipulation in the lowland gorilla', *J. Assisted Reprod. Genet.* **9**, 358–364.

LEVERAGE, W. E., VALERIO, D. A., SCHULTZ, A. P., KINGSBURY, E. and DOREY, C. (1972) 'Comparative study on the freeze preservation of spermatozoa. Primate, bovine and human', *Lab. Anim. Sci.* **22**, 882–889.

MCGANN, L. E. (1978) 'Differing actions of penetrating and non-penetrating cryoprotective agents', *Cryobiology* **15**, 382–390.

MAHONE, J. P. and DUKELOW, W. R. (1978) 'Semen preservation in *Macaca fascicularis'*, *Lab. Anim. Sci.* **28**, 556–561.

MAHONE, J. P. and DUKELOW, W. R. (1979) 'Seasonal variation of reproductive parameters in the laboratory-housed male cynomolgus macaque (*Macaca fascicularis*)', *J. Med. Primatol.* **8**, 179–183.

MATERN, B. (1983) 'Problems and experiences in performing artificial insemination in bonobos (*Pan paniscus*)', *Zoo Biol.* **2**, 303–306.

MORRELL, J. M. (1997) 'Cryopreservation of marmoset sperm (*Callithrix jacchus*)', *Cryo-Letters* **18**, 45–54.

MORRELL, J. M., NUBBEMEYER, R., HEISTERMANN, M., ROSENBUSCH, J., KÜDERLING, I., HOLT, W. V. and HODGES, J. K. (1998) 'Artificial insemination in *Callithrix jacchus* using fresh or cryopreserved sperm', *Anim. Reprod. Sci.* **52**, 165–174.

OKAMOTO, M. (1994) 'Annual sperm concentration variation in semen collected by electroejaculation in the cynomolgus monkey (*Macaca fascicularis*)', *Exp. Anim.* **43**, 25–31.

POPE, C. E., POPE, V. Z. and BECK, L. R. (1984) 'Live birth following cryopreservation and transfer of a baboon embryo', *Fertil. Steril.* **42**, 143–145.

POPE, C. E., POPE, V. Z. and BECK, L. R. (1986) 'Cryopreservation and transfer of baboon embryos', *J. In vitro Fertil. Embryo Transfer* **3**, 33–39.

POPE, C. E., DRESSER, B. L., CHIN, N. W., LIU, J. H., LOSKUTOFF, N. M., BEHNKE, J., BROWN, C., MCRAE, M. A., SINOWAY, C. E., CAMPBELL, M. K., CAMERON, K. N., OWENS, O'D. M., JOHNSON, C. A., EVANS, R. R. and CEDARS, M. I. (1997) 'Birth of a lowland gorilla (*Gorilla gorilla gorilla*) following in vitro fertilization and embryo transfer', *Am. J. Primatol.* **41**, 247–260.

ROUSSEL, J. D. and AUSTIN, C. R. (1967) 'Preservation of primate spermatozoa by freezing', *J. Reprod. Fertil.* **13**, 333–335.

SADLEIR, R. M. F. S. (1966) 'The preservation of mammalian spermatozoa by freezing', *Lab. Pract.* **15**, 413–417.

SANKAI, T., TERAO, K., YANAGIMACHI, R., CHO, F. and YOSHIKAWA, Y. (1994) 'Cryopreservation of spermatozoa from cynomolgus monkeys *(Macaca fascicularis)*', *J. Reprod. Fertil.* **101**, 273–278.

SANKAI, T., SHIMIZU, K., CHO, F. and YOSHIKAWA, Y. (1997) 'In vitro fertilization of follicular oocytes by frozen–thawed spermatozoa in Japanese monkeys (*Macaca fuscata*)', *Lab. Anim. Sci.* **47**, 58–62.

SEIER, J. V., CONRADIE, E., OETTLE, E. E. and FINCHAM, J. E. (1993) 'Cryopreservation of vervet monkey semen and recovery of progressively motile spermatozoa', *J. Med. Primatol.* **22**, 355–359.

CHAPTER 20

SUMMERS, P. M., SHEPHARD, A. M., TAYLOR, C. T. and HEARN, J. P. (1987) 'The effects of cryopreservation and transfer on embryonic development in the common marmoset monkey, *Callithrix jacchus*', *J. Reprod. Fertil.* **79**, 241–250.

TOLLNER, T. L., VANDEVOORT, C. A., OVERSTREET, J. W. and DROBNIS, E. Z. (1990) 'Cryopreservation of spermatozoa from cynomolgus monkeys (*Macaca fascicularis*)', *J. Reprod. Fertil.* **90**, 347–352.

VALERIO, D. A. and DALGARD, D. W. (1975) 'Experiences in the laboratory breeding of non-human primates', *Lab. Anim. Handbooks* **6**, 49–62.

WICKINGS, E. J., ZAIDI, P. and NIESCHLAG, E. (1981) 'Seminal parameters in rhesus monkeys under physiological conditions and in studies for male fertility control using FSH antibodies or LH-RH agonists', *Am. J. Primatol.* **1**, 203–210.

WILTON, L. J., MARSHALL, V. S., PIERCY, E. C. and MOORE, H. D. M. (1993) '*In vitro* fertilization and embryo development in the marmoset monkey (*Callithrix jacchus*)', *J. Reprod. Fertil.* **97**, 481–486.

WOLF, D. P. and PATTON, P. E. (1989) 'Sperm cryopreservation: state of the art', *J. In Vitro Fertil. Embryo Transfer* **6**, 325–327.

WOLF, D. P., VANDEVOORT, C. A., MEYER-HAAS, G. R., ZELINSKI-WOOTEN, M. B., HESS, D. L., BAUGHMAN, W. L. and STOUFFER, R. L. (1989) 'In vitro fertilization and embryo transfer in the rhesus monkey', *Biol. Reprod.* **41**, 335–346.

YEOMAN, R. R., RICKER, R. B., HOSSAIN, A. M. and ABEE, C. R. (1997) 'Cryopreservation of spermatozoa from squirrel monkeys (*Saimiri bolivensis*)', *Am. J. Primatol* **42**, 157.

YOUNIS, A. I., TONER, M., ALBERTINI, D. F. and BIGGERS, J. D. (1996) 'Cryobiology of non-human primate oocytes', *Hum. Reprod.* **11**, 156–165.

ZAMBONI, L., CONAWAY, C. H., and VAN PELT, L. (1974) 'Seasonal changes in production of semen in free-ranging rhesus monkeys', *Biol. Reprod.* **11**, 251–267.

The Cryopreservation of Human Gametes and Embryos

P. F. WATSON

Department of Veterinary Basic Sciences, The Royal Veterinary College, London NW1 0TU, UK

Contents

21.1   INTRODUCTION

The inclusion of a chapter devoted to study of human germplasm in a book on germplasm resource banking may at first sight be surprising. There are two main arguments in defence of this chapter. First, since such material is part of the vertebrate genetic resource, it is not precluded from inclusion. Second, in the field of reproductive technology, the human has become the subject of much novel advancements and, as such, deserves to be included as a model for the non-human primate!

To this end, the relevant studies in the human are reviewed and indications for the future of this work are described. The reader is also advised to consult Chapter 3.

21.2   CONVENTIONAL CRYOPRESERVATION OF EJACULATED SPERMATOZOA

Cryopreservation of human spermatozoa has a long history, the first babies born as a result of donor artificial insemination (DI) with frozen–thawed semen dating from 1954 (Bunge *et al.*, 1954). In those days, frozen semen was a less satisfactory alternative to fresh semen for DI, but with developing concern for the prevention of viral disease transmission, the majority of countries in the developed world now have legislation in place requiring DI to be conducted only with frozen semen stored for a period of quarantine. In the UK, the donor must be demonstrated to be free of HIV antibodies both at the time of donation and six months after the donation before the semen may be released for use (HFEA, 1998). Reviews of current practice by Royere *et al.* (1996) and Holt (1998) supplement the information given in this section.

Semen is collected by masturbation; human semen is fractionated with the sperm-rich portion in the early part of the ejaculate. Shortly after ejaculation the ejaculate coagulates, but it liquefies again within about 20 minutes. Occasionally the liquefaction is not complete and a viscoid mass remains, making dilution of the spermatozoa difficult. Various methods have been proposed to liquefy this material but it can remain a problem; one such method is to isolate the sperm-rich portion which has less tendency to coagulate. A good reference for the handling of human semen, and its normal characteristics is the WHO Laboratory Manual (WHO, 1999).

A number of diluents are in use, notably TEST-yolk, Human Sperm Preservation Medium (HPSM, Mahadevan and Trounson 1983), Tris–glucose, yolk–citrate or combinations of these (McLaughlin *et al.,* 1992). In a trial of eight diluents, Weidel and Prins (1987) found that yolk–citrate–Tris gave the most satisfactory results over a range of individual samples. It is noteworthy that the TEST–yolk diluent was used as a satisfactory preservation medium for semen of novel species where there was no background information on suitable media (Graham *et al.,* 1978). Royere *et al.* (1996) gives a range of additives that have been claimed to improve post-thaw quality of spermatozoa.

The advantage of selecting (Perez-Sanchez *et al.*, 1994) and/or concentrating spermatozoa (Kobayashi *et al.*, 1991) before freezing have been demonstrated, especially in the case of poor-quality ejaculates. Human semen is generally packaged in 0.5-ml straws or in ampoules. There does not seem to be a preference for one or the other, people using what they originally became familiar with, but the straw is probably more widely used. Undoubtedly, it allows good control of the cooling and warming profile of the material contained within, but recently it has been questioned as a suitable storage container because of the danger of release of infected material into the liquid nitrogen. There are arguments being proposed for a secondary double container to be used for storage of straws (see McLaughlin *et al.*, 1999), which may be extended to the storage of non-human animal materials in liquid nitrogen in the years to come. This will add to costs and will require the development of suitable secondary containers.

Human semen is best cooled at around 10°C/min and poorer results are evident at both higher and lower cooling rates (Henry *et al.*, 1993) although there is some latitude in the optimum rate. Some people have advocated the use of programmable freezers to achieve controlled freezing rates (Henry *et al.*, 1993), while others have found cooling in the vapour phase above liquid nitrogen to be quite satisfactory (McLaughlin *et al.*, 1990). Warming is carried out rapidly by thawing straws either at room temperature or at 37°C submersed in water. A recent study found thawing at 37°C more preferable if cooling had been carried out more rapidly in nitrogen vapour whereas thawing at room temperature was better when cooling had been slower in a controlled freezing device (Verheyen *et al.*, 1993). Because of the phenomenon of cryopreserved spermatozoa acting as if capacitated (Critser *et al.*, 1988; Watson, 1995), insemination should be carried out immediately so that the spermatozoa have a greater chance of contacting the oocyte before undergoing the acrosome reaction and dying. However, studies of the optimum timing of insemination with respect to ovulation do not necessarily support this view (Brook *et al.*, 1994). Indeed, in one study the highest conception rate (20%) occurred with insemination 24–48 hours before ovulation, falling to 11% on the day of ovulation (LeLannou and Lansac, 1993). Holt (1998) suggested that this might be interpreted as evidence for selection of the 'fittest' survivors but this is still a controversial concept.

Intrauterine insemination (IUI) is considered desirable; in a survey of the outomes of ten randomized studies which compared IUI and cervical insemination, IUI was found to offer approximately double the conception rate (Ford *et al.*, 1997). The majority of inseminations are now performed by a transcervical intrauterine route *per vaginam* and involve the need to prepare an inseminate free of any seminal plasma elements remaining from the cryopreservation medium. For intrauterine DI and IVF uses, motile spermatozoa are often recovered by swim-up into a solution suitable for oocyte support such as a modified Tyrode's solution. Alternatively, Percoll (or similar) separation was used with redilution into a suitable supportive diluent. In recent years, Percoll has been withdrawn from use in andrology laboratories, and other products of a similar nature (e.g. Nycodenz, Optiprep, Nycomed Pharma Inc., Oslo, Norway) have been introduced. These products are made up as suspensions of inert polymers which have a density dependent on concentration. They are not sold as suitable for use for human semen, and thus there is a reluctance to use them in a clinical IVF situation for fear of litigation in the event of adverse outcome.

For IVF, and particularly for intracytoplasmic sperm injection (ICSI, the introduction of a single spermatozoon into the oocyte by microinjection), relatively few spermatozoa are required and their advanced capacitation state is not generally considered a problem. While this may not be a general model for the use of non-human primate semen, it may find some applications in situations where particular matings are needed.

It is generally agreed that cryopreserved spermatozoa are not as fertile as fresh spermatozoa (LeLannou *et al.*, 1995) although this has not been formally tested recently because of the legislation preventing the use of fresh semen. The overall clinical pregnancy rate per treatment cycle for (frozen) donor insemination in the UK in the year 1997/1998 was 11.6 and the live birth rate was 9.6 (HFEA, 1999). Although these figures have improved over the past few years (HFEA, 1999) , they still suggest that frozen semen does not provide optimal chances of conception.

With the successes in treating male factor infertility during the last few years, there has been a growing interest in storing spermatozoa from cancer patients, persons whose ejaculates are often of very poor quality. Ragni *et al.* (1990) described the use of a slow staged freezing method to give optimal cryopreservation in these situations. Whether the spermatozoa are used for conventional IVF (Khalifa *et al.*, 1992) or ICSI, this is an area of great interest and such studies could have implications for storage of poor-quality semen samples from non-human primates.

There is currently a debate about safe cryostorage of gamete and embryo material because of the potential risks of transfer of viruses (and other potential infectious risks) during storage (McLaughlin *et al.*, 1999; see also Chapter 5).

21.3 CONSERVATION OF IMMATURE SPERMATOZOA

In recent years, with the development of ICSI there has been an interest in addressing severe male factor infertility (oligospermia and even azoospermia) by harvesting spermatozoa from early developmental stages in the epididymis or even the testis. Because ICSI requires only few spermatozoa, small puncture recoveries or biopsies can yield sufficient spermatozoa for the procedure. Details of methodology can be found in Marmar (1998). With that has come the possibility of cryopreservation of these small or poor-quality samples with the difficulty of recovery on thawing.

Ideally, the aim is to recover viable spermatozoa for ICSI or IVF. Motility is often not a reliable indicator of fertility of a sample in this situation, but can be improved on culture (Edirisinghe *et al.*, 1996). Cryopreservation is clearly detrimental but sufficient viable spermatozoa can be recovered to make the procedures possible (Edirisinghe *et al.*, 1996; Wurfel *et al.*, 1996; Verheyen *et al.*, 1997; Marmar 1998). Testicular biopsy material should be disrupted to free the cells before cryopreservation to improve their survival (Crabbe *et al.*, 1999). The largest survey of ICSI following use of these recovery and storage techniques is presented by Van Stierteghem *et al.* (1998), in which the results over a five-year period seem very favourable compared with conventional IVF.

Cohen *et al.* (1997) describe a method of cryopreserving and recovering individual spermatozoa by injecting them into a cell-free zona pellucida before preserving then in straws. They report a 75% recovery and satisfactory fertilization rates with ICSI.

A persistent anxiety concerning the use of ICSI, and particularly ICSI of immature spermatozoa or even spermatids (see below), is the perpetuation of genetic disorders which would normally have been screened out of the population by natural selective processes. To date, there is little evidence that such is the case but in humans, obstructive azoospermia is known to be associated with the cystic fibrosis genetic disorder and patients are advised to undergo genetic screening before opting for the infertility treatment. Recent evidence, however, suggests that babies produced following ICSI have a higher prevalence of sex chromosomal abnormalities, probably relating to genetic abnormalities of the genetic fathers (Bonduelle *et al.*, 1998). Such early indicators of problems with the techniques need to be borne in mind by those working with non-human species, especially if such techniques are contemplated for use with endangered species.

21.4 CONSERVATION OF MATURE AND IMMATURE HUMAN OOCYTES

At present there are very few instances of cryopreservation of human oocytes with subsequent fertilization and successful embryo transfer (for reference, see Bernard and Fuller, 1996; Newton, 1998). The metaphase II oocyte represents a distinct cryobiological challenge. Unlike spermatozoa, the oocyte is a single cell, and cryosurvival is an all-or-none phenomenon. Moreover, whereas the spermatozoon has completed meiosis and the chromatin has been packaged in a highly condensed and stable condition, the oocyte at ovulation is in metaphase arrest in the midst of the meiosis. The chromosomes of the second division are arranged on the metaphase plate on the spindle of microtubules. Not only do its organelles have to remain functional and able to resume activation and development, but the spindle on which the cell division will take place must depolymerize and repolymerize during the cooling and rewarming cycle and the chromosomes must reattach correctly to the metaphase plate.

Moreover, the cortical granules beneath the oolemma must remain intact in order that the zona pellucida may be penetrable by spermatozoa and be able to mount the block to polyspermy in the normal way. Zona hardening as a result of cryopreservation is recognized as one of the challenges facing cryobiology. Nevertheless, results to date promise a significant proportion of mature oocytes being recovered in a morphologically normal state (Gook *et al.*, 1994; Van Blerkom and Davis, 1994). A useful summary of recent progress and the nature of the problems is given by Bernard and Fuller (1996).

Most of the developmental work has been conducted using mouse oocytes. Studies have revealed that both DMSO and PrOH are suitable cryoprotectants, and data based on human oocytes are encouraging (Hunter *et al.*, 1991; Gook *et al.*, 1993). Nevertheless, spindle abnormalities following freezing and thawing are commonplace. In general, exposure to cryoprotectants in molar concentrations is recommended at reduced temperature (0–4°C) to minimize any toxic effect. Since human oocytes are recovered from follicles approaching ovulation the actual stage of development may vary. Such oocytes need to experience a period of maturation before fertilization. Because these stages involve considerable restructuring of the genetic material there is anxiety as to whether the *in vitro* manipulation will induce aneuploidy. However, there are data to suggest that this is not inevitable (Toth *et al.*, 1994; Van Blerkom and Davis, 1994).

The cooling and warming stages are generally conducted under controlled conditions using slow cooling and rewarming. Bernard and Fuller (1996) summarize the various studies on human oocyte membrane permeability characteristics on which informed cryopreservation protocols can be established. In general, the water permeability is low and the cryoprotectant permeabilites are an order of magnitude lower, underlying the importance of slow removal of cryoprotectant or the use of an external osmotic buffer during removal to avoid membrane rupture. There are very few studies of vitrification but Hunter *et al.* (1991) found that although fertilization was possible, embryonic development was arrested.

21.5 CONSERVATION OF OVARIAN SLICES

Given the difficulty of cryopreservation of the mature or germinal vesicle stage oocyte, it is not surprising that experiments have been initiated to cryopreserve ovarian slices. Succcessful outcomes have been achieved in mice and sheep, with transplantation of the thawed material and subsequent restoration of normal fertility (see Newton, 1998). It has its application in human medicine for the restoration of fertility after the sterilizing effects of cancer therapy in young women, but its wider implications in terms of a model for germplasm banking should not be overlooked. Obviously, there are implications for immunocompatibility and/or immunosuppression in heterotransplantation but these may be less of a barrier in the future. Alternatively, *in vitro* techniques provide an alternative scenario for oocyte growth, maturation, IVF and embryo transfer which avoids the problems of graft rejection. While this is as yet not possible in humans, its potential has already been demonstrated in mice (Eppig and O'Brien, 1996).

The most important contribution in this field to date showed that, with the exception of glycerol, a range of cryoprotectants (1.5 M) could be used to sustain the follicular growth functions of the tissue after subsequent transplantation into immunodeficient mice (Newton *et al.*, 1996). The cooling rate was slow and after storage for two months, samples were thawed in water at room temperature before removal of cryoprotectant and transplantation into immunodeficient mice for evaluation. Further studies of cryoprotectant permeation found that either EG or DMSO at 4°C provided the best permeation with least toxicity (Newton *et al.*, 1998). In another study, Gook *et al.* (1999) found that single-step dehydration of thin human ovarian slices in PrOH and sucrose for 90 minutes followed by slow cooling and rapid rewarming resulted in the best recovery of normal primordial oocytes and pregranulosa cells. It is noteworthy that the cryobiological protocols are unremarkable, and this suggests that immature gametes and their supporting cells can be cryopreserved rather easier than the end-differentiated highly specialized cells during meiosis.

21.6 CONSERVATION OF EMBRYOS

Results from cycles involving ovarian stimulation show that the embryo quality is no less good than with natural cycles, and the cryopreservation success is similar. With the better pregnancy rates being achieved with IVF there is an increasing tendency to restrict the number of embryo replacements to two in any cycle, leading to a greater need to store the extra embryos to allow for a second IVF attempt without the need for further ovarian stimulation. In some situations, the immediate cycle may not be suitable for transfer and, again in this case, cryopreservation is a sensible option.

The first human embryo cryopreservation with successful transfer was achieved in the early 1980s (Trounson and Mohr, 1983; Downing *et al.*, 1985). Embryo cryopreservation is now considered a fully validated protocol in infertility treatment, implantation rates approaching those of fresh embryos being expected (Tucker *et al.*, 1995), although this is not supported in all studies (see Ludwig *et al.*, 1998). A recent large-scale survey of embryo transfer involving thousands of transfers carried out in France showed that although the pregnancy per single embryo transfer remains lower with cryopreserved (7.3%) than with fresh (9.2%) embryos, the pregnancy outcome was no different (FIVNAT, 1996). This demonstrated the advances that have been achieved in recent years. Nevertheless, the damage to embryos as a result of freezing and thawing is of the order of 30% (Testart *et al.*, 1987).

There is debate about the optimal time for cryopreservation, some people preferring cryopreservation at the pronuclear phase, others at later stages (Kattera *et al.*, 1999). This allows for the 'best' embryos to be selected for fresh embryo transfer while the remainder are then stored pending the outcome. Inevitably, this tends to bias the comparisons of fresh and cryopreserved embryo transfers in favour of fresh transfers. More recently, there has been interest in cryopreserving blastocysts, and results have been encouraging (Kaufman *et al.*, 1995). In general, the later the selection the better the result of transfer, but few qualify for selection. This relates more to the inherent embryo quality, but also allows for the sublethal cell damage resulting from cryopreservation to become manifested. However, the determination of what is a 'good' embryo is still very subjective and not necessarily related to developmental function.

Diluents are often based on tissue culture media, and contain, for normal freezing and ice formation, DMSO or PrOH at a concentration of approximately 1–2 M. Additionally, sugars are frequently included. Other cryoprotectants have been utilized but glycerol is clearly unsuitable and other alcohols are less satifactory than PrOH and DMSO. Cryopreservation cycles involve slow cooling to at least $-30°C$ before plunging to storage in liquid nitrogen, allowing for sufficient dehydration to take place to prevent intracellular ice formation. Alternatively, other protocols utilize vitrification in which ice formation is prevented by very high concentrations of cryoprotectants and rapid cooling rates. The glass formation of the medium allows long-term cryopreservation at liquid nitrogen temperatures without the dangers of ice formation (see Chapter 3).

Thawing should be carried out carefully in the presence of appropriate concentrations of non-permeating sugars in order to prevent the overhydration of the cells as the permeating cryoprotectant solutes are diluted out. Embryos are readily transferred between media by means of a pipette controlled by mouth-suction and equipped with a protective trap. It is customary to culture the embryos for 24 hours to ensure that development has resumed before transfer to the recipient.

21.7 CONSERVATION OF IMMATURE GERM CELLS

In this section, developments which are only in their experimental stages are discussed. One area that is causing much debate at present is the use of spermatids to generate embryos. Spermatids are the last stage of the germ cell differentiation before release as spermatozoa in the spermatogenic tubule of the testis. They are haploid cells which mature by changing from a round cell to a highly specialized elongate cell with nucleus packaged in the 'head' together with an acrosome, and a midpiece and tail containing the mitochondria and the motile apparatus. Cryopreserved round spermatids have been shown to support fertilization by ICSI in mice (Ogura *et al.*, 1996;

Tanemura *et al.*, 1997). Early results in humans also show successful pregnancy outcome with this technology (Antinori *et al.*, 1997; Gianaroli *et al.*, 1999) although the technology is not yet licensed for clinical application in the UK. Nogueira *et al.* (1999) have reported that the same ultrastructural injuries to plasma membrane and acrosome are seen with cryopreservation of these testicular cells as are seen in epididymal and ejaculated spermatozoa, but that the later stages (late spermatid and spermatozoa) were more commonly affected.

With the early promise of mouse oocytes cultured from promordial follicles through to fertilization (Eppig and O'Brien, 1996), there is the prospect of culturing primordial follicles from human ovarian tissue which has been cryopreserved, and obtaining IVF and embryo transfer (Oktay *et al.*, 1997). The primordial follicles are separated by the use of proteolytic enzymes and are fragile, requiring a supporting matrix. At present, this is not a practical proposition and transplantation of the primordial follicles (Carroll and Gosden, 1993) is a more realistic goal.

Spermatogonia are the most primitive diploid germ cells in the postpubescent testis. Early experiments with rodents have demonstrated the feasibility of collection and storage of spermatogonia with subsequent thawing and transplantation into recipient testes; the re-establishment of spermatogenesis was demonstrated (Avarbock *et al.*, 1996). Moreover, a suitable transplantation technique has been developed for the non-human primate (Schlatt *et al.*, 1999). These experiments have generated much interest in the possibility of restoring spermatogenesis in patients irradiated for cancer therapy, and research is ongoing in the isolation and storage of spermatogonia from young men. A general observation is the ease with which these cells can be cryopreserved using standard cell preservation techniques (Avarbock *et al.*, 1996). Their lack of differentiation and their opportunity to repair themselves after transplantation ensures a good postfreezing response. Moreover, rat spermatogonia can establish rat spermatogenesis in the seminiferous tubules of immunodeficient mice (Clouthier *et al.*, 1996). Such techniques offer radical means to preserve genetic material.

In the future, the prospect of recovering gonocytes from prepubertal testes for cryostorage and transplantation into adult testes at a later date generates much interest. The spermatogenic tubule, being a privileged immunological site, holds the prospect of relatively easy access to this technology.

21.8 CONCLUSIONS

The area of reproductive technology in infertility is raising both technological and ethical challenges. In the not too distant future, we may see germ cell autotransplants as a routine way to re-establish fertility; the prospect of heterotransplantation cannot be far away. Moreover the demonstration that rat spermatogonia could establish rat spermatogenesis in a mouse testis (Clouthier *et al.*, 1996) opens the way to the use of xenotransplants to generate spermatozoa. These provide opportunities for ICSI, or even conventional IVF if the efficiency of spermatogenesis is sufficient, which may have appeal for endangered species. Work in humans is progressing apace and does not apparently require extensive testing in animals before it can reach clinical application. Indeed at the level of gamete development and interaction, species differences are such that the value of using another species model is questionable.

REFERENCES

ANTINORI, S., VERSACI, C., DANI, G., ANTINORI, M. and SELMAN, H. A. (1997) 'Successful fertilization and pregnancy after injection of frozen thawed round spermatids into human oocytes', *Hum. Reprod.* **12**, 554–556.

AVARBOCK, M. R., BRINSTER, C. J. and BRINSTER, R. L. (1996) 'Reconstitution of spermatogenesis from frozen spermatogonial stem cells', *Nature Med.* **2**, 693–696.

BERNARD, A. and FULLER, B. J. (1996) 'Cryopreservation of human oocytes: a review of current problems and perspectives', *Hum. Reprod. Update* **2**, 193–207.

BONDUELLE, M., WILIKENS, A., BUYSSE, A., VAN ASSCHE, E., DEVROEY, P., VAN STEIRTEGHEM, A. C. and LIEBAERS, I. (1998) 'A follow-up study of children born after intracytoplasmic sperm injection (ICSI) with epididymal and testicular spermatozoa and after replacement of cryopreserved embryos obtained after ICSI', *Hum. Reprod.* **13**, 196–207.

BROOK, P. F., BARRATT, C. L. and COOKE, I. D. (1994) 'The more accurate timing of insemination with regard to ovulation does not create a significant improvement in pregnancy rates in a donor insemination program', *Fertil. Steril.* **61**, 308–313.

BUNGE, R. G., KEETEL, W., and SHERMAN, J. (1954) 'Clinical use of frozen semen. Report of four cases', *Fertil. Steril.* **5**, 520–529.

CARROLL, J. and GOSDEN, R. G. (1993) 'Transplantation of frozen-thawed mouse primordial follicles', *Hum. Reprod.* **8**, 1163–1167.

CLOUTHIER, D. E., AVARBOCK, M. R., MAIKA, S. D., HAMMA, R. E. and BRINSTER R. L. (1996) 'Rat spermatogenesis in mouse testis', *Nature, Lond.* **381**, 418–421.

COHEN, J., GARRISI, G. J., CONGEDO-FERRARA, T. A., KIECK, K. A., SCHIMMEL, T. W. and SCOTT R. T. (1997) 'Cryopreservation of single human spermatozoa', *Hum. Reprod.* **12**, 994–1001.

CRABBE, E., VERHEYEN, G., TOURNAYE, H. and VAN STEIRTEGHEM, A. (1999) 'Freezing testicular tissue as a minced suspension preserves sperm quality better that whole biopsy freezing when glycerol is used as cryoprotectant', *Int. J. Androl.* **22**, 43–48.

CRITSER, J. K., HUSE-BENDA, A. R., AAKER, D. V., ARNESON, B. W. and BALL, G. D. (1988) 'Cryopreservation of human spermatozoa. III. The effect of cryoprotectants on motility', *Fertil. Steril.* **50**, 314–320.

DOWNING, B. G., MOHR, L. R., TROUNSON, A. O., FREEMANN, L. E. and WOOD, C. (1985) 'Birth after transfer of cryopreserved embryos'. *Med. J. Aust.* **142**, 409–411.

EDIRISINGHE, W. R., JUNK, S. M., MATSON, P. L. and YOVICH, J. L. (1996) 'Changes in motility patterns during in-vitro culture of fresh and frozen/thawed testicular and epididymal spermatozoa: implications for planning treatment by intracytoplasmic sperm injection', *Hum. Reprod.* **11**, 2474–2476.

EPPIG, J. J. and O'BRIEN, M. J. (1996) 'Development *in vitro* of mouse oocytes from primordial follicles', *Biol. Reprod.* **54**, 197–207.

FIVNAT (1996) 'Bilan des transferts d'embryons congelés de 1987 à 1994', *Contracept. Fertil. Sexual.* **24**, 700–705.

FORD, W. C. L., MATHUR, R. S. and HULL, M. G. R. (1997) 'Intrauterine insemination: is it an effective treatment for male factor infertility?' *Baillière's Clin. Obstet. Gynaecol.* **11**, 1–20.

GIANAROLI, L., SELMAN, H. A., MAGLI, M. C., COLPI, G., FORTINI, D, and FERRARETTI, A. P. (1999) 'Birth of a healthy infant after conception with round spermatids isolated from cryopreserved testicular tissue', *Fertil. Steril.* **72**, 539–541.

GOOK, D. A., OSBORN, S. M. and JOHNSTON, W. I. (1993) 'Cryopreservation of mouse and human oocytes using 1,2-propanediol and the configuration of the meiotic spindle', *Hum. Reprod.* **8**, 1101–1109.

GOOK, D. A., OSBORN, S. M. and JOHNSON, W. I. (1994) 'Fertilization of human oocytes following cryopreservation: normal karyotypes and absence of stray chroomosomes', *Hum. Reprod.* **9**, 684–691.

GOOK, D. A., EDGAR, D. H. and STERN, C. (1999) 'Effect of cooling rate and dehydration regimen on the histological appearance of human ovarian cortex following cryopreservation in 1,2–propanediol', *Hum. Reprod.* **14**, 2061–2068.

GRAHAM, E. F., SCHMEHL, M. K. L., EVENSEN, B. K. and NELSON, D. S. (1978) 'Semen preservation in non-domestic mammals', in Watson, P. F. (ed.) *Artificial Breeding of Non-Domestic Animals, Symposia of the Zoological Society of London, No. 43*, London: Academic Press, pp. 153–173.

HENRY, M. A., NOILES, E. E., GAO, D. Y., MAZUR P. and CRITSER, J. K. (1993) 'Cryopreservation of human spermatozoa. IV. The effects of cooling rate and warming rate on the maintenance of motility, plasma membrane integrity, and mitochondrial function', *Fertil. Steril.* **60**, 911–918.

HFEA (1998) *Human Fertilization and Embryology Authority, Code of Practice,* 4th edn, London: HFEA, Paxton House, 30 Artillery Lane, London E1 7LS.

HFEA (1999) *Human Fertilization Authority, Eighth Annual Report (1999),* London: HFEA, Paxton House, 30 Artillery Lane, London E1 7LS.

HOLT, W. V. (1998) 'Cryopreservation of human spermatozoa for donor insemination: problems, principles and research recommendations', in Templeton A., Cooke, I., Shaunessy, P. M. and O'Brien, P. M. (eds) *Evidence-Based Fertility Treatment,* London: Royal College of Obstetricians and Gynaecologists, pp. 135–147.

HUNTER, J. E., BERNARD, A., FULLER B. J., AMSO, N. and SHAW, R. W. (1991) 'Fertilization and development of the human oocyte following exposure to cryopreservation: a comparison of two techniques', *Hum. Reprod.* 6, 1460–1465.

KATTERA, S., SHRIVASTAV, P. and CRAFT, I. (1999) 'Comparison of pregnancy outcome of pronuclear- and multicellular-stage frozen–thawed embryo transfers', *J. Assist. Reprod. Genet.* 16, 358–362.

KAUFMAN, R. A., MENEZO, Y., HAZOUT, A., NICOLLET, B., DUMONT, M. and SERVY, E. J. (1995) 'Cocultured blastocyst cryopreservation: experience of more than 500 transfer cycles', *Fertil. Steril.* 64,1125–1129.

KHALIFA, E., OEHNINGER, S., ACOSTA, A. A., MORSHEDI, M., VEECK, L., BRYZYNSKI, R. G. and MUASHER, S. J. (1992) 'Successful fertilization and pregnancy outcome in in-vitro fertilization using cryopreserved/thawed spermatozoa from patients with malignant diseases', *Hum. Reprod.* 7, 105–108.

KOBAYASHI, T., KANEKO, S., HARA I , PARK, Y. J., SATO, H., OHNO, T. and NOZAWA, S. (1991) 'Concentrating human sperm before cryopreservation', *Andrologia* 23, 25–28.

LELANNOU, D. and LANSAC, J. (1993) 'Artificial procreation with frozen donor semen: the French experience of CECOS', in Barratt, C. L. R. and Cooke, I. D. (eds) *Donor Insemination,* Cambridge: Cambridge University Press, pp. 152–169.

LELANNOU, D., GASTARD, D., GUIVARCH, A., LAURENT, M. C. and POULAIN, P. (1995) 'Strategies in frozen donor semen procreation', *Hum. Reprod.* 10, 1765–1774.

LUDWIG, M, AL-HASANI, S., FELBERBAUM, R. and DIEDRICH, K. (1998) 'No impact of cryopreservation and thawing on embryo developmental potential–one more example of or the problem of retrospective non-controlled data', *Hum. Reprod.* 13, 786–787.

MCLAUGHLIN, E. A., FORD W. C. L. and HULL, M. G. R. (1990) 'A comparison of the freezing of human semen in the uncirculated vapour above liquid nitrogen and in a commercial semi-programmable freezer', *Hum. Reprod.* 5, 724–728.

MCLAUGHLIN, E. A., FORD W. C. L. and HULL, M. G. R. (1992) 'The contribution of glycerol egg yolk citrate cryopreservative to the decline in human sperm motility during cryopreservation', *J. Reprod. Fertil.* 95, 749–754.

MCLAUGHLIN, E. A., PACEY, A. and ELLIOTT, T. (eds) (1999) *Safe Cryopreservation of Gametes and Embryos,* West Leederville, Western Australia, Ladybrook Publishing.

CHAPTER 21

MAHADEVAN, M. M. and TROUNSON, A. O. (1983) 'Effects of cryoprotective media and dilution methods on the preservation of human spermatozoa', *Andrologia* **15**, 355–366.

MARMAR, J. L. (1998) 'The emergence of specialized procedures for the acquisition, processing, and cryopreservation of epididymal and testicular sperm in connection with intracytoplasmic sperm injection', *J. Androl.* **19**, 517–526.

NEWTON, H. (1998) 'The cryopreservation of ovarian tissue as a strategy for preserving the fertility of cancer patients', *Hum. Reprod. Update* **4**, 237–247.

NEWTON, H., AUBARD, Y., RUTHERFORD, A., SHARMA, V. and GOSDEN, R. (1996) 'Low tempeature storage and grafting of human ovarian tissue', *Hum. Reprod.* **11**, 1487–1491.

NEWTON, H., FISHER, J., ARNOLD, J. R., PEGG, D. E., FADDY, M. J. and GOSDEN, R. G. (1998) 'Permeation of human ovarian tissue with cryoprotective agents in preparation for cryopreservation', *Hum. Reprod.* **13**, 376–380.

NOGUEIRA, D., BOURGAIN, C., VERHAEYAEN, G., VAN STIRTEGHEM, A. C. (1999) 'Light and electron microscopic analysis of human testicular spermatozoa and spermatids from frozen and thawed testicular biopsies', *Hum. Reprod.* **14**, 2041–2049.

OGURA, A., MATSUDA, J., ASANO, T., SUZUKI, O. and YANAGIMACHI, R. (1996) 'Mouse oocytes injected with cryopreserved round spermatids can develop into normal offspring', *J. Assist. Reprod. Genet.* **13**, 431–434.

OKTAY, K., NUGENT, D., NEWTON, H., SALHA, O., CHATTERJEE, P. and GOSDEN, R. G. (1997) 'Isolation and characterization of primordial follicles from fresh and cryopreserved human ovarian tissue', *Fertil. Steril.* **67**, 481–486.

PEREZ-SANCHEZ, F, COOPER, T. G., YEUNG, C. H. and NIESCHLAG, E. (1994) 'Improvement in quality of cryopreserved human spermatozoa by swim-up before freezing', *Int. J. Androl.* **17**, 115–120.

PRINS, G. S. and WEIDEL, L. (1986) 'A comprehensive study of buffer systems as cryo-protectants for human spermatozoa', *Fertil. Steril.* **46**, 147–149.

RAGNI, G., CCCAMO, A. M., DALLA SERRA, A. and GUERCILENA, S. (1990) 'Computerized slow-staged freezing of semen from men with testicular tumors or Hodgkin's disease preserved sperm better than standard valour freezing', *Fertil. Steril.* **53**, 1072–1075.

ROYERE, D., BARTHELEMY, C., HAMAMAH, S. and LANSAC, J. (1996) 'Cryopreservation of spermatozoa: a 1996 review', *Hum. Reprod. Update* **2**, 553–559.

SCHLATT, S., ROSIEPEN, G., WEINBAUER, G. F., ROLF, C., BROOK, P. F. and NIESCHLAG, E. (1999) 'Germ cell transfer into rat, bovine, monkey and human testes', *Hum. Reprod.* **14**, 144–150.

TANEMURA, K., WAKAYAMA, T., KURAMOTO, K., HAYASHI, Y., SATO, E and OGURA, A. (1997) 'Birth of normal young by microinsemination with frozen–thawed round spermatids collected from aged azoospermic mice', *Lab. Anim. Sci.* **47**, 203–204.

TESTART, J., LASALLE, B., BELAISCH-ALLART, J., FORMAN, R., HAZOUT, A., VOLANTE, M. and FRYDMAN, R. (1987) 'Human embryo viability related to freezing and thawing', *Am. J. Obstet. Gynecol.* **157**, 168–171.

TOTH, T. L., BAKA, S. G., VEECK, L. I., JONES, H. W., MUASHER, S. and LANZENDORF, S. E. (1994) 'Fertilization and *in vitro* development of cryopreserved human prophase I oocytes', *Fertil. Steril.* **61**, 891–894.

TROUNSON, A., MOHR, L. (1983) 'Human pregnancy following cryopreservation, thawing and transfer of an eight-cell embryo', *Nature, Lond.* **305**, 707–709.

TUCKER, M. J., MORTON, P. C., SWEITZER, C. L. and WRIGHT, G. (1995) 'Cryopreservation of human embryos and oocytes', *Curr. Opin. Obstet. Gynecol.* **7**, 188–192.

VAN BLERKOM, J. and DAVIS P. W. (1994) 'Cytogenetic, cellular, and developmental consequences of cryopresevation of immature and mature mouse and human oocytes', *Microsc. Res. Technol.* **27**, 165–193.

VAN STEIRTEGHEM, A., NAGY, P, JORIS, H., JANSSENSWILLEN, C., STAESSEN, C, VERHEYEN, G., CAMUS, M, TOURNAYE, H and DEVROEY, P. (1998) 'Results of intracytoplasmic sperm injection with ejaculated, fresh and frozen–thawed epididymal and testicular spermatozoa', *Hum. Reprod.* **13** (Suppl. 1), 134–142

VERHEYEN, G., PLETINCX, I. and VAN STEIRTEGHEM, A. (1993) 'Effect of freezing method, thawing temperature and post-thaw dilution/washing on motility (CASA) and morphology characteristics of high quality human spermatozoa', *Hum. Reprod.* **8**, 1678–1684.

VERHEYEN, G., NAGY, Z., JORIS, H., DE CROO, I., TOURNAYE, H. and VAN STIERTEGHEM, A. (1997) 'Quality of frozen–thawed testicular sperm and its preeclinical use for intracytoplasmic sperm injection into in vitro-matured geminal-vesicle stage oocytes', *Fertil. Steril.* **67**, 74–80.

WATSON, P. F. (1995) 'Recent developments and concepts in the cryopreservation of spermatozoa and the assessment of their post-thawing function'. *Reprod. Fertil. Dev.* **7**, 871–891.

WEIDEL, L. and PRINS, G. S. (1987) 'Cryosurvival of human spermatozoa frozen in eight different buffer systems', *J. Androl.* **8**, 41–47.

WHO (1999) *WHO Laboratory Manual for the Examination of Human Semen and Sperm-Cervical Mucus Interaction*, 4th edn, Cambridge: Cambridge University Press.

CHAPTER 21

WURFEL, W., KRUSMANN, G., FIEDLER, K., VON HERTWIG, I. and SCHWARTZER, U. (1996) 'Pregnancies after in vitro fertilization (IVF) and intracytoplasmic sperm injection (ICSI) of testicular spermatozoa (TESE) from frozen semen', *Zentralbl. Gynakol.* **118**, 665–668.

Postscript

W. V. HOLT

The Institute of Zoology, The Zoological Society of London,
Regent's Park, London NW1 4RY, UK

Over the last two decades the concept of genetic resource banking has received increasing attention in both scientific and popular media circles. Some of this has been thoughtful, genuinely attempting to establish a useful and realistic niche for this technology. Alongside this, however, a counter philosophy has developed, emphasizing the need to focus on habitat protection and *in-situ* conservation. Unfortunately, the two views tend to foster polarization of opinion. As a result, many GRB ideas, and even experiments, have been highly speculative and unlikely to produce a truly useful result. In this volume we have tried to explore the theoretical and practical basis of the application of GRB in the context of the scientific knowledge as it currently stands. We have attempted not only to present technical data, but also to summarize the considerable amount of strategic thinking which has been put into this topic by a number of groups around the world. Much of the credit for developing the GRB vision must go to Professor B.N. Veprintsev of the Institute of Cell Biophysics, Moscow, Russia, who, together with Dr Natalia Rott, published a series of lengthy monographs proposing the cryopreservation of germplasm from virtually all known animal species (Veprintsev and Rott, 1979). These initial ideas have been developed in several different situations.

Recently, consortia of research laboratories interested in developing the GRB concept have become organized in different parts of the world. The National Zoo in Washington, in association with the Conservation Breeding Specialist Group, has provided much of the impetus for the GRB movement and was primarily responsible for drawing up a GRB Action Plan for tiger conservation as a model for other species (Wildt *et al*, 1993). Australian research institutions and zoos have recently formed the Animal Gene Storage Resource Centre of Australia, which is encouraging collaborative research efforts and conservation especially, but not exclusively, focusing on Australian species. A southern African consortium, the Wildlife Breeding Research Centre, has also been formed recently for the collection and storage of germplasm from African species. It operates two mobile laboratories that can be used to handle gamete collection and storage in the field.

At present, there is no formal and equivalent association of laboratories and zoological parks specifically committed to genetic resource banking in Europe. However, the group of laboratories and zoos that worked together as a consortium under the auspices of a European Union-funded programme on genetic resources in the first half of the 1990s have developed considerable experience of the topic (Holt *et al*., 1996). Work continues in many laboratories, and there are examples of efforts towards applications in the field (see Chapter 8). The European consortium remains committed to the GRB concept and many of the individuals involved in it have contributed to this book.

The various research groups working in this area have approached issues of scale, organization, species choice and practicality in different ways and with different priorities. Experience gained is shared, and the amount to which research activities are coordinated is increasing all the time. The development of e-mail and the internet is a very positive influence on the development of GRB approaches to animal conservation. Once the technical issues have been addressed by suitable research, and the logistics have been agreed and developed, the actual implementation of GRB programmes is dependent upon good communications between those who manage animals and those who hold and curate the cryopreserved materials. In principle, this demands only good management and organization. In a sense, once the GRB for a given species is up and running it should be regarded as so commonplace and boring, that its successes do not elicit surprise. However, none of the groups is yet in this position. We have much to look forward to in the next few years.

Several common themes have become apparent through conducting this wide-ranging review. Perhaps the most important is the major discrepancy between the total number of wild species and the number for which suitable reproductive technologies are available. While much has been achieved in the twenty years since the first international meeting to discuss these issues (Watson, 1978), the development of satisfactory GRB techniques for wild species can probably be counted on the fingers of one hand, if methodologies for domestic and laboratory species are excluded. We are still not much further forward than choosing the nearest domesticated or laboratory animal species and hoping that the technology is appropriate. In practice this is rarely the case. There is a dearth of knowledge about reproductive biology in wild species. While information on mating systems is beginning to be developed, often through observation alone but nowadays increasingly coupled with the use of genetic markers, knowledge of physiological processes is often completely absent. This absence of data has misled researchers into commonly held, but erroneous, assumptions. For example, because AI in cattle is a highly successful technique, there was an assumption that the same would be true for all other Bovidae. We are now beginning to realize that this is perhaps not the case, not because the techniques are poor but because the very diversity we are seeking to conserve includes animals whose fertility is inherently poor.

One assumption underlying the conservation aims of GRB technology is that the intention must always be the amplification of populations through captive breeding. Emphasis is therefore mostly upon inseminations, embryo transfers and other ways to accelerate the reproductive process. Some of the greatest threats to threatened wild populations come, however, from competing species; this may be through human pressures from hunting, agriculture and urban development, but it may also be through introduced carnivores, often foxes and feral cats. There are several examples of intentional or inadvertent introductions which have so disturbed the natural ecology that other species are threatened. The development of methods for controlling populations is therefore a complementary component of wildlife conservation. Indeed, it is a truism to say that controlling the human population is probably one of the best ways of promoting wildlife conservation.

Another paradoxical feature of wildlife conservation is that because the regions of the world with the greatest degree of biodiversity, and possibly the greatest conservation needs, are mostly found in the tropics, they are also home to the poorest nations. Expensive and highly technical means of achieving conservation aims are unlikely to appeal in such situations. Indeed the justification for undertaking wildlife conservation at all has to be questioned, when investment in social development may be a more pressing need. To be meaningful, conservation in these situations will have to pay its way by offering a tangible return to the local people; eco-tourism and sustainable harvesting are probably the best ways forward here. Although it would be unrealistic to expect that GRB and reproductive technology would have a central role in such circumstances, the conservation of key genetic resources could have real value in protecting the investment against further loss of genetic diversity and sustainability. Advances in aquaculture lead the way in this respect, where major facilities have been built to hold key genetic founder stocks of wild fish such as *Tilapia*, and where strenuous efforts are underway to develop cryopreservation technologies for sea urchin and oyster embryos. These form the basis of local and sustainable fish farming industries, although based on wild species.

A final message to emerge from reviewing the wealth of cryobiological data presented in these pages is the need to find unifying principles. After decades of research, much of it empirically based, it is still impossible reliably to predict the cryobiological responses of spermatozoa from a few suitable measurements of cell membrane permeability or biochemical composition. Moreover, the logic of including egg yolk in sperm freezing diluents is still unclear, although it evidently works, and the choices of cryoprotectant and its concentration are also unpredictable.

A wealth of detailed information has been amassed in the last few years concerning the structure and function of gametes and embryos of a few species. Knowledge of membrane lipids, proteins and microstructure, however, although useful to some extent, cannot yet help to formulate a suitable technique for sperm, oocyte or embryo cryopreservation in an unstudied species. As the pace of technological development accelerates ever faster, genomics and proteomics being the watchwords of the new millennium, gamete biologists and embryologists cannot continue to solve their problems on a species-by-species basis. There must be a concerted research effort by those with the appropriate background and the right vision to apply these new techniques to solve fundamental functional questions which have an application across species groups. Gamete and embryo cryopreservation must move from its comfortable empirical approaches into fundamental hypothesis-testing of novel and overarching concepts.

REFERENCES

Holt W. V., Bennett, P. M., Volubouev, V. and Watson, P. F. (1996) 'Genetic resource banks in wildlife conservation', *J. Zool.* **238**, 531–544.

Veprintsev, B. N. and Rott, N. N. (1979). 'Conserving genetic resources'. *Nature* **280**, 633–634.

Watson, P. F. (ed.) (1978) *Artificial Breeding of Non-Domestic Animals. Symposia of the Zoological Society of London, No. 43*, London: Academic Press.

Wildt, D. E., Byers, A. P., Howard, J. G., Wiese, R., Willis, K., O'Brien, S. J., Block, J., Tilson, R. I. and Rall, W. F. (1993) *Tiger Genome Resource Banking (GRB) Action Plan. Global Need and a Plan for the North American Region,* Apple Valley, 12101 Johnny Cake Road, MA 55124, USA: CBSG.

Index

Abbreviations: GRB, genetic resource banks/banking. *Passim* means that discussion of a topic is not continuous but scattered throughout the page ranges mentioned.